The Annotated IFl

CW00796591

Standards issued at 1
reflecting changes no ~ ~ ~ ~ ~ ~ ~ ~

This edition is issued in three parts

PART B

contains the annotated illustrative examples and implementation
guidance that accompany the Standards,
together with the annotated IFRS practice statements

See also Parts A and C of this edition:

Part A

*contains the annotated text of IFRS Standards including
IAS® Standards, IFRIC® Interpretations and
SIC® Interpretations, together with the*
Conceptual Framework for Financial Reporting

Part C

*contains the annotated bases for conclusions that accompany
the Standards, the* Conceptual Framework for Financial
Reporting *and IFRS practice statements, together with the*
Constitution *and* Due Process Handbook *of the IFRS Foundation*

Contents

continued...

IASB documents published to accompany

IFRS 1

First-time Adoption of International Financial Reporting Standards

The text of the unaccompanied standard, IFRS 1, is contained in Part A of this edition. Its effective date when issued was 1 July 2009. The text of the Basis for Conclusions on IFRS 1 is contained in Part C of this edition. This part presents the following documents:

IMPLEMENTATION GUIDANCE

TABLE OF CONCORDANCE

Contents

continued...

...continued

TABLE OF CONCORDANCE

Guidance on implementing
IFRS 1 *First-time Adoption of International Financial Reporting Standards*

This guidance accompanies, but is not part of, IFRS 1.

Introduction

IG1   This implementation guidance:

(a)   explains how the requirements of the IFRS interact with the requirements of some other IFRSs (paragraphs IG2–IG62, IG64 and IG65). This explanation addresses those IFRSs that are most likely to involve questions that are specific to first-time adopters.

(b)   includes an illustrative example to show how a first-time adopter might disclose how the transition to IFRSs affected its reported financial position, financial performance and cash flows, as required by paragraphs 24(a) and (b), 25 and 26 of the IFRS (paragraph IG63).

IAS 10 *Events after the Reporting Period*

IG2   Except as described in paragraph IG3, an entity applies IAS 10 in determining whether:

(a)   its opening IFRS statement of financial position reflects an event that occurred after the date of transition to IFRSs; and

(b)   comparative amounts in its first IFRS financial statements reflect an event that occurred after the end of that comparative period.

IG3   Paragraphs 14–17 of the IFRS require some modifications to the principles in IAS 10 when a first-time adopter determines whether changes in estimates are adjusting or non-adjusting events at the date of transition to IFRSs (or, when applicable, the end of the comparative period). Cases 1 and 2 below illustrate those modifications. In case 3 below, paragraphs 14–17 of the IFRS do not require modifications to the principles in IAS 10.

(a)   Case 1—Previous GAAP required estimates of similar items for the date of transition to IFRSs, using an accounting policy that is consistent with IFRSs. In this case, the estimates in accordance with IFRSs need to be consistent with estimates made for that date in accordance with previous GAAP, unless there is objective evidence that those estimates were in error (see IAS 8 *Accounting Policies, Changes in Accounting Estimates and Errors*). The entity reports later revisions to those estimates as events of the period in which it makes the revisions, rather than as adjusting events resulting from the receipt of further evidence about conditions that existed at the date of transition to IFRSs.

[Refer: paragraphs 14 and 15]

(b)   Case 2 – Previous GAAP required estimates of similar items for the date of transition to IFRSs, but the entity made those estimates using accounting policies that are not consistent with its accounting policies in accordance with IFRSs. In this case, the estimates in accordance with IFRSs need to be consistent with the estimates required in accordance with previous GAAP for that date (unless there is objective evidence that those estimates were in error), after adjusting for the difference in accounting policies. The opening IFRS statement of financial position reflects those adjustments for the difference in accounting policies. As in case 1, the entity reports later revisions to those estimates as events of the period in which it makes the revisions.

For example, previous GAAP may have required an entity to recognise and measure provisions on a basis consistent with IAS 37 *Provisions, Contingent Liabilities and Contingent Assets*, except that the previous GAAP measurement was on an undiscounted basis. In this example, the entity uses the estimates in accordance with previous GAAP as inputs in making the discounted measurement required by IAS 37.

[Refer: paragraphs 14 and 15]

(c)   Case 3 – Previous GAAP did not require estimates of similar items for the date of transition to IFRSs. Estimates in accordance with IFRSs for that date reflect conditions existing at that date. In particular, estimates of market prices, interest rates or foreign exchange rates at the date of transition to IFRSs reflect market conditions at that date. This is consistent with the distinction in IAS 10 between adjusting events after the reporting period and non-adjusting events after the reporting period.

[Refer: paragraphs 14 and 15]

IG Example 1 Estimates
Background
Entity A's first IFRS financial statements are for a period that ends on 31 December 20X5 and include comparative information **[Refer: paragraphs 21 and 22]** for one year. In its previous GAAP financial statements for 31 December 20X3 and 20X4, entity A:
(a)   made estimates of accrued expenses and provisions at those dates;
(b)   accounted on a cash basis for a defined benefit pension plan; and
(c)   did not recognise a provision for a court case arising from events that occurred in September 20X4. When the court case was concluded on 30 June 20X5, entity A was required to pay CU1,000[(a)] and paid this on 10 July 20X5.
<div align="right">*continued...*</div>

...continued

IG Example 1 Estimates

In preparing its first IFRS financial statements, entity A concludes that its estimates in accordance with previous GAAP of accrued expenses and provisions at 31 December 20X3 and 20X4 were made on a basis consistent with its accounting policies in accordance with IFRSs. Although some of the accruals and provisions turned out to be overestimates and others to be underestimates, entity A concludes that its estimates were reasonable and that, therefore, no error had occurred. As a result, accounting for those overestimates and underestimates involves the routine adjustment of estimates in accordance with IAS 8.

Application of requirements

In preparing its opening IFRS statement of financial position at 1 January 20X4 and in its comparative statement of financial position at 31 December 20X4, entity A:

(a)   does not adjust the previous estimates for accrued expenses and provisions; and **[Refer: paragraphs 14 and 15]**

(b)   makes estimates (in the form of actuarial assumptions) necessary to account for the pension plan in accordance with IAS 19 *Employee Benefits*. Entity A's actuarial assumptions at 1 January 20X4 and 31 December 20X4 do not reflect conditions that arose after those dates. For example, entity A's:

   (i)   discount rates at 1 January 20X4 and 31 December 20X4 for the pension plan and for provisions reflect market conditions at those dates; and

   (ii)   actuarial assumptions at 1 January 20X4 and 31 December 20X4 about future employee turnover rates do not reflect conditions that arose after those dates – such as a significant increase in estimated employee turnover rates as a result of a curtailment of the pension plan in 20X5. **[Refer: paragraphs 14 and 16]**

The treatment of the court case at 31 December 20X4 depends on the reason why entity A did not recognise a provision in accordance with previous GAAP at that date.

Assumption 1 – Previous GAAP was consistent with IAS 37 *Provisions, Contingent Liabilities and Contingent Assets*. Entity A concluded that the recognition criteria were not met. **[Refer: IAS 37 paragraph 14]** In this case, entity A's assumptions in accordance with IFRSs are consistent with its assumptions in accordance with previous GAAP. Therefore, entity A does not recognise a provision at 31 December 20X4. **[Refer: paragraphs 14 and 15]**

continued...

...continued

IG Example 1 Estimates

Assumption 2 – Previous GAAP was not consistent with IAS 37. Therefore, entity A develops estimates in accordance with IAS 37. Under IAS 37, an entity determines whether an obligation exists at the end of the reporting period by taking account of all available evidence, including any additional evidence provided by events after the reporting period. **[Refer: IAS 37 paragraphs 14–16]** Similarly, in accordance with IAS 10 *Events after the Reporting Period*, the resolution of a court case after the reporting period is an adjusting event after the reporting period if it confirms that the entity had a present obligation at that date. **[Refer: IAS 10 paragraphs 8 and 9]** In this instance, the resolution of the court case confirms that entity A had a liability in September 20X4 (when the events occurred that gave rise to the court case). Therefore, entity A recognises a provision at 31 December 20X4. Entity A measures that provision by discounting the CU1,000 paid on 10 July 20X5 to its present value, using a discount rate that complies with IAS 37 and reflects market conditions at 31 December 20X4. **[Refer: IAS 37 paragraphs 36–47]**

[Refer: paragraphs 31 and 33]

(a)   In this guidance monetary amounts are denominated in 'currency units (CU)'.

IG4   Paragraphs 14–17 of the IFRS do not override requirements in other IFRSs that base classifications or measurements on circumstances existing at a particular date. Examples include:

   (a)   the distinction between finance leases and operating leases for a lessor (see IFRS 16 *Leases* **[Refer: IFRS 16 paragraphs 61–66 and B53–B57]** and paragraph IG14);

   (b)   the restrictions in IAS 38 *Intangible Assets* that prohibit capitalisation of expenditure on an internally generated intangible asset if the asset did not qualify for recognition when the expenditure was incurred; **[Refer: IAS 38 paragraphs 48–67]** and

   (c)   the distinction between financial liabilities and equity instruments (see IAS 32 *Financial Instruments: Presentation*). **[Refer: IAS 32 paragraphs 11 (definitions of a financial liability and an equity instrument), 15–32 and AG3–AG35]**

IAS 12 *Income Taxes*

IG5   An entity applies IAS 12 to temporary differences between the carrying amount of the assets and liabilities in its opening IFRS statement of financial position and their tax bases.
[Refer: paragraphs 7–9]

IG6   In accordance with IAS 12, the measurement of current and deferred tax reflects tax rates and tax laws that have been enacted or substantively enacted by the end of the reporting period. **[Refer: IAS 12 paragraphs 46–49]** An entity accounts for the effect of changes in tax rates and tax laws when those changes are enacted or substantively enacted. **[Refer: IAS 12 paragraphs 47 and 60]**

     [Refer: paragraphs 7–9]

IAS 16 *Property, Plant and Equipment*

IG7   If an entity's depreciation methods and rates in accordance with previous GAAP are acceptable in accordance with IFRSs, **[Refer: IAS 16 paragraphs 43–62]** it accounts for any change in estimated useful life or depreciation pattern prospectively from when it makes that change in estimate (paragraphs 14 and 15 of the IFRS and paragraph 61 of IAS 16). However, in some cases, an entity's depreciation methods and rates in accordance with previous GAAP may differ from those that would be acceptable in accordance with IFRSs (for example, if they were adopted solely for tax purposes and do not reflect a reasonable estimate of the asset's useful life). If those differences have a material effect on the financial statements, the entity adjusts accumulated depreciation in its opening IFRS statement of financial position retrospectively so that it complies with IFRSs. **[Refer: paragraphs 14 and 16]**

IG8   An entity may elect to use one of the following amounts as the deemed cost of an item of property, plant and equipment:

     (a)   fair value at the date of transition to IFRSs (paragraph D5 of the IFRS), in which case the entity gives the disclosures required by paragraph 30 of the IFRS;

     (b)   a revaluation in accordance with previous GAAP that meets the criteria in paragraph D6 of the IFRS;

     (c)   fair value at the date of an event such as a privatisation or initial public offering (paragraph D8 of the IFRS);

     (d)   an allocation of an amount determined under previous GAAP that meets the criteria in paragraph D8A of the IFRS; or

     (e)   the carrying amount under previous GAAP of an item of property, plant and equipment that is used, or was previously used, in operations subject to rate regulation (paragraph D8B of the IFRS).

IG9   Subsequent depreciation is based on that deemed cost and starts from the date for which the entity established the deemed cost.

IG10   If an entity chooses as its accounting policy the revaluation model in IAS 16 for some or all classes of property, plant and equipment, it presents the cumulative revaluation surplus as a separate component of equity. **[Refer: IAS 16 paragraphs 31–42]** The revaluation surplus at the date of transition to IFRSs is based on a comparison of the carrying amount of the asset at that date with its cost or deemed cost. If the deemed cost is the fair value at the date of transition to IFRSs, the entity gives the disclosures required by paragraph 30 of the IFRS.

IG11   If revaluations in accordance with previous GAAP did not satisfy the criteria in paragraph D6 or D8 of the IFRS, an entity measures the revalued assets in its opening statement of financial position on one of the following bases:

(a)   cost (or deemed cost) less any accumulated depreciation and any accumulated impairment losses under the cost model in IAS 16; **[Refer: IAS 16 paragraph 30]**

(b)   deemed cost, being the fair value at the date of transition to IFRSs (paragraph D5 of the IFRS); or

(c)   revalued amount, if the entity adopts the revaluation model in IAS 16 **[Refer: IAS 16 paragraphs 31–42]** as its accounting policy in accordance with IFRSs for all items of property, plant and equipment in the same class.

IG12   IAS 16 requires each part of an item of property, plant and equipment with a cost that is significant in relation to the total cost of the item to be depreciated separately. However, IAS 16 does not prescribe the unit of measure for recognition of an asset, ie what constitutes an item of property, plant and equipment. Thus, judgement is required in applying the recognition criteria to an entity's specific circumstances (see IAS 16 paragraphs 9 and 43).

IG13   In some cases, the construction or commissioning of an asset results in an obligation for an entity to dismantle or remove the asset and restore the site on which the asset stands. An entity applies IAS 37 *Provisions, Contingent Liabilities and Contingent Assets* in recognising and measuring any resulting provision. **[Refer: IAS 37 paragraphs 14–26 and 36–52, and example 3 in Implementation Guidance part C to IAS 37]** The entity applies IAS 16 in determining the resulting amount included in the cost of the asset, before depreciation and impairment losses. **[Refer: IAS 16 paragraph 16(c)]** Items such as depreciation and, when applicable, impairment losses cause differences between the carrying amount of the liability and the amount included in the carrying amount of the asset. An entity accounts for changes in such liabilities in accordance with IFRIC 1 *Changes in Existing Decommissioning, Restoration and Similar Liabilities*. However, paragraph D21 of IFRS 1 provides an exemption for changes that occurred before the date of transition to IFRSs, and prescribes an alternative treatment where the exemption is used. An example of the first-time adoption of IFRIC 1, which illustrates the use of this exemption, is given at paragraphs IG201–IG203.

IFRS 16 *Leases*

IG14   At the date of transition to IFRSs, a lessor classifies leases as operating leases or finance leases on the basis of circumstances existing at the inception of the lease (IFRS 16 paragraph 66). Lease classification is reassessed only if there is a lease modification. Changes in estimates (for example, changes in estimates of the economic life or of the residual value of the underlying asset) or changes in circumstances (for example, default by the lessee) do not give rise to a new classification of a lease.

[Refer:
paragraphs 7 and 10
IFRS 16 paragraph 66]

IG15   [Deleted]

IG16   [Deleted]

IFRS 15 *Revenue from Contracts with Customers*

IG17   If an entity has received amounts that do not yet qualify for recognition as revenue in accordance with IFRS 15 (for example, the proceeds of a sale that does not qualify for revenue recognition), the entity recognises a liability in its opening IFRS statement of financial position and measures that liability at the amount received, adjusted (if appropriate) for a significant financing component in accordance with IFRS 15.

[Refer: paragraphs 7–9]

IAS 19 *Employee Benefits*

IG18   [Deleted]

IG19   An entity's actuarial assumptions **[Refer: IAS 19 paragraphs 75–98]** at the date of transition to IFRSs are consistent with actuarial assumptions made for the same date in accordance with previous GAAP (after adjustments to reflect any difference in accounting policies), unless there is objective evidence that those assumptions were in error (paragraph 14 of the IFRS). The impact of any later revisions to those assumptions is an actuarial gain or loss of the period in which the entity makes the revisions.

[Refer: paragraph 15]

IG20   An entity may need to make actuarial assumptions **[Refer: IAS 19 paragraphs 75–98]** at the date of transition to IFRSs that were not necessary in accordance with its previous GAAP. Such actuarial assumptions do not reflect conditions that arose after the date of transition to IFRSs. In particular, discount rates and the fair value of plan assets at the date of transition to IFRSs reflect market conditions at that date. Similarly, the entity's actuarial assumptions at the date of transition to IFRSs about future employee turnover rates do not reflect a significant increase in estimated employee turnover rates as a result of a curtailment of the pension plan that occurred after the date of transition to IFRSs (paragraph 16 of the IFRS).

IG21   In many cases, an entity's first IFRS financial statements will reflect measurements of employee benefit obligations at three dates: the end of the first IFRS reporting period, the date of the comparative statement of financial position and the date of transition to IFRSs. IAS 19 encourages an entity to involve a qualified actuary in the measurement of all material post-employment benefit obligations. To minimise costs, an entity may request a qualified actuary to carry out a detailed actuarial valuation at one or two of these dates and roll the valuation(s) forward or back to the other date(s). Any such roll forward or roll back reflects any material transactions and other material events (including changes in market prices and interest rates) between those dates (IAS 19 paragraph 57).

IAS 21 *The Effects of Changes in Foreign Exchange Rates*

IG21A   An entity may, in accordance with previous GAAP, have treated goodwill arising on the acquisition of a foreign operation and any fair value adjustments to the carrying amounts of assets and liabilities arising on the acquisition of that foreign operation as assets and liabilities of the entity rather than as assets and liabilities of the foreign operation. If so, the entity is permitted to apply prospectively the requirements of paragraph 47 of IAS 21 to all acquisitions occurring after the date of transition to IFRSs.

[Refer: paragraphs D12 and D13]

IFRS 3 *Business Combinations*

IG22   The following examples illustrate the effect of Appendix C of the IFRS, assuming that a first-time adopter uses the exemption.

[Refer: paragraph C1]

IG Example 2 Business combination

Background

Entity B's first IFRS financial statements are for a period that ends on 31 December 20X5 and include comparative information [Refer: paragraphs 21 and 22] for 20X4 only. On 1 July 20X1, entity B acquired 100 per cent of subsidiary C. In accordance with its previous GAAP, entity B:

(a) classified the business combination as an acquisition by entity B.

(b) measured the assets acquired and liabilities assumed at the following amounts in accordance with previous GAAP at 31 December 20X3 (date of transition to IFRSs):

  (i) identifiable assets less liabilities for which IFRSs require cost-based measurement at a date after the business combination: CU200 (with a tax base of CU150 and an applicable tax rate of 30 per cent).

  (ii) pension liability (for which the present value of the defined benefit obligation measured in accordance with IAS 19 *Employee Benefits* is CU130 and the fair value of plan assets is CU100): nil (because entity B used a pay as you go cash method of accounting for pensions in accordance with its previous GAAP). The tax base of the pension liability is also nil.

  (iii) goodwill: CU180.

(c) did not, at the acquisition date, recognise deferred tax arising from temporary differences associated with the identifiable assets acquired and liabilities assumed.

continued...

...continued

IG Example 2 Business combination

Application of requirements
[Refer: paragraph C1]

In its opening (consolidated) IFRS statement of financial position, entity B:

(a) classifies the business combination as an acquisition by entity B even if the business combination would have qualified in accordance with IFRS 3 as a reverse acquisition by subsidiary C (paragraph C4(a) of the IFRS).

(b) does not adjust the accumulated amortisation of goodwill. Entity B tests the goodwill for impairment in accordance with IAS 36 *Impairment of Assets* **[Refer: IAS 36 paragraphs 80–99]** and recognises any resulting impairment loss, based on conditions that existed at the date of transition to IFRSs. If no impairment exists, the carrying amount of the goodwill remains at CU180 (paragraph C4(g) of the IFRS).

(c) for those net identifiable assets acquired for which IFRSs require cost-based measurement at a date after the business combination, treats their carrying amount in accordance with previous GAAP immediately after the business combination as their deemed cost at that date (paragraph C4(e) of the IFRS).

(d) does not restate the accumulated depreciation and amortisation of the net identifiable assets in (c), unless the depreciation methods and rates in accordance with previous GAAP result in amounts that differ materially from those required in accordance with IFRSs (for example, if they were adopted solely for tax purposes and do not reflect a reasonable estimate of the asset's useful life in accordance with IFRSs). If no such restatement is made, the carrying amount of those assets in the opening IFRS statement of financial position equals their carrying amount in accordance with previous GAAP at the date of transition to IFRSs (CU200) (paragraph IG7).
[Refer: paragraphs 14 and 15]

(e) if there is any indication that identifiable assets are impaired, tests those assets for impairment, based on conditions that existed at the date of transition to IFRSs (see IAS 36).

[Refer: Implementation Guidance paragraphs IG39–IG43]

continued...

...continued

IG Example 2 Business combination

(f)   recognises the pension liability, and measures it, at the present value of the defined benefit obligation (CU130) less the fair value of the plan assets (CU100), giving a carrying amount of CU30, with a corresponding debit of CU30 to retained earnings (paragraph C4(d) of the IFRS). However, if subsidiary C had already adopted IFRSs in an earlier period, entity B would measure the pension liability at the same amount as in subsidiary C's financial statements (paragraph D17 of the IFRS and IG Example 9).

(g)   recognises a net deferred tax liability of CU6 (CU20 at 30 per cent) arising from:

    (i)   the taxable temporary difference of CU50 (CU200 less CU150) associated with the identifiable assets acquired and non-pension liabilities assumed, less

    (ii)   the deductible temporary difference of CU30 (CU30 less nil) associated with the pension liability.

The entity recognises the resulting increase in the deferred tax liability as a deduction from retained earnings (paragraph C4(k) of the IFRS). If a taxable temporary difference arises from the initial recognition of the goodwill, entity B does not recognise the resulting deferred tax liability (paragraph 15(a) of IAS 12 *Income Taxes*).

IG Example 3 Business combination—restructuring provision

Background

Entity D's first IFRS financial statements are for a period that ends on 31 December 20X5 and include comparative information **[Refer: paragraphs 21 and 22]** for 20X4 only. On 1 July 20X3, entity D acquired 100 per cent of subsidiary E. In accordance with its previous GAAP, entity D recognised an (undiscounted) restructuring provision **[Refer: IAS 37 paragraphs 70–83]** of CU100 that would not have qualified as an identifiable liability in accordance with IFRS 3. **[Refer: IFRS 3 paragraphs 10–17]** The recognition of this restructuring provision increased goodwill by CU100. At 31 December 20X3 (date of transition to IFRSs), entity D:

(a)   had paid restructuring costs of CU60; and

(b)   estimated that it would pay further costs of CU40 in 20X4, and that the effects of discounting were immaterial. At 31 December 20X3, those further costs did not qualify for recognition as a provision in accordance with IAS 37 *Provisions, Contingent Liabilities and Contingent Assets*. **[Refer: IAS 37 paragraphs 14–26]**

continued...

...continued

IG Example 3 Business combination—restructuring provision

Application of requirements

[Refer: paragraph C1]

In its opening IFRS statement of financial position, entity D:

(a) does not recognise a restructuring provision (paragraph C4(c) of the IFRS).

(b) does not adjust the amount assigned to goodwill. However, entity D tests the goodwill for impairment in accordance with IAS 36 *Impairment of Assets*, **[Refer: IAS 36 paragraphs 80–99]** and recognises any resulting impairment loss (paragraph C4(g) of the IFRS).

(c) as a result of (a) and (b), reports retained earnings in its opening IFRS statement of financial position that are higher by CU40 (before income taxes, and before recognising any impairment loss) than in the statement of financial position at the same date in accordance with previous GAAP.

IG Example 4 Business combination—intangible assets

Background

Entity F's first IFRS financial statements are for a period that ends on 31 December 20X5 and include comparative information **[Refer: paragraphs 21 and 22]** for 20X4 only. On 1 July 20X1 entity F acquired 75 per cent of subsidiary G. In accordance with its previous GAAP, entity F assigned an initial carrying amount of CU200 to intangible assets that would not have qualified for recognition in accordance with IAS 38 *Intangible Assets*. **[Refer: IAS 38 paragraphs 9–17 and 33–41]** The tax base of the intangible assets was nil, giving rise to a deferred tax liability (at 30 per cent) of CU60.

On 31 December 20X3 (the date of transition to IFRSs) the carrying amount of the intangible assets in accordance with previous GAAP was CU160, and the carrying amount of the related deferred tax liability was CU48 (30 per cent of CU160).

continued...

...continued

IG Example 4 Business combination—intangible assets

Application of requirements
[Refer: paragraph C1]

Because the intangible assets do not qualify for recognition as separate assets in accordance with IAS 38, entity F transfers them to goodwill, together with the related deferred tax liability (CU48) and non-controlling interests (paragraph C4(g)(i) of the IFRS). The related non-controlling interests amount to CU28 (25 per cent of [CU160 − CU48 = CU112]). Thus, the increase in goodwill is CU84 — intangible assets (CU160) less deferred tax liability (CU48) less non-controlling interests (CU28).

Entity F tests the goodwill for impairment in accordance with IAS 36 *Impairment of Assets* **[Refer: IAS 36 paragraphs 80–99]** and recognises any resulting impairment loss, based on conditions that existed at the date of transition to IFRSs (paragraph C4(g)(ii) of the IFRS).

IG Example 5 Business combination—goodwill deducted from equity and treatment of related intangible assets

Background

Entity H acquired a subsidiary before the date of transition to IFRSs. In accordance with its previous GAAP, entity H:

(a) recognised goodwill as an immediate deduction from equity;

(b) recognised an intangible asset of the subsidiary that does not qualify for recognition as an asset in accordance with IAS 38 *Intangible Assets*; **[Refer: IAS 38 paragraphs 9–17 and 33–41]** and

(c) did not recognise an intangible asset of the subsidiary that would qualify in accordance with IAS 38 for recognition as an asset in the financial statements of the subsidiary. The subsidiary held the asset at the date of its acquisition by entity H.

continued...

...continued

IG Example 5 Business combination—goodwill deducted from equity and treatment of related intangible assets

Application of requirements
[Refer: paragraph C1]

In its opening IFRS statement of financial position, entity H:

(a) does not recognise the goodwill, as it did not recognise the goodwill as an asset in accordance with previous GAAP (paragraph C4(g)–(i) of the IFRS).

(b) does not recognise the intangible asset that does not qualify for recognition as an asset in accordance with IAS 38. Because entity H deducted goodwill from equity in accordance with its previous GAAP, the elimination of this intangible asset reduces retained earnings (paragraph C4(c)(ii) of the IFRS).

(c) recognises the intangible asset that qualifies in accordance with IAS 38 for recognition as an asset in the financial statements of the subsidiary, even though the amount assigned to it in accordance with previous GAAP in entity H's consolidated financial statements was nil (paragraph C4(f) of the IFRS). The recognition criteria in IAS 38 include the availability of a reliable measurement of cost (paragraphs IG45–IG48) and entity H measures the asset at cost less accumulated depreciation and less any impairment losses identified in accordance with IAS 36 *Impairment of Assets*. Because entity H deducted goodwill from equity in accordance with its previous GAAP, the recognition of this intangible asset increases retained earnings (paragraph C4(c) (ii) of the IFRS). However, if this intangible asset had been subsumed in goodwill recognised as an asset in accordance with previous GAAP, entity H would have decreased the carrying amount of that goodwill accordingly (and, if applicable, adjusted deferred tax and non-controlling interests) (paragraph C4(g)(i) of the IFRS).

IG Example 6 Business combination—subsidiary not consolidated in accordance with previous GAAP

Background

Parent J's date of transition to IFRSs is 1 January 20X4. In accordance with its previous GAAP, parent J did not consolidate its 75 per cent subsidiary K, acquired in a business combination on 15 July 20X1. On 1 January 20X4:

(a) the cost of parent J's investment in subsidiary K is CU180.

(b) in accordance with IFRSs, subsidiary K would measure its assets at CU500 and its liabilities (including deferred tax in accordance with IAS 12 *Income Taxes*) at CU300. On this basis, subsidiary K's net assets are CU200 in accordance with IFRSs.

continued...

...continued

IG Example 6 Business combination—subsidiary not consolidated in accordance with previous GAAP

Application of requirements
[Refer: paragraph C1]

Parent J consolidates subsidiary K. The consolidated statement of financial position at 1 January 20X4 includes:

(a) subsidiary K's assets at CU500 and liabilities at CU300;

(b) non-controlling interests of CU50 (25 per cent of [CU500 – CU300]); and

(c) goodwill of CU30 (cost of CU180 less 75 per cent of [CU500 – CU300]) (paragraph C4(j) of the IFRS). Parent J tests the goodwill for impairment in accordance with IAS 36 *Impairment of Assets* **[Refer: IAS 36 paragraphs 80–99]** and recognises any resulting impairment loss, based on conditions that existed at the date of transition to IFRSs (paragraph C4(g)(ii) of the IFRS).

IG Example 7 Business combination—lease in which the acquiree was a lessee not capitalised in accordance with previous GAAP

Background

Parent L's date of transition to IFRSs is 1 January 20X4. Parent L acquired subsidiary M on 15 January 20X1 and did not capitalise leases in which subsidiary M was a lessee. If subsidiary M prepared financial statements in accordance with IFRSs, it would recognise lease liabilities of CU300 and right-of-use assets of CU250 at 1 January 20X4.

Application of requirements
[Refer: paragraph C1]

Parent L has elected not to apply the transition reliefs in paragraphs D9 and D9B–D9E of this Standard. In its consolidated opening IFRS statement of financial position, parent L recognises lease liabilities of CU300 and right-of-use assets of CU250, and charges CU50 to retained earnings (paragraph C4(f)).

IAS 23 *Borrowing Costs*

IG23   On first adopting IFRSs, an entity begins capitalising borrowing costs (IAS 23 as revised in 2007). In accordance with paragraph D23 of the IFRS, an entity:
[Refer: paragraphs 7–9]

(a) capitalises borrowing costs relating to qualifying assets for which the commencement date for capitalisation is on or after 1 January 2009 or the date of transition to IFRSs (whichever is later);

(b)   may elect to designate any date before 1 January 2009 or the date of transition to IFRSs (whichever is later) and to capitalise borrowing costs relating to all qualifying assets for which the commencement date for capitalisation is on or after that date.

However, if the entity established a deemed cost for an asset, the entity does not capitalise borrowing costs incurred before the date of the measurement that established the deemed cost. **[Refer: paragraphs D5–D8]**

IG24   IAS 23 requires disclosure of interest capitalised during the period. **[Refer: IAS 23 paragraph 26(b)]** Neither IAS 23 nor the IFRS requires disclosure of the cumulative amount capitalised.

IG25   [Deleted]

IFRS 10 *Consolidated Financial Statements*

IG26   A first-time adopter consolidates all subsidiaries (as defined in IFRS 10), unless IFRS 10 requires otherwise.
[Refer:
paragraph 7
IAS 27 paragraphs 9–17]

IG27   If a first-time adopter did not consolidate a subsidiary in accordance with previous GAAP, then:

(a)   in its consolidated financial statements, the first-time adopter measures the subsidiary's assets and liabilities at the same carrying amounts as in the IFRS financial statements of the subsidiary, after adjusting for consolidation procedures **[Refer: IFRS 10 paragraphs B86–B96]** and for the effects of the business combination in which it acquired the subsidiary (paragraph D17 of the IFRS). If the subsidiary has not adopted IFRSs in its financial statements, the carrying amounts described in the previous sentence are those that IFRSs would require in those financial statements (paragraph C4(j) of the IFRS).

(b)   if the parent acquired the subsidiary in a business combination before the date of transition to IFRS, the parent recognises goodwill, as explained in IG Example 6.

(c)   if the parent did not acquire the subsidiary in a business combination because it created the subsidiary, the parent does not recognise goodwill.

[Refer: paragraphs 7–10]

IG28   When a first-time adopter adjusts the carrying amounts of assets and liabilities of its subsidiaries in preparing its opening IFRS statement of financial position, this may affect non-controlling interests and deferred tax.

IG29   IG Examples 8 and 9 illustrate paragraphs D16 and D17 of the IFRS, which address cases where a parent and its subsidiary become first-time adopters at different dates.

IG Example 8 Parent adopts IFRSs before subsidiary

Background

Parent N presents its (consolidated) first IFRS financial statements in 20X5. Its foreign subsidiary O, wholly owned by parent N since formation, prepares information in accordance with IFRSs for internal consolidation purposes from that date, but subsidiary O does not present its first IFRS financial statements until 20X7.

Application of requirements
[Refer: paragraphs D1 and D16]

If subsidiary O applies paragraph D16(a) of the IFRS, the carrying amounts of its assets and liabilities are the same in both its opening IFRS statement of financial position at 1 January 20X6 and parent N's consolidated statement of financial position (except for adjustments for consolidation procedures) **[Refer: IFRS 10 paragraphs B86–B96]** and are based on parent N's date of transition to IFRSs.

Alternatively, subsidiary O may, in accordance with paragraph D16(b) of the IFRS, measure all its assets or liabilities based on its own date of transition to IFRSs (1 January 20X6). However, the fact that subsidiary O becomes a first-time adopter in 20X7 does not change the carrying amounts of its assets and liabilities in parent N's consolidated financial statements.

IG Example 9 Subsidiary adopts IFRSs before parent

Background

Parent P presents its (consolidated) first IFRS financial statements in 20X7. Its foreign subsidiary Q, wholly owned by parent P since formation, presented its first IFRS financial statements in 20X5. Until 20X7, subsidiary Q prepared information for internal consolidation purposes in accordance with parent P's previous GAAP.

Application of requirements
[Refer: paragraphs D1 and D17]

The carrying amounts of subsidiary Q's assets and liabilities at 1 January 20X6 are the same in both parent P's (consolidated) opening IFRS statement of financial position and subsidiary Q's financial statements (except for adjustments for consolidation procedures) **[Refer: IFRS 10 paragraphs B86–B96]** and are based on subsidiary Q's date of transition to IFRSs. The fact that parent P becomes a first-time adopter in 20X7 does not change those carrying amounts (paragraph D17 of the IFRS).

IG30   Paragraphs D16 and D17 of the IFRS do not override the following requirements:

(a)   to apply Appendix C of the IFRS to assets acquired, and liabilities assumed, in a business combination that occurred before the acquirer's date of transition to IFRSs. However, the acquirer applies paragraph D17 to new assets acquired, and liabilities assumed, by the acquiree after that business combination and still held at the acquirer's date of transition to IFRSs.

(b)   to apply the rest of the IFRS in measuring all assets and liabilities for which paragraphs D16 and D17 are not relevant.

(c)   to give all disclosures required by the IFRS as of the first-time adopter's own date of transition to IFRSs.

IG31   Paragraph D16 of the IFRS applies if a subsidiary becomes a first-time adopter later than its parent, for example if the subsidiary previously prepared a reporting package in accordance with IFRSs for consolidation purposes but did not present a full set of financial statements in accordance with IFRSs. This may be relevant not only when a subsidiary's reporting package complies fully with the recognition and measurement requirements of IFRSs, but also when it is adjusted centrally for matters such as review of events after the reporting period and central allocation of pension costs. For the disclosure required by paragraph 26 of the IFRS, adjustments made centrally to an unpublished reporting package are not corrections of errors. However, paragraph D16 does not permit a subsidiary to ignore misstatements that are immaterial to the consolidated financial statements of its parent but material to its own financial statements.

IAS 29 *Financial Reporting in Hyperinflationary Economies*

IG32   An entity complies with IAS 21 *The Effects of Changes in Foreign Exchange Rates* in determining its functional currency and presentation currency. **[Refer: IAS 21 paragraphs 8–14 and 17–19]** When the entity prepares its opening IFRS statement of financial position, it applies IAS 29 to any periods during which the economy of the functional currency or presentation currency was hyperinflationary. **[Refer: IAS 29 paragraphs 1–4]**
[Refer: paragraphs 7–9]

IG33   An entity may elect to use the fair value of an item of property, plant and equipment at the date of transition to IFRSs as its deemed cost at that date (paragraph D5 of the IFRS), in which case it gives the disclosures required by paragraph 30 of the IFRS.
[Refer: paragraphs 10 and D1]

IG34   If an entity elects to use the exemptions in paragraphs D5–D8 of the IFRS, it applies IAS 29 to periods after the date for which the revalued amount or fair value was determined.

IAS 32 *Financial Instruments: Presentation*

IG35   In its opening IFRS statement of financial position, an entity applies the criteria in IAS 32 to classify financial instruments issued (or components of compound instruments issued) as either financial liabilities or equity instruments in accordance with the substance of the contractual arrangement when the instrument first satisfied the recognition criteria in IAS 32 (paragraphs 15 and 30), without considering events after that date (other than changes to the terms of the instruments).

[Refer: paragraphs 7–9]

IG36   For compound instruments outstanding at the date of transition to IFRSs, an entity determines the initial carrying amounts of the components on the basis of circumstances existing when the instrument was issued (IAS 32 paragraph 30). An entity determines those carrying amounts using the version of IAS 32 effective at the end of its first IFRS reporting period. If the liability component is no longer outstanding at the date of transition to IFRSs, a first-time adopter need not separate the initial equity component of the instrument from the cumulative interest accreted on the liability component (paragraph D18 of the IFRS).

[Refer: paragraphs 7–10]

IAS 34 *Interim Financial Reporting*

IG37   IAS 34 applies if an entity is required, or elects, to present an interim financial report in accordance with IFRSs. Accordingly, neither IAS 34 nor the IFRS requires an entity:

(a)   to present interim financial reports that comply with IAS 34; or

(b)   to prepare new versions of interim financial reports presented in accordance with previous GAAP. However, if an entity does prepare an interim financial report in accordance with IAS 34 for part of the period covered by its first IFRS financial statements, the entity restates the comparative information presented in that report so that it complies with IFRSs.

[Refer:
paragraph 2(b)
IAS 34 paragraph 1]

IG38   An entity applies the IFRS in each interim financial report that it presents in accordance with IAS 34 for part of the period covered by its first IFRS financial statements. In particular, paragraph 32 of the IFRS requires an entity to disclose various reconciliations (see IG Example 10).

[Refer: paragraphs 2(b) and 33]

IG Example 10 Interim financial reporting

Background

Entity R's first IFRS financial statements are for a period that ends on 31 December 20X5, and its first interim financial report in accordance with IAS 34 is for the quarter ended 31 March 20X5. Entity R prepared previous GAAP annual [Refer: IAS 1 paragraphs 36 and 37] financial statements for the year ended 31 December 20X4, and prepared quarterly reports throughout 20X4.

---

continued...

...continued

IG Example 10 Interim financial reporting

Application of requirements

In each quarterly interim financial report for 20X5, entity R includes reconciliations of:

(a)   its equity in accordance with previous GAAP at the end of the comparable quarter of 20X4 to its equity in accordance with IFRSs at that date; and

(b)   its total comprehensive income (or, if it did not report such a total, profit or loss) in accordance with previous GAAP for the comparable quarter of 20X4 (current and year to date) to its total comprehensive income in accordance with IFRSs.

[Refer: paragraph 32(a)]

In addition to the reconciliations required by (a) and (b) and the disclosures required by IAS 34, entity R's interim financial report for the first quarter of 20X5 includes reconciliations of (or a cross-reference to another published document that includes these reconciliations):

(a)   its equity in accordance with previous GAAP at 1 January 20X4 and 31 December 20X4 to its equity in accordance with IFRSs at those dates; and

(b)   its total comprehensive income (or, if it did not report such a total, profit or loss) for 20X4 in accordance with previous GAAP to its total comprehensive income for 20X4 in accordance with IFRSs.

[Refer: paragraphs 24(a) and (b) and 32(b)]

Each of the above reconciliations gives sufficient detail to enable users to understand the material [Refer: IAS 34 paragraphs 23–25] adjustments to the statement of financial position and statement of comprehensive income. Entity R also explains the material adjustments to the statement of cash flows. [Refer: paragraphs 25 and 32(b)]

If entity R becomes aware of errors made in accordance with previous GAAP, the reconciliations distinguish the correction of those errors from changes in accounting policies. [Refer: paragraphs 26 and 32]

If entity R did not, in its most recent annual financial statements in accordance with previous GAAP, disclose information material to an understanding of the current interim period, its interim financial reports for 20X5 disclose that information or include a cross-reference to another published document that includes it (paragraph 33 of the IFRS).

IAS 36 *Impairment of Assets* and IAS 37 *Provisions, Contingent Liabilities and Contingent Assets*

IG39   An entity applies IAS 36 in:

(a)   determining whether any impairment loss exists at the date of transition to IFRSs; and
**[Refer:
paragraphs C1 and C4(g)(ii)
IAS 36 paragraphs 7–17]**

(b)   measuring any impairment loss that exists at that date, **[Refer: IAS 36 paragraphs 18–108]** and reversing any impairment loss that no longer exists at that date. **[Refer: IAS 36 paragraphs 109–125]** An entity's first IFRS financial statements include the disclosures that IAS 36 would have required if the entity had recognised those impairment losses or reversals in the period beginning with the date of transition to IFRSs (paragraph 24(c) of the IFRS). **[Refer: IAS 36 paragraphs 126–137]**

[Refer: paragraphs 7–10]

IG40   The estimates used to determine whether an entity recognises an impairment loss or provision (and to measure any such impairment loss or provision) at the date of transition to IFRSs are consistent with estimates made for the same date in accordance with previous GAAP (after adjustments to reflect any difference in accounting policies), unless there is objective evidence that those estimates were in error (paragraphs 14 and 15 of the IFRS). The entity reports the impact of any later revisions to those estimates as an event of the period in which it makes the revisions.
**[Refer:
IAS 36
IAS 37]**

IG41   In assessing whether it needs to recognise an impairment loss or provision (and in measuring any such impairment loss or provision) at the date of transition to IFRSs, an entity may need to make estimates for that date that were not necessary in accordance with its previous GAAP. Such estimates and assumptions do not reflect conditions that arose after the date of transition to IFRSs (paragraph 16 of the IFRS).
**[Refer:
IAS 36
IAS 37]**

IG42   The transitional provisions in IAS 36 and IAS 37 do not apply to an entity's opening IFRS statement of financial position (paragraph 9 of the IFRS).

IG43   IAS 36 requires the reversal of impairment losses in some cases. **[Refer: IAS 36 paragraphs 109–125]** If an entity's opening IFRS statement of financial position reflects impairment losses, the entity recognises any later reversal of those impairment losses in profit or loss (except when IAS 36 requires the entity to treat that reversal as a revaluation). This applies to both impairment losses recognised in accordance with previous GAAP and additional impairment losses recognised on transition to IFRSs. **[Refer: IAS 36 paragraphs 117–125]**

IAS 38 *Intangible Assets*

IG44   An entity's opening IFRS statement of financial position:

   (a)   excludes all intangible assets and other intangible items that do not meet the criteria for recognition in accordance with IAS 38 at the date of transition to IFRSs; and

   (b)   includes all intangible assets that meet the recognition criteria in IAS 38 at that date, except for intangible assets acquired in a business combination that were not recognised in the acquirer's consolidated statement of financial position in accordance with previous GAAP and also would not qualify for recognition in accordance with IAS 38 in the separate statement of financial position of the acquiree (see paragraph C4(f) of the IFRS).
           [Refer: paragraphs 7–9]

IG45   The criteria in IAS 38 require an entity to recognise an intangible asset if, and only if:

   (a)   it is probable that the future economic benefits that are attributable to the asset will flow to the entity; and

   (b)   the cost of the asset can be measured reliably.
           [Refer: IAS 38 paragraph 21]

         IAS 38 supplements these two criteria with further, more specific, criteria for internally generated intangible assets.
         [Refer: IAS 38 paragraphs 51–67]

IG46   In accordance with paragraphs 65 and 71 of IAS 38, an entity capitalises the costs of creating internally generated intangible assets prospectively from the date when the recognition criteria are met. IAS 38 does not permit an entity to use hindsight to conclude retrospectively that these recognition criteria are met. Therefore, even if an entity concludes retrospectively that a future inflow of economic benefits from an internally generated intangible asset is probable and the entity is able to reconstruct the costs reliably, IAS 38 prohibits it from capitalising the costs incurred before the date when the entity both:

   (a)   concludes, based on an assessment made and documented at the date of that conclusion, that it is probable that future economic benefits from the asset will flow to the entity; and

   (b)   has a reliable system for accumulating the costs of internally generated intangible assets when, or shortly after, they are incurred.

IG47   If an internally generated intangible asset qualifies for recognition at the date of transition to IFRSs, an entity recognises the asset in its opening IFRS statement of financial position even if it had recognised the related expenditure as an expense in accordance with previous GAAP. If the asset does not qualify for recognition in accordance with IAS 38 until a later date, its cost is the sum of the expenditure incurred from that later date.

[Refer: paragraphs 7–10]

IG48 The criteria discussed in paragraph IG45 also apply to an intangible asset acquired separately. In many cases, contemporaneous documentation prepared to support the decision to acquire the asset will contain an assessment of the future economic benefits. Furthermore, as explained in paragraph 26 of IAS 38, the cost of a separately acquired intangible asset can usually be measured reliably.

IG49 For an intangible asset acquired in a business combination before the date of transition to IFRSs, its carrying amount in accordance with previous GAAP immediately after the business combination is its deemed cost in accordance with IFRSs at that date (paragraph C4(e) of the IFRS). If that carrying amount was zero, the acquirer does not recognise the intangible asset in its consolidated opening IFRS statement of financial position, unless it would qualify in accordance with IAS 38, applying the criteria discussed in paragraphs IG45–IG48, for recognition at the date of transition to IFRSs in the statement of financial position of the acquiree (paragraph C4(f) of the IFRS). If those recognition criteria are met, the acquirer measures the asset on the basis that IAS 38 would require in the statement of financial position of the acquiree. The resulting adjustment affects goodwill (paragraph C4(g)(i) of the IFRS).

IG50 A first-time adopter may elect to use the fair value of an intangible asset at the date of an event such as a privatisation or initial public offering as its deemed cost at the date of that event (paragraph D8 of the IFRS), provided that the intangible asset qualifies for recognition in accordance with IAS 38 (paragraph 10 of the IFRS). In addition, if, and only if, an intangible asset meets both the recognition criteria in IAS 38 (including reliable measurement of original cost) and the criteria in IAS 38 for revaluation (including the existence of an active market), a first-time adopter may elect to use one of the following amounts as its deemed cost (paragraph D7 of the IFRS):

(a) fair value at the date of transition to IFRSs (paragraph D5 of the IFRS), in which case the entity gives the disclosures required by paragraph 30 of the IFRS; or

(b) a revaluation in accordance with previous GAAP that meets the criteria in paragraph D6 of the IFRS.

IG51 If an entity's amortisation methods and rates in accordance with previous GAAP would be acceptable in accordance with IFRSs, the entity does not restate the accumulated amortisation in its opening IFRS statement of financial position. Instead, the entity accounts for any change in estimated useful life or amortisation pattern prospectively from the period when it makes that change in estimate (paragraph 14 of the IFRS and paragraph 104 of IAS 38). **[Refer: paragraph 15]** However, in some cases, an entity's amortisation methods and rates in accordance with previous GAAP may differ from those that would be acceptable in accordance with IFRSs (for example, if they were adopted solely for tax purposes and do not reflect a reasonable estimate of the asset's useful life). If those differences have a material effect on the financial statements, the entity adjusts the accumulated amortisation in its opening IFRS statement of financial position retrospectively so that it complies with IFRSs (paragraph 14 of the IFRS). However, if an entity uses the exemption in paragraph D8B, it uses the carrying amount of the intangible asset at the date of transition to IFRSs as deemed cost as if it had acquired an intangible asset with the same remaining service potential for that amount at the date of transition to IFRSs. Subsequent amortisation is based on that deemed cost and starts from the date of transition to IFRSs.

[Refer: paragraphs 7–10 and 16]

IFRS 9 *Financial Instruments*

IG52   An entity recognises and measures all financial assets and financial liabilities in its opening IFRS statement of financial position in accordance with IFRS 9, except as specified in paragraphs B2–B6 of the IFRS, which address derecognition and hedge accounting.

[Refer:

paragraphs 7–12

IAS 32]

Recognition

IG53   An entity recognises all financial assets and financial liabilities (including all derivatives) that qualify for recognition in accordance with IFRS 9 and have not yet qualified for derecognition in accordance with IFRS 9, except non-derivative financial assets and non-derivative financial liabilities derecognised in accordance with previous GAAP before the date of transition to IFRSs, to which the entity does not choose to apply paragraph B3 (see paragraphs B2 and B3 of the IFRS). For example, an entity that does not apply paragraph B3 does not recognise assets transferred in a securitisation, transfer or other derecognition transaction that occurred before the date of transition to IFRSs if transactions qualified for derecognition in accordance with previous GAAP. However, if the entity uses the same securitisation arrangement or other derecognition arrangement for further transfers after the date of transition to IFRSs, those further transfers qualify for derecognition only if they meet the derecognition criteria of IFRS 9.

IG54   An entity does not recognise financial assets and financial liabilities [Refer: IAS 32] that do not qualify for recognition in accordance with IFRS 9, [Refer: IFRS 9 paragraphs 3.1.1, B3.1.1 and B3.1.2] or have already qualified for derecognition in accordance with IFRS 9. [Refer: IFRS 9 sections 3.2 and 3.3] [Refer: paragraphs 7–12, B2 and B3]

Embedded derivatives

IG55   When IFRS 9 requires an entity to separate an embedded derivative from a host contract, the initial carrying amounts of the components at the date when the instrument first satisfies the recognition criteria in IFRS 9 reflect circumstances at that date (IFRS 9 paragraph 4.3.3). If the entity cannot determine the initial carrying amounts of the embedded derivative and host contract reliably, it measures the entire combined contract as at fair value through profit or loss (IFRS 9 paragraph 4.3.6).

[Refer:

paragraphs 7–12

Basis for Conclusions paragraphs BC65 and BC66]

Measurement

IG56   In preparing its opening IFRS statement of financial position, an entity applies the criteria in IFRS 9 to classify financial instruments on the basis of the facts and circumstances that exist at the date of transition to IFRSs. The resulting classifications are applied retrospectively.

IG57   For those financial assets and financial liabilities measured at amortised cost in the opening IFRS statement of financial position, an entity determines the gross carrying amount of the financial assets and the amortised cost of the financial liabilities on the basis of circumstances existing when the assets and liabilities first satisfied the recognition criteria in IFRS 9. However, if the entity acquired those financial assets and financial liabilities in a past business combination, their carrying amount in accordance with previous GAAP immediately following the business combination is their deemed cost in accordance with IFRSs at that date (paragraph C4(e) of the IFRS).

[Refer: paragraphs 7–12]

IG58   [Deleted]

Transition adjustments

IG58A   An entity shall treat an adjustment to the carrying amount of a financial asset or financial liability as a transition adjustment to be recognised in the opening balance of retained earnings (or another component of equity, as appropriate) at the date of transition to IFRSs only to the extent that it results from adopting IFRS 9. Because all derivatives, other than those that are financial guarantee contracts, a commitment to provide a loan at a below-market interest rate, a loan commitment that is subject to the impairment requirements of IFRS 9 or are designated and effective hedging instruments, are measured at fair value through profit or loss, the differences between the previous carrying amount (which may have been zero) and the fair value of the derivatives are recognised as an adjustment of the balance of retained earnings at the beginning of the financial year in which IFRS 9 is initially applied (other than for a derivative that is a financial guarantee contract, a commitment to provide a loan at a below-market interest rate or a designated and effective hedging instrument).

[Refer: paragraphs 7–12]

IG58B   IAS 8 (as revised in 2003) applies to adjustments resulting from changes in estimates. If an entity is unable to determine whether a particular portion of the adjustment is a transition adjustment or a change in estimate, it treats that portion as a change in accounting estimate in accordance with IAS 8, with appropriate disclosures (IAS 8 paragraphs 32–40).

IG59   An entity may, in accordance with its previous GAAP, have measured investments at fair value and recognised the revaluation gain outside profit or loss. If an investment is classified as at fair value through profit or loss, the pre-IFRS 9 revaluation gain that had been recognised outside profit or loss is reclassified into retained earnings on initial application of IFRS 9. If, on initial application of IFRS 9, an investment is measured at fair value through other comprehensive income in accordance with paragraph 4.1.2A of IFRS 9 or is designated at fair value through other comprehensive income in accordance with paragraph 5.7.5 of IFRS 9, then the pre-IFRS 9 revaluation gain is recognised in a separate component of equity. Subsequently, the entity recognises gains and losses on these financial assets in accordance with IFRS 9. **[Refer: paragraphs 7–12]**

Hedge accounting

IG60   Paragraphs B4–B6 of the IFRS deal with hedge accounting. The designation and documentation of a hedge relationship must be completed on or before the date of transition to IFRSs if the hedge relationship is to qualify for hedge accounting from that date. Hedge accounting can be applied prospectively only from the date that the hedge relationship is fully designated and documented. **[Refer: IFRS 9 paragraph 6.4.1]**

IG60A   An entity may, in accordance with its previous GAAP, have deferred or not recognised gains and losses on a fair value hedge **[Refer: IFRS 9 paragraphs 6.5.8–6.5.10]** of a hedged item that is not measured at fair value. For such a fair value hedge, an entity adjusts the carrying amount of the hedged item at the date of transition to IFRSs. The adjustment is the lower of:

(a)   that portion of the cumulative change in the fair value of the hedged item that was not recognised in accordance with previous GAAP; and

(b)   that portion of the cumulative change in the fair value of the hedging instrument and, in accordance with previous GAAP, was either (i) not recognised or (ii) deferred in the statement of financial position as an asset or liability.

[Refer: paragraph B4]

IG60B   An entity may, in accordance with its previous GAAP, have deferred gains and losses on a cash flow hedge **[Refer: IFRS 9 paragraphs 6.5.11–6.5.12]** of a forecast transaction. If, at the date of transition to IFRSs, the hedged forecast transaction is not highly probable, but is expected to occur, the entire deferred gain or loss is recognised in the cash flow hedge reserve within equity. Any net cumulative gain or loss that has been reclassified to the cash flow hedge reserve on initial application of IFRS 9 remains there until (a) the forecast transaction subsequently results in the recognition of a non-financial asset or non-financial liability, (b) the forecast transaction affects profit or loss or (c) subsequently circumstances change and the forecast transaction is no longer expected to occur, in which case any related net cumulative gain or loss is reclassified from the cash flow hedge reserve to profit or loss. If the hedging instrument is still held, but the hedge does not qualify as a cash flow hedge in accordance with IFRS 9, hedge accounting is no longer appropriate starting from the date of transition to IFRSs.

[Refer: paragraph B6]

IAS 40 *Investment Property*

IG61   An entity that adopts the fair value model in IAS 40 [Refer: IAS 40 paragraphs 30 and 33–55] measures its investment property at fair value at the date of transition to IFRSs. [Refer: paragraphs 7 and 8] The transitional requirements of IAS 40 do not apply (paragraph 9 of the IFRS).

IG62   An entity that adopts the cost model in IAS 40 applies [Refer: IAS 40 paragraphs 30 and 56] paragraphs IG7–IG13 on property, plant and equipment.

[Refer: paragraphs 7–12]

Explanation of transition to IFRSs

IG63   Paragraphs 24(a) and (b), 25 and 26 of the IFRS require a first-time adopter to disclose reconciliations that give sufficient detail to enable users to understand the material adjustments to the statement of financial position, statement of comprehensive income and, if applicable, statement of cash flows. Paragraph 24(a) and (b) requires specific reconciliations of equity and total comprehensive income. IG Example 11 shows one way of satisfying these requirements.

IG Example 11 Reconciliation of equity and total comprehensive income

Background

An entity first adopted IFRSs in 20X5, with a date of transition to IFRSs of 1 January 20X4. Its last financial statements in accordance with previous GAAP were for the year ended 31 December 20X4.

Application of requirements

The entity's first IFRS financial statements include the reconciliations and related notes shown below.

Among other things, this example includes a reconciliation of equity at the date of transition to IFRSs (1 January 20X4). [Refer: paragraph 24(a)(i)] The IFRS also requires a reconciliation at the end of the last period presented in accordance with previous GAAP [Refer: paragraph 24(a)(ii)] (not included in this example).

In practice, it may be helpful to include cross-references to accounting policies and supporting analyses that give further explanation of the adjustments shown in the reconciliations below.

If a first-time adopter becomes aware of errors made in accordance with previous GAAP, the reconciliations distinguish the correction of those errors from changes in accounting policies (paragraph 26 of the IFRS). This example does not illustrate disclosure of a correction of an error.

continued...

...continued

IG Example 11 Reconciliation of equity and total comprehensive income

Reconciliation of equity at 1 January 20X4 (date of transition to IFRSs)
[Refer: paragraphs 24(a) and 25]

Note		Previous GAAP	Effect of transition to IFRSs	IFRSs
		CU	CU	CU
1	Property, plant and equipment	8,299	100	8,399
2	Goodwill	1,220	150	1,370
2	Intangible assets	208	(150)	58
3	Financial assets	3,471	420	3,891
	Total non-current assets	13,198	520	13,718
	Trade and other receivables	3,710	0	3,710
4	Inventories	2,962	400	3,362
5	Other receivables	333	431	764
	Cash and cash equivalents	748	0	748
	Total current assets	7,753	831	8,584
	Total assets	20,951	1,351	22,302
	Interest-bearing loans	9,396	0	9,396
	Trade and other payables	4,124	0	4,124
6	Employee benefits	0	66	66
7	Restructuring provision	250	(250)	0
	Current tax liability	42	0	42
8	Deferred tax liability	579	460	1,039
	Total liabilities	14,391	276	14,667
	Total assets less total liabilities	6,560	1,075	7,635
	Issued capital	1,500	0	1,500
5	Cash flow hedge reserve	0	302	302
9	Retained earnings	5,060	773	5,833
	Total equity	6,560	1,075	7,635

continued...

...continued

IG Example 11 Reconciliation of equity and total comprehensive income

Notes to the reconciliation of equity at 1 January 20X4:
[Refer: paragraphs 23 and 25]

1. Depreciation was influenced by tax requirements in accordance with previous GAAP, but in accordance with IFRSs reflects the useful life of the assets. The cumulative adjustment increased the carrying amount of property, plant and equipment by 100. [Refer: IAS 16]

2. Intangible assets in accordance with previous GAAP included CU150 for items that are transferred to goodwill because they do not qualify for recognition as intangible assets in accordance with IFRSs. [Refer: IAS 38 and IFRS 3]

3. Financial assets are all classified as at fair value through profit or loss in accordance with IFRSs and are carried at their fair value of CU3,891. They were carried at cost of CU3,471 in accordance with previous GAAP. The resulting gains of CU294 (CU420, less related deferred tax of CU126) are included in retained earnings.

4. Inventories include fixed and variable production overhead of CU400 in accordance with IFRSs, but this overhead was excluded in accordance with previous GAAP. [Refer: IAS 2]

5. Unrealised gains of CU431 on unmatured forward foreign exchange contracts are recognised in accordance with IFRSs, but were not recognised in accordance with previous GAAP. The resulting gains of CU302 (CU431, less related deferred tax of CU129) are included in the cash flow hedge reserve because the contracts hedge forecast sales. [Refer: IAS 12, IAS 21, IFRS 9 and IAS 39]

6. A pension liability of CU66 is recognised in accordance with IFRSs, but was not recognised in accordance with previous GAAP, which used a cash basis. [Refer: IAS 19]

7. A restructuring provision of CU250 relating to head office activities was recognised in accordance with previous GAAP, but does not qualify for recognition as a liability in accordance with IFRSs. [Refer: IAS 37]

continued...

...continued

IG Example 11 Reconciliation of equity and total comprehensive income

8   The above changes increased the deferred tax liability as follows:
     [Refer: IAS 12]

	CU
Cash flow hedge reserve (note 5)	129
Retained earnings	331
Increase in deferred tax liability	460

Because the tax base at 1 January 20X4 of the items reclassified from intangible assets to goodwill (note 2) equalled their carrying amount at that date, the reclassification did not affect deferred tax liabilities.

9   The adjustments to retained earnings are as follows:

	CU
Depreciation (note 1)	100
Financial assets (note 3)	420
Production overhead (note 4)	400
Pension liability (note 6)	(66)
Restructuring provision (note 7)	250
Tax effect of the above	(331)
Total adjustment to retained earnings	773

continued...

...continued

IG Example 11 Reconciliation of equity and total comprehensive income				
Reconciliation of total comprehensive income for 20X4				
Note		*Previous GAAP*	*Effect of transition to IFRSs*	*IFRSs*
		CU	CU	CU
	Revenue	20,910	0	20,910
1,2,3	Cost of sales	(15,283)	(97)	(15,380)
	Gross profit	5,627	(97)	5,530
6	Other income	0	180	180
1	Distribution costs	(1,907)	(30)	(1,937)
1,4	Administrative expenses	(2,842)	(300)	(3,142)
	Finance income	1,446	0	1,446
	Finance costs	(1,902)	0	(1,902)
	Profit before tax	422	(247)	175
5	Tax expense	(158)	74	(84)
	Profit (loss) for the year	264	(173)	91
7	Cash flow hedges	0	(40)	(40)
8	Tax relating to other comprehensive income	0	(29)	(29)
	Other comprehensive income	0	(69)	(69)
	Total comprehensive income	264	(242)	22

continued...

...continued

IG Example 11 Reconciliation of equity and total comprehensive income

Notes to the reconciliation of total comprehensive income for 20X4:

1. A pension liability is recognised in accordance with IFRSs, but was not recognised in accordance with previous GAAP. The pension liability increased by CU130 during 20X4, which caused increases in cost of sales (CU50), distribution costs (CU30) and administrative expenses (CU50).

2. Cost of sales is higher by CU47 in accordance with IFRSs because inventories include fixed and variable production overhead in accordance with IFRSs but not in accordance with previous GAAP.

3. Depreciation was influenced by tax requirements in accordance with previous GAAP, but reflects the useful life of the assets in accordance with IFRSs. The effect on the profit for 20X4 was not material.

4. A restructuring provision of CU250 was recognised in accordance with previous GAAP at 1 January 20X4, but did not qualify for recognition in accordance with IFRSs until the year ended 31 December 20X4. This increases administrative expenses for 20X4 in accordance with IFRSs.

5. Adjustments 1–4 above lead to a reduction of CU128 in deferred tax expense.

6. Financial assets at fair value through profit or loss increased in value by CU180 during 20X4. They were carried at cost in accordance with previous GAAP. Fair value changes have been included in 'Other income'.

7. The fair value of forward foreign exchange contracts that are effective hedges of forecast transactions decreased by CU40 during 20X4.

8. Adjustments 6 and 7 above lead to an increase of CU29 in deferred tax expense.

Explanation of material adjustments to the statement of cash flows for 20X4:

Income taxes of CU133 paid during 20X4 are classified as operating cash flows in accordance with IFRSs, but were included in a separate category of tax cash flows in accordance with previous GAAP. There are no other material differences between the statement of cash flows presented in accordance with IFRSs and the statement of cash flows presented in accordance with previous GAAP.

IFRS 2 *Share-based Payment*

IG64   A first-time adopter is encouraged, but not required, to apply IFRS 2 *Share-based Payment* to equity instruments that were granted after 7 November 2002 that vested before the later of (a) the date of transition to IFRSs and (b) 1 January 2005.

IG65   For example, if an entity's date of transition to IFRSs is 1 January 2004, the entity applies IFRS 2 to shares, share options or other equity instruments that were granted after 7 November 2002 and had not yet vested at 1 January 2005. Conversely, if an entity's date of transition to IFRSs is 1 January 2010, the entity applies IFRS 2 to shares, share options or other equity instruments that were granted after 7 November 2002 and had not yet vested at 1 January 2010.

IAS 20 *Accounting for Government Grants and Disclosure of Government Assistance*

IG66   Paragraph B10 of the IFRS requires a first-time adopter to use its previous GAAP carrying amount of government loans existing at the date of transition to IFRS as the IFRS carrying amount of such loans at that date. A first-time adopter applies IAS 32 *Financial Instruments: Presentation* to classify such a loan as a financial liability or an equity instrument. Subsequently, the first-time adopter applies IFRS 9 to such a loan. To do so, the entity calculates the effective interest rate by comparing the carrying amount of the loan at the date of transition to IFRSs with the amount and timing of expected repayments to the government. IG Example 12 illustrates accounting for such a loan.

[Paragraphs IG67–IG200 reserved for possible guidance on future standards]

IG Example 12 Government loan at a below-market rate of interest at the date of transition to IFRSs

To encourage entities to expand their operations in a specified development zone where it is difficult for entities to obtain financing for their projects, the government provides loans at a below-market rate of interest to fund the purchase of manufacturing equipment.

Entity S's date of transition to IFRSs is 1 January 20X2.

In accordance with the development scheme, in 20X0 Entity S receives a loan at a below-market rate of interest from the government for CU100,000. Under previous GAAP, Entity S accounted for the loan as equity and the carrying amount under previous GAAP was CU100,000 at the date of transition to IFRSs. The amount repayable will be CU103,030 at 1 January 20X5.

No other payment is required under the terms of the loan and there are no future performance conditions attached to the loan. The information needed to measure the fair value of the loan was not obtained at the time of initially accounting for the loan.

The loan meets the definition of a financial liability in accordance with IAS 32. Entity S therefore reclassifies the government loan as a liability. It also uses the previous GAAP carrying amount of the loan at the date of transition to IFRSs as the carrying amount of the loan in the opening IFRS statement of financial position. Entity S therefore reclassifies the amount of CU100,000 from equity to liability in the opening IFRS statement of financial position. In order to measure the loan after the date of transition to IFRSs, the effective interest rate starting 1 January 20X2 is calculated as below:

$$= \sqrt[3]{\left(\frac{103,030}{100,000}\right)} - 1$$

$$= 0.01$$

The carrying amounts of the loan are as follows:

Date	Carrying amount	Interest expense	Interest payable
	CU	CU	CU
1 January 20X2	100,000		
31 December 20X2	101,000	1,000	1,000
31 December 20X3	102,010	1,010	2,010
31 December 20X4	103,030	1,020	3,030

IFRIC Interpretations

IFRIC 1 *Changes in Existing Decommissioning, Restoration and Similar Liabilities*

IG201   IAS 16 requires the cost of an item of property, plant and equipment to include the initial estimate of the costs of dismantling and removing the asset and restoring the site on which it is located. IAS 37 requires the liability, both initially and subsequently, to be measured at the amount required to settle the present obligation at the end of the reporting period, reflecting a current market-based discount rate. **[Refer: IAS 37 paragraphs 36–52]**

IG202   IFRIC 1 requires that, subject to specified conditions, changes in an existing decommissioning, restoration or similar liability are added to or deducted from the cost of the related asset. The resulting depreciable amount of the asset is depreciated over its useful life, and the periodic unwinding of the discount on the liability is recognised in profit or loss as it occurs. **[Refer: IFRIC 1 paragraphs 4–8]**

IG203   Paragraph D21 of IFRS 1 provides a transitional exemption. Instead of retrospectively accounting for changes in this way, entities can include in the depreciated cost of the asset an amount calculated by discounting the liability at the date of transition to IFRSs back to, and depreciating it from, when the liability was first incurred. IG Example 201 illustrates the effect of applying this exemption, assuming that the entity accounts for its property, plant and equipment using the cost model. **[Refer: IAS 16 paragraph 30]**

IG Example 201 Changes in existing decommissioning, restoration and similar liabilities

Background

An entity's first IFRS financial statements are for a period that ends on 31 December 20X5 and include comparative information **[Refer: paragraphs 21 and 22]** for 20X4 only. Its date of transition to IFRSs is therefore 1 January 20X4.

The entity acquired an energy plant on 1 January 20X1, with a life of 40 years.

As at the date of transition to IFRSs, the entity estimates the decommissioning cost in 37 years' time to be 470, and estimates that the appropriate risk-adjusted discount rate for the liability is 5 per cent. It judges that the appropriate discount rate has not changed since 1 January 20X1.

continued...

...continued

IG Example 201 Changes in existing decommissioning, restoration and similar liabilities

Application of requirements

The decommissioning liability recognised at the transition date is CU77 (CU470 discounted for 37 years at 5 per cent). **[Refer: paragraph D21(a) and IAS 37 paragraphs 36–52]**

Discounting this liability back for a further three years to 1 January 20X1 gives an estimated liability at acquisition, to be included in the cost of the asset, of CU67. **[Refer: paragraph D21(b)]** Accumulated depreciation on the asset is CU67 × 3/40 = CU5. **[Refer: paragraph D21(c)]**

The amounts recognised in the opening IFRS statement of financial position on the date of transition to IFRSs (1 January 20X4) are, in summary:

	CU
Decommissioning cost included in cost of plant	67
Accumulated depreciation	(5)
Decommissioning liability	(77)
Net assets/retained earnings	(15)

IG204–
IG206
[Deleted]

Table of Concordance

This table shows how the contents of the superseded version of IFRS 1 and the revised version of IFRS 1 correspond.

Superseded IFRS 1 paragraph	Revised IFRS 1 paragraph
1	1
2	2
3	3
4	4
5	5
6	6
7	7
8	8
9	9
10	10
11	11
12	12
13	D1
14	19
15	None
16	D5
17	D6
18	D7
19	D8
20	D10
20A	D11
21	D12
22	D13
23	D18
23A	D14
23B	D15
24	D16
25	D17
25A	D19
25B	D2

continued...

...continued

Superseded IFRS 1 paragraph	Revised IFRS 1 paragraph
25C	D3
25D	D4
25E	D21
25F	D9
25G	D20
25H	D22
25I	D23
26	B1
27	B2
27A	B3
28	B4
29	B5
30	B6
31	14
32	15
33	16
34	17
34A	None
34B	None
34C	B7
35	20
36	21
36A	None
36B	None
36C	None
37	22
38	23
39	24
40	25
41	26
42	27
43	28
43A	29

continued...

...continued

Superseded IFRS 1 paragraph	Revised IFRS 1 paragraph
44	30
44A	31
45	32
46	33
47	34
47A	None
47B	None
47C	None
47D	None
47E	None
47F	None
47G	35
47H	None
47I	36
47J	37
47K	38
47L	39
Appendix A	Appendix A
Appendix B	Appendix C
None	13, 18, 40

IASB documents published to accompany

IFRS 2

Share-based Payment

The text of the unaccompanied standard, IFRS 2, is contained in Part A of this edition. The text of the Basis for Conclusions on IFRS 2 is contained in Part C of this edition. Its effective date when issued was 1 January 2005. This part presents the following documents:

IMPLEMENTATION GUIDANCE

TABLE OF CONCORDANCE

Contents

Guidance on implementing
IFRS 2 *Share-based Payment*

This guidance accompanies, but is not part of, IFRS 2.

Definition of grant date

IG1   IFRS 2 defines grant date as the date at which the entity and the employee (or other party providing similar services) agree to a share-based payment arrangement, being when the entity and the counterparty have a shared understanding of the terms and conditions of the arrangement. At grant date the entity confers on the counterparty the right to cash, other assets, or equity instruments of the entity, provided the specified vesting conditions, if any, are met. If that agreement is subject to an approval process (for example, by shareholders), grant date is the date when that approval is obtained.

IG2   As noted above, grant date is when both parties agree to a share-based payment arrangement. The word 'agree' is used in its usual sense, which means that there must be both an offer and acceptance of that offer. Hence, the date at which one party makes an offer to another party is not grant date. The date of grant is when that other party accepts the offer. In some instances, the counterparty explicitly agrees to the arrangement, eg by signing a contract. In other instances, agreement might be implicit, eg for many share-based payment arrangements with employees, the employees' agreement is evidenced by their commencing to render services.

IG3   Furthermore, for both parties to have agreed to the share-based payment arrangement, both parties must have a shared understanding of the terms and conditions of the arrangement. Therefore, if some of the terms and conditions of the arrangement are agreed on one date, with the remainder of the terms and conditions agreed on a later date, then grant date is on that later date, when all of the terms and conditions have been agreed. For example, if an entity agrees to issue share options to an employee, but the exercise price of the options will be set by a compensation committee that meets in three months' time, grant date is when the exercise price is set by the compensation committee.

IG4   In some cases, grant date might occur after the employees to whom the equity instruments were granted have begun rendering services. For example, if a grant of equity instruments is subject to shareholder approval, grant date might occur some months after the employees have begun rendering services in respect of that grant. The IFRS requires the entity to recognise the services when received. In this situation, the entity should estimate the grant date fair value of the equity instruments (eg by estimating the fair value of the equity instruments at the end of the reporting period), for the purposes of recognising the services received during the period between service commencement date and grant date. Once the date of grant has been established, the entity should revise the earlier estimate so that the amounts recognised for services received in respect of the grant are ultimately based on the grant date fair value of the equity instruments.

Definition of vesting conditions

IG4A   IFRS 2 defines vesting conditions as the conditions that determine whether the entity receives the services that entitle the counterparty to receive cash, other assets or equity instruments of the entity under a share-based payment arrangement. The following flowchart illustrates the evaluation of whether a condition is a service or performance condition or a non-vesting condition.

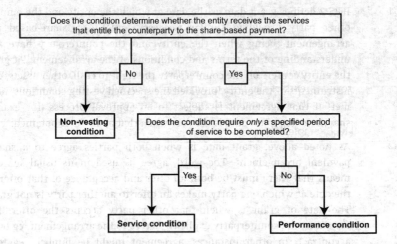

Transactions with parties other than employees

IG5   For transactions with parties other than employees (and others providing similar services) that are measured by reference to the fair value of the equity instruments granted, paragraph 13 of IFRS 2 includes a rebuttable presumption that the fair value of the goods or services received can be estimated reliably. In these situations, paragraph 13 of IFRS 2 requires the entity to measure that fair value at the date the entity obtains the goods or the counterparty renders service.

Transaction in which the entity cannot identify specifically some or all of the goods or services received

IG5A   In some cases, however, it might be difficult to demonstrate that goods or services have been (or will be) received. For example, an entity may grant shares to a charitable organisation for nil consideration. It is usually not possible to identify the specific goods or services received in return for such a transaction. A similar situation might arise in transactions with other parties.

IG5B   Paragraph 11 of IFRS 2 requires transactions in which share-based payments are made to employees to be measured by reference to the fair value of the share-based payments at grant date.[1] Hence, the entity is not required to measure directly the fair value of the employee services received.

---

1   In IFRS 2, all references to employees include others providing similar services.

IG5C It should be noted that the phrase 'the fair value of the share-based payment' refers to the fair value of the particular share-based payment concerned. For example, an entity might be required by government legislation to issue some portion of its shares to nationals of a particular country that may be transferred only to other nationals of that country. Such a transfer restriction may affect the fair value of the shares concerned, and therefore those shares may have a fair value that is less than the fair value of otherwise identical shares that do not carry such restrictions. In this situation, the phrase 'the fair value of the share-based payment' would refer to the fair value of the restricted shares, not the fair value of other, unrestricted shares.

IG5D Paragraph 13A of IFRS 2 specifies how such transactions should be measured. The following example illustrates how the entity should apply the requirements of the IFRS to a transaction in which the entity cannot identify specifically some or all of the goods or services received.

IG Example 1
Share-based payment transaction in which the entity cannot identify specifically some or all of the goods or services received
Background
An entity granted shares with a total fair value of CU100,000[a] to parties other than employees who are from a particular section of the community (historically disadvantaged individuals), as a means of enhancing its image as a good corporate citizen. The economic benefits derived from enhancing its corporate image could take a variety of forms, such as increasing its customer base, attracting or retaining employees, or improving or maintaining its ability to tender successfully for business contracts.
The entity cannot identify the specific consideration received. For example, no cash was received and no service conditions were imposed. Therefore, the identifiable consideration (nil) is less than the fair value of the equity instruments granted (CU100,000).
Application of requirements
Although the entity cannot identify the specific goods or services received, the circumstances indicate that goods or services have been (or will be) received, and therefore IFRS 2 applies.
In this situation, because the entity cannot identify the specific goods or services received, the rebuttable presumption in paragraph 13 of IFRS 2, that the fair value of the goods or services received can be estimated reliably, does not apply. The entity should instead measure the goods or services received by reference to the fair value of the equity instruments granted.
(a) In this example, and in all other examples in this guidance, monetary amounts are denominated in 'currency units (CU)'.

Measurement date for transactions with parties other than employees

IG6   If the goods or services are received on more than one date, the entity should measure the fair value of the equity instruments granted on each date when goods or services are received. The entity should apply that fair value when measuring the goods or services received on that date.

IG7   However, an approximation could be used in some cases. For example, if an entity received services continuously during a three-month period, and its share price did not change significantly during that period, the entity could use the average share price during the three-month period when estimating the fair value of the equity instruments granted.

Transitional arrangements

IG8   In paragraph 54 of IFRS 2, the entity is encouraged, but not required, to apply the requirements of the IFRS to other grants of equity instruments (ie grants other than those specified in paragraph 53 of the IFRS), if the entity has disclosed publicly the fair value of those equity instruments, measured at the measurement date. For example, such equity instruments include equity instruments for which the entity has disclosed in the notes to its financial statements the information required in the US by SFAS 123 *Accounting for Stock-based Compensation*.

Equity-settled share-based payment transactions

IG9   For equity-settled transactions measured by reference to the fair value of the equity instruments granted, paragraph 19 of IFRS 2 states that vesting conditions, other than market conditions,[2] are not taken into account when estimating the fair value of the shares or share options at the measurement date (ie grant date, for transactions with employees and others providing similar services). Instead, vesting conditions are taken into account by adjusting the number of equity instruments included in the measurement of the transaction amount so that, ultimately, the amount recognised for goods or services received as consideration for the equity instruments granted is based on the number of equity instruments that eventually vest. Hence, on a cumulative basis, no amount is recognised for goods or services received if the equity instruments granted do not vest because of failure to satisfy a vesting condition, eg the counterparty fails to complete a specified service period, or a performance condition is not satisfied. This accounting method is known as the modified grant date method, because the number of equity instruments included in the determination of the transaction amount is adjusted to reflect the outcome of the vesting conditions, but no adjustment is made to the fair value of those equity instruments. That fair value is estimated at grant date (for transactions with employees and others providing similar services) and not subsequently revised. Hence, neither increases nor decreases in the fair value of the equity instruments after grant date are taken into account when

---

2   In the remainder of this paragraph, the discussion of vesting conditions excludes market conditions, which are subject to the requirements of paragraph 21 of IFRS 2.

determining the transaction amount (other than in the context of measuring the incremental fair value transferred if a grant of equity instruments is subsequently modified).

IG10   To apply these requirements, paragraph 20 of IFRS 2 requires the entity to recognise the goods or services received during the vesting period based on the best available estimate of the number of equity instruments expected to vest and to revise that estimate, if necessary, if subsequent information indicates that the number of equity instruments expected to vest differs from previous estimates. On vesting date, the entity revises the estimate to equal the number of equity instruments that ultimately vested (subject to the requirements of paragraph 21 concerning market conditions).

IG11   In the examples below, the share options granted all vest at the same time, at the end of a specified period. In some situations, share options or other equity instruments granted might vest in instalments over the vesting period. For example, suppose an employee is granted 100 share options, which will vest in instalments of 25 share options at the end of each year over the next four years. To apply the requirements of the IFRS, the entity should treat each instalment as a separate share option grant, because each instalment has a different vesting period, and hence the fair value of each instalment will differ (because the length of the vesting period affects, for example, the likely timing of cash flows arising from the exercise of the options).

IG Example 1A
Background
An entity grants 100 share options to each of its 500 employees. Each grant is conditional upon the employee working for the entity over the next three years. **[Note: the vesting condition is a service condition of three years—service conditions are not market conditions]** The entity estimates that the fair value of each share option is CU15. **[Refer: paragraphs 11, 12 and 16–19]**
On the basis of a weighted average probability, the entity estimates that 20 per cent of employees will leave during the three-year period and therefore forfeit their rights to the share options.

continued...

...continued

IG Example 1A

Application of requirements

Scenario 1

If everything turns out exactly as expected, the entity recognises the following amounts during the vesting period, for services received as consideration for the share options.

Year	Calculation [Refer: paragraph 10]	Remuneration expense for period	Cumulative remuneration expense
		CU	CU
1	50,000 options × 80% [Refer: paragraphs 19 and 20] × CU15 [Refer: paragraphs 11, 12 and 16–19] × $^1/_3$ years [Refer: paragraph 15(a)]	200,000	200,000
2	(50,000 options × 80% × CU15 × $^2/_3$ years) – CU200,000	200,000	400,000
3	(50,000 options × 80% × CU15 × $^3/_3$ years) – CU400,000	200,000	600,000

continued...

...continued

IG Example 1A

Scenario 2

During year 1, 20 employees leave. The entity revises its estimate of total employee departures over the three-year period from 20 per cent (100 employees) to 15 per cent (75 employees). During year 2, a further 22 employees leave. The entity revises its estimate of total employee departures over the three-year period from 15 per cent to 12 per cent (60 employees). During year 3, a further 15 employees leave. Hence, a total of 57 employees forfeited their rights to the share options during the three-year period, and a total of 44,300 share options (443 employees × 100 options per employee) vested at the end of year 3.

Year	Calculation [Refer: paragraph 10]	Remuneration expense for period	Cumulative remuneration expense
		CU	CU
1	50,000 options × 85% [Refer: paragraphs 19 and 20] × CU15 [Refer: paragraphs 11, 12 and 16–19] × $1/3$ years [Refer: paragraph 15(a)]	212,500	212,500
2	(50,000 options × 88% [Refer: paragraphs 19 and 20] × CU15 × $2/3$ years) – CU212,500	227,500	440,000
3	(44,300 options [Refer: paragraphs 19 and 20] × CU15) – CU440,000	224,500	664,500

IG12 In Example 1A, the share options were granted conditionally upon the employees' completing a specified service period. In some cases, a share option or share grant might also be conditional upon the achievement of a specified performance target. Examples 2, 3 and 4 illustrate the application of the IFRS to share option or share grants with performance conditions (other than market conditions, which are discussed in paragraph IG13 and illustrated in Examples 5 and 6). In Example 2, the length of the vesting period varies, depending on when the performance condition is satisfied. Paragraph 15 of the IFRS requires the entity to estimate the length of the expected vesting period, based on the most likely outcome of the performance condition, and to revise that estimate, if necessary, if subsequent information indicates that the length of the vesting period is likely to differ from previous estimates.

IG Example 2

Grant with a performance condition, in which the length of the vesting period varies

Background

At the beginning of year 1, the entity grants 100 shares each to 500 employees, conditional upon the employees' remaining in the entity's employ during the vesting period. **[Note: this vesting condition is a service condition—service conditions are not market conditions]** The shares will vest at the end of year 1 if the entity's earnings increase by more than 18 per cent; at the end of year 2 if the entity's earnings increase by more than an average of 13 per cent per year over the two-year period; and at the end of year 3 if the entity's earnings increase by more than an average of 10 per cent per year over the three-year period. **[Note: this vesting condition is a non-market performance condition]** The shares have a fair value of CU30 per share **[Refer: paragraphs 11, 12 and 16–19]** at the start of year 1, which equals the share price at grant date. No dividends are expected to be paid over the three-year period.

By the end of year 1, the entity's earnings have increased by 14 per cent, and 30 employees have left. The entity expects that earnings will continue to increase at a similar rate in year 2, and therefore expects that the shares will vest at the end of year 2. The entity expects, on the basis of a weighted average probability, that a further 30 employees will leave during year 2, and therefore expects that 440 employees will vest in 100 shares each at the end of year 2.

By the end of year 2, the entity's earnings have increased by only 10 per cent and therefore the shares do not vest at the end of year 2. 28 employees have left during the year. The entity expects that a further 25 employees will leave during year 3, and that the entity's earnings will increase by at least 6 per cent, thereby achieving the average of 10 per cent per year.

By the end of year 3, 23 employees have left and the entity's earnings had increased by 8 per cent, resulting in an average increase of 10.67 per cent per year. Therefore, 419 employees received 100 shares at the end of year 3.

continued...

...continued

IG Example 2

Application of requirements

Year	Calculation [Refer: paragraph 10]	Remuneration expense for period	Cumulative remuneration expense
		CU	CU
1	440 employees [Refer: paragraphs 19 and 20] × 100 shares × CU30 [Refer: paragraphs 11, 12 and 16–19] × $^1/_2$ [Refer: paragraph 15(b)]	660,000	660,000
2	(417 employees [Refer: paragraphs 19 and 20] × 100 shares × CU30 × $^2/_3$ [Refer: paragraph 15(b)]) – CU660,000	174,000	834,000
3	(419 employees [Refer: paragraphs 19 and 20] × 100 shares × CU30 × $^3/_3$ [Refer: paragraph 15(b)]) – CU834,000	423,000	1,257,000

IG Example 3

Grant with a performance condition, in which the number of equity instruments varies

Background

At the beginning of year 1, Entity A grants share options to each of its 100 employees working in the sales department. The share options will vest at the end of year 3, provided that the employees remain in the entity's employ, and provided that the volume of sales of a particular product increases by at least an average of 5 per cent per year. If the volume of sales of the product increases by an average of between 5 per cent and 10 per cent per year, each employee will receive 100 share options. If the volume of sales increases by an average of between 10 per cent and 15 per cent each year, each employee will receive 200 share options. If the volume of sales increases by an average of 15 per cent or more, each employee will receive 300 share options.

[this share-based payment has two vesting conditions. The first is a service condition of three years (service conditions are not market conditions). The second is a non-market performance condition where the number of options that vest depends on the volume of sales of the product.]

On grant date, Entity A estimates that the share options have a fair value of CU20 per option. **[Refer: paragraphs 11, 12 and 16–19]** Entity A also estimates that the volume of sales of the product will increase by an average of between 10 per cent and 15 per cent per year, and therefore expects that, for each employee who remains in service until the end of year 3, 200 share options will vest. The entity also estimates, on the basis of a weighted average probability, that 20 per cent of employees will leave before the end of year 3.

By the end of year 1, seven employees have left and the entity still expects that a total of 20 employees will leave by the end of year 3. Hence, the entity expects that 80 employees will remain in service for the three-year period. Product sales have increased by 12 per cent and the entity expects this rate of increase to continue over the next 2 years.

By the end of year 2, a further five employees have left, bringing the total to 12 to date. The entity now expects only three more employees will leave during year 3, and therefore expects a total of 15 employees will have left during the three-year period, and hence 85 employees are expected to remain. Product sales have increased by 18 per cent, resulting in an average of 15 per cent over the two years to date. The entity now expects that sales will average 15 per cent or more over the three-year period, and hence expects each sales employee to receive 300 share options at the end of year 3.

By the end of year 3, a further two employees have left. Hence, 14 employees have left during the three-year period, and 86 employees remain. The entity's sales have increased by an average of 16 per cent over the three years. Therefore, each of the 86 employees receives 300 share options.

continued...

...continued

	IG Example 3		
	Application of requirements		
Year	Calculation [Refer: paragraph 10]	Remuneration expense for period	Cumulative remuneration expense
		CU	CU
1	80 employees [Refer: paragraphs 19 and 20] × 200 options [Refer: paragraphs 19 and 20] × CU20 [Refer: paragraphs 11, 12 and 16–19] × $^1/_3$ [Refer: paragraph 15(a)]	106,667	106,667
2	(85 employees [Refer: paragraphs 19 and 20] × 300 options [Refer: paragraphs 19 and 20] × CU20 × $^2/_3$) – CU106,667	233,333	340,000
3	(86 employees [Refer: paragraphs 19 and 20] × 300 options [Refer: paragraphs 19 and 20] × CU20 × $^3/_3$) – CU340,000	176,000	516,000

IG Example 4

Grant with a performance condition, in which the exercise price varies

Background

At the beginning of year 1, an entity grants to a senior executive 10,000 share options, conditional upon the executive remaining in the entity's employ until the end of year 3. **[Note: this vesting condition is a service condition —service conditions are not market conditions]** The exercise price is CU40. However, the exercise price drops to CU30 if the entity's earnings increase by at least an average of 10 per cent per year over the three-year period. **[Note: this vesting condition is a non-market performance condition]**

On grant date **[Refer: paragraph 11]**, the entity estimates that the fair value of the share options, with an exercise price of CU30, is CU16 per option. **[Refer: paragraphs 11, 12 and 16–19]** If the exercise price is CU40, the entity estimates that the share options have a fair value of CU12 per option. **[Refer: paragraphs 11, 12 and 16–19]**

continued...

...continued

IG Example 4

During year 1, the entity's earnings increased by 12 per cent, and the entity expects that earnings will continue to increase at this rate over the next two years. The entity therefore expects that the earnings target will be achieved, and hence the share options will have an exercise price of CU30.

During year 2, the entity's earnings increased by 13 per cent, and the entity continues to expect that the earnings target will be achieved.

During year 3, the entity's earnings increased by only 3 per cent, and therefore the earnings target was not achieved. The executive completes three years' service, and therefore satisfies the service condition. Because the earnings target was not achieved, the 10,000 vested share options have an exercise price of CU40.

Application of requirements

Because the exercise price varies depending on the outcome of a performance condition that is not a market condition, the effect of that performance condition (ie the possibility that the exercise price might be CU40 and the possibility that the exercise price might be CU30) is not taken into account when estimating the fair value of the share options at grant date. Instead, the entity estimates the fair value of the share options at grant date under each scenario (ie exercise price of CU40 and exercise price of CU30) and ultimately revises the transaction amount to reflect the outcome of that performance condition, as illustrated below.

Year	Calculation [Refer: paragraph 10]	Remuneration expense for period	Cumulative remuneration expense
		CU	CU
1	10,000 options [Refer: paragraphs 19 and 20] × CU16 [Refer: paragraphs 11, 12 and 16–19] × $^1/_3$ [Refer: paragraph 15(a)]	53,333	53,333
2	(10,000 options × CU16 [Refer: paragraphs 11, 12 and 16–19] × $^2/_3$) – CU53,333	53,334	106,667
3	(10,000 options × CU12 [Refer: paragraphs 11, 12 and 16–19] × $^3/_3$) – CU106,667	13,333	120,000

IG13   Paragraph 21 of the IFRS requires market conditions, such as a target share price upon which vesting (or exercisability) is conditional, to be taken into account when estimating the fair value of the equity instruments granted. Therefore, for grants of equity instruments with market conditions, the entity recognises the goods or services received from a counterparty who satisfies all other vesting conditions (eg services received from an employee who remains

in service for the specified period of service), irrespective of whether that market condition is satisfied. Example 5 illustrates these requirements.

IG Example 5

Grant with a market condition

Background

At the beginning of year 1, an entity grants to a senior executive 10,000 share options, conditional upon the executive remaining in the entity's employ until the end of year 3. **[Note: this vesting condition is a service condition —service conditions are not market conditions]** However, the share options cannot be exercised unless the share price has increased from CU50 at the beginning of year 1 to above CU65 at the end of year 3. **[Note: this vesting condition is a market condition]** If the share price is above CU65 at the end of year 3, the share options can be exercised at any time during the next seven years, ie by the end of year 10.

The entity applies a binomial option pricing model, which takes into account the possibility that the share price will exceed CU65 at the end of year 3 (and hence the share options become exercisable) and the possibility that the share price will not exceed CU65 at the end of year 3 (and hence the options will be forfeited). It estimates the fair value of the share options with this market condition to be CU24 per option. **[Refer: paragraphs 11, 12 and 16–21]**

Application of requirements

Because paragraph 21 of the IFRS requires the entity to recognise the services received from a counterparty who satisfies all other vesting conditions (eg services received from an employee who remains in service for the specified service period), irrespective of whether that market condition is satisfied, it makes no difference whether the share price target is achieved. The possibility that the share price target might not be achieved has already been taken into account when estimating the fair value of the share options at grant date. Therefore, if the entity expects the executive to complete the three-year service period, and the executive does so, the entity recognises the following amounts in years 1, 2 and 3:

continued...

...continued

	IG Example 5		
Year	Calculation [Refer: paragraph 10]	Remuneration expense for period	Cumulative remuneration expense
		CU	CU
1	10,000 options [Refer: paragraphs 19–21] × CU24 [Refer: paragraphs 11, 12 and 16–21] × ¹/₃ [Refer: paragraph 15(a)]	80,000	80,000
2	(10,000 options × CU24 × ²/₃) – CU80,000	80,000	160,000
3	(10,000 options × CU24) – CU160,000	80,000	240,000

As noted above, these amounts are recognised irrespective of the outcome of the market condition. However, if the executive left during year 2 (or year 3), the amount recognised during year 1 (and year 2) would be reversed in year 2 (or year 3). This is because the service condition, in contrast to the market condition, was not taken into account when estimating the fair value of the share options at grant date. Instead, the service condition is taken into account by adjusting the transaction amount to be based on the number of equity instruments that ultimately vest, in accordance with paragraphs 19 and 20 of the IFRS.

IG14   In Example 5, the outcome of the market condition did not change the length of the vesting period. However, if the length of the vesting period varies depending on when a performance condition is satisfied, paragraph 15 of the IFRS requires the entity to presume that the services to be rendered by the employees as consideration for the equity instruments granted will be received in the future, over the expected vesting period. The entity is required to estimate the length of the expected vesting period at grant date, based on the most likely outcome of the performance condition. If the performance condition is a market condition, the estimate of the length of the expected vesting period must be consistent with the assumptions used in estimating the fair value of the share options granted, and is not subsequently revised. Example 6 illustrates these requirements.

IG Example 6

Grant with a market condition, in which the length of the vesting period varies

Background

At the beginning of year 1, an entity grants 10,000 share options with a ten-year life to each of ten senior executives. The share options will vest and become exercisable immediately if and when the entity's share price increases from CU50 to CU70, **[Note: this vesting condition is a market condition in which the length of the vesting period varies]** provided that the executive remains in service until the share price target is achieved. **[Note: this vesting condition is a service condition—service conditions are not market conditions]**

The entity applies a binomial option pricing model, which takes into account the possibility that the share price target will be achieved during the ten-year life of the options, and the possibility that the target will not be achieved. The entity estimates that the fair value of the share options at grant date is CU25 per option **[Refer: paragraphs 11, 12 and 16–21]**. From the option pricing model, the entity determines that the mode of the distribution of possible vesting dates is five years. In other words, of all the possible outcomes, the most likely outcome of the market condition is that the share price target will be achieved at the end of year 5. Therefore, the entity estimates that the expected vesting period is five years. The entity also estimates that two executives will have left by the end of year 5, and therefore expects that 80,000 share options (10,000 share options × 8 executives) will vest at the end of year 5.

Throughout years 1–4, the entity continues to estimate that a total of two executives will leave by the end of year 5. However, in total three executives leave, one in each of years 3, 4 and 5. The share price target is achieved at the end of year 6. Another executive leaves during year 6, before the share price target is achieved.

Application of requirements

Paragraph 15 **[Refer: paragraph 15(b)]** of the IFRS requires the entity to recognise the services received over the expected vesting period, as estimated at grant date, and also requires the entity not to revise that estimate. Therefore, the entity recognises the services received from the executives over years 1–5. Hence, the transaction amount is ultimately based on 70,000 share options (10,000 share options × 7 executives who remain in service at the end of year 5). **[Note: in effect the share-based payment is treated as an option with a market condition and an expected vesting period of five years. The length of the expected vesting period is not subsequently revised because it is a market condition that affects its length—see paragraph 15(b)]**

Although another executive left during year 6, no adjustment is made, because the executive had already completed the expected vesting period of five years. **[Refer: paragraph 23]** Therefore, the entity recognises the following amounts in years 1–5:

continued...

...*continued*

		IG Example 6		
Year	Calculation [Refer: paragraph 10]		Remuneration expense for period	Cumulative remuneration expense
			CU	CU
1	80,000 options [Refer: paragraphs 19–21] × CU25 [Refer: paragraphs 11, 12 and 16–21] × $^1/_5$ [Refer: paragraph 15(b)]		400,000	400,000
2	(80,000 options × CU25 × $^2/_5$) – CU400,000		400,000	800,000
3	(80,000 options × CU25 × $^3/_5$) – CU800,000		400,000	1,200,000
4	(80,000 options × CU25 × $^4/_5$) – CU1,200,000		400,000	1,600,000
5	(70,000 [Note: the reduction by 10,000 options is as a result of the service condition not being met during the expected vesting period— paragraph BC180] options [Refer: paragraphs 19–20] × CU25) – CU1,600,000		150,000	1,750,000

IG15   Paragraphs 26–29 and B42–B44 of the IFRS set out requirements that apply if a share option is repriced (or the entity otherwise modifies the terms or conditions of a share-based payment arrangement). Examples 7–9 illustrate some of these requirements.

IG Example 7

Grant of share options that are subsequently repriced

Background

At the beginning of year 1, an entity grants 100 share options to each of its 500 employees. Each grant is conditional upon the employee remaining in service over the next three years. [Note: this vesting condition is a service condition—service conditions are not market conditions] The entity estimates that the fair value of each option is CU15. [Refer: paragraphs 11, 12 and 16–19] On the basis of a weighted average probability, the entity estimates that 100 employees will leave during the three-year period and therefore forfeit their rights to the share options.

continued...

...continued

IG Example 7

Suppose that 40 employees leave during year 1. Also suppose that by the end of year 1, the entity's share price has dropped, and the entity reprices its share options, **[Refer: paragraphs 26 and 27]** and that the repriced share options vest at the end of year 3. The entity estimates that a further 70 employees will leave during years 2 and 3, and hence the total expected employee departures over the three-year vesting period is 110 employees. During year 2, a further 35 employees leave, and the entity estimates that a further 30 employees will leave during year 3, to bring the total expected employee departures over the three-year vesting period to 105 employees. During year 3, a total of 28 employees leave, and hence a total of 103 employees ceased employment during the vesting period. For the remaining 397 employees, the share options vested at the end of year 3.

The entity estimates that, at the date of repricing, the fair value of each of the original share options granted (ie before taking into account the repricing) is CU5 and that the fair value of each repriced share option is CU8.

Application of requirements

Paragraph 27 of the IFRS requires the entity to recognise the effects of modifications that increase the total fair value of the share-based payment arrangement or are otherwise beneficial to the employee. If the modification increases the fair value of the equity instruments granted (eg by reducing the exercise price), measured immediately before and after the modification, paragraph B43(a) of Appendix B requires the entity to include the incremental fair value granted (ie the difference between the fair value of the modified equity instrument and that of the original equity instrument, both estimated as at the date of the modification) in the measurement of the amount recognised for services received as consideration for the equity instruments granted. If the modification occurs during the vesting period, the incremental fair value granted is included in the measurement of the amount recognised for services received over the period from the modification date until the date when the modified equity instruments vest, in addition to the amount based on the grant date fair value of the original equity instruments, which is recognised over the remainder of the original vesting period.

The incremental value is CU3 per share option (CU8 − CU5). This amount is recognised over the remaining two years of the vesting period, along with remuneration expense based on the original option value of CU15.

continued...

...continued

IG Example 7

The amounts recognised in years 1–3 are as follows:

Year	Calculation [Refer: paragraph 10]	Remuneration expense for period CU	Cumulative remuneration expense CU
1	(500 – 110) employees [Refer: paragraphs 19–20] × 100 options × CU15 [Refer: paragraphs 11, 12 and 16–19] × ¹/₃ [Refer: paragraph 15(a)]	195,000	195,000
2	(500 – 105) employees [Refer: paragraphs 19 and 20] × 100 options × (CU15 [Refer: paragraph 27] × ²/₃ [Refer: paragraph 27] + CU3 [Refer: paragraph B43(a)] × ¹/₂ [Refer: paragraph B43(a)]) – CU195,000	259,250	454,250
3	(500 – 103) employees [Refer: paragraphs 19 and 20] × 100 options × (CU15 + CU3) – CU454,250	260,350	714,600

IG Example 8

Grant of share options with a vesting condition that is subsequently modified

Background

At the beginning of year 1, the entity grants 1,000 share options to each member of its sales team, conditional upon the employee remaining in the entity's employ for three years, **[Note: this vesting condition is a service condition]** and the team selling more than 50,000 units of a particular product over the three-year period. **[Note: this vesting condition is a non-market performance condition]** The fair value of the share options is CU15 per option [Refer: paragraphs 11, 12 and 16–19] at the date of grant.

During year 2, the entity increases the sales target to 100,000 units. **[Note: a modification of a non-market condition—see paragraph 27]** By the end of year 3, the entity has sold 55,000 units, and the share options are forfeited. Twelve members of the sales team have remained in service for the three-year period.

continued...

...continued

IG Example 8

Application of requirements

Paragraph 20 of the IFRS requires, for a performance condition that is not a market condition, the entity to recognise the services received during the vesting period based on the best available estimate of the number of equity instruments expected to vest and to revise that estimate, if necessary, if subsequent information indicates that the number of equity instruments expected to vest differs from previous estimates. On vesting date, the entity revises the estimate to equal the number of equity instruments that ultimately vested. However, paragraph 27 of the IFRS requires, irrespective of any modifications to the terms and conditions on which the equity instruments were granted, or a cancellation or settlement of that grant of equity instruments, the entity to recognise, as a minimum, the services received, measured at the grant date fair value of the equity instruments granted, unless those equity instruments do not vest because of failure to satisfy a vesting condition (other than a market condition) that was specified at grant date. Furthermore, paragraph B44(c) of Appendix B specifies that, if the entity modifies the vesting conditions in a manner that is not beneficial to the employee, the entity does not take the modified vesting conditions into account when applying the requirements of paragraphs 19–21 of the IFRS.

Therefore, because the modification to the performance condition made it less likely that the share options will vest, which was not beneficial to the employee, the entity takes no account of the modified performance condition when recognising the services received. Instead, it continues to recognise the services received over the three-year period based on the original vesting conditions. Hence, the entity ultimately recognises cumulative remuneration expense of CU180,000 over the three-year period (12 employees × 1,000 options × CU15).

The same result would have occurred if, instead of modifying the performance target, the entity had increased the number of years of service required for the share options to vest from three years to ten years. Because such a modification would make it less likely that the options will vest, which would not be beneficial to the employees, the entity would take no account of the modified service condition when recognising the services received. Instead, it would recognise the services received from the twelve employees who remained in service over the original three-year vesting period.

IG Example 9

Grant of shares, with a cash alternative subsequently added

Background

At the beginning of year 1, the entity grants 10,000 shares with a fair value of CU33 per share to a senior executive, conditional upon the completion of three years' service. **[Note: ie this vesting condition is a service condition—service conditions are not market conditions]** By the end of year 2, the share price has dropped to CU25 per share. At that date, the entity adds a cash alternative to the grant, whereby the executive can choose whether to receive 10,000 shares or cash equal to the value of 10,000 shares on vesting date. The share price is CU22 on vesting date.

Application of requirements

Paragraph 27 of the IFRS requires, irrespective of any modifications to the terms and conditions on which the equity instruments were granted, or a cancellation or settlement of that grant of equity instruments, the entity to recognise, as a minimum, the services received measured at the grant date fair value of the equity instruments granted, unless those equity instruments do not vest because of failure to satisfy a vesting condition (other than a market condition) that was specified at grant date. Therefore, the entity recognises the services received over the three-year period, based on the grant date fair value of the shares.

Furthermore, the addition of the cash alternative at the end of year 2 creates an obligation to settle in cash. In accordance with the requirements for cash-settled share-based payment transactions (paragraphs 30–33 of the IFRS), the entity recognises the liability to settle in cash at the modification date, based on the fair value of the shares at the modification date and the extent to which the specified services have been received. Furthermore, the entity remeasures the fair value of the liability at the end of each reporting period and at the date of settlement, with any changes in fair value recognised in profit or loss for the period. Therefore, the entity recognises the following amounts:

continued...

...continued

IG Example 9				
Year	Calculation [Refer: paragraphs 10 and 30]	Expense	Equity	Liability
		CU	CU	CU
1	Remuneration expense for year: 10,000 shares [Refer: paragraphs 19 and 20] × CU33 [Refer: paragraphs 11, 12 and 16–19] × $1/3$ [Refer: paragraph 15(a)]	110,000	110,000	
2	Remuneration expense for year: (10,000 shares × CU33 × $2/3$) – CU110,000	110,000	110,000	
	Reclassify equity to liabilities [Refer: paragraph 42]: 10,000 shares × CU25 × $2/3$		(166,667)	166,667
3	Remuneration expense for year: (10,000 shares × CU33 × $3/3$) [Refer: paragraph 27] – CU220,000	110,000[a]	26,667	83,333
	Adjust liability to closing fair value: [Refer: paragraphs 30–33] (CU166,667 + CU83,333) – (CU22 × 10,000 shares)	(30,000)		(30,000)
	Total	300,000	80,000	220,000

(a) Allocated between liabilities and equity, to bring in the final third of the liability based on the fair value of the shares as at the date of the modification.

IG15A   If a share-based payment has a non-vesting condition that the counterparty can choose not to meet and the counterparty does not meet that non-vesting condition during the vesting period, paragraph 28A of the IFRS requires that event to be treated as a cancellation. Example 9A illustrates the accounting for this type of event.

IG Example 9A

Share-based payment with vesting and non-vesting conditions when the counterparty can choose whether the non-vesting condition is met

Background

An entity grants an employee the opportunity to participate in a plan in which the employee obtains share options if he agrees to save 25 per cent of his monthly salary of CU400 for a three-year period. The monthly payments are made by deduction from the employee's salary. The employee may use the accumulated savings to exercise his options at the end of three years, or take a refund of his contributions at any point during the three-year period. The estimated annual expense for the share-based payment arrangement is CU120.

After 18 months, the employee stops paying contributions to the plan and takes a refund of contributions paid to date of CU1,800.

Application of requirements

There are three components to this plan: paid salary, salary deduction paid to the savings plan and share-based payment. The entity recognises an expense in respect of each component and a corresponding increase in liability or equity as appropriate. The requirement to pay contributions to the plan is a non-vesting condition, which the employee chooses not to meet in the second year. Therefore, in accordance with paragraphs 28(b) and 28A of the IFRS, the repayment of contributions is treated as an extinguishment of the liability and the cessation of contributions in year 2 is treated as a cancellation.

continued...

...continued

IG Example 9A

YEAR 1	Expense	Cash	Liability	Equity
	CU	CU	CU	CU
Paid salary	3,600			
	(75% × 400 × 12)	(3,600)		
Salary deduction paid to the savings plan	1,200			
	(25% × 400 × 12)		(1,200)	
Share-based payment	120			(120)
Total	4,920	(3,600)	(1,200)	(120)
YEAR 2				
Paid salary	4,200			
	(75% × 400 × 6			
	+ 100% × 400 × 6)	(4,200)		
Salary deduction paid to the savings plan	600			
	(25% × 400 × 6)		(600)	
Refund of contributions to the employee		(1,800)	1,800	
Share-based payment	240			
(acceleration of remaining expense)	(120 × 3 – 120)			(240)
Total	5,040	(6,000)	1,200	(240)

IG16   Paragraph 24 of the IFRS requires that, in rare cases only, in which the IFRS requires the entity to measure an equity-settled share-based payment transaction by reference to the fair value of the equity instruments granted, but the entity is unable to estimate reliably that fair value at the specified measurement date (eg grant date, for transactions with employees), the entity shall instead measure the transaction using an intrinsic value measurement method. Paragraph 24 also contains requirements on how to apply this method. The following example illustrates these requirements.

IG Example 10

Grant of share options that is accounted for by applying the intrinsic value method

Background

At the beginning of year 1, an entity grants 1,000 share options to 50 employees. The share options will vest at the end of year 3, provided the employees remain in service until then. **[Note: this vesting condition is a non-market performance condition]** The share options have a life of 10 years. The exercise price is CU60 and the entity's share price is also CU60 at the date of grant.

At the date of grant, the entity concludes that it cannot estimate reliably the fair value of the share options granted. **[Refer: paragraph 24]**

At the end of year 1, three employees have ceased employment and the entity estimates that a further seven employees will leave during years 2 and 3. Hence, the entity estimates that 80 per cent of the share options will vest.

Two employees leave during year 2, and the entity revises its estimate of the number of share options that it expects will vest to 86 per cent.

Two employees leave during year 3. Hence, 43,000 share options vested at the end of year 3.

The entity's share price during years 1–10, and the number of share options exercised during years 4–10, are set out below. Share options that were exercised during a particular year were all exercised at the end of that year.

Year	Share price at year-end	Number of share options exercised at year-end
1	63	0
2	65	0
3	75	0
4	88	6,000
5	100	8,000
6	90	5,000
7	96	9,000
8	105	8,000
9	108	5,000
10	115	2,000

continued...

...*continued*

IG Example 10

Application of requirements

In accordance with paragraph 24 of the IFRS, the entity recognises the following amounts in years 1–10.

Year	Calculation [Refer: paragraph 24]	Expense for period CU	Cumulative expense CU
1	50,000 options × 80% [Refer: paragraph 24(b)] × (CU63 – CU60) [Refer: paragraph 24(a)] × $^1/_3$ years [Refer: paragraph 24(b)]	40,000	40,000
2	50,000 options × 86% [Refer: paragraph 24(b)] × (CU65 – CU60) [Refer: paragraph 24(a)] × $^2/_3$ years – CU40,000	103,333	143,333
3	43,000 options × (CU75 – CU60) – CU143,333	501,667	645,000
4	37,000 outstanding options × (CU88 – CU75) [Refer: paragraph 24(a)] + 6,000 exercised options × (CU88 – CU75) [Refer: paragraph 24(a)]	559,000	1,204,000
5	29,000 outstanding options × (CU100 – CU88) + 8,000 exercised options × (CU100 – CU88)	444,000	1,648,000
6	24,000 outstanding options × (CU90 – CU100) + 5,000 exercised options × (CU90 – CU100)	(290,000)	1,358,000
7	15,000 outstanding options × (CU96 – CU90) + 9,000 exercised options × (CU96 – CU90)	144,000	1,502,000
8	7,000 outstanding options × (CU105 – CU96) + 8,000 exercised options × (CU105 – CU96)	135,000	1,637,000
9	2,000 outstanding options × (CU108 – CU105) + 5,000 exercised options × (CU108 – CU105)	21,000	1,658,000
10	2,000 exercised options × (CU115 – CU108)	14,000	1,672,000

IG17   There are many different types of employee share and share option plans. The following example illustrates the application of IFRS 2 to one particular type of plan—an employee share purchase plan. Typically, an employee share purchase plan provides employees with the opportunity to purchase the

entity's shares at a discounted price. The terms and conditions under which employee share purchase plans operate differ from country to country. That is to say, not only are there many different types of employee share and share options plans, there are also many different types of employee share purchase plans. Therefore, the following example illustrates the application of IFRS 2 to one specific employee share purchase plan.

IG Example 11

Employee share purchase plan

Background

An entity offers all its 1,000 employees the opportunity to participate in an employee share purchase plan. The employees have two weeks to decide whether to accept the offer. Under the terms of the plan, the employees are entitled to purchase a maximum of 100 shares each. The purchase price will be 20 per cent less than the market price of the entity's shares at the date the offer is accepted, and the purchase price must be paid immediately upon acceptance of the offer. All shares purchased must be held in trust for the employees, and cannot be sold for five years. The employee is not permitted to withdraw from the plan during that period. For example, if the employee ceases employment during the five-year period, the shares must nevertheless remain in the plan until the end of the five-year period. Any dividends paid during the five-year period will be held in trust for the employees until the end of the five-year period.

In total, 800 employees accept the offer and each employee purchases, on average, 80 shares, ie the employees purchase a total of 64,000 shares. The weighted-average market price of the shares at the purchase date is CU30 per share, and the weighted-average purchase price is CU24 per share.

Application of requirements

For transactions with employees, IFRS 2 requires the transaction amount to be measured by reference to the fair value of the equity instruments granted (IFRS 2, paragraph 11). To apply this requirement, it is necessary first to determine the type of equity instrument granted to the employees. Although the plan is described as an employee share purchase plan (ESPP), some ESPPs include option features and are therefore, in effect, share option plans. For example, an ESPP might include a 'look-back feature', whereby the employee is able to purchase shares at a discount, and choose whether the discount is applied to the entity's share price at the date of grant or its share price at the date of purchase. Or an ESPP might specify the purchase price, and then allow the employees a significant period of time to decide whether to participate in the plan. Another example of an option feature is an ESPP that permits the participating employees to cancel their participation before or at the end of a specified period and obtain a refund of amounts previously paid into the plan.

continued...

...continued

IG Example 11
However, in this example, the plan includes no option features. The discount is applied to the share price at the purchase date, and the employees are not permitted to withdraw from the plan.

Another factor to consider is the effect of post-vesting transfer restrictions, if any. Paragraph B3 of IFRS 2 states that, if shares are subject to restrictions on transfer after vesting date, that factor should be taken into account when estimating the fair value of those shares, but only to the extent that the post-vesting restrictions affect the price that a knowledgeable, willing market participant would pay for that share. For example, if the shares are actively traded in a deep and liquid market, post-vesting transfer restrictions may have little, if any, effect on the price that a knowledgeable, willing market participant would pay for those shares.

In this example, the shares are vested when purchased, but cannot be sold for five years after the date of purchase. Therefore, the entity should consider the valuation effect of the five-year post-vesting transfer restriction. This entails using a valuation technique to estimate what the price of the restricted share would have been on the purchase date in an arm's length transaction between knowledgeable, willing parties. Suppose that, in this example, the entity estimates that the fair value of each restricted share is CU28. In this case, the fair value of the equity instruments granted is CU4 per share (being the fair value of the restricted share of CU28 less the purchase price of CU24). Because 64,000 shares were purchased, the total fair value of the equity instruments granted is CU256,000.

In this example, there is no vesting period. Therefore, in accordance with paragraph 14 of IFRS 2, the entity should recognise an expense of CU256,000 immediately.

However, in some cases, the expense relating to an ESPP might not be material. IAS 8 *Accounting Policies, Changes in Accounting Estimates and Errors* states that the accounting policies in IFRSs need not be applied when the effect of applying them is immaterial (IAS 8, paragraph 8). IAS 1 *Presentation of Financial Statements* states that information is material if omitting, misstating or obscuring it could reasonably be expected to influence decisions that the primary users of general purpose financial statements make on the basis of those financial statements, which provide financial information about a specific reporting entity. Materiality depends on the nature or magnitude of information, or both. An entity assesses whether information, either individually or in combination with other information, is material in the context of its financial statements taken as a whole (IAS 1, paragraph 7). Therefore, in this example, the entity should consider whether the expense of CU256,000 is material.

Cash-settled share-based payment transactions

IG18   Paragraphs 30–33 of the IFRS set out requirements for transactions in which an entity acquires goods or services by incurring liabilities to the supplier of those goods or services in amounts based on the price of the entity's shares or other equity instruments. The entity is required to recognise initially the goods or services acquired, and a liability to pay for those goods or services, when the entity obtains the goods or as the services are rendered, measured at the fair value of the liability. Thereafter, until the liability is settled, the entity is required to recognise changes in the fair value of the liability.

IG19   For example, an entity might grant share appreciation rights to employees as part of their remuneration package, whereby the employees will become entitled to a future cash payment (rather than an equity instrument), based on the increase in the entity's share price from a specified level over a specified period of time. If the share appreciation rights do not vest until the employees have completed a specified period of service, the entity recognises the services received, and a liability to pay for them, as the employees render service during that period. The liability is measured, initially and at the end of each reporting period until settled, at the fair value of the share appreciation rights in accordance with paragraphs 30–33D of IFRS 2. Changes in fair value are recognised in profit or loss. Therefore, if the amount recognised for the services received was included in the carrying amount of an asset recognised in the entity's statement of financial position (for example, inventory), the carrying amount of that asset is not adjusted for the effects of the liability remeasurement. Example 12 illustrates these requirements for a cash-settled share-based payment transaction that is subject to a service condition. Example 12A illustrates these requirements for a cash-settled share-based payment transaction that is subject to a performance condition.

IG Example 12

Background

An entity grants 100 cash share appreciation rights (SARs) to each of its 500 employees, on condition that the employees remain in its employ for the next three years. **[Note: a cash-settled share-based payment]**

During year 1, 35 employees leave. The entity estimates that a further 60 will leave during years 2 and 3. During year 2, 40 employees leave and the entity estimates that a further 25 will leave during year 3. During year 3, 22 employees leave. At the end of year 3, 150 employees exercise their SARs, another 140 employees exercise their SARs at the end of year 4 and the remaining 113 employees exercise their SARs at the end of year 5.

The entity estimates the fair value of the SARs at the end of each year in which a liability exists as shown below. At the end of year 3, all SARs held by the remaining employees vest. The intrinsic values of the SARs at the date of exercise (which equal the cash paid out) at the end of years 3, 4 and 5 are also shown below.

continued...

...continued

IG Example 12		
Year	Fair value	Intrinsic value
1	CU14.40	
2	CU15.50	
3	CU18.20	CU15.00
4	CU21.40	CU20.00
5		CU25.00

Application of requirements

Year	Calculation [Refer: paragraphs 30–33]	Expense CU	Liability CU
1	(500 – 95) employees × 100 SARs × CU14.40 [Refer: paragraphs 33] × $^1/_3$	194,400	194,400
2	(500 – 100) employees × 100 SARs × CU15.50 [Refer: paragraphs 33] × $^2/_3$ – CU194,400	218,933	413,333
3	(500 – 97 – 150) employees × 100 SARs × CU18.20 – CU413,333	47,127	460,460
	+ 150 employees × 100 SARs × CU15.00	225,000	
	Total	272,127	
4	(253 – 140) employees × 100 SARs × CU21.40 – CU460,460	(218,640)	241,820
	+ 140 employees × 100 SARs × CU20.00	280,000	
	Total	61,360	
5	CU0 – CU241,820	(241,820)	0
	+ 113 employees × 100 SARs × CU25.00	282,500	
	Total	40,680	
	Total	787,500	

IG Example 12A

Background

An entity grants 100 cash-settled share appreciation rights (SARs) to each of its 500 employees on the condition that the employees remain in its employ for the next three years **[ie a cash-settled share-based payment]** and the entity reaches a revenue target (CU1 billion in sales) by the end of Year 3. The entity expects all employees to remain in its employ.

For simplicity, this example assumes that none of the employees' compensation qualifies for capitalisation as part of the cost of an asset.

At the end of Year 1, the entity expects that the revenue target will not be achieved by the end of Year 3. During Year 2, the entity's revenue increased significantly and it expects that it will continue to grow. Consequently, at the end of Year 2, the entity expects that the revenue target will be achieved by the end of Year 3.

At the end of Year 3, the revenue target is achieved and 150 employees exercise their SARs. Another 150 employees exercise their SARs at the end of Year 4 and the remaining 200 employees exercise their SARs at the end of Year 5.

Using an option pricing model, the entity estimates the fair value of the SARs, ignoring the revenue target performance condition and the employment-service condition, at the end of each year until all of the cash-settled share-based payments are settled. At the end of Year 3, all of the SARs vest. The following table shows the estimated fair value of the SARs at the end of each year and the intrinsic values of the SARs at the date of exercise (which equals the cash paid out).

Year	Fair value of one SAR	Intrinsic value of one SAR
1	CU14.40	–
2	CU15.50	–
3	CU18.20	CU15.00
4	CU21.40	CU20.00
5	CU25.00	CU25.00

Application of requirements

	Number of employees expected to satisfy the service condition	Best estimate of whether the revenue target will be met
Year 1	500	No
Year 2	500	Yes
Year 3	500	Yes

continued...

...continued

IG Example 12A			
Year	Calculation	Expense CU	Liability CU
1	SARs are not expected to vest: no expense is recognised	–	–
2	SARs are expected to vest: 500 employees × 100 SARs × CU15.50 × $^2/_3$	516,667	516,667
3	(500 – 150) employees × 100 SARs × CU18.20 × $^3/_3$ – CU516,667	120,333	637,000
	+ 150 employees × 100 SARs × CU15.00	225,000	
	Total	345,333	
4	(350 – 150) employees × 100 SARs × CU21.40 – CU637,000	(209,000)	428,000
	+ 150 employees × 100 SARs × CU20.00	300,000	
	Total	91,000	
5	(200 – 200) employees × 100 SARs × CU25.00 – CU428,000	(428,000)	–
	+ 200 employees × 100 SARs × CU25.00	500,000	
	Total	72,000	
	Total	1,025,000	

Share-based payment transactions with a net settlement feature for withholding tax obligations

IG19A   Paragraphs 33E and 33F require an entity to classify an arrangement in its entirety as an equity-settled share-based payment transaction if it would have been so classified in the absence of a net settlement feature that obliges the entity to withhold an amount for an employee's tax obligation associated with a share-based payment. The entity transfers that amount, normally in cash, to the tax authority on the employee's behalf. Example 12B illustrates these requirements.

IG Example 12B

Background

The tax law in jurisdiction X requires entities to withhold an amount for an employee's tax obligation associated with a share-based payment and transfer that amount in cash to the tax authority on the employee's behalf. [Refer: paragraphs 33E–33G]

On 1 January 20X1 an entity in jurisdiction X grants an award of 100 shares to an employee; that award is conditional upon the completion of four years' service. The entity expects that the employee will complete the service period. For simplicity, this example assumes that none of the employee's compensation qualifies for capitalisation as part of the cost of an asset.

The terms and conditions of the share-based payment arrangement require the entity to withhold shares from the settlement of the award to its employee in order to settle the employee's tax obligation (that is, the share-based payment arrangement has a 'net settlement feature'). Accordingly, the entity settles the transaction on a net basis by withholding the number of shares with a fair value equal to the monetary value of the employee's tax obligation and issuing the remaining shares to the employee on completion of the vesting period.

The employee's tax obligation associated with the award is calculated based on the fair value of the shares on the vesting date. The employee's applicable tax rate is 40 per cent.

At grant date, the fair value of each share is CU2. The fair value of each share at 31 December 20X4 is CU10.

The fair value of the shares on the vesting date is CU1,000 (100 shares × CU10 per share) and therefore the employee's tax obligation is CU400 (100 shares × CU10 × 40%). Accordingly, on the vesting date, the entity issues 60 shares to the employee and withholds 40 shares (CU400 = 40 shares × CU10 per share). The entity pays the fair value of the withheld shares in cash to the tax authority on the employee's behalf. In other words, it is as if the entity had issued all 100 vested shares to the employee, and at the same time, repurchased 40 shares at their fair value.

Application of requirements

Year	Calculation	Dr. Expense CU	Cr. Equity CU	Cr. Liability CU
1	100 shares × CU2 × $^1/_4$	50	(50)	–
2	100 shares × CU2 × $^2/_4$ – CU50	50	(50)	–
3	100 shares × CU2 × $^3/_4$ – (CU50 + CU50)	50	(50)	–
4	100 shares × CU2 × $^4/_4$ – (CU50 + CU50 + CU50)	50	(50)	–
	Total	200	(200)	–

continued...

...continued

IG Example 12B

The journal entries recorded by the entity are as follows:

During the vesting period

Accumulated compensation expense recognised over the vesting period

Dr Expense   200

     Cr Equity   200

Recognition of the tax liability[a]

Dr Equity   400

     Cr Liability   400

Settlement of tax obligation

Cash paid to the tax authority on the employee's behalf at the date of settlement

Dr Liability   400

     Cr Cash   400

(a) The entity considers disclosing an estimate of the amount that it expects to transfer to the tax authority at the end of each reporting period. The entity makes such disclosure when it determines that this information is necessary to inform users about the future cash flow effects associated with the share-based payment. **[Refer: paragraph 52]**

Accounting for a modification of a share-based payment transaction that changes its classification from cash-settled to equity-settled

IG19B   The following example illustrates the application of the requirements in paragraph B44A of IFRS 2 to a modification of the terms and conditions of a cash-settled share-based payment transaction that becomes an equity-settled share-based payment transaction.

IG Example 12C

Background

On 1 January 20X1 an entity grants 100 share appreciation rights (SARs) that will be settled in cash to each of 100 employees on the condition that employees will remain employed for the next four years. **[Note: a cash-settled share-based payment]**

On 31 December 20X1 the entity estimates that the fair value of each SAR is CU10 and consequently, the total fair value of the cash-settled award is CU100,000. On 31 December 20X2 the estimated fair value of each SAR is CU12 and consequently, the total fair value of the cash-settled award is CU120,000.

continued...

...continued

IG Example 12C

On 31 December 20X2 the entity cancels the SARs and, in their place, grants 100 share options to each employee on the condition that each employee remains in its employ for the next two years. Therefore the original vesting period is not changed. On this date the fair value of each share option is CU13.20 and consequently, the total fair value of the new grant is CU132,000. All of the employees are expected to and ultimately do provide the required service. **[Refer: paragraph B44A]**

For simplicity, this example assumes that none of the employees' compensation qualifies for capitalisation as part of the cost of an asset.

Application of requirements

At the modification date (31 December 20X2), the entity applies paragraph B44A. Accordingly:

(a)   from the date of the modification, the share options are measured by reference to their modification-date fair value and, at the modification date, the share options are recognised in equity to the extent to which the employees have rendered services;

(b)   the liability for the SARs is derecognised at the modification date; and

(c)   the difference between the carrying amount of the liability derecognised and the equity amount recognised at the modification date is recognised immediately in profit or loss.

At the modification date (31 December 20X2), the entity compares the fair value of the equity-settled replacement award for services provided through to the modification date (CU132,000 × $^2/_4$ = CU66,000) with the fair value of the cash-settled original award for those services (CU120,000 × $^2/_4$ = CU60,000). The difference (CU6,000) is recognised immediately in profit or loss at the date of the modification.

The remainder of the equity-settled share-based payment (measured at its modification-date fair value) is recognised in profit or loss over the remaining two-year vesting period from the date of the modification.

continued...

...continued

		Dr. Expense	Cumulative expense	Cr. Equity	Cr. Liability
Year	Calculation	CU	CU	CU	CU
1	100 employees ×100 SARs × CU10 × $^1/_4$	25,000	–	–	25,000
2	*Remeasurement before the modification* 100 employees × 100 SARs × CU12.00 × $^2/_4$ – 25,000	35,000	60,000	–	35,000
	Derecognition of the liability, recognition of the modifica-tion-date fair value amount in equity and recognition of the effect of settlement for CU6,000 (100 employees x 100 share options × CU13.20 × $^2/_4$) – (100 employees × 100 SARs × CU12.00 × $^2/_4$)	6,000	66,000	66,000	(60,000)
3	100 employees × 100 share options × CU13.20 × $^3/_4$ – CU66,000	33,000	99,000	33,000	–
4	100 employees x 100 share options × CU13.20 × $^4/_4$ – CU99,000	33,000	132,000	33,000	–
	Total			132,000	–

IG Example 12C

Share-based payment arrangements with cash alternatives

IG20 Some employee share-based payment arrangements permit the employee to choose whether to receive cash or equity instruments. In this situation, a compound financial instrument has been granted, ie a financial instrument with debt and equity components. Paragraph 37 of the IFRS requires the entity to estimate the fair value of the compound financial instrument at grant date, by first measuring the fair value of the debt component, and then measuring the fair value of the equity component – taking into account that the employee must forfeit the right to receive cash to receive the equity instrument.

IG21   Typically, share-based payment arrangements with cash alternatives are structured so that the fair value of one settlement alternative is the same as the other. For example, the employee might have the choice of receiving share options or cash share appreciation rights. In such cases, the fair value of the equity component will be zero, and hence the fair value of the compound financial instrument will be the same as the fair value of the debt component. However, if the fair values of the settlement alternatives differ, usually the fair value of the equity component will be greater than zero, in which case the fair value of the compound financial instrument will be greater than the fair value of the debt component.

IG22   Paragraph 38 of the IFRS requires the entity to account separately for the services received in respect of each component of the compound financial instrument. For the debt component, the entity recognises the services received, and a liability to pay for those services, as the counterparty renders service, in accordance with the requirements applying to cash-settled share-based payment transactions. **[Refer: paragraphs 30–33]** For the equity component (if any), the entity recognises the services received, and an increase in equity, as the counterparty renders service, in accordance with the requirements applying to equity-settled share-based payment transactions. **[Refer: paragraphs 10–29]** Example 13 illustrates these requirements.

IG Example 13

Background

An entity grants to an employee the right to choose either 1,000 phantom shares, ie a right to a cash payment equal to the value of 1,000 shares, or 1,200 shares. **[Refer: paragraphs 34–40]** The grant is conditional upon the completion of three years' service. If the employee chooses the share alternative, the shares must be held for three years after vesting date.

At grant date, the entity's share price is CU50 per share. At the end of years 1, 2 and 3, the share price is CU52, CU55 and CU60 respectively. The entity does not expect to pay dividends in the next three years. After taking into account the effects of the post-vesting transfer restrictions, the entity estimates that the grant date fair value of the share alternative is CU48 per share.

At the end of year 3, the employee chooses:

Scenario 1: The cash alternative

Scenario 2: The equity alternative

continued...

...continued

IG Example 13

Application of requirements

The fair value of the equity alternative is CU57,600 (1,200 shares × CU48). The fair value of the cash alternative is CU50,000 (1,000 phantom shares × CU50). Therefore, the fair value of the equity component of the compound instrument is CU7,600 (CU57,600 – CU50,000). **[Refer: paragraphs 35–37]**

The entity recognises the following amounts:

Year		Expense CU	Equity CU	Liability CU
1	Liability component **[Refer: paragraph 38]**: (1,000 × CU52 × $^1/_3$) **[Refer: paragraphs 30–33]**	17,333		17,333
	Equity component **[Refer: paragraph 38]**: (CU7,600 **[Refer: paragraphs 19 and 20]** × $^1/_3$ **[Refer: paragraph 15(a)]**)	2,533	2,533	
2	Liability component: (1,000 × CU55 × $^2/_3$) **[Refer: paragraphs 30–33]** – CU17,333	19,333		19,333
	Equity component: (CU7,600 × $^1/_3$)	2,533	2,533	
3	Liability component: (1,000 × CU60) **[Refer: paragraphs 30–33]** – CU36,666	23,334		23,334
	Equity component: (CU7,600 × $^1/_3$)	2,534	2,534	
End Year 3	Scenario 1: cash of CU60,000 paid **[Refer: paragraph 40]**			
	Scenario 1 totals	67,600	7,600	0
	Scenario 2: 1,200 shares issued **[Refer: paragraph 39]**		60,000	(60,000)
	Scenario 2 totals	67,600	67,600	0

Share-based payment transactions among group entities

IG22A   Paragraphs 43A and 43B of IFRS 2 specify the accounting requirements for share-based payment transactions among group entities in the separate or individual financial statements of the entity receiving the goods or services. Example 14 illustrates the journal entries in the separate or individual financial statements for a group transaction in which a parent grants rights to its equity instruments to the employees of its subsidiary.

IG Example 14

Share-based payment transactions in which a parent grants rights to its equity instruments to the employees of its subsidiary

Background

A parent grants 200 share options to each of 100 employees of its subsidiary, conditional upon the completion of two years' service with the subsidiary. The fair value of the share options on grant date is CU30 each. At grant date, the subsidiary estimates that 80 per cent of the employees will complete the two-year service period. This estimate does not change during the vesting period. At the end of the vesting period, 81 employees complete the required two years of service. The parent does not require the subsidiary to pay for the shares needed to settle the grant of share options.

Application of requirements

As required by paragraph B53 of the IFRS, over the two-year vesting period, the subsidiary measures the services received from the employees in accordance with the requirements applicable to equity-settled share-based payment transactions. **[Refer: paragraph 43B]** Thus, the subsidiary measures the services received from the employees on the basis of the fair value of the share options at grant date. An increase in equity is recognised as a contribution from the parent in the separate or individual financial statements of the subsidiary.

The journal entries recorded by the subsidiary for each of the two years are as follows:

Year 1

Dr Remuneration expense (200 × 100 × CU30 **[Refer: paragraphs 11, 12 and 16–19]** × 0.8/2 **[Refer: paragraphs 19, 20 and 15(a)]**)	CU240,000	
Cr Equity (Contribution from the parent)		CU240,000

Year 2

Dr Remuneration expense (200 × 100 × CU30 × 0.81 **[Refer: paragraphs 19 and 20]** − 240,000)	CU246,000	
Cr Equity (Contribution from the parent)		CU246,000

Illustrative disclosures

IG23　　The following example illustrates the disclosure requirements in paragraphs 44–52 of the IFRS.[3]

Extract from the Notes to the Financial Statements of Company Z for the year ended 31 December 20X5.

Share-based Payment

During the period ended 31 December 20X5, the Company had four share-based payment arrangements, which are described below.

Type of arrangement	Senior management share option plan	General employee share option plan	Executive share plan	Senior management share appreciation cash plan
Date of grant	1 January 20X4	1 January 20X5	1 January 20X5	1 July 20X5
Number granted	50,000	75,000	50,000	25,000
Contractual life	10 years	10 years	N/A	10 years
Vesting conditions	1.5 years' service and achievement of a share price target, which was achieved.	Three years' service.	Three years' service and achievement of a target growth in earnings per share.	Three years' service and achievement of a target increase in market share.

The estimated fair value of each share option granted in the general employee share option plan is CU23.60. This was calculated by applying a binomial option pricing model. The model inputs were the share price at grant date of CU50, exercise price of CU50, expected volatility of 30 per cent, no expected dividends, contractual life of ten years, and a risk-free interest rate of 5 per cent. To allow for the effects of early exercise, it was assumed that the employees would exercise the options after vesting date when the share price was twice the exercise price. Historical volatility was 40 per cent, which includes the early years of the Company's life; the Company expects the volatility of its share price to reduce as it matures.

The estimated fair value of each share granted in the executive share plan is CU50.00, which is equal to the share price at the date of grant.

3　Note that the illustrative example is not intended to be a template or model and is therefore not exhaustive. For example, it does not illustrate the disclosure requirements in paragraphs 47(c), 48 and 49 of the IFRS.

Further details of the two share option plans are as follows:

	20X4		20X5	
	Number of options	Weighted average exercise price	Number of options	Weighted average exercise price
Outstanding at start of year	0	–	45,000	CU40
Granted	50,000	CU40	75,000	CU50
Forfeited	(5,000)	CU40	(8,000)	CU46
Exercised	0	–	(4,000)	CU40
Outstanding at end of year	45,000	CU40	108,000	CU46
Exercisable at end of year	0	CU40	38,000	CU40

The weighted average share price at the date of exercise for share options exercised during the period was CU52. The options outstanding at 31 December 20X5 had an exercise price of CU40 or CU50, and a weighted average remaining contractual life of 8.64 years.

	20X4	20X5
	CU	CU
Expense arising from share-based payment transactions	495,000	1,105,867
Expense arising from share and share option plans	495,000	1,007,000
Closing balance of liability for cash share appreciation plan	–	98,867
Expense arising from increase in fair value of liability for cash share appreciation plan	–	9,200

Summary of conditions for a counterparty to receive an equity instrument granted and of accounting treatments

IG24   The table below categorises, with examples, the various conditions that determine whether a counterparty receives an equity instrument granted and the accounting treatment of share-based payments with those conditions.

	VESTING CONDITIONS			NON-VESTING CONDITIONS		
	Service conditions	Performance conditions				
		Performance conditions that are market conditions	Other performance conditions	Neither the entity nor the counterparty can choose whether the condition is met	Counterparty can choose whether to meet the condition	Entity can choose whether to meet the condition
Example conditions	Requirement to remain in service for three years	Target based on the market price of the entity's equity instruments	Target based on a successful initial public offering with a specified service requirement	Target based on a commodity index	Paying contributions towards the exercise price of a share-based payment	Continuation of the plan by the entity
Include in grant-date fair value?	No	Yes	No	Yes	Yes	Yes[a]
Accounting treatment if the condition is not met after the grant date and during the vesting period	Forfeiture. The entity revises the expense to reflect the best available estimate of the number of equity instruments expected to vest.	No change to accounting. The entity continues to recognise the expense over the remainder of the vesting period.	Forfeiture. The entity revises the expense to reflect the best available estimate of the number of equity instruments expected to vest.	No change to accounting. The entity continues to recognise the expense over the remainder of the vesting period.	Cancellation. The entity recognises immediately the amount of the expense that would otherwise have been recognised over the remainder of the vesting period.	Cancellation. The entity recognises immediately the amount of the expense that would otherwise have been recognised over the remainder of the vesting period.
	(paragraph 19)	(paragraph 21)	(paragraph 19)	(paragraph 21A)	(paragraph 28A)	(paragraph 28A)

Summary of conditions that determine whether a counterparty receives an equity instrument granted

(a) In the calculation of the fair value of the share-based payment, the probability of continuation of the plan by the entity is assumed to be 100 per cent.

Table of Concordance

This table shows how the contents of IFRIC 8 and IFRIC 11 correspond with IFRS 2 (as amended in 2009).

IFRIC 8 paragraph	IFRS 2 (amended) paragraph	IFRIC 11 paragraph	IFRS 2 (amended) paragraph
1	2	1	B48
2, 3	IG5A, IG5B	2, 3	B51, B52
4	None	4–6	B46
5	IG5C	7	B49
6	2	8	B53
7, 8	2	9	B59
9	2	10	B61
9–12	13A	11	B55
13, 14	64	12, 13	64
IE1–IE4	IG Example 1	IE1–IE4	IG Example 14
BC1–BC5	BC18A–BC18D	BC1, BC2	None
BC6–BC12	BC128B–BC128H	BC3–BC18	None
BC13	None	BC19	BC268P
		BC20	None
		BC21, BC22	BC268Q, BC268R

IASB documents published to accompany

IFRS 3

Business Combinations

The text of the unaccompanied standard, IFRS 3, is contained in Part A of this edition. The text of the Basis for Conclusions on IFRS 3 is contained in Part C of this edition. Its effective date when issued was 1 July 2009. This part presents the following documents:

ILLUSTRATIVE EXAMPLES

APPENDIX
Amendments to the guidance on other IFRSs

Contents

...continued

APPENDIX

Amendments to guidance on other IFRSs

IFRS 3 *Business Combinations*
Illustrative Examples

These examples accompany, but are not part of, IFRS 3.

Reverse acquisitions

Illustrating the consequences of recognising a reverse acquisition by applying paragraphs B19–B27 of IFRS 3.

IE1   This example illustrates the accounting for a reverse acquisition in which Entity B, the legal subsidiary, acquires Entity A, the entity issuing equity instruments and therefore the legal parent, in a reverse acquisition on 30 September 20X6. This example ignores the accounting for any income tax effects.

IE2   The statements of financial position of Entity A and Entity B immediately before the business combination are:

	Entity A (legal parent, accounting acquiree) CU[(a)]	Entity B (legal subsidiary, accounting acquirer) CU
Current assets	500	700
Non-current assets	1,300	3,000
Total assets	1,800	3,700
Current liabilities	300	600
Non-current liabilities	400	1,100
Total liabilities	700	1,700
Shareholders' equity		
Retained earnings	800	1,400
Issued equity		
100 ordinary shares	300	
60 ordinary shares		600
Total shareholders' equity	1,100	2,000
Total liabilities and shareholders' equity	1,800	3,700

(a)   In these examples monetary amounts are denominated in 'currency units (CU)'.

IE3   This example also uses the following information:

(a)   On 30 September 20X6 Entity A issues 2.5 shares in exchange for each ordinary share of Entity B. All of Entity B's shareholders exchange their shares in Entity B. Therefore, Entity A issues 150 ordinary shares in exchange for all 60 ordinary shares of Entity B.

(b)   The fair value of each ordinary share of Entity B at 30 September 20X6 is CU40. The quoted market price of Entity A's ordinary shares at that date is CU16.

(c)   The fair values of Entity A's identifiable assets and liabilities at 30 September 20X6 are the same as their carrying amounts, except that the fair value of Entity A's non-current assets at 30 September 20X6 is CU1,500.

Calculating the fair value of the consideration transferred

IE4   As a result of Entity A (legal parent, accounting acquiree) issuing 150 ordinary shares, Entity B's shareholders own 60 per cent of the issued shares of the combined entity (ie 150 of 250 issued shares). The remaining 40 per cent are owned by Entity A's shareholders. If the business combination had taken the form of Entity B issuing additional ordinary shares to Entity A's shareholders in exchange for their ordinary shares in Entity A, Entity B would have had to issue 40 shares for the ratio of ownership interest in the combined entity to be the same. Entity B's shareholders would then own 60 of the 100 issued shares of Entity B – 60 per cent of the combined entity. As a result, the fair value of the consideration effectively transferred by Entity B and the group's interest in Entity A is CU1,600 (40 shares with a fair value per share of CU40).

IE5   The fair value of the consideration effectively transferred should be based on the most reliable measure. In this example, the quoted price of Entity A's shares in the principal (or most advantageous) market for the shares provides a more reliable basis for measuring the consideration effectively transferred than the fair value of the shares in Entity B, and the consideration is measured using the market price of Entity A's shares – 100 shares with a fair value per share of CU16.

Measuring goodwill
[Refer: paragraph B19]

IE6   Goodwill is measured as the excess of the fair value of the consideration effectively transferred (the group's interest in Entity A) over the net amount of Entity A's recognised identifiable assets and liabilities, as follows:

	CU	CU
Consideration effectively transferred		1,600
Net recognised values of Entity A's identifiable assets and liabilities		
Current assets	500	
Non-current assets	1,500	
Current liabilities	(300)	
Non-current liabilities	(400)	(1,300)
Goodwill		300

Consolidated statement of financial position at 30 September 20X6
[Refer: paragraphs B21 and B22]

IE7 The consolidated statement of financial position immediately after the business combination is:

	CU
Current assets [CU700 + CU500] **[Refer: paragraph B22(a) and (b)]**	1,200
Non-current assets [CU3,000 + CU1,500] **[Refer: paragraph B22(a) and (b)]**	4,500
Goodwill **[Refer: paragraph B19]**	300
Total assets	6,000
Current liabilities [CU600 + CU300] **[Refer: paragraph B22(a) and (b)]**	900
Non-current liabilities [CU1,100 + CU400] **[Refer: paragraph B22(a) and (b)]**	1,500
Total liabilities	2,400

continued...

...continued

	CU
Shareholders' equity	
Retained earnings	1,400
[Refer: paragraph B22(c)]	
Issued equity	
250 ordinary shares [CU600 + CU1,600]	2,200
[Refer: paragraph B22(d)]	
Total shareholders' equity	3,600
Total liabilities and shareholders' equity	6,000

IE8   The amount recognised as issued equity interests in the consolidated financial statements (CU2,200) is determined by adding the issued equity of the legal subsidiary immediately before the business combination (CU600) and the fair value of the consideration effectively transferred (CU1,600). However, the equity structure appearing in the consolidated financial statements (ie the number and type of equity interests issued) must reflect the equity structure of the legal parent, including the equity interests issued by the legal parent to effect the combination.

Earnings per share
[Refer: paragraphs B25–B27]

IE9   Assume that Entity B's earnings for the annual period ended 31 December 20X5 were CU600 and that the consolidated earnings for the annual period ended 31 December 20X6 were CU800. Assume also that there was no change in the number of ordinary shares issued by Entity B during the annual period ended 31 December 20X5 and during the period from 1 January 20X6 to the date of the reverse acquisition on 30 September 20X6. Earnings per share for the annual period ended 31 December 20X6 is calculated as follows:

Number of shares deemed to be outstanding for the period from 1 January 20X6 to the acquisition date (ie the number of ordinary shares issued by Entity A (legal parent, accounting acquiree) in the reverse acquisition) **[Refer: paragraph B26(a), ie 2.5 Entity A shares x (issued for each of) 60 Entity B shares]**	150
Number of shares outstanding from the acquisition date to 31 December 20X6 **[Refer: paragraph B26(b), ie 100 shares before the reverse acquisition + (60 x 2.5 shares = 150 shares issued in the reverse acquisition)]**	250
Weighted average number of ordinary shares outstanding [(150 **[shares]** x 9/12 **[months]**) + (250 **[shares]** x 3/12 **[months]**)] **[Refer: paragraph B26]**	175
Earnings per share [800/175]	CU4.57

IE10   Restated earnings per share for the annual period ended 31 December 20X5 is CU4.00 (calculated as the earnings of Entity B of 600 divided by the number of ordinary shares Entity A issued in the reverse acquisition (150)).

Non-controlling interest
[Refer: paragraphs B23 and B24]

IE11   Assume the same facts as above, except that only 56 of Entity B's 60 ordinary shares are exchanged. Because Entity A issues 2.5 shares in exchange for each ordinary share of Entity B, Entity A issues only 140 (rather than 150) shares. As a result, Entity B's shareholders own 58.3 per cent of the issued shares of the combined entity (140 of 240 issued shares). The fair value of the consideration transferred for Entity A, the accounting acquiree, is calculated by assuming that the combination had been effected by Entity B issuing additional ordinary shares to the shareholders of Entity A in exchange for their ordinary shares in Entity A. That is because Entity A is the accounting acquirer, and paragraph B20 of IFRS 3 requires the acquirer to measure the consideration exchanged for the accounting acquiree.

IE12   In calculating the number of shares that Entity B would have had to issue, the non-controlling interest is excluded from the calculation. The majority shareholders own 56 shares of Entity B. For that to represent a 58.3 per cent equity interest, Entity B would have had to issue an additional 40 shares. The majority shareholders would then own 56 of the 96 issued shares of Entity B and, therefore, 58.3 per cent of the combined entity. As a result, the fair value of the consideration transferred for Entity A, the accounting acquiree, is CU1,600 (ie 40 shares, each with a fair value of CU40). That is the same amount as when all 60 of Entity B's shareholders tender all 60 of its ordinary shares for exchange. The recognised amount of the group's interest in Entity A, the accounting acquiree, does not change if some of Entity B's shareholders do not participate in the exchange.

IE13   The non-controlling interest is represented by the four shares of the total 60 shares of Entity B that are not exchanged for shares of Entity A. Therefore, the non-controlling interest is 6.7 per cent. The non-controlling interest reflects the proportionate interest of the non-controlling shareholders in the pre-combination carrying amounts of the net assets of Entity B, the legal subsidiary. Therefore, the consolidated statement of financial position is adjusted to show a non-controlling interest of 6.7 per cent of the pre-combination carrying amounts of Entity B's net assets (ie CU134 or 6.7 per cent of CU2,000).

IE14   The consolidated statement of financial position at 30 September 20X6, reflecting the non-controlling interest, is as follows:

	CU
Current assets [CU700 + CU500] **[Refer: paragraph B22(a) and (b)]**	1,200
Non-current assets [CU3,000 + CU1,500] **[Refer: paragraph B22(a) and (b)]**	4,500
Goodwill **[Refer: paragraph B19]**	300
Total assets	6,000
Current liabilities [CU600 + CU300] **[Refer: paragraph B22(a) and (b)]**	900
Non-current liabilities [CU1,100 + CU400] **[Refer: paragraph 22(a) and (b)]**	1,500
Total liabilities	2,400
Shareholders' equity	
Retained earnings [CU1,400 × 93.3 per cent] **[Refer: paragraphs B22(c) and B23]**	1,306
Issued equity 240 ordinary shares [CU560 + CU1,600] **[Refer: paragraphs B22(d) and B23]**	2,160
Non-controlling interest **[Refer: paragraphs B23 and B24]**	134
Total shareholders' equity	3,600
Total liabilities and shareholders' equity	6,000

IE15   The non-controlling interest of CU134 has two components. The first component is the reclassification of the non-controlling interest's share of the accounting acquirer's retained earnings immediately before the acquisition (CU1,400 × 6.7 per cent or CU93.80). The second component represents the reclassification of the non-controlling interest's share of the accounting acquirer's issued equity (CU600 × 6.7 per cent or CU40.20).

Identifiable intangible assets

Illustrating the consequences of applying paragraphs 10–14 and B31–B40 of IFRS 3.

IE16   The following are examples of identifiable intangible assets acquired in a business combination. Some of the examples may have characteristics of assets other than intangible assets. The acquirer should account for those assets in accordance with their substance. The examples are not intended to be all-inclusive.

IE17   Intangible assets identified as having a contractual basis are those that arise from contractual or other legal rights. Those designated as having a non-contractual basis do not arise from contractual or other legal rights but are separable. Intangible assets identified as having a contractual basis might also be separable but separability is not a necessary condition for an asset to meet the contractual-legal criterion.

Marketing-related intangible assets

IE18   Marketing-related intangible assets are used primarily in the marketing or promotion of products or services. Examples of marketing-related intangible assets are:

Class	Basis
Trademarks, trade names, service marks, collective marks and certification marks	Contractual
Trade dress (unique colour, shape or package design)	Contractual
Newspaper mastheads	Contractual
Internet domain names	Contractual
Non-competition agreements	Contractual

Trademarks, trade names, service marks, collective marks and certification marks

IE19   Trademarks are words, names, symbols or other devices used in trade to indicate the source of a product and to distinguish it from the products of others. A service mark identifies and distinguishes the source of a service rather than a product. Collective marks identify the goods or services of members of a group. Certification marks certify the geographical origin or other characteristics of a good or service.

IE20   Trademarks, trade names, service marks, collective marks and certification marks may be protected legally through registration with governmental agencies, continuous use in commerce or by other means. If it is protected legally through registration or other means, a trademark or other mark acquired in a business combination is an intangible asset that meets the contractual-legal criterion. Otherwise, a trademark or other mark acquired in a business combination can be recognised separately from goodwill if the separability criterion is met, which normally it would be.

IE21   The terms *brand* and *brand name*, often used as synonyms for trademarks and other marks, are general marketing terms that typically refer to a group of complementary assets such as a trademark (or service mark) and its related trade name, formulas, recipes and technological expertise. IFRS 3 does not preclude an entity from recognising, as a single asset separately from goodwill, a group of complementary intangible assets commonly referred to as a brand if the assets that make up that group have similar useful lives.

Internet domain names

IE22   An Internet domain name is a unique alphanumeric name that is used to identify a particular numeric Internet address. Registration of a domain name creates an association between that name and a designated computer on the Internet for the period of the registration. Those registrations are renewable. A registered domain name acquired in a business combination meets the contractual-legal criterion.

Customer-related intangible assets

IE23   Examples of customer-related intangible assets are:

Class	Basis
Customer lists	Non-contractual
Order or production backlog	Contractual
Customer contracts and related customer relationships	Contractual
Non-contractual customer relationships	Non-contractual

Customer lists

IE24   A customer list consists of information about customers, such as their names and contact information. A customer list also may be in the form of a database that includes other information about the customers, such as their order histories and demographic information. A customer list does not usually arise from contractual or other legal rights. However, customer lists are often leased or exchanged. Therefore, a customer list acquired in a business combination normally meets the separability criterion.

Order or production backlog

IE25 An order or production backlog arises from contracts such as purchase or sales orders. An order or production backlog acquired in a business combination meets the contractual-legal criterion even if the purchase or sales orders can be cancelled.

Customer contracts and the related customer relationships

IE26 If an entity establishes relationships with its customers through contracts, those customer relationships arise from contractual rights. Therefore, customer contracts and the related customer relationships acquired in a business combination meet the contractual-legal criterion, even if confidentiality or other contractual terms prohibit the sale or transfer of a contract separately from the acquiree.

IE27 A customer contract and the related customer relationship may represent two distinct intangible assets. Both the useful lives and the pattern in which the economic benefits of the two assets are consumed may differ.

IE28 A customer relationship exists between an entity and its customer if (a) the entity has information about the customer and has regular contact with the customer and (b) the customer has the ability to make direct contact with the entity. Customer relationships meet the contractual-legal criterion if an entity has a practice of establishing contracts with its customers, regardless of whether a contract exists at the acquisition date. Customer relationships may also arise through means other than contracts, such as through regular contact by sales or service representatives.

IE29 As noted in paragraph IE25, an order or a production backlog arises from contracts such as purchase or sales orders and is therefore considered a contractual right. Consequently, if an entity has relationships with its customers through these types of contracts, the customer relationships also arise from contractual rights and therefore meet the contractual-legal criterion.

Examples

IE30 The following examples illustrate the recognition of customer contract and customer relationship intangible assets acquired in a business combination.

(a) Acquirer Company (AC) acquires Target Company (TC) in a business combination on 31 December 20X5. TC has a five-year agreement to supply goods to Customer. Both TC and AC believe that Customer will renew the agreement at the end of the current contract. The agreement is not separable.

The agreement, whether cancellable or not, meets the contractual-legal criterion. Additionally, because TC establishes its relationship with Customer through a contract, not only the agreement itself but also TC's customer relationship with Customer meet the contractual-legal criterion.

(b)   AC acquires TC in a business combination on 31 December 20X5. TC manufactures goods in two distinct lines of business: sporting goods and electronics. Customer purchases both sporting goods and electronics from TC. TC has a contract with Customer to be its exclusive provider of sporting goods but has no contract for the supply of electronics to Customer. Both TC and AC believe that only one overall customer relationship exists between TC and Customer.

     The contract to be Customer's exclusive supplier of sporting goods, whether cancellable or not, meets the contractual-legal criterion. Additionally, because TC establishes its relationship with Customer through a contract, the customer relationship with Customer meets the contractual-legal criterion. Because TC has only one customer relationship with Customer, the fair value of that relationship incorporates assumptions about TC's relationship with Customer related to both sporting goods and electronics. However, if AC determines that the customer relationships with Customer for sporting goods and for electronics are separate from each other, AC would assess whether the customer relationship for electronics meets the separability criterion for identification as an intangible asset.

(c)   AC acquires TC in a business combination on 31 December 20X5. TC does business with its customers solely through purchase and sales orders. At 31 December 20X5, TC has a backlog of customer purchase orders from 60 per cent of its customers, all of whom are recurring customers. The other 40 per cent of TC's customers are also recurring customers. However, as of 31 December 20X5, TC has no open purchase orders or other contracts with those customers.

     Regardless of whether they are cancellable or not, the purchase orders from 60 per cent of TC's customers meet the contractual-legal criterion. Additionally, because TC has established its relationship with 60 per cent of its customers through contracts, not only the purchase orders but also TC's customer relationships meet the contractual-legal criterion. Because TC has a practice of establishing contracts with the remaining 40 per cent of its customers, its relationship with those customers also arises through contractual rights and therefore meets the contractual-legal criterion even though TC does not have contracts with those customers at 31 December 20X5.

(d)   AC acquires TC, an insurer, in a business combination on 31 December 20X5. TC has a portfolio of one-year motor insurance contracts that are cancellable by policyholders.

     Because TC establishes its relationships with policyholders through insurance contracts, the customer relationship with policyholders meets the contractual-legal criterion. IAS 36 *Impairment of Assets* and IAS 38 *Intangible Assets* apply to the customer relationship intangible asset.

Non-contractual customer relationships

IE31   A customer relationship acquired in a business combination that does not arise from a contract may nevertheless be identifiable because the relationship is separable. Exchange transactions for the same asset or a similar asset that indicate that other entities have sold or otherwise transferred a particular type of non-contractual customer relationship would provide evidence that the relationship is separable.

Artistic-related intangible assets

IE32   Examples of artistic-related intangible assets are:

Class	Basis
Plays, operas and ballets	Contractual
Books, magazines, newspapers and other literary works	Contractual
Musical works such as compositions, song lyrics and advertising jingles	Contractual
Pictures and photographs	Contractual
Video and audiovisual material, including motion pictures or films, music videos and television programmes	Contractual

IE33   Artistic-related assets acquired in a business combination are identifiable if they arise from contractual or legal rights such as those provided by copyright. The holder can transfer a copyright, either in whole through an assignment or in part through a licensing agreement. An acquirer is not precluded from recognising a copyright intangible asset and any related assignments or licence agreements as a single asset, provided they have similar useful lives.

Contract-based intangible assets

IE34   Contract-based intangible assets represent the value of rights that arise from contractual arrangements. Customer contracts are one type of contract-based intangible asset. If the terms of a contract give rise to a liability (for example, if the terms of a customer contract are unfavourable relative to market terms), the acquirer recognises it as a liability assumed in the business combination. Examples of contract-based intangible assets are:

Class	Basis
Licensing, royalty and standstill agreements	Contractual
Advertising, construction, management, service or supply contracts	Contractual
Construction permits	Contractual
Franchise agreements	Contractual
Operating and broadcast rights	Contractual
Servicing contracts, such as mortgage servicing contracts	Contractual
Employment contracts	Contractual
Use rights, such as drilling, water, air, timber cutting and route authorities	Contractual

Servicing contracts, such as mortgage servicing contracts

IE35　Contracts to service financial assets are one type of contract-based intangible asset. Although servicing is inherent in all financial assets, it becomes a distinct asset (or liability) by one of the following:

(a)　when contractually separated from the underlying financial asset by sale or securitisation of the assets with servicing retained;

(b)　through the separate purchase and assumption of the servicing.

IE36　If mortgage loans, credit card receivables or other financial assets are acquired in a business combination with servicing retained, the inherent servicing rights are not a separate intangible asset because the fair value of those servicing rights is included in the measurement of the fair value of the acquired financial asset.

Employment contracts

IE37　Employment contracts that are beneficial contracts from the perspective of the employer because the pricing of those contracts is favourable relative to market terms are one type of contract-based intangible asset.

Use rights

IE38　Use rights include rights for drilling, water, air, timber cutting and route authorities. Some use rights are contract-based intangible assets to be accounted for separately from goodwill. Other use rights may have characteristics of tangible assets rather than of intangible assets. An acquirer should account for use rights on the basis of their nature.

Technology-based intangible assets

IE39   Examples of technology-based intangible assets are:

Class	Basis
Patented technology	Contractual
Computer software and mask works	Contractual
Unpatented technology	Non-contractual
Databases, including title plants	Non-contractual
Trade secrets, such as secret formulas, processes and recipes	Contractual

Computer software and mask works

IE40   Computer software and program formats acquired in a business combination that are protected legally, such as by patent or copyright, meet the contractual-legal criterion for identification as intangible assets.

IE41   Mask works are software permanently stored on a read-only memory chip as a series of stencils or integrated circuitry. Mask works may have legal protection. Mask works with legal protection that are acquired in a business combination meet the contractual-legal criterion for identification as intangible assets.

Databases, including title plants

IE42   Databases are collections of information, often stored in electronic form (such as on computer disks or files). A database that includes original works of authorship may be entitled to copyright protection. A database acquired in a business combination and protected by copyright meets the contractual-legal criterion. However, a database typically includes information created as a consequence of an entity's normal operations, such as customer lists, or specialised information, such as scientific data or credit information. Databases that are not protected by copyright can be, and often are, exchanged, licensed or leased to others in their entirety or in part. Therefore, even if the future economic benefits from a database do not arise from legal rights, a database acquired in a business combination meets the separability criterion.

IE43   Title plants constitute a historical record of all matters affecting title to parcels of land in a particular geographical area. Title plant assets are bought and sold, either in whole or in part, in exchange transactions or are licensed. Therefore, title plant assets acquired in a business combination meet the separability criterion.

Trade secrets, such as secret formulas, processes and recipes

IE44   A trade secret is 'information, including a formula, pattern, recipe, compilation, program, device, method, technique, or process that (a) derives independent economic value, actual or potential, from not being generally known and (b) is the subject of efforts that are reasonable under the circumstances to maintain its secrecy.'[1] If the future economic benefits from a trade secret acquired in a business combination are legally protected, that asset meets the contractual-legal criterion. Otherwise, trade secrets acquired in a business combination are identifiable only if the separability criterion is met, which is likely to be the case.

Measurement of non-controlling interest (NCI)

Illustrating the consequences of applying paragraph 19 of IFRS 3.

IE44A   The following examples illustrate the measurement of components of NCI at the acquisition date in a business combination.

Measurement of NCI including preference shares

IE44B   TC has issued 100 preference shares, which are classified as equity. The preference shares have a nominal value of CU1 each. The preference shares give their holders a right to a preferential dividend in priority to the payment of any dividend to the holders of ordinary shares. Upon liquidation of TC, the holders of the preference shares are entitled to receive out of the assets available for distribution the amount of CU1 per share in priority to the holders of ordinary shares. The holders of the preference shares do not have any further rights on liquidation.

IE44C   AC acquires all ordinary shares of TC. The acquisition gives AC control of TC. The acquisition-date fair value of the preference shares is CU120.

IE44D   Paragraph 19 of IFRS 3 states that for each business combination, the acquirer shall measure at the acquisition date components of non-controlling interest in the acquiree that are present ownership interests and entitle their holders to a proportionate share of the entity's net assets in the event of liquidation at either fair value or the present ownership instruments' proportionate share in the acquiree's recognised amounts of the identifiable net assets. All other components of non-controlling interest must be measured at their acquisition-date fair value, unless another measurement basis is required by IFRSs.

IE44E   The non-controlling interests that relate to TC's preference shares do not qualify for the measurement choice in paragraph 19 of IFRS 3 because they do not entitle their holders to a proportionate share of the entity's net assets in the event of liquidation. The acquirer measures the preference shares at their acquisition-date fair value of CU120.

First variation

IE44F   Suppose that upon liquidation of TC, the preference shares entitle their holders to receive a proportionate share of the assets available for distribution. The holders of the preference shares have equal right and ranking to the holders of ordinary shares in the event of liquidation. Assume that the

---

1   Melvin Simensky and Lanning Bryer, *The New Role of Intellectual Property in Commercial Transactions* (New York: John Wiley & Sons, 1998), page 293.

acquisition-date fair value of the preference shares is now CU160 and that the proportionate share of TC's recognised amounts of the identifiable net assets that is attributable to the preference shares is CU140.

IE44G   The preference shares qualify for the measurement choice in paragraph 19 of IFRS 3. AC can choose to measure the preference shares either at their acquisition-date fair value of CU160 or at their proportionate share in the acquiree's recognised amounts of the identifiable net assets of CU140.

Second variation

IE44H   Suppose also that TC has issued share options as remuneration to its employees. The share options are classified as equity and are vested at the acquisition date. They do not represent present ownership interest and do not entitle their holders to a proportionate share of TC's net assets in the event of liquidation. The market-based measure of the share options in accordance with IFRS 2 *Share-based Payment* at the acquisition date is CU200. The share options do not expire on the acquisition date and AC does not replace them.

IE44I   Paragraph 19 of IFRS 3 requires such share options to be measured at their acquisition-date fair value, unless another measurement basis is required by IFRSs. Paragraph 30 of IFRS 3 states that the acquirer shall measure an equity instrument related to share-based payment transactions of the acquiree in accordance with the method in IFRS 2.

IE44J   The acquirer measures the non-controlling interests that are related to the share options at their market-based measure of CU200.

Gain on a bargain purchase

Illustrating the consequences of recognising and measuring a gain from a bargain purchase by applying paragraphs 32–36 of IFRS 3.

IE45   The following example illustrates the accounting for a business combination in which a gain on a bargain purchase is recognised.

IE46   On 1 January 20X5 AC acquires 80 per cent of the equity interests of TC, a private entity, in exchange for cash of CU150. Because the former owners of TC needed to dispose of their investments in TC by a specified date, they did not have sufficient time to market TC to multiple potential buyers. The management of AC initially measures the separately recognisable identifiable assets acquired and the liabilities assumed as of the acquisition date in accordance with the requirements of IFRS 3. The identifiable assets are measured at CU250 and the liabilities assumed are measured at CU50. AC engages an independent consultant, who determines that the fair value of the 20 per cent non-controlling interest in TC is CU42.

IE47   The amount of TC's identifiable net assets (CU200, calculated as CU250 – CU50) exceeds the fair value of the consideration transferred plus the fair value of the non-controlling interest in TC. Therefore, AC reviews the procedures it used to identify and measure the assets acquired and liabilities assumed and to measure the fair value of both the non-controlling interest in

TC and the consideration transferred. After that review, AC decides that the procedures and resulting measures were appropriate. AC measures the gain on its purchase of the 80 per cent interest as follows:

	CU
Amount of the identifiable net assets acquired (CU250 – CU50)	200

		CU	
Less:	Fair value of the consideration transferred for AC's 80 per cent interest in TC; plus	150	
	Fair value of non-controlling interest in TC	42	
			192
Gain on bargain purchase of 80 per cent interest			8

IE48   AC would record its acquisition of TC in its consolidated financial statements as follows:

	CU	CU
Dr Identifiable assets acquired	250	
Cr Cash		150
Cr Liabilities assumed		50
Cr Gain on the bargain purchase		8
Cr Equity—non-controlling interest in TC		42

IE49   If the acquirer chose to measure the non-controlling interest in TC on the basis of its proportionate interest in the identifiable net assets of the acquiree, the recognised amount of the non-controlling interest would be CU40 (CU200 × 0.20). The gain on the bargain purchase then would be CU10 (CU200 – (CU150 + CU40)).

Measurement period

Illustrating the consequences of applying paragraphs 45–50 of IFRS 3.

IE50   If the initial accounting for a business combination is not complete at the end of the financial reporting period in which the combination occurs, paragraph 45 of IFRS 3 requires the acquirer to recognise in its financial statements provisional amounts for the items for which the accounting is incomplete. During the measurement period, the acquirer recognises adjustments to the provisional amounts needed to reflect new information obtained about facts and circumstances that existed as of the acquisition date and, if known, would have affected the measurement of the amounts recognised as of that date. Paragraph 49 of IFRS 3 requires the acquirer to recognise such adjustments as if the accounting for the business combination had been completed at the acquisition date. Measurement period adjustments are not included in profit or loss.

IE51   Suppose that AC acquires TC on 30 September 20X7. AC seeks an independent valuation for an item of property, plant and equipment acquired in the combination, and the valuation was not complete by the time AC authorised for issue its financial statements for the year ended 31 December 20X7. In its 20X7 annual financial statements, AC recognised a provisional fair value for the asset of CU30,000. At the acquisition date, the item of property, plant and equipment had a remaining useful life of five years. Five months after the acquisition date, AC received the independent valuation, which estimated the asset's acquisition-date fair value as CU40,000.

IE52   In its financial statements for the year ended 31 December 20X8, AC retrospectively adjusts the 20X7 prior year information as follows:

(a)   The carrying amount of property, plant and equipment as of 31 December 20X7 is increased by CU9,500. That adjustment is measured as the fair value adjustment at the acquisition date of CU10,000 less the additional depreciation that would have been recognised if the asset's fair value at the acquisition date had been recognised from that date (CU500 for three months' depreciation).

(b)   The carrying amount of goodwill as of 31 December 20X7 is decreased by CU10,000.

(c)   Depreciation expense for 20X7 is increased by CU500.

IE53   In accordance with paragraph B67 of IFRS 3, AC discloses:

(a)   in its 20X7 financial statements, that the initial accounting for the business combination has not been completed because the valuation of property, plant and equipment has not yet been received.

(b)   in its 20X8 financial statements, the amounts and explanations of the adjustments to the provisional values recognised during the current reporting period. Therefore, AC discloses that the 20X7 comparative information is adjusted retrospectively to increase the fair value of the item of property, plant and equipment at the acquisition date by CU9,500, offset by a decrease to goodwill of CU10,000 and an increase in depreciation expense of CU500.

Determining what is part of the business combination transaction

Settlement of a pre-existing relationship

Illustrating the consequences of applying paragraphs 51, 52 and B50–B53 of IFRS 3.

IE54   AC purchases electronic components from TC under a five-year supply contract at fixed rates. Currently, the fixed rates are higher than the rates at which AC could purchase similar electronic components from another supplier. The supply contract allows AC to terminate the contract before the end of the initial five-year term but only by paying a CU6 million penalty. With three years remaining under the supply contract, AC pays CU50 million to acquire TC, which is the fair value of TC based on what other market participants would be willing to pay.

IE55　Included in the total fair value of TC is CU8 million related to the fair value of the supply contract with AC. The CU8 million represents a CU3 million component that is 'at market' because the pricing is comparable to pricing for current market transactions for the same or similar items (selling effort, customer relationships and so on) and a CU5 million component for pricing that is unfavourable to AC because it exceeds the price of current market transactions for similar items. TC has no other identifiable assets or liabilities related to the supply contract, and AC has not recognised any assets or liabilities related to the supply contract before the business combination.

IE56　In this example, AC calculates a loss of CU5 million (the lesser of the CU6 million stated settlement amount and the amount by which the contract is unfavourable to the acquirer) separately from the business combination. **[Refer: paragraph B52(b)]** The CU3 million 'at-market' component of the contract is part of goodwill.

IE57　Whether AC had recognised previously an amount in its financial statements related to a pre-existing relationship will affect the amount recognised as a gain or loss for the effective settlement of the relationship. Suppose that IFRSs had required AC to recognise a CU6 million liability for the supply contract before the business combination. In that situation, AC recognises a CU1 million settlement gain on the contract in profit or loss at the acquisition date (the CU5 million measured loss on the contract less the CU6 million loss previously recognised). In other words, AC has in effect settled a recognised liability of CU6 million for CU5 million, resulting in a gain of CU1 million.

Contingent payments to employees

Illustrating the consequences of applying paragraphs 51, 52, B50, B54 and B55 of IFRS 3.

IE58　TC appointed a candidate as its new CEO under a ten-year contract. The contract required TC to pay the candidate CU5 million if TC is acquired before the contract expires. AC acquires TC eight years later. The CEO was still employed at the acquisition date and will receive the additional payment under the existing contract.

IE59　In this example, TC entered into the employment agreement before the negotiations of the combination began, and the purpose of the agreement was to obtain the services of CEO. Thus, there is no evidence that the agreement was arranged primarily to provide benefits to AC or the combined entity. Therefore, the liability to pay CU5 million is included in the application of the acquisition method.
[Refer: paragraph B50]

IE60　In other circumstances, TC might enter into a similar agreement with CEO at the suggestion of AC during the negotiations for the business combination. If so, the primary purpose of the agreement might be to provide severance pay to CEO, and the agreement may primarily benefit AC or the combined entity rather than TC or its former owners. In that situation, AC accounts for the liability to pay CEO in its post-combination financial statements separately from application of the acquisition method.

[Refer: paragraph B50]

Replacement awards

Illustrating the consequences of applying paragraphs 51, 52 and B56–B62 of IFRS 3.

IE61   The following examples illustrate replacement awards that the acquirer was obliged to issue in the following circumstances:

		Acquiree awards Has the vesting period been completed before the business combination?	
		Completed	**Not completed**
Replacement awards Are employees required to provide additional service after the acquisition date?	**Not required**	Example 1	Example 4
	Required	Example 2	Example 3

IE62   The examples assume that all awards are classified as equity.

Example 1

Acquiree awards	Vesting period **completed** before the business combination
Replacement awards	Additional employee services **are not** required after the acquisition date

IE63   AC issues replacement awards of CU110 (market-based measure) at the acquisition date for TC awards of CU100 (market-based measure) at the acquisition date. No post-combination services are required for the replacement awards and TC's employees had rendered all of the required service for the acquiree awards as of the acquisition date.

IE64   The amount attributable to pre-combination service is the market-based measure of TC's awards (CU100) at the acquisition date; that amount is included in the consideration transferred in the business combination. [Refer: paragraphs B57 and B58] The amount attributable to post-combination service is CU10, which is the difference between the total value of the replacement awards (CU110) and the portion attributable to pre-combination service (CU100). [Refer: paragraph B59] Because no post-combination service is required for the replacement awards, AC immediately recognises CU10 as remuneration cost in its post-combination financial statements.

Example 2

Acquiree awards	Vesting period **completed** before the business combination
Replacement awards	Additional employee services **are** required after the acquisition date

IE65   AC exchanges replacement awards that require one year of post-combination service for share-based payment awards of TC, for which employees had completed the vesting period before the business combination. The market-based measure of both awards is CU100 at the acquisition date. When originally granted, TC's awards had a vesting period of four years. As of the acquisition date, the TC employees holding unexercised awards had rendered a total of seven years of service since the grant date.

IE66   Even though TC employees had already rendered all of the service, AC attributes a portion of the replacement award to post-combination remuneration cost in accordance with paragraph B59 of IFRS 3, because the replacement awards require one year of post-combination service. The total vesting period is five years—the vesting period for the original acquiree award completed before the acquisition date (four years) plus the vesting period for the replacement award (one year).

IE67   The portion attributable to pre-combination services equals the market-based measure of the acquiree award (CU100) multiplied by the ratio of the pre-combination vesting period (four years) to the total vesting period (five years). Thus, CU80 (CU100 × 4/5 years) is attributed to the pre-combination vesting period and therefore included in the consideration transferred in the business combination. **[Refer: paragraph B58]** The remaining CU20 is attributed to the post-combination vesting period and is therefore recognised as remuneration cost in AC's post-combination financial statements in accordance with IFRS 2. **[Refer: paragraph B59]**

Example 3

Acquiree awards	Vesting period **not completed** before the business combination
Replacement awards	Additional employee services **are** required after the acquisition date

IE68   AC exchanges replacement awards that require one year of post-combination service for share-based payment awards of TC, for which employees had not yet rendered all of the service as of the acquisition date. The market-based measure of both awards is CU100 at the acquisition date. When originally granted, the awards of TC had a vesting period of four years. As of the acquisition date, the TC employees had rendered two years' service, and they would have been required to render two additional years of service after the acquisition date for their awards to vest. Accordingly, only a portion of the TC awards is attributable to pre-combination service.

IE69   The replacement awards require only one year of post-combination service. Because employees have already rendered two years of service, the total vesting period is three years. The portion attributable to pre-combination services equals the market-based measure of the acquiree award (CU100) multiplied by the ratio of the pre-combination vesting period (two years) to the **greater of** the total vesting period (three years) or the original vesting period of TC's award (four years). Thus, CU50 (CU100 × 2/4 years) is attributable to pre-combination service and therefore included in the consideration transferred for the acquiree. **[Refer: paragraph B58]** The remaining CU50 is attributable to post-combination service and therefore recognised as remuneration cost in AC's post-combination financial statements. **[Refer: paragraph B59]**

Example 4

Acquiree awards	Vesting period **not completed** before the business combination
Replacement awards	Additional employee services **are not** required after the acquisition date

IE70   Assume the same facts as in Example 3 above, except that AC exchanges replacement awards that require no post-combination service for share-based payment awards of TC for which employees had not yet rendered all of the service as of the acquisition date. The terms of the replaced TC awards did not eliminate any remaining vesting period upon a change in control. (If the TC awards had included a provision that eliminated any remaining vesting period upon a change in control, the guidance in Example 1 would apply.) The market-based measure of both awards is CU100. Because employees have already rendered two years of service and the replacement awards do not require any post-combination service, the total vesting period is two years.

IE71   The portion of the market-based measure of the replacement awards attributable to pre-combination services equals the market-based measure of the acquiree award (CU100) multiplied by the ratio of the pre-combination vesting period (two years) to the **greater of** the total vesting period (two years) or the original vesting period of TC's award (four years). Thus, CU50 (CU100 × 2/4 years) is attributable to pre-combination service and therefore included in the consideration transferred for the acquiree. **[Refer: paragraph B58]** The remaining CU50 is attributable to post-combination service. Because no post-combination service is required to vest in the replacement award, AC recognises the entire CU50 immediately as remuneration cost in the post-combination financial statements. **[Refer: paragraph B59]**

Disclosure requirements

Illustrating the consequences of applying the disclosure requirements in paragraphs 59–63 and B64–B67 of IFRS 3.

IE72 The following example illustrates some of the disclosure requirements of IFRS 3; it is not based on an actual transaction. The example assumes that AC is a listed entity and that TC is an unlisted entity. The illustration presents the disclosures in a tabular format that refers to the specific disclosure requirements illustrated. An actual footnote might present many of the disclosures illustrated in a simple narrative format.

Footnote X: Acquisitions

Paragraph reference	
B64(a)–(d)	On 30 June 20X0 AC acquired 15 per cent of the outstanding ordinary shares of TC. On 30 June 20X2 AC acquired 60 per cent of the outstanding ordinary shares of TC and obtained control of TC. TC is a provider of data networking products and services in Canada and Mexico. As a result of the acquisition, AC is expected to be the leading provider of data networking products and services in those markets. It also expects to reduce costs through economies of scale.
B64(e)	The goodwill of CU2,500 arising from the acquisition consists largely of the synergies and economies of scale expected from combining the operations of AC and TC.
B64(k)	None of the goodwill recognised is expected to be deductible for income tax purposes. The following table summarises the consideration paid for TC and the amounts of the assets acquired and liabilities assumed recognised at the acquisition date, as well as the fair value at the acquisition date of the non-controlling interest in TC.

At 30 June 20X2

	Consideration	CU
B64(f)(i)	Cash	5,000
B64(f)(iv)	Equity instruments (100,000 ordinary shares of AC)	4,000
B64(f)(iii); B64(g)(i)	Contingent consideration arrangement	1,000
B64(f)	**Total consideration transferred**	10,000
B64(p)(i)	**Fair value of AC's equity interest in TC held before the business combination**	2,000
		12,000
B64(m)	Acquisition-related costs (included in selling, general and administrative expenses in AC's statement of comprehensive income for the year ended 31 December 20X2)	1,250

continued...

...continued

Footnote X: Acquisitions

Paragraph reference

B64(i)	**Recognised amounts of identifiable assets acquired and liabilities assumed**	
	Financial assets	3,500
	Inventory	1,000
	Property, plant and equipment	10,000
	Identifiable intangible assets	3,300
	Financial liabilities	(4,000)
	Contingent liability	(1,000)
	Total identifiable net assets	12,800
B64(o)(i)	**Non-controlling interest in TC**	(3,300)
	Goodwill	2,500
		12,000

B64(f)(iv) The fair value of the 100,000 ordinary shares issued as part of the consideration paid for TC (CU4,000) was measured using the closing market price of AC's ordinary shares on the acquisition date.

B64(f)(iii)

B64(g)

B67(b)

The contingent consideration arrangement requires AC to pay the former owners of TC 5 per cent of the revenues of XC, an unconsolidated equity investment owned by TC, in excess of CU7,500 for 20X3, up to a maximum amount of CU2,500 (undiscounted).

The potential undiscounted amount of all future payments that AC could be required to make under the contingent consideration arrangement is between CU0 and CU2,500.

The fair value of the contingent consideration arrangement of CU1,000 was estimated by applying the income approach. The fair value measurement is based on significant inputs that are not observable in the market, which IFRS 13 *Fair Value Measurement* refers to as Level 3 inputs. Key assumptions include a discount rate range of 20–25 per cent and assumed probability-adjusted revenues in XC of CU10,000–20,000.

As of 31 December 20X2, neither the amount recognised for the contingent consideration arrangement, nor the range of outcomes or the assumptions used to develop the estimates had changed.

continued...

...continued

Footnote X: Acquisitions

Paragraph reference

B64(h)   The fair value of the financial assets acquired includes receivables under finance leases of data networking equipment with a fair value of CU2,375. The gross amount due under the contracts is CU3,100, of which CU450 is expected to be uncollectible.

B67(a)   The fair value of the acquired identifiable intangible assets of CU3,300 is provisional pending receipt of the final valuations for those assets.

B64(j)   A contingent liability of CU1,000 has been recognised for expected warran-
B67(c)   ty claims on products sold by TC during the last three years. We expect that the majority of this expenditure will be incurred in 20X3 and that all
IAS 37.84,   will be incurred by the end of 20X4. The potential undiscounted amount of
85   all future payments that AC could be required to make under the warranty arrangements is estimated to be between CU500 and CU1,500. As of 31 December 20X2, there has been no change since 30 June 20X2 in the amount recognised for the liability or any change in the range of outcomes or assumptions used to develop the estimates.

B64(o)   The fair value of the non-controlling interest in TC, an unlisted company, was estimated by applying a market approach and an income approach. The fair value measurements are based on significant inputs that are not observable in the market and thus represent a fair value measurement categorised within Level 3 of the fair value hierarchy as described in IFRS 13. Key assumptions include the following:

(a)   a discount rate range of 20–25 per cent;

(b)   a terminal value based on a range of terminal EBITDA multiples between 3 and 5 times (or, if appropriate, based on long-term sustainable growth rates ranging from 3 to 6 per cent);

(c)   financial multiples of companies deemed to be similar to TC; and

(d)   adjustments because of the lack of control or lack of marketability that market participants would consider when measuring the fair value of the non-controlling interest in TC.

B64(p)(ii)   AC recognised a gain of CU500 as a result of measuring at fair value its 15 per cent equity interest in TC held before the business combination. The gain is included in other income in AC's statement of comprehensive income for the year ending 31 December 20X2.

B64(q)(i)   The revenue included in the consolidated statement of comprehensive income since 30 June 20X2 contributed by TC was CU4,090. TC also contributed profit of CU1,710 over the same period.

continued...

...continued

Footnote X: Acquisitions

Paragraph reference	
B64(q)(ii)	Had TC been consolidated from 1 January 20X2 the consolidated statement of comprehensive income would have included revenue of CU27,670 and profit of CU12,870.

Definition of a business

IE73 The examples in paragraphs IE74–IE123 illustrate application of the guidance in paragraphs B7–B12D on the definition of a business.

[Link to Basis for Conclusions paragraph BC21R(f) for why the draft example on the acquisition of oil and gas operations was not incorporated]

Example A—acquisition of real estate

Scenario 1—Background

IE74 An entity (Purchaser) purchases a portfolio of 10 single-family homes that each have an in-place lease. The fair value of the consideration paid is equal to the aggregate fair value of the 10 single-family homes acquired. Each single-family home includes the land, building and property improvements. Each home has a different floor area and interior design. The 10 single-family homes are located in the same area and the classes of customers (eg tenants) are similar. The risks associated with operating in the real estate market of the homes acquired are not significantly different. No employees, other assets, processes or other activities are transferred.

Scenario 1—Application of requirements

IE75 Purchaser elects to apply the optional concentration test set out in paragraph B7B and concludes that:

    (a)   each single-family home is considered a single identifiable asset in accordance with paragraph B7B for the following reasons:

        (i)   the building and property improvements are attached to the land and cannot be removed without incurring significant cost; and

        (ii)   the building and the in-place lease are considered a single identifiable asset, because they would be recognised and measured as a single identifiable asset in a business combination (see paragraph B42).

    (b)   the group of 10 single-family homes is a group of similar identifiable assets because the assets (all single-family homes) are similar in nature and the risks associated with managing and creating outputs are not significantly different. This is because the types of homes and classes of customers are not significantly different.

(c)   consequently, substantially all of the fair value of the gross assets acquired is concentrated in a group of similar identifiable assets.

IE76   Therefore, Purchaser concludes that the acquired set of activities and assets is not a business.

Scenario 2—Background

IE77   Assume the same facts as in Scenario 1 except that Purchaser also purchases a multi-tenant corporate office park with six 10-storey office buildings that are fully leased. The additional set of activities and assets acquired includes the land, buildings, leases and contracts for outsourced cleaning, security and maintenance. No employees, other assets, other processes or other activities are transferred. The aggregate fair value associated with the office park is similar to the aggregate fair value associated with the 10 single-family homes. The processes performed through the contracts for outsourced cleaning and security are ancillary or minor within the context of all the processes required to create outputs.

Scenario 2—Application of requirements

IE78   Purchaser elects to apply the optional concentration test set out in paragraph B7B and concludes that the single-family homes and the office park are not similar identifiable assets, because the single-family homes and the office park differ significantly in the risks associated with operating the assets, obtaining tenants and managing tenants. In particular, the scale of operations and risks associated with the two classes of customers are significantly different. Consequently, the fair value of the gross assets acquired is not substantially all concentrated in a group of similar identifiable assets, because the fair value of the office park is similar to the aggregate fair value of the 10 single-family homes. Thus Purchaser assesses whether the set meets the minimum requirements to be considered a business in accordance with paragraphs B8–B12D.

IE79   The set of activities and assets has outputs because it generates revenue through the in-place leases. Consequently, Purchaser applies the criteria in paragraph B12C to determine whether any processes acquired are substantive.

IE80   Purchaser concludes that the criterion in paragraph B12C(a) is not met because:

(a)   the set does not include an organised workforce; and

(b)   Purchaser considers that the processes performed by the outsourced cleaning, security and maintenance personnel (the only processes acquired) are ancillary or minor within the context of all the processes required to create outputs (see paragraph B12D(c)) and, therefore, are not critical to the ability to continue producing outputs.

IE81   After considering the only processes acquired, those performed by the outsourced cleaning, security and maintenance personnel, Purchaser also concludes that the criteria in paragraph B12C(b) are not met. Either of the following reasons justifies that conclusion:

(a)   the processes do not significantly contribute to the ability to continue producing outputs.

(b)   the processes are readily accessible in the marketplace. Thus, they are not unique or scarce. In addition, they could be replaced without significant cost, effort, or delay in the ability to continue producing outputs.

IE82   Because none of the criteria in paragraph B12C is met, Purchaser concludes that the acquired set of activities and assets is not a business.

Scenario 3—Background

IE83   Assume the same facts as in Scenario 2, except that the acquired set of activities and assets also includes the employees responsible for leasing, tenant management, and managing and supervising all operational processes.

Scenario 3—Application of requirements

IE84   Purchaser elects not to apply the optional concentration test set out in paragraph B7B and therefore assesses whether the set meets the minimum requirements to be considered a business in accordance with paragraphs B8–B12D.

IE85   The acquired set of activities and assets has outputs because it generates revenue through the in-place leases. Consequently, Purchaser applies the criteria in paragraph B12C.

IE86   Purchaser concludes that the criterion in paragraph B12C(a) is met because the set includes an organised workforce with the necessary skills, knowledge or experience to perform processes (ie leasing, tenant management, and managing and supervising the operational processes) that are substantive because they are critical to the ability to continue producing outputs when applied to the acquired inputs (ie the land, buildings and in-place leases). Furthermore, Purchaser concludes that the criterion in paragraph B8 is met because those substantive processes and inputs together significantly contribute to the ability to create output. Consequently, Purchaser concludes that the acquired set of activities and assets is a business.

Example B—acquisition of a drug candidate

Scenario 1—Background

IE87   An entity (Purchaser) purchases a legal entity that contains:

   (a)   the rights to an in-process research and development project that is developing a compound to treat diabetes and is in its final testing phase (Project 1). Project 1 includes the historical know-how, formula protocols, designs and procedures expected to be needed to complete the final testing phase.

   (b)   a contract that provides outsourced clinical trials. The contract is priced at current market rates and a number of vendors in the marketplace could provide the same services. Therefore, the fair value associated with this contract is nil. Purchaser has no option to renew the contract.

   No employees, other assets, other processes or other activities are transferred.

Scenario 1—Application of requirements

IE88   Purchaser elects to apply the optional concentration test set out in paragraph B7B and concludes that:

   (a)   Project 1 is a single identifiable asset because it would be recognised and measured as a single identifiable intangible asset in a business combination.

   (b)   because the acquired contract has a fair value of nil, substantially all of the fair value of the gross assets acquired is concentrated in Project 1.

IE89   Consequently, Purchaser concludes that the acquired set of activities and assets is not a business.

Scenario 2—Background

IE90   Assume the same facts as in Scenario 1 except that the acquired set of activities and assets also includes another in-process research and development project that is developing a compound to treat Alzheimer's disease and is in its final testing phase (Project 2). Project 2 includes the historical know-how, formula protocols, designs, and procedures expected to be needed to complete the final phase of testing. The fair value associated with Project 2 is similar to the fair value associated with Project 1. No employees, other assets, processes or other activities are transferred.

Scenario 2—Application of requirements

IE91   Purchaser elects to apply the optional concentration test set out in paragraph B7B and concludes that:

   (a)   Project 1 and Project 2 are identifiable intangible assets that would each be recognised and measured as a separate identifiable asset in a business combination.

    (b)   Project 1 and Project 2 are not similar identifiable assets because significantly different risks are associated with managing and creating outputs from each asset. Each project has significantly different risks associated with developing, completing and marketing the compound to customers. The compounds are intended to treat significantly different medical conditions, and each project has a significantly different potential customer base.

    (c)   consequently, the fair value of the gross assets acquired is not substantially all concentrated in a single identifiable asset or group of similar identifiable assets. Therefore, Purchaser assesses whether the set meets the minimum requirements to be considered a business in accordance with paragraphs B8–B12D.

IE92   The acquired set of activities and assets does not have outputs because it has not started generating revenue. Thus, Purchaser applies the criteria in paragraph B12B. Purchaser concludes that those criteria are not met for the following reasons:

    (a)   the set does not include an organised workforce; and

    (b)   although the contract that provides outsourced clinical trials might give access to an organised workforce that has the necessary skills, knowledge or experience to perform processes needed to carry out the clinical trials, that organised workforce cannot develop or convert the inputs acquired by Purchaser into outputs. Successful clinical trials are a pre-condition for producing output, but carrying out those trials will not develop or convert the acquired inputs into outputs.

Consequently, Purchaser concludes that the acquired set of activities and assets is not a business.

Example C—acquisition of a biotech entity

Background

IE93   An entity (Purchaser) purchases a legal entity (Entity Biotech). Entity Biotech's operations include: research and development activities on several drug compounds that it is developing (in-process research and development projects); senior management and scientists who have the necessary skills, knowledge, or experience to perform research and development activities; and tangible assets (including a corporate headquarters, a research lab, and lab equipment). Entity Biotech does not yet have a marketable product and has not yet generated revenue. Each of the assets acquired has a similar fair value.

Application of requirements

IE94   It is evident that the fair value of the gross assets acquired is not substantially all concentrated in a single identifiable asset or group of similar identifiable assets. Thus, the optional concentration test set out in paragraph B7B would not be met. Consequently, Purchaser assesses whether the set meets the minimum requirements to be considered a business in accordance with paragraphs B8–B12D.

IE95   Purchaser first assesses whether it has acquired any processes. No process is documented. Nevertheless, the acquired organised workforce has proprietary knowledge of Biotech's ongoing projects and experience with them. Applying paragraph B7(b), Purchaser concludes that the intellectual capacity of the acquired organised workforce having the necessary skills and experience following rules and conventions provides the necessary processes that are capable of being applied to inputs to create outputs.

IE96   Purchaser next assesses whether the acquired processes are substantive. The set of activities and assets does not have outputs. Thus, Purchaser applies the criteria in paragraph B12B. Purchaser concludes that those criteria are met because:

(a)   the acquired processes are critical to the ability to develop or convert the acquired inputs into outputs; and

(b)   the inputs acquired include both:

(i)   an organised workforce that has the necessary skills, knowledge, or experience to perform the acquired processes; and

(ii)   other inputs that the organised workforce could develop or convert into outputs. Those inputs include the in-process research and development projects.

IE97   Finally, applying the criteria in paragraph B8, Purchaser concludes that the acquired substantive processes and the acquired inputs together significantly contribute to the ability to create output. Consequently, Purchaser concludes that the acquired set of activities and assets is a business.

Example D—acquisition of a television station

Background

IE98   An entity (Purchaser) purchases broadcasting assets from another entity (Seller). The acquired set of activities and assets includes only the communications licence, the broadcasting equipment and an office building. Each of the assets acquired has a similar fair value. Purchaser does not purchase the processes needed to broadcast programmes and it does not acquire any employees, other assets, other processes or other activities. Before the acquisition date, Seller stopped broadcasting using the set of activities and assets acquired by Purchaser.

Application of requirements

IE99   Purchaser elects to apply the optional concentration test set out in paragraph B7B and concludes that:

(a)   the broadcasting equipment and building are not a single identifiable asset because the equipment is not attached to the building and can be removed without significant cost or diminution in utility or fair value of either asset.

(b)   the licence is an intangible asset, whereas the broadcasting equipment and building are tangible assets in different classes. Consequently, in accordance with paragraph B7B(f), the assets are not considered similar to each other.

(c)   each of the single identifiable assets has similar fair value. Thus, the fair value of the gross assets acquired is not substantially all concentrated in a single identifiable asset or group of similar identifiable assets.

Consequently, Purchaser assesses whether the set of activities and assets meets the minimum requirements to be considered a business in accordance with paragraphs B8–B12D.

IE100   The set of activities and assets does not have outputs, because Seller has stopped broadcasting. Thus, Purchaser applies the criteria in paragraph B12B. The set does not include an organised workforce, so it does not meet those criteria. Consequently, Purchaser concludes that the acquired set of activities and assets is not a business.

Example E—acquisition of a closed manufacturing facility

Background

IE101   An entity (Purchaser) purchases a closed manufacturing facility—the land and the building—as well as the related equipment. The fair value of the equipment and the fair value of the facility are similar. To comply with local laws, Purchaser must take over the employees who worked in the facility. No other assets, processes or other activities are transferred. The acquired set of activities and assets stopped producing outputs before the acquisition date.

Application of requirements

IE102   Purchaser elects to apply the optional concentration test set out in paragraph B7B and concludes that:

(a)   the equipment and the facility are not a single identifiable asset because the equipment could be removed from the facility without significant cost or diminution in utility or fair value of either the equipment or the facility—the equipment is not attached to the facility and can be used in many other types of manufacturing facilities.

(b)   the equipment and facility are not similar identifiable assets because they are in different classes of tangible assets.

(c)   the fair values of the equipment and the facility are similar. Therefore, the fair value of the gross assets acquired is not substantially all concentrated in a single identifiable asset or group of similar identifiable assets.

Consequently, Purchaser assesses whether the set of activities and assets meets the minimum requirements to be considered a business in accordance with paragraphs B8–B12D.

IE103   The acquired set of activities and assets does not have outputs at the acquisition date because it stopped producing outputs before then. Consequently, Purchaser applies the criteria in paragraph B12B. The set includes an organised workforce that has the necessary skills, knowledge or experience to use the equipment, but it does not include another acquired input (such as intellectual property or inventories) that the organised workforce could develop or convert into outputs. The facility and the equipment cannot be developed or converted into outputs. Consequently, Purchaser concludes that the acquired set of activities and assets is not a business.

Example F—licence of distribution rights

Background

IE104   An entity (Purchaser) purchases from another entity (Seller) the exclusive sublicence to distribute Product X in a specified jurisdiction. Seller has the licence to distribute Product X worldwide. As part of this transaction, Purchaser also purchases the existing customer contracts in the jurisdiction and takes over a supply contract to purchase Product X from the producer at market rates. None of the identifiable assets acquired has a fair value that constitutes substantially all of the fair value of the gross assets acquired. No employees, other assets, processes, distribution capabilities or other activities are transferred.

Application of requirements

IE105   Purchaser elects to apply the optional concentration test set out in paragraph B7B and concludes that:

(a)   the identifiable assets that could be recognised in a business combination include the sublicence to distribute Product X, customer contracts and the supply contract;

(b)   the sublicence and customer contracts are in different classes of intangible assets, so they are not similar identifiable assets; and

(c)   consequently, the fair value of the gross assets acquired is not substantially all concentrated in a single identifiable asset or group of similar identifiable assets.

Consequently, Purchaser assesses whether the set of activities and assets meets the minimum requirements to be considered a business in accordance with paragraphs B8–B12D.

IE106   The set of activities and assets has outputs because at the acquisition date the licence was generating revenue from customers in the jurisdiction specified in the sublicence. Consequently, Purchaser applies the criteria in paragraph B12C. As explained in paragraph B12D(a), acquired contracts are an input and not a substantive process. Purchaser considers next whether the acquired supply contract provides access to an organised workforce that performs a substantive process. Because the supply contract is not providing a service that applies a process to another acquired input, Purchaser concludes that the substance of the supply contract is only that of buying Product X, without acquiring the organised workforce, processes and other inputs needed to produce Product X. Furthermore, the acquired sublicence is an input, not a process. Purchaser concludes that the set is not a business because it does not include an organised workforce and Purchaser has acquired no substantive process that could meet the criteria in paragraph B12C.

Example G—acquisition of brands

Background

IE107   Assume the same facts as in Example F, except that Purchaser purchases the worldwide rights to Product X, including all related intellectual property. The acquired set of activities and assets includes all customer contracts and customer relationships, finished goods inventories, marketing materials, customer incentive programmes, raw material supply contracts, specialised equipment specific to manufacturing Product X and documented manufacturing processes and protocols to produce Product X. No employees, other assets, other processes or other activities are transferred. None of the identifiable assets acquired has a fair value that constitutes substantially all of the fair value of the gross assets acquired.

Application of requirements

IE108   As noted in paragraphs IE105 and IE107, the fair value of the gross assets acquired is not substantially all concentrated in a single identifiable asset or group of similar identifiable assets. Thus, the optional concentration test set out in paragraph B7B would not be met. Consequently, Purchaser assesses whether the set of activities and assets meets the minimum requirements to be considered a business in accordance with paragraphs B8–B12D.

IE109   The set of activities and assets has outputs, so Purchaser applies the criteria in paragraph B12C. The set does not include an organised workforce and, therefore, does not meet the criterion in paragraph B12C(a). However, Purchaser concludes that the acquired manufacturing processes are substantive because, when applied to acquired inputs, such as the intellectual property, raw material supply contracts and specialised equipment, those processes significantly contribute to the ability to continue producing outputs and because they are unique to Product X. Consequently, the criterion in paragraph B12C(b) is met. Furthermore, Purchaser concludes that the criterion in paragraph B8 is met because those substantive processes and inputs together significantly contribute to the ability to create output. As a result, Purchaser concludes that the acquired set of activities and assets is a business.

Example H—acquisition of loan portfolio

Scenario 1—Background

IE110 An entity (Purchaser) purchases a loan portfolio from another entity (Seller). The portfolio consists of residential mortgage loans with terms, sizes and risk ratings that are not significantly different. No employees, other assets, processes or other activities are transferred.

Scenario 1—Application of requirements

IE111 Purchaser elects to apply the optional concentration test set out in paragraph B7B and concludes that:

(a) the assets (residential mortgage loans) are similar in nature;

(b) the risks associated with managing and creating outputs are not significantly different because the terms, sizes and risk ratings of the loans are not significantly different;

(c) the acquired loans are similar assets; and

(d) consequently, substantially all of the fair value of the gross assets acquired is concentrated in a group of similar identifiable assets.

Consequently, Purchaser concludes that the acquired set of activities and assets is not a business.

Scenario 2—Background

IE112 Assume the same facts as in Scenario 1 except that the portfolio of loans consists of commercial loans with terms, sizes and risk ratings that are significantly different. None of the acquired loans, and no group of loans with similar terms, sizes and risk ratings, has a fair value that constitutes substantially all of the fair value of the acquired portfolio. No employees, other assets, processes or other activities are transferred.

Scenario 2—Application of requirements

IE113 Purchaser elects to apply the optional concentration test set out in paragraph B7B and concludes that:

(a) the assets (commercial loans) are similar in nature;

(b) the risks associated with managing and creating outputs from the loans are significantly different because the terms, sizes and risk ratings of the loans are significantly different;

(c) the acquired loans are not similar identifiable assets; and

(d) consequently, the fair value of the gross assets acquired is not substantially all concentrated in a group of similar identifiable assets.

Consequently, Purchaser assesses whether the set meets the minimum requirements to be considered a business in accordance with paragraphs B8–B12D.

IE114 The portfolio of loans has outputs because it generates interest income. Consequently, Purchaser applies the criteria in paragraph B12C. Acquired contracts are not a substantive process, as explained in paragraph B12D(a). Moreover, the acquired set of activities and assets does not include an organised workforce and there are no acquired processes that could meet the criteria in paragraph B12C(b). Consequently, Purchaser concludes that the acquired set of activities and assets is not a business.

Scenario 3—Background

IE115 Assume the same facts as in Scenario 2 but Purchaser also takes over the employees of Seller (such as brokers, vendors, and risk managers) who managed the credit risk of the portfolio and the relationship with the borrowers. The consideration transferred to Seller is significantly higher than the fair value of the acquired portfolio of loans.

Scenario 3—Application of requirements

IE116 As noted in paragraph IE113, the fair value of the gross assets acquired is not substantially all concentrated in a group of similar identifiable assets. Thus, the optional concentration test set out in paragraph B7B would not be met. Consequently, Purchaser assesses whether the set meets the minimum requirements to be considered a business in accordance with paragraphs B8–B12D.

IE117 The portfolio of loans has outputs because it generates interest income. Consequently, Purchaser applies the criteria in paragraph B12C and concludes that the criterion in paragraph B12C(a) is met because the set includes an organised workforce with the necessary skills, knowledge or experience to perform processes (customer relationship management and credit risk management) critical to the ability to continue producing outputs. Furthermore, Purchaser concludes that the criterion in paragraph B8 is met because those substantive processes and the acquired inputs (the portfolio of loans) together significantly contribute to the ability to create output. Consequently, Purchaser concludes that the acquired set is a business.

Example I—determining the fair value of the gross assets acquired

Background

IE118 An entity (Purchaser) holds a 20% interest in another entity (Entity A). At a subsequent date (the acquisition date), Purchaser acquires a further 50% interest in Entity A and obtains control of it. Entity A's assets and liabilities on the acquisition date are the following:

(a) a building with a fair value of CU500;

(b) an identifiable intangible asset with a fair value of CU400;

(c) cash and cash equivalents with a fair value of CU100;

(d) financial liabilities with a fair value of CU700; and

(e)   deferred tax liabilities of CU160 arising from temporary differences associated with the building and the intangible asset.

IE119   Purchaser pays CU200 for the additional 50% interest in Entity A. Purchaser determines that at the acquisition date the fair value of Entity A is CU400, that the fair value of the non-controlling interest in Entity A is CU120 (30% x CU400) and that the fair value of the previously held interest is CU80 (20% x CU400).

Application of requirements

IE120   To perform the optional concentration test set out in paragraph B7B, Purchaser needs to determine the fair value of the gross assets acquired. Applying paragraph B7B, Purchaser determines that the fair value of the gross assets acquired is CU1,000, calculated as follows:

(a)   the fair value of the building (CU500); **[Refer: paragraph B7B(a)]** plus

(b)   the fair value of the identifiable intangible asset (CU400); **[Refer: paragraph B7B(a)]** plus

(c)   the excess (CU100) of:

    (i)   the sum (CU400) of the consideration transferred (CU200), plus the fair value of the non-controlling interest (CU120), plus the fair value of the previously held interest (CU80); over

    (ii)   the fair value of the net identifiable assets acquired (CU300 = CU500 + CU400 + CU100 − CU700).

[Refer: paragraph B7B(a) and (b)]

IE121   The excess referred to in paragraph IE120(c) is determined in a manner similar to the initial measurement of goodwill in accordance with paragraph 32 of IFRS 3. Including this amount in determining the fair value of the gross assets acquired means that the concentration test is based on an amount that is affected by the value of any substantive processes acquired.

IE122   The fair value of gross assets acquired is determined after making the following exclusions specified in paragraph B7B(a) of IFRS 3 for items that are independent of whether any substantive process was acquired:

(a)   the fair value of the gross assets acquired does not include the fair value of the cash and cash equivalents acquired (CU100) and does not include deferred tax assets (nil in this example); and

(b)   for the calculation specified in paragraph IE120(c)(ii), the deferred tax liability is not deducted in determining the fair value of the net assets acquired (CU300) and does not need to be determined. As a result, the excess (CU100) calculated by applying paragraph IE120(c) does not include goodwill resulting from the effects of deferred tax liabilities.

IE123 The fair value of the gross assets acquired (CU1,000) may also be determined as follows:

(a) the total (CU1,100) obtained by adding:

(i) the amount paid (CU200) (plus the fair value of the non-controlling interest (CU120) plus the fair value of the previously held interest (CU80)); to

(ii) the fair value of the liabilities assumed (other than deferred tax liabilities) (CU700); less

(b) the cash and cash equivalents acquired (CU100); less

(c) deferred tax assets acquired (nil in this example). In practice, it would be necessary to determine the amount of deferred tax assets to be excluded only if including the deferred tax assets could lead to the concentration test not being met.

[Refer: paragraph B7B(b)]

Appendix
Amendments to guidance on other IFRSs

The following amendments to guidance on other IFRSs are necessary in order to ensure consistency with IFRS 3 (as revised in 2008) and the related amendments to other IFRSs. In the amended paragraphs, new text is underlined and deleted text is struck through.

* * * * *

The amendments contained in this appendix when IFRS 3 was issued in 2008 have been incorporated into the text of the Guidance on Implementing IFRS 5, Appendices A and B of IAS 12 and the Illustrative Examples of IAS 36, as issued at 10 January 2008.

IASB documents published to accompany

IFRS 5

Non-current Assets Held for Sale and Discontinued Operations

The text of the unaccompanied standard, IFRS 5, is contained in Part A of this edition. The text of the Basis for Conclusions on IFRS 5 is contained in Part C of this edition. Its effective date when issued was 1 January 2005. This part presents the following document:

IMPLEMENTATION GUIDANCE

CONTENTS

**GUIDANCE ON IMPLEMENTING
IFRS 5 *NON-CURRENT ASSETS HELD FOR SALE
AND DISCONTINUED OPERATIONS***

Guidance on implementing
IFRS 5 *Non-current Assets Held for Sale and Discontinued Operations*

This guidance accompanies, but is not part of, IFRS 5.

Availability for immediate sale (paragraph 7)

To qualify for classification as held for sale, a non-current asset (or disposal group) must be available for immediate sale in its present condition subject only to terms that are usual and customary for sales of such assets (or disposal groups) (paragraph 7). A non-current asset (or disposal group) is available for immediate sale if an entity currently has the intention and ability to transfer the asset (or disposal group) to a buyer in its present condition. Examples 1–3 illustrate situations in which the criterion in paragraph 7 would or would not be met.

Example 1

An entity is committed to a plan to sell its headquarters building and has initiated actions to locate a buyer.

(a)   The entity intends to transfer the building to a buyer after it vacates the building. The time necessary to vacate the building is usual and customary for sales of such assets. The criterion in paragraph 7 would be met at the plan commitment date.

(b)   The entity will continue to use the building until construction of a new headquarters building is completed. The entity does not intend to transfer the existing building to a buyer until after construction of the new building is completed (and it vacates the existing building). The delay in the timing of the transfer of the existing building imposed by the entity (seller) demonstrates that the building is not available for immediate sale. The criterion in paragraph 7 would not be met until construction of the new building is completed, even if a firm purchase commitment for the future transfer of the existing building is obtained earlier.

Example 2

An entity is committed to a plan to sell a manufacturing facility and has initiated actions to locate a buyer. At the plan commitment date, there is a backlog of uncompleted customer orders.

(a)   The entity intends to sell the manufacturing facility with its operations. Any uncompleted customer orders at the sale date will be transferred to the buyer. The transfer of uncompleted customer orders at the sale date will not affect the timing of the transfer of the facility. The criterion in paragraph 7 would be met at the plan commitment date.

(b)   The entity intends to sell the manufacturing facility, but without its operations. The entity does not intend to transfer the facility to a buyer until after it ceases all operations of the facility and eliminates the backlog of uncompleted customer orders. The delay in the timing of the transfer of the facility imposed by the entity (seller) demonstrates that the facility is not available for immediate sale. The criterion in paragraph 7 would not be met until the operations of the facility cease, even if a firm purchase commitment for the future transfer of the facility were obtained earlier.

Example 3

An entity acquires through foreclosure a property comprising land and buildings that it intends to sell.

(a)   The entity does not intend to transfer the property to a buyer until after it completes renovations to increase the property's sales value. The delay in the timing of the transfer of the property imposed by the entity (seller) demonstrates that the property is not available for immediate sale. The criterion in paragraph 7 would not be met until the renovations are completed.

(b)   After the renovations are completed and the property is classified as held for sale [Refer: paragraphs 6–14] but before a firm purchase commitment is obtained, the entity becomes aware of environmental damage requiring remediation. The entity still intends to sell the property. However, the entity does not have the ability to transfer the property to a buyer until after the remediation is completed. The delay in the timing of the transfer of the property imposed by others before a firm purchase commitment is obtained demonstrates that the property is not available for immediate sale. The criterion in paragraph 7 would not continue to be met. The property would be reclassified as held and used in accordance with paragraph 26.

Completion of sale expected within one year (paragraph 8)

Example 4

To qualify for classification as held for sale, the sale of a non-current asset (or disposal group) must be highly probable (paragraph 7), and transfer of the asset (or disposal group) must be expected to qualify for recognition as a completed sale within one year (paragraph 8). That criterion would not be met if, for example:

(a)   an entity that is a commercial leasing and finance company is holding for sale or lease equipment that has recently ceased to be leased and the ultimate form of a future transaction (sale or lease) has not yet been determined.

(b)   an entity is committed to a plan to 'sell' a property that is in use as part of a sale and leaseback transaction, but the transfer does not qualify to be accounted for as a sale in accordance with paragraph 99 of IFRS 16 Leases and, instead, will be accounted for in accordance with paragraph 103 of IFRS 16.

Exceptions to the criterion that the sale should be expected to be completed in one year (paragraphs 8 and B1)

An exception to the one-year requirement in paragraph 8 applies in limited situations in which the period required to complete the sale of a non-current asset (or disposal group) will be (or has been) extended by events or circumstances beyond an entity's control and specified conditions are met (paragraphs 9 and B1). Examples 5–7 illustrate those situations.

Example 5

An entity in the power generating industry is committed to a plan to sell a disposal group that represents a significant portion of its regulated operations. The sale requires regulatory approval, which could extend the period required to complete the sale beyond one year. Actions necessary to obtain that approval cannot be initiated until after a buyer is known and a firm purchase commitment is obtained. However, a firm purchase commitment is highly probable within one year. In that situation, the conditions in paragraph B1(a) for an exception to the one-year requirement in paragraph 8 would be met.

Example 6

An entity is committed to a plan to sell a manufacturing facility in its present condition and classifies the facility as held for sale at that date. After a firm purchase commitment is obtained, the buyer's inspection of the property identifies environmental damage not previously known to exist. The entity is required by the buyer to make good the damage, which will extend the period required to complete the sale beyond one year. However, the entity has initiated actions to make good the damage, and satisfactory rectification of the damage is highly probable. In that situation, the conditions in paragraph B1(b) for an exception to the one-year requirement in paragraph 8 would be met.

Example 7

An entity is committed to a plan to sell a non-current asset and classifies the asset as held for sale at that date.

(a)   During the initial one-year period, the market conditions that existed at the date the asset was classified initially as held for sale deteriorate and, as a result, the asset is not sold by the end of that period. During that period, the entity actively solicited but did not receive any reasonable offers to purchase the asset and, in response, reduced the price. The asset continues to be actively marketed at a price that is reasonable given the change in market conditions, and the criteria in paragraphs 7 and 8 are therefore met. In that situation, the conditions in paragraph B1(c) for an exception to the one-year requirement in paragraph 8 would be met. At the end of the initial one-year period, the asset would continue to be classified as held for sale. [Refer: paragraphs 6–14]

(b)   During the following one-year period, market conditions deteriorate further, and the asset is not sold by the end of that period. The entity believes that the market conditions will improve and has not further reduced the price of the asset. The asset continues to be held for sale, but at a price in excess of its current fair value.

In that situation, the absence of a price reduction demonstrates that the asset is not available for immediate sale as required by paragraph 7. In addition, paragraph 8 also requires an asset to be marketed at a price that is reasonable in relation to its current fair value. Therefore, the conditions in paragraph B1(c) for an exception to the one-year requirement in paragraph 8 would not be met. The asset would be reclassified as held and used in accordance with paragraph 26.

Determining whether an asset has been abandoned

Paragraphs 13 and 14 of the IFRS specify requirements for when assets are to be treated as abandoned. Example 8 illustrates when an asset has not been abandoned.

Example 8

An entity ceases to use a manufacturing plant because demand for its product has declined. However, the plant is maintained in workable condition and it is expected that it will be brought back into use if demand picks up. The plant is not regarded as abandoned.

Presenting a discontinued operation that has been abandoned

Paragraph 13 of the IFRS prohibits assets that will be abandoned from being classified as held for sale. [Refer: paragraphs 6–14] However, if the assets to be abandoned are a major line of business or geographical area of operations, they are reported in discontinued operations at the date at which they are abandoned. Example 9 illustrates this.

Example 9

In October 20X5 an entity decides to abandon all of its cotton mills, which constitute a major line of business. All work stops at the cotton mills during the year ended 31 December 20X6. In the financial statements for the year ended 31 December 20X5, results and cash flows of the cotton mills are treated as continuing operations. In the financial statements for the year ended 31 December 20X6, the results and cash flows of the cotton mills are treated as discontinued operations and the entity makes the disclosures required by paragraphs 33 and 34 of the IFRS.

Allocation of an impairment loss on a disposal group

Paragraph 23 of the IFRS requires an impairment loss (or any subsequent gain) recognised for a disposal group to reduce (or increase) the carrying amount of the non-current assets in the group that are within the scope of the measurement requirements of the IFRS, in the order of allocation set out in paragraphs 104 and 122 of IAS 36 (as revised in 2004). Example 10 illustrates the allocation of an impairment loss on a disposal group.

Example 10

An entity plans to dispose of a group of its assets (as an asset sale). The assets form a disposal group, and are measured as follows:

	Carrying amount at the end of the reporting period before classification as held for sale	Carrying amount as remeasured immediately before classification as held for sale
	CU[(a)]	CU
Goodwill	1,500	1,500
Property, plant and equipment (carried at revalued amounts)	4,600	4,000
Property, plant and equipment (carried at cost)	5,700	5,700
Inventory	2,400	2,200
Investments in equity instruments	1,800	1,500
Total	**16,000**	**14,900**

(a) In this guidance, monetary amounts are denominated in 'currency units (CU)'.

The entity recognises the loss of CU1,100 (CU16,000 – CU14,900) immediately before classifying the disposal group as held for sale.

The entity measures the fair value less costs to sell of the disposal group as CU13,000. Because an entity measures a disposal group classified as held for sale [Refer: paragraphs 6–14] at the lower of its carrying amount and fair value less costs to sell, the entity recognises an impairment loss of CU1,900 (CU14,900 – CU13,000) when the group is initially classified as held for sale.

The impairment loss is allocated to non-current assets to which the measurement requirements of the IFRS are applicable. Therefore, no impairment loss is allocated to inventory and investments in equity instruments. The loss is allocated to the other assets in the order of allocation set out in paragraphs 104 and 122 of IAS 36 (as revised in 2004).

The allocation can be illustrated as follows:

	Carrying amount as remeasured immediately before classification as held for sale	Allocated impairment loss	Carrying amount after allocation of impairment loss
	CU	CU	CU
Goodwill	1,500	(1,500)	0
Property, plant and equipment (carried at revalued amounts)	4,000	(165)	3,835
Property, plant and equipment (carried at cost)	5,700	(235)	5,465
Inventory	2,200	–	2,200
Investments in equity instruments	1,500	–	1,500
Total	**14,900**	**(1,900)**	**13,000**

First, the impairment loss reduces any amount of goodwill. Then, the residual loss is allocated to other assets pro rata based on the carrying amounts of those assets.

Presenting discontinued operations in the statement of comprehensive income

Paragraph 33 of the IFRS requires an entity to disclose a single amount in the statement of comprehensive income for discontinued operations with an analysis in the notes or in a section of the statement of comprehensive income separate from continuing operations. Example 11 illustrates how these requirements might be met.

Example 11

XYZ GROUP – STATEMENT OF COMPREHENSIVE INCOME FOR THE YEAR ENDED 31 DECEMBER 20X2 (illustrating the classification of expenses by function)

(in thousands of currency units)	20X2	20X1
Continuing operations		
Revenue	X	X
Cost of sales	(X)	(X)
Gross profit	X	X
Other income	X	X
Distribution costs	(X)	(X)
Administrative expenses	(X)	(X)
Other expenses	(X)	(X)
Finance costs	(X)	(X)
Share of profit of associates	X	X
Profit before tax	X	X
Income tax expense	(X)	(X)
Profit for the period from continuing operations	X	X
Discontinued operations		
Profit for the period from discontinued operations[a]	X	X
Profit for the period	X	X
Attributable to:		
Owners of the parent		
Profit for the period from continuing operations	X	X
Profit for the period from discontinued operations	X	X
Profit for the period attributable to owners of the parent	X	X
Non-controlling interests		
Profit for the period from continuing operations	X	X
Profit for the period from discontinued operations	X	X
Profit for the period attributable to non-controlling interests	X	X
	X	X

(a) The required analysis would be given in the notes.

Presenting non-current assets or disposal groups classified as held for sale

Paragraph 38 of the IFRS requires an entity to present a non-current asset classified as held for sale [Refer: paragraphs 6–14] and the assets of a disposal group classified as held for sale separately from other assets in the statement of financial position. The liabilities of a disposal group classified as held for sale are also presented separately from other liabilities in the statement of financial position. Those assets and liabilities are not offset and presented as a single amount. Example 12 illustrates these requirements.

Example 12

At the end of 20X5, an entity decides to dispose of part of its assets (and directly associated liabilities). The disposal, which meets the criteria in paragraphs 7 and 8 to be classified as held for sale, [Refer: paragraphs 6–14] takes the form of two disposal groups, as follows:

	Carrying amount after classification as held for sale	
	Disposal group I: CU	Disposal group II: CU
Property, plant and equipment	4,900	1,700
Investments in equity instruments	1,400[(a)]	–
Liabilities	(2,400)	(900)
Net carrying amount of disposal group	**3,900**	**800**

(a) An amount of CU400 relating to these assets has been recognised in other comprehensive income and accumulated in equity.

The presentation in the entity's statement of financial position of the disposal groups classified as held for sale [Refer: paragraphs 6–14] can be shown as follows:

	20X5	20X4
ASSETS		
Non-current assets		
AAA	X	X
BBB	X	X
CCC	X	X
	X	X

continued...

...continued

	20X5	20X4
Current assets		
DDD	X	X
EEE	X	X
	X	X
Non-current assets classified as held for sale [Refer: paragraphs 6–14]	8,000	–
	X	X
Total assets	X	X

EQUITY AND LIABILITIES

Equity attributable to owners of the parent		
FFF	X	X
GGG	X	X
Amounts recognised in other comprehensive income and accumulated in equity relating to non-current assets held for sale	400	–
	X	X
Non-controlling interests	X	X
Total equity	X	X
Non-current liabilities		
HHH	X	X
III	X	X
JJJ	X	X
	X	X
Current liabilities		
KKK	X	X
LLL	X	X
MMM	X	X
Liabilities directly associated with non-current assets classified as held for sale	3,300	–
	X	X
Total liabilities	X	X
Total equity and liabilities	X	X

The presentation requirements for assets (or disposal groups) classified as held for sale [Refer: paragraphs 6–14] at the end of the reporting period do not apply retrospectively. The comparative statements of financial position for any previous periods are therefore not re-presented.

Measuring and presenting subsidiaries acquired with a view to resale and classified as held for sale

A subsidiary acquired with a view to sale is not exempt from consolidation in accordance with IFRS 10 *Consolidated Financial Statements*, unless the acquirer is an investment entity, as defined in IFRS 10, and is required to measure the investment in that subsidiary at fair value through profit or loss. However, if it meets the criteria in paragraph 11, it is presented as a disposal group classified as held for sale. [Refer: paragraphs 6–14] Example 13 illustrates these requirements.

Example 13

Entity A acquires an entity H, which is a holding company with two subsidiaries, S1 and S2. S2 is acquired exclusively with a view to sale and meets the criteria to be classified as held for sale. [Refer: paragraphs 6–14] In accordance with paragraph 32(c), S2 is also a discontinued operation.

The fair value less costs to sell of S2 is CU135. A accounts for S2 as follows:

- initially, A measures the identifiable liabilities of S2 at fair value, say at CU40

- initially, A measures the acquired assets as the fair value less costs to sell of S2 (CU135) plus the fair value of the identifiable liabilities (CU40), ie at CU175

- at the end of the reporting period, A remeasures the disposal group at the lower of its cost and fair value less costs to sell, say at CU130. The liabilities are remeasured in accordance with applicable IFRSs, say at CU35. The total assets are measured at CU130 + CU35, ie at CU165

- at the end of the reporting period, A presents the assets and liabilities separately from other assets and liabilities in its consolidated financial statements as illustrated in Example 12 *Presenting non-current assets or disposal groups classified as held for sale*, and

- in the statement of comprehensive income, A presents the total of the post-tax profit or loss of S2 and the post-tax gain or loss recognised on the subsequent remeasurement of S2, which equals the remeasurement of the disposal group from CU135 to CU130.

Further analysis of the assets and liabilities or of the change in value of the disposal group is not required.

IASB documents published to accompany

IFRS 7

Financial Instruments: Disclosures

The text of the unaccompanied standard, IFRS 7, is contained in Part A of this edition. The text of the Basis for Conclusions on IFRS 7 is contained in Part C of this edition. Its effective date when issued was 1 January 2007. This part presents the following documents:

IMPLEMENTATION GUIDANCE

APPENDIX
Amendments to guidance on other IFRSs

CONTENTS

© IFRS Foundation

Guidance on implementing
IFRS 7 *Financial Instruments: Disclosures*

This guidance accompanies, but is not part of, IFRS 7.

Introduction

IG1   This guidance suggests possible ways to apply some of the disclosure requirements in IFRS 7. The guidance does not create additional requirements.

IG2   For convenience, each disclosure requirement in the IFRS is discussed separately. In practice, disclosures would normally be presented as an integrated package and individual disclosures might satisfy more than one requirement. For example, information about concentrations of risk might also convey information about exposure to credit or other risk.

IG3–IG4   [Deleted]

Classes of financial instruments and level of disclosure (paragraphs 6 and B1–B3)

IG5   Paragraph B3 states that 'an entity decides in the light of its circumstances how much detail it provides to satisfy the requirements of this IFRS, how much emphasis it places on different aspects of the requirements and how it aggregates information to display the overall picture without combining information with different characteristics.' To satisfy the requirements, an entity may not need to disclose all the information suggested in this guidance.

IG6   Paragraph 17(c) of IAS 1 requires an entity to 'provide additional disclosures when compliance with the specific requirements in IFRSs is insufficient to enable users to understand the impact of particular transactions, other events and conditions on the entity's financial position and financial performance.'

Significance of financial instruments for financial position and performance (paragraphs 7–30, B4 and B5)[1]

IG7–IG11   [Deleted]

Defaults and breaches (paragraphs 18 and 19)

IG12   Paragraphs 18 and 19 require disclosures when there are any defaults or breaches of loans payable. Any defaults or breaches may affect the classification of the liability as current or non-current in accordance with IAS 1.

---

1   IFRS 9 *Financial Instruments* deleted paragraph B4 of IFRS 7.

Total interest expense (paragraph 20(b))[2]

IG13   Total interest expense disclosed in accordance with paragraph 20(b) is a component of finance costs, which paragraph 82(b) of IAS 1 requires to be presented separately in the statement of comprehensive income. The line item for finance costs may also include amounts associated with non-financial liabilities.

IG13A–
IG13B   [Deleted]

Hedge accounting (paragraphs 24A–24C)

IG13C   Paragraph 24A of IFRS 7 requires that an entity discloses amounts related to items designated as hedging instruments in a tabular format. The following example illustrates how that information might be disclosed.

	Nominal amount of the hedging instrument	Carrying amount of the hedging instrument		Line item in the statement of financial position where the hedging instrument is located	Changes in fair value used for calculating hedge ineffectiveness for 20X1
		Assets	Liabilities		
Cash flow hedges					
Commodity price risk - Forward sales contracts	xx	xx	xx	Line item XX	xx
Fair value hedges					
Interest rate risk - Interest rate swaps	xx	xx	xx	Line item XX	xx
Foreign exchange risk - Foreign currency loan	xx	xx	xx	Line item XX	xx

IG13D   Paragraph 24B of IFRS 7 requires that an entity discloses amounts related to items designated as hedged items in a tabular format. The following example illustrates how that information might be disclosed.

---

2   In *Improvements to IFRSs* issued in May 2008, the Board amended paragraph IG13 and removed 'total interest income' as a component of finance costs. This amendment removed an inconsistency with paragraph 32 of IAS 1 *Presentation of Financial Statements*, which precludes the offsetting of income and expenses (except when required or permitted by an IFRS).

     © IFRS Foundation

	Carrying amount of the hedged item		Accumulated amount of fair value hedge adjustments on the hedged item included in the carrying amount of the hedged item		Line item in the statement of financial position in which the hedged item is included	Change in value used for calculating hedge ineffec-tive-ness for 20X1	Cash flow hedge reserve
	Assets	Liabilities	Assets	Liabilities			
Cash flow hedges							
Commodity price risk							
- Forecast sales	n/a	n/a	n/a	n/a	n/a	xx	xx
- Discontinued hedges (forecast sales)	n/a	n/a	n/a	n/a	n/a	n/a	xx
Fair value hedges							
Interest rate risk							
- Loan payable	–	xx	–	xx	Line item XX	xx	n/a
- Discontinued hedges (Loan payable)	–	xx	–	xx	Line item XX	n/a	n/a
Foreign exchange risk							
- Firm commitment	xx	xx	xx	xx	Line item XX	xx	n/a

IG13E   Paragraph 24C of IFRS 7 requires that an entity discloses amounts that have affected the statement of comprehensive income as a result of applying hedge accounting in a tabular format. The following example illustrates how that information might be disclosed.

Cash flow hedges[a]	Separate line item recognised in profit or loss as a result of a hedge of a net position[b]	Change in the value of the hedging instru-ment recognised in other compre-hensive income	Hedge ineffec-tiveness recognised in profit or loss	Line item in profit or loss (that includes hedge ineffec-tiveness)	Amount reclassi-fied from the cash flow hedge reserve to profit or loss	Line item affected in profit or loss because of the reclassifi-cation
Commodity price risk Commodity X	n/a	xx	xx	Line item XX	xx	Line item XX
- Discontinued hedge	n/a	n/a	n/a	n/a	xx	Line item XX

(a) The information disclosed in the statement of changes in equity (cash flow hedge reserve) should have the same level of detail as these disclosures.

(b) This disclosure only applies to cash flow hedges of foreign currency risk.

Fair value hedges	Ineffectiveness recognised in profit or loss	Line item(s) in profit or loss (that include(s) hedge ineffectiveness)
Interest rate risk	xx	Line item XX
Foreign exchange risk	xx	Line item XX

Fair value (paragraph 28)

IG14   At initial recognition an entity measures the fair value of financial instruments that are not traded in active markets. However, when, after initial recognition, an entity will use a valuation technique that incorporates data not obtained from observable markets, there may be a difference between the transaction price at initial recognition and the amount determined at initial recognition using that valuation technique. In these circumstances, the difference will be recognised in profit or loss in subsequent periods in accordance with IFRS 9 *Financial Instruments* and the entity's accounting policy. Such recognition reflects changes in factors (including time) that market participants would take into account when pricing the asset or liability (see paragraph B5.1.2A(b) of IFRS 9). Paragraph 28 requires disclosures in these circumstances. An entity might disclose the following to comply with paragraph 28:

Background

On 1 January 20X1 an entity purchases for CU15 million financial assets that are not traded in an active market. The entity has only one class of such financial assets.

The transaction price of CU15 million is the fair value at initial recognition.

After initial recognition, the entity will apply a valuation technique to measure the financial assets' fair value. This valuation technique uses inputs other than data from observable markets.

At initial recognition, the same valuation technique would have resulted in an amount of CU14 million, which differs from fair value by CU1 million. The entity has existing differences of CU5 million at 1 January 20X1.

Application of requirements

The entity's 20X2 disclosure would include the following:

Accounting policies

The entity uses the following valuation technique to measure the fair value of financial instruments that are not traded in an active market: [description of technique, not included in this example]. Differences may arise between the fair value at initial recognition (which, in accordance with IFRS 13 and IFRS 9, is generally the transaction price) and the amount determined at initial recognition using the valuation technique. Any such differences are [description of the entity's accounting policy].

In the notes to the financial statements

As discussed in note X, the entity uses [name of valuation technique] to measure the fair value of the following financial instruments that are not traded in an active market. However, in accordance with IFRS 13 and IFRS 9, the fair value of an instrument at inception is normally the transaction price. If the transaction price differs from the amount determined at inception using the valuation technique, that difference is [description of the entity's accounting policy].

continued...

...continued

The differences yet to be recognised in profit or loss are as follows:

	31 Dec X2	31 Dec X1
	CU million	CU million
Balance at beginning of year	5.3	5.0
New transactions	–	1.0
Amounts recognised in profit or loss during the year	(0.7)	(0.8)
Other increases	–	0.2
Other decreases	(0.1)	(0.1)
Balance at end of year	4.5	5.3

Nature and extent of risks arising from financial instruments (paragraphs 31–42 and B6–B28)

Qualitative disclosures (paragraph 33)

IG15   The type of qualitative information an entity might disclose to meet the requirements in paragraph 33 includes, but is not limited to, a narrative description of:

(a)   the entity's exposures to risk and how they arose. Information about risk exposures might describe exposures both gross and net of risk transfer and other risk-mitigating transactions.

(b)   the entity's policies and processes for accepting, measuring, monitoring and controlling risk, which might include:

   (i)   the structure and organisation of the entity's risk management function(s), including a discussion of independence and accountability;

   (ii)   the scope and nature of the entity's risk reporting or measurement systems;

   (iii)   the entity's policies for hedging or mitigating risk, including its policies and procedures for taking collateral; and

   (iv)   the entity's processes for monitoring the continuing effectiveness of such hedges or mitigating devices.

(c)   the entity's policies and procedures for avoiding excessive concentrations of risk.

IG16   Information about the nature and extent of risks arising from financial instruments is more useful if it highlights any relationship between financial instruments that can affect the amount, timing or uncertainty of an entity's future cash flows. The extent to which a risk exposure is altered by such relationships might be apparent to users from the disclosures required by this Standard, but in some cases further disclosures might be useful.

IG17　In accordance with paragraph 33(c), entities disclose any change in the qualitative information from the previous period and explain the reasons for the change. Such changes may result from changes in exposure to risk or from changes in the way those exposures are managed.

Quantitative disclosures (paragraphs 34–42 and B7–B28)

IG18　Paragraph 34 requires disclosure of quantitative data about concentrations of risk. For example, concentrations of credit risk may arise from:

(a)　industry sectors. Thus, if an entity's counterparties are concentrated in one or more industry sectors (such as retail or wholesale), it would disclose separately exposure to risks arising from each concentration of counterparties.

(b)　credit rating or other measure of credit quality. Thus, if an entity's counterparties are concentrated in one or more credit qualities (such as secured loans or unsecured loans) or in one or more credit ratings (such as investment grade or speculative grade), it would disclose separately exposure to risks arising from each concentration of counterparties.

(c)　geographical distribution. Thus, if an entity's counterparties are concentrated in one or more geographical markets (such as Asia or Europe), it would disclose separately exposure to risks arising from each concentration of counterparties.

(d)　a limited number of individual counterparties or groups of closely related counterparties.

Similar principles apply to identifying concentrations of other risks, including liquidity risk and market risk. For example, concentrations of liquidity risk may arise from the repayment terms of financial liabilities, sources of borrowing facilities or reliance on a particular market in which to realise liquid assets. Concentrations of foreign exchange risk may arise if an entity has a significant net open position in a single foreign currency, or aggregate net open positions in several currencies that tend to move together.

[Refer: paragraphs 34(c) and B8]

IG19　In accordance with paragraph B8, disclosure of concentrations of risk includes a description of the shared characteristic that identifies each concentration. For example, the shared characteristic may refer to geographical distribution of counterparties by groups of countries, individual countries or regions within countries.

[Refer: paragraph 34(c)]

IG20　When quantitative information at the end of the reporting period is unrepresentative of the entity's exposure to risk during the period, paragraph 35 requires further disclosure. To meet this requirement, an entity might disclose the highest, lowest and average amount of risk to which it was exposed during the period. For example, if an entity typically has a large exposure to a particular currency, but at year-end unwinds the position, the entity might disclose a graph that shows the exposure at various times during the period, or disclose the highest, lowest and average exposures.

Credit risk (paragraphs 35A–36, B8A–B10)

IG20A   The following examples illustrate possible ways in which an entity might provide the disclosures required by paragraphs 35A–35N of IFRS 7. However, these illustrations do not address all possible ways of applying the disclosure requirements.

Illustrating the application of paragraphs 35H and 35I

IG20B   The following example illustrates one way of providing information about the changes in the loss allowance and the significant changes in the gross carrying amount of financial assets during the period that contributed to changes in the loss allowance as required by paragraphs 35H–35I. This example does not illustrate the requirements for financial assets that are purchased or originated credit-impaired.

Mortgage loans–loss allowance	12-month expected credit losses	Lifetime expected credit losses (collectively assessed)	Lifetime expected credit losses (individually assessed)	Credit-impaired financial assets (lifetime expected credit losses)
CU'000				
Loss allowance as at 1 January	X	X	X	X
Changes due to financial instruments recognised as at 1 January:				
- Transfer to lifetime expected credit losses	(X)	X	X	–
- Transfer to credit-impaired financial assets	(X)	–	(X)	X
- Transfer to 12-month expected credit losses	X	(X)	(X)	–
- Financial assets that have been derecognised during the period	(X)	(X)	(X)	(X)
New financial assets originated or purchased	X	–	–	–
Write-offs	–	–	(X)	(X)
Changes in models/risk parameters	X	X	X	X
Foreign exchange and other movements	X	X	X	X
Loss allowance as at 31 December	X	X	X	X

Significant changes in the gross carrying amount of mortgage loans that contributed to changes in the loss allowance were:

- The acquisition of the ABC prime mortgage portfolio increased the residential mortgage book by x per cent, with a corresponding increase in the loss allowance measured on a 12-month basis.

- The write off of the CUXX DEF portfolio following the collapse of the local market reduced the loss allowance for financial assets with objective evidence of impairment by CUX.

- The expected increase in unemployment in Region X caused a net increase in financial assets whose loss allowance is equal to lifetime expected credit losses and caused a net increase of CUX in the lifetime expected credit losses allowance.

The significant changes in the gross carrying amount of mortgage loans are further explained below:

Mortgage loans–gross carrying amount	12-month expected credit losses	Lifetime expected credit losses (collectively assessed)	Lifetime expected credit losses (individually assessed)	Credit-impaired financial assets (lifetime expected credit losses)
CU'000				
Gross carrying amount as at 1 January	X	X	X	X
Individual financial assets transferred to lifetime expected credit losses	(X)	–	X	–
Individual financial assets transferred to credit-impaired financial assets	(X)	–	(X)	X
Individual financial assets transferred from credit-impaired financial assets	X	–	X	(X)
Financial assets assessed on collective basis	(X)	X	–	–
New financial assets originated or purchased	X	–	–	–
Write-offs	–	–	(X)	(X)
Financial assets that have been derecognised	(X)	(X)	(X)	(X)
Changes due to modifications that did not result in derecognition	(X)	–	(X)	(X)
Other changes	X	X	X	X
Gross carrying amount as at 31 December	X	X	X	X

Illustrating the application of paragraphs 35M and 35N

IG20C   The following example illustrates some ways of providing information about an entity's credit risk exposure and significant credit risk concentrations in accordance with paragraph 35M of IFRS 7. The number of grades used to disclose the information in accordance with paragraph 35M of IFRS 7 shall be consistent with the number that the entity uses to report internally to key management personnel for internal credit risk management purposes. However, if information about credit risk rating grades is not available without undue cost or effort and an entity uses past due information to assess whether credit risk has increased significantly since initial recognition in accordance with paragraph 5.5.11 of IFRS 9, the entity shall provide an analysis by past due status for those financial assets.

Consumer loan credit risk exposure by internal rating grades				
20XX	Consumer—credit card		Consumer—automotive	
CU'000	Gross carrying amount		Gross carrying amount	
	Lifetime	12-month	Lifetime	12-month
Internal Grade 1–2	X	X	X	X
Internal Grade 3–4	X	X	X	X
Internal Grade 5–6	X	X	X	X
Internal Grade 7	X	X	X	X
Total	X	X	X	X

Corporate loan credit risk profile by external rating grades				
20XX	Corporate—equipment		Corporate—construction	
CU'000	Gross carrying amount		Gross carrying amount	
	Lifetime	12-month	Lifetime	12-month
AAA-AA	X	X	X	X
A	X	X	X	X
BBB-BB	X	X	X	X
B	X	X	X	X
CCC-CC	X	X	X	X
C	X	X	X	X
D	X	X	X	X
Total	X	X	X	X

Corporate loan risk profile by probability of default				
20XX CU'000	Corporate—unsecured Gross carrying amount		Corporate—secured Gross carrying amount	
	Lifetime	12-month	Lifetime	12-month
0.00 – 0.10	X	X	X	X
0.11 – 0.40	X	X	X	X
0.41 – 1.00	X	X	X	X
1.01 – 3.00	X	X	X	X
3.01 – 6.00	X	X	X	X
6.01 – 11.00	X	X	X	X
11.01 – 17.00	X	X	X	X
17.01 – 25.00	X	X	X	X
25.01 – 50.00	X	X	X	X
50.01+	X	X	X	X
Total	**X**	**X**	**X**	**X**

IG20D   Entity A manufactures cars and provides financing to both dealers and end customers. Entity A discloses its dealer financing and customer financing as separate classes of financial instruments and applies the simplified approach to its trade receivables so that the loss allowance is always measured at an amount equal to lifetime expected credit losses. The following table illustrates the use of a provision matrix as a risk profile disclosure under the simplified approach:

20XX CU'000	Trade receivables days past due				
Dealer financing	**Current**	**More than 30 days**	**More than 60 days**	**More than 90 days**	**Total**
Expected credit loss rate Estimated total gross carrying amount at default	0.10% CU20,777	2% CU1,416	5% CU673	13% CU235	CU23,101
Lifetime expected credit losses—dealer financing	CU21	CU28	CU34	CU31	CU114
Customer financing					
Expected credit loss rate Estimated total gross carrying amount at default	0.20% CU19,222	3% CU2,010	8% CU301	15% CU154	CU21,687
Lifetime expected credit losses— customer financing	CU38	CU60	CU24	CU23	CU145

IG21　Paragraph 36 requires an entity to disclose information about its exposure to credit risk by class of financial instrument. Financial instruments in the same class share economic characteristics with respect to the risk being disclosed (in this case, credit risk). For example, an entity might determine that residential mortgages, unsecured consumer loans, and commercial loans each have different economic characteristics.

Collateral and other credit enhancements pledged (paragraph 36(b))

IG22　Paragraph 36(b) requires an entity to describe collateral available as security for assets it holds and other credit enhancements obtained. An entity might meet this requirement by disclosing:

(a)　the policies and processes for valuing and managing collateral and other credit enhancements obtained;

(b)　a description of the main types of collateral and other credit enhancements (examples of the latter being guarantees, credit derivatives, and netting agreements that do not qualify for offset in accordance with IAS 32);

(c)　the main types of counterparties to collateral and other credit enhancements and their creditworthiness; and

(d)　information about risk concentrations within the collateral or other credit enhancements.

IG23–
IG31　[Deleted]

Liquidity risk disclosures (paragraph 39(a))

IG31A　The following examples illustrate how an entity might meet the disclosure requirement in paragraph 39(a).

Illustrating the application of paragraph 39(a)

Undiscounted cash flows: Non-derivative financial liabilities								
Maturity								
	Total	less than 1 month	1–3 months	3–6 months	6 months –1 year	1–3 years	3–5 years	more than 5 years
Bank borrowings	1,625				285	740	600	
Lease liabilities	2,300	70	140	210	400	750	620	110
[Refer: IFRS 16 paragraph 58 and IFRS 16 Basis for Conclusions paragraph BC221]								
Trade and other payables	350	70	190	90				

Illustrating the application of paragraph 39(a)

Undiscounted cash flows: Non-derivative financial liabilities									
		Maturity							
	Total	less than 1 year	1–2 years	2–3 years	3–4 years	4–5 years	5–7 years	7–10 years	more than 10 years
Bank borrowings	3,100	40	300	38	280	2,442			
Lease liabilities	4,400	500	500	480	430	430	790	800	470
[Refer: IFRS 16 paragraph 58 and IFRS 16 Basis for Conclusions paragraph BC221]									
Trade and other payables	95	95							

Illustrating the application of paragraph 39(a)

Undiscounted cash flows: Non-derivative financial liabilities							
		Maturity					
	Total	less than 1 month	1–6 months	6 months– 1 year	1–2 years	2–3 years	more than 3 years
Bonds	2,100	7	34	40	79	1,940	
Lease liabilities*	4,970			340	310	290	4,030
Trade and other payables	980	280	700				

*Further information about the maturity of lease liabilities [Refer: IFRS 16 Basis for Conclusions paragraph BC221] is provided in the table below:

		Maturity					
	Total	less than 1 year	1–5 years	5–10 years	10–15 years	15–20 years	20–25 years
Lease liabilities	4,970	340	1,200	1,110	1,050	970	300

Market risk (paragraphs 40–42 and B17–B28)

IG32 Paragraph 40(a) requires a sensitivity analysis for each type of market risk to which the entity is exposed. There are three types of market risk: interest rate risk, currency risk and other price risk. Other price risk may include risks such as equity price risk, commodity price risk, prepayment risk (ie the risk that one party to a financial asset will incur a financial loss because the other party repays earlier or later than expected), and residual value risk (eg a lessor of motor cars that writes residual value guarantees is exposed to residual value risk). Risk variables that are relevant to disclosing market risk include, but are not limited to:

(a)   the yield curve of market interest rates. It may be necessary to consider both parallel and non-parallel shifts in the yield curve.

(b)   foreign exchange rates.

(c)   prices of equity instruments.

(d)   market prices of commodities.

[Refer: paragraph B17]

IG33   Paragraph 40(a) requires the sensitivity analysis to show the effect on profit or loss and equity of reasonably possible changes in the relevant risk variable. For example, relevant risk variables might include:

(a)   prevailing market interest rates, for interest-sensitive financial instruments such as a variable-rate loan; or

(b)   currency rates and interest rates, for foreign currency financial instruments such as foreign currency bonds.

[Refer: paragraph B18]

IG34   For interest rate risk, the sensitivity analysis might show separately the effect of a change in market interest rates on:

(a)   interest income and expense;

(b)   other line items of profit or loss (such as trading gains and losses); and

(c)   when applicable, equity.

An entity might disclose a sensitivity analysis for interest rate risk for each currency in which the entity has material exposures to interest rate risk.

[Refer: paragraphs 40(a) and B17–B22]

IG35   Because the factors affecting market risk vary depending on the specific circumstances of each entity, the appropriate range to be considered in providing a sensitivity analysis of market risk varies for each entity and for each type of market risk.

[Refer: paragraphs 40–42 and B19]

IG36   The following example illustrates the application of the disclosure
        requirement in paragraph 40(a):

Interest rate risk

At 31 December 20X2, if interest rates at that date had been 10 basis points
lower with all other variables held constant, post-tax profit for the year
would have been CU1.7 million (20X1 – CU2.4 million) higher, arising mainly
as a result of lower interest expense on variable borrowings. If interest rates
had been 10 basis points higher, with all other variables held constant, post-
tax profit would have been CU1.5 million (20X1 – CU2.1 million) lower,
arising mainly as a result of higher interest expense on variable borrowings.
Profit is more sensitive to interest rate decreases than increases because of
borrowings with capped interest rates. The sensitivity is lower in 20X2 than
in 20X1 because of a reduction in outstanding borrowings that has occurred
as the entity's debt has matured (see note X).[a]

Foreign currency exchange rate risk

At 31 December 20X2, if the CU had weakened 10 per cent against the US
dollar with all other variables held constant, post-tax profit for the year
would have been CU2.8 million (20X1 – CU6.4 million) lower, and other
comprehensive income would have been CU1.2 million (20X1 – CU1.1
million) higher. Conversely, if the CU had strengthened 10 per cent against
the US dollar with all other variables held constant, post-tax profit would
have been CU2.8 million (20X1 – CU6.4 million) higher, and other
comprehensive income would have been CU1.2 million (20X1 – CU1.1
million) lower. The lower foreign currency exchange rate sensitivity in profit
in 20X2 compared with 20X1 is attributable to a reduction in foreign
currency denominated debt. Equity is more sensitive in 20X2 than in 20X1
because of the increased use of hedges of foreign currency purchases, offset
by the reduction in foreign currency debt.

(a)   Paragraph 39(a) requires disclosure of a maturity analysis of liabilities.

[Refer: Basis for Conclusions paragraph BC64]

Other market risk disclosures (paragraph 42)

IG37   Paragraph 42 requires the disclosure of additional information when the
        sensitivity analysis disclosed is unrepresentative of a risk inherent in a
        financial instrument. For example, this can occur when:

        (a)   a financial instrument contains terms and conditions whose effects are
               not apparent from the sensitivity analysis, eg options that remain out
               of (or in) the money for the chosen change in the risk variable;

               [Refer: Implementation Guidance paragraph IG38]

        (b)   financial assets are illiquid, eg when there is a low volume of
               transactions in similar assets and an entity finds it difficult to find a
               counterparty; or

               [Refer: Implementation Guidance paragraph IG39]

(c)   an entity has a large holding of a financial asset that, if sold in its entirety, would be sold at a discount or premium to the quoted market price for a smaller holding.

[Refer: Implementation Guidance paragraph IG40]

IG38   In the situation in paragraph IG37(a), additional disclosure might include:

(a)   the terms and conditions of the financial instrument (eg the options);

(b)   the effect on profit or loss if the term or condition were met (ie if the options were exercised); and

(c)   a description of how the risk is hedged.

For example, an entity may acquire a zero-cost interest rate collar that includes an out-of-the-money leveraged written option (eg the entity pays ten times the amount of the difference between a specified interest rate floor and the current market interest rate). The entity may regard the collar as an inexpensive economic hedge against a reasonably possible increase in interest rates. However, an unexpectedly large decrease in interest rates might trigger payments under the written option that, because of the leverage, might be significantly larger than the benefit of lower interest rates. Neither the fair value of the collar nor a sensitivity analysis based on reasonably possible changes in market variables would indicate this exposure. In this case, the entity might provide the additional information described above.

IG39   In the situation described in paragraph IG37(b), additional disclosure might include the reasons for the lack of liquidity and how the entity hedges the risk.

IG40   In the situation described in paragraph IG37(c), additional disclosure might include:

(a)   the nature of the security (eg entity name);

(b)   the extent of holding (eg 15 per cent of the issued shares);

(c)   the effect on profit or loss; and

(d)   how the entity hedges the risk.

Derecognition (paragraphs 42D and 42E)

IG40A   The following examples illustrate some possible ways to meet the quantitative disclosure requirements in paragraphs 42D and 42E.

IG40B   The following examples illustrate how an entity that has adopted IFRS 9 might meet the quantitative disclosure requirements in paragraphs 42D and 42E.

Transferred financial assets that are not derecognised in their entirety

Illustrating the application of paragraph 42D(d) and (e)

	Financial assets at fair value through profit or loss		Financial assets at amortised cost		Financial assets at fair value through other comprehensive income
	CU million		CU million		CU million
	Trading assets	Derivatives	Mortgages	Consumer loans	Equity investments
Carrying amount of assets	X	X	X	X	X
Carrying amount of associated liabilities	(X)	(X)	(X)	(X)	(X)
For those liabilities that have recourse only to the transferred assets:					
Fair value of assets	X	X	X	X	X
Fair value of associated liabilities	(X)	(X)	(X)	(X)	(X)
Net position	X	X	X	X	X

Transferred financial assets that are derecognised in their entirety

Illustrating the application of paragraph 42E(a)–(d)

	Cash outflows to repurchase transferred (derecognised) assets	Carrying amount of continuing involvement in statement of financial position			Fair value of continuing involvement		Maximum exposure to loss
	CU million	CU million			CU million		CU million
Type of continuing involvement		Financial assets at fair value through profit or loss	Financial assets at fair value through other comprehensive income	Financial liabilities at fair value through profit or loss	Assets	Liabilities	
Written put options	(X)			(X)		(X)	X
Purchased call options	(X)	X			X		X
Securities lending	(X)			(X)	X	(X)	X
Total		X		(X)	X	(X)	X

Illustrating the application of paragraph 42E(e)

Undiscounted cash flows to repurchase transferred assets								
		Maturity of continuing involvement CU million						
Type of continuing involvement	Total	less than 1 month	1–3 months	3–6 months	6 months –1 year	1–3 years	3–5 years	more than 5 years
Written put options	X		X	X	X	X		
Purchased call options	X			X	X	X		X
Securities lending	X	X	X					

IG40C The following examples illustrate how an entity that has not adopted IFRS 9 might meet the quantitative disclosure requirements in paragraphs 42D and 42E.

Transferred financial assets that are not derecognised in their entirety

Illustrating the application of paragraph 42D(d) and (e)

	Financial assets at fair value through profit or loss CU million		Loans and receivables CU million		Available-for-sale financial assets CU million
	Trading securities	Derivatives	Mortgages	Consumer loans	Equity investments
Carrying amount of assets	X	X	X	X	X
Carrying amount of associated liabilities	(X)	(X)	(X)	(X)	(X)
For those liabilities that have recourse only to the transferred assets:					
Fair value of assets	X	X	X	X	X
Fair value of associated liabilities	(X)	(X)	(X)	(X)	(X)
Net position	X	X	X	X	X

Transferred financial assets that are derecognised in their entirety

Illustrating the application of paragraph 42E(a)–(d)

Type of continuing involvement	Cash outflows to repurchase transferred (derecognised) assets CU million	Carrying amount of continuing involvement in statement of financial position CU million			Fair value of continuing involvement CU million		Maximum exposure to loss CU million
		Held for trading	Available-for-sale financial assets	Financial liabilities at fair value through profit or loss	Assets	Liabilities	
Written put options	(X)			(X)		(X)	X
Purchased call options	(X)	X			X		X
Securities lending	(X)		X	(X)	X	(X)	X
Total		X	X	(X)	X	(X)	X

Illustrating the application of paragraph 42E(e)

Undiscounted cash flows to repurchase transferred assets								
Maturity of continuing involvement CU million								
Type of continuing involvement	Total	less than 1 month	1–3 months	3–6 months	6 months –1 year	1–3 years	3–5 years	more than 5 years
Written put options	X			X	X	X	X	
Purchased call options	X				X	X	X	X
Securities lending	X	X	X					

Disclosures (paragraphs 13A–13F and B40–B53)

IG40D   The following examples illustrate ways in which an entity might provide the quantitative disclosures required by paragraph 13C. However, these illustrations do not address all possible ways of applying the disclosure requirements as set out in paragraphs 13B–13E.

Background

An entity has entered into transactions subject to an enforceable master netting arrangement or similar agreement with the following counterparties. The entity has the following recognised financial assets and financial liabilities resulting from those transactions that meet the scope of the disclosure requirements in paragraph 13A.

Counterparty A:

The entity has a derivative asset (fair value of CU100 million) and a derivative liability (fair value of CU80 million) with Counterparty A that meet the offsetting criteria in paragraph 42 of IAS 32. Consequently, the gross derivative liability is set off against the gross derivative asset, resulting in the presentation of a net derivative asset of CU20 million in the entity's statement of financial position. Cash collateral has also been received from Counterparty A for a portion of the net derivative asset (CU10 million). The cash collateral of CU10 million does not meet the offsetting criteria in paragraph 42 of IAS 32, but it can be set off against the net amount of the derivative asset and derivative liability in the case of default and insolvency or bankruptcy, in accordance with an associated collateral arrangement.

Counterparty B:

The entity has a derivative asset (fair value of CU100 million) and a derivative liability (fair value of CU80 million) with Counterparty B that do not meet the offsetting criteria in paragraph 42 of IAS 32, but which the entity has the right to set off in the case of default and insolvency or bankruptcy. Consequently, the gross amount of the derivative asset (CU100 million) and the gross amount of the derivative liability (CU80 million) are presented separately in the entity's statement of financial position. Cash collateral has also been received from Counterparty B for the net amount of the derivative asset and derivative liability (CU20 million). The cash collateral of CU20 million does not meet the offsetting criteria in paragraph 42 of IAS 32, but it can be set off against the net amount of the derivative asset and derivative liability in the case of default and insolvency or bankruptcy, in accordance with an associated collateral arrangement.

continued...

...continued

Counterparty C:

The entity has entered into a sale and repurchase agreement with Counterparty C that is accounted for as a collateralised borrowing. The carrying amount of the financial assets (bonds) used as collateral and posted by the entity for the transaction is CU79 million and their fair value is CU85 million. The carrying amount of the collateralised borrowing (repo payable) is CU80 million.

The entity has also entered into a reverse sale and repurchase agreement with Counterparty C that is accounted for as a collateralised lending. The fair value of the financial assets (bonds) received as collateral (and not recognised in the entity's statement of financial position) is CU105 million. The carrying amount of the collateralised lending (reverse repo receivable) is CU90 million.

The transactions are subject to a global master repurchase agreement with a right of set-off only in default and insolvency or bankruptcy and therefore do not meet the offsetting criteria in paragraph 42 of IAS 32. Consequently, the related repo payable and repo receivable are presented separately in the entity's statement of financial position.

Illustrating the application of paragraph 13C(a)–(e) by type of financial instrument

Financial assets subject to offsetting, enforceable master netting arrangements and similar agreements

CU million

As at 31 December 20XX	(a)	(b)	(c)=(a)-(b)	(d)		(e)=(c)-(d)
				Related amounts not set off in the statement of financial position		
	Gross amounts of recognised financial assets	Gross amounts of recognised financial liabilities set off in the statement of financial position	Net amounts of financial assets presented in the statement of financial position	(d)(i), (d)(ii) Financial instruments	(d)(ii) Cash collateral received	Net amount
Description						
Derivatives	200	(80)	120	(80)	(30)	10
Reverse repurchase, securities borrowing and similar agreements	90	–	90	(90)	–	–
Other financial instruments	–		–	–	–	–
Total	290	(80)	210	(170)	(30)	10

Financial liabilities subject to offsetting, enforceable master netting arrangements and similar agreements

CU million

As at 31 December 20XX	(a)	(b)	(c)=(a)-(b)	(d)		(e)=(c)-(d)
				Related amounts not set off in the statement of financial position		
	Gross amounts of recognised financial liabilities	Gross amounts of recognised financial assets set off in the statement of financial position	Net amounts of financial liabilities presented in the statement of financial position	(d)(i), (d)(ii) Financial instruments	(d)(ii) Cash collateral pledged	Net amount
Description						
Derivatives	160	(80)	80	(80)	–	–
Repurchase, securities lending and similar agreements	80	–	80	(80)	–	–
Other financial instruments	–	–	–	–	–	–
Total	240	(80)	160	(160)	–	–

Illustrating the application of paragraph 13C(a)–(c) by type of financial instrument and paragraph 13C(c)–(e) by counterparty

Financial assets subject to offsetting, enforceable master netting arrangements and similar agreements

CU million

As at 31 December 20XX	(a)	(b)	(c)=(a)-(b)
	Gross amounts of recognised financial assets	Gross amounts of recognised financial liabilities set off in the statement of financial position	Net amounts of financial assets presented in the statement of financial position
Description			
Derivatives	200	(80)	120
Reverse repurchase, securities borrowing and similar agreements	90	–	90
Other financial instruments	–	–	–
Total	290	(80)	210

Net financial assets subject to enforceable master netting arrangements and similar agreements, by counterparty

CU million

As at 31 December 20XX	(c)	(d)		(e)=(c)-(d)
		Related amounts not set off in the statement of financial position		
	Net amounts of financial assets presented in the statement of financial position	(d)(i), (d)(ii) Financial instruments	(d)(ii) Cash collateral received	Net amount
Counterparty A	20	–	(10)	10
Counterparty B	100	(80)	(20)	–
Counterparty C	90	(90)	–	–
Other	–	–	–	–
Total	210	(170)	(30)	10

Financial liabilities subject to offsetting, enforceable master netting arrangements and similar agreements

CU million

As at 31 December 20XX	(a)	(b)	(c)=(a)-(b)
	Gross amounts of recognised financial liabilities	Gross amounts of recognised financial assets set off in the statement of financial position	Net amounts of financial liabilities presented in the statement of financial position
Description			
Derivatives	160	(80)	80
Repurchase, securities lending and similar agreements	80	–	80
Other financial instruments	–	–	–
Total	240	(80)	160

Net financial liabilities subject to enforceable master netting arrangements and similar agreements, by counterparty

CU million

As at 31 December 20XX	(c)	(d)		(e)=(c)-(d)
		Related amounts not set off in the statement of financial position		
	Net amounts of financial liabilities presented in the statement of financial position	(d)(i), (d)(ii) Financial instruments	(d)(ii) Cash collateral pledged	Net amount
Counterparty A	–	–	–	–
Counterparty B	80	(80)	–	–
Counterparty C	80	(80)	–	–
Other	–	–	–	–
Total	160	(160)	–	–

Transition from IAS 39 to IFRS 9 (paragraphs 42K–42O)

IG40E   The following illustration is an example of one possible way to meet the quantitative disclosure requirements in paragraphs 42K–42O of IFRS 7 at the date of initial application of IFRS 9. However, this illustration does not address all possible ways of applying the disclosure requirements of this IFRS.

Reconciliation of statement of financial position balances from IAS 39 to IFRS 9 at 1 January 2018

Financial assets	(i)	(ii)	(iii)	(iv) = (i) + (ii) + (iii)	(v) = (iii)
	IAS 39 carrying amount 31 December 2017 (1)	Reclassifications	Remeasurements	IFRS 9 carrying amount 1 January 2018	Retained earnings effect on 1 January 2018 (2), (3)
Fair value through profit or loss					
Additions:					
From available for sale (IAS 39)		(a)			(c)
From amortised cost (IAS 39) – required reclassification		(b)			
From amortised cost (IAS 39) – fair value option elected at 1 January 2018					

continued...

...continued

Reconciliation of statement of financial position balances from IAS 39 to IFRS 9 at 1 January 2018

Financial assets	(i)	(ii)	(iii)	(iv) = (i) + (ii) + (iii)	(v) = (iii)
	IAS 39 carrying amount 31 December 2017 (1)	Reclassifications	Remeasurements	IFRS 9 carrying amount 1 January 2018	Retained earnings effect on 1 January 2018 (2), (3)
Subtractions:					
To amortised cost (IFRS 9)					
To fair value through other comprehensive income – debt instruments (IFRS 9)					
To fair value through other comprehensive income – equity instruments (IFRS 9)					
Total change to fair value through profit or loss					
Fair value through other comprehensive income					
Additions – debt instruments:					
From available for sale (IAS 39)					(g)
From amortised cost (IAS 39)					(h)
From fair value through profit or loss (IAS 39) – required reclassification based on classification criteria					(i)
From fair value through profit or loss (fair value option under IAS 39) – fair value option criteria not met at 1 January 2018					(j)
From fair value through profit or loss (IAS 39) – fair value option revoked at 1 January 2018 by choice					(k)

continued...

...continued

Reconciliation of statement of financial position balances from IAS 39 to IFRS 9 at 1 January 2018

Financial assets	(i)	(ii)	(iii)	(iv) = (i) + (ii) + (iii)	(v) = (iii)
	IAS 39 carrying amount 31 December 2017 (1)	Reclassifications	Remeasurements	IFRS 9 carrying amount 1 January 2018	Retained earnings effect on 1 January 2018 (2), (3)
Additions – equity instruments:					
From available-for-sale (IAS 39)					
From fair value through profit or loss (fair value option under IAS 39)–fair value through other comprehensive income elected at 1 January 2018					
From cost (IAS 39)					
Subtractions – debt and equity instruments:					
Available for sale (IAS 39) to fair value through profit or loss (IFRS 9) – required reclassification based on classification criteria					
Available for sale (IAS 39) to fair value through profit or loss (IFRS 9) – fair value option elected at 1 January 2018					
Available for sale (IAS 39) to amortised cost (IFRS 9)					
Total change to fair value through other comprehensive income					

continued...

...continued

Reconciliation of statement of financial position balances from IAS 39 to IFRS 9 at 1 January 2018

Financial assets	(i)	(ii)	(iii)	(iv) = (i) + (ii) + (iii)	(v) = (iii)
	IAS 39 carrying amount 31 December 2017 (1)	Reclassifications	Remeasurements	IFRS 9 carrying amount 1 January 2018	Retained earnings effect on 1 January 2018 (2), (3)
Amortised cost					
Additions:					
From available for sale (IAS 39)					(f)
From fair value through profit or loss (IAS 39) – required reclassification					
From fair value through profit or loss (fair value option under IAS 39) – fair value option criteria not met at 1 January 2018					
From fair value through profit or loss (IAS 39) – fair value option revoked at 1 January 2018 by choice					

continued...

...continued

Reconciliation of statement of financial position balances from IAS 39 to IFRS 9 at 1 January 2018

Financial assets	(i)	(ii)	(iii)	(iv) = (i) + (ii) + (iii)	(v) = (iii)
	IAS 39 carrying amount 31 December 2017 (1)	Reclassifications	Remeasurements	IFRS 9 carrying amount 1 January 2018	Retained earnings effect on 1 January 2018 (2), (3)
Subtractions:					
To fair value through other comprehensive income (IFRS 9)					(l)
To fair value through profit or loss (IFRS 9) – required reclassification based on classification criteria					
To fair value through profit or loss (IFRS 9)–fair value option elected at 1 January 2018					
Total change to amortised cost					
Total financial asset balances, reclassifications and remeasurements at 1 January 2018	(i)	Total (ii) = 0	(iii)	(iv) = (i) + (ii) + (iii)	

1   Includes the effect of reclassifying hybrid instruments that were bifurcated under IAS 39 with host contract components of (a), which had associated embedded derivatives with a fair value of X at 31 December 2017, and (b), which had associated embedded derivatives with a fair value of Y at 31 December 2017.

2   Includes (c), (d), (e) and (f), which are amounts reclassified from other comprehensive income to retained earnings at the date of initial application.

3   Includes (g), (h), (i), (j), (k) and (l), which are amounts reclassified from retained earnings to accumulated other comprehensive income at the date of initial application.

Transition (paragraph 44)

IG41   The following table summarises the effect of the exemption from presenting comparative accounting and risk disclosures for accounting periods beginning before 1 January 2006, before 1 January 2007, and on or after 1 January 2007. In this table:

   (a)   a **first-time adopter** is an entity preparing its first IFRS financial statements (see IFRS 1 *First-time Adoption of International Financial Reporting Standards*).

   (b)   an **existing IFRS user** is an entity preparing its second or subsequent IFRS financial statements.

	Accounting disclosures (paragraphs 7–30)	Risk disclosures (paragraphs 31–42)
Accounting periods beginning before 1 January 2006		
First-time adopter not applying IFRS 7 early	*Applies IAS 32 but exempt from providing IAS 32 comparative information*	*Applies IAS 32 but exempt from providing IAS 32 comparative information*
First-time adopter applying IFRS 7 early	**Exempt from presenting IFRS 7 comparative information**	**Exempt from presenting IFRS 7 comparative information**
Existing IFRS user not applying IFRS 7 early	Applies IAS 32. Provides full IAS 32 comparative information	Applies IAS 32. Provides full IAS 32 comparative information
Existing IFRS user applying IFRS 7 early	Provides full IFRS 7 comparative information	**Exempt from presenting IFRS 7 comparative information**[a]
Accounting periods beginning on or after 1 January 2006 and before 1 January 2007		
First-time adopter not applying IFRS 7 early	Applies IAS 32. Provides full IAS 32 comparative information	Applies IAS 32. Provides full IAS 32 comparative information
First-time adopter applying IFRS 7 early	Provides full IFRS 7 comparative information	Provides full IFRS 7 comparative information
Existing IFRS user not applying IFRS 7 early	Applies IAS 32. Provides full IAS 32 comparative information	Applies IAS 32. Provides full IAS 32 comparative information
Existing IFRS user applying IFRS 7 early	Provides full IFRS 7 comparative information	Provides full IFRS 7 comparative information
Accounting periods beginning on or after 1 January 2007 (mandatory application of IFRS 7)		
First-time adopter	Provides full IFRS 7 comparative information	Provides full IFRS 7 comparative information
Existing IFRS user	Provides full IFRS 7 comparative information	Provides full IFRS 7 comparative information
(a) See paragraph 44 of IFRS 7		

Appendix
Amendments to guidance on other IFRSs

The following amendments to guidance on IFRSs other than IFRS 4 are necessary in order to ensure consistency with IFRS 7. Amendments to the Guidance on Implementing IFRS 4 will be published at a later date. In the amended paragraphs, new text is underlined and deleted text is struck through.

******

The amendments contained in this appendix when IFRS 7 was issued in 2005 have been incorporated into the text of the Guidance on Implementing IAS 39 as issued at 18 August 2005. The revised Guidance on Implementing IFRS 4 was published in December 2005.

IASB documents published to accompany

IFRS 8

Operating Segments

The text of the unaccompanied standard, IFRS 8, is contained in Part A of this edition. The text of the Basis for Conclusions on IFRS 8 is contained in Part C of this edition. Its effective date when issued was 1 January 2009. This part presents the following documents:

IMPLEMENTATION GUIDANCE

APPENDIX
Amendments to other Implementation Guidance

CONTENTS

Guidance on implementing
IFRS 8 *Operating Segments*

This guidance accompanies, but is not part of, IFRS 8.

Introduction

IG1   This implementation guidance provides examples that illustrate the disclosures required by IFRS 8 and a diagram to assist in identifying reportable segments. The formats in the illustrations are not requirements. The Board encourages a format that provides the information in the most understandable manner in the specific circumstances. The following illustrations are for a single hypothetical entity referred to as Diversified Company.

Descriptive information about an entity's reportable segments

IG2   The following illustrates the disclosure of descriptive information about an entity's reportable segments (the paragraph references are to the relevant requirements in the IFRS).

Description of the types of products and services from which each reportable segment derives its revenues (paragraph 22(b))

Diversified Company has five reportable segments: car parts, motor vessels, software, electronics and finance. The car parts segment produces replacement parts for sale to car parts retailers. The motor vessels segment produces small motor vessels to serve the offshore oil industry and similar businesses. The software segment produces application software for sale to computer manufacturers and retailers. The electronics segment produces integrated circuits and related products for sale to computer manufacturers. The finance segment is responsible for portions of the company's financial operations including financing customer purchases of products from other segments and property lending operations.

Measurement of operating segment profit or loss, assets and liabilities (paragraph 27)

The accounting policy information about operating segments is the same as that described as part of the material accounting policy information, except that pension expense for each operating segment is recognised and measured on the basis of cash payments to the pension plan. Diversified Company evaluates performance on the basis of profit or loss from operations before tax expense not including non-recurring gains and losses and foreign exchange gains and losses.

Diversified Company accounts for intersegment sales and transfers as if the sales or transfers were to third parties, ie at current market prices.

Factors that management used to identify the entity's reportable segments (paragraph 22(a))

Diversified Company's reportable segments are strategic business units that offer different products and services. They are managed separately because each business requires different technology and marketing strategies. Most of the businesses were acquired as individual units, and the management at the time of the acquisition was retained.

Information about reportable segment profit or loss, assets and liabilities

IG3   The following table illustrates a suggested format for disclosing information about reportable segment profit or loss, assets and liabilities (paragraphs 23 and 24). The same type of information is required for each year for which a statement of comprehensive income is presented. Diversified Company does not allocate tax expense (tax income) or non-recurring gains and losses to reportable segments. In addition, not all reportable segments have material non-cash items other than depreciation and amortisation in profit or loss. The amounts in this illustration, denominated as 'currency units (CU)', are assumed to be the amounts in reports used by the chief operating decision maker.

	Car parts	Motor vessels	Software	Electronics	Finance	All other	Totals
	CU	CU	CU	CU	CU	CU	CU
Revenues from external customers	3,000	5,000	9,500	12,000	5,000	1,000[a]	35,500
Intersegment revenues	–	–	3,000	1,500	–	–	4,500
Interest revenue	450	800	1,000	1,500	–	–	3,750
Interest expense	350	600	700	1,100	–	–	2,750
Net interest revenue[b]	–	–	–	–	1,000	–	1,000
Depreciation and amortisation	200	100	50	1,500	1,100	–	2,950
Reportable segment profit	200	70	900	2,300	500	100	4,070
Other material non-cash items:							
Impairment of assets	–	200	–	–	–	–	200
Reportable segment assets	2,000	5,000	3,000	12,000	57,000	2,000	81,000
Expenditures for reportable segment non-current assets	300	700	500	800	600	–	2,900
Reportable segment liabilities	1,050	3,000	1,800	8,000	30,000	–	43,850

(a) Revenues from segments below the quantitative thresholds are attributable to four operating segments of Diversified Company. Those segments include a small property business, an electronics equipment rental business, a software consulting practice and a warehouse leasing operation. None of those segments has ever met any of the quantitative thresholds for determining reportable segments.
(b) The finance segment derives a majority of its revenue from interest. Management primarily relies on net interest revenue, not the gross revenue and expense amounts, in managing that segment. Therefore, as permitted by paragraph 23, only the net amount is disclosed.

Reconciliations of reportable segment revenues, profit or loss, assets and liabilities

IG4   The following illustrate reconciliations of reportable segment revenues, profit or loss, assets and liabilities to the entity's corresponding amounts (paragraph 28(a)–(d)). Reconciliations also are required to be shown for every other material item of information disclosed (paragraph 28(e)). The entity's financial statements are assumed not to include discontinued operations. As discussed in paragraph IG2, the entity recognises and measures pension expense of its reportable segments on the basis of cash payments to the pension plan, and it does not allocate certain items to its reportable segments.

Revenues	CU
Total revenues for reportable segments	39,000
Other revenues	1,000
Elimination of intersegment revenues	(4,500)
Entity's revenues	35,500

Profit or loss	CU
Total profit or loss for reportable segments	3,970
Other profit or loss	100
Elimination of intersegment profits	(500)
Unallocated amounts:	
Litigation settlement received	500
Other corporate expenses	(750)
Adjustment to pension expense in consolidation	(250)
Income before income tax expense	3,070

Assets	CU
Total assets for reportable segments	79,000
Other assets	2,000
Elimination of receivable from corporate headquarters	(1,000)
Other unallocated amounts	1,500
Entity's assets	81,500

Liabilities	CU
Total liabilities for reportable segments	43,850
Unallocated defined benefit pension liabilities	25,000
Entity's liabilities	68,850

Other material items	Reportable segment totals	Adjustments	Entity totals
	CU	CU	CU
Interest revenue	3,750	75	3,825
Interest expense	2,750	(50)	2,700
Net interest revenue (finance segment only)	1,000	–	1,000
Expenditures for assets	2,900	1,000	3,900
Depreciation and amortisation	2,950	–	2,950
Impairment of assets	200	–	200

The reconciling item to adjust expenditures for assets is the amount incurred for the corporate headquarters building, which is not included in segment information. None of the other adjustments are material.

Geographical information

IG5 The following illustrates the geographical information required by paragraph 33. (Because Diversified Company's reportable segments are based on differences in products and services, no additional disclosures of revenue information about products and services are required (paragraph 32).)

Geographical information	Revenues[a]	Non-current assets
	CU	CU
United States	19,000	11,000
Canada	4,200	–
China	3,400	6,500
Japan	2,900	3,500
Other countries	6,000	3,000
Total	35,500	24,000

(a) Revenues are attributed to countries on the basis of the customer's location.

Information about major customers

IG6 The following illustrates the information about major customers required by paragraph 34. Neither the identity of the customer nor the amount of revenues for each operating segment is required.

Revenues from one customer of Diversified Company's software and electronics segments represent approximately CU5,000 of the Company's total revenues.

Diagram to assist in identifying reportable segments

IG7   The following diagram illustrates how to apply the main provisions for identifying reportable segments as defined in the IFRS. The diagram is a visual supplement to the IFRS. It should not be interpreted as altering or adding to any requirements of the IFRS nor should it be regarded as a substitute for the requirements.

Diagram for identifying reportable segments

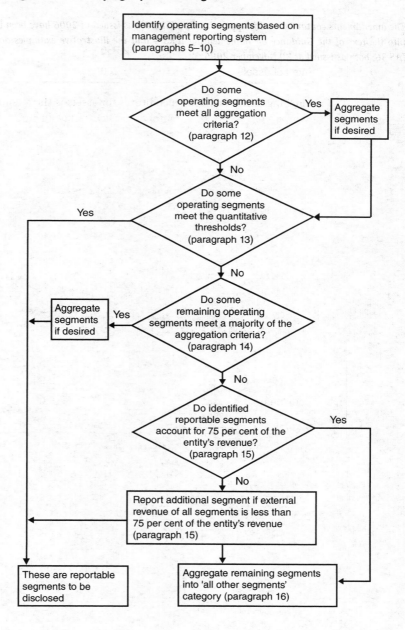

Appendix
Amendments to other Implementation Guidance

This appendix contains amendments to guidance on other IFRSs that are necessary in order to ensure consistency with IFRS 8. In the amended paragraphs, new text is underlined and deleted text is struck through.

* * * * *

The amendments contained in this appendix when IFRS 8 was issued in 2006 have been incorporated into the text of the Guidance on Implementing IFRS 4 and the illustrative examples accompanying IAS 36, both as issued at 30 November 2006.

IASB documents published to accompany

IFRS 9

Financial Instruments

The text of the unaccompanied standard, IFRS 9, is contained in Part A of this edition. The text of the Basis for Conclusions on IFRS 9 is contained in Part C of this edition. Its effective date when issued was 1 January 2018. This part presents the following documents:

ILLUSTRATIVE EXAMPLES

GUIDANCE ON IMPLEMENTING IFRS 9 *FINANCIAL INSTRUMENTS*

APPENDIX

Amendments to the guidance on other Standards

CONTENTS

IFRS 9 *Financial Instruments*
Illustrative Examples

These examples accompany, but are not part of, IFRS 9.

Financial liabilities at fair value through profit or loss

IE1　The following example illustrates the calculation that an entity might perform in accordance with paragraph B5.7.18 of IFRS 9.

IE2　On 1 January 20X1 an entity issues a 10-year bond with a par value of CU150,000[1] and an annual fixed coupon rate of 8 per cent, which is consistent with market rates for bonds with similar characteristics.

IE3　The entity uses LIBOR as its observable (benchmark) interest rate. At the date of inception of the bond, LIBOR is 5 per cent. At the end of the first year:

(a)　LIBOR has decreased to 4.75 per cent.

(b)　the fair value for the bond is CU153,811, consistent with an interest rate of 7.6 per cent.[2]

IE4　The entity assumes a flat yield curve, all changes in interest rates result from a parallel shift in the yield curve, and the changes in LIBOR are the only relevant changes in market conditions.

IE5　The entity estimates the amount of change in the fair value of the bond that is not attributable to changes in market conditions that give rise to market risk as follows:

[paragraph B5.7.18(a)] First, the entity computes the liability's internal rate of return at the start of the period using the observed market price of the liability and the liability's contractual cash flows at the start of the period. It deducts from this rate of return the observed (benchmark) interest rate at the start of the period, to arrive at an instrument-specific component of the internal rate of return.	At the start of the period of a 10-year bond with a coupon of 8 per cent, the bond's internal rate of return is 8 per cent.
	Because the observed (benchmark) interest rate (LIBOR) is 5 per cent, the instrument-specific component of the internal rate of return is 3 per cent.

continued...

1　In this guidance monetary amounts are denominated in 'currency units' (CU).

2　This reflects a shift in LIBOR from 5 per cent to 4.75 per cent and a movement of 0.15 per cent which, in the absence of other relevant changes in market conditions, is assumed to reflect changes in credit risk of the instrument.

...continued

[paragraph B5.7.18(b)]	The contractual cash flows of the instrument at the end of the period are:
Next, the entity calculates the present value of the cash flows associated with the liability using the liability's contractual cash flows at the end of the period and a discount rate equal to the sum of (i) the observed (benchmark) interest rate at the end of the period and (ii) the instrument-specific component of the internal rate of return as determined in accordance with paragraph B5.7.18(a).	• interest: CU12,000[a] per year for each of years 2–10. • principal: CU150,000 in year 10. The discount rate to be used to calculate the present value of the bond is thus 7.75 per cent, which is the end of period LIBOR rate of 4.75 per cent, plus the 3 per cent instrument-specific component. This gives a present value of CU152,367.[b]
[paragraph B5.7.18(c)] The difference between the observed market price of the liability at the end of the period and the amount determined in accordance with paragraph B5.7.18(b) is the change in fair value that is not attributable to changes in the observed (benchmark) interest rate. This is the amount to be presented in other comprehensive income in accordance with paragraph 5.7.7(a).	The market price of the liability at the end of the period is CU153,811.[c] Thus, the entity presents CU1,444 in other comprehensive income, which is CU153,811 – CU152,367, as the increase in fair value of the bond that is not attributable to changes in market conditions that give rise to market risk.

(a) CU150,000 × 8% = CU12,000.

(b) PV = [CU12,000 × (1 − (1 + 0.0775)$^{-9}$)/0.0775] + CU150,000 × (1 + 0.0775)$^{-9}$.

(c) market price = [CU12,000 × (1 − (1 + 0.076)$^{-9}$)/0.076] + CU150,000 × (1 + 0.076)$^{-9}$.

Impairment (Section 5.5)

Assessing significant increases in credit risk since initial recognition

IE6   The following examples illustrate possible ways to assess whether there have been significant increases in credit risk since initial recognition. For simplicity of illustration, the following examples only show one aspect of the credit risk analysis. However, the assessment of whether lifetime expected credit losses should be recognised is a multifactor and holistic analysis that considers reasonable and supportable information that is available without undue cost or effort and that is relevant for the particular financial instrument being assessed.

Example 1—significant increase in credit risk

[Refer:
paragraphs 5.5.3–5.5.5, 5.5.9 and B5.5.7–B5.5.17
Basis for Conclusions paragraphs BC5.143–BC5.194]

IE7   Company Y has a funding structure that includes a senior secured loan facility with different tranches[3]. Bank X provides a tranche of that loan facility to Company Y. At the time of origination of the loan by Bank X, although Company Y's leverage was relatively high compared with other issuers with similar credit risk, it was expected that Company Y would be able to meet the covenants for the life of the instrument. In addition, the generation of revenue and cash flow was expected to be stable in Company Y's industry over the term of the senior facility. However, there was some business risk related to the ability to grow gross margins within its existing businesses.

IE8   At initial recognition, because of the considerations outlined in paragraph IE7, Bank X considers that despite the level of credit risk at initial recognition, the loan is not an originated credit-impaired loan because it does not meet the definition of a credit-impaired financial asset in Appendix A of IFRS 9.

IE9   Subsequent to initial recognition, macroeconomic changes have had a negative effect on total sales volume and Company Y has underperformed on its business plan for revenue generation and net cash flow generation. Although spending on inventory has increased, anticipated sales have not materialised. To increase liquidity, Company Y has drawn down more on a separate revolving credit facility, thereby increasing its leverage ratio. Consequently, Company Y is now close to breaching its covenants on the senior secured loan facility with Bank X.

IE10   Bank X makes an overall assessment of the credit risk on the loan to Company Y at the reporting date by taking into consideration all reasonable and supportable information that is available without undue cost or effort and that is relevant for assessing the extent of the increase in credit risk since initial recognition. This may include factors such as:

(a)   Bank X's expectation that the deterioration in the macroeconomic environment may continue in the near future, which is expected to have a further negative impact on Company Y's ability to generate cash flows and to deleverage.

(b)   Company Y is closer to breaching its covenants, which may result in a need to restructure the loan or reset the covenants.

(c)   Bank X's assessment that the trading prices for Company Y's bonds have decreased and that the credit margin on newly originated loans have increased reflecting the increase in credit risk, and that these changes are not explained by changes in the market environment (for

---

3   The security on the loan affects the loss that would be realised if a default occurs, but does not affect the risk of a default occurring, so it is not considered when determining whether there has been a significant increase in credit risk since initial recognition as required by paragraph 5.5.3 of IFRS 9.

example, benchmark interest rates have remained unchanged). A further comparison with the pricing of Company Y's peers shows that reductions in the price of Company Y's bonds and increases in credit margin on its loans have probably been caused by company-specific factors.

(d)   Bank X has reassessed its internal risk grading of the loan on the basis of the information that it has available to reflect the increase in credit risk.

IE11   Bank X determines that there has been a significant increase in credit risk since initial recognition of the loan in accordance with paragraph 5.5.3 of IFRS 9. Consequently, Bank X recognises lifetime expected credit losses on its senior secured loan to Company Y. Even if Bank X has not yet changed the internal risk grading of the loan it could still reach this conclusion—the absence or presence of a change in risk grading in itself is not determinative of whether credit risk has increased significantly since initial recognition.

Example 2—no significant increase in credit risk

[Refer:
paragraphs 5.5.3–5.5.5, 5.5.9 and B5.5.7–B5.5.17
Basis for Conclusions paragraphs BC5.143–BC5.194]

IE12   Company C, is the holding company of a group that operates in a cyclical production industry. Bank B provided a loan to Company C. At that time, the prospects for the industry were positive, because of expectations of further increases in global demand. However, input prices were volatile and given the point in the cycle, a potential decrease in sales was anticipated.

IE13   In addition, in the past Company C has been focused on external growth, acquiring majority stakes in companies in related sectors. As a result, the group structure is complex and has been subject to change, making it difficult for investors to analyse the expected performance of the group and to forecast the cash that will be available at the holding company level. Even though leverage is at a level that is considered acceptable by Company C's creditors at the time that Bank B originates the loan, its creditors are concerned about Company C's ability to refinance its debt because of the short remaining life until the maturity of the current financing. There is also concern about Company C's ability to continue to service interest using the dividends it receives from its operating subsidiaries.

IE14   At the time of the origination of the loan by Bank B, Company C's leverage was in line with that of other customers with similar credit risk and based on projections over the expected life of the loan, the available capacity (ie headroom) on its coverage ratios before triggering a default event, was high. Bank B applies its own internal rating methods to determine credit risk and allocates a specific internal rating score to its loans. Bank B's internal rating categories are based on historical, current and forward-looking information and reflect the credit risk for the tenor of the loans. On initial recognition, Bank B determines that the loan is subject to considerable credit risk, has speculative elements and that the uncertainties affecting Company C, including the group's uncertain prospects for cash generation, could lead to default. However, Bank B does not consider the loan to be originated credit-impaired because it does not meet the definition of a purchased or originated credit-impaired financial asset in Appendix A of IFRS 9.

IE15   Subsequent to initial recognition, Company C has announced that three of its five key subsidiaries had a significant reduction in sales volume because of deteriorated market conditions but sales volumes are expected to improve in line with the anticipated cycle for the industry in the following months. The sales of the other two subsidiaries were stable. Company C has also announced a corporate restructure to streamline its operating subsidiaries. This restructuring will increase the flexibility to refinance existing debt and the ability of the operating subsidiaries to pay dividends to Company C.

IE16   Despite the expected continuing deterioration in market conditions, Bank B determines, in accordance with paragraph 5.5.3 of IFRS 9, that there has not been a significant increase in the credit risk on the loan to Company C since initial recognition. This is demonstrated by factors that include:

(a)   Although current sale volumes have fallen, this was as anticipated by Bank B at initial recognition. Furthermore, sales volumes are expected to improve, in the following months.

(b)   Given the increased flexibility to refinance the existing debt at the operating subsidiary level and the increased availability of dividends to Company C, Bank B views the corporate restructure as being credit enhancing. This is despite some continued concern about the ability to refinance the existing debt at the holding company level.

(c)   Bank B's credit risk department, which monitors Company C, has determined that the latest developments are not significant enough to justify a change in its internal credit risk rating.

IE17   As a consequence, Bank B does not recognise a loss allowance at an amount equal to lifetime expected credit losses on the loan. However, it updates its measurement of the 12-month expected credit losses for the increased risk of a default occurring in the next 12 months and for current expectations of the credit losses that would arise if a default were to occur.

Example 3—highly collateralised financial asset

[Refer:
paragraphs 5.5.3–5.5.5, 5.5.9, B5.5.7–B5.5.17 and B5.5.55
Basis for Conclusions paragraphs BC5.143–BC5.194]

IE18   Company H owns real estate assets which are financed by a five-year loan from Bank Z with a loan-to-value (LTV) ratio of 50 per cent. The loan is secured by a first-ranking security over the real estate assets. At initial recognition of the loan, Bank Z does not consider the loan to be originated credit-impaired as defined in Appendix A of IFRS 9.

IE19   Subsequent to initial recognition, the revenues and operating profits of Company H have decreased because of an economic recession. Furthermore, expected increases in regulations have the potential to further negatively affect revenue and operating profit. These negative effects on Company H's operations could be significant and ongoing.

IE20   As a result of these recent events and expected adverse economic conditions, Company H's free cash flow is expected to be reduced to the point that the coverage of scheduled loan payments could become tight. Bank Z estimates that a further deterioration in cash flows may result in Company H missing a contractual payment on the loan and becoming past due.

IE21   Recent third party appraisals have indicated a decrease in the value of the real estate properties, resulting in a current LTV ratio of 70 per cent.

IE22   At the reporting date, the loan to Company H is not considered to have low credit risk in accordance with paragraph 5.5.10 of IFRS 9. Bank Z therefore needs to assess whether there has been a significant increase in credit risk since initial recognition in accordance with paragraph 5.5.3 of IFRS 9, irrespective of the value of the collateral it holds. It notes that the loan is subject to considerable credit risk at the reporting date because even a slight deterioration in cash flows could result in Company H missing a contractual payment on the loan. As a result, Bank Z determines that the credit risk (ie the risk of a default occurring) has increased significantly since initial recognition. Consequently, Bank Z recognises lifetime expected credit losses on the loan to Company H.

IE23   Although lifetime expected credit losses should be recognised, the measurement of the expected credit losses will reflect the recovery expected from the collateral (adjusting for the costs of obtaining and selling the collateral) on the property as required by paragraph B5.5.55 of IFRS 9 and may result in the expected credit losses on the loan being very small.

Example 4—public investment-grade bond

[Refer:
paragraphs 5.5.3–5.5.5, 5.5.9, 5.5.10 and B5.5.22–B5.5.24
Basis for Conclusions paragraphs BC5.180–BC5.189]

IE24   Company A is a large listed national logistics company. The only debt in the capital structure is a five-year public bond with a restriction on further borrowing as the only bond covenant. Company A reports quarterly to its shareholders. Entity B is one of many investors in the bond. Entity B considers the bond to have low credit risk at initial recognition in accordance with paragraph 5.5.10 of IFRS 9. This is because the bond has a low risk of default and Company A is considered to have a strong capacity to meet its obligations in the near term. Entity B's expectations for the longer term are that adverse changes in economic and business conditions may, but will not necessarily, reduce Company A's ability to fulfil its obligations on the bond. In addition, at initial recognition the bond had an internal credit rating that is correlated to a global external credit rating of investment grade.

IE25   At the reporting date, Entity B's main credit risk concern is the continuing pressure on the total volume of sales that has caused Company A's operating cash flows to decrease.

IE26   Because Entity B relies only on quarterly public information and does not have access to private credit risk information (because it is a bond investor), its assessment of changes in credit risk is tied to public announcements and information, including updates on credit perspectives in press releases from rating agencies.

IE27   Entity B applies the low credit risk simplification in paragraph 5.5.10 of IFRS 9. Accordingly, at the reporting date, Entity B evaluates whether the bond is considered to have low credit risk using all reasonable and supportable information that is available without undue cost or effort. In making that evaluation, Entity B reassesses the internal credit rating of the bond and concludes that the bond is no longer equivalent to an investment grade rating because:

(a)   The latest quarterly report of Company A revealed a quarter-on-quarter decline in revenues of 20 per cent and in operating profit by 12 per cent.

(b)   Rating agencies have reacted negatively to a profit warning by Company A and put the credit rating under review for possible downgrade from investment grade to non-investment grade. However, at the reporting date the external credit risk rating was unchanged.

(c)   The bond price has also declined significantly, which has resulted in a higher yield to maturity. Entity B assesses that the bond prices have been declining as a result of increases in Company A's credit risk. This is because the market environment has not changed (for example, benchmark interest rates, liquidity etc are unchanged) and comparison with the bond prices of peers shows that the reductions are probably company specific (instead of being, for example, changes in benchmark interest rates that are not indicative of company-specific credit risk).

IE28   While Company A currently has the capacity to meet its commitments, the large uncertainties arising from its exposure to adverse business and economic conditions have increased the risk of a default occurring on the bond. As a result of the factors described in paragraph IE27, Entity B determines that the bond does not have low credit risk at the reporting date. As a result, Entity B needs to determine whether the increase in credit risk since initial recognition has been significant. On the basis of its assessment, Company B determines that the credit risk has increased significantly since initial recognition and that a loss allowance at an amount equal to lifetime expected credit losses should be recognised in accordance with paragraph 5.5.3 of IFRS 9.

Example 5—responsiveness to changes in credit risk

[Refer:
paragraphs 5.5.4 and B5.5.1–B5.5.6
Basis for Conclusions paragraphs BC5.136–BC5.142]

IE29   Bank ABC provides mortgages to finance residential real estate in three different regions. The mortgage loans are originated across a wide range of LTV criteria and a wide range of income groups. As part of the mortgage application process, customers are required to provide information such as the industry within which the customer is employed and the post code of the property that serves as collateral on the mortgage.

IE30   Bank ABC sets its acceptance criteria based on credit scores. Loans with a credit score above the 'acceptance level' are approved because these borrowers are considered to be able to meet contractual payment obligations. When new mortgage loans are originated, Bank ABC uses the credit score to determine the risk of a default occurring as at initial recognition.

IE31   At the reporting date Bank ABC determines that economic conditions are expected to deteriorate significantly in all regions. Unemployment levels are expected to increase while the value of residential property is expected to decrease, causing the LTV ratios to increase. As a result of the expected deterioration in economic conditions, Bank ABC expects default rates on the mortgage portfolio to increase.

Individual assessment

IE32   In Region One, Bank ABC assesses each of its mortgage loans on a monthly basis by means of an automated behavioural scoring process. Its scoring models are based on current and historical past due statuses, levels of customer indebtedness, LTV measures, customer behaviour on other financial instruments with Bank ABC, the loan size and the time since the origination of the loan. Bank ABC updates the LTV measures on a regular basis through an automated process that re-estimates property values using recent sales in each post code area and reasonable and supportable forward-looking information that is available without undue cost or effort.

IE33   Bank ABC has historical data that indicates a strong correlation between the value of residential property and the default rates for mortgages. That is, when the value of residential property declines, a customer has less economic incentive to make scheduled mortgage repayments, increasing the risk of a default occurring.

IE34   Through the impact of the LTV measure in the behavioural scoring model, an increased risk of a default occurring due to an expected decline in residential property value adjusts the behavioural scores. The behavioural score can be adjusted as a result of expected declines in property value even when the mortgage loan is a bullet loan with the most significant payment obligations at maturity (and beyond the next 12 months). Mortgages with a high LTV ratio are more sensitive to changes in the value of the residential property and Bank ABC is able to identify significant increases in credit risk since initial recognition on individual customers before a mortgage becomes past due if there has been a deterioration in the behavioural score.

IE35   When the increase in credit risk has been significant, a loss allowance at an amount equal to lifetime expected credit losses is recognised. Bank ABC measures the loss allowance by using the LTV measures to estimate the severity of the loss, ie the loss given default (LGD). The higher the LTV measure, the higher the expected credit losses all else being equal.

IE36   If Bank ABC was unable to update behavioural scores to reflect the expected declines in property prices, it would use reasonable and supportable information that is available without undue cost or effort to undertake a collective assessment to determine the loans on which there has been a significant increase in credit risk since initial recognition and recognise lifetime expected credit losses for those loans.

Collective assessment

IE37   In Regions Two and Three, Bank ABC does not have an automated scoring capability. Instead, for credit risk management purposes, Bank ABC tracks the risk of a default occurring by means of past due statuses. It recognises a loss allowance at an amount equal to lifetime expected credit losses for all loans that have a past due status of more than 30 days past due. Although Bank ABC uses past due status information as the only borrower-specific information, it also considers other reasonable and supportable forward-looking information that is available without undue cost or effort to assess whether lifetime expected credit losses should be recognised on loans that are not more than 30 days past due. This is necessary in order to meet the objective in paragraph 5.5.4 of IFRS 9 of recognising lifetime expected credit losses for all significant increases in credit risk.

Region Two

IE38   Region Two includes a mining community that is largely dependent on the export of coal and related products. Bank ABC becomes aware of a significant decline in coal exports and anticipates the closure of several coal mines. Because of the expected increase in the unemployment rate, the risk of a default occurring on mortgage loans to borrowers who are employed by the coal mines is determined to have increased significantly, even if those customers are not past due at the reporting date. Bank ABC therefore segments its mortgage portfolio by the industry within which customers are employed (using the information recorded as part of the mortgage application process) to identify customers that rely on coal mining as the dominant source of employment (ie a 'bottom up' approach in which loans are identified based on a common risk characteristic). For those mortgages, Bank ABC recognises a loss allowance at an amount equal to lifetime expected credit losses while it continues to recognise a loss allowance at an amount equal to 12-month expected credit losses for all other mortgages in Region Two.[4] Newly

---

4   Except for those mortgages that are determined to have significantly increased in credit risk based on an individual assessment, such as those that are more than 30 days past due. Lifetime expected credit losses would also be recognised on those mortgages.

originated mortgages to borrowers who rely on the coal mines for employment in this community would, however, have a loss allowance at an amount equal to 12-month expected credit losses because they would not have experienced significant increases in credit risk since initial recognition. However, some of these mortgages may experience significant increases in credit risk soon after initial recognition because of the expected closure of the coal mines.

Region Three

IE39   In Region Three, Bank ABC anticipates the risk of a default occurring and thus an increase in credit risk, as a result of an expected increase in interest rates during the expected life of the mortgages. Historically, an increase in interest rates has been a lead indicator of future defaults on mortgages in Region Three—especially when customers do not have a fixed interest rate mortgage. Bank ABC determines that the variable interest-rate portfolio of mortgages in Region Three is homogenous and that unlike for Region Two, it is not possible to identify particular sub portfolios on the basis of shared risk characteristics that represent customers who are expected to have increased significantly in credit risk. However, as a result of the homogenous nature of the mortgages in Region Three, Bank ABC determines that an assessment can be made of a proportion of the overall portfolio that has significantly increased in credit risk since initial recognition (ie a 'top down' approach can be used). Based on historical information, Bank ABC estimates that an increase in interest rates of 200 basis points will cause a significant increase in credit risk on 20 per cent of the variable interest-rate portfolio. Therefore, as a result of the anticipated increase in interest rates, Bank ABC determines that the credit risk on 20 per cent of mortgages in Region Three has increased significantly since initial recognition. Accordingly Bank ABC recognises lifetime expected credit losses on 20 per cent of the variable rate mortgage portfolio and a loss allowance at an amount equal to 12-month expected credit losses for the remainder of the portfolio.[5]

Example 6—comparison to maximum initial credit risk

[Refer:
paragraphs 5.5.3–5.5.5, 5.5.9 and B5.5.7–B5.5.17
Basis for Conclusions paragraph BC5.161]

IE40   Bank A has two portfolios of automobile loans with similar terms and conditions in Region W. Bank A's policy on financing decisions for each loan is based on an internal credit rating system that considers a customer's credit history, payment behaviour on other products with Bank A and other factors, and assigns an internal credit risk rating from 1 (lowest credit risk) to 10 (highest credit risk) to each loan on origination. The risk of a default occurring increases exponentially as the credit risk rating deteriorates so, for example, the difference between credit risk rating grades 1 and 2 is smaller than the

---

5   Except for those mortgages that are determined to have significantly increased in credit risk based on an individual assessment, such as those that are more than 30 days past due. Lifetime expected credit losses would also be recognised on those mortgages.

difference between credit risk rating grades 2 and 3. Loans in Portfolio 1 were only offered to existing customers with a similar internal credit risk rating and at initial recognition all loans were rated 3 or 4 on the internal rating scale. Bank A determines that the maximum initial credit risk rating at initial recognition it would accept for Portfolio 1 is an internal rating of 4. Loans in Portfolio 2 were offered to customers that responded to an advertisement for automobile loans and the internal credit risk ratings of these customers range between 4 and 7 on the internal rating scale. Bank A never originates an automobile loan with an internal credit risk rating worse than 7 (ie with an internal rating of 8–10).

IE41   For the purposes of assessing whether there have been significant increases in credit risk, Bank A determines that all loans in Portfolio 1 had a similar initial credit risk. It determines that given the risk of default reflected in its internal risk rating grades, a change in internal rating from 3 to 4 would not represent a significant increase in credit risk but that there has been a significant increase in credit risk on any loan in this portfolio that has an internal rating worse than 5. This means that Bank A does not have to know the initial credit rating of each loan in the portfolio to assess the change in credit risk since initial recognition. It only has to determine whether the credit risk is worse than 5 at the reporting date to determine whether lifetime expected credit losses should be recognised in accordance with paragraph 5.5.3 of IFRS 9.

IE42   However, determining the maximum initial credit risk accepted at initial recognition for Portfolio 2 at an internal credit risk rating of 7, would not meet the objective of the requirements as stated in paragraph 5.5.4 of IFRS 9. This is because Bank A determines that significant increases in credit risk arise not only when credit risk increases above the level at which an entity would originate new financial assets (ie when the internal rating is worse than 7). Although Bank A never originates an automobile loan with an internal credit rating worse than 7, the initial credit risk on loans in Portfolio 2 is not of sufficiently similar credit risk at initial recognition to apply the approach used for Portfolio 1. This means that Bank A cannot simply compare the credit risk at the reporting date with the lowest credit quality at initial recognition (for example, by comparing the internal credit risk rating of loans in Portfolio 2 with an internal credit risk rating of 7) to determine whether credit risk has increased significantly because the initial credit quality of loans in the portfolio is too diverse. For example, if a loan initially had a credit risk rating of 4 the credit risk on the loan may have increased significantly if its internal credit risk rating changes to 6.

Example 7—counterparty assessment of credit risk

[Refer:
paragraphs 5.5.3–5.5.5, 5.5.9 and B5.5.7–B5.5.17
Basis for Conclusions paragraphs BC5.166–BC5.168]

Scenario 1

IE43   In 20X0 Bank A granted a loan of CU10,000 with a contractual term of 15 years to Company Q when the company had an internal credit risk rating of 4 on a scale of 1 (lowest credit risk) to 10 (highest credit risk). The risk of a default occurring increases exponentially as the credit risk rating deteriorates so, for example, the difference between credit risk rating grades 1 and 2 is smaller than the difference between credit risk rating grades 2 and 3. In 20X5, when Company Q had an internal credit risk rating of 6, Bank A issued another loan to Company Q for CU5,000 with a contractual term of 10 years. In 20X7 Company Q fails to retain its contract with a major customer and correspondingly experiences a large decline in its revenue. Bank A considers that as a result of losing the contract, Company Q will have a significantly reduced ability to meet its loan obligations and changes its internal credit risk rating to 8.

IE44   Bank A assesses credit risk on a counterparty level for credit risk management purposes and determines that the increase in Company Q's credit risk is significant. Although Bank A did not perform an individual assessment of changes in the credit risk on each loan since its initial recognition, assessing the credit risk on a counterparty level and recognising lifetime expected credit losses on all loans granted to Company Q, meets the objective of the impairment requirements as stated in paragraph 5.5.4 of IFRS 9. This is because, even since the most recent loan was originated (in 20X7) when Company Q had the highest credit risk at loan origination, its credit risk has increased significantly. The counterparty assessment would therefore achieve the same result as assessing the change in credit risk for each loan individually.

Scenario 2

IE45   Bank A granted a loan of CU150,000 with a contractual term of 20 years to Company X in 20X0 when the company had an internal credit risk rating of 4. During 20X5 economic conditions deteriorate and demand for Company X's products has declined significantly. As a result of the reduced cash flows from lower sales, Company X could not make full payment of its loan instalment to Bank A. Bank A re-assesses Company X's internal credit risk rating, and determines it to be 7 at the reporting date. Bank A considered the change in credit risk on the loan, including considering the change in the internal credit risk rating, and determines that there has been a significant increase in credit risk and recognises lifetime expected credit losses on the loan of CU150,000.

IE46   Despite the recent downgrade of the internal credit risk rating, Bank A grants another loan of CU50,000 to Company X in 20X6 with a contractual term of 5 years, taking into consideration the higher credit risk at that date.

IE47   The fact that Company X's credit risk (assessed on a counterparty basis) has previously been assessed to have increased significantly, does not result in lifetime expected credit losses being recognised on the new loan. This is because the credit risk on the new loan has not increased significantly since the loan was initially recognised. If Bank A only assessed credit risk on a counterparty level, without considering whether the conclusion about changes in credit risk applies to all individual financial instruments provided to the same customer, the objective in paragraph 5.5.4 of IFRS 9 would not be met.

Recognition and measurement of expected credit losses

IE48   The following examples illustrate the application of the recognition and measurement requirements in accordance with Section 5.5 of IFRS 9, as well as the interaction with the hedge accounting requirements.

Example 8—12-month expected credit loss measurement using an explicit 'probability of default' approach

[Refer:
paragraphs 5.5.3–5.5.5, 5.5.9 and B5.5.12
Basis for Conclusions paragraphs BC5.156–BC5.157]

Scenario 1

IE49   Entity A originates a single 10 year amortising loan for CU1 million. Taking into consideration the expectations for instruments with similar credit risk (using reasonable and supportable information that is available without undue cost or effort), the credit risk of the borrower, and the economic outlook for the next 12 months, Entity A estimates that the loan at initial recognition has a probability of default (PD) of 0.5 per cent over the next 12 months. Entity A also determines that changes in the 12-month PD are a reasonable approximation of the changes in the lifetime PD for determining whether there has been a significant increase in credit risk since initial recognition.

IE50   At the reporting date (which is before payment on the loan is due[6]), there has been no change in the 12-month PD and Entity A determines that there was no significant increase in credit risk since initial recognition. Entity A determines that 25 per cent of the gross carrying amount will be lost if the loan defaults (ie the LGD is 25 per cent).[7] Entity A measures the loss allowance at an amount equal to 12-month expected credit losses using the 12-month PD of 0.5 per cent. Implicit in that calculation is the 99.5 per cent probability that there is no default. At the reporting date the loss allowance for the 12 month expected credit losses is CU1,250 (0.5% × 25% × CU1,000,000).

---

6   Thus for simplicity of illustration it is assumed there is no amortisation of the loan.

7   Because the LGD represents a percentage of the present value of the gross carrying amount, this example does not illustrate the time value of money.

Scenario 2

IE51   Entity B acquires a portfolio of 1,000 five year bullet loans for CU1,000 each (ie CU1million in total) with an average 12-month PD of 0.5 per cent for the portfolio. Entity B determines that because the loans only have significant payment obligations beyond the next 12 months, it would not be appropriate to consider changes in the 12-month PD when determining whether there have been significant increases in credit risk since initial recognition. At the reporting date Entity B therefore uses changes in the lifetime PD to determine whether the credit risk of the portfolio has increased significantly since initial recognition.

IE52   Entity B determines that there has not been a significant increase in credit risk since initial recognition and estimates that the portfolio has an average LGD of 25 per cent. Entity B determines that it is appropriate to measure the loss allowance on a collective basis in accordance with IFRS 9. The 12-month PD remains at 0.5 per cent at the reporting date. Entity B therefore measures the loss allowance on a collective basis at an amount equal to 12-month expected credit losses based on the average 0.5 per cent 12-month PD. Implicit in the calculation is the 99.5 per cent probability that there is no default. At the reporting date the loss allowance for the 12-month expected credit losses is CU1,250 (0.5% × 25% × CU1,000,000).

Example 9—12-month expected credit loss measurement based on a loss rate approach

[Refer:
paragraphs B5.5.12 and B5.5.53
Basis for Conclusions paragraph BC5.266]

IE53   Bank A originates 2,000 bullet loans with a total gross carrying amount of CU500,000. Bank A segments its portfolio into borrower groups (Groups X and Y) on the basis of shared credit risk characteristics at initial recognition. Group X comprises 1,000 loans with a gross carrying amount per client of CU200, for a total gross carrying amount of CU200,000. Group Y comprises 1,000 loans with a gross carrying amount per client of CU300, for a total gross carrying amount of CU300,000. There are no transaction costs and the loan contracts include no options (for example, prepayment or call options), premiums or discounts, points paid, or other fees.

IE54   Bank A measures expected credit losses on the basis of a loss rate approach for Groups X and Y. In order to develop its loss rates, Bank A considers samples of its own historical default and loss experience for those types of loans. In addition, Bank A considers forward-looking information, and updates its historical information for current economic conditions as well as reasonable and supportable forecasts of future economic conditions. Historically, for a population of 1,000 loans in each group, Group X's loss rates are 0.3 per cent, based on four defaults, and historical loss rates for Group Y are 0.15 per cent, based on two defaults.

	Number of clients in sample	Estimated per client gross carrying amount at default	Total estimated gross carrying amount at default	Historic per annum average defaults	Estimated total gross carrying amount at default	Present value of observed loss[a]	Loss rate
Group	A	B	C = A × B	D	E = B × D	F	G = F ÷ C
X	1,000	CU200	CU200,000	4	CU800	CU600	0.3%
Y	1,000	CU300	CU300,000	2	CU600	CU450	0.15%

(a) In accordance with paragraph 5.5.17(b) expected credit losses should be discounted using the effective interest rate. However, for purposes of this example, the present value of the observed loss is assumed.

IE55 At the reporting date, Bank A expects an increase in defaults over the next 12 months compared to the historical rate. As a result, Bank A estimates five defaults in the next 12 months for loans in Group X and three for loans in Group Y. It estimates that the present value of the observed credit loss per client will remain consistent with the historical loss per client.

IE56 On the basis of the expected life of the loans, Bank A determines that the expected increase in defaults does not represent a significant increase in credit risk since initial recognition for the portfolios. On the basis of its forecasts, Bank A measures the loss allowance at an amount equal to 12-month expected credit losses on the 1,000 loans in each group amounting to CU750 and CU675 respectively. This equates to a loss rate in the first year of 0.375 per cent for Group X and 0.225 per cent for Group Y.

	Number of clients in sample	Estimated per client gross carrying amount at default	Total estimated gross carrying amount at default	Expected defaults	Estimated total gross carrying amount at default	Present value of observed loss	Loss rate
Group	A	B	C = A × B	D	E = B × D	F	G = F ÷ C
X	1,000	CU200	CU200,000	5	CU1,000	CU750	0.375%
Y	1,000	CU300	CU300,000	3	CU900	CU675	0.225%

IE57 Bank A uses the loss rates of 0.375 per cent and 0.225 per cent respectively to estimate 12-month expected credit losses on new loans in Group X and Group Y originated during the year and for which credit risk has not increased significantly since initial recognition.

Example 10—revolving credit facilities

[Refer:
paragraphs 5.5.20, B5.5.31, B5.5.39 and B5.5.40
Basis for Conclusions paragraphs BC5.254–BC5.261]

IE58 Bank A provides co-branded credit cards to customers in conjunction with a local department store. The credit cards have a one-day notice period after which Bank A has the contractual right to cancel the credit card (both the drawn and undrawn components). However, Bank A does not enforce its contractual right to cancel the credit cards in the normal day-to-day management of the instruments and only cancels facilities when it becomes aware of an increase in credit risk and starts to monitor customers on an individual basis. Bank A therefore does not consider the contractual right to cancel the credit cards to limit its exposure to credit losses to the contractual notice period.

IE59   For credit risk management purposes Bank A considers that there is only one set of contractual cash flows from customers to assess and does not distinguish between the drawn and undrawn balances at the reporting date. The portfolio is therefore managed and expected credit losses are measured on a facility level.

IE60   At the reporting date the outstanding balance on the credit card portfolio is CU60,000 and the available undrawn facility is CU40,000. Bank A determines the expected life of the portfolio by estimating the period over which it expects to be exposed to credit risk on the facilities at the reporting date, taking into account:

(a)   the period over which it was exposed to credit risk on a similar portfolio of credit cards;

(b)   the length of time for related defaults to occur on similar financial instruments; and

(c)   past events that led to credit risk management actions because of an increase in credit risk on similar financial instruments, such as the reduction or removal of undrawn credit limits.

IE61   On the basis of the information listed in paragraph IE60, Bank A determines that the expected life of the credit card portfolio is 30 months.

IE62   At the reporting date Bank A assesses the change in the credit risk on the portfolio since initial recognition and determines in accordance with paragraph 5.5.3 of IFRS 9 that the credit risk on a portion of the credit card facilities representing 25 per cent of the portfolio, has increased significantly since initial recognition. The outstanding balance on these credit facilities for which lifetime expected credit losses should be recognised is CU20,000 and the available undrawn facility is CU10,000.

IE63   When measuring the expected credit losses in accordance with paragraph 5.5.20 of IFRS 9, Bank A considers its expectations about future draw-downs over the expected life of the portfolio (ie 30 months) in accordance with paragraph B5.5.31 and estimates what it expects the outstanding balance (ie exposure at default) on the portfolio would be if customers were to default. By using its credit risk models Bank A determines that the exposure at default on the credit card facilities for which lifetime expected credit losses should be recognised, is CU25,000 (ie the drawn balance of CU20,000 plus further draw-downs of CU5,000 from the available undrawn commitment). The exposure at default of the credit card facilities for which 12-month expected credit losses are recognised, is CU45,000 (ie the outstanding balance of CU40,000 and an additional draw-down of CU5,000 from the undrawn commitment over the next 12 months).

IE64   The exposure at default and expected life determined by Bank A are used to measure the lifetime expected credit losses and 12-month expected credit losses on its credit card portfolio.

IE65   Bank A measures expected credit losses on a facility level and therefore cannot separately identify the expected credit losses on the undrawn commitment component from those on the loan component. It recognises expected credit losses for the undrawn commitment together with the loss allowance for the loan component in the statement of financial position. To the extent that the combined expected credit losses exceed the gross carrying amount of the financial asset, the expected credit losses should be presented as a provision (in accordance with IFRS 7 *Financial Instruments: Disclosure*).

Example 11—modification of contractual cash flows

[Refer:
paragraphs 5.4.3, 5.5.3–5.5.5, 5.5.9, 5.5.12 and B5.5.25–B5.5.27
Basis for Conclusions paragraphs BC5.227–BC5.241]

IE66   Bank A originates a five-year loan that requires the repayment of the outstanding contractual amount in full at maturity. Its contractual par amount is CU1,000 with an interest rate of 5 per cent payable annually. The effective interest rate is 5 per cent. At the end of the first reporting period (Period 1), Bank A recognises a loss allowance at an amount equal to 12-month expected credit losses because there has not been a significant increase in credit risk since initial recognition. A loss allowance balance of CU20 is recognised.

IE67   In the subsequent reporting period (Period 2), Bank A determines that the credit risk on the loan has increased significantly since initial recognition. As a result of this increase, Bank A recognises lifetime expected credit losses on the loan. The loss allowance balance is CU30.

IE68   At the end of the third reporting period (Period 3), following significant financial difficulty of the borrower, Bank A modifies the contractual cash flows on the loan. It extends the contractual term of the loan by one year so that the remaining term at the date of the modification is three years. The modification does not result in the derecognition of the loan by Bank A.

IE69   As a result of that modification, Bank A recalculates the gross carrying amount of the financial asset as the present value of the modified contractual cash flows discounted at the loan's original effective interest rate of 5 per cent. In accordance with paragraph 5.4.3 of IFRS 9, the difference between this recalculated gross carrying amount and the gross carrying amount before the modification is recognised as a modification gain or loss. Bank A recognises the modification loss (calculated as CU300) against the gross carrying amount of the loan, reducing it to CU700, and a modification loss of CU300 in profit or loss.

IE70   Bank A also remeasures the loss allowance, taking into account the modified contractual cash flows and evaluates whether the loss allowance for the loan shall continue to be measured at an amount equal to lifetime expected credit losses. Bank A compares the current credit risk (taking into consideration the modified cash flows) to the credit risk (on the original unmodified cash flows) at initial recognition. Bank A determines that the loan is not credit-impaired at the reporting date but that credit risk has still significantly increased compared to the credit risk at initial recognition and continues to measure the loss allowance at an amount equal to lifetime expected credit losses. The loss allowance balance for lifetime expected credit losses is CU100 at the reporting date.

Period	Beginning gross carrying amount	Impairment (loss)/gain	Modification (loss)/gain	Interest revenue	Cash flows	Ending gross carrying amount	Loss allowance	Ending amortised cost amount
	A	B	C	D Gross: A × 5%	E	F = A + C + D - E	G	H = F - G
1	CU1,000	(CU20)		CU50	CU50	CU1,000	CU20	CU980
2	CU1,000	(CU10)		CU50	CU50	CU1,000	CU30	CU970
3	CU1,000	(CU70)	(CU300)	CU50	CU50	CU700	CU100	CU600

IE71   At each subsequent reporting date, Bank A evaluates whether there is a significant increase in credit risk by comparing the loan's credit risk at initial recognition (based on the original, unmodified cash flows) with the credit risk at the reporting date (based on the modified cash flows), in accordance with paragraph 5.5.12 of IFRS 9.

IE72   Two reporting periods after the loan modification (Period 5), the borrower has outperformed its business plan significantly compared to the expectations at the modification date. In addition, the outlook for the business is more positive than previously envisaged. An assessment of all reasonable and supportable information that is available without undue cost or effort indicates that the overall credit risk on the loan has decreased and that the risk of a default occurring over the expected life of the loan has decreased, so Bank A adjusts the borrower's internal credit rating at the end of the reporting period.

IE73   Given the positive overall development, Bank A re-assesses the situation and concludes that the credit risk of the loan has decreased and there is no longer a significant increase in credit risk since initial recognition. As a result, Bank A once again measures the loss allowance at an amount equal to 12-month expected credit losses.

Example 12—provision matrix

[Refer:
paragraphs 5.5.15, 5.5.17 and B5.5.35
Basis for Conclusions paragraphs BC5.129, BC5.225 and BC5.242]

IE74   Company M, a manufacturer, has a portfolio of trade receivables of CU30 million in 20X1 and operates only in one geographical region. The customer base consists of a large number of small clients and the trade receivables are categorised by common risk characteristics that are representative of the customers' abilities to pay all amounts due in accordance with the contractual terms. The trade receivables do not have a significant financing component in accordance with IFRS 15 *Revenue from Contracts with Customers*. In accordance with paragraph 5.5.15 of IFRS 9 the loss allowance for such trade receivables is always measured at an amount equal to lifetime time expected credit losses.

IE75   To determine the expected credit losses for the portfolio, Company M uses a provision matrix. The provision matrix is based on its historical observed default rates over the expected life of the trade receivables and is adjusted for forward-looking estimates. At every reporting date the historical observed default rates are updated and changes in the forward-looking estimates are analysed. In this case it is forecast that economic conditions will deteriorate over the next year.

IE76   On that basis, Company M estimates the following provision matrix:

	Current	1–30 days past due	31–60 days past due	61–90 days past due	More than 90 days past due
Default rate	0.3%	1.6%	3.6%	6.6%	10.6%

IE77   The trade receivables from the large number of small customers amount to CU30 million and are measured using the provision matrix.

	Gross carrying amount	Lifetime expected credit loss allowance (Gross carrying amount x lifetime expected credit loss rate)
Current	CU15,000,000	CU45,000
1–30 days past due	CU7,500,000	CU120,000
31–60 days past due	CU4,000,000	CU144,000
61–90 days past due	CU2,500,000	CU165,000
More than 90 days past due	CU1,000,000	CU106,000
	CU30,000,000	**CU580,000**

Example 13—debt instrument measured at fair value through other comprehensive income

[Refer:
paragraph 5.5.2
Basis for Conclusions paragraphs BC5.119–BC5.124]

IE78   An entity purchases a debt instrument with a fair value of CU1,000 on 15 December 20X0 and measures the debt instrument at fair value through other comprehensive income. The instrument has an interest rate of 5 per cent over the contractual term of 10 years, and has a 5 per cent effective interest rate. At initial recognition the entity determines that the asset is not purchased or originated credit-impaired.

	Debit	Credit
Financial asset—FVOCI[(a)]	CU1,000	
Cash		CU1,000
(To recognise the debt instrument measured at its fair value)		
(a) FVOCI means fair value through other comprehensive income.		

IE79   On 31 December 20X0 (the reporting date), the fair value of the debt instrument has decreased to CU950 as a result of changes in market interest rates. The entity determines that there has not been a significant increase in credit risk since initial recognition and that expected credit losses should be measured at an amount equal to 12-month expected credit losses, which amounts to CU30. For simplicity, journal entries for the receipt of interest revenue are not provided.

	Debit	Credit
Impairment loss (profit or loss)	CU30	
Other comprehensive income[(a)]	CU20	
Financial asset—FVOCI		CU50
(To recognise 12-month expected credit losses and other fair value changes on the debt instrument)		
(a) The cumulative loss in other comprehensive income at the reporting date was CU20. That amount consists of the total fair value change of CU50 (ie CU1,000 – CU950) offset by the change in the accumulated impairment amount representing 12-month expected credit losses that was recognised (CU30).		

IE80   Disclosure would be provided about the accumulated impairment amount of CU30.

IE81   On 1 January 20X1, the entity decides to sell the debt instrument for CU950, which is its fair value at that date.

	Debit	Credit
Cash	CU950	
Financial asset—FVOCI		CU950
Loss (profit or loss)	CU20	
Other comprehensive income		CU20
(To derecognise the fair value through other comprehensive income asset and recycle amounts accumulated in other comprehensive income to profit or loss)		

Example 14—interaction between the fair value through other comprehensive income measurement category and foreign currency denomination, fair value hedge accounting and impairment

IE82   This example illustrates the accounting relating to a debt instrument denominated in a foreign currency, measured at fair value through other comprehensive income and designated in a fair value hedge accounting relationship. The example illustrates the interaction with accounting for impairment.

IE83   An entity purchases a debt instrument (a bond) denominated in a foreign currency (FC) for its fair value of FC100,000 on 1 January 20X0 and classifies the bond as measured at fair value through other comprehensive income. The bond has five years remaining to maturity and a fixed coupon of 5 per cent over its contractual life on the contractual par amount of FC100,000. On initial recognition the bond has a 5 per cent effective interest rate. The entity's functional currency is its local currency (LC). The exchange rate is FC1 to LC1 on 1 January 20X0. At initial recognition the entity determines that the bond is not purchased or originated credit-impaired. In addition, as at 1 January 20X0 the 12-month expected credit losses are determined to be FC1,200. Its amortised cost in FC as at 1 January 20X0 is equal to its gross carrying amount of FC100,000 less the 12-month expected credit losses (FC100,000 − FC1,200).

IE84   The entity has the following risk exposures:

(a)   fair value interest rate risk in FC: the exposure that arises as a result of purchasing a fixed interest rate instrument; and

(b)   foreign exchange risk: the exposure to changes in foreign exchange rates measured in LC.

IE85   The entity hedges its risk exposures using the following risk management strategy:

    (a)   for fixed interest rate risk (in FC) the entity decides to link its interest receipts in FC to current variable interest rates in FC. Consequently, the entity uses interest rate swaps denominated in FC under which it pays fixed interest and receives variable interest in FC; and

    (b)   for foreign exchange risk the entity decides not to hedge against any variability in LC arising from changes in foreign exchange rates.

IE86   The entity designates the following hedge relationship:[8] a fair value hedge of the bond in FC as the hedged item with changes in benchmark interest rate risk in FC as the hedged risk. The entity enters into an on-market swap that pays fixed and receives variable interest on the same day and designates the swap as the hedging instrument. The tenor of the swap matches that of the hedged item (ie five years).

IE87   For simplicity, in this example it is assumed that no hedge ineffectiveness arises in the hedge accounting relationship. This is because of the assumptions made in order to better focus on illustrating the accounting mechanics in a situation that entails measurement at fair value through other comprehensive income of a foreign currency financial instrument that is designated in a fair value hedge relationship, and also to focus on the recognition of impairment gains or losses on such an instrument.

IE88   The entity makes the following journal entries to recognise the bond and the swap on 1 January 20X0:

	Debit LC	Credit LC
Financial asset—FVOCI	100,000	
Cash		100,000
(To recognise the bond at its fair value)		
Impairment loss (profit or loss)	1,200	
Other comprehensive income		1,200
(To recognise the 12-month expected credit losses)(a)		
Swap	—	
Cash		—
(To recognise the swap at its fair value)		
(a) In case of items measured in the functional currency of an entity the journal entry recognising expected credit losses will usually be made at the reporting date.		

---

8   This example assumes that all qualifying criteria for hedge accounting are met (see paragraph 6.4.1 of IFRS 9). The following description of the designation is solely for the purpose of understanding this example (ie it is not an example of the complete formal documentation required in accordance with paragraph 6.4.1 of IFRS 9).

        © IFRS Foundation

IE89   As of 31 December 20X0 (the reporting date), the fair value of the bond decreased from FC100,000 to FC96,370 because of an increase in market interest rates. The fair value of the swap increased to FC1,837. In addition, as at 31 December 20X0 the entity determines that there has been no change to the credit risk on the bond since initial recognition and continues to carry a loss allowance for 12-month expected credit losses at FC1,200.[9] As at 31 December 20X0, the exchange rate is FC1 to LC1.4. This is reflected in the following table:

	1 January 20X0	31 December 20X0
Bond		
Fair value (FC)	100,000	96,370
Fair value (LC)	100,000	134,918
Amortised cost (FC)	98,800	98,800
Amortised cost (LC)	98,800	138,320
Interest rate swap		
Interest rate swap (FC)	–	1,837
Interest rate swap (LC)	–	2,572
Impairment – loss allowance		
Loss allowance (FC)	1,200	1,200
Loss allowance (LC)	1,200	1,680
FX rate (FC:LC)	1:1	1:1.4

IE90   The bond is a monetary asset. Consequently, the entity recognises the changes arising from movements in foreign exchange rates in profit or loss in accordance with paragraphs 23(a) and 28 of IAS 21 *The Effects of Changes in Foreign Exchange Rates* and recognises other changes in accordance with IFRS 9. For the purposes of applying paragraph 28 of IAS 21 the asset is treated as an asset measured at amortised cost in the foreign currency.

IE91   As shown in the table, on 31 December 20X0 the fair value of the bond is LC134,918 (FC96,370 × 1.4) and its amortised cost is LC138,320 (FC(100,000–1,200) × 1.4).

IE92   The gain recognised in profit or loss that is due to the changes in foreign exchange rates is LC39,520 (LC138,320 – LC98,800), ie the change in the amortised cost of the bond during 20X0 in LC. The change in the fair value of the bond in LC, which amounts to LC34,918, is recognised as an adjustment to the carrying amount. The difference between the fair value of the bond and its amortised cost in LC is LC3,402 (LC134,918 – LC138,320). However, the change

---

9   For the purposes of simplicity the example ignores the impact of discounting when computing expected credit losses.

in the cumulative gain or loss recognised in other comprehensive income during 20X0 as a reduction is LC 4,602 (LC3,402 + LC1,200).

IE93   A gain of LC2,572 (FC1,837 × 1.4) on the swap is recognised in profit or loss and, because it is assumed that there is no hedge ineffectiveness, an equivalent amount is recycled from other comprehensive income in the same period. For simplicity, journal entries for the recognition of interest revenue are not provided. It is assumed that interest accrued is received in the period.

IE94   The entity makes the following journal entries on 31 December 20X0:

	Debit LC	Credit LC
Financial asset—FVOCI	34,918	
Other comprehensive income	4,602	
Profit or loss		39,520
(To recognise the foreign exchange gain on the bond, the adjustment to its carrying amount measured at fair value in LC and the movement in the accumulated impairment amount due to changes in foreign exchange rates)		
Swap	2,572	
Profit or loss		2,572
(To remeasure the swap at fair value)		
Profit or loss	2,572	
Other comprehensive income		2,572
(To recognise in profit or loss the change in fair value of the bond due to a change in the hedged risk)		

IE95   In accordance with paragraph 16A of IFRS 7, the loss allowance for financial assets measured at fair value through other comprehensive income is not presented separately as a reduction of the carrying amount of the financial asset. However, disclosure would be provided about the accumulated impairment amount recognised in other comprehensive income.

IE96   As at 31 December 20X1 (the reporting date), the fair value of the bond decreased to FC87,114 because of an increase in market interest rates and an increase in the credit risk of the bond. The fair value of the swap increased by FC255 to FC2,092. In addition, as at 31 December 20X1 the entity determines that there has been a significant increase in credit risk on the bond since initial recognition, so a loss allowance at an amount equal to lifetime expected credit losses is recognised.[10] The estimate of lifetime expected credit losses as at 31 December 20X1 is FC9,700. As at 31 December 20X1, the exchange rate is FC1 to LC1.25. This is reflected in the following table:

---

10 For simplicity this example assumes that credit risk does not dominate the fair value hedge relationship.

	31 December 20X0	31 December 20X1
Bond		
Fair value (FC)	96,370	87,114
Fair value (LC)	134,918	108,893
Amortised cost (FC)	98,800	90,300
Amortised cost (LC)	138,320	112,875
Interest rate swap		
Interest rate swap (FC)	1,837	2,092
Interest rate swap (LC)	2,572	2,615
Impairment – loss allowance		
Loss allowance (FC)	1,200	9,700
Loss allowance (LC)	1,680	12,125
FX rate (FC:LC)	1:1.4	1:1.25

IE97   As shown in the table, as at 31 December 20X1 the fair value of the bond is LC108,893 (FC87,114 × 1.25) and its amortised cost is LC112,875 (FC(100,000 − 9,700) × 1.25).

IE98   The lifetime expected credit losses on the bond are measured as FC9,700 as of 31 December 20X1. Thus the impairment loss recognised in profit or loss in LC is LC10,625 (FC(9,700 − 1,200) x 1.25).

IE99   The loss recognised in profit or loss because of the changes in foreign exchange rates is LC14,820 (LC112,875 − LC138,320 + LC10,625), which is the change in the gross carrying amount of the bond on the basis of amortised cost during 20X1 in LC, adjusted for the impairment loss. The difference between the fair value of the bond and its amortised cost in the functional currency of the entity on 31 December 20X1 is LC3,982 (LC108,893 − LC112,875). However, the change in the cumulative gain or loss recognised in other comprehensive income during 20X1 as a reduction in other comprehensive income is LC11,205 (LC3,982 − LC3,402 + LC10,625).

IE100   A gain of LC43 (LC2,615 − LC2,572) on the swap is recognised in profit or loss and, because it is assumed that there is no hedge ineffectiveness, an equivalent amount is recycled from other comprehensive income in the same period.

IE101   The entity makes the following journal entries on 31 December 20X1:

	Debit LC	Credit LC
Financial asset—FVOCI		26,025
Other comprehensive income	11,205	
Profit or loss	14,820	
(To recognise the foreign exchange gain on the bond, the adjustment to its carrying amount measured at fair value in LC and the movement in the accumulated impairment amount due to changes in foreign exchange rates)		
Swap	43	
Profit or loss		43
(To remeasure the swap at fair value)		
Profit or loss	43	
Other comprehensive income		43
(To recognise in profit or loss the change in fair value of the bond due to a change in the hedged risk)		
Profit or loss (impairment loss)	10,625	
Other comprehensive income (accumulated impairment amount)		10,625
(To recognise lifetime expected credit losses)		

IE102   On 1 January 20X2, the entity decides to sell the bond for FC 87,114, which is its fair value at that date and also closes out the swap at fair value. The foreign exchange rate is the same as at 31 December 20X1. The journal entries to derecognise the bond and reclassify the gains and losses that have accumulated in other comprehensive income would be as follows:

	Debit LC	Credit LC
Cash	108,893	
Financial asset—FVOCI		108,893
Loss on sale (profit or loss)	1,367[(a)]	
Other comprehensive income		1,367
(To derecognise the bond)		
Swap		2,615
Cash	2,615	
(To close out the swap)		

(a) This amount consists of the changes in fair value of the bond, the accumulated impairment amount and the changes in foreign exchange rates recognised in other comprehensive income (LC2,572 + LC1,200 + LC43 + LC10,625 − LC4,602 − LC11,205 = -LC1,367, which is recycled as a loss in profit or loss).

Application of the impairment requirements on a reporting date

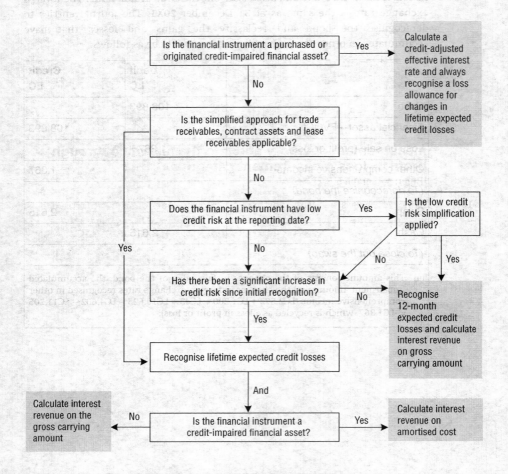

Reclassification of financial assets (Section 5.6)

IE103   This example illustrates the accounting requirements for the reclassification of financial assets between measurement categories in accordance with Section 5.6 of IFRS 9. The example illustrates the interaction with the impairment requirements in Section 5.5 of IFRS 9.

Example 15—reclassification of financial assets

[Refer: paragraphs 4.4.1, 5.6.1 and B4.4.1–B4.4.3]

IE104   An entity purchases a portfolio of bonds for its fair value (gross carrying amount) of CU500,000.

IE105   The entity changes the business model for managing the bonds in accordance with paragraph 4.4.1 of IFRS 9. The fair value of the portfolio of bonds at the reclassification date is CU490,000.

IE106   If the portfolio was measured at amortised cost or at fair value through other comprehensive income immediately prior to reclassification, the loss allowance recognised at the date of reclassification would be CU6,000 (reflecting a significant increase in credit risk since initial recognition and thus the measurement of lifetime expected credit losses).

IE107   The 12-month expected credit losses at the reclassification date are CU4,000.

IE108   For simplicity, journal entries for the recognition of interest revenue are not provided.

Scenario 1: Reclassification out of the amortised cost measurement category and into the fair value through profit or loss measurement category
[Refer: paragraph 5.6.2]

IE109   Bank A reclassifies the portfolio of bonds out of the amortised cost measurement category and into the fair value through profit or loss measurement category. At the reclassification date, the portfolio of bonds is measured at fair value. Any gain or loss arising from a difference between the previous amortised cost amount of the portfolio of bonds and the fair value of the portfolio of bonds is recognised in profit or loss on reclassification.

	Debit	Credit
Bonds (FVPL assets)	CU490,000	
Bonds (gross carrying amount of the amortised cost assets)		CU500,000
Loss allowance	CU6,000	
Reclassification loss (profit or loss)	CU4,000	
(To recognise the reclassification of bonds from amortised cost to fair value through profit or loss and to derecognise the loss allowance.)		

Scenario 2: Reclassification out of the fair value through profit or loss measurement category and into the amortised cost measurement category
[Refer: paragraphs 5.6.3 and B5.6.2]

IE110   Bank A reclassifies the portfolio of bonds out of the fair value through profit or loss measurement category and into the amortised cost measurement category. At the reclassification date, the fair value of the portfolio of bonds becomes the new gross carrying amount and the effective interest rate is determined based on that gross carrying amount. The impairment requirements apply to the bond from the reclassification date. For the purposes of recognising expected credit losses, the credit risk of the portfolio of bonds at the reclassification date becomes the credit risk against which future changes in credit risk shall be compared.

	Debit	Credit
Bonds (gross carrying amount of the amortised cost assets)	CU490,000	
Bonds (FVPL assets)		CU490,000
Impairment loss (profit or loss)	CU4,000	
Loss allowance		CU4,000
(To recognise reclassification of bonds from fair value through profit or loss to amortised cost including commencing accounting for impairment.)		

Scenario 3: Reclassification out of the amortised cost measurement category and into the fair value through other comprehensive income measurement category
[Refer: paragraphs 5.6.4 and B5.6.1]

IE111 Bank A reclassifies the portfolio of bonds out of the amortised cost measurement category and into the fair value through other comprehensive income measurement category. At the reclassification date, the portfolio of bonds is measured at fair value. Any gain or loss arising from a difference between the previous amortised cost amount of the portfolio of bonds and the fair value of the portfolio of bonds is recognised in other comprehensive income. The effective interest rate and the measurement of expected credit losses are not adjusted as a result of the reclassification. The credit risk at initial recognition continues to be used to assess changes in credit risk. From the reclassification date the loss allowance ceases to be recognised as an adjustment to the gross carrying amount of the bond and is recognised as an accumulated impairment amount, which would be disclosed.

	Debit	Credit
Bonds (FVOCI assets)	CU490,000	
Bonds (gross carrying amount of amortised cost assets)		CU500,000
Loss allowance	CU6,000	
Other comprehensive income[a]	CU4,000	
(To recognise the reclassification from amortised cost to fair value through other comprehensive income. The measurement of expected credit losses is however unchanged.)		

(a) For simplicity, the amount related to impairment is not shown separately. If it had been, this journal entry (ie DR CU4,000) would be split into the following two entries: DR Other comprehensive income CU10,000 (fair value changes) and CR other comprehensive income CU6,000 (accumulated impairment amount).

Scenario 4: Reclassification out of the fair value through other comprehensive income measurement category and into the amortised cost measurement category
[Refer: paragraphs 5.6.5 and B5.6.1]

IE112 Bank A reclassifies the portfolio of bonds out of the fair value through other comprehensive income measurement category and into the amortised cost measurement category. The portfolio of bonds is reclassified at fair value. However, at the reclassification date, the cumulative gain or loss previously recognised in other comprehensive income is removed from equity and adjusted against the fair value of the portfolio of bonds. As a result, the portfolio of bonds is measured at the reclassification date as if it had always been measured at amortised cost. The effective interest rate and the measurement of expected credit losses are not adjusted as a result of the reclassification. The credit risk at initial recognition continues to be used to assess changes in the credit risk on the bonds. The loss allowance is recognised as an adjustment to the gross carrying amount of the bond (to reflect the amortised cost amount) from the reclassification date.

	Debit	Credit
Bonds (gross carrying value of the amortised cost assets)	CU490,000	
Bonds (FVOCI assets)		CU490,000
Bonds (gross carrying value of the amortised cost assets)	CU10,000	
Loss allowance		CU6,000
Other comprehensive income[a]		CU4,000

(To recognise the reclassification from fair value through other comprehensive income to amortised cost including the recognition of the loss allowance deducted to determine the amortised cost amount. The measurement of expected credit losses is however unchanged.)

(a) The cumulative loss in other comprehensive income at the reclassification date was CU4,000. That amount consists of the total fair value change of CU10,000 (ie CU500,000 – 490,000) offset by the accumulated impairment amount recognised (CU6,000) while the assets were measured at fair value through other comprehensive income.

Scenario 5: Reclassification out of the fair value through profit or loss measurement category and into the fair value through other comprehensive income measurement category
[Refer: paragraphs 5.6.6 and B5.6.2]

IE113 Bank A reclassifies the portfolio of bonds out of the fair value through profit or loss measurement category and into the fair value through other comprehensive measurement category. The portfolio of bonds continues to be measured at fair value. However, for the purposes of applying the effective interest method, the fair value of the portfolio of bonds at the reclassification date becomes the new gross carrying amount and the effective interest rate is determined based on that new gross carrying amount. The impairment requirements apply from the reclassification date. For the purposes of recognising expected credit losses, the credit risk of the portfolio of bonds at the reclassification date becomes the credit risk against which future changes in credit risk shall be compared.

	Debit	Credit
Bonds (FVOCI assets)	CU490,000	
Bonds (FVPL assets)		CU490,000
Impairment loss (profit or loss)	CU4,000	
Other comprehensive income		CU4,000
(To recognise the reclassification of bonds from fair value through profit or loss to fair value through other comprehensive income including commencing accounting for impairment. The other comprehensive income amount reflects the loss allowance at the date of reclassification (an accumulated impairment amount relevant for disclosure purposes) of CU4,000.)		

Scenario 6: Reclassification out of the fair value through other comprehensive income measurement category and into the fair value through profit or loss measurement category
[Refer: paragraph 5.6.7]

IE114   Bank A reclassifies the portfolio of bonds out of the fair value through other comprehensive income measurement category and into the fair value through profit or loss measurement category. The portfolio of bonds continues to be measured at fair value. However, the cumulative gain or loss previously recognised in other comprehensive income is reclassified from equity to profit or loss as a reclassification adjustment (see IAS 1 *Presentation of Financial Statements*).

	Debit	Credit
Bonds (FVPL assets)	CU490,000	
Bonds (FVOCI assets)		CU490,000
Reclassification loss (profit or loss)	CU4,000	
Other comprehensive income[a]		CU4,000
(To recognise the reclassification of bonds from fair value through other comprehensive income to fair value through profit or loss.)		

(a)   The cumulative loss in other comprehensive income at the reclassification date was CU4,000. That amount consists of the total fair value change of CU10,000 (ie CU500,000 – 490,000) offset by the loss allowance that was recognised (CU6,000) while the assets were measured at fair value through other comprehensive income.

Hedge accounting for aggregated exposures

IE115 The following examples illustrate the mechanics of hedge accounting for aggregated exposures.

[Refer: paragraph 6.3.4]

Example 16—combined commodity price risk and foreign currency risk hedge (cash flow hedge/cash flow hedge combination)

Fact pattern

IE116 Entity A wants to hedge a highly probable forecast coffee purchase (which is expected to occur at the end of Period 5). Entity A's functional currency is its Local Currency (LC). Coffee is traded in Foreign Currency (FC). Entity A has the following risk exposures:

(a) commodity price risk: the variability in cash flows for the purchase price, which results from fluctuations of the spot price of coffee in FC; and

(b) foreign currency (FX) risk: the variability in cash flows that result from fluctuations of the spot exchange rate between LC and FC.

IE117 Entity A hedges its risk exposures using the following risk management strategy:

(a) Entity A uses benchmark commodity forward contracts, which are denominated in FC, to hedge its coffee purchases four periods before delivery. The coffee price that Entity A actually pays for its purchase is different from the benchmark price because of differences in the type of coffee, the location and delivery arrangement.[11] This gives rise to the risk of changes in the relationship between the two coffee prices (sometimes referred to as 'basis risk'), which affects the effectiveness of the hedging relationship. Entity A does not hedge this risk because it is not considered economical under cost/benefit considerations.

(b) Entity A also hedges its FX risk. However, the FX risk is hedged over a different horizon—only three periods before delivery. Entity A considers the FX exposure from the variable payments for the coffee purchase in FC and the gain or loss on the commodity forward contract in FC as one aggregated FX exposure. Hence, Entity A uses one single FX forward contract to hedge the FX cash flows from a forecast coffee purchase and the related commodity forward contract.

IE118 The following table sets out the parameters used for Example 16 (the 'basis spread' is the differential, expressed as a percentage, between the price of the coffee that Entity A actually buys and the price for the benchmark coffee):

---

11 For the purpose of this example it is assumed that the hedged risk is not designated based on a benchmark coffee price risk component. Consequently, the entire coffee price risk is hedged.

Example 16—Parameters					
Period	1	2	3	4	5
Interest rates for remaining maturity [FC]	0.26%	0.21%	0.16%	0.06%	0.00%
Interest rates for remaining maturity [LC]	1.12%	0.82%	0.46%	0.26%	0.00%
Forward price [FC/lb]	1.25	1.01	1.43	1.22	2.15
Basis spread	-5.00%	-5.50%	-6.00%	-3.40%	-7.00%
FX rate (spot) [FC/LC]	1.3800	1.3300	1.4100	1.4600	1.4300

Accounting mechanics

IE119   Entity A designates as cash flow hedges the following two hedging relationships:[12]

(a)   A commodity price risk hedging relationship between the coffee price related variability in cash flows attributable to the forecast coffee purchase in FC as the hedged item and a commodity forward contract denominated in FC as the hedging instrument (the 'first level relationship'). This hedging relationship is designated at the end of Period 1 with a term to the end of Period 5. Because of the basis spread between the price of the coffee that Entity A actually buys and the price for the benchmark coffee, Entity A designates a volume of 112,500 pounds (lbs) of coffee as the hedging instrument and a volume of 118,421 lbs as the hedged item.[13]

(b)   An FX risk hedging relationship between the aggregated exposure as the hedged item and an FX forward contract as the hedging instrument (the 'second level relationship'). This hedging relationship is designated at the end of Period 2 with a term to the end of Period 5. The aggregated exposure that is designated as the hedged item represents the FX risk that is the effect of exchange rate changes, compared to the forward FX rate at the end of Period 2 (ie the time of designation of the FX risk hedging relationship), on the combined FX cash flows in FC of the two items designated in the commodity price risk hedging relationship, which are the forecast coffee purchase and the commodity forward contract. Entity A's long-term view of the basis spread between the price of the coffee that it actually buys and the price for the benchmark coffee has not changed from the end of

---

12   This example assumes that all qualifying criteria for hedge accounting are met (see paragraph 6.4.1 of IFRS 9). The following description of the designation is solely for the purpose of understanding this example (ie it is not an example of the complete formal documentation required in accordance with IFRS 9.6.4.1(b)).

13   In this example, the current basis spread at the time of designation is coincidentally the same as Entity A's long-term view of the basis spread (-5 per cent) that determines the volume of coffee purchases that it actually hedges. Also, this example assumes that Entity A designates the hedging instrument in its entirety and designates as much of its highly probable forecast purchases as it regards as hedged. That results in a hedge ratio of 1/(100%-5%). Other entities might follow different approaches when determining what volume of their exposure they actually hedge, which can result in a different hedge ratio and also designating less than a hedging instrument in its entirety (see paragraph 6.4.1 of IFRS 9).

Period 1. Consequently, the actual volume of hedging instrument that Entity A enters into (the nominal amount of the FX forward contract of FC140,625) reflects the cash flow exposure associated with a basis spread that had remained at -5 per cent. However, Entity A's actual aggregated exposure is affected by changes in the basis spread. Because the basis spread has moved from -5 per cent to -5.5 per cent during Period 2, Entity A's actual aggregated exposure at the end of Period 2 is FC140,027.

IE120   The following table sets out the fair values of the derivatives, the changes in the value of the hedged items and the calculation of the cash flow hedge reserves and hedge ineffectiveness:[14]

Example 16—Calculations						
Period		**1**	**2**	**3**	**4**	**5**
Commodity price risk hedging relationship (first level relationship)						
Forward purchase contract for coffee						
Volume (lbs)	112,500					
Forward price [FC/lb]	1.25 Price (fwd) [FC/lb]	1.25	1.01	1.43	1.22	2.15
	Fair value [FC]	0	(26,943)	20,219	(3,373)	101,250
	Fair value [LC]	0	(20,258)	14,339	(2,310)	70,804
	Change in fair value [LC]		(20,258)	34,598	(16,650)	73,114
Hedged forecast coffee purchase						
Hedge ratio	105.26% Basis spread	-5.00%	-5.50%	-6.00%	-3.40%	-7.00%
Hedged volume	118,421 Price (fwd) [FC/lb]	1.19	0.95	1.34	1.18	2.00
Implied forward price	1.1875 Present value [FC]	0	27,540	(18,528)	1,063	(96,158)
	Present value [LC]	0	20,707	(13,140)	728	(67,243)
	Change in present value [LC]		20,707	(33,847)	13,868	(67,971)
Accounting		LC	LC	LC	LC	LC
Derivative		0	(20,258)	14,339	(2,310)	70,804
Cash flow hedge reserve		0	(20,258)	13,140	(728)	67,243
Change in cash flow hedge reserve			(20,258)	33,399	(13,868)	67,971
Profit or loss			0	1,199	(2,781)	5,143
Retained earnings		0	0	1,199	(1,582)	3,561

continued...

14 In the following table for the calculations all amounts (including the calculations for accounting purposes of amounts for assets, liabilities, equity and profit or loss) are in the format of positive (plus) and negative (minus) numbers (eg a profit or loss amount that is a negative number is a loss).

...continued

Example 16—Calculations

Period		1	2	3	4	5
FX risk hedging relationship (second level relationship)						
FX rate [FC/LC]	Spot	1.3800	1.3300	1.4100	1.4600	1.4300
	Forward	1.3683	1.3220	1.4058	1.4571	1.4300
FX forward contract (buy FC/sell LC)						
Volume [FC]	140,625					
Forward rate (in P_2)	1.3220	Fair value [LC]		0	(6,313)	(9,840)	(8,035)
		Change in fair value [LC]			(6,313)	(3,528)	1,805
Hedged FX risk						
Aggregated FX exposure		Hedged volume [FC]		140,027	138,932	142,937	135,533
		Present value [LC]		0	6,237	10,002	7,744
		Change in present value [LC]			6,237	3,765	(2,258)
Accounting			LC	LC	LC	LC
Derivative				0	(6,313)	(9,840)	(8,035)
Cash flow hedge reserve				0	(6,237)	(9,840)	(7,744)
Change in cash flow hedge reserve					(6,237)	(3,604)	2,096
Profit or loss					(76)	76	(291)
Retained earnings				0	(76)	0	(291)

IE121   The commodity price risk hedging relationship is a cash flow hedge of a highly probable forecast transaction that starts at the end of Period 1 and remains in place when the FX risk hedging relationship starts at the end of Period 2, ie the first level relationship continues as a separate hedging relationship.

IE122   The volume of the aggregated FX exposure (in FC), which is the hedged volume of the FX risk hedging relationship, is the total of:[15]

   (a)   the hedged coffee purchase volume multiplied by the current forward price (this represents the expected spot price of the actual coffee purchase); and

---

15   For example, at the end of Period 3 the aggregated FX exposure is determined as: 118,421 lbs × 1.34 FC/lb = FC159,182 for the expected price of the actual coffee purchase and 112,500 lbs × (1.25 [FC/lb] - 1.43 [FC/lb]) = FC(20,250) for the expected price differential under the commodity forward contract, which gives a total of FC138,932 — the volume of the aggregated FX exposure at the end of Period 3.

(b)   the volume of the hedging instrument (designated nominal amount) multiplied by the difference between the contractual forward rate and the current forward rate (this represents the expected price differential from benchmark coffee price movements in FC that Entity A will receive or pay under the commodity forward contract).

IE123   The present value (in LC) of the hedged item of the FX risk hedging relationship (ie the aggregated exposure) is calculated as the hedged volume (in FC) multiplied by the difference between the forward FX rate at the measurement date and the forward FX rate at the designation date of the hedging relationship (ie the end of Period 2).[16]

IE124   Using the present value of the hedged item and the fair value of the hedging instrument, the cash flow hedge reserve and the hedge ineffectiveness are then determined (see paragraph 6.5.11 of IFRS 9).

IE125   The following table shows the effect on Entity A's statement of profit or loss and other comprehensive income and its statement of financial position (for the sake of transparency the line items[17] are disaggregated on the face of the statements by the two hedging relationships, ie for the commodity price risk hedging relationship and the FX risk hedging relationship):

---

16   For example, at the end of Period 3 the present value of the hedged item is determined as the volume of the aggregated exposure at the end of Period 3 (FC138,932) multiplied by the difference between the forward FX rate at the end of Period 3 (1/1.4058) and the forward FX rate and the time of designation (ie the end of Period 2: 1/1.3220) and then discounted using the interest rate (in LC) at the end of Period 3 with a term of 2 periods (ie until the end of Period 5 – 0.46%). The calculation is: FC138,932 × (1/(1.4058[FC/LC]) - 1/(1.3220 [FC/LC]))/(1 + 0.46%) = LC6,237.

17   The line items used in this example are a possible presentation. Different presentation formats using different line items (including line items that include the amounts shown here) are also possible (IFRS 7 sets out disclosure requirements for hedge accounting that include disclosures about hedge ineffectiveness, the carrying amount of hedging instruments and the cash flow hedge reserve).

Example 16—Overview of effect on statements of financial performance and financial position

[All amounts in LC]

Period	1	2	3	4	5
Statement of profit or loss and other comprehensive income					
Hedge ineffectiveness					
Commodity hedge		0	(1,199)	2,781	(5,143)
FX hedge		0	76	(76)	291
Profit or loss	0	0	(1,123)	2,705	(4,852)
Other comprehensive income (OCI)					
Commodity hedge		20,258	(33,399)	13,868	(67,971)
FX hedge		0	6,237	3,604	(2,096)
Total other comprehensive income	0	20,258	(27,162)	17,472	(70,067)
Comprehensive income	0	20,258	(28,285)	20,177	(74,920)
Statement of financial position					
Commodity forward	0	(20,258)	14,339	(2,310)	70,804
FX forward		0	(6,313)	(9,840)	(8,035)
Total net assets	0	(20,258)	8,027	(12,150)	62,769
Equity					
Accumulated OCI					
Commodity hedge	0	20,258	(13,140)	728	(67,243)
FX hedge		0	6,237	9,840	7,744
	0	20,258	(6,904)	10,568	(59,499)
Retained earnings					
Commodity hedge	0	0	(1,199)	1,582	(3,561)
FX hedge		0	76	0	291
	0	0	(1,123)	1,582	(3,270)
Total equity	0	20,258	(8,027)	12,150	(62,769)

IE126   The total cost of inventory after hedging is as follows:[18]

Cost of inventory [all amounts in LC]	
Cash price (at spot for commodity price risk and FX risk)	165,582
Gain/loss from CFHR for commodity price risk	(67,243)
Gain/loss from CFHR for FX risk	7,744
Cost of inventory	106,083

IE127   The total overall cash flow from all transactions (the actual coffee purchase at the spot price and the settlement of the two derivatives) is LC102,813. It differs from the hedge adjusted cost of inventory by LC3,270, which is the net amount of cumulative hedge ineffectiveness from the two hedging relationships. This hedge ineffectiveness has a cash flow effect but is excluded from the measurement of the inventory.

Example 17—combined interest rate risk and foreign currency risk hedge (fair value hedge/cash flow hedge combination)

Fact pattern

IE128   Entity B wants to hedge a fixed rate liability that is denominated in Foreign Currency (FC). The liability has a term of four periods from the start of Period 1 to the end of Period 4. Entity B's functional currency is its Local Currency (LC). Entity B has the following risk exposures:

(a)   fair value interest rate risk and FX risk: the changes in fair value of the fixed rate liability attributable to interest rate changes, measured in LC.

(b)   cash flow interest rate risk: the exposure that arises as a result of swapping the combined fair value interest rate risk and FX risk exposure associated with the fixed rate liability (see (a) above) into a variable rate exposure in LC in accordance with Entity B's risk management strategy for FC denominated fixed rate liabilities (see paragraph IE129(a) below).

IE129   Entity B hedges its risk exposures using the following risk management strategy:

(a)   Entity B uses cross-currency interest rate swaps to swap its FC denominated fixed rate liabilities into a variable rate exposure in LC. Entity B hedges its FC denominated liabilities (including the interest) for their entire life. Consequently, Entity B enters into a cross-currency interest rate swap at the same time as it issues an FC denominated liability. Under the cross-currency interest rate swap Entity B receives fixed interest in FC (used to pay the interest on the liability) and pays variable interest in LC.

---

18   'CFHR' is the cash flow hedge reserve, ie the amount accumulated in other comprehensive income for a cash flow hedge.

(b)   Entity B considers the cash flows on a hedged liability and on the related cross-currency interest rate swap as one aggregated variable rate exposure in LC. From time to time, in accordance with its risk management strategy for variable rate interest rate risk (in LC), Entity B decides to lock in its interest payments and hence swaps its aggregated variable rate exposure in LC into a fixed rate exposure in LC. Entity B seeks to obtain as a fixed rate exposure a single blended fixed coupon rate (ie the uniform forward coupon rate for the hedged term that exists at the start of the hedging relationship).[19] Consequently, Entity B uses interest rate swaps (denominated entirely in LC) under which it receives variable interest (used to pay the interest on the pay leg of the cross-currency interest rate swap) and pays fixed interest.

---

19   An entity may have a different risk management strategy whereby it seeks to obtain a fixed rate exposure that is not a single blended rate but a series of forward rates that are each fixed for the respective individual interest period. For such a strategy the hedge effectiveness is measured based on the difference between the forward rates that existed at the start of the hedging relationship and the forward rates that exist at the effectiveness measurement date for the individual interest periods. For such a strategy a series of forward contracts corresponding with the individual interest periods would be more effective than an interest rate swap (that has a fixed payment leg with a single blended fixed rate).

       © IFRS Foundation

IE130   The following table sets out the parameters used for Example 17:

Example 17—Parameters

	t_0	Period 1	Period 2	Period 3	Period 4
FX spot rate [LC/FC]	1.2000	1.0500	1.4200	1.5100	1.3700
Interest curves (vertical presentation of rates for each quarter of a period on a p.a. basis)					
LC	2.50%	5.02%	6.18%	0.34%	[N/A]
	2.75%	5.19%	6.26%	0.49%	
	2.91%	5.47%	6.37%	0.94%	
	3.02%	5.52%	6.56%	1.36%	
	2.98%	5.81%	6.74%		
	3.05%	5.85%	6.93%		
	3.11%	5.91%	7.19%		
	3.15%	6.06%	7.53%		
	3.11%	6.20%			
	3.14%	6.31%			
	3.27%	6.36%			
	3.21%	6.40%			
	3.21%				
	3.25%				
	3.29%				
	3.34%				

continued...

...continued

Example 17—Parameters

		t_0	Period 1	Period 2	Period 3	Period 4
FC		3.74%	4.49%	2.82%	0.70%	[N/A]
		4.04%	4.61%	2.24%	0.79%	
		4.23%	4.63%	2.00%	1.14%	
		4.28%	4.34%	2.18%	1.56%	
		4.20%	4.21%	2.34%		
		4.17%	4.13%	2.53%		
		4.27%	4.07%	2.82%		
		4.14%	4.09%	3.13%		
		4.10%	4.17%			
		4.11%	4.13%			
		4.11%	4.24%			
		4.13%	4.34%			
		4.14%				
		4.06%				
		4.12%				
		4.19%				

Accounting mechanics

IE131 Entity B designates the following hedging relationships:[20]

(a) As a fair value hedge, a hedging relationship for fair value interest rate risk and FX risk between the FC denominated fixed rate liability (fixed rate FX liability) as the hedged item and a cross-currency interest rate swap as the hedging instrument (the 'first level relationship'). This hedging relationship is designated at the beginning of Period 1 (ie t_0) with a term to the end of Period 4.

(b) As a cash flow hedge, a hedging relationship between the aggregated exposure as the hedged item and an interest rate swap as the hedging instrument (the 'second level relationship'). This hedging relationship is designated at the end of Period 1, when Entity B decides to lock in its interest payments and hence swaps its aggregated variable rate exposure in LC into a fixed rate exposure in LC, with a term to the end of Period 4. The aggregated exposure that is designated as the hedged item represents, in LC, the variability in cash flows that is the effect of changes in the combined cash flows of the two items designated in the

---

20 This example assumes that all qualifying criteria for hedge accounting are met (see paragraph 6.4.1 of IFRS 9). The following description of the designation is solely for the purpose of understanding this example (ie it is not an example of the complete formal documentation required in accordance with paragraph 6.4.1(b) of IFRS 9).

fair value hedge of the fair value interest rate risk and FX risk (see (a) above), compared to the interest rates at the end of Period 1 (ie the time of designation of the hedging relationship between the aggregated exposure and the interest rate swap).

IE132   The following table[21] sets out the overview of the fair values of the derivatives, the changes in the value of the hedged items and the calculation of the cash flow hedge reserve and hedge ineffectiveness.[22] In this example, hedge ineffectiveness arises on both hedging relationships.[23]

Example 17—Calculations	t_0	Period 1	Period 2	Period 3	Period 4
Fixed rate FX liability					
Fair value [FC]	(1,000,000)	(995,522)	(1,031,008)	(1,030,193)	(1,000,000)
Fair value [LC]	(1,200,000)	(1,045,298)	(1,464,031)	(1,555,591)	(1,370,000)
Change in fair value [LC]		154,702	(418,733)	(91,560)	185,591
CCIRS (receive fixed FC/pay variable LC)					
Fair value [LC]	0	(154,673)	264,116	355,553	170,000
Change in fair value [LC]		(154,673)	418,788	91,437	(185,553)
IRS (receive variable/pay fixed)					
Fair value [LC]		0	18,896	(58,767)	0
Change in fair value [LC]			18,896	(77,663)	(58,767)
CF variability of the aggregated exposure					
Present value [LC]		0	(18,824)	58,753	0
Change in present value [LC]			(18,824)	77,577	(58,753)
CFHR					
Balance (end of period) [LC]		0	18,824	(58,753)	0
Change [LC]			18,824	(77,577)	58,753

21 Tables in this example use the following acronyms: 'CCIRS' for cross-currency interest rate swap, 'CF(s)' for cash flow(s), 'CFH' for cash flow hedge, 'CFHR' for cash flow hedge reserve, 'FVH' for fair value hedge, 'IRS' for interest rate swap and 'PV' for present value.

22 In the following table for the calculations all amounts (including the calculations for accounting purposes of amounts for assets, liabilities and equity) are in the format of positive (plus) and negative (minus) numbers (eg an amount in the cash flow hedge reserve that is in brackets is a loss).

23 For a situation such as in this example, hedge ineffectiveness can result from various factors, for example credit risk, differences in the day count method or, depending on whether it is included in the designation of the hedging instrument, the charge for exchanging different currencies that is included in cross-currency interest rate swaps (commonly referred to as the 'currency basis').

IE133   The hedging relationship between the fixed rate FX liability and the cross-currency interest rate swap starts at the beginning of Period 1 (ie t_0) and remains in place when the hedging relationship for the second level relationship starts at the end of Period 1, ie the first level relationship continues as a separate hedging relationship.

IE134   The cash flow variability of the aggregated exposure is calculated as follows:

(a)   At the point in time from which the cash flow variability of the aggregated exposure is hedged (ie the start of the second level relationship at the end of Period 1), all cash flows expected on the fixed rate FX liability and the cross-currency interest rate swap over the hedged term (ie until the end of Period 4) are mapped out and equated to a single blended fixed coupon rate so that the total present value (in LC) is nil. This calculation establishes the single blended fixed coupon rate (reference rate) that is used at subsequent dates as the reference point to measure the cash flow variability of the aggregated exposure since the start of the hedging relationship. This calculation is illustrated in the following table:

Example 17—Cash flow variability of the aggregated exposure (calibration)

		Variability in cash flows of the aggregated exposure						
		FX liability		CCIRS FC leg		CCIRS LC leg		Calibration	PV
		CF(s)	PV	CF(s)	PV	CF(s)	PV	1,200,000 Nominal 5.6963% Rate 4 Frequency	
		[FC]	[FC]	[FC]	[FC]	[LC]	[LC]	[LC]	[LC]
	Time								
	t_0								
	t_1								
Period 1	t_2								
	t_3								
	t_4								
	t_5	0	0	0	0	(14,771)	(14,591)	17,089	16,881
	t_6	(20,426)	(19,977)	20,246	19,801	(15,271)	(14,896)	17,089	16,669
Period 2	t_7	0	0	0	0	(16,076)	(15,473)	17,089	16,449
	t_8	(20,426)	(19,543)	20,582	19,692	(16,241)	(15,424)	17,089	16,229
	t_9	0	0	0	0	(17,060)	(15,974)	17,089	16,002
	t_{10}	(20,426)	(19,148)	20,358	19,084	(17,182)	(15,862)	17,089	15,776
Period 3	t_{11}	0	0	0	0	(17,359)	(15,797)	17,089	15,551
	t_{12}	(20,426)	(18,769)	20,582	18,912	(17,778)	(15,942)	17,089	15,324

continued...

...continued

Example 17—Cash flow variability of the aggregated exposure (calibration)							
				Variability in cash flows of the aggregated exposure			
	FX liability		CCIRS FC leg		CCIRS LC leg		Calibration	PV
	CF(s)	PV	CF(s)	PV	CF(s)	PV	1,200,000 Nominal 5.6963% Rate 4 Frequency	
	[FC]	[FC]	[FC]	[FC]	[LC]	[LC]	[LC]	[LC]
Period 4 t_{13}	0	0	0	0	(18,188)	(16,066)	17,089	15,095
t_{14}	(20,426)	(18,391)	20,246	18,229	(18,502)	(16,095)	17,089	14,866
t_{15}	0	0	0	0	(18,646)	(15,972)	17,089	14,638
t_{16}	(1,020,426)	(899,695)	1,020,582	899,832	(1,218,767)	(1,027,908)	1,217,089	1,026,493
Totals		(995,522)		995,550		(1,200,000)		1,199,971
Totals in LC		(1,045,298)		1,045,327		(1,200,000)		1,199,971
PV of all CF(s) [LC]	0 ←				Σ			

The nominal amount that is used for the calibration of the reference rate is the same as the nominal amount of aggregated exposure that creates the variable cash flows in LC (LC1,200,000), which coincides with the nominal amount of the cross-currency interest rate swap for the variable rate leg in LC. This results in a reference rate of 5.6963 per cent (determined by iteration so that the present value of all cash flows in total is nil).

(b) At subsequent dates, the cash flow variability of the aggregated exposure is determined by comparison to the reference point established at the end of Period 1. For that purpose, all remaining cash flows expected on the fixed rate FX liability and the cross-currency interest rate swap over the remainder of the hedged term (ie from the effectiveness measurement date until the end of Period 4) are updated (as applicable) and then discounted. Also, the reference rate of 5.6963 per cent is applied to the nominal amount that was used for the calibration of that rate at the end of Period 1 (LC1,200,000) in order to generate a set of cash flows over the remainder of the hedged term that is then also discounted. The total of all those present values represents the cash flow variability of the aggregated exposure. This calculation is illustrated in the following table for the end of Period 2:

Example 17—Cash flow variability of the aggregated exposure (at the end of Period 2)

		Variability in cash flows of the aggregated exposure						
		FX liability		CCIRS FC leg		CCIRS LC leg		Calibration	PV
		CF(s)	PV	CF(s)	PV	CF(s)	PV	1,200,000 Nominal 5.6963% Rate 4 Frequency	
		[FC]	[FC]	[FC]	[FC]	[LC]	[LC]	[LC]	[LC]
	Time								
	t_0								
	t_1								
Period 1	t_2								
	t_3								
	t_4								
	t_5	0	0	0	0	0	0	0	0
	t_6	0	0	0	0	0	0	0	0
Period 2	t_7	0	0	0	0	0	0	0	0
	t_8	0	0	0	0	0	0	0	0
	t_9	0	0	0	0	(18,120)	(17,850)	17,089	16,835
	t_{10}	(20,426)	(20,173)	20,358	20,106	(18,360)	(17,814)	17,089	16,581
Period 3	t_{11}	0	0	0	0	(18,683)	(17,850)	17,089	16,327
	t_{12}	(20,426)	(19,965)	20,582	20,117	(19,203)	(18,058)	17,089	16,070
	t_{13}	0	0	0	0	(19,718)	(18,243)	17,089	15,810
	t_{14}	(20,426)	(19,726)	20,246	19,553	(20,279)	(18,449)	17,089	15,547
Period 4	t_{15}	0	0	0	0	(21,014)	(18,789)	17,089	15,280
	t_{16}	(1,020,426)	(971,144)	1,020,582	971,292	(1,221,991)	(1,072,947)	1,217,089	1,068,643
Totals			(1,031,008)		1,031,067		(1,200,000)		1,181,092
Totals in LC			(1,464,031)		1,464,116		(1,200,000)		1,181,092
PV of all CF(s) [LC]		(18,824)	←			Σ			

The changes in interest rates and the exchange rate result in a change of the cash flow variability of the aggregated exposure between the end of Period 1 and the end of Period 2 that has a present value of LC-18,824.[24]

IE135 Using the present value of the hedged item and the fair value of the hedging instrument, the cash flow hedge reserve and the hedge ineffectiveness are then determined (see paragraph 6.5.11 of IFRS 9).

IE136 The following table shows the effect on Entity B's statement of profit or loss and other comprehensive income and its statement of financial position (for the sake of transparency some line items[25] are disaggregated on the face of the statements by the two hedging relationships, ie for the fair value hedge of the fixed rate FX liability and the cash flow hedge of the aggregated exposure):[26]

Example 17—Overview of effect on statements of financial performance and financial position

[All amounts in LC]

	t_0	Period 1	Period 2	Period 3	Period 4
Statement of profit or loss and other comprehensive income					
Interest expense					
FX liability		45,958	50,452	59,848	58,827
FVH adjustment		(12,731)	11,941	14,385	(49,439)
		33,227	62,393	74,233	9,388
Reclassifications (CFH)			5,990	(5,863)	58,982
Total interest expense		33,227	68,383	68,370	68,370

continued...

24 This is the amount that is included in the table with the overview of the calculations (see paragraph IE132) as the present value of the cash flow variability of the aggregated exposure at the end of Period 2.

25 The line items used in this example are a possible presentation. Different presentation formats using different line items (including line items that include the amounts shown here) are also possible (IFRS 7 sets out disclosure requirements for hedge accounting that include disclosures about hedge ineffectiveness, the carrying amount of hedging instruments and the cash flow hedge reserve).

26 For Period 4 the values in the table with the overview of the calculations (see paragraph IE132) differ from those in the following table. For Periods 1 to 3 the 'dirty' values (ie including interest accruals) equal the 'clean' values (ie excluding interest accruals) because the period end is a settlement date for all legs of the derivatives and the fixed rate FX liability. At the end of Period 4 the table with the overview of the calculations uses clean values in order to calculate the value changes consistently over time. For the following table the dirty values are presented, ie the maturity amounts including accrued interest immediately before the instruments are settled (this is for illustrative purposes as otherwise all carrying amounts other than cash and retained earnings would be nil).

...continued

Example 17—Overview of effect on statements of financial performance and financial position

[All amounts in LC]

	t₀	Period 1	Period 2	Period 3	Period 4
Other gains/losses					
Change in fair value of the CCIRS		154,673	(418,788)	(91,437)	185,553
FVH adjustment (FX liability)		(154,702)	418,733	91,560	(185,591)
Hedge ineffectiveness		0	(72)	(54)	(19)
Total other gains/losses		(29)	(127)	68	(57)
Profit or loss		33,198	68,255	68,438	68,313
Other comprehensive income (OCI)					
Effective CFH gain/loss			(12,834)	71,713	229
Reclassifications			(5,990)	5,863	(58,982)
Total other comprehensive income			(18,842)	77,577	(58,753)
Comprehensive income		33,198	49,432	146,015	9,560
Statement of financial position					
FX liability	(1,200,000)	(1,045,298)	(1,464,031)	(1,555,591)	(1,397,984)
CCIRS	0	(154,673)	264,116	355,553	194,141
IRS		0	18,896	(58,767)	(13,004)
Cash	1,200,000	1,166,773	1,098,390	1,030,160	978,641
Total net assets	0	(33,198)	(82,630)	(228,645)	(238,205)
Equity					
Accumulated OCI		0	(18,824)	58,753	0
Retained earnings	0	33,198	101,454	169,892	238,205
Total equity	0	33,198	82,630	228,645	238,205

IE137   The total interest expense in profit or loss reflects Entity B's interest expense that results from its risk management strategy:

    (a)   In Period 1 the risk management strategy results in interest expense reflecting variable interest rates in LC after taking into account the effect of the cross-currency interest rate swap, including a difference between the cash flows on the fixed rate FX liability and the fixed leg of the cross-currency interest rate swap that were settled during Period 1 (this means the interest expense does not exactly equal the variable interest expense that would arise in LC on a borrowing of LC1,200,000). There is also some hedge ineffectiveness that results from a difference in the changes in value for the fixed rate FX liability (as represented by the fair value hedge adjustment) and the cross-currency interest rate swap.

(b)   For Periods 2 to 4 the risk management strategy results in interest expense that reflects, after taking into account the effect of the interest rate swap entered into at the end of Period 1, fixed interest rates in LC (ie locking in a single blended fixed coupon rate for a three-period term based on the interest rate environment at the end of Period 1). However, Entity B's interest expense is affected by the hedge ineffectiveness that arises on its hedging relationships. In Period 2 the interest expense is slightly higher than the fixed rate payments locked in with the interest rate swap because the variable payments received under the interest rate swap are less than the total of the cash flows resulting from the aggregated exposure.[27] In Periods 3 and 4 the interest expense is equal to the locked in rate because the variable payments received under the swap are more than the total of the cash flows resulting from the aggregated exposure.[28]

Example 18—combined interest rate risk and foreign currency risk hedge (cash flow hedge/fair value hedge combination)

Fact pattern

IE138   Entity C wants to hedge a variable rate liability that is denominated in Foreign Currency (FC). The liability has a term of four periods from the start of Period 1 to the end of Period 4. Entity C's functional currency is its Local Currency (LC). Entity C has the following risk exposures:

(a)   cash flow interest rate risk and FX risk: the changes in cash flows of the variable rate liability attributable to interest rate changes, measured in LC.

(b)   fair value interest rate risk: the exposure that arises as a result of swapping the combined cash flow interest rate risk and FX risk exposure associated with the variable rate liability (see (a) above) into a fixed rate exposure in LC in accordance with Entity C's risk management strategy for FC denominated variable rate liabilities (see paragraph IE139(a) below).

---

27   In other words, the cash flow variability of the interest rate swap was lower than, and therefore did not fully offset, the cash flow variability of the aggregated exposure as a whole (sometimes called an 'underhedge' situation). In those situations the cash flow hedge does not contribute to the hedge ineffectiveness that is recognised in profit or loss because the hedge ineffectiveness is not recognised (see paragraph 6.5.11 of IFRS 9). The hedge ineffectiveness arising on the fair value hedge affects profit or loss in all periods.

28   In other words, the cash flow variability of the interest rate swap was higher than, and therefore more than fully offset, the cash flow variability of the aggregated exposure as a whole (sometimes called an 'overhedge' situation). In those situations the cash flow hedge contributes to the hedge ineffectiveness that is recognised in profit or loss (see paragraph 6.5.11 of IFRS 9). The hedge ineffectiveness arising on the fair value hedge affects profit or loss in all periods.

IE139   Entity C hedges its risk exposures using the following risk management strategy:

(a)   Entity C uses cross-currency interest rate swaps to swap its FC denominated variable rate liabilities into a fixed rate exposure in LC. Entity C hedges its FC denominated liabilities (including the interest) for their entire life. Consequently, Entity C enters into a cross-currency interest rate swap at the same time as it issues an FC denominated liability. Under the cross-currency interest rate swap Entity C receives variable interest in FC (used to pay the interest on the liability) and pays fixed interest in LC.

(b)   Entity C considers the cash flows on a hedged liability and on the related cross-currency interest rate swap as one aggregated fixed rate exposure in LC. From time to time, in accordance with its risk management strategy for fixed rate interest rate risk (in LC), Entity C decides to link its interest payments to current variable interest rate levels and hence swaps its aggregated fixed rate exposure in LC into a variable rate exposure in LC. Consequently, Entity C uses interest rate swaps (denominated entirely in LC) under which it receives fixed interest (used to pay the interest on the pay leg of the cross-currency interest rate swap) and pays variable interest.

IE140   The following table sets out the parameters used for Example 18:

Example 18—Parameter overview

	t_0	Period 1	Period 2	Period 3	Period 4
FX spot rate [LC/FC]	1.2	1.05	1.42	1.51	1.37
Interest curves (vertical presentation of rates for each quarter of a period on a p.a. basis)					
LC	2.50%	1.00%	3.88%	0.34%	[N/A]
	2.75%	1.21%	4.12%	0.49%	
	2.91%	1.39%	4.22%	0.94%	
	3.02%	1.58%	5.11%	1.36%	
	2.98%	1.77%	5.39%		
	3.05%	1.93%	5.43%		
	3.11%	2.09%	5.50%		
	3.15%	2.16%	5.64%		
	3.11%	2.22%			
	3.14%	2.28%			
	3.27%	2.30%			
	3.21%	2.31%			
	3.21%				
	3.25%				
	3.29%				
	3.34%				

continued...

...continued

Example 18—Parameter overview					
	t_0	Period 1	Period 2	Period 3	Period 4
FC	3.74%	4.49%	2.82%	0.70%	[N/A]
	4.04%	4.61%	2.24%	0.79%	
	4.23%	4.63%	2.00%	1.14%	
	4.28%	4.34%	2.18%	1.56%	
	4.20%	4.21%	2.34%		
	4.17%	4.13%	2.53%		
	4.27%	4.07%	2.82%		
	4.14%	4.09%	3.13%		
	4.10%	4.17%			
	4.11%	4.13%			
	4.11%	4.24%			
	4.13%	4.34%			
	4.14%				
	4.06%				
	4.12%				
	4.19%				

Accounting mechanics

IE141   Entity C designates the following hedging relationships:[29]

(a)   As a cash flow hedge, a hedging relationship for cash flow interest rate risk and FX risk between the FC denominated variable rate liability (variable rate FX liability) as the hedged item and a cross-currency interest rate swap as the hedging instrument (the 'first level relationship'). This hedging relationship is designated at the beginning of Period 1 (ie t_0) with a term to the end of Period 4.

(b)   As a fair value hedge, a hedging relationship between the aggregated exposure as the hedged item and an interest rate swap as the hedging instrument (the 'second level relationship'). This hedging relationship is designated at the end of Period 1, when Entity C decides to link its interest payments to current variable interest rate levels and hence swaps its aggregated fixed rate exposure in LC into a variable rate exposure in LC, with a term to the end of Period 4. The aggregated exposure that is designated as the hedged item represents, in LC, the change in value that is the effect of changes in the value of the

---

29 This example assumes that all qualifying criteria for hedge accounting are met (see paragraph 6.4.1 of IFRS 9). The following description of the designation is solely for the purpose of understanding this example (ie it is not an example of the complete formal documentation required in accordance with paragraph 6.4.1(b) of IFRS 9).

combined cash flows of the two items designated in the cash flow hedge of the cash flow interest rate risk and FX risk (see (a) above), compared to the interest rates at the end of Period 1 (ie the time of designation of the hedging relationship between the aggregated exposure and the interest rate swap).

IE142   The following table[30] sets out the overview of the fair values of the derivatives, the changes in the value of the hedged items and the calculation of the cash flow hedge reserve.[31] In this example no hedge ineffectiveness arises on either hedging relationship because of the assumptions made.[32]

Example 18—Calculations					
	t_0	Period 1	Period 2	Period 3	Period 4
Variable rate FX liability					
Fair value [FC]	(1,000,000)	(1,000,000)	(1,000,000)	(1,000,000)	(1,000,000)
Fair value [LC]	(1,200,000)	(1,050,000)	(1,420,000)	(1,510,000)	(1,370,000)
Change in fair value [LC]		150,000	(370,000)	(90,000)	140,000
PV of change in variable CF(s) [LC]	0	192,310	(260,346)	(282,979)	(170,000)
Change in PV [LC]		192,310	(452,656)	(22,633)	112,979
CCIRS (receive variable FC/pay fixed LC)					
Fair value [LC]	0	(192,310)	260,346	282,979	170,000
Change in fair value [LC]		(192,310)	452,656	22,633	(112,979)

continued...

---

30   Tables in this example use the following acronyms: 'CCIRS' for cross-currency interest rate swap, 'CF(s)' for cash flow(s), 'CFH' for cash flow hedge, 'CFHR' for cash flow hedge reserve, 'FVH' for fair value hedge, 'IRS' for interest rate swap and 'PV' for present value.

31   In the following table for the calculations all amounts (including the calculations for accounting purposes of amounts for assets, liabilities and equity) are in the format of positive (plus) and negative (minus) numbers (eg an amount in the cash flow hedge reserve that is a negative number is a loss).

32   Those assumptions have been made for didactical reasons, in order to better focus on illustrating the accounting mechanics in a cash flow hedge/fair value hedge combination. The measurement and recognition of hedge ineffectiveness has already been demonstrated in Example 16 and Example 17. However, in reality such hedges are typically not perfectly effective because hedge ineffectiveness can result from various factors, for example credit risk, differences in the day count method or, depending on whether it is included in the designation of the hedging instrument, the charge for exchanging different currencies that is included in cross-currency interest rate swaps (commonly referred to as the 'currency basis').

...continued

Example 18—Calculations	t_0	Period 1	Period 2	Period 3	Period 4
CFHR					
Opening balance	0	0	(42,310)	(28,207)	(14,103)
Reclassification FX risk		153,008	(378,220)	(91,030)	140,731
Reclassification (current period CF)		(8,656)	(18,410)	2,939	21,431
Effective CFH gain/loss		(186,662)	(479,286)	20,724	(135,141)
Reclassification for interest rate risk		0	(82,656)	67,367	(27,021)
Amortisation of CFHR		0	14,103	14,103	14,103
Ending balance		(42,103)	(28,207)	(14,103)	0
IRS (receive fixed/pay variable)					
Fair value [LC]		0	(82,656)	(15,289)	(42,310)
Change in fair value			(82,656)	67,367	(27,021)
Change in present value of the aggregated exposure					
Present value [LC]		(1,242,310)	(1,159,654)	(1,227,021)	(1,200,000)
Change in present value [LC]			82,656	(67,367)	27,021

IE143   The hedging relationship between the variable rate FX liability and the cross-currency interest rate swap starts at the beginning of Period 1 (ie t_0) and remains in place when the hedging relationship for the second level relationship starts at the end of Period 1, ie the first level relationship continues as a separate hedging relationship. However, the hedge accounting for the first level relationship is affected by the start of hedge accounting for the second level relationship at the end of Period 1. The fair value hedge for the second level relationship affects the timing of the reclassification to profit or loss of amounts from the cash flow hedge reserve for the first level relationship:

      (a)   The fair value interest rate risk that is hedged by the fair value hedge is included in the amount that is recognised in other comprehensive income as a result of the cash flow hedge for the first level hedging relationship (ie the gain or loss on the cross-currency interest rate swap that is determined to be an effective hedge).[33] This means that from the end of Period 1 the part of the effective cash flow hedging gain or loss that represents the fair value interest rate risk (in LC), and is recognised in other comprehensive income in a first step, is in a

---

33   As a consequence of hedging its exposure to cash flow interest rate risk by entering into the cross-currency interest rate swap that changed the cash flow interest rate risk of the variable rate FX liability into a fixed rate exposure (in LC), Entity C in effect assumed an exposure to fair value interest rate risk (see paragraph IE139).

second step immediately (ie in the same period) transferred from the cash flow hedge reserve to profit or loss. That reclassification adjustment offsets the gain or loss on the interest rate swap that is recognised in profit or loss.[34] In the context of accounting for the aggregated exposure as the hedged item, that reclassification adjustment is the equivalent of a fair value hedge adjustment because in contrast to a hedged item that is a fixed rate debt instrument (in LC) at amortised cost, the aggregated exposure is already remeasured for changes regarding the hedged risk but the resulting gain or loss is recognised in other comprehensive income because of applying cash flow hedge accounting for the first level relationship. Consequently, applying fair value hedge accounting with the aggregated exposure as the hedged item does not result in changing the hedged item's measurement but instead affects where the hedging gains and losses are recognised (ie reclassification from the cash flow hedge reserve to profit or loss).

(b) The amount in the cash flow hedge reserve at the end of Period 1 (LC42,310) is amortised over the remaining life of the cash flow hedge for the first level relationship (ie over Periods 2 to 4).[35]

IE144 The change in value of the aggregated exposure is calculated as follows:

(a) At the point in time from which the change in value of the aggregated exposure is hedged (ie the start of the second level relationship at the end of Period 1), all cash flows expected on the variable rate FX liability and the cross-currency interest rate swap over the hedged term (ie until the end of Period 4) are mapped out and their combined present value, in LC, is calculated. This calculation establishes the present value that is used at subsequent dates as the reference point to measure the change in present value of the aggregated exposure since the start of the hedging relationship. This calculation is illustrated in the following table:

---

34 In the table with the overview of the calculations (see paragraph IE142) this reclassification adjustment is the line item "Reclassification for interest rate risk" in the reconciliation of the cash flow hedge reserve (eg at the end of Period 2 a reclassification of a gain of LC82,656 from the cash flow hedge reserve to profit or loss—see paragraph IE144 for how that amount is calculated).
35 In the table with the overview of the calculations (see paragraph IE142) this amortisation results in a periodic reclassification adjustment of LC14,103 that is included in the line item "Amortisation of CFHR" in the reconciliation of the cash flow hedge reserve.

Example 18—Present value of the aggregated exposure (starting point)

	Present value of the aggregated exposure					
	FX liability		CCIRS FC leg		CCIRS LC leg	
	CF(s)	PV	CF(s)	PV	CF(s)	PV
	[FC]	[FC]	[FC]	[FC]	[LC]	[LC]
Time						
t_0						
t_1						
t_2						
Period 1						
t_3						
t_4						
t_5	(11,039)	(10,918)	11,039	10,918	(9,117)	(9,094)
t_6	(11,331)	(11,082)	11,331	11,082	(9,117)	(9,067)
Period 2						
t_7	(11,375)	(11,000)	11,375	11,000	(9,117)	(9,035)
t_8	(10,689)	(10,227)	10,689	10,227	(9,117)	(9,000)
t_9	(10,375)	(9,824)	10,375	9,824	(9,117)	(8,961)
t_{10}	(10,164)	(9,528)	10,164	9,528	(9,117)	(8,918)
Period 3						
t_{11}	(10,028)	(9,307)	10,028	9,307	(9,117)	(8,872)
t_{12}	(10,072)	(9,255)	10,072	9,255	(9,117)	(8,825)
t_{13}	(10,256)	(9,328)	10,256	9,328	(9,117)	(8,776)
t_{14}	(10,159)	(9,147)	10,159	9,147	(9,117)	(8,727)
Period 4						
t_{15}	(10,426)	(9,290)	10,426	9,290	(9,117)	(8,678)
t_{16}	(1,010,670)	(891,093)	1,010,670	891,093	(1,209,117)	(1,144,358)
Totals		(1,000,000)		1,000,000		(1,242,310)
Totals in LC		(1,050,000)		1,050,000		(1,242,310)
PV of aggregated exposure [LC]		(1,242,310) ←		Σ		

The present value of all cash flows expected on the variable rate FX liability and the cross-currency interest rate swap over the hedged term at the end of Period 1 is LC-1,242,310.[36]

---

36 In this example no hedge ineffectiveness arises on either hedging relationship because of the assumptions made (see paragraph IE142). Consequently, the absolute values of the variable rate FX liability and the FC denominated leg of the cross-currency interest rate are equal (but with opposite signs). In situations in which hedge ineffectiveness arises, those absolute values would not be equal so that the remaining net amount would affect the present value of the aggregated exposure.

(b)   At subsequent dates, the present value of the aggregated exposure is determined in the same way as at the end of Period 1 but for the remainder of the hedged term. For that purpose, all remaining cash flows expected on the variable rate FX liability and the cross-currency interest rate swap over the remainder of the hedged term (ie from the effectiveness measurement date until the end of Period 4) are updated (as applicable) and then discounted. The total of those present values represents the present value of the aggregated exposure. This calculation is illustrated in the following table for the end of Period 2:

Example 18—Present value of the aggregated exposure (at the end of Period 2)						
		Present value of the aggregated exposure				
		FX liability		CCIRS FC leg		CCIRS LC leg	
		CF(s) [FC]	PV [FC]	CF(s) [FC]	PV [FC]	CF(s) [LC]	PV [LC]
Period 1	Time						
	t_0						
	t_1						
	t_2						
	t_3						
	t_4						
Period 2	t_5	0	0	0	0	0	0
	t_6	0	0	0	0	0	0
	t_7	0	0	0	0	0	0
	t_8	0	0	0	0	0	0
Period 3	t_9	(6,969)	(6,921)	6,969	6,921	(9,117)	(9,030)
	t_{10}	(5,544)	(5,475)	5,544	5,475	(9,117)	(8,939)
	t_{11}	(4,971)	(4,885)	4,971	4,885	(9,117)	(8,847)
	t_{12}	(5,401)	(5,280)	5,401	5,280	(9,117)	(8,738)
Period 4	t_{13}	(5,796)	(5,632)	5,796	5,632	(9,117)	(8,624)
	t_{14}	(6,277)	(6,062)	6,277	6,062	(9,117)	(8,511)
	t_{15}	(6,975)	(6,689)	6,975	6,689	(9,117)	(8,397)
	t_{16}	(1,007,725)	(959,056)	1,007,725	956,056	(1,209,117)	(1,098,568)
Totals			(1,000,000)		1,000,000		(1,159,654)
Totals in LC			(1,420,000)		1,420,000		(1,159,654)
PV of aggregated exposure [LC]			(1,159,654)		Σ		

The changes in interest rates and the exchange rate result in a present value of the aggregated exposure at the end of Period 2 of LC-1,159,654. Consequently, the change in the present value of the aggregated exposure between the end of Period 1 and the end of Period 2 is a gain of LC82,656.[37]

IE145   Using the change in present value of the hedged item (ie the aggregated exposure) and the fair value of the hedging instrument (ie the interest rate swap), the related reclassifications from the cash flow hedge reserve to profit or loss (reclassification adjustments) are then determined.

IE146   The following table shows the effect on Entity C's statement of profit or loss and other comprehensive income and its statement of financial position (for the sake of transparency some line items[38] are disaggregated on the face of the statements by the two hedging relationships, ie for the cash flow hedge of the variable rate FX liability and the fair value hedge of the aggregated exposure):[39]

---

37 This is the amount that is included in the table with the overview of the calculations (see paragraph IE142) as the change in present value of the aggregated exposure at the end of Period 2.

38 The line items used in this example are a possible presentation. Different presentation formats using different line items (including line items that include the amounts shown here) are also possible (IFRS 7 sets out disclosure requirements for hedge accounting that include disclosures about hedge ineffectiveness, the carrying amount of hedging instruments and the cash flow hedge reserve).

39 For Period 4 the values in the table with the overview of the calculations (see paragraph IE142) differ from those in the following table. For Periods 1 to 3 the 'dirty' values (ie including interest accruals) equal the 'clean' values (ie excluding interest accruals) because the period end is a settlement date for all legs of the derivatives and the fixed rate FX liability. At the end of Period 4 the table with the overview of the calculations uses clean values in order to calculate the value changes consistently over time. For the following table the dirty values are presented, ie the maturity amounts including accrued interest immediately before the instruments are settled (this is for illustrative purposes as otherwise all carrying amounts other than cash and retained earnings would be nil).

Example 18—Overview of effect on statements of financial performance and financial position
[All amounts in LC]

	t_0	Period 1	Period 2	Period 3	Period 4
Statement of profit or loss and other comprehensive income					
Interest expense					
FX liability		45,122	54,876	33,527	15,035
FVH adjustment		0	(20,478)	16,517	(26,781)
		45,122	34,398	50,045	(11,746)
Reclassifications (CFH)		(8,656)	(18,410)	2,939	21,431
		36,466	15,989	52,983	9,685
Amortisation of CFHR		0	14,103	14,103	14,103
Total interest expense		36,466	30,092	67,087	23,788
Other gains/losses					
IRS		0	82,656	(67,367)	27,021
FX gain/loss (liability)		(150,000)	370,000	90,000	(140,000)
FX gain/loss (interest)		(3,008)	8,220	1,030	(731)
Reclassification for FX risk		153,008	(378,220)	(91,030)	140,731
Reclassification for interest rate risk		0	(82,656)	67,367	(27,021)
Total other gains/losses		0	0	0	0
Profit or loss		36,466	30,092	67,087	23,788
Other comprehensive income (OCI)					
Effective gain/loss		186,662	(479,286)	(20,724)	135,141
Reclassification (current period CF)		8,656	18,410	(2,939)	(21,431)
Reclassification for FX risk		(153,008)	378,220	91,030	(140,731)
Reclassification for interest rate risk		0	82,656	(67,367)	27,021
Amortisation of CFHR		0	(14,103)	(14,103)	(14,103)
Total other comprehensive income		42,310	(14,103)	(14,103)	(14,103)
Comprehensive income		78,776	15,989	52,983	9,685

continued...

...continued

Example 18—Overview of effect on statements of financial performance and financial position

[All amounts in LC]

	t_0	Period 1	Period 2	Period 3	Period 4
Statement of financial position					
FX liability	(1,200,000)	(1,050,000)	(1,420,000)	(1,510,000)	(1,375,306)
CCIRS	0	(192,310)	260,346	282,979	166,190
IRS		0	(82,656)	(15,289)	(37,392)
Cash	1,200,000	1,163,534	1,147,545	1,094,562	1,089,076
Total net assets	0	(78,776)	(94,765)	(147,748)	(157,433)
Accumulated OCI	0	42,310	28,207	14,103	0
Retained earnings	0	36,466	66,558	133,645	157,433
Total equity	0	78,776	94,765	147,748	157,433

IE147   The total interest expense in profit or loss reflects Entity C's interest expense that results from its risk management strategy:

(a)   In Period 1 the risk management strategy results in interest expense reflecting fixed interest rates in LC after taking into account the effect of the cross-currency interest rate swap.

(b)   For Periods 2 to 4, after taking into account the effect of the interest rate swap entered into at the end of Period 1, the risk management strategy results in interest expense that changes with variable interest rates in LC (ie the variable interest rate prevailing in each period). However, the amount of the total interest expense is not equal to the amount of the variable rate interest because of the amortisation of the amount that was in the cash flow hedge reserve for the first level relationship at the end of Period 1.[40]

---

40 See paragraph IE143(b). That amortisation becomes an expense that has an effect like a spread on the variable interest rate.

CONTENTS

...continued

Guidance on implementing
IFRS 9 *Financial Instruments*

This guidance accompanies, but is not part of, IFRS 9. The numbers used for the questions are carried forward from the implementation guidance accompanying IAS 39 Financial Instruments: Recognition and Measurement.

Section A Scope

A.1 Practice of settling net: forward contract to purchase a commodity
[Refer:

paragraphs 2.4–2.6

Basis for Conclusions paragraphs BCZ2.18–BCZ2.38]

Entity XYZ enters into a fixed price forward contract to purchase 1 million kilograms of copper in accordance with its expected usage requirements. The contract permits XYZ to take physical delivery of the copper at the end of twelve months or to pay or receive a net settlement in cash, based on the change in fair value of copper. Is the contract accounted for as a derivative?

While such a contract meets the definition of a derivative, it is not necessarily accounted for as a derivative. The contract is a derivative instrument because there is no initial net investment, the contract is based on the price of copper, and it is to be settled at a future date. However, if XYZ intends to settle the contract by taking delivery and has no history for similar contracts of settling net in cash or of taking delivery of the copper and selling it within a short period after delivery for the purpose of generating a profit from short-term fluctuations in price or dealer's margin, the contract is not accounted for as a derivative under IFRS 9. Instead, it is accounted for as an executory contract (unless the entity irrevocably designates it as measured at fair value through profit or loss in accordance with paragraph 2.5 of IFRS 9).

A.2 Option to put a non-financial asset
[Refer:

paragraphs 2.4–2.7

Basis for Conclusions paragraphs BCZ2.18–BCZ2.38]

Entity XYZ owns an office building. XYZ enters into a put option with an investor that permits XYZ to put the building to the investor for CU150 million. The current value of the building is CU175 million.[1] The option expires in five years. The option, if exercised, may be settled through physical delivery or net cash, at XYZ's option. How do both XYZ and the investor account for the option?

XYZ's accounting depends on XYZ's intention and past practice for settlement. Although the contract meets the definition of a derivative, XYZ does not account for it as a derivative if XYZ intends to settle the contract by delivering the building if XYZ exercises its option and there is no past practice of settling net (paragraph 2.4 of IFRS 9; but see also paragraph 2.5 of IFRS 9).

---

1   In this guidance, monetary amounts are denominated in 'currency units' (CU).

The investor, however, cannot conclude that the option was entered into to meet the investor's expected purchase, sale or usage requirements because the investor does not have the ability to require delivery (IFRS 9, paragraph 2.7). In addition, the option may be settled net in cash. Therefore, the investor has to account for the contract as a derivative. Regardless of past practices, the investor's intention does not affect whether settlement is by delivery or in cash. The investor has written an option, and a written option in which the holder has a choice of physical settlement or net cash settlement can never satisfy the normal delivery requirement for the exemption from IFRS 9 because the option writer does not have the ability to require delivery.

However, if the contract were a forward contract instead of an option, and if the contract required physical delivery and the reporting entity had no past practice of settling net in cash or of taking delivery of the building and selling it within a short period after delivery for the purpose of generating a profit from short-term fluctuations in price or dealer's margin, the contract would not be accounted for as a derivative. (But see also paragraph 2.5 of IFRS 9).

Section B Definitions

B.1 Definition of a financial instrument: gold bullion

Is gold bullion a financial instrument (like cash) or is it a commodity?

It is a commodity. Although bullion is highly liquid, there is no contractual right to receive cash or another financial asset inherent in bullion.

B.2 Definition of a derivative: examples of derivatives and underlyings
[Refer: paragraphs BA.1–BA.5]

What are examples of common derivative contracts and the identified underlying?

IFRS 9 defines a derivative as follows:

A derivative is a financial instrument or other contract within the scope of this Standard with all three of the following characteristics.

(a)   Its value changes in response to the change in a specified interest rate, financial instrument price, commodity price, foreign exchange rate, index of prices or rates, credit rating or credit index, or other variable, provided in the case of a nonfinancial variable that the variable is not specific to a party to the contract (sometimes called the 'underlying').

(b)   It requires no initial net investment or an initial net investment that is smaller than would be required for other types of contracts that would be expected to have a similar response to changes in market factors.

(c)   It is settled at a future date.

Type of contract	Main pricing-settlement variable (underlying variable)
Interest rate swap	Interest rates
Currency swap (foreign exchange swap)	Currency rates
Commodity swap	Commodity prices
Equity swap	Equity prices (equity of another entity)
Credit swap	Credit rating, credit index or credit price
Total return swap	Total fair value of the reference asset and interest rates
Purchased or written treasury bond option (call or put)	Interest rates
Purchased or written currency option (call or put)	Currency rates
Purchased or written commodity option (call or put)	Commodity prices
Purchased or written stock option (call or put)	Equity prices (equity of another entity)
Interest rate futures linked to government debt (treasury futures)	Interest rates
Currency futures	Currency rates
Commodity futures	Commodity prices
Interest rate forward linked to government debt (treasury forward)	Interest rates
Currency forward	Currency rates
Commodity forward	Commodity prices
Equity forward	Equity prices (equity of another entity)

The above list provides examples of contracts that normally qualify as derivatives under IFRS 9. The list is not exhaustive. Any contract that has an underlying may be a derivative. Moreover, even if an instrument meets the definition of a derivative contract, special provisions may apply, for example, if it is a weather derivative (see paragraph B2.1 of IFRS 9), a contract to buy or sell a non-financial item such as commodity (see paragraphs 2.5–2.7 and BA.2 of IFRS 9) or a contract settled in an entity's own shares (see paragraphs 21–24 of IAS 32). Therefore, an entity must evaluate the contract to determine whether the other characteristics of a derivative are present and whether special provisions apply.

B.3 Definition of a derivative: settlement at a future date, interest rate swap with net or gross settlement
[Refer: paragraphs BA.1–BA.3]

For the purpose of determining whether an interest rate swap is a derivative financial instrument under IFRS 9, does it make a difference whether the parties pay the interest payments to each other (gross settlement) or settle on a net basis?

No. The definition of a derivative does not depend on gross or net settlement.

To illustrate: Entity ABC enters into an interest rate swap with a counterparty (XYZ) that requires ABC to pay a fixed rate of 8 per cent and receive a variable amount based on three-month LIBOR, reset on a quarterly basis. The fixed and variable amounts are determined on the basis of a CU100 million notional amount. ABC and XYZ do not exchange the notional amount. ABC pays or receives a net cash amount each quarter based on the difference between 8 per cent and three-month LIBOR. Alternatively, settlement may be on a gross basis.

The contract meets the definition of a derivative regardless of whether there is net or gross settlement because its value changes in response to changes in an underlying variable (LIBOR), there is no initial net investment, and settlements occur at future dates.

B.4 Definition of a derivative: prepaid interest rate swap (fixed rate payment obligation prepaid at inception or subsequently)
[Refer: paragraphs BA.1 and BA.3]

If a party prepays its obligation under a pay-fixed, receive-variable interest rate swap at inception, is the swap a derivative financial instrument?

Yes. To illustrate: Entity S enters into a CU100 million notional amount five-year pay-fixed, receive-variable interest rate swap with Counterparty C. The interest rate of the variable part of the swap is reset on a quarterly basis to three-month LIBOR. The interest rate of the fixed part of the swap is 10 per cent per year. Entity S prepays its fixed obligation under the swap of CU50 million (CU100 million × 10% × 5 years) at inception, discounted using market interest rates, while retaining the right to receive interest payments on the CU100 million reset quarterly based on three-month LIBOR over the life of the swap.

The initial net investment in the interest rate swap is significantly less than the notional amount on which the variable payments under the variable leg will be calculated. The contract requires an initial net investment that is smaller than would be required for other types of contracts that would be expected to have a similar response to changes in market factors, such as a variable rate bond. Therefore, the contract fulfils the 'no initial net investment or an initial net investment that is smaller than would be required for other types of contracts that would be expected to have a similar response to changes in market factors' provision of IFRS 9. Even though Entity S has no future performance obligation, the ultimate settlement of the contract is at a future date and the value of the contract changes in response to changes in the LIBOR index. Accordingly, the contract is regarded as a derivative contract.

Would the answer change if the fixed rate payment obligation is prepaid subsequent to initial recognition?

If the fixed leg is prepaid during the term, that would be regarded as a termination of the old swap and an origination of a new instrument that is evaluated under IFRS 9.

B.5 Definition of a derivative: prepaid pay-variable, receive-fixed interest rate swap
[Refer: paragraph BA.3]

If a party prepays its obligation under a pay-variable, receive-fixed interest rate swap at inception of the contract or subsequently, is the swap a derivative financial instrument?

No. A prepaid pay-variable, receive-fixed interest rate swap is not a derivative if it is prepaid at inception and it is no longer a derivative if it is prepaid after inception because it provides a return on the prepaid (invested) amount comparable to the return on a debt instrument with fixed cash flows. The prepaid amount fails the 'no initial net investment or an initial net investment that is smaller than would be required for other types of contracts that would be expected to have a similar response to changes in market factors' criterion of a derivative.

To illustrate: Entity S enters into a CU100 million notional amount five-year pay-variable, receive-fixed interest rate swap with Counterparty C. The variable leg of the swap is reset on a quarterly basis to three-month LIBOR. The fixed interest payments under the swap are calculated as 10 per cent times the swap's notional amount, ie CU10 million per year. Entity S prepays its obligation under the variable leg of the swap at inception at current market rates, while retaining the right to receive fixed interest payments of 10 per cent on CU100 million per year.

The cash inflows under the contract are equivalent to those of a financial instrument with a fixed annuity stream since Entity S knows it will receive CU10 million per year over the life of the swap. Therefore, all else being equal, the initial investment in the contract should equal that of other financial instruments that consist of fixed annuities. Thus, the initial net investment in the pay-variable, receive-fixed interest rate swap is equal to the investment required in a non-derivative contract that has a similar response to changes in market conditions. For this reason, the instrument fails the 'no initial net investment or an initial net investment that is smaller than would be required for other types of contracts that would be expected to have a similar response to changes in market factors' criterion of IFRS 9. Therefore, the contract is not accounted for as a derivative under IFRS 9. By discharging the obligation to pay variable interest rate payments, Entity S in effect provides a loan to Counterparty C.

B.6 Definition of a derivative: offsetting loans[E1]

[Refer: paragraph BA.3]

E1 [IFRIC® *Update*, March 2014, Agenda Decision, 'IAS 39 *Financial instruments: Recognition and Measurement*—accounting for term-structured repo transactions'

The Interpretations Committee received a request to clarify: (Issue 1) whether an entity (Entity A) should account for three transactions separately or aggregate and treat them as a single derivative; and (Issue 2) how to apply paragraph B.6 of Guidance on Implementing IAS 39 *Financial Instruments: Recognition and Measurement* ('IG B.6 of IAS 39') [paragraph B.6 of Guidance on Implementing IFRS 9] in addressing Issue 1. Some key features of the three transactions are as follows:

a. Transaction 1 (bond purchase): Entity A purchases a bond (the bond) from another entity (Entity B).

b. Transaction 2 (interest rate swap): Entity A enters into interest rate swap contract(s) with Entity B. Entity A pays a fixed rate of interest equal to the fixed coupon rate of the purchased bond in Transaction 1 and receives a variable rate of interest.

c. Transaction 3 (repurchase agreement): Entity A enters into a repurchase agreement with Entity B, in which Entity A sells the same bond in Transaction 1 on the same day it purchases the bond and agrees to buy back the bond at the maturity date of the bond.

The Interpretations Committee noted that in order to determine whether Entity A should aggregate and account for the three transactions above as a single derivative, reference should be made to paragraphs B.6 and C.6 of Guidance on Implementing IAS 39 and paragraph AG39 of IAS 32 *Financial Instruments: Presentation*.

The Interpretations Committee also discussed Issue 2, ie, how to apply paragraph IG B.6 of IAS 39 in addressing Issue 1. The Interpretations Committee noted that application of the guidance in paragraph IG B.6 of IAS 39 requires judgement. It also noted that the indicators in paragraph IG B.6 of IAS 39 may help an entity to determine the substance of the transaction, but that the presence or absence of any single specific indicator alone may not be conclusive.

The Interpretations Committee noted that providing additional guidance would result in the Interpretations Committee attempting to specify the accounting for a specific transaction, and that this would not be appropriate.

On the basis of the analysis above, the Interpretations Committee determined that, in the light of the existing IFRS requirements, neither an Interpretation nor an amendment to a Standard was necessary and consequently decided not to add this issue to its agenda.]

Entity A makes a five-year fixed rate loan to Entity B, while B at the same time makes a five-year variable rate loan for the same amount to A. There are no transfers of contractual par amount at inception of the two loans, since A and B have a netting agreement. Is this a derivative under IFRS 9?

Yes. This meets the definition of a derivative (that is to say, there is an underlying variable, no initial net investment or an initial net investment that is smaller than would be required for other types of contracts that would be expected to have a similar response to changes in market factors, and future settlement). The contractual effect of the loans is the equivalent of an interest rate swap arrangement with no initial net investment. Non-derivative transactions are aggregated and treated as a derivative when the transactions result, in substance, in a derivative. Indicators of this would include:

• they are entered into at the same time and in contemplation of one another

• they have the same counterparty

• they relate to the same risk

- there is no apparent economic need or substantive business purpose for structuring the transactions separately that could not also have been accomplished in a single transaction.

The same answer would apply if Entity A and Entity B did not have a netting agreement, because the definition of a derivative instrument in IFRS 9 does not require net settlement.

B.7 Definition of a derivative: option not expected to be exercised

The definition of a derivative in IFRS 9 requires that the instrument 'is settled at a future date'. Is this criterion met even if an option is expected not to be exercised, for example, because it is out of the money?

Yes. An option is settled upon exercise or at its maturity. Expiry at maturity is a form of settlement even though there is no additional exchange of consideration.

B.8 Definition of a derivative: foreign currency contract based on sales volume
[Refer: paragraphs BA.1 and BA.3]

Entity XYZ, whose functional currency is the US dollar, sells products in France denominated in euro. XYZ enters into a contract with an investment bank to convert euro to US dollars at a fixed exchange rate. The contract requires XYZ to remit euro based on its sales volume in France in exchange for US dollars at a fixed exchange rate of 6.00. Is that contract a derivative?

Yes. The contract has two underlying variables (the foreign exchange rate and the volume of sales), no initial net investment or an initial net investment that is smaller than would be required for other types of contracts that would be expected to have a similar response to changes in market factors, and a payment provision. IFRS 9 does not exclude from its scope derivatives that are based on sales volume.

B.9 Definition of a derivative: prepaid forward
[Refer: paragraph BA.3]

An entity enters into a forward contract to purchase shares of stock in one year at the forward price. It prepays at inception based on the current price of the shares. Is the forward contract a derivative?

No. The forward contract fails the 'no initial net investment or an initial net investment that is smaller than would be required for other types of contracts that would be expected to have a similar response to changes in market factors' test for a derivative.

To illustrate: Entity XYZ enters into a forward contract to purchase 1 million T ordinary shares in one year. The current market price of T is CU50 per share; the one-year forward price of T is CU55 per share. XYZ is required to prepay the forward contract at inception with a CU50 million payment. The initial investment in the forward contract of CU50 million is less than the notional amount applied to the underlying, 1 million shares at the forward price of CU55 per share, ie CU55 million. However, the initial net investment approximates the investment that would be required for other types of contracts that would be expected to have a similar response to changes in market factors because T's shares could be purchased at inception for the same price of CU50.

Accordingly, the prepaid forward contract does not meet the initial net investment criterion of a derivative instrument.

B.10 Definition of a derivative: initial net investment

Many derivative instruments, such as futures contracts and exchange traded written options, require margin accounts. Is the margin account part of the initial net investment?

No. The margin account is not part of the initial net investment in a derivative instrument. Margin accounts are a form of collateral for the counterparty or clearing house and may take the form of cash, securities or other specified assets, typically liquid assets. Margin accounts are separate assets that are accounted for separately.

B.11 Definition of held for trading: portfolio with a recent actual pattern of short-term profit-taking
[Refer: paragraph BA.7]

The definition of a financial asset or financial liability held for trading states that 'a financial asset or financial liability is classified as held for trading if it is ... part of a portfolio of identified financial instruments that are managed together and for which there is evidence of a recent actual pattern of short-term profit-taking'. What is a 'portfolio' for the purposes of applying this definition?

Although the term 'portfolio' is not explicitly defined in IFRS 9, the context in which it is used suggests that a portfolio is a group of financial assets or financial liabilities that are managed as part of that group (Appendix A of IFRS 9). If there is evidence of a recent actual pattern of short-term profit-taking on financial instruments included in such a portfolio, those financial instruments qualify as held for trading even though an individual financial instrument may in fact be held for a longer period of time.

B.24 Definition of gross carrying amount: perpetual debt instruments with fixed or market-based variable rate

Sometimes entities purchase or issue debt instruments that are required to be measured at amortised cost and in respect of which the issuer has no obligation to repay the gross carrying amount. The interest rate may be fixed or variable. Would the difference between the initial amount paid or received and zero ('the maturity amount') be amortised immediately on initial recognition for the purpose of determining amortised cost if the rate of interest is fixed or specified as a market-based variable rate?

No. Since there are no repayment of the gross carrying amount, there is no amortisation of the difference between the initial amount and the maturity amount if the rate of interest is fixed or specified as a market-based variable rate. Because interest payments are fixed or market-based and will be paid in perpetuity, the amortised cost (the present value of the stream of future cash payments discounted at the effective interest rate) equals the gross carrying amount in each period.

B.25 Definition of gross carrying amount: perpetual debt instruments with decreasing interest rate

If the stated rate of interest on a perpetual debt instrument decreases over time, would the gross carrying amount equal the contractual par amount in each period?

No. From an economic perspective, some or all of the contractual interest payments are repayments of the gross carrying amount. For example, the interest rate may be stated as 16 per cent for the first 10 years and as zero per cent in subsequent periods. In that case, the initial amount is amortised to zero over the first 10 years using the effective interest method, since a portion of the contractual interest payments represents repayments of the gross carrying amount. The gross carrying amount is zero after Year 10 because the present value of the stream of future cash payments in subsequent periods is zero (there are no further contractual cash payments in subsequent periods).

B.26 Example of calculating the gross carrying amount: financial asset

How is the gross carrying amount calculated for financial assets measured at amortised cost in accordance with IFRS 9?

The gross carrying amount is calculated using the effective interest method. The effective interest rate inherent in a financial instrument is the rate that exactly discounts the estimated cash flows associated with the financial instrument through the expected life of the instrument or, where appropriate, a shorter period to the gross carrying amount at initial recognition. The computation includes all fees and points paid or received that are an integral part of the effective interest rate, directly attributable transaction costs and all other premiums or discounts.

The following example illustrates how the gross carrying amount is calculated using the effective interest method. Entity A purchases a debt instrument with five years remaining to maturity for its fair value of CU1,000 (including transaction costs). The instrument has a contractual par amount of CU1,250 and carries fixed interest of 4.7 per cent that is paid annually (CU1,250 × 4.7% = CU59 per year). The contract also specifies that the borrower has an option to prepay the instrument at par and that no penalty will be charged for prepayment. At inception, the entity expects the borrower not to prepay (and, therefore, the entity determines that the fair value of the prepayment feature is insignificant when the financial asset is initially recognised).

It can be shown that in order to allocate interest receipts and the initial discount over the term of the debt instrument at a constant rate on the carrying amount, they must be accrued at the rate of 10 per cent annually. The table below provides information about the gross carrying amount, interest revenue and cash flows of the debt instrument in each reporting period.

Year	(a) Gross carrying amount at the beginning of the year	(b = a × 10%) Interest revenue	(c) Cash flows	(d = a + b − c) Gross carrying amount at the end of the year
20X0	1,000	100	59	1,041
20X1	1,041	104	59	1,086
20X2	1,086	109	59	1,136
20X3	1,136	113	59	1,190
20X4	1,190	119	1,250 + 59	–

On the first day of 20X2 the entity revises its estimate of cash flows. It now expects that 50 per cent of the contractual par amount will be prepaid at the end of 20X2 and the remaining 50 per cent at the end of 20X4. In accordance with paragraph B5.4.6 of IFRS 9, the gross carrying amount of the debt instrument in 20X2 is adjusted. The gross carrying amount is recalculated by discounting the amount the entity expects to receive in 20X2 and subsequent years using the original effective interest rate (10 per cent). This results in the new gross carrying amount in 20X2 of CU1,138. The adjustment of CU52 (CU1,138 − CU1,086) is recorded in profit or loss in 20X2. The table below provides information about the gross carrying amount, interest revenue and cash flows as they would be adjusted taking into account the change in estimate.

Year	(a) Gross carrying amount at the beginning of the year	(b = a × 10%) Interest revenue	(c) Cash flows	(d = a + b − c) Gross carrying amount at the end of the year
20X0	1,000	100	59	1,041
20X1	1,041	104	59	1,086
20X2	1,086 + 52	114	625 + 59	568
20X3	568	57	30	595
20X4	595	60	625 + 30	–

B.27 Example of calculating the gross carrying amount: debt instruments with stepped interest payments

Sometimes entities purchase or issue debt instruments with a predetermined rate of interest that increases or decreases progressively ('stepped interest') over the term of the debt instrument. If a debt instrument with stepped interest is issued at CU1,250 and has a maturity amount of CU1,250, would the gross carrying amount equal CU1,250 in each reporting period over the term of the debt instrument?

No. Although there is no difference between the initial amount and maturity amount, an entity uses the effective interest method to allocate interest payments over the term of the debt instrument to achieve a constant rate on the carrying amount.

The following example illustrates how the gross carrying amount is calculated using the effective interest method for an instrument with a predetermined rate of interest that increases or decreases over the term of the debt instrument ('stepped interest').

On 1 January 20X0, Entity A issues a debt instrument for a price of CU1,250. The contractual par amount is CU1,250 and the debt instrument is repayable on 31 December 20X4. The rate of interest is specified in the debt agreement as a percentage of the contractual par amount as follows: 6.0 per cent in 20X0 (CU75), 8.0 per cent in 20X1 (CU100), 10.0 per cent in 20X2 (CU125), 12.0 per cent in 20X3 (CU150), and 16.4 per cent in 20X4 (CU205). In this case, the interest rate that exactly discounts the stream of future cash payments through maturity is 10 per cent. Therefore, cash interest payments are reallocated over the term of the debt instrument for the purposes of determining the gross carrying amount in each period. In each period, the gross carrying amount at the beginning of the period is multiplied by the effective interest rate of 10 per cent and added to the gross carrying amount. Any cash payments in the period are deducted from the resulting number. Accordingly, the gross carrying amount in each period is as follows:

Year	(a) Gross carrying amount at the beginning of the year	(b = a × 10%) Interest revenue	(c) Cash flows	(d = a + b − c) Gross carrying amount at the end of the year
20X0	1,250	125	75	1,300
20X1	1,300	130	100	1,330
20X2	1,330	133	125	1,338
20X3	1,338	134	150	1,322
20X4	1,322	133	1,250 + 205	–

B.28 Regular way contracts: no established market
[Refer: paragraphs B3.1.3–B3.1.6]

Can a contract to purchase a financial asset be a regular way contract if there is no established market for trading such a contract?

Yes. IFRS 9 refers to terms that require delivery of the asset within the time frame established generally by regulation or convention in the marketplace concerned. Marketplace is not limited to a formal stock exchange or organised over-the-counter market. Instead, it means the environment in which the financial asset is customarily exchanged. An acceptable time frame would be the period reasonably and customarily required for the parties to complete the transaction and prepare and execute closing documents.

For example, a market for private issue financial instruments can be a marketplace.

B.29 Regular way contracts: forward contract
[Refer: paragraphs B3.1.3–B3.1.6]

Entity ABC enters into a forward contract to purchase 1 million of M's ordinary shares in two months for CU10 per share. The contract is with an individual and is not an exchange-traded contract. The contract requires ABC to take physical delivery of the shares and pay the counterparty CU10 million in cash. M's shares trade in an active public market at an average of 100,000 shares a day. Regular way delivery is three days. Is the forward contract regarded as a regular way contract?

No. The contract must be accounted for as a derivative because it is not settled in the way established by regulation or convention in the marketplace concerned.

B.30 Regular way contracts: which customary settlement provisions apply?
[Refer: paragraphs B3.1.3–B3.1.6]

If an entity's financial instruments trade in more than one active market, and the settlement provisions differ in the various active markets, which provisions apply in assessing whether a contract to purchase those financial instruments is a regular way contract?

The provisions that apply are those in the market in which the purchase actually takes place.

To illustrate: Entity XYZ purchases 1 million shares of Entity ABC on a US stock exchange, for example, through a broker. The settlement date of the contract is six business days later. Trades for equity shares on US exchanges customarily settle in three business days. Because the trade settles in six business days, it does not meet the exemption as a regular way trade.

However, if XYZ did the same transaction on a foreign exchange that has a customary settlement period of six business days, the contract would meet the exemption for a regular way trade.

B.31 Regular way contracts: share purchase by call option
[Refer: paragraphs B3.1.3–B3.1.6]

Entity A purchases a call option in a public market permitting it to purchase 100 shares of Entity XYZ at any time over the next three months at a price of CU100 per share. If Entity A exercises its option, it has 14 days to settle the transaction according to regulation or convention in the options market. XYZ shares are traded in an active public market that requires three-day settlement. Is the purchase of shares by exercising the option a regular way purchase of shares?

Yes. The settlement of an option is governed by regulation or convention in the marketplace for options and, therefore, upon exercise of the option it is no longer accounted for as a derivative because settlement by delivery of the shares within 14 days is a regular way transaction.

B.32 Recognition and derecognition of financial liabilities using trade date or settlement date accounting
[Refer: paragraphs B3.1.3–B3.1.6]

IFRS 9 has special rules about recognition and derecognition of financial assets using trade date or settlement date accounting. Do these rules apply to transactions in financial instruments that are classified as financial liabilities, such as transactions in deposit liabilities and trading liabilities?

No. IFRS 9 does not contain any specific requirements about trade date accounting and settlement date accounting in the case of transactions in financial instruments that are classified as financial liabilities. Therefore, the general recognition and derecognition requirements in paragraphs 3.1.1 and 3.3.1 of IFRS 9 apply. Paragraph 3.1.1 of IFRS 9 states that financial liabilities are recognised on the date the entity 'becomes a party to the contractual provisions of the instrument'. Such contracts generally are not recognised unless one of the parties has performed or the contract is a derivative contract not exempted from the scope of IFRS 9. Paragraph 3.3.1 of IFRS 9 specifies that financial liabilities are derecognised only when they are extinguished, ie when the obligation specified in the contract is discharged or cancelled or expires.

Section C Embedded derivatives

C.1 Embedded derivatives: separation of host debt instrument
[Refer: paragraphs 4.3.1, 4.3.3 and B4.3.3]

If an embedded non-option derivative is required to be separated from a host debt instrument, how are the terms of the host debt instrument and the embedded derivative identified? For example, would the host debt instrument be a fixed rate instrument, a variable rate instrument or a zero coupon instrument?

The terms of the host debt instrument reflect the stated or implied substantive terms of the hybrid contract. In the absence of implied or stated terms, the entity makes its own judgement of the terms. However, an entity may not identify a component that is not specified or may not establish terms of the host debt instrument in a manner that would result in the separation of an embedded derivative that is not already clearly present in the hybrid contract, that is to say, it cannot create a cash flow that does not exist. For example, if a five-year debt instrument has fixed interest payments of CU40,000 annually and a contractual payment at maturity of CU1,000,000 multiplied by the change in an equity price index, it would be inappropriate to identify a floating rate host contract and an embedded equity swap that has an offsetting floating rate leg in lieu of identifying a fixed rate host. In that example, the host contract is a fixed rate debt instrument that pays CU40,000 annually because there are no floating interest rate cash flows in the hybrid contract.

In addition, the terms of an embedded non-option derivative, such as a forward or swap, must be determined so as to result in the embedded derivative having a fair value of zero at the inception of the hybrid contract. If it were permitted to separate embedded non-option derivatives on other terms, a single hybrid contract could be decomposed into an infinite variety of combinations of host debt instruments and embedded derivatives, for example, by separating embedded derivatives with terms that create leverage, asymmetry or some other risk exposure not already present in the hybrid contract. Therefore, it is inappropriate to separate an embedded non-option derivative on terms that result in a fair value other than zero at the inception of the hybrid contract. The determination of the terms of the embedded derivative is based on the conditions existing when the financial instrument was issued.

C.2 Embedded derivatives: separation of embedded option
[Refer: paragraphs 4.3.3 and B4.3.3]

The response to Question C.1 states that the terms of an embedded non-option derivative should be determined so as to result in the embedded derivative having a fair value of zero at the initial recognition of the hybrid contract. When an embedded option-based derivative is separated, must the terms of the embedded option be determined so as to result in the embedded derivative having either a fair value of zero or an intrinsic value of zero (that is to say, be at the money) at the inception of the hybrid contract?

No. The economic behaviour of a hybrid contract with an option-based embedded derivative depends critically on the strike price (or strike rate) specified for the option feature in the hybrid contract, as discussed below. Therefore, the separation of an option-based embedded derivative (including any embedded put, call, cap, floor, caption, floortion or swaption feature in a hybrid contract) should be based on the stated terms of the option feature documented in the hybrid contract. As a result, the embedded derivative would not necessarily have a fair value or intrinsic value equal to zero at the initial recognition of the hybrid contract.

If an entity were required to identify the terms of an embedded option-based derivative so as to achieve a fair value of the embedded derivative of zero, the strike price (or strike rate) generally would have to be determined so as to result in the option being infinitely out of the money. This would imply a zero probability of the option feature being exercised. However, since the probability of the option feature in a hybrid contract being exercised generally is not zero, it would be inconsistent with the likely economic behaviour of the hybrid contract to assume an initial fair value of zero. Similarly, if an entity were required to identify the terms of an embedded option-based derivative so as to achieve an intrinsic value of zero for the embedded derivative, the strike price (or strike rate) would have to be assumed to equal the price (or rate) of the underlying variable at the initial recognition of the hybrid contract. In this case, the fair value of the option would consist only of time value. However, such an assumption would not be consistent with the likely economic behaviour of the hybrid contract, including the probability of the option feature being exercised, unless the agreed strike price was indeed equal to the price (or rate) of the underlying variable at the initial recognition of the hybrid contract.

The economic nature of an option-based embedded derivative is fundamentally different from a forward-based embedded derivative (including forwards and swaps), because the terms of a forward are such that a payment based on the difference between the price of the underlying and the forward price will occur at a specified date, while the terms of an option are such that a payment based on the difference between the price of the underlying and the strike price of the option may or may not occur depending on the relationship between the agreed strike price and the price of the underlying at a specified date or dates in the future. Adjusting the strike price of an option-based embedded derivative, therefore, alters the nature of the hybrid contract. On the other hand, if the terms of a non-option embedded derivative in a host debt instrument were determined so as to result in a fair value of any amount other than zero at the inception of the hybrid contract, that amount would essentially represent a borrowing or lending. Accordingly, as discussed in the answer to Question C.1, it is not appropriate to separate a non-option embedded derivative in a host debt instrument on terms that result in a fair value other than zero at the initial recognition of the hybrid contract.

C.4 Embedded derivatives: equity kicker
[Refer: paragraph 4.3.1]

In some instances, venture capital entities providing subordinated loans agree that if and when the borrower lists its shares on a stock exchange, the venture capital entity is entitled to receive shares of the borrowing entity free of charge or at a very low price (an 'equity kicker') in addition to the contractual payments. As a result of the equity kicker feature, the interest on the subordinated loan is lower than it would otherwise be. Assuming that the subordinated loan is not measured at fair value with changes in fair value recognised in profit or loss (paragraph 4.3.3(c) of IFRS 9), does the equity kicker feature meet the definition of an embedded derivative even though it is contingent upon the future listing of the borrower?

Yes. The economic characteristics and risks of an equity return are not closely related to the economic characteristics and risks of a host debt instrument (paragraph 4.3.3(a) of IFRS 9). The equity kicker meets the definition of a derivative because it has a value that changes in response to the change in the price of the shares of the borrower, it requires no initial net investment or an initial net investment that is smaller than would be required for other types of contracts that would be expected to have a similar response to changes in market factors, and it is settled at a future date (paragraph 4.3.3(b) and Appendix A of IFRS 9). The equity kicker feature meets the definition of a derivative even though the right to receive shares is contingent upon the future listing of the borrower. Paragraph BA.1 of IFRS 9 states that a derivative could require a payment as a result of some future event that is unrelated to a notional amount. An equity kicker feature is similar to such a derivative except that it does not give a right to a fixed payment, but an option right, if the future event occurs.

C.6 Embedded derivatives: synthetic instruments
[Refer: paragraphs 4.3.1 and 4.3.3]

Entity A issues a five-year floating rate debt instrument. At the same time, it enters into a five-year pay-fixed, receive-variable interest rate swap with Entity B. Entity A regards the combination of the debt instrument and swap as a synthetic fixed rate instrument. Entity A contends that separate accounting for the swap is inappropriate since paragraph B4.3.8(a) of IFRS 9 requires an embedded derivative to be classified together with its host instrument if the derivative is linked to an interest rate that can change the amount of contractual interest that would otherwise be paid or received on the host debt contract. Is the entity's analysis correct?

No. Embedded derivative instruments are terms and conditions that are included in non-derivative host contracts. It is generally inappropriate to treat two or more separate financial instruments as a single combined instrument ('synthetic instrument' accounting) for the purpose of applying IFRS 9. Each of the financial instruments has its own terms and conditions and each may be transferred or settled separately. Therefore, the debt instrument and the swap are classified separately. The transactions described here differ from the transactions discussed in Question B.6, which had no substance apart from the resulting interest rate swap.

C.7 Embedded derivatives: purchases and sales contracts in foreign currency instruments
[Refer: paragraphs 4.3.1, 4.3.3 and B4.3.8(d)]

A supply contract provides for payment in a currency other than (a) the functional currency of either party to the contract, (b) the currency in which the product is routinely denominated in commercial transactions around the world and (c) the currency that is commonly used in contracts to purchase or sell non-financial items in the economic environment in which the transaction takes place. Is there an embedded derivative that should be separated under IFRS 9?

Yes. To illustrate: a Norwegian entity agrees to sell oil to an entity in France. The oil contract is denominated in Swiss francs, although oil contracts are routinely denominated in US dollars in commercial transactions around the world, and Norwegian krone are commonly used in contracts to purchase or sell non-financial items in Norway. Neither entity carries out any significant activities in Swiss francs. In this case, the Norwegian entity regards the supply contract as a host contract with an embedded foreign currency forward to purchase Swiss francs. The French entity regards the supply contact as a host contract with an embedded foreign currency forward to sell Swiss francs. Each entity includes fair value changes on the currency forward in profit or loss unless the reporting entity designates it as a cash flow hedging instrument, if appropriate.

C.8 Embedded foreign currency derivatives: unrelated foreign currency provision
[Refer: paragraph 4.3.3]

Entity A, which measures items in its financial statements on the basis of the euro (its functional currency), enters into a contract with Entity B, which has the Norwegian krone as its functional currency, to purchase oil in six months for 1,000 US dollars. The host oil contract is not within the scope of IFRS 9 because it was entered into and continues to be for the purpose of delivery of a non-financial item in accordance with the entity's expected purchase, sale or usage requirements (paragraphs 2.4 and BA.2 of IFRS 9) and the entity has not irrevocably designated it as measured at fair value through profit or loss in accordance with paragraph 2.5 of IFRS 9. The oil contract includes a leveraged foreign exchange provision that states that the parties, in addition to the provision of, and payment for, oil will exchange an amount equal to the fluctuation in the exchange rate of the US dollar and Norwegian krone applied to a notional amount of 100,000 US dollars. Under paragraph 4.3.3 of IFRS 9, is that embedded derivative (the leveraged foreign exchange provision) regarded as closely related to the host oil contract?

No, that leveraged foreign exchange provision is separated from the host oil contract because it is not closely related to the host oil contract (paragraph B4.3.8(d) of IFRS 9).

The payment provision under the host oil contract of 1,000 US dollars can be viewed as a foreign currency derivative because the US dollar is neither Entity A's nor Entity B's functional currency. This foreign currency derivative would not be separated because it follows from paragraph B4.3.8(d) of IFRS 9 that a crude oil contract that requires payment in US dollars is not regarded as a host contract with a foreign currency derivative.

The leveraged foreign exchange provision that states that the parties will exchange an amount equal to the fluctuation in the exchange rate of the US dollar and Norwegian krone applied to a notional amount of 100,000 US dollars is in addition to the required payment for the oil transaction. It is unrelated to the host oil contract and therefore separated from the host oil contract and accounted for as an embedded derivative under paragraph 4.3.3 of IFRS 9.

C.9 Embedded foreign currency derivatives: currency of international commerce
[Refer: paragraph 4.3.3]

Paragraph B4.3.8(d) of IFRS 9 refers to the currency in which the price of the related goods or services is routinely denominated in commercial transactions around the world. Could it be a currency that is used for a certain product or service in commercial transactions within the local area of one of the substantial parties to the contract?

No. The currency in which the price of the related goods or services is routinely denominated in commercial transactions around the world is only a currency that is used for similar transactions all around the world, not just in one local area. For example, if cross-border transactions in natural gas in North America are routinely denominated in US dollars and such transactions are routinely denominated in euro in Europe, neither the US dollar nor the euro is a currency in which the goods or services are routinely denominated in commercial transactions around the world.

C.10 Embedded derivatives: holder permitted, but not required, to settle without recovering substantially all of its recognised investment
[Refer: paragraph 4.3.3]

If the terms of a combined contract permit, but do not require, the holder to settle the combined contract in a manner that causes it not to recover substantially all of its recognised investment and the issuer does not have such a right (for example, a puttable debt instrument), does the contract satisfy the condition in paragraph B4.3.8(a) of IFRS 9 that the holder would not recover substantially all of its recognised investment?

No. The condition that 'the holder would not recover substantially all of its recognised investment' is not satisfied if the terms of the combined contract permit, but do not require, the investor to settle the combined contract in a manner that causes it not to recover substantially all of its recognised investment and the issuer has no such right. Accordingly, an interest-bearing host contract with an embedded interest rate derivative with such terms is regarded as closely related to the host contract. The condition that 'the holder would not recover substantially all of its recognised investment' applies to situations in which the holder can be forced to accept settlement at an amount that causes the holder not to recover substantially all of its recognised investment.

Section D Recognition and derecognition

D.1 Initial recognition

D.1.1 Recognition: cash collateral
[Refer: paragraphs 3.1.1 and B3.1.2(a)]

Entity B transfers cash to Entity A as collateral for another transaction with Entity A (for example, a securities borrowing transaction). The cash is not legally segregated from Entity A's assets. Should Entity A recognise the cash collateral it has received as an asset?

Yes. The ultimate realisation of a financial asset is its conversion into cash and, therefore, no further transformation is required before the economic benefits of the cash transferred by Entity B can be realised by Entity A. Therefore, Entity A recognises the cash as an asset and a payable to Entity B while Entity B derecognises the cash and recognises a receivable from Entity A.

D.2 Regular way purchase or sale of a financial asset

D.2.1 Trade date vs settlement date: amounts to be recorded for a purchase
[Refer: paragraphs 3.1.2, 5.1.2, B3.1.3, B3.1.5 and B3.1.6]

How are the trade date and settlement date accounting principles in IFRS 9 applied to a purchase of a financial asset?

The following example illustrates the application of the trade date and settlement date accounting principles in IFRS 9 for a purchase of a financial asset. On 29 December 20X1, an entity commits itself to purchase a financial asset for CU1,000, which is its fair value on commitment (trade) date. Transaction costs are immaterial. On 31 December 20X1 (financial year-end) and on 4 January 20X2 (settlement date) the fair value of the asset is CU1,002 and CU1,003, respectively. The amounts to be recorded for the asset will depend on how it is classified and whether trade date or settlement date accounting is used, as shown in the two tables below.

Settlement date accounting			
Balances	**Financial assets measured at amortised cost**	**Financial assets measured at fair value through other comprehensive income**	**Financial assets measured at fair value through profit or loss**
29 December 20X1			
Financial asset	–	–	–
Financial liability	–	–	–
31 December 20X1			
Receivable	–	2	2
Financial asset	–	–	–
Financial liability	–	–	–
Other comprehensive income (fair value adjustment)	–	(2)	–
Retained earnings (through profit or loss)	–	–	(2)
4 January 20X2			
Receivable	–	–	–
Financial asset	1,000	1,003	1,003
Financial liability	–	–	–
Other comprehensive income (fair value adjustment)	–	(3)	–
Retained earnings (through profit or loss)	–	–	(3)

Balances	Trade date accounting		
	Financial assets measured at amortised cost	Financial assets measured at fair value through other comprehensive income	Financial assets measured at fair value through profit or loss
29 December 20X1			
Financial asset	1,000	1,000	1,000
Financial liability	(1,000)	(1,000)	(1,000)
31 December 20X1			
Receivable	–	–	–
Financial asset	1,000	1,002	1,002
Financial liability	(1,000)	(1,000)	(1,000)
Other comprehensive income (fair value adjustment)	–	(2)	–
Retained earnings (through profit or loss)	–	–	(2)
4 January 20X2			
Receivable	–	–	–
Financial asset	1,000	1,003	1,003
Financial liability	–	–	–
Other comprehensive income (fair value adjustment)	–	(3)	–
Retained earnings (through profit or loss)	–	–	(3)

D.2.2 Trade date vs settlement date: amounts to be recorded for a sale
[Refer: paragraphs 3.1.2, B3.1.3, B3.1.5 and B3.1.6]

How are the trade date and settlement date accounting principles in IFRS 9 applied to a sale of a financial asset?

The following example illustrates the application of the trade date and settlement date accounting principles in IFRS 9 for a sale of a financial asset. On 29 December 20X2 (trade date) an entity enters into a contract to sell a financial asset for its current fair value of CU1,010. The asset was acquired one year earlier for CU1,000 and its gross carrying amount is CU1,000. On 31 December 20X2 (financial year-end), the fair value of the asset is CU1,012. On 4 January 20X3 (settlement date), the fair value is CU1,013. The amounts to be recorded will depend on how the asset is classified and whether trade date or settlement date accounting is used as shown in the two tables below (any loss allowance or interest revenue on the financial asset is disregarded for the purpose of this example).

A change in the fair value of a financial asset that is sold on a regular way basis is not recorded in the financial statements between trade date and settlement date even if the entity applies settlement date accounting because the seller's right to changes in the fair value ceases on the trade date.

Settlement date accounting			
Balances	Financial assets measured at amortised cost	Financial assets measured at fair value through other comprehensive income	Financial assets measured at fair value through profit or loss
29 December 20X2			
Receivable	–	–	–
Financial asset	1,000	1,010	1,010
Other comprehensive income (fair value adjustment)	–	10	–
Retained earnings (through profit or loss)	–	–	10
31 December 20X2			
Receivable	–	–	–
Financial asset	1,000	1,010	1,010
Other comprehensive income (fair value adjustment)	–	10	–
Retained earnings (through profit or loss)	–	–	10
4 January 20X3			
Other comprehensive income (fair value adjustment)	–	–	–
Retained earnings (through profit or loss)	10	10	10

Trade date accounting			
Balances	**Financial assets measured at amortised cost**	**Financial assets measured at fair value through other comprehensive income**	**Financial assets measured at fair value through profit or loss**
29 December 20X2			
Receivable	1,010	1,010	1,010
Financial asset	–	–	–
Other comprehensive income (fair value adjustment)	–	–	–
Retained earnings (through profit or loss)	10	10	10
31 December 20X2			
Receivable	1,010	1,010	1,010
Financial asset	–	–	–
Other comprehensive income (fair value adjustment)	–	–	–
Retained earnings (through profit or loss)	10	10	10
4 January 20X3			
Other comprehensive income (fair value adjustment)	–	–	–
Retained earnings (through profit or loss)	10	10	10

D.2.3 Settlement date accounting: exchange of non-cash financial assets
[Refer: paragraphs 3.1.2, B3.1.3, B3.1.5 and B3.1.6]

If an entity recognises sales of financial assets using settlement date accounting, would a change in the fair value of a financial asset to be received in exchange for the non-cash financial asset that is sold be recognised in accordance with paragraph 5.7.4 of IFRS 9?

It depends. Any change in the fair value of the financial asset to be received would be accounted for under paragraph 5.7.4 of IFRS 9 if the entity applies settlement date accounting for that category of financial assets. However, if the entity classifies the financial asset to be received in a category for which it applies trade date accounting, the asset to be received is recognised on the trade date as described in paragraph B3.1.5 of IFRS 9. In that case, the entity recognises a liability of an amount equal to the carrying amount of the financial asset to be delivered on settlement date.

To illustrate: on 29 December 20X2 (trade date) Entity A enters into a contract to sell Note Receivable A, which is measured at amortised cost, in exchange for Bond B, which meets the definition of held for trading and is measured at fair value. Both assets have a fair value of CU1,010 on 29 December, while the amortised cost of Note Receivable A is CU1,000. Entity A uses settlement date accounting for financial assets measured at amortised cost and trade date accounting for assets that meet the definition of held for trading. On 31 December 20X2 (financial year-end), the fair value of Note Receivable A is CU1,012 and the fair value of Bond B is CU1,009. On 4 January 20X3, the fair value of Note Receivable A is CU1,013 and the fair value of Bond B is CU1,007. The following entries are made:

29 December 20X2

Dr	Bond B	CU1,010	
	Cr Payable		CU1,010

31 December 20X2

Dr	Trading loss	CU1	
	Cr Bond B		CU1

4 January 20X3

Dr	Payable	CU1,010	
Dr	Trading loss	CU2	
	Cr Note Receivable A		CU1,000
	Cr Bond B		CU2
	Cr Realisation gain		CU10

Section E Measurement

E.1 Initial measurement of financial assets and financial liabilities

E.1.1 Initial measurement: transaction costs
[Refer: paragraph 5.1.1]

Transaction costs should be included in the initial measurement of financial assets and financial liabilities other than those at fair value through profit or loss. How should this requirement be applied in practice?

For financial assets not measured at fair value through profit or loss, transaction costs are added to the fair value at initial recognition. For financial liabilities, transaction costs are deducted from the fair value at initial recognition.

For financial instruments that are measured at amortised cost, transaction costs are subsequently included in the calculation of amortised cost using the effective interest method and, in effect, amortised through profit or loss over the life of the instrument.

For financial instruments that are measured at fair value through other comprehensive income in accordance with either paragraphs 4.1.2A and 5.7.10 or paragraphs 4.1.4 and 5.7.5 of IFRS 9, transaction costs are recognised in other comprehensive income as part of a change in fair value at the next remeasurement. If the financial asset is measured in accordance with paragraphs 4.1.2A and 5.7.10 of IFRS 9, those transaction costs are amortised to profit or loss using the effective interest method and, in effect, amortised through profit or loss over the life of the instrument.

Transaction costs expected to be incurred on transfer or disposal of a financial instrument are not included in the measurement of the financial instrument.

E.3 Gains and losses

E.3.2 IFRS 9 and IAS 21—financial assets measured at fair value through other comprehensive income: separation of currency component
[Refer:

paragraphs 4.1.2A, 5.7.10, B5.7.2 and B5.7.2A

IAS 21 paragraphs 22, 23(a) and 28]

A financial asset measured at fair value through other comprehensive income in accordance with paragraph 4.1.2A of IFRS 9 is treated as a monetary item. Therefore, the entity recognises changes in the carrying amount relating to changes in foreign exchange rates in profit or loss in accordance with paragraphs 23(a) and 28 of IAS 21 and other changes in the carrying amount in other comprehensive income in accordance with IFRS 9. How is the cumulative gain or loss that is recognised in other comprehensive income determined?

It is the difference between the amortised cost of the financial asset[2] and the fair value of the financial asset in the functional currency of the reporting entity. For the purpose of applying paragraph 28 of IAS 21 the asset is treated as an asset measured at amortised cost in the foreign currency.

To illustrate: on 31 December 20X1 Entity A acquires a bond denominated in a foreign currency (FC) for its fair value of FC1,000. The bond has five years remaining to maturity and a contractual par amount of FC1,250, carries fixed interest of 4.7 per cent that is paid annually (FC1,250 × 4.7% = FC59 per year), and has an effective interest rate of 10 per cent. Entity A classifies the bond as subsequently measured at fair value through other comprehensive income in accordance with paragraph 4.1.2A of IFRS 9, and thus recognises gains and losses in other comprehensive income. The entity's functional currency is its local currency (LC). The exchange rate is FC1 to LC1.5 and the carrying amount of the bond is LC1,500 (= FC1,000 × 1.5).

Dr Bond	LC1,500	
Cr Cash		LC1,500

---

2 The objective of this example is to illustrate the separation of the currency component for a financial asset that is measured at fair value through other comprehensive income in accordance with paragraph 4.1.2A of IFRS 9. Consequently, for simplicity, this example does not reflect the effect of the impairment requirements in Section 5.5 of IFRS 9.

On 31 December 20X2, the foreign currency has appreciated and the exchange rate is FC1 to LC2. The fair value of the bond is FC1,060 and thus the carrying amount is LC2,120 (= FC1,060 × 2). The amortised cost is FC1,041 (= LC2,082). In this case, the cumulative gain or loss to be recognised in other comprehensive income and accumulated in equity is the difference between the fair value and the amortised cost on 31 December 20X2, ie LC38 (= LC2,120 − LC2,082).

Interest received on the bond on 31 December 20X2 is FC59 (= LC118). Interest revenue determined in accordance with the effective interest method is FC100 (= FC1,000 × 10 per cent). The average exchange rate during the year is FC1 to LC1.75. For the purpose of this question, it is assumed that the use of the average exchange rate provides a reliable approximation of the spot rates applicable to the accrual of interest revenue during the year (see paragraph 22 of IAS 21). Thus, reported interest revenue is LC175 (= FC100 × 1.75) including accretion of the initial discount of LC72 (= [FC100 − FC59] × 1.75). Accordingly, the exchange difference on the bond that is recognised in profit or loss is LC510 (= LC2,082 − LC1,500 − LC72). Also, there is an exchange gain on the interest receivable for the year of LC15 (= FC59 × [2.00 − 1.75]).

Dr	Bond		LC620	
Dr	Cash		LC118	
	Cr	Interest revenue		LC175
	Cr	Exchange gain		LC525
	Cr	Fair value change in other comprehensive income		LC38

On 31 December 20X3, the foreign currency has appreciated further and the exchange rate is FC1 to LC2.50. The fair value of the bond is FC1,070 and thus the carrying amount is LC2,675 (= FC1,070 × 2.50). The amortised cost is FC1,086 (= LC2,715). The cumulative gain or loss to be accumulated in other comprehensive income is the difference between the fair value and the amortised cost on 31 December 20X3, ie negative LC40 (= LC2,675 − LC2,715). Thus, the amount recognised in other comprehensive income equals the change in the difference during 20X3 of LC78 (= LC40 + LC38).

Interest received on the bond on 31 December 20X3 is FC59 (= LC148). Interest revenue determined in accordance with the effective interest method is FC104 (= FC1,041 × 10%). The average exchange rate during the year is FC1 to LC2.25. For the purpose of this question, it is assumed that the use of the average exchange rate provides a reliable approximation of the spot rates applicable to the accrual of interest revenue during the year (see paragraph 22 of IAS 21). Thus, recognised interest revenue is LC234 (= FC104 × 2.25) including accretion of the initial discount of LC101 (= [FC104 − FC59] × 2.25). Accordingly, the exchange difference on the bond that is recognised in profit or loss is LC532 (= LC2,715 − LC2,082 − LC101). Also, there is an exchange gain on the interest receivable for the year of LC15 (= FC59 × [2.50 − 2.25]).

Dr	Bond	LC555	
Dr	Cash	LC148	
Dr	Fair value change in other comprehensive income	LC78	
	Cr Interest revenue		LC234
	Cr Exchange gain		LC547

E.3.3 IFRS 9 and IAS 21—exchange differences arising on translation of foreign entities: other comprehensive income or profit or loss?
[Refer:
paragraphs 5.7.10–5.7.11 and B5.7.2–B5.7.2A
IAS 21 paragraphs 22, 32, 39 and 48]

Paragraphs 32 and 48 of IAS 21 state that all exchange differences resulting from translating the financial statements of a foreign operation should be recognised in other comprehensive income until disposal of the net investment. This would include exchange differences arising from financial instruments carried at fair value, which would include both financial assets measured at fair value through profit or loss and financial assets that are measured at fair value through other comprehensive income in accordance with IFRS 9.

IFRS 9 requires that changes in fair value of financial assets measured at fair value through profit or loss should be recognised in profit or loss and changes in fair value of financial assets measured at fair value through other comprehensive income should be recognised in other comprehensive income.

If the foreign operation is a subsidiary whose financial statements are consolidated with those of its parent, in the consolidated financial statements how are IFRS 9 and paragraph 39 of IAS 21 applied?

IFRS 9 applies in the accounting for financial instruments in the financial statements of a foreign operation and IAS 21 applies in translating the financial statements of a foreign operation for incorporation in the financial statements of the reporting entity.

To illustrate: Entity A is domiciled in Country X and its functional currency and presentation currency are the local currency of Country X (LCX). A has a foreign subsidiary (Entity B) in Country Y whose functional currency is the local currency of Country Y (LCY). B is the owner of a debt instrument, which meets the definition of held for trading and is therefore measured at fair value through profit or loss in accordance with IFRS 9.

In B's financial statements for year 20X0, the fair value and carrying amount of the debt instrument is LCY100 in the local currency of Country Y. In A's consolidated financial statements, the asset is translated into the local currency of Country X at the spot exchange rate applicable at the end of the reporting period (2.00). Thus, the carrying amount is LCX200 (= LCY100 × 2.00) in the consolidated financial statements.

At the end of year 20X1, the fair value of the debt instrument has increased to LCY110 in the local currency of Country Y. B recognises the trading asset at LCY110 in its statement of financial position and recognises a fair value gain of LCY10 in its profit or loss. During the year, the spot exchange rate has increased from 2.00 to 3.00 resulting in an increase in the fair value of the instrument from LCX200 to LCX330 (= LCY110 × 3.00) in the currency of Country X. Therefore, Entity A recognises the trading asset at LCX330 in its consolidated financial statements.

Entity A translates the statement of comprehensive income of B 'at the exchange rates at the dates of the transactions' (paragraph 39(b) of IAS 21). Since the fair value gain has accrued through the year, A uses the average rate as a practical approximation ([3.00 + 2.00] / 2 = 2.50, in accordance with paragraph 22 of IAS 21). Therefore, while the fair value of the trading asset has increased by LCX130 (= LCX330 − LCX200), Entity A recognises only LCX25 (= LCY10 × 2.5) of this increase in consolidated profit or loss to comply with paragraph 39(b) of IAS 21. The resulting exchange difference, ie the remaining increase in the fair value of the debt instrument (LCX130 − LCX25 = LCX105), is accumulated in other comprehensive income until the disposal of the net investment in the foreign operation in accordance with paragraph 48 of IAS 21.

E.3.4 IFRS 9 and IAS 21—interaction between IFRS 9 and IAS 21
[Refer:
paragraphs 5.7.5, 5.7.10, B5.7.2, B5.7.2A and B5.7.3
IAS 21 paragraphs 23–24, 28 and 32]

IFRS 9 includes requirements about the measurement of financial assets and financial liabilities and the recognition of gains and losses on remeasurement in profit or loss. IAS 21 includes rules about the reporting of foreign currency items and the recognition of exchange differences in profit or loss. In what order are IAS 21 and IFRS 9 applied?

Statement of financial position

Generally, the measurement of a financial asset or financial liability at fair value or amortised cost is first determined in the foreign currency in which the item is denominated in accordance with IFRS 9. Then, the foreign currency amount is translated into the functional currency using the closing rate or a historical rate in accordance with IAS 21 (paragraph B5.7.2 of IFRS 9). For example, if a monetary financial asset (such as a debt instrument) is measured at amortised cost in accordance with IFRS 9, amortised cost is calculated in the currency of denomination of that financial asset. Then, the foreign currency amount is recognised using the closing rate in the entity's financial statements (paragraph 23 of IAS 21). That applies regardless of whether a monetary item is measured at amortised cost or fair value in the foreign currency (paragraph 24 of IAS 21). A non-monetary financial asset (such as an investment in an equity instrument) that is measured at fair value in the foreign currency is translated using the closing rate (paragraph 23(c) of IAS 21).

As an exception, if the financial asset or financial liability is designated as a hedged item in a fair value hedge of the exposure to changes in foreign currency rates under IFRS 9 (or IAS 39 if an entity chooses as it accounting policy to continue to apply the hedge accounting requirements in IAS 39), the hedged item is remeasured for changes in foreign currency rates even if it would otherwise have been recognised using a historical rate under IAS 21 (paragraph 6.5.8 of IFRS 9 or paragraph 89 of IAS 39), ie the foreign currency amount is recognised using the closing rate. This exception applies to non-monetary items that are carried in terms of historical cost in the foreign currency and are hedged against exposure to foreign currency rates (paragraph 23(b) of IAS 21).

Profit or loss

The recognition of a change in the carrying amount of a financial asset or financial liability in profit or loss depends on a number of factors, including whether it is an exchange difference or other change in carrying amount, whether it arises on a monetary item (for example, most debt instruments) or non-monetary item (such as most equity investments), whether the associated asset or liability is designated as a cash flow hedge of an exposure to changes in foreign currency rates, and whether it results from translating the financial statements of a foreign operation. The issue of recognising changes in the carrying amount of a financial asset or financial liability held by a foreign operation is addressed in a separate question (see Question E.3.3).

Any exchange difference arising on recognising *a monetary item* at a rate different from that at which it was initially recognised during the period, or recognised in previous financial statements, is recognised in profit or loss in accordance with IAS 21 (paragraph B5.7.2 of IFRS 9, paragraphs 28 and 32 of IAS 21), unless the monetary item is designated as a cash flow hedge of a highly probable forecast transaction in foreign currency, in which case the requirements for recognition of gains and losses on cash flow hedges apply (paragraph 6.5.11 of IFRS 9 or paragraph 95 of IAS 39). Differences arising from recognising a monetary item at a foreign currency amount different from that at which it was previously recognised are accounted for in a similar manner, since all changes in the carrying amount relating to foreign currency movements should be treated consistently. All other changes in the statement of financial position measurement of a monetary item are recognised in profit or loss in accordance with IFRS 9. For example, although an entity recognises gains and losses on financial assets measured at fair value through other comprehensive income in other comprehensive income (paragraphs 5.7.10 and B5.7.2A of IFRS 9), the entity nevertheless recognises the changes in the carrying amount relating to changes in foreign exchange rates in profit or loss (paragraph 23(a) of IAS 21).

Any changes in the carrying amount of a *non-monetary item* are recognised in profit or loss or in other comprehensive income in accordance with IFRS 9. For example, for an investment in an equity instrument that is presented in accordance with paragraph 5.7.5 of IFRS 9, the entire change in the carrying amount, including the effect of changes in foreign currency rates, is presented in other comprehensive income (paragraph B5.7.3 of IFRS 9). If the non-monetary item is designated as a cash flow hedge of an unrecognised firm commitment or a highly probable forecast transaction in foreign currency, the requirements for recognition of gains and losses on cash flow hedges apply (paragraph 6.5.11 of IFRS 9 or paragraph 95 of IAS 39).

When some portion of the change in carrying amount is recognised in other comprehensive income and some portion is recognised in profit or loss, for example, if the amortised cost of a foreign currency bond measured at fair value through other comprehensive income has increased in foreign currency (resulting in a gain in profit or loss) but its fair value has decreased in foreign currency (resulting in a loss recognised in other comprehensive income), an entity cannot offset those two components for the purposes of determining gains or losses that should be recognised in profit or loss or in other comprehensive income.

Section G Other

G.2 IFRS 9 and IAS 7—hedge accounting: statements of cash flows

How should cash flows arising from hedging instruments be classified in statements of cash flows?

Cash flows arising from hedging instruments are classified as operating, investing or financing activities, on the basis of the classification of the cash flows arising from the hedged item. While the terminology in IAS 7 has not been updated to reflect IFRS 9, the classification of cash flows arising from hedging instruments in the statement of cash flows should be consistent with the classification of these instruments as hedging instruments under IFRS 9.

Appendix
Amendments to guidance on other Standards

The amendments in this appendix to the guidance on other Standards are necessary in order to ensure consistency with IFRS 9 and the related amendments to other Standards.

* * * * *

The amendments contained in this appendix when IFRS 9 was issued in 2014 have been incorporated into the guidance on the relevant Standards included in this volume.

IASB documents published to accompany

IFRS 10

Consolidated Financial Statements

The text of the unaccompanied standard, IFRS 10, is contained in Part A of this edition. The text of the Basis for Conclusions on IFRS 10 is contained in Part C of this edition. Its effective date when issued was 1 January 2013. This part presents the following documents:

ILLUSTRATIVE EXAMPLES

AMENDMENTS TO GUIDANCE ON OTHER IFRSS

Illustrative Examples

These examples accompany, but are not part of, the IFRS.

Example 1

IE1   An entity, Limited Partnership, is formed in 20X1 as a limited partnership with a 10-year life. The offering memorandum states that Limited Partnership's purpose is to invest in entities with rapid growth potential, with the objective of realising capital appreciation over their life. Entity GP (the general partner of Limited Partnership) provides 1 per cent of the capital to Limited Partnership and has the responsibility of identifying suitable investments for the partnership. Approximately 75 limited partners, who are unrelated to Entity GP, provide 99 per cent of the capital to the partnership.

IE2   Limited Partnership begins its investment activities in 20X1. However, no suitable investments are identified by the end of 20X1. In 20X2 Limited Partnership acquires a controlling interest in one entity, ABC Corporation. Limited Partnership is unable to close another investment transaction until 20X3, at which time it acquires equity interests in five additional operating companies. Other than acquiring these equity interests, Limited Partnership conducts no other activities. Limited Partnership measures and evaluates its investments on a fair value basis and this information is provided to Entity GP and the external investors.

IE3   Limited Partnership has plans to dispose of its interests in each of its investees during the 10-year stated life of the partnership. Such disposals include the outright sale for cash, the distribution of marketable equity securities to investors following the successful public offering of the investees' securities and the disposal of investments to the public or other unrelated entities.

Conclusion

IE4   From the information provided, Limited Partnership meets the definition of an investment entity from formation in 20X1 to 31 December 20X3 because the following conditions exist:

    (a)   Limited Partnership has obtained funds from the limited partners and is providing those limited partners with investment management services; **[Refer: paragraph 27(a)]**

    (b)   Limited Partnership's only activity is acquiring equity interests in operating companies with the purpose of realising capital appreciation over the life of the investments. Limited Partnership has identified and documented exit strategies for its investments, all of which are equity investments **[Refer: paragraphs 27(b) and B85B–B85J]**; and

    (c)   Limited Partnership measures and evaluates its investments on a fair value basis and reports this financial information to its investors. **[Refer: paragraphs 27(c) and B85K–B85M]**

IE5   In addition, Limited Partnership displays the following typical characteristics of an investment entity:

(a)   Limited Partnership is funded by many investors; **[Refer: paragraphs 28(b) and B85Q–B85S]**

(b)   its limited partners are unrelated to Limited Partnership **[Refer: paragraphs 28(c) and B85T–B85U]**; and

(c)   ownership in Limited Partnership is represented by units of partnership interests acquired through a capital contribution. **[Refer: paragraphs 28(d) and B85V–B85W]**

IE6   Limited Partnership does not hold more than one investment throughout the period. However, this is because it was still in its start-up period and had not identified suitable investment opportunities. **[Refer: paragraphs 28(a) and B85O–B85P]**

Example 2

IE7   High Technology Fund was formed by Technology Corporation to invest in technology start-up companies for capital appreciation. Technology Corporation holds a 70 per cent interest in High Technology Fund and controls High Technology Fund; the other 30 per cent ownership interest in High Technology Fund is owned by 10 unrelated investors. Technology Corporation holds options to acquire investments held by High Technology Fund, at their fair value, which would be exercised if the technology developed by the investees would benefit the operations of Technology Corporation. No plans for exiting the investments have been identified by High Technology Fund. High Technology Fund is managed by an investment adviser that acts as agent for the investors in High Technology Fund.

Conclusion

IE8   Even though High Technology Fund's business purpose is investing for capital appreciation and it provides investment management services to its investors **[Refer: paragraph 27(b)]**, High Technology Fund is not an investment entity because of the following arrangements and circumstances:

(a)   Technology Corporation, the parent of High Technology Fund, holds options to acquire investments in investees held by High Technology Fund if the assets developed by the investees would benefit the operations of Technology Corporation. This provides a benefit in addition to capital appreciation or investment income; and **[Refer: paragraphs 27(b) and B85I]**

(b)   the investment plans of High Technology Fund do not include exit strategies for its investments, which are equity investments. The options held by Technology Corporation are not controlled by High Technology Fund and do not constitute an exit strategy. **[Refer: paragraphs B85F–B85H]**

Example 3

IE9   Real Estate Entity was formed to develop, own and operate retail, office and other commercial properties. Real Estate Entity typically holds its property in separate wholly-owned subsidiaries, which have no other substantial assets or liabilities other than borrowings used to finance the related investment property. Real Estate Entity and each of its subsidiaries report their investment properties at fair value in accordance with IAS 40 *Investment Property*. Real Estate Entity does not have a set time frame for disposing of its property investments, but uses fair value to help identify the optimal time for disposal. Although fair value is one performance indicator, Real Estate Entity and its investors use other measures, including information about expected cash flows, rental revenues and expenses, to assess performance and to make investment decisions. The key management personnel of Real Estate Entity do not consider fair value information to be the primary measurement attribute to evaluate the performance of its investments but rather a part of a group of equally relevant key performance indicators.

IE10   Real Estate Entity undertakes extensive property and asset management activities, including property maintenance, capital expenditure, redevelopment, marketing and tenant selection, some of which it outsources to third parties. This includes the selection of properties for refurbishment, development and the negotiation with suppliers for the design and construction work to be done to develop such properties. This development activity forms a separate substantial part of Real Estate Entity's business activities.

Conclusion

IE11   Real Estate Entity does not meet the definition of an investment entity because:

    (a)   Real Estate Entity has a separate substantial business activity that involves the active management of its property portfolio, including lease negotiations, refurbishments and development activities, and marketing of properties to provide benefits other than capital appreciation, investment income, or both; **[Refer: paragraphs 27(b) and B85B]**

    (b)   the investment plans of Real Estate Entity do not include specified exit strategies for its investments. As a result, Real Estate Entity plans to hold those property investments indefinitely **[Refer: paragraphs B85F–B85H]**; and

    (c)   although Real Estate Entity reports its investment properties at fair value in accordance with IAS 40, fair value is not the primary measurement attribute used by management to evaluate the performance of its investments. Other performance indicators are used to evaluate performance and make investment decisions. **[Refer: paragraphs 27(c) and B85K]**

Example 4

IE12   An entity, Master Fund, is formed in 20X1 with a 10-year life. The equity of Master Fund is held by two related feeder funds. The feeder funds are established in connection with each other to meet legal, regulatory, tax or similar requirements. The feeder funds are capitalised with a 1 per cent investment from the general partner and 99 per cent from equity investors that are unrelated to the general partner (with no party holding a controlling financial interest).

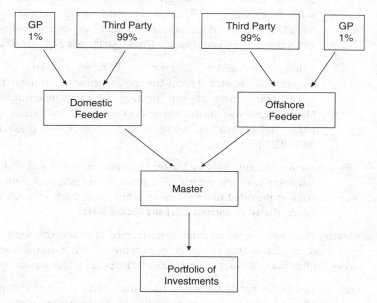

IE13   The purpose of Master Fund is to hold a portfolio of investments in order to generate capital appreciation and investment income (such as dividends, interest or rental income). The investment objective communicated to investors is that the sole purpose of the Master-Feeder structure is to provide investment opportunities for investors in separate market niches to invest in a large pool of assets. Master Fund has identified and documented exit strategies for the equity and non-financial investments that it holds. Master Fund holds a portfolio of short- and medium-term debt investments, some of which will be held until maturity and some of which will be traded but Master Fund has not specifically identified which investments will be held and which will be traded. Master Fund measures and evaluates substantially all of its investments, including its debt investments, on a fair value basis. In addition, investors receive periodic financial information, on a fair value basis, from the feeder funds. Ownership in both Master Fund and the feeder funds is represented through units of equity.

Conclusion

IE14   Master Fund and the feeder funds each meet the definition of an investment entity. The following conditions exist:

(a)   both Master Fund and the feeder funds have obtained funds for the purpose of providing investors with investment management services; **[Refer: paragraph 27(a)]**

(b)   the Master-Feeder structure's business purpose, which was communicated directly to investors of the feeder funds, is investing solely for capital appreciation and investment income and Master Fund has identified and documented potential exit strategies for its equity and non-financial investments. **[Refer: paragraphs 27(b) and B85F–B85H]**

(c)   although the feeder funds do not have an exit strategy for their interests in Master Fund, the feeder funds can nevertheless be considered to have an exit strategy for their investments because Master Fund was formed in connection with the feeder funds and holds investments on behalf of the feeder funds **[Refer: paragraphs B85F–B85H]**; and

(d)   the investments held by Master Fund are measured and evaluated on a fair value basis and information about the investments made by Master Fund is provided to investors on a fair value basis through the feeder funds. **[Refer: paragraphs 27(c) and B85K–B85M]**

IE15   Master Fund and the feeder funds were formed in connection with each other for legal, regulatory, tax or similar requirements. When considered together, they display the following typical characteristics of an investment entity:

(a)   the feeder funds indirectly hold more than one investment because Master Fund holds a portfolio of investments; **[Refer: paragraphs 28(a) and B85O]**

(b)   although Master Fund is wholly capitalised by the feeder funds, the feeder funds are funded by many investors who are unrelated to the feeder funds (and to the general partner) **[Refer: paragraphs 28(b), 28(c), B85R and B85T]**; and

(c)   ownership in the feeder funds is represented by units of equity interests acquired through a capital contribution. **[Refer: paragraphs 28(d) and B85V]**

Amendments to guidance on other IFRSs

The following amendments to guidance on IFRSs are necessary in order to ensure consistency with IFRS 10 and the related amendments to other IFRSs. Amended paragraphs are shown with new text underlined and deleted text struck through.

* * * * *

The amendments contained in this appendix when IFRS 10 was issued in 2011 have been incorporated into the guidance on the relevant IFRSs published in this volume.

IASB documents published to accompany

IFRS 11

Joint Arrangements

The text of the unaccompanied standard, IFRS 11, is contained in Part A of this edition. The text of the Basis for Conclusions on IFRS 11 is contained in Part C of this edition. Its effective date when issued was 1 January 2013. This part presents the following document:

ILLUSTRATIVE EXAMPLES

Contents

IFRS 11 *Joint Arrangements*
Illustrative Examples

These examples accompany, but are not part of, IFRS 11. They illustrate aspects of IFRS 11 but are not intended to provide interpretative guidance.

IE1   These examples portray hypothetical situations illustrating the judgements that might be used when applying IFRS 11 in different situations. Although some aspects of the examples may be present in actual fact patterns, all relevant facts and circumstances of a particular fact pattern would need to be evaluated when applying IFRS 11.

Example 1 – Construction services

IE2   A and B (the parties) are two companies whose businesses are the provision of many types of public and private construction services. They set up a contractual arrangement to work together for the purpose of fulfilling a contract with a government for the design and construction of a road between two cities. The contractual arrangement determines the participation shares of A and B and establishes joint control of the arrangement, the subject matter of which is the delivery of the road.

IE3   The parties set up a separate vehicle (entity Z) through which to conduct the arrangement. Entity Z, on behalf of A and B, enters into the contract with the government. In addition, the assets and liabilities relating to the arrangement are held in entity Z. The main feature of entity Z's legal form is that the parties, not entity Z, have rights to the assets, and obligations for the liabilities, of the entity.

IE4   The contractual arrangement between A and B additionally establishes that:

   (a)   the rights to all the assets needed to undertake the activities of the arrangement are shared by the parties on the basis of their participation shares in the arrangement;

   (b)   the parties have several and joint responsibility for all operating and financial obligations relating to the activities of the arrangement on the basis of their participation shares in the arrangement; and

   (c)   the profit or loss resulting from the activities of the arrangement is shared by A and B on the basis of their participation shares in the arrangement.

IE5   For the purposes of co-ordinating and overseeing the activities, A and B appoint an operator, who will be an employee of one of the parties. After a specified time, the role of the operator will rotate to an employee of the other party. A and B agree that the activities will be executed by the operator's employees on a 'no gain or loss' basis.

IE6   In accordance with the terms specified in the contract with the government, entity Z invoices the construction services to the government on behalf of the parties.

Analysis

IE7 The joint arrangement is carried out through a separate vehicle whose legal form does not confer separation between the parties and the separate vehicle (ie the assets and liabilities held in entity Z are the parties' assets and liabilities). **[Refer: paragraph B24]** This is reinforced by the terms agreed by the parties in their contractual arrangement, which state that A and B have rights to the assets, and obligations for the liabilities, relating to the arrangement that is conducted through entity Z. **[Refer: paragraphs B25 and B28]** The joint arrangement is a joint operation. **[Refer: paragraph 15]**

IE8 A and B each recognise in their financial statements their share of the assets (eg property, plant and equipment, accounts receivable) and their share of any liabilities resulting from the arrangement (eg accounts payable to third parties) on the basis of their agreed participation share. Each also recognises its share of the revenue and expenses resulting from the construction services provided to the government through entity Z.
[Refer: paragraph 20]

Example 2 – Shopping centre operated jointly

IE9 Two real estate companies (the parties) set up a separate vehicle (entity X) for the purpose of acquiring and operating a shopping centre. The contractual arrangement between the parties establishes joint control of the activities that are conducted in entity X. The main feature of entity X's legal form is that the entity, not the parties, has rights to the assets, and obligations for the liabilities, relating to the arrangement. These activities include the rental of the retail units, managing the car park, maintaining the centre and its equipment, such as lifts, and building the reputation and customer base for the centre as a whole.

IE10 The terms of the contractual arrangement are such that:

(a) entity X owns the shopping centre. The contractual arrangement does not specify that the parties have rights to the shopping centre.

(b) the parties are not liable in respect of the debts, liabilities or obligations of entity X. If entity X is unable to pay any of its debts or other liabilities or to discharge its obligations to third parties, the liability of each party to any third party will be limited to the unpaid amount of that party's capital contribution.

(c) the parties have the right to sell or pledge their interests in entity X.

(d) each party receives a share of the income from operating the shopping centre (which is the rental income net of the operating costs) in accordance with its interest in entity X.

Analysis

IE11 The joint arrangement is carried out through a separate vehicle whose legal form causes the separate vehicle to be considered in its own right (ie the assets and liabilities held in the separate vehicle are the assets and liabilities of the separate vehicle and not the assets and liabilities of the parties). **[Refer: paragraph B23]** In addition, the terms of the contractual arrangement do not specify that the parties have rights to the assets, or obligations for the liabilities, relating to the arrangement. Instead, the terms of the contractual arrangement establish that the parties have rights to the net assets of entity X. **[Refer: paragraph B25]**

IE12 On the basis of the description above, there are no other facts and circumstances that indicate that the parties have rights to substantially all the economic benefits of the assets relating to the arrangement, and that the parties have an obligation for the liabilities relating to the arrangement. **[Refer: paragraphs B29–B33]** The joint arrangement is a joint venture. **[Refer: paragraph 16]**

IE13 The parties recognise their rights to the net assets of entity X as investments and account for them using the equity method. **[Refer: paragraph 24]**

Example 3 – Joint manufacturing and distribution of a product

IE14 Companies A and B (the parties) have set up a strategic and operating agreement (the framework agreement) in which they have agreed the terms according to which they will conduct the manufacturing and distribution of a product (product P) in different markets.

IE15 The parties have agreed to conduct manufacturing and distribution activities by establishing joint arrangements, as described below:

(a) Manufacturing activity: the parties have agreed to undertake the manufacturing activity through a joint arrangement (the manufacturing arrangement). The manufacturing arrangement is structured in a separate vehicle (entity M) whose legal form causes it to be considered in its own right (ie the assets and liabilities held in entity M are the assets and liabilities of entity M and not the assets and liabilities of the parties). In accordance with the framework agreement, the parties have committed themselves to purchasing the whole production of product P manufactured by the manufacturing arrangement in accordance with their ownership interests in entity M. The parties subsequently sell product P to another arrangement, jointly controlled by the two parties themselves, that has been established exclusively for the distribution of product P as described below. Neither the framework agreement nor the contractual arrangement between A and B dealing with the manufacturing activity specifies that the parties have rights to the assets, and obligations for the liabilities, relating to the manufacturing activity.

(b) Distribution activity: the parties have agreed to undertake the distribution activity through a joint arrangement (the distribution arrangement). The parties have structured the distribution arrangement in a separate vehicle (entity D) whose legal form causes it to be considered in its own right (ie the assets and liabilities held in entity D are the assets and liabilities of entity D and not the assets and liabilities of the parties). In accordance with the framework agreement, the distribution arrangement orders its requirements for product P from the parties according to the needs of the different markets where the distribution arrangement sells the product. Neither the framework agreement nor the contractual arrangement between A and B dealing with the distribution activity specifies that the parties have rights to the assets, and obligations for the liabilities, relating to the distribution activity.

IE16 In addition, the framework agreement establishes:

(a) that the manufacturing arrangement will produce product P to meet the requirements for product P that the distribution arrangement places on the parties;

(b) the commercial terms relating to the sale of product P by the manufacturing arrangement to the parties. The manufacturing arrangement will sell product P to the parties at a price agreed by A and B that covers all production costs incurred. Subsequently, the parties sell the product to the distribution arrangement at a price agreed by A and B.

(c) that any cash shortages that the manufacturing arrangement may incur will be financed by the parties in accordance with their ownership interests in entity M.

Analysis

IE17 The framework agreement sets up the terms under which parties A and B conduct the manufacturing and distribution of product P. These activities are undertaken through joint arrangements whose purpose is either the manufacturing or the distribution of product P.

IE18 The parties carry out the manufacturing arrangement through entity M whose legal form confers separation between the parties and the entity. [Refer: paragraph B23] In addition, neither the framework agreement nor the contractual arrangement dealing with the manufacturing activity specifies that the parties have rights to the assets, and obligations for the liabilities, relating to the manufacturing activity. [Refer: paragraphs B25–B28] However, when considering the following facts and circumstances [Refer: paragraphs B29–B33] the parties have concluded that the manufacturing arrangement is a joint operation: [Refer: paragraph 15]

(a) The parties have committed themselves to purchasing the whole production of product P manufactured by the manufacturing arrangement. Consequently, A and B have rights to substantially all the economic benefits of the assets of the manufacturing arrangement. **[Refer: paragraph B31]**

(b) The manufacturing arrangement manufactures product P to meet the quantity and quality needs of the parties so that they can fulfil the demand for product P of the distribution arrangement. The exclusive dependence of the manufacturing arrangement upon the parties for the generation of cash flows and the parties' commitments to provide funds when the manufacturing arrangement incurs any cash shortages indicate that the parties have an obligation for the liabilities of the manufacturing arrangement, because those liabilities will be settled through the parties' purchases of product P or by the parties' direct provision of funds. **[Refer: paragraph B32]**

IE19 The parties carry out the distribution activities through entity D, whose legal form confers separation between the parties and the entity. In addition, neither the framework agreement nor the contractual arrangement dealing with the distribution activity specifies that the parties have rights to the assets, and obligations for the liabilities, relating to the distribution activity. **[Refer: paragraph B29]**

IE20 There are no other facts and circumstances that indicate that the parties have rights to substantially all the economic benefits of the assets relating to the distribution arrangement or that the parties have an obligation for the liabilities relating to that arrangement. **[Refer: paragraphs B29 and B31–B33]** The distribution arrangement is a joint venture. **[Refer: paragraph 16]**

IE21 A and B each recognise in their financial statements their share of the assets (eg property, plant and equipment, cash) and their share of any liabilities resulting from the manufacturing arrangement (eg accounts payable to third parties) on the basis of their ownership interest in entity M. Each party also recognises its share of the expenses resulting from the manufacture of product P incurred by the manufacturing arrangement and its share of the revenues relating to the sales of product P to the distribution arrangement. **[Refer: paragraph 20]**

IE22 The parties recognise their rights to the net assets of the distribution arrangement as investments and account for them using the equity method. **[Refer: paragraph 24]**

Variation

IE23 Assume that the parties agree that the manufacturing arrangement described above is responsible not only for manufacturing product P, but also for its distribution to third-party customers.

IE24 The parties also agree to set up a distribution arrangement like the one described above to distribute product P exclusively to assist in widening the distribution of product P in additional specific markets.

IE25   The manufacturing arrangement also sells product P directly to the distribution arrangement. No fixed proportion of the production of the manufacturing arrangement is committed to be purchased by, or to be reserved to, the distribution arrangement.

Analysis

IE26   The variation has affected neither the legal form of the separate vehicle in which the manufacturing activity is conducted nor the contractual terms relating to the parties' rights to the assets, and obligations for the liabilities, relating to the manufacturing activity. However, it causes the manufacturing arrangement to be a self-financed arrangement because it is able to undertake trade on its own behalf, distributing product P to third-party customers and, consequently, assuming demand, inventory and credit risks. Even though the manufacturing arrangement might also sell product P to the distribution arrangement, in this scenario the manufacturing arrangement is not dependent on the parties to be able to carry out its activities on a continuous basis. [Refer: paragraphs B29 and B31–B33] In this case, the manufacturing arrangement is a joint venture. [Refer: paragraph 16]

IE27   The variation has no effect on the classification of the distribution arrangement as a joint venture.

IE28   The parties recognise their rights to the net assets of the manufacturing arrangement and their rights to the net assets of the distribution arrangement as investments and account for them using the equity method. [Refer: paragraph 24]

Example 4 – Bank operated jointly

IE29   Banks A and B (the parties) agreed to combine their corporate, investment banking, asset management and services activities by establishing a separate vehicle (bank C). Both parties expect the arrangement to benefit them in different ways. Bank A believes that the arrangement could enable it to achieve its strategic plans to increase its size, offering an opportunity to exploit its full potential for organic growth through an enlarged offering of products and services. Bank B expects the arrangement to reinforce its offering in financial savings and market products.

IE30   The main feature of bank C's legal form is that it causes the separate vehicle to be considered in its own right (ie the assets and liabilities held in the separate vehicle are the assets and liabilities of the separate vehicle and not the assets and liabilities of the parties). Banks A and B each have a 40 per cent ownership interest in bank C, with the remaining 20 per cent being listed and widely held. The shareholders' agreement between bank A and bank B establishes joint control of the activities of bank C. [Refer: paragraphs 4 and 5]

IE31   In addition, bank A and bank B entered into an irrevocable agreement under which, even in the event of a dispute, both banks agree to provide the necessary funds in equal amount and, if required, jointly and severally, to ensure that bank C complies with the applicable legislation and banking regulations, and honours any commitments made to the banking authorities. This commitment represents the assumption by each party of 50 per cent of any funds needed to ensure that bank C complies with legislation and banking regulations.

Analysis

IE32   The joint arrangement is carried out through a separate vehicle whose legal form confers separation between the parties and the separate vehicle. **[Refer: paragraph B23]** The terms of the contractual arrangement do not specify that the parties have rights to the assets, or obligations for the liabilities, of bank C, but it establishes that the parties have rights to the net assets of bank C. The commitment by the parties to provide support if bank C is not able to comply with the applicable legislation and banking regulations is not by itself a determinant that the parties have an obligation for the liabilities of bank C. **[Refer: paragraph B25]** There are no other facts and circumstances that indicate that the parties have rights to substantially all the economic benefits of the assets of bank C and that the parties have an obligation for the liabilities of bank C. **[Refer: paragraphs B29–B33]** The joint arrangement is a joint venture. **[Refer: paragraph 16]**

IE33   Both banks A and B recognise their rights to the net assets of bank C as investments and account for them using the equity method. **[Refer: paragraph 24]**

Example 5 – Oil and gas exploration, development and production activities

IE34   Companies A and B (the parties) set up a separate vehicle (entity H) and a Joint Operating Agreement (JOA) to undertake oil and gas exploration, development and production activities in country O. The main feature of entity H's legal form is that it causes the separate vehicle to be considered in its own right (ie the assets and liabilities held in the separate vehicle are the assets and liabilities of the separate vehicle and not the assets and liabilities of the parties).

IE35   Country O has granted entity H permits for the oil and gas exploration, development and production activities to be undertaken in a specific assigned block of land (fields).

IE36   The shareholders' agreement and JOA agreed by the parties establish their rights and obligations relating to those activities. The main terms of those agreements are summarised below.

Shareholders' agreement

IE37   The board of entity H consists of a director from each party. Each party has a 50 per cent shareholding in entity H. The unanimous consent of the directors is required for any resolution to be passed.

Joint Operating Agreement (JOA)

IE38 The JOA establishes an Operating Committee. This Committee consists of one representative from each party. Each party has a 50 per cent participating interest in the Operating Committee.

IE39 The Operating Committee approves the budgets and work programmes relating to the activities, which also require the unanimous consent of the representatives of each party. One of the parties is appointed as operator and is responsible for managing and conducting the approved work programmes.

IE40 The JOA specifies that the rights and obligations arising from the exploration, development and production activities shall be shared among the parties in proportion to each party's shareholding in entity H. In particular, the JOA establishes that the parties share:

(a) the rights and the obligations arising from the exploration and development permits granted to entity H (eg the permits, rehabilitation liabilities, any royalties and taxes payable);

(b) the production obtained; and

(c) all costs associated with all work programmes.

IE41 The costs incurred in relation to all the work programmes are covered by cash calls on the parties. If either party fails to satisfy its monetary obligations, the other is required to contribute to entity H the amount in default. The amount in default is regarded as a debt owed by the defaulting party to the other party.

Analysis

IE42 The parties carry out the joint arrangement through a separate vehicle whose legal form confers separation between the parties and the separate vehicle. **[Refer: paragraph B23]** The parties have been able to reverse the initial assessment of their rights and obligations arising from the legal form of the separate vehicle in which the arrangement is conducted. They have done this by agreeing terms in the JOA that entitle them to rights to the assets (eg exploration and development permits, production, and any other assets arising from the activities) and obligations for the liabilities (eg all costs and obligations arising from the work programmes) that are held in entity H. **[Refer: paragraphs B26 and B28]** The joint arrangement is a joint operation. **[Refer: paragraph 15]**

IE43 Both company A and company B recognise in their financial statements their own share of the assets and of any liabilities resulting from the arrangement on the basis of their agreed participating interest. On that basis, each party also recognises its share of the revenue (from the sale of their share of the production) and its share of the expenses. **[Refer: paragraph 20]**

Example 6 – Liquefied natural gas arrangement

IE44   Company A owns an undeveloped gas field that contains substantial gas resources. Company A determines that the gas field will be economically viable only if the gas is sold to customers in overseas markets. To do so, a liquefied natural gas (LNG) facility must be built to liquefy the gas so that it can be transported by ship to the overseas markets.

IE45   Company A enters into a joint arrangement with company B in order to develop and operate the gas field and the LNG facility. Under that arrangement, companies A and B (the parties) agree to contribute the gas field and cash, respectively, to a new separate vehicle, entity C. In exchange for those contributions, the parties each take a 50 per cent ownership interest in entity C. The main feature of entity C's legal form is that it causes the separate vehicle to be considered in its own right (ie the assets and liabilities held in the separate vehicle are the assets and liabilities of the separate vehicle and not the assets and liabilities of the parties).

IE46   The contractual arrangement between the parties specifies that:

(a)   companies A and B must each appoint two members to the board of entity C. The board of directors must unanimously agree the strategy and investments made by entity C.

(b)   day-to-day management of the gas field and LNG facility, including development and construction activities, will be undertaken by the staff of company B in accordance with the directions jointly agreed by the parties. Entity C will reimburse B for the costs it incurs in managing the gas field and LNG facility.

(c)   entity C is liable for taxes and royalties on the production and sale of LNG as well as for other liabilities incurred in the ordinary course of business, such as accounts payable, site restoration and decommissioning liabilities.

(d)   companies A and B have equal shares in the profit from the activities carried out in the arrangement and, as such, are entitled to equal shares of any dividends distributed by entity C.

IE47   The contractual arrangement does not specify that either party has rights to the assets, or obligations for the liabilities, of entity C.

IE48   The board of entity C decides to enter into a financing arrangement with a syndicate of lenders to help fund the development of the gas field and construction of the LNG facility. The estimated total cost of the development and construction is CU1,000 million.[1]

IE49   The lending syndicate provides entity C with a CU700 million loan. The arrangement specifies that the syndicate has recourse to companies A and B only if entity C defaults on the loan arrangement during the development of the field and construction of the LNG facility. The lending syndicate agrees that it will not have recourse to companies A and B once the LNG facility is in

---

1   In these examples monetary amounts are denominated in 'currency units (CU)'.

production because it has assessed that the cash inflows that entity C should generate from LNG sales will be sufficient to meet the loan repayments. Although at this time the lenders have no recourse to companies A and B, the syndicate maintains protection against default by entity C by taking a lien on the LNG facility.

Analysis

IE50   The joint arrangement is carried out through a separate vehicle whose legal form confers separation between the parties and the separate vehicle. **[Refer: paragraph B23]** The terms of the contractual arrangement do not specify that the parties have rights to the assets, or obligations for the liabilities, of entity C, but they establish that the parties have rights to the net assets of entity C. **[Refer: paragraphs B25–B27]** The recourse nature of the financing arrangement during the development of the gas field and construction of the LNG facility (ie companies A and B providing separate guarantees during this phase) does not, by itself, impose on the parties an obligation for the liabilities of entity C (ie the loan is a liability of entity C). Companies A and B have separate liabilities, which are their guarantees to repay that loan if entity C defaults during the development and construction phase. **[Refer: IAS 37]**

IE51   There are no other facts and circumstances that indicate that the parties have rights to substantially all the economic benefits of the assets of entity C and that the parties have an obligation for the liabilities of entity C. **[Refer: paragraphs B29–B33]** The joint arrangement is a joint venture. **[Refer: paragraph 16]**

IE52   The parties recognise their rights to the net assets of entity C as investments and account for them using the equity method. **[Refer: paragraph 24]**

Example 7—Accounting for acquisitions of interests in joint operations in which the activity constitutes a business

[Refer: paragraphs 21A and B33A]

IE53   Companies A, B and C have joint control of Joint Operation D whose activity constitutes a business, as defined in IFRS 3 *Business Combinations* **[Refer: IFRS 3 Appendix A (definition of a business) and paragraphs B7–B12]**.

IE54   Company E acquires company A's 40 per cent ownership interest in Joint Operation D at a cost of CU300 and incurs acquisition-related costs of CU50.

IE55   The contractual arrangement between the parties that Company E joined as part of the acquisition establishes that Company E's shares in several assets and liabilities differ from its ownership interest in Joint Operation D. The following table sets out Company E's share in the assets and liabilities related to Joint Operation D as established in the contractual arrangement between the parties:

	Company E's share in the assets and liabilities related to Joint Operation D
Property, plant and equipment	48%
Intangible assets (excluding goodwill)	90%
Accounts receivable	40%
Inventory	40%
Retirement benefit obligations	15%
Accounts payable	40%
Contingent liabilities	56%

Analysis

IE56 Company E recognises in its financial statements its share of the assets and liabilities resulting from the contractual arrangement (see paragraph 20).

IE57 It applies the principles on business combinations accounting in IFRS 3 and other IFRSs for identifying, recognising, measuring and classifying the assets acquired, and the liabilities assumed, on the acquisition of the interest in Joint Operation D. This is because Company E acquired an interest in a joint operation in which the activity constitutes a business (see paragraph 21A).

IE58 However, Company E does not apply the principles on business combinations accounting in IFRS 3 and other IFRSs that conflict with the guidance in this IFRS. Consequently, in accordance with paragraph 20, Company E recognises, and therefore measures, in relation to its interest in Joint Operation D, only its share in each of the assets that are jointly held and in each of the liabilities that are incurred jointly, as stated in the contractual arrangement. Company E does not include in its assets and liabilities the shares of the other parties in Joint Operation D.

IE59 IFRS 3 requires the acquirer to measure the identifiable assets acquired and the liabilities assumed at their acquisition-date fair values with limited exceptions; for example, deferred tax assets and deferred tax liabilities are not measured at fair value but are measured in accordance with IAS 12 *Income Taxes*. Such measurement does not conflict with this IFRS and thus those requirements apply.

IE60 Consequently, Company E determines the fair value, or other measure specified in IFRS 3, of its share in the identifiable assets and liabilities related to Joint Operation D. The following table sets out the fair value or other measure specified by IFRS 3 of Company E's shares in the identifiable assets and liabilities related to Joint Operation D:

	Fair value or other measure specified by IFRS 3 for Company E's shares in the identifiable assets and liabilities of Joint Operation D CU
Property, plant and equipment	138
Intangible assets (excluding goodwill)	72
Accounts receivable	84
Inventory	70
Retirement benefit obligations	(12)
Accounts payable	(48)
Contingent liabilities	(52)
Deferred tax liability	(24)
Net assets	**228**

IE61 In accordance with IFRS 3, the excess of the consideration transferred over the amount allocated to Company E's shares in the net identifiable assets is recognised as goodwill:

Consideration transferred	CU300
Company E's shares in the identifiable assets and liabilities relating to its interest in the joint operation	CU228
Goodwill	**CU72**

IE62 Acquisition-related costs of CU50 are not considered to be part of the consideration transferred for the interest in the joint operation. They are recognised as expenses in profit or loss in the period that the costs are incurred and the services are received (see paragraph 53 of IFRS 3).

Example 8—Contributing the right to use know-how to a joint operation in which the activity constitutes a business

[Refer: paragraphs 21A and B33A]

IE63 Companies A and B are two companies whose business is the construction of high performance batteries for diverse applications.

IE64 In order to develop batteries for electric vehicles they set up a contractual arrangement (Joint Operation Z) to work together. Companies A and B share joint control of Joint Operation Z. This arrangement is a joint operation in which the activity constitutes a business, as defined in IFRS 3.

IE65   After several years, the joint operators (Companies A and B) concluded that it is feasible to develop a battery for electric vehicles using Material M. However, processing Material M requires specialist know-how and thus far, Material M has only been used in the production of cosmetics.

IE66   In order to get access to existing know-how in processing Material M, Companies A and B arrange for Company C to join as another joint operator by acquiring an interest in Joint Operation Z from Companies A and B and becoming a party to the contractual arrangements.

IE67   Company C's business so far has been solely the development and production of cosmetics. It has long-standing and extensive knowledge in processing Material M.

IE68   In exchange for its share in Joint Operation Z, Company C pays cash to Companies A and B and grants the right to use its know-how in processing Material M for the purposes of Joint Operation Z. In addition, Company C seconds some of its employees who are experienced in processing Material M to Joint Operation Z. However, Company C does not transfer control of the know-how to Companies A and B or Joint Operation Z because it retains all the rights to it. In particular, Company C is entitled to withdraw the right to use its know-how in processing Material M and to withdraw its seconded employees without any restrictions or compensation to Companies A and B or Joint Operation Z if it ceases its participation in Joint Operation Z.

IE69   The fair value of Company C's know-how on the date of the acquisition of the interest in the joint operation is CU1,000. Immediately before the acquisition, the carrying amount of the know-how in the financial statements of Company C was CU300.

Analysis

IE70   Company C has acquired an interest in Joint Operation Z in which the activity of the joint operation constitutes a business, as defined in IFRS 3.

IE71   In accounting for the acquisition of its interest in the joint operation, Company C applies all the principles on business combinations accounting in IFRS 3 and other IFRSs that do not conflict with the guidance in this IFRS (see paragraph 21A). Company C therefore recognises in its financial statements its share of the assets and liabilities resulting from the contractual arrangement (see paragraph 20).

IE72   Company C granted the right to use its know-how in processing Material M to Joint Operation Z as part of joining Joint Operation Z as a joint operator. However, Company C retains control of this right because it is entitled to withdraw the right to use its know-how in processing Material M and to withdraw its seconded employees without any restrictions or any compensation to Companies A and B or Joint Operation Z if it ceases its participation in Joint Operation Z.

IE73   Consequently, Company C continues to recognise the know-how in processing Material M after the acquisition of the interest in Joint Operation Z because it retains all the rights to it. This means that Company C will continue to recognise the know-how based on its carrying amount of CU300. As a consequence of retaining control of the right to use the know-how that it granted to the joint operation, Company C has granted the right to use the know-how to itself. Consequently, Company C does not remeasure the know-how, and it does not recognise a gain or loss on the grant of the right to use it.

IASB documents published to accompany

IFRS 13

Fair Value Measurement

The text of the unaccompanied standard, IFRS 13, is contained in Part A of this edition. The text of the Basis for Conclusions on IFRS 13 is contained in Part C of this edition. Its effective date when issued was 1 January 2013. This part presents the following documents:

ILLUSTRATIVE EXAMPLES

APPENDIX

Amendments to the guidance on other IFRSs

CONTENTS

IFRS 13 *Fair Value Measurement*
Illustrative Examples

These examples accompany, but are not part of, IFRS 13. They illustrate aspects of IFRS 13 but are not intended to provide interpretative guidance.

IE1   These examples portray hypothetical situations illustrating the judgements that might apply when an entity measures assets and liabilities at fair value in different valuation situations. Although some aspects of the examples may be present in actual fact patterns, all relevant facts and circumstances of a particular fact pattern would need to be evaluated when applying IFRS 13.

Highest and best use and valuation premise

IE2   Examples 1–3 illustrate the application of the highest and best use and valuation premise concepts for non-financial assets. **[Refer: paragraphs 27–33 and B3]**

Example 1—Asset group

IE3   An entity acquires assets and assumes liabilities in a business combination **[Refer: IFRS 3]**. One of the groups of assets acquired comprises Assets A, B and C. Asset C is billing software integral to the business developed by the acquired entity for its own use in conjunction with Assets A and B (ie the related assets) **[Refer: paragraph B3(e)]**. The entity measures the fair value of each of the assets individually, consistently with the specified unit of account for the assets. The entity determines that the highest and best use of the assets is their current use and that each asset would provide maximum value to market participants principally through its use in combination with other assets or with other assets and liabilities (ie its complementary assets and the associated liabilities). **[Refer: paragraph 31(a)]** There is no evidence to suggest that the current use of the assets is not their highest and best use. **[Refer: paragraph 29]**

IE4   In this situation, the entity would sell the assets in the market in which it initially acquired the assets (ie the entry and exit markets from the perspective of the entity are the same). **[Refer: paragraph 16]** Market participant **[Refer: paragraphs 22 and 23]** buyers with whom the entity would enter into a transaction in that market have characteristics **[Refer: paragraph 23]** that are generally representative of both strategic buyers (such as competitors) and financial buyers (such as private equity or venture capital firms that do not have complementary investments) and include those buyers that initially bid for the assets. Although market participant buyers might be broadly classified as strategic or financial buyers, in many cases there will be differences among the market participant buyers within each of those groups, reflecting, for example, different uses for an asset and different operating strategies.

IE5   As discussed below, differences between the indicated fair values of the individual assets relate principally to the use of the assets by those market participants within different asset groups:

(a)   Strategic buyer asset group. The entity determines that strategic buyers have related assets that would enhance the value of the group within which the assets would be used (ie market participant synergies). Those assets include a substitute asset for Asset C (the billing software), which would be used for only a limited transition period and could not be sold on its own at the end of that period. Because strategic buyers have substitute assets, Asset C would not be used for its full remaining economic life. The indicated fair values of Assets A, B and C within the strategic buyer asset group (reflecting the synergies resulting from the use of the assets within that group) are CU360,[1] CU260 and CU30, respectively. The indicated fair value of the assets as a group within the strategic buyer asset group is CU650.

(b)   Financial buyer asset group. The entity determines that financial buyers do not have related or substitute assets that would enhance the value of the group within which the assets would be used. Because financial buyers do not have substitute assets, Asset C (ie the billing software) would be used for its full remaining economic life. The indicated fair values of Assets A, B and C within the financial buyer asset group are CU300, CU200 and CU100, respectively. The indicated fair value of the assets as a group within the financial buyer asset group is CU600.

IE6   The fair values of Assets A, B and C would be determined on the basis of the use of the assets as a group within the strategic buyer group (CU360, CU260 and CU30). **[Refer: paragraph 31(a)]** Although the use of the assets within the strategic buyer group does not maximise the fair value of each of the assets individually, it maximises the fair value of the assets as a group (CU650).

Example 2—Land

IE7   An entity acquires land in a business combination **[Refer: IFRS 3]**. The land is currently developed for industrial use as a site for a factory. The current use of land is presumed to be its highest and best use unless market or other factors suggest a different use **[Refer: paragraph 29]**. Nearby sites have recently been developed for residential use as sites for high-rise apartment buildings. On the basis of that development and recent zoning and other changes to facilitate that development, the entity determines that the land currently used as a site for a factory could be developed as a site for residential use (ie for high-rise apartment buildings) because market participants would take into account the potential to develop the site for residential use when pricing the land. **[Refer: paragraph 29]**

IE8   The highest and best use of the land would be determined by comparing both of the following:

(a)   the value of the land as currently developed for industrial use (ie the land would be used in combination with other assets, such as the factory, or with other assets and liabilities).

---

1   In these examples, monetary amounts are denominated in 'currency units (CU)'.

(b) the value of the land as a vacant site for residential use, taking into account the costs of demolishing the factory and other costs (including the uncertainty about whether the entity would be able to convert the asset to the alternative use) necessary to convert the land to a vacant site (ie the land is to be used by market participants on a stand-alone basis **[Refer: paragraph 31(b)]**).

The highest and best use of the land would be determined on the basis of the higher of those values **[Refer: paragraphs 27–30]**. In situations involving real estate appraisal, the determination of highest and best use might take into account factors relating to the factory operations, including its assets and liabilities **[Refer: paragraph 31(a)]**.

Example 3—Research and development project

IE9 An entity acquires a research and development (R&D) project in a business combination **[Refer: IFRS 3]**. The entity does not intend to complete the project. If completed, the project would compete with one of its own projects (to provide the next generation of the entity's commercialised technology). Instead, the entity intends to hold (ie lock up) the project to prevent its competitors from obtaining access to the technology. In doing this the project is expected to provide defensive value **[Refer: paragraph 30]**, principally by improving the prospects for the entity's own competing technology. To measure the fair value of the project at initial recognition, the highest and best use of the project would be determined on the basis of its use by market participants. **[Refer: paragraphs 22, 23 and 29]** For example:

(a) The highest and best use **[Refer: paragraphs 27–30]** of the R&D project would be to continue development if market participants would continue to develop the project and that use would maximise the value of the group of assets or of assets and liabilities in which the project would be used (ie the asset would be used in combination with other assets or with other assets and liabilities). **[Refer: paragraph 31(a)]** That might be the case if market participants do not have similar technology, either in development or commercialised. The fair value of the project would be measured on the basis of the price that would be received in a current transaction to sell the project, assuming that the R&D would be used with its complementary assets and the associated liabilities and that those assets and liabilities would be available to market participants.

(b) The highest and best use of the R&D project would be to cease development if, for competitive reasons, market participants would lock up the project and that use would maximise the value of the group of assets or of assets and liabilities in which the project would be used. **[Refer: paragraph 31(a)]** That might be the case if market participants have technology in a more advanced stage of development that would compete with the project if completed and the project would be expected to improve the prospects for their own competing technology if locked up. The fair value of the project would be measured on the basis of the price that would be received in a current transaction to sell the project, assuming that the R&D would be used (ie locked up) with its complementary assets and the associated liabilities and that those assets and liabilities would be available to market participants.

(c) The highest and best use of the R&D project would be to cease development if market participants would discontinue its development. That might be the case if the project is not expected to provide a market rate of return if completed and would not otherwise provide defensive value if locked up. The fair value of the project would be measured on the basis of the price that would be received in a current transaction to sell the project on its own (which might be zero). [Refer: paragraph 31(b)]

Use of multiple valuation techniques

IE10   The IFRS notes that a single valuation technique will be appropriate in some cases. In other cases multiple valuation techniques will be appropriate. Examples 4 and 5 illustrate the use of multiple valuation techniques. [Refer: paragraphs 61–66 and B5–B30]

Example 4—Machine held and used

IE11   An entity acquires a machine in a business combination [Refer: IFRS 3]. The machine will be held and used in its operations. The machine was originally purchased by the acquired entity from an outside vendor and, before the business combination, was customised by the acquired entity for use in its operations. However, the customisation of the machine was not extensive. The acquiring entity determines that the asset would provide maximum value to market participants through its use in combination with other assets or with other assets and liabilities (as installed or otherwise configured for use). There is no evidence to suggest that the current use of the machine is not its highest and best use [Refer: paragraph 29]. Therefore, the highest and best use of the machine is its current use in combination with other assets or with other assets and liabilities. [Refer: paragraph 31(b)]

IE12   The entity determines that sufficient data are available to apply the cost approach [Refer: paragraphs B8 and B9] and, because the customisation of the machine was not extensive, the market approach [Refer: paragraphs B5–B7]. The income approach [Refer: paragraphs B10 and B11] is not used because the machine does not have a separately identifiable income stream from which to develop reliable estimates of future cash flows. Furthermore, information about short-term and intermediate-term lease rates for similar used machinery that otherwise could be used to project an income stream (ie lease payments over remaining service lives) is not available. The market and cost approaches are applied as follows:

(a) The market approach [Refer: paragraphs B5–B7] is applied using quoted prices for similar machines adjusted for differences between the machine (as customised) and the similar machines. The measurement reflects the price that would be received for the machine in its current condition (used) and location (installed and configured for use). The fair value indicated by that approach ranges from CU40,000 to CU48,000.

(b) The cost approach **[Refer: paragraphs B8 and B9]** is applied by estimating the amount that would be required currently to construct a substitute (customised) machine of comparable utility. The estimate takes into account the condition of the machine and the environment in which it operates, including physical wear and tear (ie physical deterioration), improvements in technology (ie functional obsolescence), conditions external to the condition of the machine such as a decline in the market demand for similar machines (ie economic obsolescence) and installation costs. The fair value indicated by that approach ranges from CU40,000 to CU52,000.

IE13 The entity determines that the higher end of the range indicated by the market approach is most representative of fair value and, therefore, ascribes more weight to the results of the market approach **[Refer: paragraph 63]**. That determination is made on the basis of the relative subjectivity of the inputs, taking into account the degree of comparability between the machine and the similar machines. In particular:

(a) the inputs used in the market approach (quoted prices for similar machines) require fewer and less subjective adjustments than the inputs used in the cost approach.

(b) the range indicated by the market approach overlaps with, but is narrower than, the range indicated by the cost approach.

(c) there are no known unexplained differences (between the machine and the similar machines) within that range.

Accordingly, the entity determines that the fair value of the machine is CU48,000.

IE14 If customisation of the machine was extensive or if there were not sufficient data available to apply the market approach (eg because market data reflect transactions for machines used on a stand-alone basis, such as a scrap value for specialised assets, rather than machines used in combination with other assets or with other assets and liabilities), the entity would apply the cost approach. When an asset is used in combination with other assets or with other assets and liabilities, the cost approach assumes the sale of the machine to a market participant buyer with the complementary assets and the associated liabilities **[Refer: paragraph 31(b)]**. The price received for the sale of the machine (ie an exit price) would not be more than either of the following:

(a) the cost that a market participant buyer would incur to acquire or construct a substitute machine of comparable utility; or

(b) the economic benefit that a market participant buyer would derive from the use of the machine.

Example 5—Software asset

IE15   An entity acquires a group of assets **[Refer: IAS 16 paragraph 24]**. The asset group includes an income-producing software asset internally developed for licensing to customers and its complementary assets (including a related database with which the software asset is used) and the associated liabilities. To allocate the cost of the group to the individual assets acquired, the entity measures the fair value of the software asset. The entity determines that the software asset would provide maximum value to market participants **[Refer: paragraphs 22 and 23]** through its use in combination with other assets or with other assets and liabilities (ie its complementary assets and the associated liabilities **[Refer: paragraph 31(a)]**). There is no evidence to suggest that the current use of the software asset is not its highest and best use **[Refer: paragraph 29]**. Therefore, the highest and best use of the software asset is its current use. (In this case the licensing of the software asset, in and of itself, does not indicate that the fair value of the asset would be maximised through its use by market participants on a stand-alone basis. **[Refer: paragraph 31(b)]**)

IE16   The entity determines that, in addition to the income approach **[Refer: paragraphs B10 and B11]**, sufficient data might be available to apply the cost approach **[Refer: paragraphs B8 and B9]** but not the market approach **[Refer: paragraphs B5–B7]**. Information about market transactions for comparable software assets is not available. The income and cost approaches are applied as follows:

(a)   The income approach is applied using a present value technique **[Refer: paragraphs B12–B30]**. The cash flows used in that technique reflect the income stream expected to result from the software asset (licence fees from customers) over its economic life. The fair value indicated by that approach is CU15 million.

(b)   The cost approach is applied by estimating the amount that currently would be required to construct a substitute software asset of comparable utility (ie taking into account functional and economic obsolescence). The fair value indicated by that approach is CU10 million.

IE17   Through its application of the cost approach, the entity determines that market participants would not be able to construct a substitute software asset of comparable utility. Some characteristics of the software asset are unique, having been developed using proprietary information, and cannot be readily replicated. The entity determines that the fair value of the software asset is CU15 million, as indicated by the income approach. **[Refer: paragraph 63]**

Principal (or most advantageous) market

IE18   Example 6 illustrates the use of Level 1 inputs to measure the fair value of an asset that trades in different active markets at different prices. **[Refer: paragraphs 15–21 and 76–80]**

Example 6—Level 1 principal (or most advantageous) market
[Refer: paragraphs 16 and 76–80]

IE19   An asset is sold in two different active markets at different prices. An entity enters into transactions in both markets [Refer: paragraph 17] and can access [Refer: paragraph 76] the price in those markets for the asset at the measurement date. In Market A, the price that would be received is CU26, transaction costs [Refer: paragraph 25 and Appendix A] in that market [Refer: paragraph 26] are CU3 and the costs to transport the asset to that market are CU2 (ie the net amount that would be received is CU21). In Market B, the price that would be received is CU25, transaction costs in that market are CU1 and the costs to transport the asset to that market are CU2 (ie the net amount that would be received in Market B is CU22).

IE20   If Market A is the principal market [Refer: paragraph 16(a)] for the asset (ie the market with the greatest volume and level of activity for the asset), the fair value of the asset would be measured using the price that would be received in that market, after taking into account transport costs (CU24).

IE21   If neither market is the principal market for the asset, the fair value of the asset would be measured using the price in the most advantageous market. [Refer: paragraph 16(b)] The most advantageous market is the market that maximises the amount that would be received to sell the asset, after taking into account transaction costs and transport costs (ie the net amount that would be received in the respective markets).

IE22   Because the entity would maximise the net amount that would be received for the asset in Market B (CU22), the fair value of the asset would be measured using the price in that market (CU25), less transport costs (CU2), resulting in a fair value measurement of CU23. Although transaction costs are taken into account when determining which market is the most advantageous market, the price used to measure the fair value of the asset is not adjusted for those costs (although it is adjusted for transport costs).

Transaction prices and fair value at initial recognition

IE23   The IFRS clarifies that in many cases the transaction price, ie the price paid (received) for a particular asset (liability), will represent the fair value of that asset (liability) at initial recognition, but not presumptively. Example 7 illustrates when the price in a transaction involving a derivative instrument might (and might not) equal the fair value of the instrument at initial recognition. [Refer: paragraphs 57–60, 64 and B4]

Example 7—Interest rate swap at initial recognition

IE24   Entity A (a retail counterparty) enters into an interest rate swap in a retail market with Entity B (a dealer) for no initial consideration (ie the transaction price is zero). Entity A can access only the retail market. Entity B can access both the retail market (ie with retail counterparties) and the dealer market (ie with dealer counterparties).

IE25　　From the perspective of Entity A, the retail market in which it initially entered into the swap is the principal market [Refer: paragraph 16(a)] for the swap. If Entity A were to transfer its rights and obligations under the swap, it would do so with a dealer counterparty in that retail market. In that case the transaction price (zero) would represent the fair value of the swap to Entity A at initial recognition, ie the price that Entity A would receive to sell or pay to transfer the swap in a transaction with a dealer counterparty in the retail market (ie an exit price). That price would not be adjusted for any incremental (transaction) costs [Refer: paragraph 25] that would be charged by that dealer counterparty.

IE26　　From the perspective of Entity B, the dealer market (not the retail market) is the principal market for the swap. If Entity B were to transfer its rights and obligations under the swap, it would do so with a dealer in that market. Because the market in which Entity B initially entered into the swap is different from the principal market for the swap, the transaction price (zero) would not necessarily represent the fair value of the swap to Entity B at initial recognition. If the fair value differs from the transaction price (zero), Entity B applies IAS 39 *Financial Instruments: Recognition and Measurement* or IFRS 9 *Financial Instruments* [Refer: IFRS 9 paragraphs 5.1.1A and B5.1.2A] to determine whether it recognises that difference as a gain or loss at initial recognition.

Restricted assets

IE27　　The effect on a fair value measurement arising from a restriction on the sale or use of an asset by an entity will differ depending on whether the restriction would be taken into account by market participants when pricing the asset. Examples 8 and 9 illustrate the effect of restrictions when measuring the fair value of an asset. [Refer: paragraphs 11(b) and 75]

Example 8—Restriction on the sale of an equity instrument

IE28　　An entity holds an equity instrument (a financial asset) for which sale is legally or contractually restricted for a specified period. (For example, such a restriction could limit sale to qualifying investors.) The restriction is a characteristic of the instrument and, therefore, would be transferred to market participants. [Refer: paragraph 11(b)] In that case the fair value of the instrument would be measured on the basis of the quoted price for an otherwise identical unrestricted equity instrument of the same issuer that trades in a public market, adjusted to reflect the effect of the restriction. The adjustment would reflect the amount market participants would demand because of the risk relating to the inability to access a public market for the instrument for the specified period. The adjustment will vary depending on all the following:

(a)　　the nature and duration of the restriction;

(b)　　the extent to which buyers are limited by the restriction (eg there might be a large number of qualifying investors); and

(c)   qualitative and quantitative factors specific to both the instrument and the issuer.

Example 9—Restrictions on the use of an asset
[Refer: paragraphs 11(b) and 75]

IE29   A donor contributes land in an otherwise developed residential area to a not-for-profit neighbourhood association. The land is currently used as a playground. The donor specifies that the land must continue to be used by the association as a playground in perpetuity. Upon review of relevant documentation (eg legal and other), the association determines that the fiduciary responsibility to meet the donor's restriction would not be transferred to market participants if the association sold the asset, ie the donor restriction on the use of the land is specific to the association. Furthermore, the association is not restricted from selling the land. Without the restriction on the use of the land by the association, the land could be used as a site for residential development. In addition, the land is subject to an easement (ie a legal right that enables a utility to run power lines across the land). Following is an analysis of the effect on the fair value measurement of the land arising from the restriction and the easement:

(a)   *Donor restriction on use of land.* Because in this situation the donor restriction on the use of the land is specific to the association, the restriction would not be transferred to market participants. [Refer: paragraphs 22 and 23] Therefore, the fair value of the land would be the higher of its fair value used as a playground (ie the fair value of the asset would be maximised through its use by market participants in combination with other assets or with other assets and liabilities [Refer: paragraph 31(a)]) and its fair value as a site for residential development (ie the fair value of the asset would be maximised through its use by market participants on a stand-alone basis [Refer: paragraph 31(b)]), regardless of the restriction on the use of the land by the association.

(b)   *Easement for utility lines.* Because the easement for utility lines is specific to (ie a characteristic of) the land, it would be transferred to market participants with the land. Therefore, the fair value measurement of the land would take into account the effect of the easement, regardless of whether the highest and best use [Refer: paragraphs 27–30] is as a playground or as a site for residential development.

Measuring liabilities

IE30   A fair value measurement of a liability [Refer: paragraphs 34–36] assumes that the liability, whether it is a financial liability or a non-financial liability, is transferred to a market participant [Refer: paragraphs 22 and 23] at the measurement date (ie the liability would remain outstanding and the market participant transferee would be required to fulfil the obligation; it would not be settled with the counterparty or otherwise extinguished on the measurement date [Refer: paragraph 34(a)]).

IE31   The fair value of a liability reflects the effect of non-performance risk **[Refer: paragraphs 42–44]**. Non-performance risk relating to a liability includes, but may not be limited to, the entity's own credit risk. An entity takes into account the effect of its credit risk (credit standing) on the fair value of the liability in all periods in which the liability is measured at fair value because those that hold the entity's obligations as assets would take into account the effect of the entity's credit standing when estimating the prices they would be willing to pay.

IE32   For example, assume that Entity X and Entity Y each enter into a contractual obligation to pay cash (CU500) to Entity Z in five years. Entity X has a AA credit rating and can borrow at 6 per cent, and Entity Y has a BBB credit rating and can borrow at 12 per cent. Entity X will receive about CU374 in exchange for its promise (the present value of CU500 in five years at 6 per cent). Entity Y will receive about CU284 in exchange for its promise (the present value of CU500 in five years at 12 per cent). The fair value of the liability to each entity (ie the proceeds) incorporates that entity's credit standing.

IE33   Examples 10–13 illustrate the measurement of liabilities and the effect of non-performance risk (including an entity's own credit risk) on a fair value measurement.

Example 10—Structured note
[Refer: paragraphs 37–39 and 42–44]

IE34   On 1 January 20X7 Entity A, an investment bank with a AA credit rating, issues a five-year fixed rate note to Entity B. The contractual principal amount to be paid by Entity A at maturity is linked to an equity index. No credit enhancements are issued in conjunction with or otherwise related to the contract (ie no collateral is posted and there is no third-party guarantee **[Refer: paragraph 44]**). Entity A designated this note as at fair value through profit or loss. The fair value of the note (ie the obligation of Entity A) during 20X7 is measured using an expected present value technique **[Refer: paragraphs B23–B30]**. Changes in fair value are as follows:

(a)   *Fair value at 1 January 20X7.* The expected cash flows used in the expected present value technique are discounted at the risk-free rate using the government bond curve at 1 January 20X7, plus the current market observable AA corporate bond spread to government bonds, if non-performance risk is not already reflected in the cash flows **[Refer: paragraph B14(c)]**, adjusted (either up or down) for Entity A's specific credit risk (ie resulting in a credit-adjusted risk-free rate). Therefore, the fair value of Entity A's obligation at initial recognition takes into account non-performance risk, including that entity's credit risk, which presumably is reflected in the proceeds.

(b)   *Fair value at 31 March 20X7.* During March 20X7 the credit spread for AA corporate bonds widens, with no changes to the specific credit risk of Entity A. The expected cash flows used in the expected present value technique are discounted at the risk-free rate using the government bond curve at 31 March 20X7, plus the current market observable AA corporate bond spread to government bonds, if non-performance risk is not already reflected in the cash flows [Refer: paragraph B14(c)], adjusted for Entity A's specific credit risk (ie resulting in a credit-adjusted risk-free rate). Entity A's specific credit risk is unchanged from initial recognition. Therefore, the fair value of Entity A's obligation changes as a result of changes in credit spreads generally. Changes in credit spreads reflect current market participant assumptions about changes in non-performance risk generally, changes in liquidity risk and the compensation required for assuming those risks.

(c)   *Fair value at 30 June 20X7.* As of 30 June 20X7 there have been no changes to the AA corporate bond spreads. However, on the basis of structured note issues corroborated with other qualitative information, Entity A determines that its own specific creditworthiness has strengthened within the AA credit spread. The expected cash flows [Refer: paragraph B14(c)] used in the expected present value technique are discounted at the risk-free rate using the government bond yield curve at 30 June 20X7, plus the current market observable AA corporate bond spread to government bonds (unchanged from 31 March 20X7), if non-performance risk is not already reflected in the cash flows, adjusted for Entity A's specific credit risk (ie resulting in a credit-adjusted risk-free rate). Therefore, the fair value of the obligation of Entity A changes as a result of the change in its own specific credit risk within the AA corporate bond spread.

Example 11—Decommissioning liability
[Refer: paragraphs 40–46, B31–B33 and B36(d)]

IE35   On 1 January 20X1 Entity A assumes a decommissioning liability in a business combination [Refer: IFRS 3]. The entity is legally required to dismantle and remove an offshore oil platform at the end of its useful life, which is estimated to be 10 years.

IE36   On the basis of paragraphs B23–B30 of the IFRS, Entity A uses the expected present value technique to measure the fair value of the decommissioning liability.

IE37   If Entity A was contractually allowed to transfer its decommissioning liability to a market participant [Refer: paragraphs 22 and 23], Entity A concludes that a market participant would use all the following inputs, probability-weighted as appropriate, when estimating the price it would expect to receive:

(a)   labour costs;

(b)   allocation of overhead costs;

(c)   the compensation that a market participant would require for undertaking the activity and for assuming the risk associated with the obligation to dismantle and remove the asset. Such compensation includes both of the following:

(i)   profit on labour and overhead costs; and

(ii)   the risk that the actual cash outflows might differ from those expected, excluding inflation;

(d)   effect of inflation on estimated costs and profits;

(e)   time value of money, represented by the risk-free rate; and

(f)   non-performance risk relating to the risk that Entity A will not fulfil the obligation, including Entity A's own credit risk.

IE38   The significant assumptions used by Entity A to measure fair value are as follows:

(a)   Labour costs are developed on the basis of current marketplace wages, adjusted for expectations of future wage increases, required to hire contractors to dismantle and remove offshore oil platforms. Entity A assigns probability assessments to a range of cash flow estimates as follows:

Cash flow estimate (CU)	Probability assessment	Expected cash flows (CU)
100,000	25%	25,000
125,000	50%	62,500
175,000	25%	43,750
		CU131,250

The probability assessments are developed on the basis of Entity A's experience with fulfilling obligations of this type and its knowledge of the market.

(b)   Entity A estimates allocated overhead and equipment operating costs using the rate it applies to labour costs (80 per cent of expected labour costs). This is consistent with the cost structure of market participants.

(c)   Entity A estimates the compensation that a market participant would require for undertaking the activity and for assuming the risk associated with the obligation [Refer: paragraphs B31–B33] to dismantle and remove the asset as follows:

(i)   A third-party contractor typically adds a mark-up on labour and allocated internal costs to provide a profit margin on the job. The profit margin used (20 per cent) represents Entity A's understanding of the operating profit that contractors in the industry generally earn to dismantle and remove offshore oil platforms. Entity A concludes that this rate is consistent with the rate that a market participant would require as compensation for undertaking the activity.

(ii) A contractor would typically require compensation for the risk that the actual cash outflows might differ from those expected because of the uncertainty inherent in locking in today's price for a project that will not occur for 10 years. Entity A estimates the amount of that premium to be 5 per cent of the expected cash flows, including the effect of inflation.

(d) Entity A assumes a rate of inflation of 4 per cent over the 10-year period on the basis of available market data.

(e) The risk-free rate of interest for a 10-year maturity on 1 January 20X1 is 5 per cent. Entity A adjusts that rate by 3.5 per cent to reflect its risk of non-performance (ie the risk that it will not fulfil the obligation), including its credit risk [Refer: paragraph 43]. Therefore, the discount rate used to compute the present value of the cash flows is 8.5 per cent.

IE39 Entity A concludes that its assumptions would be used by market participants [Refer: paragraphs 69 and 87]. In addition, Entity A does not adjust its fair value measurement for the existence of a restriction preventing it from transferring the liability [Refer: paragraphs 45 and 46]. As illustrated in the following table, Entity A measures the fair value of its decommissioning liability as CU194,879.

	Expected cash flows (CU) 1 January 20X1
Expected labour costs	131,250
Allocated overhead and equipment costs (0.80 × CU131,250)	105,000
Contractor's profit mark-up [0.20 × (CU131,250 + CU105,000)]	47,250
Expected cash flows before inflation adjustment	283,500
Inflation factor (4% for 10 years)	1.4802
Expected cash flows adjusted for inflation	419,637
Market risk premium (0.05 × CU419,637)	20,982
Expected cash flows adjusted for market risk	440,619
Expected present value using discount rate of 8.5% for 10 years	194,879

Example 12—Debt obligation: quoted price
[Refer: paragraphs 37–39, 42–44 and 72–90]

IE40 On 1 January 20X1 Entity B issues at par a CU2 million BBB-rated exchange-traded five-year fixed rate debt instrument with an annual 10 per cent coupon. Entity B designated this financial liability as at fair value through profit or loss.

IE41   On 31 December 20X1 the instrument is trading as an asset in an active market [Refer: Appendix A (definition of an active market)] at CU929 per CU1,000 of par value after payment of accrued interest. Entity B uses the quoted price of the asset in an active market as its initial input into the fair value measurement of its liability (CU929 × [CU2 million ÷ CU1,000] = CU1,858,000).

IE42   In determining whether the quoted price of the asset in an active market represents the fair value of the liability, Entity B evaluates whether the quoted price of the asset includes the effect of factors not applicable to the fair value measurement of a liability, for example, whether the quoted price of the asset includes the effect of a third-party credit enhancement if that credit enhancement [Refer: paragraph 39(b)] would be separately accounted for from the perspective of the issuer. Entity B determines that no adjustments are required to the quoted price of the asset. Accordingly, Entity B concludes that the fair value of its debt instrument at 31 December 20X1 is CU1,858,000. Entity B categorises and discloses the fair value measurement of its debt instrument within Level 1 [Refer: paragraphs 76–80] of the fair value hierarchy. [Refer: paragraphs 72–90]

Example 13—Debt obligation: present value technique
[Refer: paragraphs 37–39, 42–44 and B12–B30]

IE43   On 1 January 20X1 Entity C issues at par in a private placement a CU2 million BBB-rated five-year fixed rate debt instrument with an annual 10 per cent coupon. Entity C designated this financial liability as at fair value through profit or loss.

IE44   At 31 December 20X1 Entity C still carries a BBB credit rating. Market conditions, including available interest rates, credit spreads for a BBB-quality credit rating and liquidity, remain unchanged from the date the debt instrument was issued. However, Entity C's credit spread has deteriorated by 50 basis points because of a change in its risk of non-performance [Refer: paragraphs 42–43]. After taking into account all market conditions, Entity C concludes that if it was to issue the instrument at the measurement date, the instrument would bear a rate of interest of 10.5 per cent or Entity C would receive less than par in proceeds from the issue of the instrument.

IE45   For the purpose of this example, the fair value of Entity C's liability is calculated using a present value technique [Refer: paragraphs B12–B30]. Entity C concludes that a market participant would use all the following inputs (consistently with paragraphs B12–B30 of the IFRS) when estimating the price the market participant would expect to receive to assume Entity C's obligation:

(a)   the terms of the debt instrument, including all the following:

   (i)   coupon of 10 per cent;

   (ii)   principal amount of CU2 million; and

   (iii)   term of four years.

(b)   the market rate of interest of 10.5 per cent (which includes a change of 50 basis points in the risk of non-performance from the date of issue).

IE46   On the basis of its present value technique **[Refer: paragraphs B12–B30]**, Entity C concludes that the fair value of its liability at 31 December 20X1 is CU1,968,641.

IE47   Entity C does not include any additional input into its present value technique for risk or profit that a market participant might require for compensation for assuming the liability **[Refer: paragraph 41(a)]**. Because Entity C's obligation is a financial liability, Entity C concludes that the interest rate already captures the risk or profit that a market participant would require as compensation for assuming the liability **[Refer: paragraph B32]**. Furthermore, Entity C does not adjust its present value technique for the existence of a restriction preventing it from transferring the liability. **[Refer: paragraphs 45 and 46]**

Measuring fair value when the volume or level of activity for an asset or a liability has significantly decreased

IE48   Example 14 **[Refer: paragraphs B37–B47]** illustrates the use of judgement when measuring the fair value of a financial asset when there has been a significant decrease in the volume or level of activity for the asset when compared with normal market activity for the asset (or similar assets).

Example 14—Estimating a market rate of return when the volume or level of activity for an asset has significantly decreased

IE49   Entity A invests in a junior AAA-rated tranche of a residential mortgage-backed security on 1 January 20X8 (the issue date of the security). The junior tranche is the third most senior of a total of seven tranches. The underlying collateral for the residential mortgage-backed security is unguaranteed non-conforming residential mortgage loans that were issued in the second half of 20X6.

IE50   At 31 March 20X9 (the measurement date) the junior tranche is now A-rated. This tranche of the residential mortgage-backed security was previously traded through a brokered market. However, trading volume in that market was infrequent, with only a few transactions taking place per month from 1 January 20X8 to 30 June 20X8 and little, if any, trading activity during the nine months before 31 March 20X9.

IE51   Entity A takes into account the factors in paragraph B37 of the IFRS to determine whether there has been a significant decrease in the volume or level of activity for the junior tranche of the residential mortgage-backed security in which it has invested. After evaluating the significance and relevance of the factors, Entity A concludes that the volume and level of activity of the junior tranche of the residential mortgage-backed security have significantly decreased **[Refer: paragraph B37]**. Entity A supported its judgement primarily on the basis that there was little, if any, trading activity for an extended period before the measurement date.

IE52   Because there is little, if any, trading activity to support a valuation technique using a market approach, Entity A decides to use an income approach using the discount rate adjustment technique described in paragraphs B18–B22 of the IFRS to measure the fair value of the residential mortgage-backed security at the measurement date. Entity A uses the contractual cash flows from the residential mortgage-backed security (see also paragraphs 67 and 68 of the IFRS).

IE53   Entity A then estimates a discount rate (ie a market rate of return) to discount those contractual cash flows **[Refer: paragraph B13(c) and (d)]**. The market rate of return is estimated using both of the following:

(a)   the risk-free rate of interest.

(b)   estimated adjustments **[Refer: paragraphs 87 and 88]** for differences between the available market data and the junior tranche of the residential mortgage-backed security in which Entity A has invested. Those adjustments reflect available market data about expected non-performance and other risks (eg default risk, collateral value risk and liquidity risk) that market participants would take into account when pricing the asset in an orderly transaction at the measurement date under current market conditions.

IE54   Entity A took into account the following information when estimating the adjustments in paragraph IE53(b):

(a)   the credit spread for the junior tranche of the residential mortgage-backed security at the issue date as implied by the original transaction price.

(b)   the change in the credit spread implied by any observed transactions from the issue date to the measurement date for comparable residential mortgage-backed securities or on the basis of relevant indices.

(c)   the characteristics of the junior tranche of the residential mortgage-backed security compared with comparable residential mortgage-backed securities or indices, including all the following:

(i)   the quality of the underlying assets, ie information about the performance of the underlying mortgage loans such as delinquency and foreclosure rates, loss experience and prepayment rates;

(ii)   the seniority or subordination of the residential mortgage-backed security tranche held; and

(iii)   other relevant factors.

(d)   relevant reports issued by analysts and rating agencies.

(e)   quoted prices from third parties such as brokers or pricing services.

IE55   Entity A estimates that one indication of the market rate of return that market participants would use when pricing the junior tranche of the residential mortgage-backed security is 12 per cent (1,200 basis points). This market rate of return was estimated as follows:

(a)   Begin with 300 basis points for the relevant risk-free rate of interest at 31 March 20X9.

(b)   Add 250 basis points for the credit spread over the risk-free rate when the junior tranche was issued in January 20X8.

(c)   Add 700 basis points for the estimated change in the credit spread over the risk-free rate of the junior tranche between 1 January 20X8 and 31 March 20X9. This estimate was developed on the basis of the change in the most comparable index available for that time period.

(d)   Subtract 50 basis points (net) to adjust for differences between the index used to estimate the change in credit spreads and the junior tranche. The referenced index consists of subprime mortgage loans, whereas Entity A's residential mortgage-backed security consists of similar mortgage loans with a more favourable credit profile (making it more attractive to market participants). However, the index does not reflect an appropriate liquidity risk premium for the junior tranche under current market conditions. Thus, the 50 basis point adjustment is the net of two adjustments:

(i)   the first adjustment is a 350 basis point subtraction, which was estimated by comparing the implied yield from the most recent transactions for the residential mortgage-backed security in June 20X8 with the implied yield in the index price on those same dates. There was no information available that indicated that the relationship between Entity A's security and the index has changed.

(ii)   the second adjustment is a 300 basis point addition, which is Entity A's best estimate of the additional liquidity risk inherent in its security (a cash position) when compared with the index (a synthetic position). This estimate was derived after taking into account liquidity risk premiums implied in recent cash transactions for a range of similar securities.

IE56   As an additional indication of the market rate of return, Entity A takes into account two recent indicative quotes (ie non-binding quotes) provided by reputable brokers for the junior tranche of the residential mortgage-backed security that imply yields of 15–17 per cent. Entity A is unable to evaluate the valuation technique(s) [Refer: paragraphs 61–66] or inputs [Refer: paragraphs 67–71] used to develop the quotes [Refer: paragraphs B45–B47]. However, Entity A is able to confirm that the quotes do not reflect the results of transactions.

IE57   Because Entity A has multiple indications of the market rate of return that market participants would take into account when measuring fair value, it evaluates and weights the respective indications of the rate of return, considering the reasonableness of the range indicated by the results.

IE58   Entity A concludes that 13 per cent is the point within the range of indications that is most representative of fair value under current market conditions. Entity A places more weight on the 12 per cent indication (ie its own estimate of the market rate of return) for the following reasons:

       (a)   Entity A concluded that its own estimate appropriately incorporated the risks (eg default risk, collateral value risk and liquidity risk) that market participants would use when pricing the asset in an orderly transaction under current market conditions. **[Refer: paragraphs 24 and 88]**

       (b)   The broker quotes were non-binding and did not reflect the results of transactions, and Entity A was unable to evaluate the valuation technique(s) or inputs used to develop the quotes **[Refer: paragraphs B46 and B47]**.

Fair value disclosures

IE59   Examples 15–19 illustrate the disclosures required by paragraphs 92, 93(a), (b) and (d)–(h)(i) and 99 of the IFRS.

Example 15—Assets measured at fair value

IE60   For assets and liabilities measured at fair value at the end of the reporting period, the IFRS requires quantitative disclosures about the fair value measurements for each class of assets and liabilities **[Refer: paragraph 94]**. An entity might disclose the following for assets to comply with paragraph 93(a) and (b) of the IFRS:

(CU in millions)		Fair value measurements at the end of the reporting period using [Refer: paragraph 72]			
Description	31/12/X9	Quoted prices in active markets for identical assets (Level 1)	Significant other observable inputs (Level 2)	Significant unobservable inputs (Level 3)	Total gains (losses)
Recurring fair value measurements **[Refer: paragraph 93(a)]**					
Trading equity securities:[a]					
Real estate industry	93	70	23		
Oil and gas industry	45	45			
Other	15	15			
Total trading equity securities	153	130	23		
Other equity securities:[a]					
Financial services industry	150	150			
Healthcare industry	163	110		53	
Energy industry	32			32	
Private equity fund investments[b]	25			25	
Other	15	15			
Total other equity securities	385	275		110	
Debt securities:					
Residential mortgage-backed securities	149		24	125	
Commercial mortgage-backed securities	50			50	
Collateralised debt obligations	35			35	
Risk-free government securities	85	85			
Corporate bonds	93	9	84		
Total debt securities	412	94	108	210	

continued...

...*continued*

(CU in millions)		Fair value measurements at the end of the reporting period using [Refer: paragraph 72]			
Description	31/12/X9	Quoted prices in active markets for identical assets (Level 1)	Significant other observable inputs (Level 2)	Significant unobservable inputs (Level 3)	Total gains (losses)
Hedge fund investments:					
Equity long/short	55		55		
Global opportunities	35		35		
High-yield debt securities	90			90	
Total hedge fund investments	180		90	90	
Derivatives:					
Interest rate contracts	57		57		
Foreign exchange contracts	43		43		
Credit contracts	38			38	
Commodity futures contracts	78	78			
Commodity forward contracts	20		20		
Total derivatives	236	78	120	38	
Investment properties:					
Commercial—Asia	31			31	
Commercial—Europe	27			27	
Total investment properties	58			58	
Total recurring fair value measurements	1,424	577	341	506	

continued...

...continued

(CU in millions)		Fair value measurements at the end of the reporting period using [Refer: paragraph 72]			
Description	31/12/X9	Quoted prices in active markets for identical assets (Level 1)	Significant other observable inputs (Level 2)	Significant unobservable inputs (Level 3)	Total gains (losses)
Non-recurring fair value measurements **[Refer: paragraph 93(a)]**					
Assets held for sale(c)	26			26	15
Total non-recurring fair value measurements	26			26	15

(Note: A similar table would be presented for liabilities unless another format is deemed more appropriate by the entity.)

[Refer: paragraph 99]

(a) On the basis of its analysis of the nature, characteristics and risks of the securities, the entity has determined that presenting them by industry is appropriate.

(b) On the basis of its analysis of the nature, characteristics and risks of the investments, the entity has determined that presenting them as a single class is appropriate.

(c) In accordance with IFRS 5, **[Refer: IFRS 5 paragraph 15]** assets held for sale with a carrying amount of CU35 million were written down to their fair value of CU26 million, less costs to sell of CU6 million (or CU20 million), resulting in a loss of CU15 million, which was included in profit or loss for the period.

Example 16—Reconciliation of fair value measurements categorised within Level 3 of the fair value hierarchy

IE61   For recurring fair value measurements categorised within Level 3 of the fair value hierarchy **[Refer: paragraphs 72, 73 and 86]**, the IFRS requires a reconciliation from the opening balances to the closing balances for each class of assets and liabilities. An entity might disclose the following for assets to comply with paragraph 93(e) and (f) of the IFRS:

(CU in millions)	Other equity securities			Debt securities			Hedge fund investments	Derivatives	Investment properties		Total
	Healthcare industry	Energy industry	Private equity fund	Residential mortgage-backed securities	Commercial mortgage-backed securities	Collateralised debt obligations	High-yield debt securities	Credit contracts	Asia	Europe	
Opening balance	49	28	20	105	39	25	145	30	28	26	495
Transfers into Level 3				60 (a),(b)							60
Transfers out of Level 3				(5) (b),(c)							(5)
Total gains or losses for the period											
Included in profit or loss			5	(23)	(5)	(7)	7	5	3	1	(14)
Included in other comprehensive income	3	1									4

continued...

...continued

	Fair value measurements using significant unobservable inputs (Level 3)										
Purchases, issues, sales and settlements											
Purchases	1	3			16	17		18			55
Issues			5								5
Sales				(12)			(62)				(74)
Settlements								(15)			(15)
Closing balance	53	32	25	125	50	35	90	38	31	27	506
Change in unrealised gains or losses for the period included in profit or loss for assets held at the end of the reporting period **[Refer: Basis for Conclusions paragraph BC198]**				(3)	(5)	(7)	2	3		1	(9)

(Note: A similar table would be presented for liabilities unless another format is deemed more appropriate by the entity.)

[Refer: paragraph 99]

(a) Transferred from Level 2 to Level 3 because of a lack of observable market data, resulting from a decrease in market activity for the securities.

(b) The entity's policy is to recognise transfers into and transfers out of Level 3 as of the date of the event or change in circumstances that caused the transfer. **[Refer: paragraph 95]**

(c) Transferred from Level 3 to Level 2 because observable market data became available for the securities. **[Refer: paragraph 93(e)(iv)]**

IE62 Gains and losses included in profit or loss for the period (above) are presented in financial income and in non-financial income as follows:

	Financial income	Non-financial income
(CU in millions)		
Total gains or losses for the period included in profit or loss **[Refer: paragraph 93(e)(i)]**	(18)	4
Change in unrealised gains or losses for the **[Refer: Basis for Conclusions paragraph BC198]** period included in profit or loss for assets held at the end of the reporting period **[Refer: paragraph 93(f)]**	(13)	4
(Note: A similar table would be presented for liabilities unless another format is deemed more appropriate by the entity.) **[Refer: paragraph 99]**		

Example 17—Valuation techniques and inputs

IE63 For fair value measurements categorised within Level 2 and Level 3 of the fair value hierarchy, the IFRS requires an entity to disclose a description of the valuation technique(s) **[Refer: paragraphs 61–66]** and the inputs **[Refer: paragraphs 67–71]** used in the fair value measurement **[Refer: paragraph 93(d)]**. For fair value measurements categorised within Level 3 of the fair value hierarchy **[Refer: paragraphs 72, 73 and 86]**, information about the significant unobservable inputs used must be quantitative **[Refer: paragraph 93(d)]**. An entity might disclose the following for assets to comply with the requirement to disclose the significant unobservable inputs used in the fair value measurement in accordance with paragraph 93(d) of the IFRS:

Quantitative information about fair value measurements using significant unobservable inputs (Level 3)				
(CU in millions)				
Description	Fair value at 31/12/X9	Valuation technique(s)	Unobservable input	Range (weighted average)
Other equity securities:				
Healthcare industry	53	Discounted cash flow	weighted average cost of capital	7%–16% (12.1%)
			long-term revenue growth rate	2%–5% (4.2%)
			long-term pre-tax operating margin	3%–20% (10.3%)
			discount for lack of marketability[a]	5%–20% (17%)
			control premium[a]	10%–30% (20%)
		Market comparable companies	EBITDA multiple[b]	10–13 (11.3)
			revenue multiple[b]	1.5–2.0 (1.7)
			discount for lack of marketability[a]	5%–20% (17%)
			control premium[a]	10%–30% (20%)
Energy industry	32	Discounted cash flow	weighted average cost of capital	8%–12% (11.1%)
			long-term revenue growth rate	3%–5.5% (4.2%)
			long-term pre-tax operating margin	7.5%–13% (9.2%)
			discount for lack of marketability[a]	5%–20% (10%)
			control premium[a]	10%–20% (12%)
		Market comparable companies	EBITDA multiple[b]	6.5–12 (9.5)
			revenue multiple[b]	1.0–3.0 (2.0)
			discount for lack of marketability[a]	5%–20% (10%)
			control premium[a]	10%–20% (12%)
Private equity fund investments	25	Net asset value[c]	n/a	n/a

continued...

...continued

Quantitative information about fair value measurements using significant unobservable inputs (Level 3)				
(CU in millions)				
Description	Fair value at 31/12/X9	Valuation technique(s)	Unobservable input	Range (weighted average)
Debt securities:				
Residential mortgage-backed securities	125	Discounted cash flow	constant prepayment rate	3.5%–5.5% (4.5%)
			probability of default	5%–50% (10%)
			loss severity	40%–100% (60%)
Commercial mortgage-backed securities	50	Discounted cash flow	constant prepayment rate	3%–5% (4.1%)
			probability of default	2%–25% (5%)
			loss severity	10%–50% (20%)
Collateralised debt obligations	35	Consensus pricing	offered quotes	20–45
			comparability adjustments (%)	-10% – +15% (+5%)
Hedge fund investments:				
High-yield debt securities	90	Net asset value[c]	n/a	n/a
Derivatives:				
Credit contracts	38	Option model	annualised volatility of credit[d]	10%–20%
			counterparty credit risk[e]	0.5%–3.5%
			own credit risk[e]	0.3%–2.0%

continued...

...continued

Quantitative information about fair value measurements using significant unobservable inputs (Level 3)				
(CU in millions)				
Description	Fair value at 31/12/X9	Valuation technique(s)	Unobservable input	Range (weighted average)
Investment properties:				
Commercial—Asia	31	Discounted cash flow	long-term net operating income margin	18%–32% (20%)
			cap rate	0.08–0.12 (0.10)
		Market comparable approach	price per square metre (USD)	$3,000–$7,000 ($4,500)
Commercial—Europe	27	Discounted cash flow	long-term net operating income margin	15%–25% (18%)
			cap rate	0.06–0.10 (0.08)
		Market comparable approach	price per square metre (EUR)	€4,000–€12,000 (€8,500)

(Note: A similar table would be presented for liabilities unless another format is deemed more appropriate by the entity.)

[Refer: paragraph 99]

(a) Represents amounts used when the entity has determined that market participants would take into account these premiums and discounts when pricing the investments. **[Refer: paragraph 69]**

(b) Represents amounts used when the entity has determined that market participants would use such multiples when pricing the investments. **[Refer: paragraphs 82(a), 82(b), 89 and B35(h)]**

(c) The entity has determined that the reported net asset value represents fair value at the end of the reporting period.

(d) Represents the range of the volatility curves used in the valuation analysis that the entity has determined market participants would use when the pricing contracts. **[Refer: paragraphs 82(c) (ii) and B35(d)]**

(e) Represents the range of the credit default swap spread curves used in the valuation analysis that the entity has determined market participants would use when pricing the contracts. **[Refer: paragraphs 82(c)(i), B35(a) and B36(a)]**

IE64   In addition, an entity should provide additional information that will help users of its financial statements to evaluate the quantitative information disclosed **[Refer: paragraphs 91 and 92]**. An entity might disclose some or all the following to comply with paragraph 92 of the IFRS:

   (a)   the nature of the item being measured at fair value, including the characteristics **[Refer: paragraph 11]** of the item being measured that are taken into account in the determination of relevant inputs. For example, for residential mortgage-backed securities, an entity might disclose the following:

      (i)   the types of underlying loans (eg prime loans or sub-prime loans)

      (ii)   collateral

      (iii)   guarantees or other credit enhancements

      (iv)   seniority level of the tranches of securities

    (v)   the year of issue

    (vi)   the weighted-average coupon rate of the underlying loans and the securities

    (vii)   the weighted-average maturity of the underlying loans and the securities

    (viii) the geographical concentration of the underlying loans

    (ix)   information about the credit ratings of the securities.

(b)   how third-party information such as broker quotes, pricing services, net asset values and relevant market data was taken into account when measuring fair value. **[Refer: paragraphs B45–B47]**

Example 18—Valuation processes

IE65   For fair value measurements categorised within Level 3 **[Refer: paragraphs 73 and 86]** of the fair value hierarchy, the IFRS requires an entity to disclose a description of the valuation processes used by the entity **[Refer: paragraph 93(g)]**. An entity might disclose the following to comply with paragraph 93(g) of the IFRS:

(a)   for the group within the entity that decides the entity's valuation policies and procedures:

    (i)   its description;

    (ii)   to whom that group reports; and

    (iii)   the internal reporting procedures in place (eg whether and, if so, how pricing, risk management or audit committees discuss and assess the fair value measurements);

(b)   the frequency and methods for calibration **[Refer: paragraph 64]**, back testing and other testing procedures of pricing models;

(c)   the process for analysing changes in fair value measurements from period to period;

(d)   how the entity determined that third-party information, such as broker quotes or pricing services, used in the fair value measurement was developed in accordance with the IFRS; **[Refer: paragraph B45]** and

(e)   the methods used to develop and substantiate the unobservable inputs used in a fair value measurement.

Example 19—Information about sensitivity to changes in significant unobservable inputs

IE66   For recurring fair value measurements categorised within Level 3 of the fair value hierarchy **[Refer: paragraphs 72, 73 and 86]**, the IFRS requires an entity to provide a narrative description of the sensitivity of the fair value measurement to changes in significant unobservable inputs and a description of any interrelationships between those unobservable inputs. An entity might

                  © IFRS Foundation

disclose the following about its residential mortgage-backed securities to comply with paragraph 93(h)(i) of the IFRS:

> The significant unobservable inputs used in the fair value measurement of the entity's residential mortgage-backed securities are prepayment rates, probability of default and loss severity in the event of default. Significant increases (decreases) in any of those inputs in isolation would result in a significantly lower (higher) fair value measurement. Generally, a change in the assumption used for the probability of default is accompanied by a directionally similar change in the assumption used for the loss severity and a directionally opposite change in the assumption used for prepayment rates.

Appendix
Amendments to guidance on other IFRSs

The following amendments to guidance on other IFRSs are necessary in order to ensure consistency with IFRS 13 Fair Value Measurement and the related amendments to other IFRSs. Amended paragraphs are shown with new text underlined and deleted text struck through.

* * * * *

The amendments contained in this appendix when IFRS 13 was issued in 2011 have been incorporated into the guidance on the relevant IFRSs published in this volume.

IASB documents published to accompany

IFRS 14

Regulatory Deferral Accounts

The text of the unaccompanied standard, IFRS 14, is contained in Part A of this edition. The text of the Basis for Conclusions on IFRS 14 is contained in Part C of this edition. Its effective date when issued was 1 January 2016. This part presents the following document:

ILLUSTRATIVE EXAMPLES

IFRS 14 *Regulatory Deferral Accounts*
Illustrative Examples

These examples accompany, but are not part of, IFRS 14.

Regulatory deferral account balances

Example 1—Illustrative presentation of financial statements

IE1   Paragraphs 20–25 of this Standard require an entity to present regulatory deferral account debit balances and credit balances and any related deferred tax asset (liability) and the net movement in those balances as separate line items in the statement of financial position and the statement(s) of profit or loss and other comprehensive income respectively. Sub-totals are drawn before the regulatory line items are presented. In addition, paragraph 26 requires an entity to present additional basic and diluted earnings per share, which are calculated by excluding the net movement in regulatory deferral account balances, when the entity presents earnings per share in accordance with IAS 33 *Earnings per Share*. Example 1 illustrates how these requirements might be met, but is not intended to illustrate all aspects of this Standard or IFRS more generally.

XYZ Group—Statement of financial position as at 31 December 20X7
(in currency units)
[Refer: paragraphs 20, 21, 24 and B11 and Basis for Conclusions paragraphs BC40–BC47]

	31 Dec 20X7	31 Dec 20X6
ASSETS		
Non-current assets		
Property, plant and equipment	350,700	360,020
Goodwill	80,800	91,200
Other intangible assets	227,470	227,470
Investments in associates	100,150	110,770
Investments in equity instruments	129,790	146,460
	888,910	935,920
Current assets		
Inventories	135,230	132,500
Trade receivables	91,600	110,800
Other current assets	25,650	12,540
Cash and cash equivalents	212,160	220,570
	464,640	476,410
Total assets	**1,353,550**	**1,412,330**
Regulatory deferral account debit balances and related deferred tax asset	112,950	111,870
Total assets and regulatory deferral account debit balances	**1,466,500**	**1,524,200**

Note: The aggregated total that is presented for regulatory deferral account debit balances and the related deferred tax asset includes the sum of the regulatory deferral account debit balances of CU100,240 (20X6 – CU102,330) plus the deferred tax asset that is related to the recognition of regulatory deferral account balances of CU12,710 (20X6 – CU9,540). This aggregated presentation is permitted by paragraphs 24 and B11 of this Standard. An alternative disaggregated presentation is illustrated in Example 2.

XYZ Group—Statement of financial position as at 31 December 20X7
(in currency units)
[Refer: paragraphs 20, 21, 24 and B11 and Basis for Conclusions paragraphs BC40–BC47]

	31 Dec 20X7	31 Dec 20X6
EQUITY AND LIABILITIES		
Equity attributable to owners of the parent		
Share capital	650,000	600,000
Retained earnings	243,500	164,500
Other components of equity	10,200	21,200
	903,700	785,700
Non-controlling interests	70,050	45,800
Total equity	**973,750**	**831,500**
Non-current liabilities		
Long-term borrowings	120,000	160,000
Deferred tax	28,800	26,040
Long-term provisions	28,850	52,240
	177,650	238,280
Current liabilities		
Trade and other payables	87,140	111,150
Short-term borrowings	80,000	200,000
Current portion of long-term borrowings	10,000	20,000
Current tax payable	35,000	42,000
Short-term provisions	5,000	4,800
	217,140	377,950
Total liabilities	**394,790**	**616,230**
Total equity and liabilities	**1,368,540**	**1,447,730**
Regulatory deferral account credit balances	97,960	76,470
Total equity, liabilities and regulatory deferral account credit balances	**1,466,500**	**1,524,200**

continued...

...continued

Note: regulatory deferral account balances are not described as assets or liabilities for the purposes of this Standard. The sub-totals described as "Total assets" and "Total liabilities" are comparable to those that would be presented if the regulatory deferral account balances were not recognised. The difference between these two sub-totals represents the net balance of all regulatory deferral account balances recognised and any related deferred tax asset (liability) that arises as a result of recognising regulatory deferral account balances, which would otherwise be recognised within retained earnings or other components of equity.

XYZ Group—Statement of profit or loss and other comprehensive income for the year ended 31 December 20X7
(illustrating the presentation of profit or loss and other comprehensive income in one statement and the classification of expenses within profit or loss by function)
(in currency units)
[Refer: paragraphs 22–24, 26 and B12–B14 and Basis for Conclusions paragraphs BC44–BC46]

	20X7	20X6
Revenue	390,000	358,784
Cost of sales	(237,062)	(230,000)
Gross profit	152,938	128,784
Other income	44,247	16,220
Distribution costs	(9,000)	(13,700)
Administrative expenses	(20,000)	(31,500)
Other expenses	(2,100)	(1,200)
Finance costs	(8,000)	(7,500)
Share of profit of associates	35,100	15,100
Profit before tax	**193,185**	**106,204**
Income tax expense	(43,587)	(44,320)
Profit for the year before net movements in regulatory deferral account balances	**149,598**	**61,884**
Net movement in regulatory deferral account balances related to profit or loss and the related deferred tax movement	(27,550)	3,193
Profit for the year and net movements in regulatory deferral account balances	**122,048**	**65,077**
Other comprehensive income: Items that will not be reclassified to profit or loss		
Remeasurement of defined benefit pension plans	(7,938)	(3,784)
Net movement in regulatory deferral account balances related to other comprehensive income	7,140	4,207
Other comprehensive income for the year, net of income tax	(798)	423
TOTAL COMPREHENSIVE INCOME FOR THE YEAR	**121,250**	**65,500**
Profit and net movements in regulatory deferral account balances attributable to:		
Owners of the parent	97,798	51,977
Non-controlling interests	24,250	13,100
	122,048	65,077

continued...

...continued

Total comprehensive income attributable to

Owners of the parent	97,000	52,400
Non-controlling interests	24,250	13,100
	121,250	65,500

Earnings per share (in currency units):

Basic and diluted	0.61	0.35
Basic and diluted including net movement in regulatory deferral account balances	0.46	0.30

Notes:

(1) To simplify the example, it is assumed that all regulatory deferral account balances relate to activities that are carried out in wholly-owned subsidiaries and thus no amounts are attributable to non-controlling interests.

(2) The aggregated total that is presented for the net movement in regulatory deferral account balances related to profit or loss and the related deferred tax movement includes the net movement in regulatory deferral account balances of CU30,720 **[Refer: paragraph IE2 Note (5)]** (20X6 – CU9,127) and the movement in the related deferred tax asset that is related to the recognition of regulatory deferral account balances, which is CU3,170 **[Refer: CU12,710 less CU9,540]** (20X6 – CU12,320). This aggregated presentation is permitted by paragraphs 24 and B12 of this Standard. An alternative disaggregated presentation is illustrated in Example 2.

IE2   For each type of rate-regulated activity, paragraph 33 requires an entity to present, for each class of regulatory deferral account balance, a reconciliation of the carrying amount at the beginning and the end of the period. This example illustrates how that requirement may be met for an entity with two types of rate-regulated activity (electricity distribution and gas distribution), but is not intended to illustrate all aspects of this Standard or IFRS more generally.

Regulatory deferral account balances

Regulatory deferral account debit balances	20X6	Balances arising in the period	Recovery/ reversal	20X7	Remaining recovery/ reversal period (years)
Electricity distribution					
Construction costs	18,720	5,440	(80)	24,080	4–10
Storm damage	64,410	–	(12,060)	52,350	4
Other regulatory accounts	6,270	2,320	(950)	7,640	4–10
Gas distribution					
Pension costs	5,130	10,120	(2,980)	12,270	N/A
Gas cost variances	7,800	–	(3,900)	3,900	1
	102,330	**17,880**	**(19,970)**	**100,240**	

Regulatory deferral account credit balances					
Electricity distribution					
Land disposal	–	19,000	–	19,000	10
Income tax	6,360	3,207	(1,093)	8,474	1–10
Gas distribution					
Gas cost variances	600	4,000	(200)	4,400	2–3
Income tax	3,180	1,603	(547)	4,236	1–10
Decommissioning costs	66,330	(2,030)	(2,450)	61,850	3–20
	76,470	**25,780**	**(4,290)**	**97,960**	

Notes:

(1)   Construction costs consist of costs that are not permitted to be included in the cost of property, plant and equipment in accordance with IAS 16 *Property, Plant and Equipment*. **[Refer: Basis for Conclusions paragraphs BC40–BC43 and BC45]**

(2)   Other regulatory accounts include regulatory deferral account debit balances that are individually immaterial.

continued...

...*continued*

(3) The net movement in the pension costs regulatory deferral account balance of CU7,140 (CU12,270 – CU5,130) relates to the remeasurement of the defined benefit pension plan, which is presented in other comprehensive income in accordance with IAS 19 *Employee Benefits*. In accordance with paragraph 22 of this Standard, the related movement in the regulatory deferral account balance is also presented in other comprehensive income.

(4) The recovery from, or refund to, customers of future income taxes through future rates is recognised as a regulatory deferral account balance. The company has recognised a deferred tax asset of CU12,710 (20X6 – CU9,540) arising from the recognition of regulatory deferral account balances and a corresponding regulatory deferral account credit balance of CU12,710 (20X6 – CU9,540). The deferred tax asset balance is presented within the total regulatory deferral account debit balances presented in the statement of financial position. **[Refer: paragraph 24 and Appendix B paragraph B11(a)]**

(5) The net movement of CU30,720 in the remaining regulatory deferral account balances is presented in the profit or loss section of the statement of profit or loss and other comprehensive income, net of the movement in the deferred tax asset related to the regulatory deferral account balances of CU3,170 [CU (8,474 – 6,360) + CU(4,236 – 3,180)]. **[Refer: paragraphs 23 and 24 and Appendix B paragraph B12(a)]** The remaining net movement of CU30,720 consists of:

Decrease in regulatory deferral account debit balances (CU100,240 – CU102,330)	(2,090)
Less: increase in pension cost regulatory deferral account debit balance presented in other comprehensive income (CU12,270 – CU5,130)	(7,140)
	(9,230)
Increase in regulatory deferral account credit balances (CU97,960 – CU76,470)	(21,490)
Net movement in regulatory deferral account balances presented in profit or loss	30,720

Example 2—Discontinued operations and taxation

IE3 Paragraphs 25 and 34 of this Standard require an entity to disclose the regulatory deferral account debit and credit balances and the net movement in those balances that relate to discontinued operations and disposal groups and to deferred taxes respectively. Paragraphs B19–B22 provide additional guidance relating to these disclosures. In particular, paragraphs B20–B21 permit an entity to present the regulatory deferral account amounts that are related to discontinued operations or disposal groups alongside the other regulatory deferral account amounts that are presented in the statement of financial position or the statement of profit or loss and other comprehensive income, or disclose them in the table that is required by paragraph 33. Example 2 illustrates how these requirements might be met, but is not intended to illustrate all aspects of this Standard or IFRS more generally.

IE4   In this example, the entity is in the process of disposing of one of its wholly-owned, rate-regulated subsidiaries and, consequently, is presenting the assets and liabilities of that subsidiary as a disposal group in the statement of financial position in accordance with IFRS 5 *Non-current Assets Held for Sale and Discontinued Operations*. In addition, the results of that subsidiary are presented in a single line item in the statement of profit or loss as a discontinued operation. The entity has decided that the amounts related to the regulatory deferral account balances included in the disposal group should be presented separately in the statement of financial position as permitted by paragraph B20.

IE5   In addition, the entity has decided to present separately the deferred tax asset balance that relates to the recognition of regulatory deferral account balances that are expected to be recovered (reversed) through future rates by presenting additional line items for the deferred tax asset balance and the movement in it, as permitted by paragraphs 24 and B11–B12.

XYZ Group—Statement of financial position as at 31 December 20X7 (extract)
(in currency units)
[Refer: paragraphs 20, 21, 24 and B11 and Basis for Conclusions paragraphs BC40–BC47]

	31 Dec 20X7	31 Dec 20X6
ASSETS		
Non-current assets		
AAA	x	x
	888,910	935,920
Current assets		
BBB	x	x
	x	x
Disposal group assets	15,200	–
	464,640	476,410
Total assets	1,353,550	1,412,330
Regulatory deferral account debit balances directly related to disposal group	9,800	–
Other regulatory deferral account debit balances	90,440	102,330
Deferred tax asset associated with regulatory deferral account balances	12,710	9,540
Total assets and regulatory deferral account debit balances	1,466,500	1,524,200

XYZ Group—Statement of financial position as at 31 December 20X7 (extract)
(in currency units)
[Refer: paragraphs 20, 21, 24 and B11 and Basis for Conclusions paragraphs BC40–BC47]

	31 Dec 20X7	31 Dec 20X6
EQUITY AND LIABILITIES		
Equity attributable to owners of the parent	x	x
Non-controlling interests	x	x
Total equity	973,750	831,500
Non-current liabilities		
DDD	x	x
	177,650	238,280
Current liabilities		
EEE	x	x
	x	x
Disposal group liabilities	2,540	–
	217,140	377,950
Total liabilities	394,790	616,230
Total equity and liabilities	1,368,540	1,447,730
Regulatory deferral account credit balances directly related to disposal group	17,460	–
Other regulatory deferral account credit balances	80,500	76,470
Total equity, liabilities and regulatory deferral account credit balances	1,466,500	1,524,200

Note: regulatory deferral account balances are not described as assets or liabilities for the purposes of this Standard. The sub-totals described as "Total assets" and "Total liabilities" are comparable to those that would be presented if the regulatory deferral account balances were not recognised. The difference between these two sub-totals represents the net balance of all regulatory deferral account balances recognised and any related deferred tax asset (liability) that arises as a result of recognising regulatory deferral account balances, which would otherwise be recognised within retained earnings or other components of equity.

XYZ Group—Statement of profit or loss and other comprehensive income for the year ended 31 December 20X7 (extract)
(illustrating the presentation of profit or loss and other comprehensive income in one statement)
(in currency units)
[Refer: paragraphs 22–24 and B12 and Basis for Conclusions paragraphs BC44–BC46]

	20X7	20X6
Revenue	390,000	358,784
FFF	x	x
Profit before tax	196,685	106,204
Income tax expense	(43,587)	(44,320)
Profit for the year from continuing operations	153,098	61,884
Loss for the year from discontinued operations	(3,500)	–
Profit for the year before net movements in regulatory deferral account balances	**149,598**	**61,884**
Net movement in regulatory deferral account balances related to profit or loss	(30,720)	(9,127)
Net movement in the deferred tax asset arising from regulatory deferral account balances related to profit or loss	3,170	12,320
Profit for the year and net movements in regulatory deferral account balances	**122,048**	**65,077**
Other comprehensive income: Items that will not be reclassified to profit or loss		
Remeasurement of defined benefit pension plans	(7,938)	(3,784)
Net movement in regulatory deferral account balances related to other comprehensive income	7,140	4,207
Other comprehensive income for the year, net of income tax	(798)	423
TOTAL COMPREHENSIVE INCOME FOR THE YEAR	121,250	65,500

Regulatory deferral account balances

Regulatory deferral account debit balances	20X6	Balances arising in the period	Recovery/ reversal	Other movements	20X7	Remaining recovery/ reversal period (years)
Electricity distribution						
Construction costs	18,720	5,440	(80)	–	24,080	4–10
Storm damage	64,410	–	(12,060)	(9,800)	42,550	4
Other regulatory balances	6,270	2,320	(950)	–	7,640	4–10
Gas distribution						
Pension costs	5,130	10,120	(2,980)	–	12,270	N/A
Gas cost variances	7,800	–	(3,900)	–	3,900	1
	102,330	**17,880**	**(19,970)**	**(9,800)**	**90,440**	
Disposal group	–	–	–	9,800	9,800	
	102,330	**17,880**	**(19,970)**	–	**100,240**	
Regulatory deferral account credit balances						
Electricity distribution						
Land disposal	–	19,000	–	–	19,000	10
Income tax	6,360	3,207	(1,093)	–	8,474	1–10
Gas distribution						
Gas cost variances	600	4,000	(200)	–	4,400	2–3
Income tax	3,180	1,603	(547)	–	4,236	1–10
Decommissioning costs	66,330	(2,030)	(2,450)	(17,460)	44,390	3–20
	76,470	**25,780**	**(4,290)**	**(17,460)**	**80,500**	
Disposal group	–	–	–	17,460	17,460	
	76,470	**25,780**	**(4,290)**	–	**97,960**	

[Refer: paragraph 33(a)]

Notes:

(1) The net movement in the pension costs regulatory deferral account balance of CU7,140 (CU12,270 – CU5,130) relates to the remeasurement of the defined benefit pension plan, which is presented in other comprehensive income in accordance with IAS 19 *Employee Benefits*. In accordance with paragraph 22 of this Standard, the related movement in the regulatory deferral account balance is also presented in other comprehensive income.

continued...

...continued

(2) The recovery from, or refund to, customers of future income taxes through future rates is recognised as a regulatory deferral account balance. The company has recognised a deferred tax asset of CU12,710 (20X6 – CU9,540) arising from the recognition of regulatory deferral account balances and a corresponding regulatory deferral account credit balance of CU12,710 (20X6 – CU9,540). The deferred tax asset balance is presented separately alongside the total of regulatory deferral account debit balances in the statement of financial position. **[Refer: paragraph 24 and Appendix B paragraph B11(b)]** Similarly, the net movement in the deferred tax asset related to the regulatory deferral account balances of CU3,170 [CU(8,474 - 6,360) + CU(4,236 – 3,180)] is presented separately in the statement of profit or loss.
[Refer: paragraph 24 and Appendix B paragraph B12(b)]

(3) The net movement of CU30,720 in the remaining regulatory deferral account balances is presented in the profit or loss section of the statement of profit or loss and other comprehensive income. **[Refer: paragraph 23]** This remaining net movement consists of:

Decrease in regulatory deferral account debit balances (CU100,240 – CU102,330)	(2,090)
Less: increase in pension cost regulatory deferral account debit balance presented in other comprehensive income (CU12,270 – CU5,130)	(7,140)
	(9,230)
Increase in regulatory deferral account credit balances (CU97,960 – CU76,470)	(21,490)
Net movement in regulatory deferral account balances presented in profit or loss	(30,720)

(4) In this example, the other movements represent transfers to the disposal group and have been shown separately in accordance with paragraph 33(a)(iii). If there are other movements that require separate disclosure, such as those caused by impairments or the effects of changes in foreign exchange rates or discount rates, these could be shown in a separate column or another method of disclosure, such as a footnote to the table.

IASB documents published to accompany

IFRS 15

Revenue from Contracts with Customers

The text of the unaccompanied standard, IFRS 15, is contained in Part A of this edition. The text of the Basis for Conclusions on IFRS 15 is contained in Part C of this edition. Its effective date when issued was 1 January 2017. In September 2015 the Board issued *Effective Date of IFRS 15* which deferred the effective date to 1 January 2018. This part presents the following documents:

ILLUSTRATIVE EXAMPLES

APPENDIX

Amendments to the guidance on other Standards

Contents

continued...

continued...

...continued

IFRS 15 *Revenue from Contracts with Customers* Illustrative Examples

These examples accompany, but are not part of, IFRS 15. They illustrate aspects of IFRS 15 but are not intended to provide interpretative guidance.

IE1 These examples portray hypothetical situations illustrating how an entity might apply some of the requirements in IFRS 15 to particular aspects of a contract with a customer on the basis of the limited facts presented. The analysis in each example is not intended to represent the only manner in which the requirements could be applied, nor are the examples intended to apply only to the specific industry illustrated. Although some aspects of the examples may be present in actual fact patterns, all relevant facts and circumstances of a particular fact pattern would need to be evaluated when applying IFRS 15.

Identifying the contract

IE2 Examples 1–4 illustrate the requirements in paragraphs 9–16 of IFRS 15 on identifying the contract. In addition, the following requirements are illustrated in these examples:

 (a) the interaction of paragraph 9 of IFRS 15 with paragraphs 47 and 52 of IFRS 15 on estimating variable consideration (Examples 2–3); and

 (b) paragraph B63 of IFRS 15 on consideration in the form of sales-based or usage-based royalties on licences of intellectual property (Example 4).

Example 1—Collectability of the consideration

IE3 An entity, a real estate developer, enters into a contract with a customer for the sale of a building for CU1 million.[1] The customer intends to open a restaurant in the building. The building is located in an area where new restaurants face high levels of competition and the customer has little experience in the restaurant industry.

IE4 The customer pays a non-refundable deposit of CU50,000 at inception of the contract and enters into a long-term financing agreement with the entity for the remaining 95 per cent of the promised consideration. The financing arrangement is provided on a non-recourse basis, which means that if the customer defaults, the entity can repossess the building, but cannot seek further compensation from the customer, even if the collateral does not cover the full value of the amount owed. The entity's cost of the building is CU600,000. The customer obtains control of the building at contract inception.

---

1 In these examples monetary amounts are denominated in 'currency units' (CU).

IE5   In assessing whether the contract meets the criteria in paragraph 9 of IFRS 15, the entity concludes that the criterion in paragraph 9(e) of IFRS 15 is not met because it is not probable that the entity will collect the consideration to which it is entitled in exchange for the transfer of the building. In reaching this conclusion, the entity observes that the customer's ability and intention to pay may be in doubt because of the following factors:

(a)   the customer intends to repay the loan (which has a significant balance) primarily from income derived from its restaurant business (which is a business facing significant risks because of high competition in the industry and the customer's limited experience);

(b)   the customer lacks other income or assets that could be used to repay the loan; and

(c)   the customer's liability under the loan is limited because the loan is non-recourse.

IE6   Because the criteria in paragraph 9 of IFRS 15 are not met, the entity applies paragraphs 15–16 of IFRS 15 to determine the accounting for the non-refundable deposit of CU50,000. The entity observes that none of the events described in paragraph 15 have occurred—that is, the entity has not received substantially all of the consideration and it has not terminated the contract. Consequently, in accordance with paragraph 16, the entity accounts for the non-refundable CU50,000 payment as a deposit liability. The entity continues to account for the initial deposit, as well as any future payments of principal and interest, as a deposit liability, until such time that the entity concludes that the criteria in paragraph 9 are met (ie the entity is able to conclude that it is probable that the entity will collect the consideration) or one of the events in paragraph 15 has occurred. The entity continues to assess the contract in accordance with paragraph 14 to determine whether the criteria in paragraph 9 are subsequently met or whether the events in paragraph 15 of IFRS 15 have occurred.

Example 2—Consideration is not the stated price— implicit price concession

IE7   An entity sells 1,000 units of a prescription drug to a customer for promised consideration of CU1 million. This is the entity's first sale to a customer in a new region, which is experiencing significant economic difficulty. Thus, the entity expects that it will not be able to collect from the customer the full amount of the promised consideration. Despite the possibility of not collecting the full amount, the entity expects the region's economy to recover over the next two to three years and determines that a relationship with the customer could help it to forge relationships with other potential customers in the region.

IE8   When assessing whether the criterion in paragraph 9(e) of IFRS 15 is met, the entity also considers paragraphs 47 and 52(b) of IFRS 15. Based on the assessment of the facts and circumstances, the entity determines that it expects to provide a price concession and accept a lower amount of consideration from the customer. Accordingly, the entity concludes that the transaction price is not CU1 million and, therefore, the promised consideration is variable. The entity estimates the variable consideration and determines that it expects to be entitled to CU400,000.

IE9　　The entity considers the customer's ability and intention to pay the consideration and concludes that even though the region is experiencing economic difficulty, it is probable that it will collect CU400,000 from the customer. Consequently, the entity concludes that the criterion in paragraph 9(e) of IFRS 15 is met based on an estimate of variable consideration of CU400,000. In addition, on the basis of an evaluation of the contract terms and other facts and circumstances, the entity concludes that the other criteria in paragraph 9 of IFRS 15 are also met. Consequently, the entity accounts for the contract with the customer in accordance with the requirements in IFRS 15.

Example 3—Implicit price concession

IE10　　An entity, a hospital, provides medical services to an uninsured patient in the emergency room. The entity has not previously provided medical services to this patient but is required by law to provide medical services to all emergency room patients. Because of the patient's condition upon arrival at the hospital, the entity provides the services immediately and, therefore, before the entity can determine whether the patient is committed to perform its obligations under the contract in exchange for the medical services provided. Consequently, the contract does not meet the criteria in paragraph 9 of IFRS 15 and, in accordance with paragraph 14 of IFRS 15, the entity will continue to assess its conclusion based on updated facts and circumstances.

IE11　　After providing services, the entity obtains additional information about the patient including a review of the services provided, standard rates for such services and the patient's ability and intention to pay the entity for the services provided. During the review, the entity notes its standard rate for the services provided in the emergency room is CU10,000. The entity also reviews the patient's information and to be consistent with its policies designates the patient to a customer class based on the entity's assessment of the patient's ability and intention to pay.

IE12　　Before reassessing whether the criteria in paragraph 9 of IFRS 15 have been met, the entity considers paragraphs 47 and 52(b) of IFRS 15. Although the standard rate for the services is CU10,000 (which may be the amount invoiced to the patient), the entity expects to accept a lower amount of consideration in exchange for the services. Accordingly, the entity concludes that the transaction price is not CU10,000 and, therefore, the promised consideration is variable. The entity reviews its historical cash collections from this customer class and other relevant information about the patient. The entity estimates the variable consideration and determines that it expects to be entitled to CU1,000.

IE13   In accordance with paragraph 9(e) of IFRS 15, the entity evaluates the patient's ability and intention to pay (ie the credit risk of the patient). On the basis of its collection history from patients in this customer class, the entity concludes it is probable that the entity will collect CU1,000 (which is the estimate of variable consideration). In addition, on the basis of an assessment of the contract terms and other facts and circumstances, the entity concludes that the other criteria in paragraph 9 of IFRS 15 are also met. Consequently, the entity accounts for the contract with the patient in accordance with the requirements in IFRS 15.

Example 4—Reassessing the criteria for identifying a contract

IE14   An entity licences a patent to a customer in exchange for a usage-based royalty. At contract inception, the contract meets all the criteria in paragraph 9 of IFRS 15 and the entity accounts for the contract with the customer in accordance with the requirements in IFRS 15. The entity recognises revenue when the customer's subsequent usage occurs in accordance with paragraph B63 of IFRS 15.

IE15   Throughout the first year of the contract, the customer provides quarterly reports of usage and pays within the agreed-upon period.

IE16   During the second year of the contract, the customer continues to use the entity's patent, but the customer's financial condition declines. The customer's current access to credit and available cash on hand are limited. The entity continues to recognise revenue on the basis of the customer's usage throughout the second year. The customer pays the first quarter's royalties but makes nominal payments for the usage of the patent in Quarters 2–4. The entity accounts for any impairment of the existing receivable in accordance with IFRS 9 *Financial Instruments*.

IE17   During the third year of the contract, the customer continues to use the entity's patent. However, the entity learns that the customer has lost access to credit and its major customers and thus the customer's ability to pay significantly deteriorates. The entity therefore concludes that it is unlikely that the customer will be able to make any further royalty payments for ongoing usage of the entity's patent. As a result of this significant change in facts and circumstances, in accordance with paragraph 13 of IFRS 15, the entity reassesses the criteria in paragraph 9 of IFRS 15 and determines that they are not met because it is no longer probable that the entity will collect the consideration to which it will be entitled. Accordingly, the entity does not recognise any further revenue associated with the customer's future usage of its patent. The entity accounts for any impairment of the existing receivable in accordance with IFRS 9 *Financial Instruments*.

Contract modifications

IE18   Examples 5–9 illustrate the requirements in paragraphs 18–21 of IFRS 15 on contract modifications. In addition, the following requirements are illustrated in these examples:

(a) paragraphs 22–30 of IFRS 15 on identifying performance obligations (Examples 7–8);

(b) paragraphs 56–58 of IFRS 15 on constraining estimates of variable consideration (Examples 6 and 8–9); and

(c) paragraphs 87–90 of IFRS 15 on changes in the transaction price (Example 6).

Example 5—Modification of a contract for goods

IE19   An entity promises to sell 120 products to a customer for CU12,000 (CU100 per product). The products are transferred to the customer over a six-month period. The entity transfers control of each product at a point in time. After the entity has transferred control of 60 products to the customer, the contract is modified to require the delivery of an additional 30 products (a total of 150 identical products) to the customer. The additional 30 products were not included in the initial contract.

Case A—Additional products for a price that reflects the stand-alone selling price

IE20   When the contract is modified, the price of the contract modification for the additional 30 products is an additional CU2,850 or CU95 per product. The pricing for the additional products reflects the stand-alone selling price of the products at the time of the contract modification and the additional products are distinct (in accordance with paragraph 27 of IFRS 15) from the original products.

IE21   In accordance with paragraph 20 of IFRS 15, the contract modification for the additional 30 products is, in effect, a new and separate contract for future products that does not affect the accounting for the existing contract. The entity recognises revenue of CU100 per product for the 120 products in the original contract and CU95 per product for the 30 products in the new contract.

Case B—Additional products for a price that does not reflect the stand-alone selling price

IE22   During the process of negotiating the purchase of an additional 30 products, the parties initially agree on a price of CU80 per product. However, the customer discovers that the initial 60 products transferred to the customer contained minor defects that were unique to those delivered products. The entity promises a partial credit of CU15 per product to compensate the customer for the poor quality of those products. The entity and the customer agree to incorporate the credit of CU900 (CU15 credit × 60 products) into the price that the entity charges for the additional 30 products. Consequently, the contract modification specifies that the price of the additional 30 products is CU1,500 or CU50 per product. That price comprises the agreed-upon price for the additional 30 products of CU2,400, or CU80 per product, less the credit of CU900.

IE23   At the time of modification, the entity recognises the CU900 as a reduction of the transaction price and, therefore, as a reduction of revenue for the initial 60 products transferred. In accounting for the sale of the additional 30 products, the entity determines that the negotiated price of CU80 per product does not reflect the stand-alone selling price of the additional products. Consequently, the contract modification does not meet the conditions in paragraph 20 of IFRS 15 to be accounted for as a separate contract. Because the remaining products to be delivered are distinct from those already transferred, the entity applies the requirements in paragraph 21(a) of IFRS 15 and accounts for the modification as a termination of the original contract and the creation of a new contract.

IE24   Consequently, the amount recognised as revenue for each of the remaining products is a blended price of CU93.33 {[(CU100 × 60 products not yet transferred under the original contract) + (CU80 × 30 products to be transferred under the contract modification)] ÷ 90 remaining products}.

Example 6—Change in the transaction price after a contract modification

IE25   On 1 July 20X0, an entity promises to transfer two distinct products to a customer. Product X transfers to the customer at contract inception and Product Y transfers on 31 March 20X1. The consideration promised by the customer includes fixed consideration of CU1,000 and variable consideration that is estimated to be CU200. The entity includes its estimate of variable consideration in the transaction price because it concludes that it is highly probable that a significant reversal in cumulative revenue recognised will not occur when the uncertainty is resolved. **[Refer: paragraph 56]**

IE26   The transaction price of CU1,200 is allocated equally to the performance obligation for Product X and the performance obligation for Product Y. This is because both products have the same stand-alone selling prices and the variable consideration does not meet the criteria in paragraph 85 that requires allocation of the variable consideration to one but not both of the performance obligations.

IE27   When Product X transfers to the customer at contract inception, the entity recognises revenue of CU600.

IE28   On 30 November 20X0, the scope of the contract is modified to include the promise to transfer Product Z (in addition to the undelivered Product Y) to the customer on 30 June 20X1 and the price of the contract is increased by CU300 (fixed consideration), which does not represent the stand-alone selling price of Product Z. The stand-alone selling price of Product Z is the same as the stand-alone selling prices of Products X and Y.

IE29   The entity accounts for the modification as if it were the termination of the existing contract and the creation of a new contract. This is because the remaining Products Y and Z are distinct from Product X, which had transferred to the customer before the modification, and the promised consideration for the additional Product Z does not represent its stand-alone selling price. Consequently, in accordance with paragraph 21(a) of IFRS 15, the consideration to be allocated to the remaining performance obligations comprises the consideration that had been allocated to the performance obligation for Product Y (which is measured at an allocated transaction price amount of CU600) and the consideration promised in the modification (fixed consideration of CU300). The transaction price for the modified contract is CU900 and that amount is allocated equally to the performance obligation for Product Y and the performance obligation for Product Z (ie CU450 is allocated to each performance obligation).

IE30   After the modification but before the delivery of Products Y and Z, the entity revises its estimate of the amount of variable consideration to which it expects to be entitled to CU240 (rather than the previous estimate of CU200). The entity concludes that the change in estimate of the variable consideration can be included in the transaction price, because it is highly probable that a significant reversal in cumulative revenue recognised will not occur when the uncertainty is resolved. Even though the modification was accounted for as if it were the termination of the existing contract and the creation of a new contract in accordance with paragraph 21(a) of IFRS 15, the increase in the transaction price of CU40 is attributable to variable consideration promised before the modification. Therefore, in accordance with paragraph 90 of IFRS 15, the change in the transaction price is allocated to the performance obligations for Product X and Product Y on the same basis as at contract inception. Consequently, the entity recognises revenue of CU20 for Product X in the period in which the change in the transaction price occurs. Because Product Y had not transferred to the customer before the contract modification, the change in the transaction price that is attributable to Product Y is allocated to the remaining performance obligations at the time of the contract modification. This is consistent with the accounting that would have been required by paragraph 21(a) of IFRS 15 if that amount of variable consideration had been estimated and included in the transaction price at the time of the contract modification.

IE31   The entity also allocates the CU20 increase in the transaction price for the modified contract equally to the performance obligations for Product Y and Product Z. This is because the products have the same stand-alone selling prices and the variable consideration does not meet the criteria in paragraph 85 that require allocation of the variable consideration to one but not both of the performance obligations. Consequently, the amount of the transaction price allocated to the performance obligations for Product Y and Product Z increases by CU10 to CU460 each.

IE32   On 31 March 20X1, Product Y is transferred to the customer and the entity recognises revenue of CU460. On 30 June 20X1, Product Z is transferred to the customer and the entity recognises revenue of CU460.

Example 7—Modification of a services contract

IE33   An entity enters into a three-year contract to clean a customer's offices on a weekly basis. The customer promises to pay CU100,000 per year. The stand-alone selling price of the services at contract inception is CU100,000 per year. The entity recognises revenue of CU100,000 per year during the first two years of providing services. At the end of the second year, the contract is modified and the fee for the third year is reduced to CU80,000. In addition, the customer agrees to extend the contract for three additional years for consideration of CU200,000 payable in three equal annual instalments of CU66,667 at the beginning of years 4, 5 and 6. After the modification, the contract has four years remaining in exchange for total consideration of CU280,000. The stand-alone selling price of the services at the beginning of the third year is CU80,000 per year. The entity's stand-alone selling price at the beginning of the third year, multiplied by the remaining number of years to provide services, is deemed to be an appropriate estimate of the stand-alone selling price of the multi-year contract (ie the stand-alone selling price is 4 years × CU80,000 per year = CU320,000).

IE34 At contract inception, the entity assesses that each week of cleaning service is distinct in accordance with paragraph 27 of IFRS 15. Notwithstanding that each week of cleaning service is distinct, the entity accounts for the cleaning contract as a single performance obligation in accordance with paragraph 22(b) of IFRS 15. This is because the weekly cleaning services are a series of distinct services that are substantially the same and have the same pattern of transfer to the customer (the services transfer to the customer over time and use the same method to measure progress—that is, a time-based measure of progress).

IE35 At the date of the modification, the entity assesses the remaining services to be provided and concludes that they are distinct. However, the amount of remaining consideration to be paid (CU280,000) does not reflect the stand-alone selling price of the services to be provided (CU320,000).

IE36 Consequently, the entity accounts for the modification in accordance with paragraph 21(a) of IFRS 15 as a termination of the original contract and the creation of a new contract with consideration of CU280,000 for four years of cleaning service. The entity recognises revenue of CU70,000 per year (CU280,000 ÷ 4 years) as the services are provided over the remaining four years.

Example 8—Modification resulting in a cumulative catch-up adjustment to revenue

IE37 An entity, a construction company, enters into a contract to construct a commercial building for a customer on customer-owned land for promised consideration of CU1 million and a bonus of CU200,000 if the building is completed within 24 months. The entity accounts for the promised bundle of goods and services as a single performance obligation satisfied over time in accordance with paragraph 35(b) of IFRS 15 because the customer controls the building during construction. At the inception of the contract, the entity expects the following:

	CU
Transaction price	1,000,000
Expected costs	700,000
Expected profit (30%)	300,000

IE38   At contract inception, the entity excludes the CU200,000 bonus from the transaction price because it cannot conclude that it is highly probable that a significant reversal in the amount of cumulative revenue recognised will not occur. Completion of the building is highly susceptible to factors outside the entity's influence, including weather and regulatory approvals. In addition, the entity has limited experience with similar types of contracts.

[Refer: paragraphs 56 and 57]

IE39   The entity determines that the input measure, on the basis of costs incurred, provides an appropriate measure of progress towards complete satisfaction of the performance obligation. By the end of the first year, the entity has satisfied 60 per cent of its performance obligation on the basis of costs incurred to date (CU420,000) relative to total expected costs (CU700,000). The entity reassesses the variable consideration and concludes that the amount is still constrained in accordance with paragraphs 56–58 of IFRS 15. Consequently, the cumulative revenue and costs recognised for the first year are as follows:

	CU
Revenue	600,000
Costs	420,000
Gross profit	180,000

IE40   In the first quarter of the second year, the parties to the contract agree to modify the contract by changing the floor plan of the building. As a result, the fixed consideration and expected costs increase by CU150,000 and CU120,000, respectively. Total potential consideration after the modification is CU1,350,000 (CU1,150,000 fixed consideration + CU200,000 completion bonus). In addition, the allowable time for achieving the CU200,000 bonus is extended by 6 months to 30 months from the original contract inception date. At the date of the modification, on the basis of its experience and the remaining work to be performed, which is primarily inside the building and not subject to weather conditions, the entity concludes that it is highly probable that including the bonus in the transaction price will not result in a significant reversal in the amount of cumulative revenue recognised in accordance with paragraph 56 of IFRS 15 and includes the CU200,000 in the transaction price. In assessing the contract modification, the entity evaluates paragraph 27(b) of IFRS 15 and concludes (on the basis of the factors in paragraph 29 of IFRS 15) that the remaining goods and services to be provided using the modified contract are not distinct from the goods and services transferred on or before the date of contract modification; that is, the contract remains a single performance obligation.

IE41 Consequently, the entity accounts for the contract modification as if it were part of the original contract (in accordance with paragraph 21(b) of IFRS 15). The entity updates its measure of progress and estimates that it has satisfied 51.2 per cent of its performance obligation (CU420,000 actual costs incurred ÷ CU820,000 total expected costs). The entity recognises additional revenue of CU91,200 [(51.2 per cent complete × CU1,350,000 modified transaction price) – CU600,000 revenue recognised to date] at the date of the modification as a cumulative catch-up adjustment.

Example 9—Unapproved change in scope and price

IE42 An entity enters into a contract with a customer to construct a building on customer-owned land. The contract states that the customer will provide the entity with access to the land within 30 days of contract inception. However, the entity was not provided access until 120 days after contract inception because of storm damage to the site that occurred after contract inception. The contract specifically identifies any delay (including force majeure) in the entity's access to customer-owned land as an event that entitles the entity to compensation that is equal to actual costs incurred as a direct result of the delay. The entity is able to demonstrate that the specific direct costs were incurred as a result of the delay in accordance with the terms of the contract and prepares a claim. The customer initially disagreed with the entity's claim.

IE43 The entity assesses the legal basis of the claim and determines, on the basis of the underlying contractual terms, that it has enforceable rights. Consequently, it accounts for the claim as a contract modification in accordance with paragraphs 18–21 of IFRS 15. The modification does not result in any additional goods and services being provided to the customer. In addition, all of the remaining goods and services after the modification are not distinct and form part of a single performance obligation. Consequently, the entity accounts for the modification in accordance with paragraph 21(b) of IFRS 15 by updating the transaction price and the measure of progress towards complete satisfaction of the performance obligation. The entity considers the constraint on estimates of variable consideration in paragraphs 56–58 of IFRS 15 when estimating the transaction price.

Identifying performance obligations

IE44 Examples 10–12 illustrate the requirements in paragraphs 22–30 of IFRS 15 on identifying performance obligations.

Example 10—Goods and services are not distinct

Case A—Significant integration service

IE45 An entity, a contractor, enters into a contract to build a hospital for a customer. The entity is responsible for the overall management of the project and identifies various promised goods and services, including engineering, site clearance, foundation, procurement, construction of the structure, piping and wiring, installation of equipment and finishing.

IE46   The promised goods and services are capable of being distinct in accordance with paragraph 27(a) of IFRS 15. That is, the customer can benefit from the goods and services either on their own or together with other readily available resources. This is evidenced by the fact that the entity, or competitors of the entity, regularly sells many of these goods and services separately to other customers. In addition, the customer could generate economic benefit from the individual goods and services by using, consuming, selling or holding those goods or services.

IE47   However, the promises to transfer the goods and services are not separately identifiable in accordance with paragraph 27(b) of IFRS 15 (on the basis of the factors in paragraph 29 of IFRS 15). This is evidenced by the fact that the entity provides a significant service of integrating the goods and services (the inputs) into the hospital (the combined output) for which the customer has contracted.

IE48   Because both criteria in paragraph 27 of IFRS 15 are not met, the goods and services are not distinct. The entity accounts for all of the goods and services in the contract as a single performance obligation.

Case B—Significant integration service
[Refer: Basis for Conclusions paragraph BC116Q]

IE48A   An entity enters into a contract with a customer that will result in the delivery of multiple units of a highly complex, specialised device. The terms of the contract require the entity to establish a manufacturing process in order to produce the contracted units. The specifications are unique to the customer, based on a custom design that is owned by the customer and that were developed under the terms of a separate contract that is not part of the current negotiated exchange. The entity is responsible for the overall management of the contract, which requires the performance and integration of various activities including procurement of materials, identifying and managing subcontractors, and performing manufacturing, assembly and testing.

IE48B   The entity assesses the promises in the contract and determines that each of the promised devices is capable of being distinct in accordance with paragraph 27(a) of IFRS 15 because the customer can benefit from each device on its own. This is because each unit can function independently of the other units.

IE48C   The entity observes that the nature of its promise is to establish and provide a service of producing the full complement of devices for which the customer has contracted in accordance with the customer's specifications. The entity considers that it is responsible for overall management of the contract and for providing a significant service of integrating various goods and services (the inputs) into its overall service and the resulting devices (the combined output) and, therefore, the devices and the various promised goods and services inherent in producing those devices are not separately identifiable in accordance with paragraph 27(b) and paragraph 29 of IFRS 15. In this case, the manufacturing process provided by the entity is specific to its contract with the customer. In addition, the nature of the entity's performance and, in particular, the significant integration service of the various activities means that a change in one of the entity's activities to produce the devices has a significant effect on the other activities required to produce the highly complex, specialised devices such that the entity's activities are highly interdependent and highly interrelated. Because the criterion in paragraph 27(b) of IFRS 15 is not met, the goods and services that will be provided by the entity are not separately identifiable and, therefore, are not distinct. The entity accounts for all of the goods and services promised in the contract as a single performance obligation.

Example 11—Determining whether goods or services are distinct

Case A—Distinct goods or services

IE49   An entity, a software developer, enters into a contract with a customer to transfer a software licence, perform an installation service and provide unspecified software updates and technical support (online and telephone) for a two-year period. The entity sells the licence, installation service and technical support separately. The installation service includes changing the web screen for each type of user (for example, marketing, inventory management and information technology). The installation service is routinely performed by other entities and does not significantly modify the software. The software remains functional without the updates and the technical support.

IE50   The entity assesses the goods and services promised to the customer to determine which goods and services are distinct in accordance with paragraph 27 of IFRS 15. The entity observes that the software is delivered before the other goods and services and remains functional without the updates and the technical support. The customer can benefit from the updates together with the software licence transferred at the start of the contract. Thus, the entity concludes that the customer can benefit from each of the goods and services either on their own or together with the other goods and services that are readily available and the criterion in paragraph 27(a) of IFRS 15 is met.

IE51   The entity also considers the principle and the factors in paragraph 29 of IFRS 15 and determines that the promise to transfer each good and service to the customer is separately identifiable from each of the other promises (thus the criterion in paragraph 27(b) of IFRS 15 is met). In reaching this determination, the entity considers that, although it integrates the software into the customer's system, the installation services do not significantly affect the customer's ability to use and benefit from the software licence because the installation services are routine and can be obtained from alternative providers. The software updates do not significantly affect the customer's ability to use and benefit from the software licence during the licence period. The entity further observes that none of the promised goods or services significantly modify or customise one another, nor is the entity providing a significant service of integrating the software and the services into a combined output. Lastly, the entity concludes that the software and the services do not significantly affect each other and, therefore, are not highly interdependent or highly interrelated, because the entity would be able to fulfil its promise to transfer the initial software licence independently from its promise to subsequently provide the installation service, software updates or technical support.

IE52   On the basis of this assessment, the entity identifies four performance obligations in the contract for the following goods or services:

(a)   the software licence;

(b)   an installation service;

(c)   software updates; and

(d)   technical support.

IE53   The entity applies paragraphs 31–38 of IFRS 15 to determine whether each of the performance obligations for the installation service, software updates and technical support are satisfied at a point in time or over time. The entity also assesses the nature of the entity's promise to transfer the software licence in accordance with paragraph B58 of IFRS 15 (see Example 54 in paragraphs IE276–IE277).

Case B—Significant customisation

IE54   The promised goods and services are the same as in Case A, except that the contract specifies that, as part of the installation service, the software is to be substantially customised to add significant new functionality to enable the software to interface with other customised software applications used by the customer. The customised installation service can be provided by other entities.

IE55   The entity assesses the goods and services promised to the customer to determine which goods and services are distinct in accordance with paragraph 27 of IFRS 15. The entity first assesses whether the criterion in paragraph 27(a) has been met. For the same reasons as in Case A, the entity determines that the software licence, installation, software updates and technical support each meet that criterion. The entity next assesses whether the criterion in paragraph 27(b) has been met by evaluating the principle and the factors in paragraph 29 of IFRS 15. The entity observes that the terms of the contract result in a promise to provide a significant service of integrating the licenced software into the existing software system by performing a customised installation service as specified in the contract. In other words, the entity is using the licence and the customised installation service as inputs to produce the combined output (ie a functional and integrated software system) specified in the contract (see paragraph 29(a) of IFRS 15). The software is significantly modified and customised by the service (see paragraph 29(b) of IFRS 15). Consequently, the entity determines that the promise to transfer the licence is not separately identifiable from the customised installation service and, therefore, the criterion in paragraph 27(b) of IFRS 15 is not met. Thus, the software licence and the customised installation service are not distinct.

IE56   On the basis of the same analysis as in Case A, the entity concludes that the software updates and technical support are distinct from the other promises in the contract.

IE57   On the basis of this assessment, the entity identifies three performance obligations in the contract for the following goods or services:

(a)   software customisation (which comprises the licence for the software and the customised installation service);

(b)   software updates; and

(c)   technical support.

IE58   The entity applies paragraphs 31–38 of IFRS 15 to determine whether each performance obligation is satisfied at a point in time or over time.

Case C—Promises are separately identifiable (installation)

IE58A   An entity contracts with a customer to sell a piece of equipment and installation services. The equipment is operational without any customisation or modification. The installation required is not complex and is capable of being performed by several alternative service providers.

IE58B   The entity identifies two promised goods and services in the contract: (a) equipment and (b) installation. The entity assesses the criteria in paragraph 27 of IFRS 15 to determine whether each promised good or service is distinct. The entity determines that the equipment and the installation each meet the criterion in paragraph 27(a) of IFRS 15. The customer can benefit from the equipment on its own, by using it or reselling it for an amount greater than scrap value, or together with other readily available resources (for example, installation services available from alternative providers). The customer also can benefit from the installation services together with other resources that the customer will already have obtained from the entity (ie the equipment).

IE58C   The entity further determines that its promises to transfer the equipment and to provide the installation services are each separately identifiable (in accordance with paragraph 27(b) of IFRS 15). The entity considers the principle and the factors in paragraph 29 of IFRS 15 in determining that the equipment and the installation services are not inputs to a combined item in this contract. In this case, each of the factors in paragraph 29 of IFRS 15 contributes to, but is not individually determinative of, the conclusion that the equipment and the installation services are separately identifiable as follows:

(a)   The entity is not providing a significant integration service. That is, the entity has promised to deliver the equipment and then install it; the entity would be able to fulfil its promise to transfer the equipment separately from its promise to subsequently install it. The entity has not promised to combine the equipment and the installation services in a way that would transform them into a combined output.

(b)   The entity's installation services will not significantly customise or significantly modify the equipment.

(c)   Although the customer can benefit from the installation services only after it has obtained control of the equipment, the installation services do not significantly affect the equipment because the entity would be able to fulfil its promise to transfer the equipment independently of its promise to provide the installation services. Because the equipment and the installation services do not each significantly affect the other, they are not highly interdependent or highly interrelated.

On the basis of this assessment, the entity identifies two performance obligations in the contract for the following goods or services:

(i)   the equipment; and

(ii)   installation services.

IE58D   The entity applies paragraphs 31–38 of IFRS 15 to determine whether each performance obligation is satisfied at a point in time or over time.

Case D—Promises are separately identifiable (contractual restrictions)
[Refer: Basis for Conclusions paragraph BC116O]

IE58E   Assume the same facts as in Case C, except that the customer is contractually required to use the entity's installation services.

IE58F   The contractual requirement to use the entity's installation services does not change the evaluation of whether the promised goods and services are distinct in this case. This is because the contractual requirement to use the entity's installation services does not change the characteristics of the goods or services themselves, nor does it change the entity's promises to the customer. Although the customer is required to use the entity's installation services, the equipment and the installation services are capable of being distinct (ie they each meet the criterion in paragraph 27(a) of IFRS 15) and the entity's promises to provide the equipment and to provide the installation services are each separately identifiable, ie they each meet the criterion in paragraph 27(b) of IFRS 15. The entity's analysis in this regard is consistent with that in Case C.

Case E—Promises are separately identifiable (consumables)
[Refer: Basis for Conclusions paragraph BC116K]

IE58G   An entity enters into a contract with a customer to provide a piece of off-the-shelf equipment (ie the equipment is operational without any significant customisation or modification) and to provide specialised consumables for use in the equipment at predetermined intervals over the next three years. The consumables are produced only by the entity, but are sold separately by the entity.

IE58H   The entity determines that the customer can benefit from the equipment together with the readily available consumables. The consumables are readily available in accordance with paragraph 28 of IFRS 15, because they are regularly sold separately by the entity (ie through refill orders to customers that previously purchased the equipment). The customer can benefit from the consumables that will be delivered under the contract together with the delivered equipment that is transferred to the customer initially under the contract. Therefore, the equipment and the consumables are each capable of being distinct in accordance with paragraph 27(a) of IFRS 15.

IE58I   The entity determines that its promises to transfer the equipment and to provide consumables over a three-year period are each separately identifiable in accordance with paragraph 27(b) of IFRS 15. In determining that the equipment and the consumables are not inputs to a combined item in this contract, the entity considers that it is not providing a significant integration service that transforms the equipment and consumables into a combined output. In addition, neither the equipment nor the consumables are significantly customised or modified by the other. Lastly, the entity concludes that the equipment and the consumables are not highly interdependent or highly interrelated because they do not significantly affect each other. Although the customer can benefit from the consumables in this contract only after it has obtained control of the equipment (ie the consumables would have no use without the equipment) and the consumables are required for the equipment to function, the equipment and the consumables do not each significantly affect the other. This is because the entity would be able to fulfil each of its promises in the contract independently of the other. That is, the entity would be able to fulfil its promise to transfer the equipment even if the customer did not purchase any consumables and would be able to fulfil its promise to provide the consumables, even if the customer acquired the equipment separately.

IE58J   On the basis of this assessment, the entity identifies two performance obligations in the contract for the following goods or services:

(a)   the equipment; and

(b)   the consumables.

IE58K   The entity applies paragraphs 31–38 of IFRS 15 to determine whether each performance obligation is satisfied at a point in time or over time.

Example 12—Explicit and implicit promises in a contract

IE59   An entity, a manufacturer, sells a product to a distributor (ie its customer) who will then resell it to an end customer.

Case A—Explicit promise of service

IE60   In the contract with the distributor, the entity promises to provide maintenance services for no additional consideration (ie 'free') to any party (ie the end customer) that purchases the product from the distributor. The entity outsources the performance of the maintenance services to the distributor and pays the distributor an agreed-upon amount for providing those services on the entity's behalf. If the end customer does not use the maintenance services, the entity is not obliged to pay the distributor.

IE61   The contract with the customer includes two promised goods or services—(a) the product and (b) the maintenance services. The promise of maintenance services is a promise to transfer goods or services in the future and is part of the negotiated exchange between the entity and the distributor. The entity assesses whether each good or service is distinct in accordance with paragraph 27 of IFRS 15. The entity determines that both the product and the maintenance services meet the criterion in paragraph 27(a) of IFRS 15. The entity regularly sells the product on a stand-alone basis, which indicates that the customer can benefit from the product on its own. The customer can benefit from the maintenance services together with a resource the customer already has obtained from the entity (ie the product).

IE61A   The entity further determines that its promises to transfer the product and to provide the maintenance services are separately identifiable (in accordance with paragraph 27(b) of IFRS 15) on the basis of the principle and the factors in paragraph 29 of IFRS 15. The product and the maintenance services are not inputs to a combined item in the contract. The entity is not providing a significant integration service because the presence of the product and the services together in this contract do not result in any additional or combined functionality. In addition, neither the product nor the services modify or customise the other. Lastly, the product and the maintenance services are not highly interdependent or highly interrelated because the entity would be able to fulfil each of the promises in the contract independently of its efforts to fulfil the other (ie the entity would be able to transfer the product even if the customer declined maintenance services and would be able to provide maintenance services in relation to products sold previously through other distributors). The entity also observes, in applying the principle in paragraph 29 of IFRS 15, that the entity's promise to provide maintenance is not necessary for the product to continue to provide significant benefit to the customer. Consequently, the entity allocates a portion of the transaction price to each of the two performance obligations (ie the product and the maintenance services) in the contract.

Case B—Implicit promise of service

IE62   The entity has historically provided maintenance services for no additional consideration (ie 'free') to end customers that purchase the entity's product from the distributor. The entity does not explicitly promise maintenance services during negotiations with the distributor and the final contract between the entity and the distributor does not specify terms or conditions for those services.

IE63   However, on the basis of its customary business practice, the entity determines at contract inception that it has made an implicit promise to provide maintenance services as part of the negotiated exchange with the distributor. That is, the entity's past practices of providing these services create valid expectations of the entity's customers (ie the distributor and end customers) in accordance with paragraph 24 of IFRS 15. Consequently, the entity assesses whether the promise of maintenance services is a performance obligation. For the same reasons as in Case A, the entity determines that the product and maintenance services are separate performance obligations.

Case C—Services are not a promised service

IE64　In the contract with the distributor, the entity does not promise to provide any maintenance services. In addition, the entity typically does not provide maintenance services and, therefore, the entity's customary business practices, published policies and specific statements at the time of entering into the contract have not created an implicit promise to provide goods or services to its customers. The entity transfers control of the product to the distributor and, therefore, the contract is completed. However, before the sale to the end customer, the entity makes an offer to provide maintenance services to any party that purchases the product from the distributor for no additional promised consideration.

IE65　The promise of maintenance is not included in the contract between the entity and the distributor at contract inception. That is, in accordance with paragraph 24 of IFRS 15, the entity does not explicitly or implicitly promise to provide maintenance services to the distributor or the end customers. Consequently, the entity does not identify the promise to provide maintenance services as a performance obligation. Instead, the obligation to provide maintenance services is accounted for in accordance with IAS 37 *Provisions, Contingent Liabilities and Contingent Assets*.

IE65A　Although the maintenance services are not a promised service in the current contract, in future contracts with customers the entity would assess whether it has created a business practice resulting in an implied promise to provide maintenance services.

Performance obligations satisfied over time

IE66　Examples 13–17 illustrate the requirements in paragraphs 35–37 and B2–B13 of IFRS 15 on performance obligations satisfied over time. In addition, the following requirements are illustrated in these examples:

(a)　paragraphs 35(a) and B3–B4 of IFRS 15 on when a customer simultaneously receives and consumes the benefits provided by the entity's performance as the entity performs (Examples 13–14);

(b)　paragraphs 35(c), 36–37 and B6–B13 of IFRS 15 on an entity's performance that does not create an asset with an alternative use and an entity's enforceable right to payment for performance completed to date (Examples 14–17); and

(c)　paragraph 38 of IFRS 15 on performance obligations satisfied at a point in time (Example 17).

Example 13—Customer simultaneously receives and consumes the benefits

IE67　An entity enters into a contract to provide monthly payroll processing services to a customer for one year.

IE68 The promised payroll processing services are accounted for as a single performance obligation in accordance with paragraph 22(b) of IFRS 15. The performance obligation is satisfied over time in accordance with paragraph 35(a) of IFRS 15 because the customer simultaneously receives and consumes the benefits of the entity's performance in processing each payroll transaction as and when each transaction is processed. The fact that another entity would not need to re-perform payroll processing services for the service that the entity has provided to date also demonstrates that the customer simultaneously receives and consumes the benefits of the entity's performance as the entity performs. (The entity disregards any practical limitations on transferring the remaining performance obligation, including setup activities that would need to be undertaken by another entity.) The entity recognises revenue over time by measuring its progress towards complete satisfaction of that performance obligation in accordance with paragraphs 39–45 and B14–B19 of IFRS 15.

Example 14—Assessing alternative use and right to payment

IE69 An entity enters into a contract with a customer to provide a consulting service that results in the entity providing a professional opinion to the customer. The professional opinion relates to facts and circumstances that are specific to the customer. If the customer were to terminate the consulting contract for reasons other than the entity's failure to perform as promised, the contract requires the customer to compensate the entity for its costs incurred plus a 15 per cent margin. The 15 per cent margin approximates the profit margin that the entity earns from similar contracts.

IE70 The entity considers the criterion in paragraph 35(a) of IFRS 15 and the requirements in paragraphs B3 and B4 of IFRS 15 to determine whether the customer simultaneously receives and consumes the benefits of the entity's performance. If the entity were to be unable to satisfy its obligation and the customer hired another consulting firm to provide the opinion, the other consulting firm would need to substantially re-perform the work that the entity had completed to date, because the other consulting firm would not have the benefit of any work in progress performed by the entity. The nature of the professional opinion is such that the customer will receive the benefits of the entity's performance only when the customer receives the professional opinion. Consequently, the entity concludes that the criterion in paragraph 35(a) of IFRS 15 is not met.

IE71 However, the entity's performance obligation meets the criterion in paragraph 35(c) of IFRS 15 and is a performance obligation satisfied over time because of both of the following factors:

 (a) in accordance with paragraphs 36 and B6–B8 of IFRS 15, the development of the professional opinion does not create an asset with alternative use to the entity because the professional opinion relates to facts and circumstances that are specific to the customer. Therefore, there is a practical limitation on the entity's ability to readily direct the asset to another customer.

(b)   in accordance with paragraphs 37 and B9–B13 of IFRS 15, the entity has an enforceable right to payment for its performance completed to date for its costs plus a reasonable margin, which approximates the profit margin in other contracts.

IE72   Consequently, the entity recognises revenue over time by measuring the progress towards complete satisfaction of the performance obligation in accordance with paragraphs 39–45 and B14–B19 of IFRS 15.

Example 15—Asset has no alternative use to the entity

IE73   An entity enters into a contract with a customer, a government agency, to build a specialised satellite. The entity builds satellites for various customers, such as governments and commercial entities. The design and construction of each satellite differ substantially, on the basis of each customer's needs and the type of technology that is incorporated into the satellite.

IE74   At contract inception, the entity assesses whether its performance obligation to build the satellite is a performance obligation satisfied over time in accordance with paragraph 35 of IFRS 15.

IE75   As part of that assessment, the entity considers whether the satellite in its completed state will have an alternative use to the entity. Although the contract does not preclude the entity from directing the completed satellite to another customer, the entity would incur significant costs to rework the design and function of the satellite to direct that asset to another customer. Consequently, the asset has no alternative use to the entity (see paragraphs 35(c), 36 and B6–B8 of IFRS 15) because the customer-specific design of the satellite limits the entity's practical ability to readily direct the satellite to another customer.

IE76   For the entity's performance obligation to be satisfied over time when building the satellite, paragraph 35(c) of IFRS 15 also requires the entity to have an enforceable right to payment for performance completed to date. This condition is not illustrated in this example.

Example 16—Enforceable right to payment for performance completed to date

IE77   An entity enters into a contract with a customer to build an item of equipment. The payment schedule in the contract specifies that the customer must make an advance payment at contract inception of 10 per cent of the contract price, regular payments throughout the construction period (amounting to 50 per cent of the contract price) and a final payment of 40 per cent of the contract price after construction is completed and the equipment has passed the prescribed performance tests. The payments are non-refundable unless the entity fails to perform as promised. If the customer terminates the contract, the entity is entitled only to retain any progress payments received from the customer. The entity has no further rights to compensation from the customer.

IE78   At contract inception, the entity assesses whether its performance obligation to build the equipment is a performance obligation satisfied over time in accordance with paragraph 35 of IFRS 15.

IE79   As part of that assessment, the entity considers whether it has an enforceable right to payment for performance completed to date in accordance with paragraphs 35(c), 37 and B9–B13 of IFRS 15 if the customer were to terminate the contract for reasons other than the entity's failure to perform as promised. Even though the payments made by the customer are non-refundable, the cumulative amount of those payments is not expected, at all times throughout the contract, to at least correspond to the amount that would be necessary to compensate the entity for performance completed to date. This is because at various times during construction the cumulative amount of consideration paid by the customer might be less than the selling price of the partially completed item of equipment at that time. Consequently, the entity does not have a right to payment for performance completed to date.

IE80   Because the entity does not have a right to payment for performance completed to date, the entity's performance obligation is not satisfied over time in accordance with paragraph 35(c) of IFRS 15. Accordingly, the entity does not need to assess whether the equipment would have an alternative use to the entity. The entity also concludes that it does not meet the criteria in paragraph 35(a) or (b) of IFRS 15 and thus, the entity accounts for the construction of the equipment as a performance obligation satisfied at a point in time in accordance with paragraph 38 of IFRS 15.

Example 17—Assessing whether a performance obligation is satisfied at a point in time or over time

IE81   An entity is developing a multi-unit residential complex. A customer enters into a binding sales contract with the entity for a specified unit that is under construction. Each unit has a similar floor plan and is of a similar size, but other attributes of the units are different (for example, the location of the unit within the complex).

Case A—Entity does not have an enforceable right to payment for performance completed to date

IE82   The customer pays a deposit upon entering into the contract and the deposit is refundable only if the entity fails to complete construction of the unit in accordance with the contract. The remainder of the contract price is payable on completion of the contract when the customer obtains physical possession of the unit. If the customer defaults on the contract before completion of the unit, the entity only has the right to retain the deposit.

IE83   At contract inception, the entity applies paragraph 35(c) of IFRS 15 to determine whether its promise to construct and transfer the unit to the customer is a performance obligation satisfied over time. The entity determines that it does not have an enforceable right to payment for performance completed to date because, until construction of the unit is complete, the entity only has a right to the deposit paid by the customer.

Because the entity does not have a right to payment for work completed to date, the entity's performance obligation is not a performance obligation satisfied over time in accordance with paragraph 35(c) of IFRS 15. Instead, the entity accounts for the sale of the unit as a performance obligation satisfied at a point in time in accordance with paragraph 38 of IFRS 15.

Case B—Entity has an enforceable right to payment for performance completed to date

IE84   The customer pays a non-refundable deposit upon entering into the contract and will make progress payments during construction of the unit. The contract has substantive terms that preclude the entity from being able to direct the unit to another customer. In addition, the customer does not have the right to terminate the contract unless the entity fails to perform as promised. If the customer defaults on its obligations by failing to make the promised progress payments as and when they are due, the entity would have a right to all of the consideration promised in the contract if it completes the construction of the unit. The courts have previously upheld similar rights that entitle developers to require the customer to perform, subject to the entity meeting its obligations under the contract.

IE85   At contract inception, the entity applies paragraph 35(c) of IFRS 15 to determine whether its promise to construct and transfer the unit to the customer is a performance obligation satisfied over time. The entity determines that the asset (unit) created by the entity's performance does not have an alternative use to the entity because the contract precludes the entity from transferring the specified unit to another customer. The entity does not consider the possibility of a contract termination in assessing whether the entity is able to direct the asset to another customer.

IE86   The entity also has a right to payment for performance completed to date in accordance with paragraphs 37 and B9–B13 of IFRS 15. This is because if the customer were to default on its obligations, the entity would have an enforceable right to all of the consideration promised under the contract if it continues to perform as promised.

IE87   Therefore, the terms of the contract and the practices in the legal jurisdiction indicate that there is a right to payment for performance completed to date. Consequently, the criteria in paragraph 35(c) of IFRS 15 are met and the entity has a performance obligation that it satisfies over time. To recognise revenue for that performance obligation satisfied over time, the entity measures its progress towards complete satisfaction of its performance obligation in accordance with paragraphs 39–45 and B14–B19 of IFRS 15.

IE88   In the construction of a multi-unit residential complex, the entity may have many contracts with individual customers for the construction of individual units within the complex. The entity would account for each contract separately. However, depending on the nature of the construction, the entity's performance in undertaking the initial construction works (ie the foundation and the basic structure), as well as the construction of common areas, may need to be reflected when measuring its progress towards complete satisfaction of its performance obligations in each contract.

Case C—Entity has an enforceable right to payment for performance completed to date

IE89   The same facts as in Case B apply to Case C, except that in the event of a default by the customer, either the entity can require the customer to perform as required under the contract or the entity can cancel the contract in exchange for the asset under construction and an entitlement to a penalty of a proportion of the contract price.

IE90   Notwithstanding that the entity could cancel the contract (in which case the customer's obligation to the entity would be limited to transferring control of the partially completed asset to the entity and paying the penalty prescribed), the entity has a right to payment for performance completed to date because the entity could also choose to enforce its rights to full payment under the contract. The fact that the entity may choose to cancel the contract in the event the customer defaults on its obligations would not affect that assessment (see paragraph B11 of IFRS 15), provided that the entity's rights to require the customer to continue to perform as required under the contract (ie pay the promised consideration) are enforceable.

Measuring progress towards complete satisfaction of a performance obligation

IE91   Examples 18–19 illustrate the requirements in paragraphs 39–45 of IFRS 15 on measuring progress towards complete satisfaction of a performance obligation satisfied over time. Example 19 also illustrates the requirements in paragraph B19 of IFRS 15 on uninstalled materials when costs incurred are not proportionate to the entity's progress in satisfying a performance obligation.
        [Refer: Illustrative Examples, example 58]

Example 18—Measuring progress when making goods or services available

IE92   An entity, an owner and manager of health clubs, enters into a contract with a customer for one year of access to any of its health clubs. The customer has unlimited use of the health clubs and promises to pay CU100 per month.

IE93   The entity determines that its promise to the customer is to provide a service of making the health clubs available for the customer to use as and when the customer wishes. This is because the extent to which the customer uses the health clubs does not affect the amount of the remaining goods and services to which the customer is entitled. The entity concludes that the customer simultaneously receives and consumes the benefits of the entity's performance as it performs by making the health clubs available. Consequently, the entity's performance obligation is satisfied over time in accordance with paragraph 35(a) of IFRS 15.

IE94   The entity also determines that the customer benefits from the entity's service of making the health clubs available evenly throughout the year. (That is, the customer benefits from having the health clubs available, regardless of whether the customer uses it or not.) Consequently, the entity concludes that the best measure of progress towards complete satisfaction of the performance obligation over time is a time-based measure and it recognises revenue on a straight-line basis throughout the year at CU100 per month.

Example 19—Uninstalled materials

IE95　In November 20X2, an entity contracts with a customer to refurbish a 3-storey building and install new elevators for total consideration of CU5 million. The promised refurbishment service, including the installation of elevators, is a single performance obligation satisfied over time. Total expected costs are CU4 million, including CU1.5 million for the elevators. The entity determines that it acts as a principal in accordance with paragraphs B34–B38 of IFRS 15, because it obtains control of the elevators before they are transferred to the customer.

IE96　A summary of the transaction price and expected costs is as follows:

	CU
Transaction price	5,000,000
Expected costs:	
Elevators	1,500,000
Other costs	2,500,000
Total expected costs	4,000,000

IE97　The entity uses an input method based on costs incurred to measure its progress towards complete satisfaction of the performance obligation. The entity assesses whether the costs incurred to procure the elevators are proportionate to the entity's progress in satisfying the performance obligation, in accordance with paragraph B19 of IFRS 15. The customer obtains control of the elevators when they are delivered to the site in December 20X2, although the elevators will not be installed until June 20X3. The costs to procure the elevators (CU1.5 million) are significant relative to the total expected costs to completely satisfy the performance obligation (CU4 million). The entity is not involved in designing or manufacturing the elevators.

IE98　The entity concludes that including the costs to procure the elevators in the measure of progress would overstate the extent of the entity's performance. Consequently, in accordance with paragraph B19 of IFRS 15, the entity adjusts its measure of progress to exclude the costs to procure the elevators from the measure of costs incurred and from the transaction price. The entity recognises revenue for the transfer of the elevators in an amount equal to the costs to procure the elevators (ie at a zero margin).

IE99　As of 31 December 20X2 the entity observes that:

(a)　other costs incurred (excluding elevators) are CU500,000; and

(b)　performance is 20 per cent complete (ie CU500,000 ÷ CU2,500,000).

IE100 Consequently, at 31 December 20X2, the entity recognises the following:

	CU
Revenue	2,200,000[a]
Cost of goods sold	2,000,000[b]
Profit	200,000

(a) Revenue recognised is calculated as (20 per cent × CU3,500,000) + CU1,500,000. (CU3,500,000 is CU5,000,000 transaction price – CU1,500,000 costs of elevators.)

(b) Cost of goods sold is CU500,000 of costs incurred + CU1,500,000 costs of elevators.

Variable consideration

IE101 Examples 20–21 illustrate the requirements in paragraphs 50–54 of IFRS 15 on identifying variable consideration.

Example 20—Penalty gives rise to variable consideration

IE102 An entity enters into a contract with a customer to build an asset for CU1 million. In addition, the terms of the contract include a penalty of CU100,000 if the construction is not completed within three months of a date specified in the contract.

IE103 The entity concludes that the consideration promised in the contract includes a fixed amount of CU900,000 and a variable amount of CU100,000 (arising from the penalty).

IE104 The entity estimates the variable consideration in accordance with paragraphs 50–54 of IFRS 15 and considers the requirements in paragraphs 56–58 of IFRS 15 on constraining estimates of variable consideration.

Example 21—Estimating variable consideration

IE105 An entity enters into a contract with a customer to build a customised asset. The promise to transfer the asset is a performance obligation that is satisfied over time. The promised consideration is CU2.5 million, but that amount will be reduced or increased depending on the timing of completion of the asset. Specifically, for each day after 31 March 20X7 that the asset is incomplete, the promised consideration is reduced by CU10,000. For each day before 31 March 20X7 that the asset is complete, the promised consideration increases by CU10,000.

IE106 In addition, upon completion of the asset, a third party will inspect the asset and assign a rating based on metrics that are defined in the contract. If the asset receives a specified rating, the entity will be entitled to an incentive bonus of CU150,000.

IE107 In determining the transaction price, the entity prepares a separate estimate for each element of variable consideration to which the entity will be entitled using the estimation methods described in paragraph 53 of IFRS 15:

(a)   the entity decides to use the expected value method to estimate the variable consideration associated with the daily penalty or incentive (ie CU2.5 million, plus or minus CU10,000 per day). This is because it is the method that the entity expects to better predict the amount of consideration to which it will be entitled.

(b)   the entity decides to use the most likely amount to estimate the variable consideration associated with the incentive bonus. This is because there are only two possible outcomes (CU150,000 or CU0) and it is the method that the entity expects to better predict the amount of consideration to which it will be entitled.

IE108   The entity considers the requirements in paragraphs 56–58 of IFRS 15 on constraining estimates of variable consideration to determine whether the entity should include some or all of its estimate of variable consideration in the transaction price.

Constraining estimates of variable consideration

IE109   Examples 22–25 illustrate the requirements in paragraphs 56–58 of IFRS 15 on constraining estimates of variable consideration. In addition, the following requirements are illustrated in these examples:

(a)   paragraph 55 of IFRS 15 on refund liabilities (Example 22);

(b)   paragraphs B20–B27 of IFRS 15 on sales with a right of return (Example 22); and

(c)   paragraphs 84–86 of IFRS 15 on allocating variable consideration to performance obligations (Example 25).

Example 22—Right of return

IE110   An entity enters into 100 contracts with customers. Each contract includes the sale of one product for CU100 (100 total products × CU100 = CU10,000 total consideration). Cash is received when control of a product transfers. The entity's customary business practice is to allow a customer to return any unused product within 30 days and receive a full refund. The entity's cost of each product is CU60.

IE111   The entity applies the requirements in IFRS 15 to the portfolio of 100 contracts because it reasonably expects that, in accordance with paragraph 4, the effects on the financial statements from applying these requirements to the portfolio would not differ materially from applying the requirements to the individual contracts within the portfolio.

IE112   Because the contract allows a customer to return the products, the consideration received from the customer is variable. To estimate the variable consideration to which the entity will be entitled, the entity decides to use the expected value method (see paragraph 53(a) of IFRS 15) because it is the method that the entity expects to better predict the amount of consideration to which it will be entitled. Using the expected value method, the entity estimates that 97 products will not be returned.

IE113   The entity also considers the requirements in paragraphs 56–58 of IFRS 15 on constraining estimates of variable consideration to determine whether the estimated amount of variable consideration of CU9,700 (CU100 × 97 products not expected to be returned) can be included in the transaction price. The entity considers the factors in paragraph 57 of IFRS 15 and determines that although the returns are outside the entity's influence, it has significant experience in estimating returns for this product and customer class. In addition, the uncertainty will be resolved within a short time frame (ie the 30-day return period). Thus, the entity concludes that it is highly probable that a significant reversal in the cumulative amount of revenue recognised (ie CU9,700) will not occur as the uncertainty is resolved (ie over the return period).

IE114   The entity estimates that the costs of recovering the products will be immaterial and expects that the returned products can be resold at a profit.

IE115   Upon transfer of control of the 100 products, the entity does not recognise revenue for the three products that it expects to be returned. Consequently, in accordance with paragraphs 55 and B21 of IFRS 15, the entity recognises the following:

(a)   revenue of CU9,700 (CU100 × 97 products not expected to be returned);

(b)   a refund liability of CU300 (CU100 refund × 3 products expected to be returned); and

(c)   an asset of CU180 (CU60 × 3 products for its right to recover products from customers on settling the refund liability).

Example 23—Price concessions

IE116   An entity enters into a contract with a customer, a distributor, on 1 December 20X7. The entity transfers 1,000 products at contract inception for a price stated in the contract of CU100 per product (total consideration is CU100,000). Payment from the customer is due when the customer sells the products to the end customers. The entity's customer generally sells the products within 90 days of obtaining them. Control of the products transfers to the customer on 1 December 20X7.

IE117   On the basis of its past practices and to maintain its relationship with the customer, the entity anticipates granting a price concession to its customer because this will enable the customer to discount the product and thereby move the product through the distribution chain. Consequently, the consideration in the contract is variable.

Case A—Estimate of variable consideration is not constrained

IE118   The entity has significant experience selling this and similar products. The observable data indicate that historically the entity grants a price concession of approximately 20 per cent of the sales price for these products. Current market information suggests that a 20 per cent reduction in price will be sufficient to move the products through the distribution chain. The entity has not granted a price concession significantly greater than 20 per cent in many years.

IE119   To estimate the variable consideration to which the entity will be entitled, the entity decides to use the expected value method (see paragraph 53(a) of IFRS 15) because it is the method that the entity expects to better predict the amount of consideration to which it will be entitled. Using the expected value method, the entity estimates the transaction price to be CU80,000 (CU80 × 1,000 products).

IE120   The entity also considers the requirements in paragraphs 56–58 of IFRS 15 on constraining estimates of variable consideration to determine whether the estimated amount of variable consideration of CU80,000 can be included in the transaction price. The entity considers the factors in paragraph 57 of IFRS 15 and determines that it has significant previous experience with this product and current market information that supports its estimate. In addition, despite some uncertainty resulting from factors outside its influence, based on its current market estimates, the entity expects the price to be resolved within a short time frame. Thus, the entity concludes that it is highly probable that a significant reversal in the cumulative amount of revenue recognised (ie CU80,000) will not occur when the uncertainty is resolved (ie when the total amount of price concessions is determined). Consequently, the entity recognises CU80,000 as revenue when the products are transferred on 1 December 20X7.

Case B—Estimate of variable consideration is constrained

IE121   The entity has experience selling similar products. However, the entity's products have a high risk of obsolescence and the entity is experiencing high volatility in the pricing of its products. The observable data indicate that historically the entity grants a broad range of price concessions ranging from 20–60 per cent of the sales price for similar products. Current market information also suggests that a 15–50 per cent reduction in price may be necessary to move the products through the distribution chain.

IE122   To estimate the variable consideration to which the entity will be entitled, the entity decides to use the expected value method (see paragraph 53(a) of IFRS 15) because it is the method that the entity expects to better predict the amount of consideration to which it will be entitled. Using the expected value method, the entity estimates that a discount of 40 per cent will be provided and, therefore, the estimate of the variable consideration is CU60,000 (CU60 × 1,000 products).

IE123   The entity also considers the requirements in paragraphs 56–58 of IFRS 15 on constraining estimates of variable consideration to determine whether some or all of the estimated amount of variable consideration of CU60,000 can be included in the transaction price. The entity considers the factors in paragraph 57 of IFRS 15 and observes that the amount of consideration is highly susceptible to factors outside the entity's influence (ie risk of obsolescence) and it is likely that the entity may be required to provide a broad range of price concessions to move the products through the distribution chain. Consequently, the entity cannot include its estimate of

CU60,000 (ie a discount of 40 per cent) in the transaction price because it cannot conclude that it is highly probable that a significant reversal in the amount of cumulative revenue recognised will not occur. Although the entity's historical price concessions have ranged from 20–60 per cent, market information currently suggests that a price concession of 15–50 per cent will be necessary. The entity's actual results have been consistent with then-current market information in previous, similar transactions. Consequently, the entity concludes that it is highly probable that a significant reversal in the cumulative amount of revenue recognised will not occur if the entity includes CU50,000 in the transaction price (CU100 sales price and a 50 per cent price concession) and therefore, recognises revenue at that amount. Therefore, the entity recognises revenue of CU50,000 when the products are transferred and reassesses the estimates of the transaction price at each reporting date until the uncertainty is resolved in accordance with paragraph 59 of IFRS 15.

Example 24—Volume discount incentive

IE124 An entity enters into a contract with a customer on 1 January 20X8 to sell Product A for CU100 per unit. If the customer purchases more than 1,000 units of Product A in a calendar year, the contract specifies that the price per unit is retrospectively reduced to CU90 per unit. Consequently, the consideration in the contract is variable.

IE125 For the first quarter ended 31 March 20X8, the entity sells 75 units of Product A to the customer. The entity estimates that the customer's purchases will not exceed the 1,000-unit threshold required for the volume discount in the calendar year.

IE126 The entity considers the requirements in paragraphs 56–58 of IFRS 15 on constraining estimates of variable consideration, including the factors in paragraph 57 of IFRS 15. The entity determines that it has significant experience with this product and with the purchasing pattern of the entity. Thus, the entity concludes that it is highly probable that a significant reversal in the cumulative amount of revenue recognised (ie CU100 per unit) will not occur when the uncertainty is resolved (ie when the total amount of purchases is known). Consequently, the entity recognises revenue of CU7,500 (75 units × CU100 per unit) for the quarter ended 31 March 20X8.

IE127 In May 20X8, the entity's customer acquires another company and in the second quarter ended 30 June 20X8 the entity sells an additional 500 units of Product A to the customer. In the light of the new fact, the entity estimates that the customer's purchases will exceed the 1,000-unit threshold for the calendar year and therefore it will be required to retrospectively reduce the price per unit to CU90.

IE128 Consequently, the entity recognises revenue of CU44,250 for the quarter ended 30 June 20X8. That amount is calculated from CU45,000 for the sale of 500 units (500 units × CU90 per unit) less the change in transaction price of CU750 (75 units × CU10 price reduction) for the reduction of revenue relating to units sold for the quarter ended 31 March 20X8 (see paragraphs 87 and 88 of IFRS 15).

Example 25—Management fees subject to the constraint

IE129　On 1 January 20X8, an entity enters into a contract with a client to provide asset management services for five years. The entity receives a two per cent quarterly management fee based on the client's assets under management at the end of each quarter. In addition, the entity receives a performance-based incentive fee of 20 per cent of the fund's return in excess of the return of an observable market index over the five-year period. Consequently, both the management fee and the performance fee in the contract are variable consideration.

IE130　The entity accounts for the services as a single performance obligation in accordance with paragraph 22(b) of IFRS 15, because it is providing a series of distinct services that are substantially the same and have the same pattern of transfer (the services transfer to the customer over time and use the same method to measure progress—that is, a time-based measure of progress).

IE131　At contract inception, the entity considers the requirements in paragraphs 50–54 of IFRS 15 on estimating variable consideration and the requirements in paragraphs 56–58 of IFRS 15 on constraining estimates of variable consideration, including the factors in paragraph 57 of IFRS 15. The entity observes that the promised consideration is dependent on the market and thus is highly susceptible to factors outside the entity's influence. In addition, the incentive fee has a large number and a broad range of possible consideration amounts. The entity also observes that although it has experience with similar contracts, that experience is of little predictive value in determining the future performance of the market. Therefore, at contract inception, the entity cannot conclude that it is highly probable that a significant reversal in the cumulative amount of revenue recognised would not occur if the entity included its estimate of the management fee or the incentive fee in the transaction price.

IE132　At each reporting date, the entity updates its estimate of the transaction price. Consequently, at the end of each quarter, the entity concludes that it can include in the transaction price the actual amount of the quarterly management fee because the uncertainty is resolved. However, the entity concludes that it cannot include its estimate of the incentive fee in the transaction price at those dates. This is because there has not been a change in its assessment from contract inception—the variability of the fee based on the market index indicates that the entity cannot conclude that it is highly probable that a significant reversal in the cumulative amount of revenue recognised would not occur if the entity included its estimate of the incentive fee in the transaction price. At 31 March 20X8, the client's assets under management are CU100 million. Therefore, the resulting quarterly management fee and the transaction price is CU2 million.

IE133　At the end of each quarter, the entity allocates the quarterly management fee to the distinct services provided during the quarter in accordance with paragraphs 84(b) and 85 of IFRS 15. This is because the fee relates specifically to the entity's efforts to transfer the services for that quarter, which are distinct from the services provided in other quarters, and the resulting allocation will be consistent with the allocation objective in paragraph 73 of IFRS 15. Consequently, the entity recognises CU2 million as revenue for the quarter ended 31 March 20X8.

The existence of a significant financing component in the contract

IE134   Examples 26–30 illustrate the requirements in paragraphs 60–65 of IFRS 15 on the existence of a significant financing component in the contract. In addition, the following requirements are illustrated in Example 26:

(a)   paragraphs 56–58 of IFRS 15 on constraining estimates of variable consideration; and

(b)   paragraphs B20–B27 of IFRS 15 on sales with a right of return.

Example 26—Significant financing component and right of return

IE135   An entity sells a product to a customer for CU121 that is payable 24 months after delivery. The customer obtains control of the product at contract inception. The contract permits the customer to return the product within 90 days. The product is new and the entity has no relevant historical evidence of product returns or other available market evidence.

IE136   The cash selling price of the product is CU100, which represents the amount that the customer would pay upon delivery for the same product sold under otherwise identical terms and conditions as at contract inception. The entity's cost of the product is CU80.

IE137   The entity does not recognise revenue when control of the product transfers to the customer. This is because the existence of the right of return and the lack of relevant historical evidence means that the entity cannot conclude that it is highly probable that a significant reversal in the amount of cumulative revenue recognised will not occur in accordance with paragraphs 56–58 of IFRS 15. Consequently, revenue is recognised after three months when the right of return lapses.

IE138   The contract includes a significant financing component, in accordance with paragraphs 60–62 of IFRS 15. This is evident from the difference between the amount of promised consideration of CU121 and the cash selling price of CU100 at the date that the goods are transferred to the customer.

IE139   The contract includes an implicit interest rate of 10 per cent (ie the interest rate that over 24 months discounts the promised consideration of CU121 to the cash selling price of CU100). The entity evaluates the rate and concludes that it is commensurate with the rate that would be reflected in a separate financing transaction between the entity and its customer at contract inception. The following journal entries illustrate how the entity accounts for this contract in accordance with paragraphs B20–B27 of IFRS 15.

(a)   When the product is transferred to the customer, in accordance with paragraph B21 of IFRS 15:

Asset for right to recover product to be returned	CU80[a]
Inventory	CU80

(a) This example does not consider expected costs to recover the asset.

(b) During the three-month right of return period, no interest is recognised in accordance with paragraph 65 of IFRS 15 because no contract asset or receivable has been recognised.

(c) When the right of return lapses (the product is not returned):

Receivable	CU100[a]
Revenue	CU100
Cost of sales	CU80
Asset for product to be returned	CU80

(a) The receivable recognised would be measured in accordance with IFRS 9. This example assumes there is no material difference between the fair value of the receivable at contract inception and the fair value of the receivable when it is recognised at the time the right of return lapses. In addition, this example does not consider the impairment accounting for the receivable.

IE140 Until the entity receives the cash payment from the customer, interest revenue would be recognised in accordance with IFRS 9. In determining the effective interest rate in accordance with IFRS 9, the entity would consider the remaining contractual term.

Example 27—Withheld payments on a long-term contract

IE141 An entity enters into a contract for the construction of a building that includes scheduled milestone payments for the performance by the entity throughout the contract term of three years. The performance obligation will be satisfied over time and the milestone payments are scheduled to coincide with the entity's expected performance. The contract provides that a specified percentage of each milestone payment is to be withheld (ie retained) by the customer throughout the arrangement and paid to the entity only when the building is complete.

IE142 The entity concludes that the contract does not include a significant financing component. The milestone payments coincide with the entity's performance and the contract requires amounts to be retained for reasons other than the provision of finance in accordance with paragraph 62(c) of IFRS 15. The withholding of a specified percentage of each milestone payment is intended to protect the customer from the contractor failing to adequately complete its obligations under the contract.

Example 28—Determining the discount rate

IE143   An entity enters into a contract with a customer to sell equipment. Control of the equipment transfers to the customer when the contract is signed. The price stated in the contract is CU1 million plus a five per cent contractual rate of interest, payable in 60 monthly instalments of CU18,871.

Case A—Contractual discount rate reflects the rate in a separate financing transaction

IE144   In evaluating the discount rate in the contract that contains a significant financing component, the entity observes that the five per cent contractual rate of interest reflects the rate that would be used in a separate financing transaction between the entity and its customer at contract inception (ie the contractual rate of interest of five per cent reflects the credit characteristics of the customer).

IE145   The market terms of the financing mean that the cash selling price of the equipment is CU1 million. This amount is recognised as revenue and as a loan receivable when control of the equipment transfers to the customer. The entity accounts for the receivable in accordance with IFRS 9.

Case B—Contractual discount rate does not reflect the rate in a separate financing transaction

IE146   In evaluating the discount rate in the contract that contains a significant financing component, the entity observes that the five per cent contractual rate of interest is significantly lower than the 12 per cent interest rate that would be used in a separate financing transaction between the entity and its customer at contract inception (ie the contractual rate of interest of five per cent does not reflect the credit characteristics of the customer). This suggests that the cash selling price is less than CU1 million.

IE147   In accordance with paragraph 64 of IFRS 15, the entity determines the transaction price by adjusting the promised amount of consideration to reflect the contractual payments using the 12 per cent interest rate that reflects the credit characteristics of the customer. Consequently, the entity determines that the transaction price is CU848,357 (60 monthly payments of CU18,871 discounted at 12 per cent). The entity recognises revenue and a loan receivable for that amount. The entity accounts for the loan receivable in accordance with IFRS 9.

Example 29—Advance payment and assessment of discount rate

IE148   An entity enters into a contract with a customer to sell an asset. Control of the asset will transfer to the customer in two years (ie the performance obligation will be satisfied at a point in time). The contract includes two alternative payment options: payment of CU5,000 in two years when the customer obtains control of the asset or payment of CU4,000 when the contract is signed. The customer elects to pay CU4,000 when the contract is signed.

IE149   The entity concludes that the contract contains a significant financing component because of the length of time between when the customer pays for the asset and when the entity transfers the asset to the customer, as well as the prevailing interest rates in the market.

IE150   The interest rate implicit in the transaction is 11.8 per cent, which is the interest rate necessary to make the two alternative payment options economically equivalent. However, the entity determines that, in accordance with paragraph 64 of IFRS 15, the rate that should be used in adjusting the promised consideration is six per cent, which is the entity's incremental borrowing rate.

IE151   The following journal entries illustrate how the entity would account for the significant financing component:

    (a)   recognise a contract liability for the CU4,000 payment received at contract inception:

Cash	CU4,000	
Contract liability		CU4,000

    (b)   during the two years from contract inception until the transfer of the asset, the entity adjusts the promised amount of consideration (in accordance with paragraph 65 of IFRS 15) and accretes the contract liability by recognising interest on CU4,000 at six per cent for two years:

Interest expense	CU494[a]	
Contract liability		CU494

        (a)   CU494 = CU4,000 contract liability × (6 per cent interest per year for two years).

    (c)   recognise revenue for the transfer of the asset:

Contract liability	CU4,494	
Revenue		CU4,494

Example 30—Advance payment

IE152   An entity, a technology product manufacturer, enters into a contract with a customer to provide global telephone technology support and repair coverage for three years along with its technology product. The customer purchases this support service at the time of buying the product. Consideration for the service is an additional CU300. Customers electing to buy this service must pay for it upfront (ie a monthly payment option is not available).

IE153   To determine whether there is a significant financing component in the contract, the entity considers the nature of the service being offered and the purpose of the payment terms. The entity charges a single upfront amount, not with the primary purpose of obtaining financing from the customer but, instead, to maximise profitability, taking into consideration the risks associated with providing the service. Specifically, if customers could pay monthly, they would be less likely to renew and the population of customers that continue to use the support service in the later years may become smaller and less diverse over time (ie customers that choose to renew historically are those that make greater use of the service, thereby increasing the entity's costs). In addition, customers tend to use services more if they pay monthly rather than making an upfront payment. Finally, the entity would incur higher administration costs such as the costs related to administering renewals and collection of monthly payments.

IE154   In assessing the requirements in paragraph 62(c) of IFRS 15, the entity determines that the payment terms were structured primarily for reasons other than the provision of finance to the entity. The entity charges a single upfront amount for the services because other payment terms (such as a monthly payment plan) would affect the nature of the risks assumed by the entity to provide the service and may make it uneconomical to provide the service. As a result of its analysis, the entity concludes that there is not a significant financing component.

Non-cash consideration

IE155   Example 31 illustrates the requirements in paragraphs 66–69 of IFRS 15 on non-cash consideration. In addition, the following requirements are illustrated in this example:

(a)   paragraph 22 of IFRS 15 on identifying performance obligations; and

(b)   paragraphs 56–58 of IFRS 15 on constraining estimates of variable consideration.

Example 31—Entitlement to non-cash consideration

IE156   An entity enters into a contract with a customer to provide a weekly service for one year. The contract is signed on 1 January 20X1 and work begins immediately. The entity concludes that the service is a single performance obligation in accordance with paragraph 22(b) of IFRS 15. This is because the entity is providing a series of distinct services that are substantially the same and have the same pattern of transfer (the services transfer to the customer over time and use the same method to measure progress – that is, a time-based measure of progress).

IE157   In exchange for the service, the customer promises 100 shares of its common stock per week of service (a total of 5,200 shares for the contract). The terms in the contract require that the shares must be paid upon the successful completion of each week of service.

IE158   The entity measures its progress towards complete satisfaction of the performance obligation as each week of service is complete. To determine the transaction price (and the amount of revenue to be recognised), the entity measures the fair value of 100 shares that are received upon completion of each weekly service. The entity does not reflect any subsequent changes in the fair value of the shares received (or receivable) in revenue.

Consideration payable to a customer

IE159   Example 32 illustrates the requirements in paragraphs 70–72 of IFRS 15 on consideration payable to a customer.

Example 32—Consideration payable to a customer

IE160   An entity that manufactures consumer goods enters into a one-year contract to sell goods to a customer that is a large global chain of retail stores. The customer commits to buy at least CU15 million of products during the year. The contract also requires the entity to make a non-refundable payment of CU1.5 million to the customer at the inception of the contract. The CU1.5 million payment will compensate the customer for the changes it needs to make to its shelving to accommodate the entity's products.

IE161   The entity considers the requirements in paragraphs 70–72 of IFRS 15 and concludes that the payment to the customer is not in exchange for a distinct good or service that transfers to the entity. This is because the entity does not obtain control of any rights to the customer's shelves. Consequently, the entity determines that, in accordance with paragraph 70 of IFRS 15, the CU1.5 million payment is a reduction of the transaction price.

IE162   The entity applies the requirements in paragraph 72 of IFRS 15 and concludes that the consideration payable is accounted for as a reduction in the transaction price when the entity recognises revenue for the transfer of the goods. Consequently, as the entity transfers goods to the customer, the entity reduces the transaction price for each good by 10 per cent (CU1.5 million ÷ CU15 million). Therefore, in the first month in which the entity transfers goods to the customer, the entity recognises revenue of CU1.8 million (CU2.0 million invoiced amount less CU0.2 million of consideration payable to the customer).

Allocating the transaction price to performance obligations

IE163   Examples 33–35 illustrate the requirements in paragraphs 73–86 of IFRS 15 on allocating the transaction price to performance obligations. In addition, the following requirements are illustrated in Example 35:

          (a)   paragraph 53 of IFRS 15 on variable consideration; and

          (b)   paragraph B63 of IFRS 15 on consideration in the form of sales-based or usage-based royalties on licences of intellectual property.

Example 33—Allocation methodology

IE164   An entity enters into a contract with a customer to sell Products A, B and C in exchange for CU100. The entity will satisfy the performance obligations for each of the products at different points in time. The entity regularly sells Product A separately and therefore the stand-alone selling price is directly observable. The stand-alone selling prices of Products B and C are not directly observable.

IE165   Because the stand-alone selling prices for Products B and C are not directly observable, the entity must estimate them. To estimate the stand-alone selling prices, the entity uses the adjusted market assessment approach for Product B and the expected cost plus a margin approach for Product C. In making those estimates, the entity maximises the use of observable inputs (in accordance with paragraph 78 of IFRS 15). The entity estimates the stand-alone selling prices as follows:

Product	Stand-alone selling price	Method
	CU	
Product A	50	Directly observable (see paragraph 77 of IFRS 15)
Product B	25	Adjusted market assessment approach (see paragraph 79(a) of IFRS 15)
Product C	75	Expected cost plus a margin approach (see paragraph 79(b) of IFRS 15)
Total	150	

IE166   The customer receives a discount for purchasing the bundle of goods because the sum of the stand-alone selling prices (CU150) exceeds the promised consideration (CU100). The entity considers whether it has observable evidence about the performance obligation to which the entire discount belongs (in accordance with paragraph 82 of IFRS 15) and concludes that it does not. Consequently, in accordance with paragraphs 76 and 81 of IFRS 15, the discount is allocated proportionately across Products A, B and C. The discount, and therefore the transaction price, is allocated as follows:

Product	Allocated transaction price
	CU
Product A	33 (CU50 ÷ CU150 × CU100)
Product B	17 (CU25 ÷ CU150 × CU100)
Product C	50 (CU75 ÷ CU150 × CU100)
Total	100

Example 34—Allocating a discount

IE167   An entity regularly sells Products A, B and C individually, thereby establishing the following stand-alone selling prices:

Product	Stand-alone selling price
	CU
Product A	40
Product B	55
Product C	45
Total	140

IE168   In addition, the entity regularly sells Products B and C together for CU60.

Case A—Allocating a discount to one or more performance obligations

IE169   The entity enters into a contract with a customer to sell Products A, B and C in exchange for CU100. The entity will satisfy the performance obligations for each of the products at different points in time.

IE170   The contract includes a discount of CU40 on the overall transaction, which would be allocated proportionately to all three performance obligations when allocating the transaction price using the relative stand-alone selling price method (in accordance with paragraph 81 of IFRS 15). However, because the entity regularly sells Products B and C together for CU60 and Product A for CU40, it has evidence that the entire discount should be allocated to the promises to transfer Products B and C in accordance with paragraph 82 of IFRS 15.

IE171   If the entity transfers control of Products B and C at the same point in time, then the entity could, as a practical matter, account for the transfer of those products as a single performance obligation. That is, the entity could allocate CU60 of the transaction price to the single performance obligation and recognise revenue of CU60 when Products B and C simultaneously transfer to the customer.

IE172   If the contract requires the entity to transfer control of Products B and C at different points in time, then the allocated amount of CU60 is individually allocated to the promises to transfer Product B (stand-alone selling price of CU55) and Product C (stand-alone selling price of CU45) as follows:

Product	Allocated transaction price
	CU
Product B	33 (CU55 ÷ CU100 total stand-alone selling price × CU60)
Product C	27 (CU45 ÷ CU100 total stand-alone selling price × CU60)
Total	60

Case B—Residual approach is appropriate

IE173   The entity enters into a contract with a customer to sell Products A, B and C as described in Case A. The contract also includes a promise to transfer Product D. Total consideration in the contract is CU130. The stand-alone selling price for Product D is highly variable (see paragraph 79(c) of IFRS 15) because the entity sells Product D to different customers for a broad range of amounts (CU15–CU45). Consequently, the entity decides to estimate the stand-alone selling price of Product D using the residual approach.

IE174   Before estimating the stand-alone selling price of Product D using the residual approach, the entity determines whether any discount should be allocated to the other performance obligations in the contract in accordance with paragraphs 82 and 83 of IFRS 15.

IE175   As in Case A, because the entity regularly sells Products B and C together for CU60 and Product A for CU40, it has observable evidence that CU100 should be allocated to those three products and a CU40 discount should be allocated to the promises to transfer Products B and C in accordance with paragraph 82 of IFRS 15. Using the residual approach, the entity estimates the stand-alone selling price of Product D to be CU30 as follows:

Product	Stand-alone selling price	Method
	CU	
Product A	40	Directly observable (see paragraph 77 of IFRS 15)
Products B and C	60	Directly observable with discount (see paragraph 82 of IFRS 15)
Product D	30	Residual approach (see paragraph 79(c) of IFRS 15)
Total	130	

IE176   The entity observes that the resulting CU30 allocated to Product D is within the range of its observable selling prices (CU15–CU45). Therefore, the resulting allocation (see above table) is consistent with the allocation objective in paragraph 73 of IFRS 15 and the requirements in paragraph 78 of IFRS 15.

Case C—Residual approach is inappropriate

IE177   The same facts as in Case B apply to Case C except the transaction price is CU105 instead of CU130. Consequently, the application of the residual approach would result in a stand-alone selling price of CU5 for Product D (CU105 transaction price less CU100 allocated to Products A, B and C). The entity concludes that CU5 would not faithfully depict the amount of consideration to which the entity expects to be entitled in exchange for satisfying its performance obligation to transfer Product D, because CU5 does not approximate the stand-alone selling price of Product D, which ranges from CU15–CU45. Consequently, the entity reviews its observable data, including sales and margin reports, to estimate the stand-alone selling price of

Product D using another suitable method. The entity allocates the transaction price of CU105 to Products A, B, C and D using the relative stand-alone selling prices of those products in accordance with paragraphs 73–80 of IFRS 15.

Example 35—Allocation of variable consideration

IE178   An entity enters into a contract with a customer for two intellectual property licences (Licences X and Y), which the entity determines to represent two performance obligations each satisfied at a point in time. The stand-alone selling prices of Licences X and Y are CU800 and CU1,000, respectively.

Case A—Variable consideration allocated entirely to one performance obligation

IE179   The price stated in the contract for Licence X is a fixed amount of CU800 and for Licence Y the consideration is three per cent of the customer's future sales of products that use Licence Y. For purposes of allocation, the entity estimates its sales-based royalties (ie the variable consideration) to be CU1,000, in accordance with paragraph 53 of IFRS 15.

IE180   To allocate the transaction price, the entity considers the criteria in paragraph 85 of IFRS 15 and concludes that the variable consideration (ie the sales-based royalties) should be allocated entirely to Licence Y. The entity concludes that the criteria in paragraph 85 of IFRS 15 are met for the following reasons:

(a)   the variable payment relates specifically to an outcome from the performance obligation to transfer Licence Y (ie the customer's subsequent sales of products that use Licence Y).

(b)   allocating the expected royalty amounts of CU1,000 entirely to Licence Y is consistent with the allocation objective in paragraph 73 of IFRS 15. This is because the entity's estimate of the amount of sales-based royalties (CU1,000) approximates the stand-alone selling price of Licence Y and the fixed amount of CU800 approximates the stand-alone selling price of Licence X. The entity allocates CU800 to Licence X in accordance with paragraph 86 of IFRS 15. This is because, based on an assessment of the facts and circumstances relating to both licences, allocating to Licence Y some of the fixed consideration in addition to all of the variable consideration would not meet the allocation objective in paragraph 73 of IFRS 15.

IE181   The entity transfers Licence Y at inception of the contract and transfers Licence X one month later. Upon the transfer of Licence Y, the entity does not recognise revenue because the consideration allocated to Licence Y is in the form of a sales-based royalty. Therefore, in accordance with paragraph B63 of IFRS 15, the entity recognises revenue for the sales-based royalty when those subsequent sales occur.

IE182   When Licence X is transferred, the entity recognises as revenue the CU800 allocated to Licence X.

Case B—Variable consideration allocated on the basis of stand-alone selling prices

IE183   The price stated in the contract for Licence X is a fixed amount of CU300 and for Licence Y the consideration is five per cent of the customer's future sales of products that use Licence Y. The entity's estimate of the sales-based royalties (ie the variable consideration) is CU1,500 in accordance with paragraph 53 of IFRS 15.

IE184   To allocate the transaction price, the entity applies the criteria in paragraph 85 of IFRS 15 to determine whether to allocate the variable consideration (ie the sales-based royalties) entirely to Licence Y. In applying the criteria, the entity concludes that even though the variable payments relate specifically to an outcome from the performance obligation to transfer Licence Y (ie the customer's subsequent sales of products that use Licence Y), allocating the variable consideration entirely to Licence Y would be inconsistent with the principle for allocating the transaction price. Allocating CU300 to Licence X and CU1,500 to Licence Y does not reflect a reasonable allocation of the transaction price on the basis of the stand-alone selling prices of Licences X and Y of CU800 and CU1,000, respectively. Consequently, the entity applies the general allocation requirements in paragraphs 76–80 of IFRS 15.

IE185   The entity allocates the transaction price of CU300 to Licences X and Y on the basis of relative stand-alone selling prices of CU800 and CU1,000, respectively. The entity also allocates the consideration related to the sales-based royalty on a relative stand-alone selling price basis. However, in accordance with paragraph B63 of IFRS 15, when an entity licenses intellectual property in which the consideration is in the form of a sales-based royalty, the entity cannot recognise revenue until the later of the following events: the subsequent sales occur or the performance obligation is satisfied (or partially satisfied).

IE186   Licence Y is transferred to the customer at the inception of the contract and Licence X is transferred three months later. When Licence Y is transferred, the entity recognises as revenue the CU167 (CU1,000 ÷ CU1,800 × CU300) allocated to Licence Y. When Licence X is transferred, the entity recognises as revenue the CU133 (CU800 ÷ CU1,800 × CU300) allocated to Licence X.

IE187   In the first month, the royalty due from the customer's first month of sales is CU200. Consequently, in accordance with paragraph B63 of IFRS 15, the entity recognises as revenue the CU111 (CU1,000 ÷ CU1,800 × CU200) allocated to Licence Y (which has been transferred to the customer and is therefore a satisfied performance obligation). The entity recognises a contract liability for the CU89 (CU800 ÷ CU1,800 × CU200) allocated to Licence X. This is because although the subsequent sale by the entity's customer has occurred, the performance obligation to which the royalty has been allocated has not been satisfied.

Contract costs

IE188   Examples 36–37 illustrate the requirements in paragraphs 91–94 of IFRS 15 on incremental costs of obtaining a contract, paragraphs 95–98 of IFRS 15 on costs to fulfil a contract and paragraphs 99–104 of IFRS 15 on amortisation and impairment of contract costs.

Example 36—Incremental costs of obtaining a contract

IE189   An entity, a provider of consulting services, wins a competitive bid to provide consulting services to a new customer. The entity incurred the following costs to obtain the contract:

	CU
External legal fees for due diligence	15,000
Travel costs to deliver proposal	25,000
Commissions to sales employees	10,000
Total costs incurred	50,000

IE190   In accordance with paragraph 91 of IFRS 15, the entity recognises an asset for the CU10,000 incremental costs of obtaining the contract arising from the commissions to sales employees because the entity expects to recover those costs through future fees for the consulting services. The entity also pays discretionary annual bonuses to sales supervisors based on annual sales targets, overall profitability of the entity and individual performance evaluations. In accordance with paragraph 91 of IFRS 15, the entity does not recognise an asset for the bonuses paid to sales supervisors because the bonuses are not incremental to obtaining a contract. The amounts are discretionary and are based on other factors, including the profitability of the entity and the individuals' performance. The bonuses are not directly attributable to identifiable contracts.

IE191   The entity observes that the external legal fees and travel costs would have been incurred regardless of whether the contract was obtained. Therefore, in accordance with paragraph 93 of IFRS 15, those costs are recognised as expenses when incurred, unless they are within the scope of another Standard, in which case, the relevant provisions of that Standard apply.

Example 37—Costs that give rise to an asset

IE192   An entity enters into a service contract to manage a customer's information technology data centre for five years. The contract is renewable for subsequent one-year periods. The average customer term is seven years. The entity pays an employee a CU10,000 sales commission upon the customer signing the contract. Before providing the services, the entity designs and builds a technology platform for the entity's internal use that interfaces with the customer's systems. That platform is not transferred to the customer, but will be used to deliver services to the customer.

Incremental costs of obtaining a contract

IE193   In accordance with paragraph 91 of IFRS 15, the entity recognises an asset for the CU10,000 incremental costs of obtaining the contract for the sales commission because the entity expects to recover those costs through future fees for the services to be provided. The entity amortises the asset over seven years in accordance with paragraph 99 of IFRS 15, because the asset relates to the services transferred to the customer during the contract term of five years and the entity anticipates that the contract will be renewed for two subsequent one-year periods.

Costs to fulfil a contract

IE194   The initial costs incurred to set up the technology platform are as follows:

	CU
Design services	40,000
Hardware	120,000
Software	90,000
Migration and testing of data centre	100,000
Total costs	350,000

IE195   The initial setup costs relate primarily to activities to fulfil the contract but do not transfer goods or services to the customer. The entity accounts for the initial setup costs as follows:

(a)   hardware costs—accounted for in accordance with IAS 16 *Property, Plant and Equipment*.

(b)   software costs—accounted for in accordance with IAS 38 *Intangible Assets*.

(c)   costs of the design, migration and testing of the data centre—assessed in accordance with paragraph 95 of IFRS 15 to determine whether an asset can be recognised for the costs to fulfil the contract. Any resulting asset would be amortised on a systematic basis over the seven-year period (ie the five-year contract term and two anticipated one-year renewal periods) that the entity expects to provide services related to the data centre.

IE196   In addition to the initial costs to set up the technology platform, the entity also assigns two employees who are primarily responsible for providing the service to the customer. Although the costs for these two employees are incurred as part of providing the service to the customer, the entity concludes that the costs do not generate or enhance resources of the entity (see paragraph 95(b) of IFRS 15). Therefore, the costs do not meet the criteria in paragraph 95 of IFRS 15 and cannot be recognised as an asset using IFRS 15. In accordance with paragraph 98, the entity recognises the payroll expense for these two employees when incurred.

Presentation

IE197   Examples 38–40 illustrate the requirements in paragraphs 105–109 of IFRS 15 on the presentation of contract balances.

Example 38—Contract liability and receivable

Case A—Cancellable contract

IE198   On 1 January 20X9, an entity enters into a cancellable contract to transfer a product to a customer on 31 March 20X9. The contract requires the customer to pay consideration of CU1,000 in advance on 31 January 20X9. The customer pays the consideration on 1 March 20X9. The entity transfers the product on 31 March 20X9. The following journal entries illustrate how the entity accounts for the contract:

(a)   The entity receives cash of CU1,000 on 1 March 20X9 (cash is received in advance of performance):

Cash	CU1,000	
Contract liability		CU1,000

(b)   The entity satisfies the performance obligation on 31 March 20X9:

Contract liability	CU1,000	
Revenue		CU1,000

Case B—Non-cancellable contract

IE199   The same facts as in Case A apply to Case B except that the contract is non-cancellable. The following journal entries illustrate how the entity accounts for the contract:

(a)   The amount of consideration is due on 31 January 20X9 (which is when the entity recognises a receivable because it has an unconditional right to consideration):

Receivable	CU1,000	
Contract liability		CU1,000

(b)   The entity receives the cash on 1 March 20X9:

Cash	CU1,000	
Receivable		CU1,000

(c)   The entity satisfies the performance obligation on 31 March 20X9:

Contract liability	CU1,000	
Revenue		CU1,000

IE200   If the entity issued the invoice before 31 January 20X9 (the due date of the consideration), the entity would not present the receivable and the contract liability on a gross basis in the statement of financial position because the entity does not yet have a right to consideration that is unconditional.

Example 39—Contract asset recognised for the entity's performance

IE201   On 1 January 20X8, an entity enters into a contract to transfer Products A and B to a customer in exchange for CU1,000. The contract requires Product A to be delivered first and states that payment for the delivery of Product A is conditional on the delivery of Product B. In other words, the consideration of CU1,000 is due only after the entity has transferred both Products A and B to the customer. Consequently, the entity does not have a right to consideration that is unconditional (a receivable) until both Products A and B are transferred to the customer.

IE202   The entity identifies the promises to transfer Products A and B as performance obligations and allocates CU400 to the performance obligation to transfer Product A and CU600 to the performance obligation to transfer Product B on the basis of their relative stand-alone selling prices. The entity recognises revenue for each respective performance obligation when control of the product transfers to the customer.

IE203   The entity satisfies the performance obligation to transfer Product A:

Contract asset	CU400	
Revenue		CU400

IE204   The entity satisfies the performance obligation to transfer Product B and to recognise the unconditional right to consideration:

Receivable	CU1,000	
Contract asset		CU400
Revenue		CU600

Example 40—Receivable recognised for the entity's performance

IE205   An entity enters into a contract with a customer on 1 January 20X9 to transfer products to the customer for CU150 per product. If the customer purchases more than 1 million products in a calendar year, the contract indicates that the price per unit is retrospectively reduced to CU125 per product.

IE206   Consideration is due when control of the products transfer to the customer. Therefore, the entity has an unconditional right to consideration (ie a receivable) for CU150 per product until the retrospective price reduction applies (ie after 1 million products are shipped).

IE207   In determining the transaction price, the entity concludes at contract inception that the customer will meet the 1 million products threshold and therefore estimates that the transaction price is CU125 per product. Consequently, upon the first shipment to the customer of 100 products the entity recognises the following:

Receivable	CU15,000[(a)]
Revenue	CU12,500[(b)]
Refund liability (contract liability)	CU2,500

(a) CU150 per product × 100 products.

(b) CU125 transaction price per product × 100 products.

IE208   The refund liability (see paragraph 55 of IFRS 15) represents a refund of CU25 per product, which is expected to be provided to the customer for the volume-based rebate (ie the difference between the CU150 price stated in the contract that the entity has an unconditional right to receive and the CU125 estimated transaction price).

Disclosure

IE209   Example 41 illustrates the requirements in paragraphs 114–115 and B87–B89 of IFRS 15 on the disaggregation of revenue disclosure. Examples 42–43 illustrate the requirements in paragraphs 120–122 of IFRS 15 for the disclosure of the transaction price allocated to the remaining performance obligations. In addition, the following requirements are illustrated in Example 42:

(a)   paragraph 57 of IFRS 15 on constraining estimates of variable consideration; and

(b)   paragraph B16 of IFRS 15 on methods for measuring progress towards complete satisfaction of a performance obligation.

Example 41—Disaggregation of revenue—quantitative disclosure

IE210   An entity reports the following segments: consumer products, transportation and energy, in accordance with IFRS 8 *Operating Segments*. When the entity prepares its investor presentations, it disaggregates revenue into primary geographical markets, major product lines and timing of revenue recognition (ie goods transferred at a point in time or services transferred over time).

IE211   The entity determines that the categories used in the investor presentations can be used to meet the objective of the disaggregation disclosure requirement in paragraph 114 of IFRS 15, which is to disaggregate revenue from contracts with customers into categories that depict how the nature, amount, timing and uncertainty of revenue and cash flows are affected by economic factors. The following table illustrates the disaggregation disclosure by primary geographical market, major product line and timing of revenue recognition, including a reconciliation of how the disaggregated revenue ties in with the consumer products, transportation and energy segments, in accordance with paragraph 115 of IFRS 15.

Segments	Consumer products	Transport	Energy	Total
	CU	CU	CU	CU
Primary geographical markets				
North America	990	2,250	5,250	8,490
Europe	300	750	1,000	2,050
Asia	700	260	–	960
	1,990	3,260	6,250	11,500
Major goods/service lines				
Office supplies	600	–	–	600
Appliances	990	–	–	990
Clothing	400	–	–	400
Motorcycles	–	500	–	500
Automobiles	–	2,760	–	2,760
Solar panels	–	–	1,000	1,000
Power plant	–	–	5,250	5,250
	1,990	3,260	6,250	11,500
Timing of revenue recognition				
Goods transferred at a point in time	1,990	3,260	1,000	6,250
Services transferred over time	–	–	5,250	5,250
	1,990	3,260	6,250	11,500

Example 42—Disclosure of the transaction price allocated to the remaining performance obligations

IE212 On 30 June 20X7, an entity enters into three contracts (Contracts A, B and C) with separate customers to provide services. Each contract has a two-year non-cancellable term. The entity considers the requirements in paragraphs 120–122 of IFRS 15 in determining the information in each contract to be included in the disclosure of the transaction price allocated to the remaining performance obligations at 31 December 20X7.

Contract A

IE213 Cleaning services are to be provided over the next two years typically at least once per month. For services provided, the customer pays an hourly rate of CU25.

IE214 Because the entity bills a fixed amount for each hour of service provided, the entity has a right to invoice the customer in the amount that corresponds directly with the value of the entity's performance completed to date in accordance with paragraph B16 of IFRS 15. Consequently, no disclosure is necessary if the entity elects to apply the practical expedient in paragraph 121(b) of IFRS 15.

Contract B

IE215 Cleaning services and lawn maintenance services are to be provided as and when needed with a maximum of four visits per month over the next two years. The customer pays a fixed price of CU400 per month for both services. The entity measures its progress towards complete satisfaction of the performance obligation using a time-based measure.

IE216 The entity discloses the amount of the transaction price that has not yet been recognised as revenue in a table with quantitative time bands that illustrates when the entity expects to recognise the amount as revenue. The information for Contract B included in the overall disclosure is as follows:

	20X8	20X9	Total
	CU	CU	CU
Revenue expected to be recognised on this contract as of 31 December 20X7	4,800[a]	2,400[b]	7,200

(a) CU4,800 = CU400 × 12 months.
(b) CU2,400 = CU400 × 6 months.

Contract C

IE217 Cleaning services are to be provided as and when needed over the next two years. The customer pays fixed consideration of CU100 per month plus a one-time variable consideration payment ranging from CU0–CU1,000 corresponding to a one-time regulatory review and certification of the customer's facility (ie a performance bonus). The entity estimates that it will be entitled to CU750 of the variable consideration. On the basis of the entity's assessment of the factors in paragraph 57 of IFRS 15, the entity includes its estimate of CU750 of variable consideration in the transaction price because it is highly probable that a significant reversal in the amount of cumulative revenue recognised will not occur. The entity measures its progress towards complete satisfaction of the performance obligation using a time-based measure.

IE218 The entity discloses the amount of the transaction price that has not yet been recognised as revenue in a table with quantitative time bands that illustrates when the entity expects to recognise the amount as revenue. The entity also includes a qualitative discussion about any significant variable consideration that is not included in the disclosure. The information for Contract C included in the overall disclosure is as follows:

	20X8	20X9	Total
	CU	CU	CU
Revenue expected to be recognised on this contract as of 31 December 20X7	1,575[(a)]	788[(b)]	2,363

(a) Transaction price = CU3,150 (CU100 × 24 months + CU750 variable consideration) recognised evenly over 24 months at CU1,575 per year.

(b) CU1,575 ÷ 2 = CU788 (ie for 6 months of the year).

IE219 In addition, in accordance with paragraph 122 of IFRS 15, the entity discloses qualitatively that part of the performance bonus has been excluded from the disclosure because it was not included in the transaction price. That part of the performance bonus was excluded from the transaction price in accordance with the requirements for constraining estimates of variable consideration.

Example 43—Disclosure of the transaction price allocated to the remaining performance obligations—qualitative disclosure

IE220 On 1 January 20X2, an entity enters into a contract with a customer to construct a commercial building for fixed consideration of CU10 million. The construction of the building is a single performance obligation that the entity satisfies over time. As of 31 December 20X2, the entity has recognised CU3.2 million of revenue. The entity estimates that construction will be completed in 20X3, but it is possible that the project will be completed in the first half of 20X4.

IE221 At 31 December 20X2, the entity discloses the amount of the transaction price that has not yet been recognised as revenue in its disclosure of the transaction price allocated to the remaining performance obligations. The entity also discloses an explanation of when the entity expects to recognise that amount as revenue. The explanation can be disclosed either on a quantitative basis using time bands that are most appropriate for the duration of the remaining performance obligation or by providing a qualitative explanation. Because the entity is uncertain about the timing of revenue recognition, the entity discloses this information qualitatively as follows:

> 'As of 31 December 20X2, the aggregate amount of the transaction price allocated to the remaining performance obligation is CU6.8 million and the entity will recognise this revenue as the building is completed, which is expected to occur over the next 12–18 months.'

Warranties

IE222 Example 44 illustrates the requirements in paragraphs B28–B33 of IFRS 15 on warranties. In addition, Example 44 illustrates the requirements in paragraphs 27–29 of IFRS 15 on identifying performance obligations.

Example 44—Warranties

IE223   An entity, a manufacturer, provides its customer with a warranty with the purchase of a product. The warranty provides assurance that the product complies with agreed-upon specifications and will operate as promised for one year from the date of purchase. The contract also provides the customer with the right to receive up to 20 hours of training services on how to operate the product at no additional cost.

IE224   The entity assesses the goods and services in the contract to determine whether they are distinct and therefore give rise to separate performance obligations.

IE225   The product and training services are each capable of being distinct in accordance with paragraphs 27(a) and 28 of IFRS 15, because the customer can benefit from the product on its own without the training services and can benefit from the training services together with the product that already has been transferred by the entity. The entity regularly sells the product separately without the training services.

IE226   The entity next assesses whether its promises to transfer the product and to provide the training services are separately identifiable in accordance with paragraphs 27(b) and 29 of IFRS 15. The entity does not provide a significant service of integrating the training services with the product (see paragraph 29(a) of IFRS 15). The training services and product do not significantly modify or customise each other (see paragraph 29(b) of IFRS 15). The product and the training services are not highly interdependent or highly interrelated (see paragraph 29(c) of IFRS 15). The entity would be able to fulfil its promise to transfer the product independently of its efforts to subsequently provide the training services, and would be able to provide training services to any customer that had previously acquired its product. Consequently, the entity concludes that its promise to transfer the product and its promise to provide training services are not inputs to a combined item, and, therefore, are each separately identifiable.

IE227   The product and training services are each distinct in accordance with paragraph 27 of IFRS 15 and therefore give rise to two separate performance obligations.

IE228   Finally, the entity assesses the promise to provide a warranty and observes that the warranty provides the customer with the assurance that the product will function as intended for one year. The entity concludes, in accordance with paragraphs B28–B33 of IFRS 15, that the warranty does not provide the customer with a good or service in addition to that assurance and, therefore, the entity does not account for it as a performance obligation. The entity accounts for the assurance-type warranty in accordance with the requirements in IAS 37.

IE229   As a result, the entity allocates the transaction price to the two performance obligations (the product and the training services) and recognises revenue when (or as) those performance obligations are satisfied.

Principal versus agent considerations

IE230　Examples 45–48A illustrate the requirements in paragraphs B34–B38 of IFRS 15 on principal versus agent considerations.

Example 45—Arranging for the provision of goods or services (entity is an agent)

IE231　An entity operates a website that enables customers to purchase goods from a range of suppliers who deliver the goods directly to the customers. Under the terms of the entity's contracts with suppliers, when a good is purchased via the website, the entity is entitled to a commission that is equal to 10 per cent of the sales price. The entity's website facilitates payment between the supplier and the customer at prices that are set by the supplier. The entity requires payment from customers before orders are processed and all orders are non-refundable. The entity has no further obligations to the customer after arranging for the products to be provided to the customer.

IE232　To determine whether the entity's performance obligation is to provide the specified goods itself (ie the entity is a principal) or to arrange for those goods to be provided by the supplier (ie the entity is an agent), the entity identifies the specified good or service to be provided to the customer and assesses whether it controls that good or service before the good or service is transferred to the customer.

IE232A　The website operated by the entity is a marketplace in which suppliers offer their goods and customers purchase the goods that are offered by the suppliers. Accordingly, the entity observes that the specified goods to be provided to customers that use the website are the goods provided by the suppliers, and no other goods or services are promised to customers by the entity.

IE232B　The entity concludes that it does not control the specified goods before they are transferred to customers that order goods using the website. The entity does not at any time have the ability to direct the use of the goods transferred to customers. For example, it cannot direct the goods to parties other than the customer or prevent the supplier from transferring those goods to the customer. The entity does not control the suppliers' inventory of goods used to fulfil the orders placed by customers using the website.

IE232C　As part of reaching that conclusion, the entity considers the following indicators in paragraph B37 of IFRS 15. The entity concludes that these indicators provide further evidence that it does not control the specified goods before they are transferred to the customers:

(a)　the supplier is primarily responsible for fulfilling the promise to provide the goods to the customer. The entity is neither obliged to provide the goods if the supplier fails to transfer the goods to the customer, nor responsible for the acceptability of the goods.

(b)   the entity does not take inventory risk at any time before or after the goods are transferred to the customer. The entity does not commit itself to obtain the goods from the supplier before the goods are purchased by the customer, and does not accept responsibility for any damaged or returned goods.

(c)   the entity does not have discretion in establishing prices for the supplier's goods. The sales price is set by the supplier.

IE233   Consequently, the entity concludes that it is an agent and its performance obligation is to arrange for the provision of goods by the supplier. When the entity satisfies its promise to arrange for the goods to be provided by the supplier to the customer (which, in this example, is when goods are purchased by the customer), the entity recognises revenue in the amount of the commission to which it is entitled.

Example 46—Promise to provide goods or services (entity is a principal)

IE234   An entity enters into a contract with a customer for equipment with unique specifications. The entity and the customer develop the specifications for the equipment, which the entity communicates to a supplier that the entity contracts with to manufacture the equipment. The entity also arranges to have the supplier deliver the equipment directly to the customer. Upon delivery of the equipment to the customer, the terms of the contract require the entity to pay the supplier the price agreed to by the entity and the supplier for manufacturing the equipment.

IE235   The entity and the customer negotiate the selling price and the entity invoices the customer for the agreed-upon price with 30-day payment terms. The entity's profit is based on the difference between the sales price negotiated with the customer and the price charged by the supplier.

IE236   The contract between the entity and the customer requires the customer to seek remedies for defects in the equipment from the supplier under the supplier's warranty. However, the entity is responsible for any corrections to the equipment required resulting from errors in specifications.

IE237   To determine whether the entity's performance obligation is to provide the specified goods or services itself (ie the entity is a principal) or to arrange for those goods or services to be provided by another party (ie the entity is an agent), the entity identifies the specified good or service to be provided to the customer and assesses whether it controls that good or service before the good or service is transferred to the customer.

IE237A   The entity concludes that it has promised to provide the customer with specialised equipment designed by the entity. Although the entity has subcontracted the manufacturing of the equipment to the supplier, the entity concludes that the design and manufacturing of the equipment are not distinct, because they are not separately identifiable (ie there is a single performance obligation). The entity is responsible for the overall management of the contract (for example, by ensuring that the manufacturing service

© IFRS Foundation

conforms to the specifications) and, thus, provides a significant service of integrating those items into the combined output—the specialised equipment —for which the customer has contracted. In addition, those activities are highly interrelated. If necessary modifications to the specifications are identified as the equipment is manufactured, the entity is responsible for developing and communicating revisions to the supplier and for ensuring that any associated rework required conforms with the revised specifications. Accordingly, the entity identifies the specified good to be provided to the customer as the specialised equipment.

IE237B The entity concludes that it controls the specialised equipment before that equipment is transferred to the customer (see paragraph B35A(c)). The entity provides the significant integration service necessary to produce the specialised equipment and, therefore, controls the specialised equipment before it is transferred to the customer. The entity directs the use of the supplier's manufacturing service as an input in creating the combined output that is the specialised equipment. In reaching the conclusion that it controls the specialised equipment before that equipment is transferred to the customer, the entity also observes that, even though the supplier delivers the specialised equipment to the customer, the supplier has no ability to direct its use (ie the terms of the contract between the entity and the supplier preclude the supplier from using the specialised equipment for another purpose or directing that equipment to another customer). The entity also obtains the remaining benefits from the specialised equipment by being entitled to the consideration in the contract from the customer.

IE238 Thus, the entity concludes that it is a principal in the transaction. The entity does not consider the indicators in paragraph B37 of IFRS 15 because the evaluation above is conclusive without consideration of the indicators. The entity recognises revenue in the gross amount of consideration to which it is entitled from the customer in exchange for the specialised equipment.

Example 46A—Promise to provide goods or services (entity is a principal)

IE238A An entity enters into a contract with a customer to provide office maintenance services. The entity and the customer define and agree on the scope of the services and negotiate the price. The entity is responsible for ensuring that the services are performed in accordance with the terms and conditions in the contract. The entity invoices the customer for the agreed-upon price on a monthly basis with 10-day payment terms.

IE238B The entity regularly engages third-party service providers to provide office maintenance services to its customers. When the entity obtains a contract from a customer, the entity enters into a contract with one of those service providers, directing the service provider to perform office maintenance services for the customer. The payment terms in the contracts with the service providers are generally aligned with the payment terms in the entity's contracts with customers. However, the entity is obliged to pay the service provider even if the customer fails to pay.

IE238C   To determine whether the entity is a principal or an agent, the entity identifies the specified good or service to be provided to the customer and assesses whether it controls that good or service before the good or service is transferred to the customer.

IE238D   The entity observes that the specified services to be provided to the customer are the office maintenance services for which the customer contracted, and that no other goods or services are promised to the customer. While the entity obtains a right to office maintenance services from the service provider after entering into the contract with the customer, that right is not transferred to the customer. That is, the entity retains the ability to direct the use of, and obtain substantially all the remaining benefits from, that right. For example, the entity can decide whether to direct the service provider to provide the office maintenance services for that customer, or for another customer, or at its own facilities. The customer does not have a right to direct the service provider to perform services that the entity has not agreed to provide. Therefore, the right to office maintenance services obtained by the entity from the service provider is not the specified good or service in its contract with the customer.

IE238E   The entity concludes that it controls the specified services before they are provided to the customer. The entity obtains control of a right to office maintenance services after entering into the contract with the customer but before those services are provided to the customer. The terms of the entity's contract with the service provider give the entity the ability to direct the service provider to provide the specified services on the entity's behalf (see paragraph B35A(b)). In addition, the entity concludes that the following indicators in paragraph B37 of IFRS 15 provide further evidence that the entity controls the office maintenance services before they are provided to the customer:

(a)   the entity is primarily responsible for fulfilling the promise to provide office maintenance services. Although the entity has hired a service provider to perform the services promised to the customer, it is the entity itself that is responsible for ensuring that the services are performed and are acceptable to the customer (ie the entity is responsible for fulfilment of the promise in the contract, regardless of whether the entity performs the services itself or engages a third-party service provider to perform the services).

(b)   the entity has discretion in setting the price for the services to the customer.

IE238F   The entity observes that it does not commit itself to obtain the services from the service provider before obtaining the contract with the customer. Thus, the entity has mitigated inventory risk with respect to the office maintenance services. Nonetheless, the entity concludes that it controls the office maintenance services before they are provided to the customer on the basis of the evidence in paragraph IE238E.

IE238G   Thus, the entity is a principal in the transaction and recognises revenue in the amount of consideration to which it is entitled from the customer in exchange for the office maintenance services.

Example 47—Promise to provide goods or services (entity is a principal)

IE239   An entity negotiates with major airlines to purchase tickets at reduced rates compared with the price of tickets sold directly by the airlines to the public. The entity agrees to buy a specific number of tickets and must pay for those tickets regardless of whether it is able to resell them. The reduced rate paid by the entity for each ticket purchased is negotiated and agreed in advance.

IE240   The entity determines the prices at which the airline tickets will be sold to its customers. The entity sells the tickets and collects the consideration from customers when the tickets are purchased.

IE241   The entity also assists the customers in resolving complaints with the service provided by the airlines. However, each airline is responsible for fulfilling obligations associated with the ticket, including remedies to a customer for dissatisfaction with the service.

IE242   To determine whether the entity's performance obligation is to provide the specified goods or services itself (ie the entity is a principal) or to arrange for those goods or services to be provided by another party (ie the entity is an agent), the entity identifies the specified good or service to be provided to the customer and assesses whether it controls that good or service before the good or service is transferred to the customer.

IE242A   The entity concludes that, with each ticket that it commits itself to purchase from the airline, it obtains control of a right to fly on a specified flight (in the form of a ticket) that the entity then transfers to one of its customers (see paragraph B35A(a)). Consequently, the entity determines that the specified good or service to be provided to its customer is that right (to a seat on a specific flight) that the entity controls. The entity observes that no other goods or services are promised to the customer.

IE242B   The entity controls the right to each flight before it transfers that specified right to one of its customers because the entity has the ability to direct the use of that right by deciding whether to use the ticket to fulfil a contract with a customer and, if so, which contract it will fulfil. The entity also has the ability to obtain the remaining benefits from that right by either reselling the ticket and obtaining all of the proceeds from the sale or, alternatively, using the ticket itself.

IE242C   The indicators in paragraphs B37(b)–(c) of IFRS 15 also provide relevant evidence that the entity controls each specified right (ticket) before it is transferred to the customer. The entity has inventory risk with respect to the ticket because the entity committed itself to obtain the ticket from the airline before obtaining a contract with a customer to purchase the ticket. This is because the entity is obliged to pay the airline for that right regardless of whether it is able to obtain a customer to resell the ticket to or whether it can obtain a favourable price for the ticket. The entity also establishes the price that the customer will pay for the specified ticket.

IE243   Thus, the entity concludes that it is a principal in the transactions with customers. The entity recognises revenue in the gross amount of consideration to which it is entitled in exchange for the tickets transferred to the customers.

Example 48—Arranging for the provision of goods or services (entity is an agent)

IE244   An entity sells vouchers that entitle customers to future meals at specified restaurants. The sales price of the voucher provides the customer with a significant discount when compared with the normal selling prices of the meals (for example, a customer pays CU100 for a voucher that entitles the customer to a meal at a restaurant that would otherwise cost CU200). The entity does not purchase or commit itself to purchase vouchers in advance of the sale of a voucher to a customer; instead, it purchases vouchers only as they are requested by the customers. The entity sells the vouchers through its website and the vouchers are non-refundable.

IE245   The entity and the restaurants jointly determine the prices at which the vouchers will be sold to customers. Under the terms of its contracts with the restaurants, the entity is entitled to 30 per cent of the voucher price when it sells the voucher.

IE246   The entity also assists the customers in resolving complaints about the meals and has a buyer satisfaction programme. However, the restaurant is responsible for fulfilling obligations associated with the voucher, including remedies to a customer for dissatisfaction with the service.

IE247   To determine whether the entity is a principal or an agent, the entity identifies the specified good or service to be provided to the customer and assesses whether it controls the specified good or service before that good or service is transferred to the customer.

IE247A   A customer obtains a voucher for the restaurant that it selects. The entity does not engage the restaurants to provide meals to customers on the entity's behalf as described in the indicator in paragraph B37(a) of IFRS 15. Therefore, the entity observes that the specified good or service to be provided to the customer is the right to a meal (in the form of a voucher) at a specified restaurant or restaurants, which the customer purchases and then can use itself or transfer to another person. The entity also observes that no other goods or services (other than the vouchers) are promised to the customers.

IE247B   The entity concludes that it does not control the voucher (right to a meal) at any time. In reaching this conclusion, the entity principally considers the following:

(a) the vouchers are created only at the time that they are transferred to the customers and, thus, do not exist before that transfer. Therefore, the entity does not at any time have the ability to direct the use of the vouchers, or obtain substantially all of the remaining benefits from the vouchers, before they are transferred to customers.

(b) the entity neither purchases, nor commits itself to purchase, vouchers before they are sold to customers. The entity also has no responsibility to accept any returned vouchers. Therefore, the entity does not have inventory risk with respect to the vouchers as described in the indicator in paragraph B37(b) of IFRS 15.

IE248 Thus, the entity concludes that it is an agent with respect to the vouchers. The entity recognises revenue in the net amount of consideration to which the entity will be entitled in exchange for arranging for the restaurants to provide vouchers to customers for the restaurants' meals, which is the 30 per cent commission it is entitled to upon the sale of each voucher.

Example 48A—Entity is a principal and an agent in the same contract

IE248A An entity sells services to assist its customers in more effectively targeting potential recruits for open job positions. The entity performs several services itself, such as interviewing candidates and performing background checks. As part of the contract with a customer, the customer agrees to obtain a licence to access a third party's database of information on potential recruits. The entity arranges for this licence with the third party, but the customer contracts directly with the database provider for the licence. The entity collects payment on behalf of the third-party database provider as part of the entity's overall invoicing to the customer. The database provider sets the price charged to the customer for the licence, and is responsible for providing technical support and credits to which the customer may be entitled for service down time or other technical issues.

IE248B To determine whether the entity is a principal or an agent, the entity identifies the specified goods or services to be provided to the customer, and assesses whether it controls those goods or services before they are transferred to the customer.

IE248C For the purpose of this example, it is assumed that the entity concludes that its recruitment services and the database access licence are each distinct on the basis of its assessment of the requirements in paragraphs 27–30 of IFRS 15. Accordingly, there are two specified goods or services to be provided to the customer—access to the third party's database and recruitment services.

IE248D The entity concludes that it does not control the access to the database before it is provided to the customer. The entity does not at any time have the ability to direct the use of the licence because the customer contracts for the licence directly with the database provider. The entity does not control access to the provider's database—it cannot, for example, grant access to the database to a party other than the customer, or prevent the database provider from providing access to the customer.

IE248E   As part of reaching that conclusion, the entity also considers the indicators in paragraph B37 of IFRS 15. The entity concludes that these indicators provide further evidence that it does not control access to the database before that access is provided to the customer:

(a)   the entity is not responsible for fulfilling the promise to provide the database access service. The customer contracts for the licence directly with the third-party database provider and the database provider is responsible for the acceptability of the database access (for example, by providing technical support or service credits).

(b)   the entity does not have inventory risk because it does not purchase, or commit itself to purchase, the database access before the customer contracts for database access directly with the database provider.

(c)   the entity does not have discretion in setting the price for the database access with the customer because the database provider sets that price.

IE248F   Thus, the entity concludes that it is an agent in relation to the third party's database service. In contrast, the entity concludes that it is the principal in relation to the recruitment services because the entity performs those services itself and no other party is involved in providing those services to the customer.

Customer options for additional goods or services

IE249   Examples 49–52 illustrate the requirements in paragraphs B39–B43 of IFRS 15 on customer options for additional goods or services. Example 50 illustrates the requirements in paragraphs 27–29 of IFRS 15 on identifying performance obligations. Example 52 illustrates a customer loyalty programme. That example may not apply to all customer loyalty arrangements because the terms and conditions may differ. In particular, when there are more than two parties to the arrangement, an entity should consider all facts and circumstances to determine the customer in the transaction that gives rise to the award credits.

Example 49—Option that provides the customer with a material right (discount voucher)

IE250   An entity enters into a contract for the sale of Product A for CU100. As part of the contract, the entity gives the customer a 40 per cent discount voucher for any future purchases up to CU100 in the next 30 days. The entity intends to offer a 10 per cent discount on all sales during the next 30 days as part of a seasonal promotion. The 10 per cent discount cannot be used in addition to the 40 per cent discount voucher.

IE251   Because all customers will receive a 10 per cent discount on purchases during the next 30 days, the only discount that provides the customer with a material right is the discount that is incremental to that 10 per cent (ie the additional 30 per cent discount). The entity accounts for the promise to provide the incremental discount as a performance obligation in the contract for the sale of Product A.

IE252   To estimate the stand-alone selling price of the discount voucher in accordance with paragraph B42 of IFRS 15, the entity estimates an 80 per cent likelihood that a customer will redeem the voucher and that a customer will, on average, purchase CU50 of additional products. Consequently, the entity's estimated stand-alone selling price of the discount voucher is CU12 (CU50 average purchase price of additional products × 30 per cent incremental discount × 80 per cent likelihood of exercising the option). The stand-alone selling prices of Product A and the discount voucher and the resulting allocation of the CU100 transaction price are as follows:

Performance obligation	Stand-alone selling price
	CU
Product A	100
Discount voucher	12
Total	112

Performance obligation	Allocated transaction price	
Product A	89	(CU100 ÷ CU112 × CU100)
Discount voucher	11	(CU12 ÷ CU112 × CU100)
Total	100	

IE253   The entity allocates CU89 to Product A and recognises revenue for Product A when control transfers. The entity allocates CU11 to the discount voucher and recognises revenue for the voucher when the customer redeems it for goods or services or when it expires.

Example 50—Option that does not provide the customer with a material right (additional goods or services)

IE254   An entity in the telecommunications industry enters into a contract with a customer to provide a handset and monthly network service for two years. The network service includes up to 1,000 call minutes and 1,500 text messages each month for a fixed monthly fee. The contract specifies the price for any additional call minutes or texts that the customer may choose to purchase in any month. The prices for those services are equal to their stand-alone selling prices.

IE255   The entity determines that the promises to provide the handset and network service are each separate performance obligations. This is because the customer can benefit from the handset and network service either on their own or together with other resources that are readily available to the customer in accordance with the criterion in paragraph 27(a) of IFRS 15. In addition, the handset and network service are separately identifiable in accordance with the criterion in paragraph 27(b) of IFRS 15 (on the basis of the factors in paragraph 29 of IFRS 15).

IE256   The entity determines that the option to purchase the additional call minutes and texts does not provide a material right that the customer would not receive without entering into the contract (see paragraph B41 of IFRS 15). This is because the prices of the additional call minutes and texts reflect the stand-alone selling prices for those services. Because the option for additional call minutes and texts does not grant the customer a material right, the entity concludes it is not a performance obligation in the contract. Consequently, the entity does not allocate any of the transaction price to the option for additional call minutes or texts. The entity will recognise revenue for the additional call minutes or texts if and when the entity provides those services.

Example 51—Option that provides the customer with a material right (renewal option)

IE257   An entity enters into 100 separate contracts with customers to provide one year of maintenance services for CU1,000 per contract. The terms of the contracts specify that at the end of the year, each customer has the option to renew the maintenance contract for a second year by paying an additional CU1,000. Customers who renew for a second year are also granted the option to renew for a third year for CU1,000. The entity charges significantly higher prices for maintenance services to customers that do not sign up for the maintenance services initially (ie when the products are new). That is, the entity charges CU3,000 in Year 2 and CU5,000 in Year 3 for annual maintenance services if a customer does not initially purchase the service or allows the service to lapse.

IE258   The entity concludes that the renewal option provides a material right to the customer that it would not receive without entering into the contract, because the price for maintenance services are significantly higher if the customer elects to purchase the services only in Year 2 or 3. Part of each customer's payment of CU1,000 in the first year is, in effect, a non-refundable prepayment of the services to be provided in a subsequent year. Consequently, the entity concludes that the promise to provide the option is a performance obligation.

IE259   The renewal option is for a continuation of maintenance services and those services are provided in accordance with the terms of the existing contract. Instead of determining the stand-alone selling prices for the renewal options directly, [Refer: paragraph B42] the entity allocates the transaction price by determining the consideration that it expects to receive in exchange for all the services that it expects to provide, in accordance with paragraph B43 of IFRS 15.

IE260   The entity expects 90 customers to renew at the end of Year 1 (90 per cent of contracts sold) and 81 customers to renew at the end of Year 2 (90 per cent of the 90 customers that renewed at the end of Year 1 will also renew at the end of Year 2, that is 81 per cent of contracts sold).

IE261   At contract inception, the entity determines the expected consideration for each contract is CU2,710 [CU1,000 + (90 per cent × CU1,000) + (81 per cent × CU1,000)]. The entity also determines that recognising revenue on the basis of costs incurred relative to the total expected costs depicts the transfer of services to the customer. Estimated costs for a three-year contract are as follows:

	CU
	CU
Year 1	600
Year 2	750
Year 3	1,000

IE262   Accordingly, the pattern of revenue recognition expected at contract inception for each contract is as follows:

	Expected costs adjusted for likelihood of contract renewal	Allocation of consideration expected
	CU	**CU**
Year 1	600 (CU600 × 100%)	780 [(CU600 ÷ CU2,085) × CU2,710]
Year 2	675 (CU750 × 90%)	877 [(CU675 ÷ CU2,085) × CU2,710]
Year 3	810 (CU1,000 × 81%)	1,053 [(CU810 ÷ CU2,085) × CU2,710]
Total	2,085	2,710

IE263   Consequently, at contract inception, the entity allocates to the option to renew at the end of Year 1 CU22,000 of the consideration received to date [cash of CU100,000 – revenue to be recognised in Year 1 of CU78,000 (CU780 × 100)].

IE264   Assuming there is no change in the entity's expectations and the 90 customers renew as expected, at the end of the first year, the entity has collected cash of CU190,000 [(100 × CU1,000) + (90 × CU1,000)], has recognised revenue of CU78,000 (CU780 × 100) and has recognised a contract liability of CU112,000.

IE265   Consequently, upon renewal at the end of the first year, the entity allocates CU24,300 to the option to renew at the end of Year 2 [cumulative cash of CU190,000 less cumulative revenue recognised in Year 1 and to be recognised in Year 2 of CU165,700 (CU78,000 + CU877 × 100)].

IE266   If the actual number of contract renewals was different than what the entity expected, the entity would update the transaction price and the revenue recognised accordingly.

Example 52—Customer loyalty programme

IE267 An entity has a customer loyalty programme that rewards a customer with one customer loyalty point for every CU10 of purchases. Each point is redeemable for a CU1 discount on any future purchases of the entity's products. During a reporting period, customers purchase products for CU100,000 and earn 10,000 points that are redeemable for future purchases. The consideration is fixed and the stand-alone selling price of the purchased products is CU100,000. The entity expects 9,500 points to be redeemed. The entity estimates a stand-alone selling price of CU0.95 per point (totalling CU9,500) on the basis of the likelihood of redemption in accordance with paragraph B42 of IFRS 15.

IE268 The points provide a material right to customers that they would not receive without entering into a contract. Consequently, the entity concludes that the promise to provide points to the customer is a performance obligation. [Refer: paragraph 27] The entity allocates the transaction price (CU100,000) to the product and the points on a relative stand-alone selling price basis as follows:

	CU	
Product	91,324	[CU100,000 × (CU100,000 stand-alone selling price ÷ CU109,500)]
Points	8,676	[CU100,000 × (CU9,500 stand-alone selling price ÷ CU109,500)]

IE269 At the end of the first reporting period, 4,500 points have been redeemed and the entity continues to expect 9,500 points to be redeemed in total. The entity recognises revenue for the loyalty points of CU4,110 [(4,500 points ÷ 9,500 points) × CU8,676] and recognises a contract liability of CU4,566 (CU8,676 – CU4,110) for the unredeemed points at the end of the first reporting period.

IE270 At the end of the second reporting period, 8,500 points have been redeemed cumulatively. The entity updates its estimate of the points that will be redeemed and now expects that 9,700 points will be redeemed. The entity recognises revenue for the loyalty points of CU3,493 {[(8,500 total points redeemed ÷ 9,700 total points expected to be redeemed) × CU8,676 initial allocation] – CU4,110 recognised in the first reporting period}. The contract liability balance is CU1,073 (CU8,676 initial allocation – CU7,603 of cumulative revenue recognised).

Non-refundable upfront fees

IE271 Example 53 illustrates the requirements in paragraphs B48–B51 of IFRS 15 on non-refundable upfront fees.

Example 53—Non-refundable upfront fee

IE272 An entity enters into a contract with a customer for one year of transaction processing services. The entity's contracts have standard terms that are the same for all customers. The contract requires the customer to pay an upfront fee to set up the customer on the entity's systems and processes. The fee is a nominal amount and is non-refundable. The customer can renew the contract each year without paying an additional fee.

IE273 The entity's setup activities do not transfer a good or service to the customer and, therefore, do not give rise to a performance obligation.

IE274 The entity concludes that the renewal option does not provide a material right to the customer that it would not receive without entering into that contract (see paragraph B40 of IFRS 15). The upfront fee is, in effect, an advance payment for the future transaction processing services. Consequently, the entity determines the transaction price, which includes the non-refundable upfront fee, and recognises revenue for the transaction processing services as those services are provided in accordance with paragraph B49 of IFRS 15.

Licensing

IE275 Examples 54–61 illustrate the requirements in paragraphs 22–30 of IFRS 15 for identifying performance obligations and paragraphs B52–B63B of IFRS 15 on licensing. These examples also illustrate other requirements as follows:

(a) paragraphs 39–45 of IFRS 15 on measuring progress towards complete satisfaction of a performance obligation (Example 58);

(b) paragraphs 84–86 of IFRS 15 on allocating variable consideration to performance obligations (Example 57); and

(c) paragraphs B63–B63B of IFRS 15 on consideration in the form of sales-based or usage-based royalties on licences of intellectual property (Examples 57 and 61).

Example 54—Right to use intellectual property

IE276 Using the same facts as in Case A in Example 11 (see paragraphs IE49–IE53), the entity identifies four performance obligations in a contract:

(a) the software licence;

(b) installation services;

(c) software updates; and

(d) technical support.

IE277　The entity assesses the nature of its promise to transfer the software licence in accordance with paragraph B58 of IFRS 15. The entity does not consider in its assessment of the criteria in paragraph B58 of IFRS 15 the promise to provide software updates, because they result in the transfer of an additional good or service to the customer (see paragraph B58(c)). The entity also observes that it does not have any contractual or implied obligations (independent of the updates and technical support) to undertake activities that will change the functionality of the software during the licence period. The entity observes that the software remains functional without the updates and the technical support and, therefore, the ability of the customer to obtain the benefits of the software is not substantially derived from, or dependent on, the entity's ongoing activities. The entity therefore determines that the contract does not require, and the customer does not reasonably expect, the entity to undertake activities that significantly affect the software (independent of the updates and technical support). The entity concludes that the software to which the licence relates has significant stand-alone functionality and none of the criteria in paragraph B58 of IFRS 15 are met. The entity further concludes that the nature of the entity's promise in transferring the licence is to provide a right to use the entity's intellectual property as it exists at a point in time. Consequently, the entity accounts for the licence as a performance obligation satisfied at a point in time.

Example 55—Licence of intellectual property
[Refer: Basis for Conclusions paragraph BC116P]

IE278　An entity enters into a contract with a customer to licence (for a period of three years) intellectual property related to the design and production processes for a good. The contract also specifies that the customer will obtain any updates to that intellectual property for new designs or production processes that may be developed by the entity. The updates are integral to the customer's ability to derive benefit from the licence during the licence period, because the intellectual property is used in an industry in which technologies change rapidly.

IE279　The entity assesses the goods and services promised to the customer to determine which goods and services are distinct in accordance with paragraph 27 of IFRS 15. The entity determines that the customer can benefit from (a) the licence on its own without the updates; and (b) the updates together with the initial licence. Although the benefit the customer can derive from the licence on its own (ie without the updates) is limited because the updates are integral to the customer's ability to continue to use the intellectual property in an industry in which technologies change rapidly, the licence can be used in a way that generates some economic benefits. Therefore, the criterion in paragraph 27(a) of IFRS 15 is met for the licence and the updates.

IE279A　The fact that the benefit the customer can derive from the licence on its own (ie without the updates) is limited (because the updates are integral to the customer's ability to continue to use the licence in the rapidly changing technological environment) is also considered in assessing whether the criterion in paragraph 27(b) of IFRS 15 is met. Because the benefit that the customer could obtain from the licence over the three-year term without the updates would be significantly limited, the entity's promises to grant the licence and to provide the expected updates are, in effect, inputs that together fulfil a single promise to deliver a combined item to the customer. That is, the nature of the entity's promise in the contract is to provide ongoing access to the entity's intellectual property related to the design and production processes for a good for the three-year term of the contract. The promises within that combined item (ie to grant the licence and to provide when-and-if-available updates) are, therefore, not separately identifiable in accordance with the criterion in paragraph 27(b) of IFRS 15.

IE280   The nature of the combined good or service that the entity promised to transfer to the customer is ongoing access to the entity's intellectual property related to the design and production processes for a good for the three-year term of the contract. On the basis of this conclusion, the entity applies paragraphs 31–38 of IFRS 15 to determine whether single the performance obligation is satisfied at a point in time or over time. The entity concludes that because the customer simultaneously receives and consumes the benefits of the entity's performance as it occurs, the performance obligation is satisfied over time in accordance with paragraph 35(a) of IFRS 15.

Example 56—Identifying a distinct licence

IE281   An entity, a pharmaceutical company, licenses to a customer its patent rights to an approved drug compound for 10 years and also promises to manufacture the drug for the customer. The drug is a mature product; therefore the entity will not undertake any activities to support the drug, which is consistent with its customary business practices.

Case A—Licence is not distinct

IE282   In this case, no other entity can manufacture this drug because of the highly specialised nature of the manufacturing process. As a result, the licence cannot be purchased separately from the manufacturing services.

IE283   The entity assesses the goods and services promised to the customer to determine which goods and services are distinct in accordance with paragraph 27 of IFRS 15. The entity determines that the customer cannot benefit from the licence without the manufacturing service; therefore, the criterion in paragraph 27(a) of IFRS 15 is not met. Consequently, the licence and the manufacturing service are not distinct and the entity accounts for the licence and the manufacturing service as a single performance obligation.

IE284   The entity applies paragraphs 31–38 of IFRS 15 to determine whether the performance obligation (ie the bundle of the licence and the manufacturing services) is a performance obligation satisfied at a point in time or over time.

Case B—Licence is distinct

IE285   In this case, the manufacturing process used to produce the drug is not unique or specialised and several other entities can also manufacture the drug for the customer.

IE286   The entity assesses the goods and services promised to the customer to determine which goods and services are distinct, and it concludes that the criteria in paragraph 27 of IFRS 15 are met for each of the licence and the manufacturing service. The entity concludes that the criterion in paragraph 27(a) of IFRS 15 is met because the customer can benefit from the licence together with readily available resources other than the entity's manufacturing service (because there are other entities that can provide the manufacturing service), and can benefit from the manufacturing service together with the licence transferred to the customer at the start of the contract.

IE286A   The entity also concludes that its promises to grant the licence and to provide the manufacturing service are separately identifiable (ie the criterion in paragraph 27(b) of IFRS 15 is met). The entity concludes that the licence and the manufacturing service are not inputs to a combined item in this contract on the basis of the principle and the factors in paragraph 29 of IFRS 15. In reaching this conclusion, the entity considers that the customer could separately purchase the licence without significantly affecting its ability to benefit from the licence. Neither the licence, nor the manufacturing service, is significantly modified or customised by the other and the entity is not providing a significant service of integrating those items into a combined output. The entity further considers that the licence and the manufacturing service are not highly interdependent or highly interrelated because the entity would be able to fulfil its promise to transfer the licence independently of fulfilling its promise to subsequently manufacture the drug for the customer. Similarly, the entity would be able to manufacture the drug for the customer even if the customer had previously obtained the licence and initially utilised a different manufacturer. Thus, although the manufacturing service necessarily depends on the licence in this contract (ie the entity would not provide the manufacturing service without the customer having obtained the licence), the licence and the manufacturing service do not significantly affect each other. Consequently, the entity concludes that its promises to grant the licence and to provide the manufacturing service are distinct and that there are two performance obligations:

(a)   licence of patent rights; and

(b)   manufacturing service.

IE287   The entity assesses, in accordance with paragraph B58 of IFRS 15, the nature of the entity's promise to grant the licence. The drug is a mature product (ie it has been approved, is currently being manufactured and has been sold commercially for the last several years). For these types of mature products, the entity's customary business practices are not to undertake any activities to support the drug. The drug compound has significant stand-alone functionality (ie its ability to produce a drug that treats a disease or condition).

Consequently, the customer obtains a substantial portion of the benefits of the drug compound from that functionality, rather than from the entity's ongoing activities. The entity concludes that the criteria in paragraph B58 of IFRS 15 are not met because the contract does not require, and the customer does not reasonably expect, the entity to undertake activities that significantly affect the intellectual property to which the customer has rights. In its assessment of the criteria in paragraph B58 of IFRS 15, the entity does not take into consideration the separate performance obligation of promising to provide a manufacturing service. Consequently, the nature of the entity's promise in transferring the licence is to provide a right to use the entity's intellectual property in the form and the functionality with which it exists at the point in time that it is granted to the customer. Consequently, the entity accounts for the licence as a performance obligation satisfied at a point in time.

IE288 The entity applies paragraphs 31–38 of IFRS 15 to determine whether the manufacturing service is a performance obligation satisfied at a point in time or over time.

Example 57—Franchise rights

IE289 An entity enters into a contract with a customer and promises to grant a franchise licence that provides the customer with the right to use the entity's trade name and sell the entity's products for 10 years. In addition to the licence, the entity also promises to provide the equipment necessary to operate a franchise store. In exchange for granting the licence, the entity receives a sales-based royalty of five per cent of the customer's monthly sales. The fixed consideration for the equipment is CU150,000 payable when the equipment is delivered.

Identifying performance obligations

IE290 The entity assesses the goods and services promised to the customer to determine which goods and services are distinct in accordance with paragraph 27 of IFRS 15. The entity observes that the entity, as a franchisor, has developed a customary business practice to undertake activities such as analysing consumers' changing preferences and implementing product improvements, pricing strategies, marketing campaigns and operational efficiencies to support the franchise name. However, the entity concludes that these activities do not directly transfer goods or services to the customer because they are part of the entity's promise to grant a licence.

IE291 The entity determines that it has two promises to transfer goods or services: a promise to grant a licence and a promise to transfer equipment. In addition, the entity concludes that the promise to grant the licence and the promise to transfer the equipment are each distinct. This is because the customer can benefit from each good or service (ie the licence and the equipment) on its own or together with other resources that are readily available (see paragraph 27(a) of IFRS 15). The customer can benefit from the licence together with the equipment that is delivered before the opening of the franchise and the equipment can be used in the franchise or sold for an amount other than scrap value. The entity also determines that the promises to grant the franchise licence and to transfer the equipment are separately identifiable, in accordance with the criterion in paragraph 27(b) of IFRS 15. The entity concludes that the licence and the equipment are not inputs to a combined item (ie they are not fulfilling what is, in effect, a single promise to the customer). In reaching this conclusion, the entity considers that it is not providing a significant service of integrating the licence and the equipment into a combined item (ie the licensed intellectual property is not a component of, and does not significantly modify, the equipment). In addition, the licence and the equipment are not highly interdependent or highly interrelated because the entity would be able to fulfil each promise (ie to license the franchise or to transfer the equipment) independently of the other. Consequently, the entity has two performance obligations:

(a)   the franchise licence; and

(b)   the equipment.

Allocating the transaction price

IE292   The entity determines that the transaction price includes fixed consideration of CU150,000 and variable consideration (five per cent of customer sales). The stand-alone selling price of the equipment is CU150,000 and the entity regularly licenses franchises in exchange for five per cent of customer sales.

IE293   The entity applies paragraph 85 of IFRS 15 to determine whether the variable consideration should be allocated entirely to the performance obligation to transfer the franchise licence. The entity concludes that the variable consideration (ie the sales-based royalty) should be allocated entirely to the franchise licence because the variable consideration relates entirely to the entity's promise to grant the franchise licence. In addition, the entity observes that allocating CU150,000 to the equipment and the sales-based royalty to the franchise licence would be consistent with an allocation based on the entity's relative stand-alone selling prices in similar contracts. Consequently, the entity concludes that the variable consideration (ie the sales-based royalty) should be allocated entirely to the performance obligation to grant the franchise licence.

Application guidance: licensing

IE294   The entity assesses, in accordance with paragraph B58 of IFRS 15, the nature of the entity's promise to grant the franchise licence. The entity concludes that the criteria in paragraph B58 of IFRS 15 are met and the nature of the entity's promise is to provide access to the entity's intellectual property in its current form throughout the licence period. This is because:

(a)   the entity concludes that the customer would reasonably expect that the entity will undertake activities that will significantly affect the intellectual property to which the customer has rights. The ability of the customer to obtain benefit from the intellectual property to which the customer has rights is substantially derived from, or dependent upon, the expected activities of the entity. This is on the basis of the entity's customary business practice to undertake activities such as analysing the consumers' changing preferences and implementing product improvements, pricing strategies, marketing campaigns and operational efficiencies. In addition, the entity observes that because part of its compensation is dependent on the success of the franchisee (as evidenced through the sales-based royalty), the entity has a shared economic interest with the customer that indicates that the customer will expect the entity to undertake those activities to maximise earnings.

(b)   the entity also observes that the franchise licence requires the customer to implement any changes that result from those activities and thus exposes the customer to any positive or negative effects of those activities.

(c)   the entity also observes that even though the customer may benefit from the activities through the rights granted by the licence, they do not transfer a good or service to the customer as those activities occur.

IE295   Because the criteria in paragraph B58 of IFRS 15 are met, the entity concludes that the promise to transfer the licence is a performance obligation satisfied over time in accordance with paragraph 35(a) of IFRS 15.

IE296   The entity also concludes that because the consideration that is in the form of a sales-based royalty relates specifically to the franchise licence (see paragraph B63A), the entity applies paragraph B63 of IFRS 15. After the transfer of the franchise licence, the entity recognises revenue as and when the customer's sales occur because the entity concludes that this reasonably depicts the entity's progress towards complete satisfaction of the franchise licence performance obligation.

Example 58—Access to intellectual property

IE297   An entity, a creator of comic strips, licenses the use of the images and names of its comic strip characters in three of its comic strips to a customer for a four-year term. There are main characters involved in each of the comic strips. However, newly created characters appear regularly and the images of the characters evolve over time. The customer, an operator of cruise ships, can use the entity's characters in various ways, such as in shows or parades, within reasonable guidelines. The contract requires the customer to use the latest images of the characters.

IE298   In exchange for granting the licence, the entity receives a fixed payment of CU1 million in each year of the four-year term.

IE299   In accordance with paragraph 27 of IFRS 15, the entity assesses the goods and services promised to the customer to determine which goods and services are distinct. The entity concludes that it has no other performance obligations other than the promise to grant a licence. That is, the additional activities associated with the licence do not directly transfer a good or service to the customer because they are part of the entity's promise to grant a licence.

IE300   The entity assesses the nature of the entity's promise to transfer the licence in accordance with paragraph B58 of IFRS 15. In assessing the criteria the entity considers the following:

(a)   the customer reasonably expects (arising from the entity's customary business practices) that the entity will undertake activities that will significantly affect the intellectual property to which the customer has rights (ie the characters). This is because the entity's activities (ie development of the characters) change the form of the intellectual property to which the customer has rights. In addition, the ability of the customer to obtain benefit from the intellectual property to which the customer has rights is substantially derived from, or dependent upon, the entity's ongoing activities (ie the publishing of the comic strip).

(b)   the rights granted by the licence directly expose the customer to any positive or negative effects of the entity's activities because the contract requires the customer to use the latest characters.

(c)   even though the customer may benefit from those activities through the rights granted by the licence, they do not transfer a good or service to the customer as those activities occur.

IE301   Consequently, the entity concludes that the criteria in paragraph B58 of IFRS 15 are met and that the nature of the entity's promise to transfer the licence is to provide the customer with access to the entity's intellectual property as it exists throughout the licence period. Consequently, the entity accounts for the promised licence as a performance obligation satisfied over time (ie the criterion in paragraph 35(a) of IFRS 15 is met).

IE302   The entity applies paragraphs 39–45 of IFRS 15 to identify the method that best depicts its performance in the licence. Because the contract provides the customer with unlimited use of the licensed characters for a fixed term, the entity determines that a time-based method would be the most appropriate measure of progress towards complete satisfaction of the performance obligation.

Example 59—Right to use intellectual property

IE303   An entity, a music record label, licenses to a customer a 1975 recording of a classical symphony by a noted orchestra. The customer, a consumer products company, has the right to use the recorded symphony in all commercials, including television, radio and online advertisements for two years in Country A. In exchange for providing the licence, the entity receives fixed consideration of CU10,000 per month. The contract does not include any other goods or services to be provided by the entity. The contract is non-cancellable.

IE304   The entity assesses the goods and services promised to the customer to determine which goods and services are distinct in accordance with paragraph 27 of IFRS 15. The entity concludes that its only performance obligation is to grant the licence. The entity determines that the term of the licence (two years), its geographical scope (the customer's right to use the recording only in Country A), and the defined permitted use for the recording (in commercials) are all attributes of the promised licence in the contract.

IE305 In accordance with paragraph B58 of IFRS 15, the entity assesses the nature of the entity's promise to grant the licence. The entity does not have any contractual or implied obligations to change the licensed recording. The licensed recording has significant stand-alone functionality (ie the ability to be played) and, therefore, the ability of the customer to obtain the benefits of the recording is not substantially derived from the entity's ongoing activities. The entity therefore determines that the contract does not require, and the customer does not reasonably expect, the entity to undertake activities that significantly affect the licensed recording (ie the criterion in paragraph B58(a) is not met). Consequently, the entity concludes that the nature of its promise in transferring the licence is to provide the customer with a right to use the entity's intellectual property as it exists at the point in time that it is granted. Therefore, the promise to grant the licence is a performance obligation satisfied at a point in time. The entity recognises all of the revenue at the point in time when the customer can direct the use of, and obtain substantially all of the remaining benefits from, the licensed intellectual property.

IE306 Because of the length of time between the entity's performance (at the beginning of the period) and the customer's monthly payments over two years (which are non-cancellable), the entity considers the requirements in paragraphs 60–65 of IFRS 15 to determine whether a significant financing component exists.

Example 60—Sales-based royalty for a licence of intellectual property

IE307 An entity, a movie distribution company, licenses Movie XYZ to a customer. The customer, an operator of cinemas, has the right to show the movie in its cinemas for six weeks. Additionally, the entity has agreed to (a) provide memorabilia from the filming to the customer for display at the customer's cinemas before the beginning of the six-week screening period; and (b) sponsor radio advertisements for Movie XYZ on popular radio stations in the customer's geographical area throughout the six-week screening period. In exchange for providing the licence and the additional promotional goods and services, the entity will receive a portion of the operator's ticket sales for Movie XYZ (ie variable consideration in the form of a sales-based royalty).

IE308 The entity concludes that the licence to show Movie XYZ is the predominant item to which the sales-based royalty relates because the entity has a reasonable expectation that the customer would ascribe significantly more value to the licence than to the related promotional goods or services. The entity recognises revenue from the sales-based royalty, the only consideration to which the entity is entitled under the contract, wholly in accordance with paragraph B63. If the licence, the memorabilia and the advertising activities are separate performance obligations, the entity would allocate the sales-based royalty to each performance obligation.

Example 61—Access to intellectual property

IE309 An entity, a well-known sports team, licenses the use of its name and logo to a customer. The customer, an apparel designer, has the right to use the sports team's name and logo on items including t-shirts, caps, mugs and towels for one year. In exchange for providing the licence, the entity will receive fixed consideration of CU2 million and a royalty of five per cent of the sales price of any items using the team name or logo. The customer expects that the entity will continue to play games and provide a competitive team.

IE310 The entity assesses the goods and services promised to the customer to determine which goods and services are distinct in accordance with paragraph 27 of IFRS 15. The entity concludes that its only performance obligation is to transfer the licence. The additional activities associated with the licence (ie continuing to play games and provide a competitive team) do not directly transfer a good or service to the customer because they are part of the entity's promise to grant the licence.

IE311 The entity assesses the nature of the entity's promise to transfer the licence in accordance with paragraph B58 of IFRS 15. In assessing the criteria the entity considers the following:

(a) the entity concludes that the customer would reasonably expect that the entity will undertake activities that will significantly affect the intellectual property (ie the team name and logo) to which the customer has rights. This is on the basis of the entity's customary business practice to undertake activities that support and maintain the value of the name and logo such as continuing to play and providing a competitive team. The entity determines that the ability of the customer to obtain benefit from the name and logo is substantially derived from, or dependent upon, the expected activities of the entity. In addition, the entity observes that because some of its consideration is dependent on the success of the customer (through the sales-based royalty), the entity has a shared economic interest with the customer, which indicates that the customer will expect the entity to undertake those activities to maximise earnings.

(b) the entity observes that the rights granted by the licence (ie the use of the team's name and logo) directly expose the customer to any positive or negative effects of the entity's activities.

(c) the entity also observes that even though the customer may benefit from the activities through the rights granted by the licence, they do not transfer a good or service to the customer as those activities occur.

IE312 The entity concludes that the criteria in paragraph B58 of IFRS 15 are met and the nature of the entity's promise to grant the licence is to provide the customer with access to the entity's intellectual property as it exists throughout the licence period. Consequently, the entity accounts for the promised licence as a performance obligation satisfied over time (ie the criterion in paragraph 35(a) of IFRS 15 is met).

IE313   The entity then applies paragraphs 39–45 of IFRS 15 to determine a measure of progress that will depict the entity's performance. For the consideration that is in the form of a sales-based royalty, paragraph B63 of IFRS 15 applies because the sales-based royalty relates solely to the licence, which is the only performance obligation in the contract. The entity concludes that recognition of the CU2 million fixed consideration as revenue rateably over time plus recognition of the royalty as revenue as and when the customer's sales of items using the team name or logo occur reasonably depicts the entity's progress towards complete satisfaction of the licence performance obligation.

Repurchase agreements

IE314   Example 62 illustrates the requirements in paragraphs B64–B76 of IFRS 15 on repurchase agreements.

Example 62—Repurchase agreements

IE315   An entity enters into a contract with a customer for the sale of a tangible asset on 1 January 20X7 for CU1 million.

Case A—Call option: financing

IE316   The contract includes a call option that gives the entity the right to repurchase the asset for CU1.1 million on or before 31 December 20X7.

IE317   Control of the asset does not transfer to the customer on 1 January 20X7 because the entity has a right to repurchase the asset and therefore the customer is limited in its ability to direct the use of, and obtain substantially all of the remaining benefits from, the asset. Consequently, in accordance with paragraph B66(b) of IFRS 15, the entity accounts for the transaction as a financing arrangement, because the exercise price is more than the original selling price. In accordance with paragraph B68 of IFRS 15, the entity does not derecognise the asset and instead recognises the cash received as a financial liability. The entity also recognises interest expense for the difference between the exercise price (CU1.1 million) and the cash received (CU1 million), which increases the liability.

IE318   On 31 December 20X7, the option lapses unexercised; therefore, the entity derecognises the liability and recognises revenue of CU1.1 million.

Case B—Put option: lease

IE319   Instead of having a call option, the contract includes a put option that obliges the entity to repurchase the asset at the customer's request for CU900,000 on or before 31 December 20X7. The market value is expected to be CU750,000 on 31 December 20X7.

IE320   At the inception of the contract, the entity assesses whether the customer has a significant economic incentive to exercise the put option, to determine the accounting for the transfer of the asset (see paragraphs B70–B76 of IFRS 15). The entity concludes that the customer has a significant economic incentive to exercise the put option because the repurchase price significantly exceeds the expected market value of the asset at the date of repurchase. The entity determines there are no other relevant factors to consider when assessing whether the customer has a significant economic incentive to exercise the put option. Consequently, the entity concludes that control of the asset does not transfer to the customer, because the customer is limited in its ability to direct the use of, and obtain substantially all of the remaining benefits from, the asset.

IE321   In accordance with paragraphs B70–B71 of IFRS 15, the entity accounts for the transaction as a lease in accordance with IFRS 16 *Leases*.

Bill-and-hold arrangements

IE322   Example 63 illustrates the requirements in paragraphs B79–B82 of IFRS 15 on bill-and-hold arrangements.

Example 63—Bill-and-hold arrangement

IE323   An entity enters into a contract with a customer on 1 January 20X8 for the sale of a machine and spare parts. The manufacturing lead time for the machine and spare parts is two years.

IE324   Upon completion of manufacturing, the entity demonstrates that the machine and spare parts meet the agreed-upon specifications in the contract. The promises to transfer the machine and spare parts are distinct [Refer: paragraph 27] and result in two performance obligations that each will be satisfied at a point in time. On 31 December 20X9, the customer pays for the machine and spare parts, but only takes physical possession of the machine. Although the customer inspects and accepts the spare parts, the customer requests that the spare parts be stored at the entity's warehouse because of its close proximity to the customer's factory. The customer has legal title to the spare parts and the parts can be identified as belonging to the customer. Furthermore, the entity stores the spare parts in a separate section of its warehouse and the parts are ready for immediate shipment at the customer's request. The entity expects to hold the spare parts for two to four years and the entity does not have the ability to use the spare parts or direct them to another customer.

IE325   The entity identifies the promise to provide custodial services as a performance obligation because it is a service provided to the customer and it is distinct from the machine and spare parts. Consequently, the entity accounts for three performance obligations in the contract (the promises to provide the machine, the spare parts and the custodial services). The transaction price is allocated to the three performance obligations and revenue is recognised when (or as) control transfers to the customer.

IE326   Control of the machine transfers to the customer on 31 December 20X9 when the customer takes physical possession. The entity assesses the indicators in paragraph 38 of IFRS 15 to determine the point in time at which control of the spare parts transfers to the customer, noting that the entity has received payment, the customer has legal title to the spare parts and the customer has inspected and accepted the spare parts. In addition, the entity concludes that all of the criteria in paragraph B81 of IFRS 15 are met, which is necessary for the entity to recognise revenue in a bill-and-hold arrangement. The entity recognises revenue for the spare parts on 31 December 20X9 when control transfers to the customer.

IE327   The performance obligation to provide custodial services is satisfied over time as the services are provided. The entity considers whether the payment terms include a significant financing component in accordance with paragraphs 60–65 of IFRS 15.

Appendix
Amendments to guidance on other Standards

The amendments in this appendix to the guidance on other Standards are necessary in order to ensure consistency with IFRS 15 and the related amendments to other Standards.

* * * * *

The amendments contained in this appendix when IFRS 15 was issued in 2014 have been incorporated into the guidance on the relevant Standards included in this volume.

IASB documents published to accompany

IFRS 16

Leases

The text of the unaccompanied standard, IFRS 16, is contained in Part A of this edition. Its effective date when issued was 1 January 2019. The text of the Basis for Conclusions on IFRS 16 is contained in Part C of this edition. This part presents the following documents:

ILLUSTRATIVE EXAMPLES

APPENDIX TO THE ILLUSTRATIVE EXAMPLES

Amendments to guidance on other Standards

CONTENTS

...continued

SALE AND LEASEBACK TRANSACTIONS

Example 24—Sale and leaseback transaction

APPENDIX

Amendments to guidance on other Standards

IFRS 16 *Leases*
Illustrative Examples

These examples accompany, but are not part of, IFRS 16. They illustrate aspects of IFRS 16 but are not intended to provide interpretative guidance.

IE1   These examples portray hypothetical situations illustrating how an entity might apply some of the requirements in IFRS 16 to particular aspects of a lease (or other contracts) on the basis of the limited facts presented. The analysis in each example is not intended to represent the only manner in which the requirements could be applied, nor are the examples intended to apply only to the specific industry illustrated. Although some aspects of the examples may be present in actual fact patterns, all relevant facts and circumstances of a particular fact pattern would need to be evaluated when applying IFRS 16.

Identifying a lease (paragraphs 9–11 and B9–B30)

IE2   The following examples illustrate how an entity determines whether a contract is, or contains, a lease.

> **Example 1—Rail cars**
>
> *Example 1A: a contract between Customer and a freight carrier (Supplier) provides Customer with the use of 10 rail cars of a particular type for five years. The contract specifies the rail cars; the cars are owned by Supplier. Customer determines when, where and which goods are to be transported using the cars. When the cars are not in use, they are kept at Customer's premises. Customer can use the cars for another purpose (for example, storage) if it so chooses. However, the contract specifies that Customer cannot transport particular types of cargo (for example, explosives). If a particular car needs to be serviced or repaired, Supplier is required to substitute a car of the same type. Otherwise, and other than on default by Customer, Supplier cannot retrieve the cars during the five-year period.*
>
> *The contract also requires Supplier to provide an engine and a driver when requested by Customer. Supplier keeps the engines at its premises and provides instructions to the driver detailing Customer's requests to transport goods. Supplier can choose to use any one of a number of engines to fulfil each of Customer's requests, and one engine could be used to transport not only Customer's goods, but also the goods of other customers (ie if other customers require the transportation of goods to destinations close to the destination requested by Customer and within a similar timeframe, Supplier can choose to attach up to 100 rail cars to the engine).*
>
> continued...

...continued

Example 1—Rail cars

The contract contains leases of rail cars. Customer has the right to use 10 rail cars for five years.

There are 10 identified cars. The cars are explicitly specified in the contract. Once delivered to Customer, the cars can be substituted only when they need to be serviced or repaired (see paragraph B18). The engine used to transport the rail cars is not an identified asset because it is neither explicitly specified nor implicitly specified in the contract.
[Refer: paragraph B13]

Customer has the right to control the use of the 10 rail cars throughout the five-year period of use because:

(a)   Customer has the right to obtain substantially all of the economic benefits from use of the cars over the five-year period of use. Customer has exclusive use of the cars throughout the period of use, including when they are not being used to transport Customer's goods. [Refer: paragraph B21]

(b)   Customer has the right to direct the use of the cars because the conditions in paragraph B24(a) exist. The contractual restrictions on the cargo that can be transported by the cars are protective rights of Supplier and define the scope of Customer's right to use the cars. [Refer: paragraph B30] Within the scope of its right of use defined in the contract, Customer makes the relevant decisions about how and for what purpose the cars are used by being able to decide when and where the rail cars will be used and which goods are transported using the cars. Customer also determines whether and how the cars will be used when not being used to transport its goods (for example, whether and when they will be used for storage). Customer has the right to change these decisions during the five-year period of use. [Refer: paragraphs B25 and B26]

Although having an engine and driver (controlled by Supplier) to transport the rail cars is essential to the efficient use of the cars, Supplier's decisions in this regard do not give it the right to direct how and for what purpose the rail cars are used. Consequently, Supplier does not control the use of the cars during the period of use. [Refer: paragraph B27]

continued...

...continued

Example 1—Rail cars

Example 1B: the contract between Customer and Supplier requires Supplier to transport a specified quantity of goods by using a specified type of rail car in accordance with a stated timetable for a period of five years. The timetable and quantity of goods specified are equivalent to Customer having the use of 10 rail cars for five years. Supplier provides the rail cars, driver and engine as part of the contract. The contract states the nature and quantity of the goods to be transported (and the type of rail car to be used to transport the goods). Supplier has a large pool of similar cars that can be used to fulfil the requirements of the contract. Similarly, Supplier can choose to use any one of a number of engines to fulfil each of Customer's requests, and one engine could be used to transport not only Customer's goods, but also the goods of other customers. The cars and engines are stored at Supplier's premises when not being used to transport goods.

The contract does not contain a lease of rail cars or of an engine.

The rail cars and the engines used to transport Customer's goods are not identified assets. Supplier has the substantive right to substitute the rail cars and engine because:

(a) Supplier has the practical ability to substitute each car and the engine throughout the period of use (see paragraph B14(a)). Alternative cars and engines are readily available to Supplier and Supplier can substitute each car and the engine without Customer's approval.

(b) Supplier would benefit economically from substituting each car and the engine (see paragraph B14(b)). There would be minimal, if any, cost associated with substituting each car or the engine because the cars and engines are stored at Supplier's premises
[Refer: paragraph B17] and Supplier has a large pool of similar cars and engines. Supplier benefits from substituting each car or the engine in contracts of this nature because substitution allows Supplier to, for example, (i) use cars or an engine to fulfil a task for which the cars or engine are already positioned to perform (for example, a task at a rail yard close to the point of origin) or (ii) use cars or an engine that would otherwise be sitting idle because they are not being used by a customer.

Accordingly, Customer does not direct the use, nor have the right to obtain substantially all of the economic benefits from use, of an identified car or an engine. Supplier directs the use of the rail cars and engine by selecting which cars and engine are used for each particular delivery and obtains substantially all of the economic benefits from use of the rail cars and engine. Supplier is only providing freight capacity.

Example 2—Concession space

A coffee company (Customer) enters into a contract with an airport operator (Supplier) to use a space in the airport to sell its goods for a three-year period. The contract states the amount of space and that the space may be located at any one of several boarding areas within the airport. Supplier has the right to change the location of the space allocated to Customer at any time during the period of use. There are minimal costs to Supplier associated with changing the space for the Customer: Customer uses a kiosk (that it owns) that can be moved easily to sell its goods. There are many areas in the airport that are available and that would meet the specifications for the space in the contract.

The contract does not contain a lease.

Although the amount of space Customer uses is specified in the contract, there is no identified asset. Customer controls its owned kiosk. However, the contract is for space in the airport, and this space can change at the discretion of Supplier. Supplier has the substantive right to substitute the space Customer uses because:

(a)   Supplier has the practical ability to change the space used by Customer throughout the period of use (see paragraph B14(a)). There are many areas in the airport that meet the specifications for the space in the contract, and Supplier has the right to change the location of the space to other space that meets the specifications at any time without Customer's approval.

(b)   Supplier would benefit economically from substituting the space (see paragraph B14(b)). There would be minimal cost associated with changing the space used by Customer because the kiosk can be moved easily. Supplier benefits from substituting the space in the airport because substitution allows Supplier to make the most effective use of the space at boarding areas in the airport to meet changing circumstances.

Example 3—Fibre-optic cable

Example 3A: Customer enters into a 15-year contract with a utilities company (Supplier) for the right to use three specified, physically distinct dark fibres within a larger cable connecting Hong Kong to Tokyo. Customer makes the decisions about the use of the fibres by connecting each end of the fibres to its electronic equipment (ie Customer 'lights' the fibres and decides what data, and how much data, those fibres will transport). If the fibres are damaged, Supplier is responsible for the repairs and maintenance. Supplier owns extra fibres, but can substitute those for Customer's fibres only for reasons of repairs, maintenance or malfunction (and is obliged to substitute the fibres in these cases).

The contract contains a lease of dark fibres. Customer has the right to use the three dark fibres for 15 years.

There are three identified fibres. The fibres are explicitly specified in the contract and are physically distinct from other fibres within the cable. **[Refer: paragraph B20]** Supplier cannot substitute the fibres other than for reasons of repairs, maintenance or malfunction (see paragraph B18).

Customer has the right to control the use of the fibres throughout the 15-year period of use because:

(a)   Customer has the right to obtain substantially all of the economic benefits from use of the fibres over the 15-year period of use. Customer has exclusive use of the fibres throughout the period of use. **[Refer: paragraph B21]**

(b)   Customer has the right to direct the use of the fibres because the conditions in paragraph B24(a) exist. Customer makes the relevant decisions about how and for what purpose the fibres are used by deciding (i) when and whether to light the fibres and (ii) when and how much output the fibres will produce (ie what data, and how much data, those fibres will transport). Customer has the right to change these decisions during the 15-year period of use. **[Refer: paragraphs B25 and B26]**

Although Supplier's decisions about repairing and maintaining the fibres are essential to their efficient use, those decisions do not give Supplier the right to direct how and for what purpose the fibres are used. Consequently, Supplier does not control the use of the fibres during the period of use. **[Refer: paragraph B27]**

continued...

...continued

Example 3—Fibre-optic cable

Example 3B: Customer enters into a 15-year contract with Supplier for the right to use a specified amount of capacity within a cable connecting Hong Kong to Tokyo. The specified amount is equivalent to Customer having the use of the full capacity of three fibre strands within the cable (the cable contains 15 fibres with similar capacities). Supplier makes decisions about the transmission of data (ie Supplier lights the fibres, makes decisions about which fibres are used to transmit Customer's traffic and makes decisions about the electronic equipment that Supplier owns and connects to the fibres).

The contract does not contain a lease.

Supplier makes all decisions about the transmission of its customers' data, which requires the use of only a portion of the capacity of the cable for each customer. The capacity portion that will be provided to Customer is not physically distinct from the remaining capacity of the cable and does not represent substantially all of the capacity of the cable (see paragraph B20). Consequently, Customer does not have the right to use an identified asset.

Example 4—Retail unit

Customer enters into a contract with a property owner (Supplier) to use Retail Unit A for a five-year period. Retail Unit A is part of a larger retail space with many retail units.

Customer is granted the right to use Retail Unit A. Supplier can require Customer to relocate to another retail unit. In that case, Supplier is required to provide Customer with a retail unit of similar quality and specifications to Retail Unit A and to pay for Customer's relocation costs. Supplier would benefit economically from relocating Customer only if a major new tenant were to decide to occupy a large amount of retail space at a rate sufficiently favourable to cover the costs of relocating Customer and other tenants in the retail space. However, although it is possible that those circumstances will arise, at inception of the contract, it is not likely that those circumstances will arise.

The contract requires Customer to use Retail Unit A to operate its well-known store brand to sell its goods during the hours that the larger retail space is open. Customer makes all of the decisions about the use of the retail unit during the period of use. For example, Customer decides on the mix of goods sold from the unit, the pricing of the goods sold and the quantities of inventory held. Customer also controls physical access to the unit throughout the five-year period of use.

The contract requires Customer to make fixed payments to Supplier, as well as variable payments that are a percentage of sales from Retail Unit A.

Supplier provides cleaning and security services, as well as advertising services, as part of the contract.

continued...

...continued

Example 4—Retail unit

The contract contains a lease of retail space. Customer has the right to use Retail Unit A for five years.

Retail Unit A is an identified asset. It is explicitly specified in the contract. **[Refer: paragraph B13]** Supplier has the practical ability to substitute the retail unit, but could benefit economically from substitution only in specific circumstances. Supplier's substitution right is not substantive because, at inception of the contract, those circumstances are not considered likely to arise (see paragraph B16).

Customer has the right to control the use of Retail Unit A throughout the five-year period of use because:

(a)   Customer has the right to obtain substantially all of the economic benefits from use of Retail Unit A over the five-year period of use. Customer has exclusive use of Retail Unit A throughout the period of use. Although a portion of the cash flows derived from sales from Retail Unit A will flow from Customer to Supplier, this represents consideration that Customer pays Supplier for the right to use the retail unit. It does not prevent Customer from having the right to obtain substantially all of the economic benefits from use of Retail Unit A. **[Refer: paragraph B23]**

(b)   Customer has the right to direct the use of Retail Unit A because the conditions in paragraph B24(a) exist. The contractual restrictions on the goods that can be sold from Retail Unit A, and when Retail Unit A is open, define the scope of Customer's right to use Retail Unit A. Within the scope of its right of use defined in the contract, Customer makes the relevant decisions about how and for what purpose Retail Unit A is used by being able to decide, for example, the mix of products that will be sold in the retail unit and the sale price for those products. Customer has the right to change these decisions during the five-year period of use. **[Refer: paragraphs B25 and B26]**

Although cleaning, security, and advertising services are essential to the efficient use of Retail Unit A, Supplier's decisions in this regard do not give it the right to direct how and for what purpose Retail Unit A is used. Consequently, Supplier does not control the use of Retail Unit A during the period of use and Supplier's decisions do not affect Customer's control of the use of Retail Unit A.

Example 5—Truck rental

Customer enters into a contract with Supplier for the use of a truck for one week to transport cargo from New York to San Francisco. Supplier does not have substitution rights. Only cargo specified in the contract is permitted to be transported on this truck for the period of the contract. The contract specifies a maximum distance that the truck can be driven. Customer is able to choose the details of the journey (speed, route, rest stops, etc.) within the parameters of the contract. Customer does not have the right to continue using the truck after the specified trip is complete.

The cargo to be transported, and the timing and location of pick-up in New York and delivery in San Francisco, are specified in the contract.

Customer is responsible for driving the truck from New York to San Francisco.

The contract contains a lease of a truck. Customer has the right to use the truck for the duration of the specified trip.

There is an identified asset. The truck is explicitly specified in the contract, and Supplier does not have the right to substitute the truck.
[Refer: paragraphs B13 and B14]

Customer has the right to control the use of the truck throughout the period of use because:

(a)   Customer has the right to obtain substantially all of the economic benefits from use of the truck over the period of use. Customer has exclusive use of the truck throughout the period of use.
[Refer: paragraph B21]

(b)   Customer has the right to direct the use of the truck because the conditions in B24(b)(i) exist. How and for what purpose the truck will be used (ie the transportation of specified cargo from New York to San Francisco within a specified timeframe) is predetermined in the contract. Customer directs the use of the truck because it has the right to operate the truck (for example, speed, route, rest stops) throughout the period of use. Customer makes all of the decisions about the use of the truck that can be made during the period of use through its control of the operations of the truck.

Because the duration of the contract is one week, this lease meets the definition of a short-term lease.
[Refer: paragraph 5]

Example 6—Ship

Example 6A: Customer enters into a contract with a ship owner (Supplier) for the transportation of cargo from Rotterdam to Sydney on a specified ship. The ship is explicitly specified in the contract and Supplier does not have substitution rights. The cargo will occupy substantially all of the capacity of the ship. The contract specifies the cargo to be transported on the ship and the dates of pickup and delivery.

Supplier operates and maintains the ship and is responsible for the safe passage of the cargo on board the ship. Customer is prohibited from hiring another operator for the ship or operating the ship itself during the term of the contract.

The contract does not contain a lease.

There is an identified asset. The ship is explicitly specified in the contract and Supplier does not have the right to substitute that specified ship. **[Refer: paragraphs B13 and B14]**

Customer has the right to obtain substantially all of the economic benefits from use of the ship over the period of use. Its cargo will occupy substantially all of the capacity of the ship, thereby preventing other parties from obtaining economic benefits from use of the ship. **[Refer: paragraph B20]**

However, Customer does not have the right to control the use of the ship because it does not have the right to direct its use. Customer does not have the right to direct how and for what purpose the ship is used. **[Refer: paragraphs B25–B27]** How and for what purpose the ship will be used (ie the transportation of specified cargo from Rotterdam to Sydney within a specified timeframe) is predetermined in the contract. Customer has no right to change how and for what purpose the ship is used during the period of use. Customer has no other decision-making rights about the use of the ship during the period of use (for example, it does not have the right to operate the ship) and did not design the ship. Customer has the same rights regarding the use of the ship as if it were one of many customers transporting cargo on the ship.

continued...

...continued

Example 6—Ship

Example 6B: Customer enters into a contract with Supplier for the use of a specified ship for a five-year period. The ship is explicitly specified in the contract and Supplier does not have substitution rights.

Customer decides what cargo will be transported, and whether, when and to which ports the ship will sail, throughout the five-year period of use, subject to restrictions specified in the contract. Those restrictions prevent Customer from sailing the ship into waters at a high risk of piracy or carrying hazardous materials as cargo.

Supplier operates and maintains the ship and is responsible for the safe passage of the cargo on board the ship. Customer is prohibited from hiring another operator for the ship of the contract or operating the ship itself during the term of the contract.

The contract contains a lease. Customer has the right to use the ship for five years.

There is an identified asset. The ship is explicitly specified in the contract, and Supplier does not have the right to substitute that specified ship. **[Refer: paragraphs B13 and B14]**

Customer has the right to control the use of the ship throughout the five-year period of use because:

(a)   Customer has the right to obtain substantially all of the economic benefits from use of the ship over the five-year period of use. Customer has exclusive use of the ship throughout the period of use. **[Refer: paragraph B21]**

(b)   Customer has the right to direct the use of the ship because the conditions in paragraph B24(a) exist. The contractual restrictions about where the ship can sail and the cargo to be transported by the ship define the scope of Customer's right to use the ship. They are protective rights that protect Supplier's investment in the ship and Supplier's personnel. **[Refer: paragraph B30]** Within the scope of its right of use, Customer makes the relevant decisions about how and for what purpose the ship is used throughout the five-year period of use because it decides whether, where and when the ship sails, as well as the cargo it will transport. Customer has the right to change these decisions throughout the five-year period of use. **[Refer: paragraphs B25 and B26]**

Although the operation and maintenance of the ship are essential to its efficient use, Supplier's decisions in this regard do not give it the right to direct how and for what purpose the ship is used. Instead, Supplier's decisions are dependent upon Customer's decisions about how and for what purpose the ship is used. **[Refer: paragraph B27]**

Example 7—Aircraft

Customer enters into a contract with an aircraft owner (Supplier) for the use of an explicitly specified aircraft for a two-year period. The contract details the interior and exterior specifications for the aircraft.

There are contractual and legal restrictions in the contract on where the aircraft can fly. Subject to those restrictions, Customer determines where and when the aircraft will fly, and which passengers and cargo will be transported on the aircraft. Supplier is responsible for operating the aircraft, using its own crew. Customer is prohibited from hiring another operator for the aircraft or operating the aircraft itself during the term of the contract.

Supplier is permitted to substitute the aircraft at any time during the two-year period and must substitute the aircraft if it is not working. Any substitute aircraft must meet the interior and exterior specifications in the contract. There are significant costs involved in outfitting an aircraft in Supplier's fleet to meet Customer's specifications.

The contract contains a lease. Customer has the right to use the aircraft for two years.

There is an identified asset. The aircraft is explicitly specified in the contract **[Refer: paragraph B13]** and, although Supplier can substitute the aircraft, its substitution right is not substantive because the conditions in paragraph B14(b) do not exist. Supplier's substitution right is not substantive because of the significant costs involved in outfitting another aircraft to meet the specifications required by the contract such that Supplier is not expected to benefit economically from substituting the aircraft.

Customer has the right to control the use of the aircraft throughout the two-year period of use because:

(a)   Customer has the right to obtain substantially all of the economic benefits from use of the aircraft over the two-year period of use. Customer has exclusive use of the aircraft throughout the period of use. **[Refer: paragraph B21]**

(b)   Customer has the right to direct the use of the aircraft because the conditions in paragraph B24(a) exist. The restrictions on where the aircraft can fly define the scope of Customer's right to use the aircraft. Within the scope of its right of use, Customer makes the relevant decisions about how and for what purpose the aircraft is used throughout the two-year period of use because it decides whether, where and when the aircraft travels as well as the passengers and cargo it will transport. Customer has the right to change these decisions throughout the two-year period of use. **[Refer: paragraphs B25 and B26]**

continued...

...continued

Example 7—Aircraft

Although the operation of the aircraft is essential to its efficient use, Supplier's decisions in this regard do not give it the right to direct how and for what purpose the aircraft is used. Consequently, Supplier does not control the use of the aircraft during the period of use and Supplier's decisions do not affect Customer's control of the use of the aircraft. **[Refer: paragraph B27]**

Example 8—Contract for shirts

Customer enters into a contract with a manufacturer (Supplier) to purchase a particular type, quality and quantity of shirts for a three-year period. The type, quality and quantity of shirts are specified in the contract.

Supplier has only one factory that can meet the needs of Customer. Supplier is unable to supply the shirts from another factory or source the shirts from a third party supplier. The capacity of the factory exceeds the output for which Customer has contracted (ie Customer has not contracted for substantially all of the capacity of the factory).

Supplier makes all decisions about the operations of the factory, including the production level at which to run the factory and which customer contracts to fulfil with the output of the factory that is not used to fulfil Customer's contract.

The contract does not contain a lease.

The factory is an identified asset. The factory is implicitly specified because Supplier can fulfil the contract only through the use of this asset. **[Refer: paragraph B13]**

Customer does not control the use of the factory because it does not have the right to obtain substantially all of the economic benefits from use of the factory. This is because Supplier could decide to use the factory to fulfil other customer contracts during the period of use. **[Refer: paragraph B21]**

Customer also does not control the use of the factory because it does not have the right to direct the use of the factory. Customer does not have the right to direct how and for what purpose the factory is used during the three-year period of use. Customer's rights are limited to specifying output from the factory in the contract with Supplier. Customer has the same rights regarding the use of the factory as other customers purchasing shirts from the factory. Supplier has the right to direct the use of the factory because Supplier can decide how and for what purpose the factory is used (ie Supplier has the right to decide the production level at which to run the factory and which customer contracts to fulfil with the output produced). **[Refer: paragraph B25]**

Either the fact that Customer does not have the right to obtain substantially all of the economic benefits from use of the factory, or that Customer does not have the right to direct the use of the factory, would be sufficient in isolation to conclude that Customer does not control the use of the factory.

Example 9—Contract for energy/power

Example 9A: a utility company (Customer) enters into a contract with a power company (Supplier) to purchase all of the electricity produced by a new solar farm for 20 years. The solar farm is explicitly specified in the contract and Supplier has no substitution rights. The solar farm is owned by Supplier and the energy cannot be provided to Customer from another asset. Customer designed the solar farm before it was constructed—Customer hired experts in solar energy to assist in determining the location of the farm and the engineering of the equipment to be used. Supplier is responsible for building the solar farm to Customer's specifications, and then operating and maintaining it. There are no decisions to be made about whether, when or how much electricity will be produced because the design of the asset has predetermined those decisions. Supplier will receive tax credits relating to the construction and ownership of the solar farm, while Customer receives renewable energy credits that accrue from use of the solar farm.

The contract contains a lease. Customer has the right to use the solar farm for 20 years.

There is an identified asset because the solar farm is explicitly specified in the contract, and Supplier does not have the right to substitute the specified solar farm. **[Refer: paragraphs B13 and B14]**

Customer has the right to control the use of the solar farm throughout the 20-year period of use because:

(a)   Customer has the right to obtain substantially all of the economic benefits from use of the solar farm over the 20-year period of use. Customer has exclusive use of the solar farm; it takes all of the electricity produced by the farm over the 20-year period of use as well as the renewable energy credits that are a by-product from use of the solar farm. Although Supplier will receive economic benefits from the solar farm in the form of tax credits, those economic benefits relate to the ownership of the solar farm rather than the use of the solar farm and, thus, are not considered in this assessment. **[Refer: paragraph B21]**

continued...

...continued

Example 9—Contract for energy/power

(b)   Customer has the right to direct the use of the solar farm because the conditions in paragraph B24(b)(ii) exist. Neither Customer, nor Supplier, decides how and for what purpose the solar farm is used during the period of use because those decisions are predetermined by the design of the asset (ie the design of the solar farm has, in effect, programmed into the asset any relevant decision-making rights about how and for what purpose the solar farm is used throughout the period of use). Customer does not operate the solar farm; Supplier makes the decisions about the operation of the solar farm. However, Customer's design of the solar farm has given it the right to direct the use of the farm. Because the design of the solar farm has predetermined how and for what purpose the asset will be used throughout the period of use, Customer's control over that design is substantively no different from Customer controlling those decisions. [Refer: paragraph B28]

Example 9B: Customer enters into a contract with Supplier to purchase all of the power produced by an explicitly specified power plant for three years. The power plant is owned and operated by Supplier. Supplier is unable to provide power to Customer from another plant. The contract sets out the quantity and timing of power that the power plant will produce throughout the period of use, which cannot be changed in the absence of extraordinary circumstances (for example, emergency situations). Supplier operates and maintains the plant on a daily basis in accordance with industry-approved operating practices. Supplier designed the power plant when it was constructed some years before entering into the contract with Customer—Customer had no involvement in that design.

The contract does not contain a lease.

There is an identified asset because the power plant is explicitly specified in the contract, and Supplier does not have the right to substitute the specified plant. [Refer: paragraphs B13 and B14]

Customer has the right to obtain substantially all of the economic benefits from use of the identified power plant over the three-year period of use. Customer will take all of the power produced by the power plant over the three-year period of use.

continued...

...continued

Example 9—Contract for energy/power

However, Customer does not have the right to control the use of the power plant because it does not have the right to direct its use. Customer does not have the right to direct how and for what purpose the plant is used. **[Refer: paragraph B24]** How and for what purpose the plant is used (ie whether, when and how much power the plant will produce) is predetermined in the contract. Customer has no right to change how and for what purpose the plant is used during the period of use. Customer has no other decision-making rights about the use of the power plant during the period of use (for example, it does not operate the power plant) and did not design the plant. Supplier is the only party that can make decisions about the plant during the period of use by making the decisions about how the plant is operated and maintained. Customer has the same rights regarding the use of the plant as if it were one of many customers obtaining power from the plant. **[Refer: paragraph B25]**

Example 9C: Customer enters into a contract with Supplier to purchase all of the power produced by an explicitly specified power plant for 10 years. The contract states that Customer has rights to all of the power produced by the plant (ie Supplier cannot use the plant to fulfil other contracts).

Customer issues instructions to Supplier about the quantity and timing of the delivery of power. If the plant is not producing power for Customer, it does not operate.

Supplier operates and maintains the plant on a daily basis in accordance with industry-approved operating practices.

The contract contains a lease. Customer has the right to use the power plant for 10 years.

There is an identified asset. The power plant is explicitly specified in the contract and Supplier does not have the right to substitute the specified plant. **[Refer: paragraphs B13 and B14]**

continued...

...continued

Example 9—Contract for energy/power

Customer has the right to control the use of the power plant throughout the 10-year period of use because:

(a)   Customer has the right to obtain substantially all of the economic benefits from use of the power plant over the 10-year period of use. Customer has exclusive use of the power plant; it has rights to all of the power produced by the power plant throughout the 10-year period of use. **[Refer: paragraph B21]**

(b)   Customer has the right to direct the use of the power plant because the conditions in paragraph B24(a) exist. Customer makes the relevant decisions about how and for what purpose the power plant is used because it has the right to determine whether, when and how much power the plant will produce (ie the timing and quantity, if any, of power produced) throughout the period of use. Because Supplier is prevented from using the power plant for another purpose, Customer's decision-making about the timing and quantity of power produced, in effect, determines when, and whether, the plant produces output. **[Refer: paragraph B25]**

Although the operation and maintenance of the power plant are essential to its efficient use, Supplier's decisions in this regard do not give it the right to direct how and for what purpose the power plant is used.
[Refer: paragraph B27] Consequently, Supplier does not control the use of the power plant during the period of use. Instead, Supplier's decisions are dependent upon Customer's decisions about how and for what purpose the power plant is used.

Example 10—Contract for network services

Example 10A: Customer enters into a contract with a telecommunications company (Supplier) for network services for two years. The contract requires Supplier to supply network services that meet a specified quality level. In order to provide the services, Supplier installs and configures servers at Customer's premises—Supplier determines the speed and quality of data transportation in the network using the servers. Supplier can reconfigure or replace the servers when needed to continuously provide the quality of network services defined in the contract. Customer does not operate the servers or make any significant decisions about their use.

The contract does not contain a lease. Instead, the contract is a service contract in which Supplier uses the equipment to meet the level of network services determined by Customer.

There is no need to assess whether the servers installed at Customer's premises are identified assets. This assessment would not change the analysis of whether the contract contains a lease because Customer does not have the right to control the use of the servers.

continued...

...continued

Example 10—Contract for network services

Customer does not control the use of the servers because Customer's only decision-making rights relate to deciding upon the level of network services (the output of the servers) before the period of use—the level of network services cannot be changed during the period of use without modifying the contract. For example, even though Customer produces the data to be transported, that activity does not directly affect the configuration of the network services and, thus, it does not affect how and for what purpose the servers are used. **[Refer: paragraph B24]**

Supplier is the only party that can make relevant decisions about the use of the servers during the period of use. Supplier has the right to decide how data is transported using the servers, whether to reconfigure the servers and whether to use the servers for another purpose. Accordingly, Supplier controls the use of the servers in providing network services to Customer.

Example 10B: Customer enters into a contract with an information technology company (Supplier) for the use of an identified server for three years. Supplier delivers and installs the server at Customer's premises in accordance with Customer's instructions, and provides repair and maintenance services for the server, as needed, throughout the period of use. **[Refer: paragraph B33]** *Supplier substitutes the server only in the case of malfunction. Customer decides which data to store on the server and how to integrate the server within its operations. Customer can change its decisions in this regard throughout the period of use.*

The contract contains a lease. Customer has the right to use the server for three years.

There is an identified asset. The server is explicitly specified in the contract. **[Refer: paragraph B13]** Supplier can substitute the server only if it is malfunctioning (see paragraph B18).

Customer has the right to control the use of the server throughout the three-year period of use because:

(a)   Customer has the right to obtain substantially all of the economic benefits from use of the server over the three-year period of use. Customer has exclusive use of the server throughout the period of use. **[Refer: paragraph B21]**

(b)   Customer has the right to direct the use of the server (because the conditions in paragraph B24(a) exist). Customer makes the relevant decisions about how and for what purpose the server is used because it has the right to decide which aspect of its operations the server is used to support and which data it stores on the server. Customer is the only party that can make decisions about the use of the server during the period of use. **[Refer: paragraph B25]**

Leases of low-value assets and portfolio application (paragraphs 5–6, B1 and B3–B8)

IE3   The following example illustrates how a lessee might (a) apply paragraphs B3–B8 of IFRS 16 to leases of low-value assets; and (b) determine portfolios of leases to which it would apply the requirements in IFRS 16.

Example 11—Leases of low-value assets and portfolio application

A lessee in the pharmaceutical manufacturing and distribution industry (Lessee) has the following leases:

(a)   *leases of real estate (both office buildings and warehouses).*

(b)   *leases of manufacturing equipment.*

(c)   *leases of company cars, both for sales personnel and senior management and of varying quality, specification and value.*

(d)   *leases of trucks and vans used for delivery purposes, of varying size and value.*

(e)   *leases of IT equipment for use by individual employees (such as laptop computers, desktop computers, hand held computer devices, desktop printers and mobile phones).*

(f)   *leases of servers, including many individual modules that increase the storage capacity of those servers. The modules have been added to the mainframe servers over time as Lessee has needed to increase the storage capacity of the servers.*

(g)   *leases of office equipment:*

    (i)   *office furniture (such as chairs, desks and office partitions);*

    (ii)   *water dispensers; and*

    (iii)   *high-capacity multifunction photocopier devices.*

Leases of low-value assets

Lessee determines that the following leases qualify as leases of low-value assets on the basis that the underlying assets, when new, are individually of low value:

(a)   leases of IT equipment for use by individual employees; and

(b)   leases of office furniture and water dispensers.

[Refer: paragraphs 5, B3, B4, B6 and B8]

Lessee elects to apply the requirements in paragraph 6 of IFRS 16 in accounting for all of those leases.

continued...

...*continued*

Example 11—Leases of low-value assets and portfolio application

Although each module within the servers, if considered individually, might be an asset of low value, the leases of modules within the servers do not qualify as leases of low-value assets. This is because each module is highly interrelated with other parts of the servers. Lessee would not lease the modules without also leasing the servers. **[Refer: paragraph B5]**

Portfolio application
[Refer: paragraph B1]

As a result, Lessee applies the recognition and measurement requirements in IFRS 16 to its leases of real estate, manufacturing equipment, company cars, trucks and vans, servers and high-capacity multifunction photocopier devices. In doing so, Lessee groups its company cars, trucks and vans into portfolios.

Lessee's company cars are leased under a series of master lease agreements. Lessee uses eight different types of company car, which vary by price and are assigned to staff on the basis of seniority and territory. Lessee has a master lease agreement for each different type of company car. The individual leases within each master lease agreement are all similar (including similar start and end dates), but the terms and conditions generally vary from one master lease agreement to another. Because the individual leases within each master lease agreement are similar to each other, Lessee reasonably expects that applying the requirements of IFRS 16 to each master lease agreement would not result in a materially different effect than applying the requirements of IFRS 16 to each individual lease within the master lease agreement. Consequently, Lessee concludes that it can apply the requirements of IFRS 16 to each master lease agreement as a portfolio. In addition, Lessee concludes that two of the eight master lease agreements are similar and cover substantially similar types of company cars in similar territories. Lessee reasonably expects that the effect of applying IFRS 16 to the combined portfolio of leases within the two master lease agreements would not differ materially from applying IFRS 16 to each lease within that combined portfolio. Lessee, therefore, concludes that it can further combine those two master lease agreements into a single lease portfolio.

Lessee's trucks and vans are leased under individual lease agreements. There are 6,500 leases in total. All of the truck leases have similar terms, as do all of the van leases. The truck leases are generally for four years and involve similar models of truck. The van leases are generally for five years and involve similar models of van. Lessee reasonably expects that applying the requirements of IFRS 16 to portfolios of truck leases and van leases, grouped by type of underlying asset, territory and the quarter of the year within which the lease was entered into, would not result in a materially different effect from applying those requirements to each individual truck or van lease. Consequently, Lessee applies the requirements of IFRS 16 to different portfolios of truck and van leases, rather than to 6,500 individual leases.

Allocating consideration to components of a contract (paragraphs 12–16 and B32–B33)

IE4   The following example illustrates the allocation of consideration in a contract to lease and non-lease components by a lessee.

Example 12—Lessee allocation of consideration to lease and non-lease components of a contract

Lessor leases a bulldozer, a truck and a long-reach excavator to Lessee to be used in Lessee's mining operations for four years. Lessor also agrees to maintain each item of equipment throughout the lease term. The total consideration in the contract is CU600,000[(a)], payable in annual instalments of CU150,000, and a variable amount that depends on the hours of work performed in maintaining the long-reach excavator. The variable payment is capped at 2 per cent of the replacement cost of the long-reach excavator. The consideration includes the cost of maintenance services for each item of equipment.

Lessee accounts for the non-lease components (maintenance services) separately from each lease of equipment applying paragraph 12 of IFRS 16. Lessee does not elect the practical expedient in paragraph 15 of IFRS 16. Lessee considers the requirements in paragraph B32 of IFRS 16 and concludes that the lease of the bulldozer, the lease of the truck and the lease of the long-reach excavator are each separate lease components. This is because:

(a)   Lessee can benefit from use of each of the three items of equipment on its own or together with other readily available resources (for example, Lessee could readily lease or purchase an alternative truck or excavator to use in its operations); and

(b)   although Lessee is leasing all three items of equipment for one purpose (ie to engage in mining operations), the machines are neither highly dependent on, nor highly interrelated with, each other. Lessee's ability to derive benefit from the lease of each item of equipment is not significantly affected by its decision to lease, or not lease, the other equipment from Lessor.

Consequently, Lessee concludes that there are three lease components and three non-lease components (maintenance services) in the contract. Lessee applies the guidance in paragraphs 13–14 of IFRS 16 to allocate the consideration in the contract to the three lease components and the non-lease components.

continued...

...*continued*

Example 12—Lessee allocation of consideration to lease and non-lease components of a contract

Several suppliers provide maintenance services for a similar bulldozer and a similar truck. Accordingly, there are observable standalone prices for the maintenance services for those two items of leased equipment. Lessee is able to establish observable stand-alone prices for the maintenance of the bulldozer and the truck of CU32,000 and CU16,000, respectively, assuming similar payment terms to those in the contract with Lessor. The long-reach excavator is highly specialised and, accordingly, other suppliers do not lease or provide maintenance services for similar excavators. Nonetheless, Lessor provides four-year maintenance service contracts to customers that purchase similar long-reach excavators from Lessor. The observable consideration for those four-year maintenance service contracts is a fixed amount of CU56,000, payable over four years, and a variable amount that depends on the hours of work performed in maintaining the long-reach excavator. That variable payment is capped at 2 per cent of the replacement cost of the long-reach excavator. Consequently, Lessee estimates the stand-alone price of the maintenance services for the long-reach excavator to be CU56,000 plus any variable amounts. Lessee is able to establish observable stand-alone prices for the leases of the bulldozer, the truck and the long-reach excavator of CU170,000, CU102,000 and CU224,000, respectively.

Lessee allocates the fixed consideration in the contract (CU600,000) to the lease and non-lease components as follows:

CU	Bulldozer	Truck	Long-reach excavator	Total
Lease	170,000	102,000	224,000	496,000
Non-lease				104,000
Total fixed consideration				600,000

Lessee allocates all of the variable consideration to the maintenance of the long-reach excavator, and, thus, to the non-lease components of the contract. Lessee then accounts for each lease component applying the guidance in IFRS 16, treating the allocated consideration as the lease payments for each lease component.

(a) In these Illustrative Examples, currency amounts are denominated in 'currency units' (CU).

Lessee measurement (paragraphs 18–41 and B34–B41)

IE5 The following example illustrates how a lessee measures right-of-use assets and lease liabilities. It also illustrates how a lessee accounts for a change in the lease term.

Example 13—Measurement by a lessee and accounting for a change in the lease term

Part 1 — Initial measurement of the right-of-use asset and the lease liability

Lessee enters into a 10-year lease of a floor of a building, with an option to extend for five years. Lease payments are CU50,000 per year during the initial term and CU55,000 per year during the optional period, all payable at the beginning of each year. To obtain the lease, Lessee incurs initial direct costs of CU20,000, of which CU15,000 relates to a payment to a former tenant occupying that floor of the building and CU5,000 relates to a commission paid to the real estate agent that arranged the lease. As an incentive to Lessee for entering into the lease, Lessor agrees to reimburse to Lessee the real estate commission of CU5,000.

At the commencement date, Lessee concludes that it is not reasonably certain to exercise the option to extend the lease and, therefore, determines that the lease term is 10 years.
[Refer: paragraph 18]

The interest rate implicit in the lease is not readily determinable. Lessee's incremental borrowing rate is 5 per cent per annum, which reflects the fixed rate at which Lessee could borrow an amount similar to the value of the right-of-use asset, in the same currency, for a 10-year term, and with similar collateral.

At the commencement date, Lessee makes the lease payment for the first year, incurs initial direct costs, receives the lease incentive from Lessor and measures the lease liability at the present value of the remaining nine payments of CU50,000, discounted at the interest rate of 5 per cent per annum, **[Refer: paragraph 26]** which is CU355,391.

Lessee initially recognises assets and liabilities in relation to the lease as follows.

Right-of-use asset	CU405,391	
Lease liability		CU355,391
Cash (lease payment for the first year)		CU50,000
Right-of-use asset	CU20,000	
Cash (initial direct costs)		CU20,000
Cash (lease incentive)	CU5,000	
Right-of-use asset		CU5,000

continued...

...continued

Example 13—Measurement by a lessee and accounting for a change in the lease term

Part 2 — Subsequent measurement and accounting for a change in the lease term

In the sixth year of the lease, Lessee acquires Entity A. Entity A has been leasing a floor in another building. The lease entered into by Entity A contains a termination option that is exercisable by Entity A. Following the acquisition of Entity A, Lessee needs two floors in a building suitable for the increased workforce. To minimise costs, Lessee (a) enters into a separate eight-year lease of another floor in the building leased that will be available for use at the end of Year 7 and (b) terminates early the lease entered into by Entity A with effect from the beginning of Year 8.

Moving Entity A's staff to the same building occupied by Lessee creates an economic incentive for Lessee to extend its original lease at the end of the non-cancellable period of 10 years. The acquisition of Entity A and the relocation of Entity A's staff is a significant event that is within the control of Lessee and affects whether Lessee is reasonably certain to exercise the extension option not previously included in its determination of the lease term. **[Refer: paragraph 20]** This is because the original floor has greater utility (and thus provides greater benefits) to Lessee than alternative assets that could be leased for a similar amount to the lease payments for the optional period — Lessee would incur additional costs if it were to lease a similar floor in a different building because the workforce would be located in different buildings. Consequently, at the end of Year 6, Lessee concludes that it is now reasonably certain to exercise the option to extend its original lease as a result of its acquisition and planned relocation of Entity A.

Lessee's incremental borrowing rate at the end of Year 6 is 6 per cent per annum, which reflects the fixed rate at which Lessee could borrow an amount similar to the value of the right-of-use asset, in the same currency, for a nine-year term, and with similar collateral. Lessee expects to consume the right-of-use asset's future economic benefits evenly over the lease term and, thus, depreciates the right-of-use asset on a straight-line basis.

The right-of-use asset and the lease liability from Year 1 to Year 6 are as follows.

	Lease liability				Right-of-use asset		
Year	Beginning balance CU	Lease payment CU	5% interest expense CU	Ending balance CU	Beginning balance CU	Depreciation charge CU	Ending balance CU
1	355,391	-	17,770	373,161	420,391	(42,039)	378,352
2	373,161	(50,000)	16,158	339,319	378,352	(42,039)	336,313
3	339,319	(50,000)	14,466	303,785	336,313	(42,039)	294,274
4	303,785	(50,000)	12,689	266,474	294,274	(42,039)	252,235
5	266,474	(50,000)	10,823	227,297	252,235	(42,039)	210,196
6	227,297	(50,000)	8,865	186,162	210,196	(42,039)	168,157

continued...

...continued

Example 13—Measurement by a lessee and accounting for a change in the lease term

At the end of the sixth year, before accounting for the change in the lease term, the lease liability is CU186,162 (the present value of four remaining payments of CU50,000, discounted at the original interest rate of 5 per cent per annum). Interest expense of CU8,865 is recognised in Year 6. Lessee's right-of-use asset is CU168,157.

Lessee remeasures the lease liability at the present value of four payments of CU50,000 followed by five payments of CU55,000, all discounted at the revised discount rate of 6 per cent per annum, which is CU378,174. **[Refer: paragraph 40]** Lessee increases the lease liability by CU192,012, which represents the difference between the remeasured liability of CU378,174 and its previous carrying amount of CU186,162. The corresponding adjustment is made to the right-of-use asset to reflect the cost of the additional right of use, **[Refer: paragraph 39]** recognised as follows.

Right-of-use asset   CU192,012

     Lease liability   CU192,012

Following the remeasurement, the carrying amount of Lessee's right-of-use asset is CU360,169 (ie CU168,157 + CU192,012). From the beginning of Year 7 Lessee calculates the interest expense on the lease liability at the revised discount rate of 6 per cent per annum.

The right-of-use asset and the lease liability from Year 7 to Year 15 are as follows.

	Lease liability				Right-of-use asset		
Year	Beginning balance CU	Lease payment CU	6% interest expense CU	Ending balance CU	Beginning balance CU	Depreciation charge CU	Ending balance CU
7	378,174	(50,000)	19,690	347,864	360,169	(40,019)	320,150
8	347,864	(50,000)	17,872	315,736	320,150	(40,019)	280,131
9	315,736	(50,000)	15,944	281,680	280,131	(40,019)	240,112
10	281,680	(50,000)	13,901	245,581	240,112	(40,019)	200,093
11	245,581	(55,000)	11,435	202,016	200,093	(40,019)	160,074
12	202,016	(55,000)	8,821	155,837	160,074	(40,019)	120,055
13	155,837	(55,000)	6,050	106,887	120,055	(40,019)	80,036
14	106,887	(55,000)	3,113	55,000	80,036	(40,018)	40,018
15	55,000	(55,000)	-	-	40,018	(40,018)	-

Variable lease payments (paragraphs 27, 39, 42(b) and 43)

IE6   The following example illustrates how a lessee accounts for variable lease payments that depend on an index and variable lease payments not included in the measurement of the lease liability.

Example 14—Variable lease payments dependent on an index and variable lease payments linked to sales

Example 14A — Lessee enters into a 10-year lease of property with annual lease payments of CU50,000, payable at the beginning of each year. The contract specifies that lease payments will increase every two years on the basis of the increase in the Consumer Price Index for the preceding 24 months. The Consumer Price Index at the commencement date is 125. This example ignores any initial direct costs. The rate implicit in the lease is not readily determinable. Lessee's incremental borrowing rate is 5 per cent per annum, which reflects the fixed rate at which Lessee could borrow an amount similar to the value of the right-of-use asset, in the same currency, for a 10-year term, and with similar collateral.

At the commencement date, Lessee makes the lease payment for the first year and measures the lease liability at the present value of the remaining nine payments of CU50,000, discounted at the interest rate of 5 per cent per annum, **[Refer: paragraph 26]** which is CU355,391.

Lessee initially recognises assets and liabilities in relation to the lease as follows.

Right-of-use asset	CU405,391	
Lease liability		CU355,391
Cash (lease payment for the first year)		CU50,000

Lessee expects to consume the right-of-use asset's future economic benefits evenly over the lease term and, thus, depreciates the right-of-use asset on a straight-line basis.

During the first two years of the lease, Lessee recognises in aggregate the following related to the lease.

Interest expense	CU33,928	
Lease liability		CU33,928
Depreciation charge	CU81,078 (CU405,391 ÷ 10 × 2 years)	
Right-of-use asset		CU81,078

continued...

...continued

Example 14—Variable lease payments dependent on an index and variable lease payments linked to sales

At the beginning of the second year, Lessee makes the lease payment for the second year and recognises the following.

Lease liability	CU50,000	
Cash		CU50,000

At the beginning of the third year, before accounting for the change in future lease payments resulting from a change in the Consumer Price Index and making the lease payment for the third year, the lease liability is CU339,319 (the present value of eight payments of CU50,000 discounted at the interest rate of 5 per cent per annum = CU355,391 + CU33,928 – CU50,000).

At the beginning of the third year of the lease the Consumer Price Index is 135.

The payment for the third year, adjusted for the Consumer Price Index, is CU54,000 (CU50,000 × 135 ÷ 125). Because there is a change in the future lease payments resulting from a change in the Consumer Price Index used to determine those payments, Lessee remeasures the lease liability to reflect those revised lease payments, ie the lease liability now reflects eight annual lease payments of CU54,000. **[Refer: paragraph 42(b)]**

At the beginning of the third year, Lessee remeasures the lease liability at the present value of eight payments of CU54,000 discounted at an unchanged discount rate of 5 per cent per annum, **[Refer: paragraph 43]** which is CU366,464. Lessee increases the lease liability by CU27,145, which represents the difference between the remeasured liability of CU366,464 and its previous carrying amount of CU339,319. The corresponding adjustment is made to the right-of-use asset, **[Refer: paragraph 39]** recognised as follows.

Right-of-use asset	CU27,145	
Lease liability		CU27,145

At the beginning of the third year, Lessee makes the lease payment for the third year and recognises the following.

Lease liability	CU54,000	
Cash		CU54,000

continued...

...continued

Example 14—Variable lease payments dependent on an index and variable lease payments linked to sales

Example 14B — Assume the same facts as Example 14A except that Lessee is also required to make variable lease payments for each year of the lease, which are determined as 1 per cent of Lessee's sales generated from the leased property.

At the commencement date, Lessee measures the right-of-use asset and the lease liability recognised at the same amounts as in Example 14A. This is because the additional variable lease payments are linked to future sales and, thus, do not meet the definition of lease payments. Consequently, those payments are not included in the measurement of the asset and liability.

Right-of-use asset	CU405,391
Lease liability	CU355,391
Cash (lease payment for the first year)	CU50,000

Lessee prepares financial statements on an annual basis. During the first year of the lease, Lessee generates sales of CU800,000 from the leased property.

Lessee incurs an additional expense related to the lease of CU8,000 (CU800,000 × 1 per cent), which Lessee recognises in profit or loss in the first year of the lease. **[Refer: paragraph 38(b)]**

Lease modifications (paragraphs 44–46)

IE7　Examples 15–19 illustrate the requirements of IFRS 16 regarding lease modifications for a lessee.

Example 15—Modification that is a separate lease

Lessee enters into a 10-year lease for 2,000 square metres of office space. At the beginning of Year 6, Lessee and Lessor agree to amend the original lease for the remaining five years to include an additional 3,000 square metres of office space in the same building. The additional space is made available for use by Lessee at the end of the second quarter of Year 6. The increase in total consideration for the lease is commensurate with the current market rate for the new 3,000 square metres of office space, adjusted for the discount that Lessee receives reflecting that Lessor does not incur costs that it would otherwise have incurred if leasing the same space to a new tenant (for example, marketing costs).

continued...

...continued

Example 15—Modification that is a separate lease

Lessee accounts for the modification as a separate lease, separate from the original 10-year lease. **[Refer: paragraph 44]** This is because the modification grants Lessee an additional right to use an underlying asset, and the increase in consideration for the lease is commensurate with the stand-alone price of the additional right-of-use adjusted to reflect the circumstances of the contract. In this example, the additional underlying asset is the new 3,000 square metres of office space. Accordingly, at the commencement date of the new lease (at the end of the second quarter of Year 6), Lessee recognises a right-of-use asset and a lease liability relating to the lease of the additional 3,000 square metres of office space. Lessee does not make any adjustments to the accounting for the original lease of 2,000 square metres of office space as a result of this modification.

Example 16—Modification that increases the scope of the lease by extending the contractual lease term

Lessee enters into a 10-year lease for 5,000 square metres of office space. The annual lease payments are CU100,000 payable at the end of each year. The interest rate implicit in the lease cannot be readily determined. Lessee's incremental borrowing rate at the commencement date is 6 per cent per annum. At the beginning of Year 7, Lessee and Lessor agree to amend the original lease by extending the contractual lease term by four years. The annual lease payments are unchanged (ie CU100,000 payable at the end of each year from Year 7 to Year 14). Lessee's incremental borrowing rate at the beginning of Year 7 is 7 per cent per annum.

At the effective date of the modification (at the beginning of Year 7), Lessee remeasures the lease liability based on: (a) an eight-year remaining lease term, (b) annual payments of CU100,000 and (c) Lessee's incremental borrowing rate of 7 per cent per annum. **[Refer: paragraph 45]** The modified lease liability equals CU597,130. The lease liability immediately before the modification (including the recognition of the interest expense until the end of Year 6) is CU346,511. Lessee recognises the difference between the carrying amount of the modified lease liability and the carrying amount of the lease liability immediately before the modification (CU250,619) as an adjustment to the right-of-use asset. **[Refer: paragraph 46(b)]**

Example 17—Modification that decreases the scope of the lease

Lessee enters into a 10-year lease for 5,000 square metres of office space. The annual lease payments are CU50,000 payable at the end of each year. The interest rate implicit in the lease cannot be readily determined. Lessee's incremental borrowing rate at the commencement date is 6 per cent per annum. At the beginning of Year 6, Lessee and Lessor agree to amend the original lease to reduce the space to only 2,500 square metres of the original space starting from the end of the first quarter of Year 6. The annual fixed lease payments (from Year 6 to Year 10) are CU30,000. Lessee's incremental borrowing rate at the beginning of Year 6 is 5 per cent per annum.

continued...

...continued

Example 17—Modification that decreases the scope of the lease

At the effective date of the modification (at the beginning of Year 6), Lessee remeasures the lease liability based on: (a) a five-year remaining lease term, (b) annual payments of CU30,000 and (c) Lessee's incremental borrowing rate of 5 per cent per annum. This equals CU129,884. **[Refer: paragraph 45]**

Lessee determines the proportionate decrease in the carrying amount of the right-of-use asset on the basis of the remaining right-of-use asset (ie 2,500 square metres corresponding to 50 per cent of the original right-of-use asset).

50 per cent of the pre-modification right-of-use asset (CU184,002) is CU92,001. Fifty per cent of the pre-modification lease liability (CU210,618) is CU105,309. Consequently, Lessee reduces the carrying amount of the right-of-use asset by CU92,001 and the carrying amount of the lease liability by CU105,309. Lessee recognises the difference between the decrease in the lease liability and the decrease in the right-of-use asset (CU105,309 − CU92,001 = CU13,308) as a gain in profit or loss at the effective date of the modification (at the beginning of Year 6). **[Refer: paragraph 46(a)]**

Lessee recognises the difference between the remaining lease liability of CU105,309 and the modified lease liability of CU129,884 (which equals CU24,575) as an adjustment to the right-of-use asset reflecting the change in the consideration paid for the lease and the revised discount rate.

Example 18—Modification that both increases and decreases the scope of the lease

Lessee enters into a 10-year lease for 2,000 square metres of office space. The annual lease payments are CU100,000 payable at the end of each year. The interest rate implicit in the lease cannot be readily determined. Lessee's incremental borrowing rate at the commencement date is 6 per cent per annum. At the beginning of Year 6, Lessee and Lessor agree to amend the original lease to (a) include an additional 1,500 square metres of space in the same building starting from the beginning of Year 6 and (b) reduce the lease term from 10 years to eight years. The annual fixed payment for the 3,500 square metres is CU150,000 payable at the end of each year (from Year 6 to Year 8). Lessee's incremental borrowing rate at the beginning of Year 6 is 7 per cent per annum.

The consideration for the increase in scope of 1,500 square metres of space is not commensurate with the stand-alone price for that increase adjusted to reflect the circumstances of the contract. Consequently, Lessee does not account for the increase in scope that adds the right to use an additional 1,500 square metres of space as a separate lease.

continued...

...continued

Example 18—Modification that both increases and decreases the scope of the lease

The pre-modification right-of-use asset and the pre-modification lease liability in relation to the lease are as follows.

	Lease liability				Right-of-use asset		
Year	Beginning balance	6% interest expense	Lease payment	Ending balance	Beginning balance	Deprecia-tion charge	Ending balance
	CU	CU	CU	CU	CU	CU	CU
1	736,009	44,160	(100,000)	680,169	736,009	(73,601)	662,408
2	680,169	40,810	(100,000)	620,979	662,408	(73,601)	588,807
3	620,979	37,259	(100,000)	558,238	588,807	(73,601)	515,206
4	558,238	33,494	(100,000)	491,732	515,206	(73,601)	441,605
5	491,732	29,504	(100,000)	421,236	441,605	(73,601)	368,004
6	421,236				368,004		

At the effective date of the modification (at the beginning of Year 6), Lessee remeasures the lease liability on the basis of: (a) a three-year remaining lease term, (b) annual payments of CU150,000 and (c) Lessee's incremental borrowing rate of 7 per cent per annum. **[Refer: paragraph 45]** The modified liability equals CU393,647, of which (a) CU131,216 relates to the increase of CU50,000 in the annual lease payments from Year 6 to Year 8 and (b) CU262,431 relates to the remaining three annual lease payments of CU100,000 from Year 6 to Year 8.

Decrease in the lease term

At the effective date of the modification (at the beginning of Year 6), the pre-modification right-of-use asset is CU368,004. Lessee determines the proportionate decrease in the carrying amount of the right-of-use asset based on the remaining right-of-use asset for the original 2,000 square metres of office space (ie a remaining three-year lease term rather than the original five-year lease term). The remaining right-of-use asset for the original 2,000 square metres of office space is CU220,802 (ie CU368,004 ÷ 5 × 3 years).

At the effective date of the modification (at the beginning of Year 6), the pre-modification lease liability is CU421,236. The remaining lease liability for the original 2,000 square metres of office space is CU267,301 (ie present value of three annual lease payments of CU100,000, discounted at the original discount rate of 6 per cent per annum).

continued...

...continued

Example 18—Modification that both increases and decreases the scope of the lease

Consequently, Lessee reduces the carrying amount of the right-of-use asset by CU147,202 (CU368,004 – CU220,802), and the carrying amount of the lease liability by CU153,935 (CU421,236 – CU267,301). Lessee recognises the difference between the decrease in the lease liability and the decrease in the right-of-use asset (CU153,935 – CU147,202 = CU6,733) as a gain in profit or loss at the effective date of the modification (at the beginning of Year 6). **[Refer: paragraph 46(a)]**

Lease liability	CU153,935
Right-of-use asset	CU147,202
Gain	CU6,733

At the effective date of the modification (at the beginning of Year 6), Lessee recognises the effect of the remeasurement of the remaining lease liability reflecting the revised discount rate of 7 per cent per annum, **[Refer: paragraph 45(c)]** which is CU4,870 (CU267,301 – CU262,431), as an adjustment to the right-of-use asset.

Lease liability	CU4,870
Right-of-use asset	CU4,870

Increase in the leased space

At the commencement date of the lease for the additional 1,500 square metres of space (at the beginning of Year 6), Lessee recognises the increase in the lease liability related to the increase in scope of CU131,216 (ie present value of three annual lease payments of CU50,000, discounted at the revised interest rate of 7 per cent per annum **[Refer: paragraph 45(c)]**) as an adjustment to the right-of-use asset. **[Refer: paragraph 46(b)]**

Right-of-use asset	CU131,216
Lease liability	CU131,216

The modified right-of-use asset and the modified lease liability in relation to the modified lease are as follows.

	Lease liability				Right-of-use asset		
	Beginning balance	7% interest expense	Lease payment	Ending balance	Beginning balance	Depreciation charge	Ending balance
Year	CU	CU	CU	CU	CU	CU	CU
6	393,647	27,556	(150,000)	271,203	347,148	(115,716)	231,432
7	271,203	18,984	(150,000)	140,187	231,432	(115,716)	115,716
8	140,187	9,813	(150,000)	-	115,716	(115,716)	-

Example 19—Modification that is a change in consideration only

Lessee enters into a 10-year lease for 5,000 square metres of office space. At the beginning of Year 6, Lessee and Lessor agree to amend the original lease for the remaining five years to reduce the lease payments from CU100,000 per year to CU95,000 per year. The interest rate implicit in the lease cannot be readily determined. Lessee's incremental borrowing rate at the commencement date is 6 per cent per annum. Lessee's incremental borrowing rate at the beginning of Year 6 is 7 per cent per annum. The annual lease payments are payable at the end of each year.

At the effective date of the modification (at the beginning of Year 6), Lessee remeasures the lease liability based on: (a) a five-year remaining lease term, (b) annual payments of CU95,000 and (c) Lessee's incremental borrowing rate of 7 per cent per annum **[Refer: paragraph 45(c)]**. Lessee recognises the difference between the carrying amount of the modified liability (CU389,519) and the lease liability immediately before the modification (CU421,236) of CU31,717 as an adjustment to the right-of-use asset. **[Refer: paragraph 46(b)]**

Subleases (paragraph B58)

IE8   Examples 20–21 illustrate the application of the requirements in IFRS 16 for an intermediate lessor that enters into a head lease and a sublease of the same underlying asset.

Example 20—Sublease classified as a finance lease

Head lease — An intermediate lessor enters into a five-year lease for 5,000 square metres of office space (the head lease) with Entity A (the head lessor).

Sublease — At the beginning of Year 3, the intermediate lessor subleases the 5,000 square metres of office space for the remaining three years of the head lease to a sublessee.

The intermediate lessor classifies the sublease by reference to the right-of-use asset arising from the head lease. The intermediate lessor classifies the sublease as a finance lease, having considered the requirements in paragraphs 61–66 of IFRS 16.

When the intermediate lessor enters into the sublease, the intermediate lessor:

(a)   derecognises the right-of-use asset relating to the head lease that it transfers to the sublessee and recognises the net investment in the sublease;

(b)   recognises any difference between the right-of-use asset and the net investment in the sublease in profit or loss; and

(c)   retains the lease liability relating to the head lease in its statement of financial position, which represents the lease payments owed to the head lessor.

continued...

...continued

Example 20—Sublease classified as a finance lease
During the term of the sublease, the intermediate lessor recognises both finance income on the sublease and interest expense on the head lease.

Example 21—Sublease classified as an operating lease
Head lease — An intermediate lessor enters into a five-year lease for 5,000 square metres of office space (the head lease) with Entity A (the head lessor).
Sublease — At commencement of the head lease, the intermediate lessor subleases the 5,000 square metres of office space for two years to a sublessee.
The intermediate lessor classifies the sublease by reference to the right-of-use asset arising from the head lease. The intermediate lessor classifies the sublease as an operating lease, having considered the requirements in paragraphs 61–66 of IFRS 16.
When the intermediate lessor enters into the sublease, the intermediate lessor retains the lease liability and the right-of-use asset relating to the head lease in its statement of financial position.
During the term of the sublease, the intermediate lessor:
(a) recognises a depreciation charge for the right-of-use asset and interest on the lease liability; and
(b) recognises lease income from the sublease.

Lessee disclosure (paragraphs 59 and B49–B50)

IE9　　Example 22 illustrates how a lessee with different types of lease portfolios might comply with the disclosure requirements described in paragraphs 59 and B49 of IFRS 16 about variable lease payments. This example shows only current period information. IAS 1 *Presentation of Financial Statements* requires an entity to present comparative information.

Example 22—Variable payment terms
Lessee with a high volume of leases with some consistent payment terms
Example 22A: a retailer (Lessee) operates a number of different branded retail stores — A, B, C and D. Lessee has a high volume of property leases. Lessee's group policy is to negotiate variable payment terms for newly established stores. Lessee concludes that information about variable lease payments is relevant to users of its financial statements and is not available elsewhere in its financial statements. In particular, Lessee concludes that information about the proportion of total lease payments that arise from variable payments, and the sensitivity of those variable lease payments to changes in sales, is the information that is relevant to users of its financial statements. This information is similar to that reported to Lessee's senior management about variable lease payments.

continued...

© IFRS Foundation

...continued

Example 22—Variable payment terms

Some of the property leases within the group contain variable payment terms that are linked to sales generated from the store. Variable payment terms are used, when possible, in newly established stores in order to link rental payments to store cash flows and minimise fixed costs. Fixed and variable rental payments by store brand for the period ended 31 December 20X0 are summarised below.

	Stores	Fixed payments	Variable payments	Total payments	Estimated annual impact on total brand rent of a 1% increase in sales
	No.	CU	CU	CU	%
Brand A	4,522	3,854	120	3,974	0.03%
Brand B	965	865	105	970	0.11%
Brand C	124	26	163	189	0.86%
Brand D	652	152	444	596	0.74%
	6,263	**4,897**	**832**	**5,729**	**0.15%**

Refer to the management commentary for store information presented on a like-for-like basis and to Note X for segmental information applying IFRS 8 *Operating Segments* relating to Brands A–D.

Example 22B: a retailer (Lessee) has a high volume of property leases of retail stores. Many of these leases contain variable payment terms linked to sales from the store. Lessee's group policy sets out the circumstances in which variable payment terms are used and all lease negotiations must be approved centrally. Lease payments are monitored centrally. Lessee concludes that information about variable lease payments is relevant to users of its financial statements and is not available elsewhere in its financial statements. In particular, Lessee concludes that information about the different types of contractual terms it uses with respect to variable lease payments, the effect of those terms on its financial performance and the sensitivity of variable lease payments to changes in sales is the information that is relevant to users of its financial statements. This is similar to the information that is reported to Lessee's senior management about variable lease payments.

Many of the property leases within the group contain variable payment terms that are linked to the volume of sales made from leased stores. These terms are used, when possible, in order to match lease payments with stores generating higher cash flows. For individual stores, up to 100 per cent of lease payments are on the basis of variable payment terms and there is a wide range of sales percentages applied. In some cases, variable payment terms also contain minimum annual payments and caps.

Lease payments and terms for the period ended 31 December 20X0 are summarised below.

continued...

...continued

Example 22—Variable payment terms

	Stores	Fixed payments	Variable payments	Total payments
	No.	CU	CU	CU
Fixed rent only	1,490	1,153	-	1,153
Variable rent with no minimum	986	-	562	562
Variable rent with minimum	3,089	1,091	1,435	2,526
	5,565	2,244	1,997	4,241

A 1 per cent increase in sales across all stores in the group would be expected to increase total lease payments by approximately 0.6–0.7 per cent. A 5 per cent increase in sales across all stores in the group would be expected to increase total lease payments by approximately 2.6–2.8 per cent.

Lessee with a high volume of leases with a wide range of different payment terms

Example 22C: a retailer (Lessee) has a high volume of property leases of retail stores. These leases contain a wide range of different variable payment terms. Lease terms are negotiated and monitored by local management. Lessee concludes that information about variable lease payments is relevant to users of its financial statements and is not available elsewhere in its financial statements. Lessee concludes that information about how its property lease portfolio is managed is the information that is relevant to users of its financial statements. Lessee also concludes that information about the expected level of variable lease payments in the coming year (similar to that reported internally to senior management) is also relevant to users of its financial statements.

Many of the property leases within the group contain variable payment terms. Local management are responsible for store margins. Accordingly, lease terms are negotiated by local management and contain a wide range of payment terms. Variable payment terms are used for a variety of reasons, including minimising the fixed cost base for newly established stores or for reasons of margin control and operational flexibility. Variable lease payment terms vary widely across the group:

(a)   the majority of variable payment terms are based on a range of percentages of store sales;

(b)   lease payments based on variable terms range from 0–20 per cent of total lease payments on an individual property; and

(c)   some variable payment terms include minimum or cap clauses.

The overall financial effect of using variable payment terms is that higher rental costs are incurred by stores with higher sales. This facilitates the management of margins across the group.

continued...

...continued

<table>
<tr><td>Example 22—Variable payment terms</td></tr>
<tr><td>Variable rent expenses are expected to continue to represent a similar proportion of store sales in future years.</td></tr>
</table>

IE10   Example 23 illustrates how a lessee with different types of lease portfolios might comply with the disclosure requirements described in paragraphs 59 and B50 of IFRS 16 about extension options and termination options. This example shows only current period information. IAS 1 requires an entity to present comparative information.

Example 23—Extension options and termination options

Lessee with a high volume of leases, that have a wide range of different terms and conditions, which are not managed centrally

Example 23A: Lessee has a high volume of equipment leases with a wide range of different terms and conditions. Lease terms are negotiated and monitored by local management. Lessee concludes that information about how it manages the use of termination and extension options is the information that is relevant to users of its financial statements and is not available elsewhere in its financial statements. Lessee also concludes that information about (a) the financial effect of reassessing options and (b) the proportion of its short-term lease portfolio resulting from leases with annual break clauses is also relevant to users of its financial statements.

Extension and termination options are included in a number of equipment leases across the group. Local teams are responsible for managing their leases and, accordingly, lease terms are negotiated on an individual basis and contain a wide range of different terms and conditions. Extension and termination options are included, when possible, to provide local management with greater flexibility to align its need for access to equipment with the fulfilment of customer contracts. The individual terms and conditions used vary across the group.

The majority of extension and termination options held are exercisable only by Lessee and not by the respective lessors. In cases in which Lessee is not reasonably certain to use an optional extended lease term, payments associated with the optional period are not included within lease liabilities.

During 20X0, the financial effect of revising lease terms to reflect the effect of exercising extension and termination options was an increase in recognised lease liabilities of CU489.

In addition, Lessee has a number of lease arrangements containing annual break clauses at no penalty. These leases are classified as short-term leases and are not included within lease liabilities. The short-term lease expense of CU30 recognised during 20X0 included CU27 relating to leases with an annual break clause.

continued...

...continued

Example 23—Extension options and termination options

Lessee with a high volume of leases with some consistent terms and options

Example 23B: a restaurateur (Lessee) has a high volume of property leases containing penalty-free termination options that are exercisable at the option of Lessee. Lessee's group policy is to have termination options in leases of more than five years, whenever possible. Lessee has a central property team that negotiates leases. Lessee concludes that information about termination options is relevant to users of its financial statements and is not available elsewhere in its financial statements. In particular, Lessee concludes that information about (a) the potential exposure to future lease payments that are not included in the measurement of lease liabilities and (b) the proportion of termination options that have been exercised historically is the information that is relevant to users of its financial statements. Lessee also notes that presenting this information on the basis of the same restaurant brands for which segment information is disclosed applying IFRS 8 is relevant to users of its financial statements. This is similar to the information that is reported to Lessee's senior management about termination options.

Many of the property leases across the group contain termination options. These options are used to limit the period to which the group is committed to individual lease contracts and to maximise operational flexibility in terms of opening and closing individual restaurants. For most leases of restaurants, recognised lease liabilities do not include potential future rental payments after the exercise date of termination options because Lessee is not reasonably certain to extend the lease beyond that date. This is the case for most leases for which a longer lease period can be enforced only by Lessee and not by the landlord, and for which there is no penalty associated with the option.

Potential future rental payments relating to periods following the exercise date of termination options are summarised below.

Business segment	Lease liabilities recognised (discounted)	Potential future lease payments not included in lease liabilities (undiscounted)		
		Payable during 20X1–20X5	Payable during 20X6–20Y0	Total
	CU	CU	CU	CU
Brand A	569	71	94	165
Brand B	2,455	968	594	1,562
Brand C	269	99	55	154
Brand D	1,002	230	180	410
Brand E	914	181	321	502
	5,209	**1,549**	**1,244**	**2,793**

continued...

...*continued*

Example 23—Extension options and termination options

The table below summarises the rate of exercise of termination options during 20X0.

Business segment	Termination option exercisable during 20X0	Termination option not exercised	Termination option exercised
	No. of leases	No. of leases	No. of leases
Brand A	33	30	3
Brand B	86	69	17
Brand C	19	18	1
Brand D	30	5	25
Brand E	66	40	26
	234	**162**	**72**

Example 23C: Lessee has a high volume of large equipment leases containing extension options that are exercisable by Lessee during the lease. Lessee's group policy is to use extension options to align, when possible, committed lease terms for large equipment with the initial contractual term of associated customer contracts, whilst retaining flexibility to manage its large equipment and reallocate assets across contracts. Lessee concludes that information about extension options is relevant to users of its financial statements and is not available elsewhere in its financial statements. In particular, Lessee concludes that (a) information about the potential exposure to future lease payments that are not included in the measurement of lease liabilities and (b) information about the historical rate of exercise of extension options is the information that is relevant to users of its financial statements. This is similar to the information that is reported to Lessee's senior management about extension options.

Many of the large equipment leases across the group contain extension options. These terms are used to maximise operational flexibility in terms of managing contracts. These terms are not reflected in measuring lease liabilities in many cases because the options are not reasonably certain to be exercised. This is generally the case when the underlying large equipment has not been allocated for use on a particular customer contract after the exercise date of an extension option. The table below summarises potential future rental payments relating to periods following the exercise dates of extension options.

continued...

...continued

Example 23—Extension options and termination options

Business segment	Lease liabilities recognised (discounted)	Potential future lease payments not included in lease liabilities (discounted)	Historical rate of exercise of extension options
	CU	CU	%
Segment A	569	799	52%
Segment B	2,455	269	69%
Segment C	269	99	75%
Segment D	1,002	111	41%
Segment E	914	312	76%
	5,209	1,590	67%

Sale and leaseback transactions (paragraphs 98–103)

IE11   Example 24 illustrates the application of the requirements in paragraphs 99–102 of IFRS 16 for a seller-lessee and a buyer-lessor.

Example 24—Sale and leaseback transaction

An entity (Seller-lessee) sells a building to another entity (Buyer-lessor) for cash of CU2,000,000. Immediately before the transaction, the building is carried at a cost of CU1,000,000. At the same time, Seller-lessee enters into a contract with Buyer-lessor for the right to use the building for 18 years, with annual payments of CU120,000 payable at the end of each year. The terms and conditions of the transaction are such that the transfer of the building by Seller-lessee satisfies the requirements for determining when a performance obligation is satisfied in IFRS 15 Revenue from Contracts with Customers. **[Refer: paragraph 99]** *Accordingly, Seller-lessee and Buyer-lessor account for the transaction as a sale and leaseback. This example ignores any initial direct costs.*

The fair value of the building at the date of sale is CU1,800,000. Because the consideration for the sale of the building is not at fair value, Seller-lessee and Buyer-lessor make adjustments to measure the sale proceeds at fair value. The amount of the excess sale price of CU200,000 (CU2,000,000 − CU1,800,000) is recognised as additional financing provided by Buyer-lessor to Seller-lessee.

[Refer: paragraph 101(b)]

The interest rate implicit in the lease is 4.5 per cent per annum, which is readily determinable by Seller-lessee. The present value of the annual payments (18 payments of CU120,000, discounted at 4.5 per cent per annum) amounts to CU1,459,200, of which CU200,000 relates to the additional financing and CU1,259,200 relates to the lease—corresponding to 18 annual payments of CU16,447 and CU103,553, respectively.

Buyer-lessor classifies the lease of the building as an operating lease.

continued...

© IFRS Foundation

...continued

Example 24—Sale and leaseback transaction

Seller-lessee

At the commencement date, Seller-lessee measures the right-of-use asset arising from the leaseback of the building at the proportion of the previous carrying amount of the building that relates to the right of use retained by Seller-lessee, which is CU699,555. **[Refer: paragraph 100(a)]** This is calculated as: CU1,000,000 (the carrying amount of the building) ÷ CU1,800,000 (the fair value of the building) × CU1,259,200 (the discounted lease payments for the 18-year right-of-use asset).

Seller-lessee recognises only the amount of the gain that relates to the rights transferred to Buyer-lessor **[Refer: paragraph 100(a)]** of CU240,355 calculated as follows. The gain on sale of building amounts to CU800,000 (CU1,800,000 − CU1,000,000), of which:

(a)   CU559,645 (CU800,000 ÷ CU1,800,000 × CU1,259,200) relates to the right to use the building retained by Seller-lessee; and

(b)   CU240,355 (CU800,000 ÷ CU1,800,000 × (CU1,800,000 − CU1,259,200)) relates to the rights transferred to Buyer-lessor.

At the commencement date, Seller-lessee accounts for the transaction as follows.

Cash	CU2,000,000	
Right-of-use asset	CU699,555	
Building		CU1,000,000
Financial liability		CU1,459,200
Gain on rights transferred		CU240,355

Buyer-lessor

At the commencement date, Buyer-lessor accounts for the transaction **[Refer: paragraph 100(b)]** as follows.

Building	CU1,800,000	
Financial asset	CU200,000 (18 payments of CU16,447, discounted at 4.5 per cent per annum)	
Cash		CU2,000,000

After the commencement date, Buyer-lessor accounts for the lease by treating CU103,553 of the annual payments of CU120,000 as lease payments. The remaining CU16,447 of annual payments received from Seller-lessee are accounted for as (a) payments received to settle the financial asset of CU200,000 and (b) interest revenue.

Appendix
Amendments to guidance on other Standards

This appendix describes the amendments to guidance on other Standards that the IASB made when it finalised IFRS 16.

★ ★ ★ ★ ★

The amendments contained in this appendix when this Standard was issued in 2016 have been incorporated into the guidance on the relevant Standards included in this volume.

IASB documents published to accompany

IFRS 17

Insurance Contracts

The text of the unaccompanied standard, IFRS 17, is contained in Part A of this edition. Its effective date when issued was 1 January 2021. In June 2020 the Board issued *Amendments to IFRS 17* which deferred the effective date to 1 January 2023. The text of the Basis for Conclusions on IFRS 17 is contained in Part C of this edition. This part presents the following documents:

ILLUSTRATIVE EXAMPLES

APPENDIX

Amendments to guidance on other Standards

IFRS 17 SUPPORTING MATERIAL

One-page summary of the accounting model in IFRS 17 *Insurance Contracts* published by the staff of the IFRS Foundation in January 2018

CONTENTS

© IFRS Foundation

...*continued*

IFRS 17 *Insurance Contracts*
Illustrative Examples

These examples accompany, but are not part of, IFRS 17. They illustrate aspects of IFRS 17 but are not intended to provide interpretative guidance.

Introduction

IE1   These examples portray hypothetical situations illustrating how an entity might apply some of the requirements in IFRS 17 to particular aspects of the accounting for contracts within the scope of IFRS 17 based on the limited facts presented. The analysis in each example is not intended to represent the only manner in which the requirements could be applied, nor are the examples intended to apply only to the specific product illustrated. Although some aspects of the examples may be presented in actual fact patterns, fact patterns in those examples are simplified and all relevant facts and circumstances of a particular fact pattern would need to be evaluated when applying IFRS 17.

IE2   These examples address specific requirements in IFRS 17:

   (a)   main features of the accounting for insurance contracts (see Examples 1–3); and

   (b)   specific requirements in IFRS 17 (see Examples 4–18).

IE3   In these examples:

   (a)   credit amounts are presented as positive and debit amounts are presented as negative (in brackets);

   (b)   amounts are denominated in currency units (CU);

   (c)   all paragraph numbers are related to IFRS 17, unless specified otherwise;

   (d)   some numbers include a rounding difference; and

   (e)   the insurance contracts are assumed to meet the conditions in paragraphs 14–23 to be assessed together and to be combined into a group on initial recognition. It is assumed that applying paragraph 24, the entity:

      (i)   establishes the groups on initial recognition of the contracts, and does not reassess the composition of the groups subsequently; and

      (ii)   may estimate the fulfilment cash flows at a higher level of aggregation than the group, provided the entity is able to include the appropriate fulfilment cash flows in the measurement of the group by allocating such estimates to groups of contracts.

IE3A   In June 2020, the International Accounting Standards Board (Board) amended
       IFRS 17 and made the following amendments to these examples:

   (a)   Example 12C was added;

   (b)   Examples 4, 6, 7, 9, 11, 12, 13, 14 and 16 were amended; and

   (c)   some amendments were made to improve the explanations in
         Examples 2B, 3B, 6, 8 and 9.

Key features of accounting for groups of insurance contracts

Example 1—Measurement on initial recognition (paragraphs 32, 38 and 47)

IE4   This example illustrates how an entity measures a group of insurance
       contracts on initial recognition that is onerous on initial recognition, and a
       group of insurance contracts that is not onerous on initial recognition.

Assumptions

IE5   An entity issues 100 insurance contracts with a coverage period of three years.
       The coverage period starts when the insurance contracts are issued. It is
       assumed, for simplicity, that no contracts will lapse before the end of the
       coverage period.

IE6   The entity expects to receive premiums of CU900 immediately after initial
       recognition; therefore, the estimate of the present value of the future cash
       inflows is CU900.

IE7   The entity estimates the annual cash outflows at the end of each year as
       follows:

   (a)   in Example 1A, the annual future cash outflows are CU200 (total
         CU600). The entity estimates the present value of the future cash flows
         to be CU545 using a discount rate of 5 per cent a year that reflects the
         characteristics of those cash flows determined applying paragraph 36.

   (b)   in Example 1B, the annual future cash outflows are CU400 (total
         CU1,200). The entity estimates the present value of the future cash
         flows to be CU1,089 using a discount rate of 5 per cent a year that
         reflects the characteristics of those cash flows determined applying
         paragraph 36.

IE8   The entity estimates the risk adjustment for non-financial risk on initial
       recognition as CU120.

IE9   In this example all other amounts are ignored, for simplicity.

Analysis

IE10 The measurement of the group of insurance contracts on initial recognition is as follows:

	Example 1A	Example 1B
	CU	CU
Estimates of the present value of future cash inflows	(900)	(900)
Estimates of the present value of future cash outflows	545	1,089
Estimates of the present value of future cash flows	(355)	189
Risk adjustment for non-financial risk	120	120
Fulfilment cash flows[(a)]	(235)	309
Contractual service margin	235 [(b)]	– [(c)]
Insurance contract (asset) / liability on initial recognition[(d)]	–	309 [(c)]
The effect on profit or loss on initial recognition is as follows:		
Insurance service expenses	–	(309) [(c)]
Loss recognised in the year	– [(b)]	**(309)**

(a) Paragraph 32 requires that the fulfilment cash flows comprise estimates of future cash flows, adjusted to reflect the time value of money and the financial risk related to those future cash flows and a risk adjustment for non-financial risk.

(b) Applying paragraph 38, the entity measures the contractual service margin on initial recognition of a group of insurance contracts at an amount that results in no income or expenses arising from the initial recognition of the fulfilment cash flows. Consequently, the contractual service margin equals CU235.

(c) Applying paragraph 47, the entity concludes that these insurance contracts on initial recognition are onerous because the fulfilment cash flows on initial recognition are a net outflow. Applying paragraph 16(a), the entity will group those contracts separately from contracts that are not onerous. The entity recognises a loss in profit or loss for the net outflow, resulting in the carrying amount of the liability for the group being equal to the fulfilment cash flows, and the contractual service margin of the group being zero.

(d) Applying paragraph 32, the entity measures the group of insurance contracts on initial recognition at the total of the fulfilment cash flows and the contractual service margin.

IE11   Immediately after initial recognition, the entity receives the premium of CU900 and the carrying amount of the group of insurance contracts changes as follows:

	Example 1A	Example 1B
	CU	CU
Estimates of the present value of future cash inflows	–	–
Estimates of the present value of future cash outflows	545	1,089
Estimates of the present value of future cash flows	545	1,089
Risk adjustment for non-financial risk	120	120
Fulfilment cash flows	665	1,209
Contractual service margin	235	–
Insurance contract (asset) / liability immediately after initial recognition	**900**	**1,209**

Example 2—Subsequent measurement (paragraphs 40, 44, 48, 101 and B96–B97)

IE12   This example illustrates how an entity subsequently measures a group of insurance contracts, including a situation when the group of insurance contracts becomes onerous after initial recognition.

IE13   This example also illustrates the requirement that an entity discloses a reconciliation from the opening to the closing balances of each component of the liability for the group of insurance contracts in paragraph 101.

Assumptions

IE14   Example 2 uses the same fact pattern as Example 1A on initial recognition. In addition:

(a)   in Year 1 all events occur as expected and the entity does not change any assumptions related to future periods;

(b)   in Year 1 the discount rate that reflects the characteristics of the cash flows of the group remains at 5 per cent a year at the end of each year (those cash flows do not vary based on the returns on any underlying items);

(c)   the risk adjustment for non-financial risk is recognised in profit or loss evenly in each year of coverage; and

(d)   the expenses are expected to be paid immediately after they are incurred at the end of each year.

IE15   At the end of Year 2 the incurred expenses differ from those expected for that year. The entity also revises the fulfilment cash flows for Year 3 as follows:

(a)   in Example 2A, there are favourable changes in fulfilment cash flows and these changes increase the expected profitability of the group of insurance contracts; and

(b)   in Example 2B, there are unfavourable changes in fulfilment cash flows that exceed the remaining contractual service margin, creating an onerous group of insurance contracts.

Analysis

IE16   On initial recognition, the entity measures the group of insurance contracts and estimates the fulfilment cash flows at the end of each subsequent year as follows:

	Initial recognition	Year 1	Year 2	Year 3
	CU	CU	CU	CU
Estimates of the present value of future cash inflows	(900)	–	–	–
Estimates of the present value of future cash outflows	545	372	191	–
Estimates of the present value of future cash flows	(355)	372	191	–
Risk adjustment for non-financial risk	120	80	40	–
Fulfilment cash flows	(235)	452	231	–
Contractual service margin	235			
Insurance contract (asset) / liability on initial recognition	–			

IE17   At the end of Year 1, applying paragraphs B96–B97, the entity analyses the source of changes in the fulfilment cash flows during the year to decide whether each change adjusts the contractual service margin. Using this information, a possible format of the reconciliation of the insurance contract liability required by paragraph 101 is as follows:

	Estimates of the present value of future cash flows	Risk adjustment for non-financial risk	Contractual service margin	Insurance contract liability
	CU	CU	CU	CU
Opening balance	–	–	–	–
Changes related to future service: new contracts	(355)	120	235 (a)	–
Cash inflows	900	–	–	900
Insurance finance expenses	27 (b)	– (c)	12 (d)	39
Changes related to current service	–	(40) (c)	(82) (e)	(122)
Cash outflows	(200)	–	–	(200)
Closing balance	**372**	**80**	**165**	**617**

continued...

...continued

(a) Applying paragraph 44(a), the entity adjusts the contractual service margin of the group of contracts with any new contracts added to the group.

(b) In this example, insurance finance expenses of CU27 are calculated by multiplying CU545 (the difference between the estimates of the present value of the future cash flows at initial recognition of CU(355) and the cash inflows of CU900 received at the beginning of Year 1) by the current discount rate of 5 per cent, determined applying paragraphs 36 and B72(a).

(c) Applying paragraph 81, the entity chooses not to disaggregate the change in the risk adjustment for non-financial risk between the insurance service result and insurance finance income or expenses, therefore the entity presents the entire change in the risk adjustment for non-financial risk as part of the insurance service result in the statement of profit or loss.

(d) Applying paragraphs 44(b) and B72(b), the entity calculates interest accreted on the carrying amount of the contractual service margin of CU12 by multiplying the opening balance of CU235 by the discount rate of 5 per cent. That rate is applicable to nominal cash flows that do not vary based on the returns on any underlying items, determined on initial recognition of the group of insurance contracts.

(e) Applying paragraphs 44(e) and B119, the entity recognises in profit or loss in each period an amount of the contractual service margin for the group of insurance contracts to reflect the services provided under the group of insurance contracts in that period. The amount is determined by identifying the coverage units in the group. These coverage units reflect the quantity of benefits provided under each contract in the group and its expected coverage duration. The entity allocates the contractual service margin at the end of the period (before recognising any amounts in profit or loss) equally to each coverage unit provided in the current period and expected to be provided in the future, and recognises in profit or loss the amount allocated to the coverage units provided in the period. In this example, the service provided in each period for the group of contracts is the same because all contracts are expected to provide the same amount of benefits for all three periods of coverage. Consequently, the amount of the contractual service margin recognised in profit or loss in the period of CU82 is CU247 (CU235 + CU12) divided by three periods of coverage.

The entity could achieve the objective of the recognition of the contractual service margin on the basis of the coverage units using a different pattern. For example, the entity could allocate equally in each period the contractual service margin including the total interest expected to be accreted over the coverage period. In this example, the allocation pattern using this method would equal CU86 in each period calculated as $CU86 = CU235 \times 1.05 \div (1 + 1 \div 1.05 + 1 \div 1.05^2)$ instead of the increasing pattern of CU82 in Year 1, CU86 in Year 2 and CU91 in Year 3.

Example 6 illustrates the allocation of the contractual service margin in a situation when the entity expects contracts in a group to have different durations.

Example 2A—Changes in fulfilment cash flows that increase future profitability

Assumptions

IE18   At the end of Year 2, the following events occur:

(a)   the actual claims of CU150 are CU50 lower than originally expected for this period;

(b)   the entity revises the estimates of future cash outflows for Year 3 and expects to pay CU140, instead of CU200 (the present value is CU133 instead of CU191, a decrease in the present value of CU58); and

(c)   the entity revises the risk adjustment for non-financial risk related to estimates of future cash flows to CU30 instead of the initially estimated CU40.

Analysis

IE19   Thus, the estimates of the revised fulfilment cash flows at the end of Year 2 are as follows (the fulfilment cash flows for Year 1 and Year 3 are provided for comparison):

	Initial recognition	Year 1	Year 2	Year 3
	CU	CU	CU	CU
Estimates of the present value of future cash inflows	(900)	–	–	–
Estimates of the present value of future cash outflows	545	372	133	–
Estimates of the present value of future cash flows	(355)	372	133	–
Risk adjustment for non-financial risk	120	80	30	–
Fulfilment cash flows	**(235)**	**452**	**163**	**–**

IE20   At the end of Year 2, applying paragraphs B96–B97, the entity analyses the source of changes in the fulfilment cash flows during the year to decide whether each change adjusts the contractual service margin. Using this information, a possible format of the reconciliation of the insurance contract liability required by paragraph 101 is as follows:

	Estimates of the present value of future cash flows	Risk adjustment for non-financial risk	Contractual service margin	Insurance contract liability
	CU	CU	CU	CU
Opening balance	372	80	165	617
Insurance finance expenses	19 (a)	–	8 (a)	27
Changes related to future service	(58)	(10)	68 (b)	–
Changes related to current service	(50) (c)	(40)	(121) (a)	(211)
Cash outflows	(150)	–	–	(150)
Closing balance	**133**	**30**	**120**	**283**

(a)   For the method of calculation, see Year 1.

(b)   Applying paragraph 44(c), the entity adjusts the contractual service margin of the group of insurance contracts for changes in fulfilment cash flows relating to future service. Applying paragraph B96, the entity adjusts the contractual service margin for changes in estimates of the present value of the future cash flows measured at the discount rate determined on initial recognition of the group of insurance contracts of CU58 and changes in the risk adjustment for non-financial risk that relate to future service of CU10. Example 6 illustrates the accounting for changes in the estimates of the present value of the future cash flows when there is a change in discount rate after initial recognition of a group.

(c)   Applying paragraph B97(c), the entity does not adjust the contractual service margin for the experience adjustment of CU50 defined as the difference between the estimate at the beginning of the period of insurance service expenses expected to be incurred in the period of CU200 and the actual insurance service expenses incurred in the period of CU150. Applying paragraph 104, the entity classifies those changes as related to current service.

IE21   At the end of Year 3 the coverage period ends, so the remaining contractual service margin is recognised in profit or loss. In this example, all claims are paid when incurred; therefore, the remaining obligation is extinguished when the revised cash outflows are paid at the end of Year 3.

IE22   At the end of Year 3, applying paragraphs B96–B97, the entity analyses the source of changes in the fulfilment cash flows during the year to decide whether each change adjusts the contractual service margin. Using this information, a possible format of the reconciliation of the insurance contract liability required by paragraph 101 is as follows:

	Estimates of the present value of future cash flows	Risk adjustment for non-financial risk	Contractual service margin	Insurance contract liability
	CU	CU	CU	CU
Opening balance	133	30	120	283
Insurance finance expenses	7 (a)	–	6 (a)	13
Changes related to current service	–	(30)	(126) (a)	(156)
Cash outflows	(140)	–	–	(140)
Closing balance	–	–	–	–

(a)   For the method of calculation, see Year 1.

IE23   The amounts recognised in the statement of financial position and the statement of profit or loss summarise the amounts analysed in the tables above as follows:

Statement of financial position	Year 1	Year 2	Year 3	Total
	CU	CU	CU	CU
Cash(a)	(700)	(550)	(410)	
Insurance contract liability	617	283	–	
Equity	83	267	410	
Statement of profit or loss(b)				
Changes related to current service	122	211	156	489
Insurance finance expenses	(39)	(27)	(13)	(79)
Profit	**83**	**184**	**143**	**410**

(a)   In Year 1, the amount of cash of CU(700) equals the receipt of premiums of CU(900) and the payment of claims of CU200. There are additional payments of claims: CU150 in Year 2 and CU140 in Year 3. For simplicity, there is no interest accreted on the cash account.

(b)   This example illustrates the amounts recognised in the statement of profit or loss. Example 3A illustrates how these amounts could be presented.

Example 2B—Changes in fulfilment cash flows that create an onerous group of insurance contracts

IE24   At the end of Year 2, the following events occur:

(a)   the actual claims of CU400 are CU200 higher than originally expected in this period.

(b)   the entity revises its estimates of the future cash outflows for Year 3 to CU450, instead of CU200 (an increase in the present value of CU238). The entity also revises the risk adjustment for non-financial risk related to those future cash flows to CU88 at the end of Year 2 (CU48 higher than the originally expected CU40).

IE25   Thus, the estimates of the revised fulfilment cash flows at the end of Years 2 and 3 are as follows (the fulfilment cash flows for Year 1 are provided for comparison):

	Initial recognition	Year 1	Year 2	Year 3
	CU	CU	CU	CU
Estimates of the present value of future cash inflows	(900)	–	–	–
Estimates of the present value of future cash outflows	545	372	429	–
Estimates of the present value of future cash flows	(355)	372	429	–
Risk adjustment for non-financial risk	120	80	88	–
Fulfilment cash flows	(235)	452	517	–

IE26   At the end of Year 2, applying paragraphs B96–B97, the entity analyses the source of changes in the fulfilment cash flows during the year to decide whether each change adjusts the contractual service margin. Using this information, a possible format of the reconciliation of the insurance contract liability required by paragraph 101 is as follows:

	Estimates of the present value of future cash flows	Risk adjustment for non-financial risk	Contractual service margin	Insurance contract liability
	CU	CU	CU	CU
Opening balance	372	80	165	617
Insurance finance expenses	19 (a)	–	8 (a)	27
Changes related to future service	238	48	(173) (b)	113
Changes related to current service	200	(40)	– (c)	160
Cash outflows	(400)	–	–	(400)
Closing balance	**429**	**88**	**–**	**517**

(a) For the method of calculation, see Year 1.

(b) Applying paragraph 44(c), the entity adjusts the contractual service margin for the changes in the fulfilment cash flows relating to future service, except to the extent that such increases in the fulfilment cash flows exceed the carrying amount of the contractual service margin, giving rise to a loss.
Applying paragraph 48, the entity recognises this loss in profit or loss. Consequently, the entity accounts for the changes in the fulfilment cash flows related to future service of CU286 (estimates of the present value of the future cash outflows of CU238 plus the change in the risk adjustment for non-financial risk of CU48) as follows:

   (i) the contractual service margin is adjusted by CU173, which reduces the contractual service margin to zero; and

   (ii) the remaining change in the fulfilment cash flows of CU113 is recognised in profit or loss.

(c) Applying paragraph 44(e), the entity does not recognise any contractual service margin in profit or loss for the year because the remaining balance of the contractual service margin (before any allocation) equals zero (CU0 = CU165 + CU8 – CU173).

IE27   At the end of Year 3, the coverage period ends and the group of contracts is derecognised. Applying paragraphs B96–B97, the entity analyses the source of changes in the fulfilment cash flows during the year to decide whether each change adjusts the contractual service margin. Using this information, a possible format of the reconciliation of the insurance contract liability required by paragraph 101 is as follows:

	Estimates of the present value of future cash flows	Risk adjustment for non-financial risk	Contractual service margin	Insurance contract liability
	CU	CU	CU	CU
Opening balance	429	88	–	517
Insurance finance expenses	21 (a)	–	–	21
Changes related to current service	–	(88)	–	(88)
Cash outflows	(450)	–	–	(450)
Closing balance	–	–	–	–

(a)   For the method of calculation, see Year 1.

IE28   The amounts recognised in the statement of financial position and the statement of profit or loss summarise the amounts analysed in the tables above as follows:

Statement of financial position	Year 1	Year 2	Year 3	Total
	CU	CU	CU	CU
Cash(a)	(700)	(300)	150	
Insurance contract liability	617	517	–	
Equity	83	(217)	(150)	
Statement of profit or loss(b)				
Changes related to current service	122	(160)	88	50
Changes related to future service: loss on onerous group of contracts	–	(113)	–	(113)
Insurance finance expenses	(39)	(27)	(21)	(87)
Profit / (loss)	**83**	**(300)**	**67**	**(150)**

(a)   In Year 1, the cash of CU(700) equals the receipt of premiums of CU(900) and the payment of claims of CU200. In Year 2 and Year 3, there is a payment of claims of CU400 and CU450 respectively. For simplicity, there is no interest accreted on the cash account.

(b)   This example illustrates the amounts recognised in the statement of profit or loss. Example 3B illustrates how these amounts could be presented.

Example 3—Presentation in the statement of profit or loss (paragraphs 49–50(a), 84–85, 100 and B120–B124)

IE29   This example illustrates how an entity could present the insurance service result, comprising insurance revenue minus insurance service expenses, in the statement of profit or loss.

IE30   This example also illustrates the disclosure requirements in paragraph 100 to reconcile the carrying amount of the insurance contracts: (a) from the opening to the closing balances by each component and (b) to the line items presented in the statement of profit or loss.

Assumptions

IE31   The illustrations of presentation requirements in Examples 3A and 3B are based on Examples 2A and 2B respectively.

IE32   In both Example 3A and Example 3B, the entity estimates in each year that an investment component of CU100 is to be excluded from insurance revenue and insurance service expenses presented in profit or loss, applying paragraph 85.

Example 3A—Changes in fulfilment cash flows that increase future profitability

Analysis

IE33   At the end of Year 1, the entity provided the reconciliation required by paragraph 100 between the amounts recognised in the statement of financial position and the statement of profit or loss, separately for the liability for remaining coverage and the liability for incurred claims. A possible format for that reconciliation for Year 1 is as follows:

	Liability for remaining coverage	Liability for incurred claims	Insurance contract liability
	CU	CU	CU
Opening balance	–	–	–
Cash inflows	900	–	900
Insurance revenue	(222) (a)	–	(222)
Insurance service expenses	–	100 (b)	100
Investment component	(100) (c)	100 (c)	–
Insurance finance expenses	39 (d)	–	39
Cash outflows	–	(200)	(200)
Closing balance	**617**	–	**617**

continued...

© IFRS Foundation

...continued

(a)　Insurance revenue of CU222 is:

    (i)　determined by the entity applying paragraph B123 as the change in the liability for remaining coverage, excluding changes that do not relate to services provided in the period, for example changes resulting from cash inflows from premiums received, changes related to investment components and changes related to insurance finance income or expenses.

    Thus, in this example insurance revenue is the difference between the opening and closing carrying amounts of the liability for remaining coverage of CU617, excluding insurance finance expenses of CU39, cash inflows of CU900 and the investment component of CU100 (CU222 = CU0 − CU617 + CU39 + CU900 − CU100).

    (ii)　analysed by the entity applying paragraph B124 as the sum of the changes in the liability for remaining coverage in the period that relate to services for which the entity expects to receive consideration. Those changes are:

        1　insurance service expenses incurred in the period (measured at the amounts expected at the beginning of the period), excluding repayments of investment components;

        2　the change in the risk adjustment for non-financial risk, excluding changes that adjust the contractual service margin because they relate to future service ie the change caused by the release from risk; and

        3　the amount of contractual service margin recognised in profit or loss in the period.

    Thus, in this example insurance revenue is the sum of insurance service expenses of CU100, the change in the risk adjustment for non-financial risk caused by the release from risk of CU40 and the contractual service margin recognised in profit or loss of CU82 (CU222 = CU100 + CU40 + CU82).

(b)　Applying paragraph 84, the entity presents insurance service expenses of CU100 as the claims incurred in the period of CU200 minus the investment component of CU100.

(c)　Applying paragraph 85, the entity presents insurance revenue and insurance service expenses in profit or loss excluding amounts related to an investment component. In this example, the investment component equals CU100.

(d)　Insurance finance expenses are the same as in Example 2. The whole amount of insurance finance expenses is related to the liability for remaining coverage because the liability for incurred claims is paid immediately after the expenses are incurred (see the assumptions in Example 2).

IE34   In Year 2, the actual claims of CU150 are lower than expected. The entity also revises its estimates relating to the fulfilment cash flows in Year 3. Consequently, the entity recognises in profit or loss the effect of the revised claims relating to Year 2, and adjusts the contractual service margin for changes in the fulfilment cash flows for Year 3. This change is only related to incurred claims and does not affect the investment component.

IE35   A possible format of the reconciliation required by paragraph 100 between the amounts recognised in the statement of financial position and the statement of profit or loss for Year 2 is as follows:

	Liability for remaining coverage	Liability for incurred claims	Insurance contract liability
	CU	CU	CU
Opening balance	617	–	617
Insurance revenue	(261) (a)	–	(261)
Insurance service expenses	–	50 (b)	50
Investment component	(100)	100	–
Insurance finance expenses	27 (c)	–	27
Cash flows	–	(150)	(150)
Closing balance	**283**	–	**283**

(a)   Insurance revenue of CU261 is:

   (i)   determined by the entity applying paragraph B123 as the difference between the opening and closing carrying amounts of the liability for remaining coverage of CU334 (CU617 – CU283), excluding insurance finance expenses of CU27 and the investment component of CU100 (CU261 = CU334 + CU27 – CU100); and

   (ii)   analysed by the entity applying paragraph B124 as the sum of the insurance service expenses of CU50 adjusted for the experience adjustment of CU50, the change in the risk adjustment for non-financial risk caused by the release from risk of CU40 and the contractual service margin recognised in profit or loss of CU121 (CU261 = CU50 + CU50 + CU40 + CU121).

(b)   Applying paragraph 84, the entity presents insurance service expenses of CU50 as the claims incurred in the period of CU150 minus the investment component of CU100.

(c)   Insurance finance expenses are the same as in Example 2A. The whole amount of insurance finance expenses is related to the liability for remaining coverage because the liability for incurred claims is paid immediately after the expenses are incurred.

IE36 In Year 3, there is no further change in estimates and the entity provides a possible format of the reconciliation required by paragraph 100 between the amounts recognised in the statement of financial position and the statement of profit or loss for Year 3 as follows:

	Liability for remaining coverage	Liability for incurred claims	Insurance contract liability
	CU	CU	CU
Opening balance	283	–	283
Insurance revenue	(196) (a)	–	(196)
Insurance service expenses	–	40 (b)	40
Investment component	(100)	100	–
Insurance finance expenses	13 (c)	–	13
Cash flows	–	(140)	(140)
Closing balance	–	–	–

(a) Insurance revenue of CU196 is:

  (i) determined by the entity applying paragraph B123 as the difference between the opening and closing carrying amounts of the liability for remaining coverage of CU283 (CU283 – CU0), excluding insurance finance expenses of CU13 and the investment component of CU100 (CU196 = CU283 + CU13 – CU100); and

  (ii) analysed by the entity applying paragraph B124 as the sum of the insurance service expenses of CU40, the change in the risk adjustment for non-financial risk caused by the release from risk of CU30 and the contractual service margin recognised in profit or loss of CU126 (CU196 = CU40 + CU30 + CU126).

(b) Applying paragraph 84, the entity presents insurance service expenses of CU40 as the claims incurred in the period of CU140 minus the investment component of CU100.

(c) Insurance finance expenses are the same as in Example 2A. The whole amount of insurance finance expenses is related to the liability for remaining coverage because the liability for incurred claims is paid immediately after the expenses are incurred.

IE37 The amounts presented in the statement of profit or loss corresponding to the amounts analysed in the tables above are:

Statement of profit or loss	Year 1	Year 2	Year 3	Total
	CU	CU	CU	CU
Insurance revenue	222	261	196	679 [a]
Insurance service expenses	(100)	(50)	(40)	(190)
Insurance service result	**122**	**211**	**156**	**489**
Investment income[b]	–	–	–	–
Insurance finance expenses	(39)	(27)	(13)	(79)
Finance result	**(39)**	**(27)**	**(13)**	**(79)**
Profit	**83**	**184**	**143**	**410**

(a) Applying paragraph B120, the entity calculates the total insurance revenue for the group of insurance contracts of CU679 as the amount of premiums paid to the entity of CU900 adjusted for the financing effect of CU79 and excluding the investment component of CU300 (CU100 a year for 3 years) ie CU679 = CU900 + CU79 – CU300.

(b) For the purpose of this example, these numbers are not included because they are accounted for applying another Standard.

Example 3B—Changes in fulfilment cash flows that create an onerous group of insurance contracts

Analysis

IE38 This example uses the same assumptions for Year 1 as those in Example 3A. Consequently, the analysis of Year 1 is the same as for Example 3A. The presentation requirements for Year 1 are illustrated in Example 3A and are not repeated in Example 3B.

IE39 A possible format of the reconciliation required by paragraph 100 between the amounts recognised in the statement of financial position and the statement of profit or loss for Year 2 is as follows:

© IFRS Foundation

	Liability for remaining coverage, excluding loss component	Loss component of the liability for remaining coverage	Liability for incurred claims	Insurance contract liability
	CU	CU	CU	CU
Opening balance	617	–	–	617
Insurance revenue	(140) (a)	–	–	(140)
Insurance service expenses	–	113 (b)	300 (c)	413
Investment component	(100)	–	100	–
Insurance finance expenses	27 (d)	–	–	27
Cash outflows	–	–	(400)	(400)
Closing balance	**404**	**113**	**–**	**517**

(a)   Insurance revenue of CU140 is:

   (i)   determined by the entity applying paragraph B123 as the change in the liability for remaining coverage, excluding:

      1   changes that do not relate to services provided in the year, for example changes resulting from cash inflows from premiums received, changes related to investment components and changes related to insurance finance income or expenses; and

      2   changes that relate to services but for which the entity does not expect consideration, ie increases and decreases in the loss component of the liability for remaining coverage.

   Thus, in this example insurance revenue is the difference between the opening and closing carrying amounts of the liability for remaining coverage, excluding changes related to the loss component of CU213 (CU617 – CU404), excluding insurance finance expenses of CU27 and the repayment of the investment component of CU100, ie CU140 = CU213 + CU27 – CU100.

continued...

...continued

      (ii)   analysed by the entity applying paragraph B124 as the sum of the changes in the liability for remaining coverage in the year that relate to services for which the entity expects to receive consideration. Those changes are:

            1   insurance service expenses incurred in the period (measured at the amounts expected at the beginning of the period), excluding amounts allocated to the loss component of the liability for remaining coverage and excluding repayments of investment components;

            2   the change in the risk adjustment for non-financial risk, excluding changes that adjust the contractual service margin because they relate to future service and amounts allocated to the loss component ie the change caused by the release from risk; and

            3   the amount of contractual service margin recognised in profit or loss in the period.

      Thus, in this example insurance revenue is the sum of the insurance service expenses of CU300 including experience adjustments of CU200 and the change in the risk adjustment for non-financial risk caused by the release from risk of CU40, ie CU140 = CU300 − CU200 + CU40.

(b)   The entity revises the estimates of fulfilment cash flows for Year 3. The increase in fulfilment cash flows exceeds the carrying amount of the remaining contractual service margin, creating a loss of CU113 (see the table after paragraph IE26). Applying paragraph 49, the entity establishes the loss component of the liability for remaining coverage for an onerous group depicting that loss. The loss component determines the amounts presented in profit or loss as reversals of losses on onerous groups that are consequently excluded from determination of insurance revenue.

(c)   Applying paragraph 84, the entity presents insurance service expenses of CU300 as the claims incurred in the period of CU400 minus the investment component of CU100.

(d)   Insurance finance expenses are the same as in Example 2B. The whole amount of insurance finance expenses is related to the liability for remaining coverage because the liability for incurred claims is paid immediately after the expenses are incurred.

IE40 A possible format of the reconciliation required by paragraph 100 between the amounts recognised in the statement of financial position and the statement of profit or loss for Year 3 is as follows:

	Liability for remaining coverage, excluding loss component	Loss component of the liability for remaining coverage	Liability for incurred claims	Insurance contract liability
	CU	CU	CU	CU
Opening balance	404	113	–	517
Insurance finance expenses	16	5 (b)	–	21 (d)
Insurance revenue	(320) (a)	–	–	(320)
Insurance service expenses	–	(118) (b)	350 (c)	232
Investment component	(100)	–	100	–
Cash flows	–	–	(450)	(450)
Closing balance	–	–	–	–

(a) Insurance revenue of CU320 is:

(i) determined by the entity applying paragraph B123 as the difference between the opening and closing carrying amounts of the liability for remaining coverage, excluding changes related to the loss component of CU404 (CU404 – CU0), insurance finance expenses of CU16 and the repayment of the investment component of CU100, ie CU320 = CU404 + CU16 – CU100.

(ii) analysed by the entity applying paragraph B124 as the sum of the insurance service expenses for the incurred claims for the year of CU350 and the change in the risk adjustment for non-financial risk caused by the release from risk of CU88, excluding CU118 allocated to the loss component of the liability of remaining coverage, ie CU320 = CU350 + CU88 – CU118.

(b) Applying paragraph 50(a), the entity allocates on a systematic basis the subsequent changes in the fulfilment cash flows of the liability for remaining coverage between the loss component of the liability for remaining coverage and the liability for remaining coverage, excluding the loss component. In this example the entity allocates subsequent changes in fulfilment cash flows to the loss component of the liability for remaining coverage as follows:

continued...

...continued

    (i)   insurance finance expenses of CU5 are determined by multiplying the total insurance finance expenses of CU21 by 22 per cent. The allocation is based on the 22 per cent proportion of the loss component of the liability for remaining coverage of CU113 to the total liability for remaining coverage of CU517 (CU404 + CU113).

    (ii)   the change of the loss component of CU118 is the sum of:

        1   the estimates of the future cash flows released from the liability for remaining coverage for the year of CU94, calculated by multiplying the expected insurance service expenses for the incurred claims for the year of CU350 by 27 per cent; and

        2   the change in the risk adjustment for non-financial risk caused by the release from risk of CU24, calculated by multiplying the total such change of CU88 by 27 per cent.

The allocation of the amounts described in 1 and 2 to the loss component of CU118 is determined after the insurance finance expenses and investment component have been allocated. The insurance finance expenses are allocated as described in (i). The investment component is allocated solely to the liability for remaining coverage excluding the loss component, because it is not included in insurance revenue or insurance service expenses. After those allocations, the loss component of the liability for remaining coverage is CU118 (CU113 + CU5) and the liability for remaining coverage excluding the investment component is CU438 (CU517 + CU21 − CU100). Hence, the allocations in (ii) are determined as the ratio of CU118 to CU438, which is 27 per cent.

See Example 8 for a more detailed calculation of losses in a group of insurance contracts subsequent to initial recognition.

(c)   Applying paragraph 84, the entity presents insurance service expenses of CU350 as the claims incurred in the period of CU450 minus the investment component of CU100.

(d)   Insurance finance expenses are the same as in Example 2B. The whole amount of insurance finance expenses is related to the liability for remaining coverage because the liability for incurred claims is paid immediately after the expenses are incurred.

IE41   The amounts presented in the statement of profit or loss corresponding to the amounts analysed in the tables above are:

Statement of profit or loss	Year 1	Year 2	Year 3	Total
	CU	CU	CU	CU
Insurance revenue	222	140	320	682 [(a)]
Insurance service expenses	(100)	(413)	(232)	(745)
Insurance service result	**122**	**(273)**	**88**	**(63)**
Investment income[(b)]	–	–	–	–
Insurance finance expenses	(39)	(27)	(21)	(87)
Finance result	**(39)**	**(27)**	**(21)**	**(87)**
Profit / (loss)	**83**	**(300)**	**67**	**(150)**

(a)   Applying paragraph B120, the entity calculates the total insurance revenue for the group of insurance contracts of CU682 as the amount of premiums paid to the entity of CU900 adjusted for the financing effect of CU82 (insurance finance expenses of CU87 minus CU5 related to the loss component) and excluding the investment component of CU300 (CU100 per year for 3 years) ie CU682 = CU900 + CU82 – CU300.

(b)   For the purpose of this example, these numbers are not included because they are accounted for applying another Standard.

Separating components from an insurance contract (paragraphs B31–B35)

IE42   The following two examples illustrate the requirements in paragraphs B31–B35 for separating non-insurance components from insurance contracts.

Example 4—Separating components from a life insurance contract with an account balance

Assumptions

IE43   An entity issues a life insurance contract with an account balance. The entity receives a premium of CU1,000 when the contract is issued. The account balance is increased annually by voluntary amounts paid by the policyholder, increased or decreased by amounts calculated using the returns from specified assets and decreased by fees charged by the entity.

IE44   The contract promises to pay the following:

(a)   a death benefit of CU5,000 plus the amount of the account balance, if the insured person dies during the coverage period; and

(b)   the account balance, if the contract is cancelled (ie there are no surrender charges).

IE45 The entity has a claims processing department to process the claims received and an asset management department to manage investments.

IE46 An investment product that has equivalent terms to the account balance, but without the insurance coverage, is sold by another financial institution.

IE47 The entity considers whether to separate the non-insurance components from the insurance contract.

Analysis

Separating the account balance

IE48 The existence of an investment product with equivalent terms indicates that the components may be distinct, applying paragraph B31(b). However, if the right to death benefits provided by the insurance coverage either lapses or matures at the same time as the account balance, the insurance and investment components are highly interrelated and are therefore not distinct, applying paragraph B32(b). Consequently, the account balance would not be separated from the insurance contract and would be accounted for applying IFRS 17.

Separating the claims processing component

IE49 Claims processing activities are part of the activities the entity must undertake to fulfil the contract, and the entity does not transfer a good or service to the policyholder because the entity performs those activities. Thus, applying paragraph B33, the entity would not separate the claims processing component from the insurance contract.

Separating the asset management component

IE50 The asset management activities, similar to claims processing activities, are part of the activities the entity must undertake to fulfil the contract, and the entity does not transfer a good or service other than insurance contract services to the policyholder because the entity performs those activities. Thus, applying paragraph B33, the entity would not separate the asset management component from the insurance contract.

Example 5—Separating components from a stop-loss contract with claims processing services

Assumptions

IE51 An entity issues a stop-loss contract to an employer (the policyholder). The contract provides health coverage for the policyholder's employees and has the following features:

(a) insurance coverage of 100 per cent for the aggregate claims from employees exceeding CU25 million (the 'stop-loss threshold'). The employer will self-insure claims from employees up to CU25 million.

(b)   claims processing services for employees' claims during the next year, regardless of whether the claims have passed the stop-loss threshold of CU25 million. The entity is responsible for processing the health insurance claims of the employees on behalf of the employer.

IE52   The entity considers whether to separate the claims processing services. The entity notes that similar services to process claims on behalf of customers are sold on the market.

Analysis

Separating the claims processing services

IE53   The criteria for identifying distinct non-insurance services in paragraph B34 are met in this example:

(a)   the claims processing services, similar to the services to process the employees' claims on behalf of the employer, are sold as a standalone service without any insurance coverage; and

(b)   the claims processing services benefit the policyholder independently of the insurance coverage. Had the entity not agreed to provide those services, the policyholder would have to process its employees' medical claims itself or engage other service providers to do this.

IE54   Additionally, the criteria in paragraph B35 that establishes if the service is not distinct are not met because the cash flows associated with the claims processing services are not highly interrelated with the cash flows associated with the insurance coverage, and the entity does not provide a significant service of integrating the claims processing services with the insurance components. In addition, the entity could provide the promised claims processing services separately from the insurance coverage.

IE55   Accordingly, the entity separates the claims processing services from the insurance contract and accounts for them applying IFRS 15 *Revenue from Contracts with Customers*.

Subsequent measurement

Example 6—Additional features of the contractual service margin (paragraphs 44, 87, 101, B96–B99 and B119–B119B)

IE56   This example illustrates adjustments to the contractual service margin of insurance contracts without direct participation features for:

(a)   the changes in discretionary cash flows for insurance contracts that give an entity discretion over the cash flows expected to be paid to the policyholder, including determination of changes in those cash flows separately from changes in financial assumptions;

(b)   the adjustments related to the time value of money and financial risks in a situation when the interest rate changes; and

(c)   the amount recognised in profit or loss for the services provided in the period in a situation when the entity expects contracts in a group to have different durations.

Assumptions

IE57   An entity issues 200 insurance contracts with a coverage period of three years. The coverage period starts when the insurance contracts are issued.

IE58   The contracts in this example:

(a)   meet the definition of insurance contracts because they offer a fixed payment on death. However, to isolate the effects illustrated in this example, and for simplicity, any fixed cash flows payable on death are ignored.

(b)   do not meet the criteria for insurance contracts with direct participation features applying paragraph B101(a) because a pool of assets is not specified in the contracts.

(c)   provide an investment-return service applying paragraph B119B.

(d)   provide both insurance coverage and investment-return service evenly over the coverage period of three years.

IE59   The entity receives a single premium of CU15 at the beginning of the coverage period. Policyholders will receive the value of the account balance:

(a)   if the insured person dies during the coverage period; or

(b)   at the end of the coverage period (maturity value) if the insured person survives to the end of the coverage period.

IE60   The entity calculates the policyholder account balances at the end of each year as follows:

(a)   opening balance; plus

(b)   premiums received at the beginning of the period (if any); minus

(c)   an annual charge of 3 per cent of the sum of the account balances at the beginning of the year and premium received if any; plus

(d)   interest credited at the end of the year (the interest credited to the account balances in each year is at the discretion of the entity); minus

(e)   the value of the remaining account balances paid to policyholders when an insured person dies or the coverage period ends.

IE61   The entity specifies that its commitment under the contract is to credit interest to the policyholder's account balance at a rate equal to the return on an internally specified pool of assets minus two percentage points, applying paragraph B98.

IE62   On initial recognition of the group of contracts, the entity:

(a)   expects the return on the specified pool of assets will be 10 per cent a year.

(b) determines the discount rate applicable to nominal cash flows that do not vary based on the returns on any underlying items is 4 per cent a year.

(c) expects that two insured people will die at the end of each year. Claims are settled immediately.

(d) estimates the risk adjustment for non-financial risk to be CU30 and expects to recognise it in profit or loss evenly over the coverage period. Applying paragraph 81, the entity does not disaggregate the changes in the risk adjustment for non-financial risk between the insurance service result and insurance finance income or expenses.

IE63 In Year 1, the return on the specified pool of assets is 10 per cent, as expected. However, in Year 2 the return on the specified pool of assets is only 7 per cent. Consequently, at the end of Year 2, the entity:

(a) revises its estimate of the expected return on the specified pool of assets to 7 per cent in Year 3.

(b) exercises its discretion over the amount of interest it will credit to the policyholder account balances in Years 2 and 3. It determines that it will credit interest to the policyholder account balances at a rate equal to the return on the specified pool of assets, minus one percentage point, ie the entity forgoes spread income of one percentage point a year in Years 2 and 3.

(c) credits 6 per cent interest to the policyholder account balances (instead of the initially expected 8 per cent).

IE64 In this example all other amounts are ignored, for simplicity.

Analysis

IE65   On initial recognition, the entity measures the group of insurance contracts and estimates the fulfilment cash flows at the end of each subsequent year as follows:

	Initial recognition	Year 1	Year 2	Year 3
	CU	CU	CU	CU
Estimates of the present value of future cash inflows	(3,000)	–	–	–
Estimates of the present value of future cash outflows[(a)]	2,596	2,824	3,074	–
Estimates of the present value of future cash flows	(404)	2,824	3,074	–
Risk adjustment for non-financial risk	30	20	10	–
Fulfilment cash flows	(374)	2,844	3,084	–
Contractual service margin	374			
Insurance contract (asset) / liability on initial recognition	–			

(a)   The entity calculates the estimates of the present value of the future cash outflows using a current discount rate of 10 per cent that reflects the characteristics of the future cash flows, determined applying paragraphs 36 and B72(a).

IE66   Applying paragraphs B98–B99, to determine how to identify a change in discretionary cash flows, an entity shall specify at inception of the contract the basis on which it expects to determine its commitment under the contract, for example, based on a fixed interest rate, or on returns that vary based on specified asset returns. An entity uses this specification to distinguish between the effect of changes in assumptions that relate to financial risk on that commitment (which does not adjust the contractual service margin) and the effect of discretionary changes to that commitment (which adjusts the contractual service margin).

IE67   In this example, the entity specified at inception of the contract that its commitment under the contract is to credit interest to the policyholder account balances at a rate equal to the return on a specified pool of assets minus two percentage points. Because of the entity's decision at the end of Year 2, this spread decreased from two percentage points to one percentage point.

IE68   Consequently, at the end of Year 2, the entity analyses the changes in the policyholder account balances between the result of changes in financial assumptions and the exercise of discretion, as follows:

Policyholder account balances		As expected on initial recognition		Revised for changes in financial assumptions		Revised for changes in financial assumptions and the exercise of discretion
		CU		CU		CU
Balance at the beginning of Year 1		–		–		–
Premiums received		3,000		3,000		3,000
Annual charge[(a)]	3%	(90)	3%	(90)	3%	(90)
Interest credited[(b)]	8%	233	8%	233	8%	233
Death benefits[(c)]	2/200	(31)	2/200	(31)	2/200	(31)
Balance carried forward to Year 2		3,112		3,112		3,112
Annual charge[(a)]	3%	(93)	3%	(93)	3%	(93)
Interest credited[(b)]	8%	242	5%	151	6%	181
Death benefits[(c)]	2/198	(33)	2/198	(32)	2/198	(32)
Balance carried forward to Year 3		3,228		3,138		3,168
Annual charge[(a)]	3%	(97)	3%	(94)	3%	(95)
Interest credited[(b)]	8%	250	5%	152	6%	184
Death benefits[(c)]	2/196	(35)	2/196	(33)	2/196	(33)
Balance at the end of Year 3 (maturity value)		3,346		3,163		3,224

(a)   The annual charge equals the percentage of the balance at the beginning of each year (including premiums received at the beginning of the year). For example, in Year 1 the annual charge of CU90 is 3% × CU3,000.

(b)   Interest credited each year equals the percentage of the balance at the beginning of each year minus the annual charge. For example, in Year 1 the interest credited of CU233 is 8% × (CU3,000 – CU90).

(c)   The death benefit equals the percentage of the balance at the beginning of each year minus the annual charge plus interest credited. For example, in Year 1 the death benefit of CU31 is 2/200 × (CU3,000 – CU90 + CU233).

IE69   The entity summarises the estimates of future cash flows for Years 2 and 3 in the table below.

	As expected on initial recognition	Revised for changes in financial assumptions	Revised for changes in financial assumptions and the exercise of discretion
	CU	CU	CU
Payment on deaths in Year 2	33	32	32
Payment on deaths in Year 3	35	33	33
Maturity value paid in Year 3	3,346	3,163	3,224
Estimates of the future cash flows at the beginning of Year 2	**3,414**	**3,228**	**3,289**

IE70   Applying paragraphs B98–B99, the entity distinguishes between the effect of changes in assumptions that relate to financial risk and the effect of discretionary changes on the fulfilment cash flows as follows:

Changes in the estimates of future cash flows in Year 2	Estimates of future cash flows	Estimates of the present value of future cash flows
	CU	CU
Beginning of Year 2 (present value discounted at 10%)	3,414 [(a)]	2,824 [(b)]
The effect of changes in financial assumptions (and interest accretion)	(186) [(c)]	195 [(d)]
Revised for changes in financial assumptions (present value discounted at 7%)	3,228 [(a)]	3,019 [(b)]
The effect of the exercise of discretion (present value discounted at 7%)	61 [(e)]	57
Revised for changes in financial assumptions and the exercise of discretion (present value discounted at 7%)	3,289 [(a)]	3,076 [(b)]
Payment of cash flows	(32) [(a)]	(32)
End of Year 2	**3,257**	**3,044**

(a)   See the table after paragraph IE69.

(b)   The entity calculates the estimates of the present value of the future cash outflows using a current discount rate that reflects the characteristics of the future cash flows, determined applying paragraphs 36 and B72(a). All the cash flows — other than the death benefit payable at the end of Year 2 — are payable at the end of Year 3.

continued...

...continued

(c)   The change in estimates of future cash flows of CU186 equals the difference between the estimates of the future cash flows revised for changes in financial assumptions of CU3,228 minus the estimates of the future cash flows before the change in financial assumptions of CU3,414. Hence, it reflects only the change in financial assumptions.

(d)   The change in estimates of the present value of the future cash flows of CU195 is the difference between the estimates of the present value of the future cash flows at the end of Year 2 (revised for changes in financial assumptions) of CU3,019 and the estimates of the present value of the future cash flows at the beginning of Year 2 (before changes in financial assumptions) of CU2,824. Hence, it reflects the effect of the interest accretion during Year 2 and the effect of the change in financial assumptions.

(e)   The effect of the exercise of discretion of CU61 equals the difference between the estimates of the future cash flows revised for the exercise of discretion of CU3,289 and the estimates of the future cash flows before the effect of the exercise of discretion of CU3,228.

IE71   A possible format for the reconciliation of the insurance contract liability required by paragraph 101 for Year 2 is as follows:

	Estimates of the present value of future cash flows	Risk adjustment for non-financial risk	Contractual service margin	Insurance contract liability
	CU	CU	CU	CU
Opening balance	2,824	20	258	3,102
Insurance finance expenses	197 (a)	–	10 (b)	207
Changes related to future service: exercise of discretion	55 (c)	–	(55) (c)	–
Changes related to current service	–	(10)	(107) (d)	(117)
Cash outflows	(32)	–	–	(32)
Closing balance	**3,044**	**10**	**106**	**3,160**

continued...

...continued

(a)   Applying paragraph B97, the entity does not adjust the contractual service margin for a group of contracts for changes in fulfilment cash flows related to the effect of time value of money and financial risk and changes therein, comprising (i) the effect, if any, on estimated future cash flows; (ii) the effect, if disaggregated, on the risk adjustment for non-financial risk; and (iii) the effect of a change in discount rate. This is because such changes do not relate to future service. Applying paragraph 87, the entity recognises those changes as insurance finance expenses. Consequently, the insurance finance expenses of CU197 are the sum of:

    (i)   the effect of interest accretion and the effect of the change in financial assumptions of CU195 (see the table after paragraph IE70); and

    (ii)   the effect of the change in the assumptions related to financial risk on the change in the discretionary cash flows of CU2, which equals:

        1   CU57 of the present value of the effect of the change in discretion discounted using the current rate (see the table after paragraph IE70); minus

        2   CU55 of the present value of the change in discretion discounted using the rate determined on initial recognition of the group of insurance contracts (see footnote (c)).

(b)   Applying paragraphs 44(b) and B72(b), the entity calculates interest accreted on the carrying amount of the contractual service margin of CU10 by multiplying the opening balance of CU258 by the discount rate of 4 per cent determined on initial recognition of the group of insurance contracts. That rate is applicable to nominal cash flows that do not vary based on the returns on any underlying items.

(c)   Applying paragraphs 44(c) and B98, the entity regards changes in discretionary cash flows as relating to future service, and accordingly adjusts the contractual service margin. Applying paragraphs B96 and B72(c), the adjustment to the contractual service margin is calculated by discounting the change in the future cash flows of CU61 using the discount rate of 10 per cent, which reflects the characteristics of the cash flows determined on initial recognition of the group of insurance contracts. Consequently, the amount of discretionary cash flows that adjusts the contractual service margin of CU55 is CU61 ÷ (1 + 10%).

continued...

...*continued*

(d) Applying paragraphs 44(e) and B119, the entity recognises in profit or loss the amount of contractual service margin determined by allocating the contractual service margin at the end of the period (before recognising any amounts in profit or loss) equally to each coverage unit provided in the current period and expected to be provided in the future, as follows:

    (i) the amount of the contractual service margin immediately before allocation to profit or loss is CU213 (opening balance of CU258 plus interest of CU10 minus the change related to future service of CU55);

    (ii) the number of coverage units in this example is the total of the number of contracts in each period for which coverage is expected to be provided (because the quantity of benefits provided for each contract is the same). Hence, there are 394 coverage units to be provided over the current and final year (198 contracts in Year 2 and 196 contracts in Year 3);

    (iii) the contractual service margin per coverage unit is CU0.54 (CU213 ÷ 394 coverage units); and

    (iv) the contractual service margin recognised in profit or loss in Year 2 of CU107 is CU0.54 of contractual service margin per coverage unit multiplied by the 198 coverage units provided in Year 2.

Example 7—Insurance acquisition cash flows (paragraphs 106, B65(e) and B125)

IE72 This example illustrates the determination of insurance acquisition cash flows on initial recognition and the subsequent determination of insurance revenue, including the portion of premium related to the recovery of the insurance acquisition cash flows.

IE73 This example also illustrates the requirement to disclose the analysis of the insurance revenue recognised in the period applying paragraph 106.

Assumptions

IE74 An entity issues a group of insurance contracts with a coverage period of three years. The coverage period starts when the insurance contracts are issued.

IE75 On initial recognition, the entity determines the following:

(a) estimates of future cash inflows of CU900, paid immediately after initial recognition;

(b) estimates of future cash outflows, which comprise:

    (i) estimates of future claims of CU600 (CU200 incurred and paid each year); and

    (ii) acquisition cash flows of CU120 (of which CU90 are cash flows directly attributable to the portfolio to which the contracts belong), are paid at the beginning of the coverage period.

(c)   the risk adjustment for non-financial risk is CU15 and the entity expects to recognise the risk adjustment for non-financial risk in profit or loss evenly over the coverage period.

IE76   In this example for simplicity, it is assumed that:

(a)   all expenses are incurred as expected;

(b)   no contracts will lapse during the coverage period;

(c)   there is no investment component;

(d)   the insurance acquisition cash flows directly attributable to the portfolio to which the contracts belong of CU90 are directly attributable to the group of contracts to which the contracts belong and no renewals of those contracts are expected; and

(e)   all other amounts, including the effect of discounting, are ignored for simplicity.

Analysis

IE77   On initial recognition, the entity measures the group of insurance contracts and estimates the fulfilment cash flows at the end of each subsequent year as follows:

	Initial recognition	Year 1	Year 2	Year 3
	CU	CU	CU	CU
Estimates of the present value of future cash inflows	(900)	–	–	–
Estimates of the present value of future cash outflows	690 (a)	400	200	–
Estimates of the present value of future cash flows	(210)	400	200	–
Risk adjustment for non-financial risk	15	10	5	–
Fulfilment cash flows	(195)	410	205	–
Contractual service margin	195			
Insurance contract (asset) / liability on initial recognition	–			

(a)   Applying paragraph B65(e), estimates of the present value of the future cash flows of CU690 comprise expected claims of CU600 and an allocation of insurance acquisition cash flows directly attributable to the portfolio to which the contracts belong of CU90.

IE78   The entity recognises the contractual service margin and insurance acquisition cash flows in profit or loss for each year as follows:

Recognised in profit or loss each year	Year 1	Year 2	Year 3	Total
	CU	CU	CU	CU
Contractual service margin[a]	65	65	65	195
Insurance acquisition cash flows[b]	30	30	30	90

(a)   Applying paragraphs 44(e) and B119, the entity recognises in profit or loss in each period an amount of the contractual service margin for a group of insurance contracts to reflect the transfer of services provided in that period. The amount recognised in each period is determined by the allocation of the contractual service margin remaining at the end of the reporting period (before any allocation) over the current and remaining coverage periods. In this example, the coverage provided in each period is the same because the number of contracts for which the coverage is provided in each period is the same. Consequently, the contractual service margin of CU195 is allocated equally in each year of coverage (ie CU65 = CU195 ÷ 3 years).

(b)   Applying paragraph B125, the entity determines the insurance revenue related to insurance acquisition cash flows by allocating the portion of the premiums that relates to recovering those cash flows to each accounting period in a systematic way on the basis of the passage of time. The entity recognises the same amount as insurance service expenses. In this example, the coverage period of the contracts is three years, therefore the expenses recognised in profit or loss each year are CU30 (CU90 ÷ 3 years).

IE79   The entity recognises the following amounts in profit or loss:

Statement of profit or loss	Year 1	Year 2	Year 3	Total
	CU	CU	CU	CU
Insurance revenue[a]	300	300	300	900
Insurance service expenses[b]	(230)	(230)	(230)	(690)
Insurance service result	70	70	70	210
Other expenses[c]	(30)	–	–	(30)
Profit	40	70	70	180

(a)   See the table after paragraph IE80 for more details on the components of insurance revenue.

continued...

...continued

(b) Applying paragraph 84, the entity presents insurance service expenses as incurred claims of CU200 in each year plus insurance acquisition cash flows of CU30 allocated to each year.

(c) Other expenses include acquisition cash flows that are not directly attributable to the portfolio of insurance contracts to which the contracts belong. They are calculated as the difference between the acquisition cash flows of CU120 and directly attributable insurance acquisition cash flows of CU90.

IE80 A possible format for the analysis of the insurance revenue required by paragraph 106 is as follows:

	Year 1	Year 2	Year 3	Total
	CU	CU	CU	CU
Amounts relating to the changes in the liability for remaining coverage:				
– Insurance service expenses incurred[(a)]	200	200	200	600
– Contractual service margin recognised in profit or loss	65	65	65	195
– Change in the risk adjustment for non-financial risk caused by the release from risk	5	5	5	15
Allocation of recovery of insurance acquisition cash flows	30	30	30	90
Insurance revenue[(b)]	300	300	300	900

(a) Applying paragraph B124, the entity measures those amounts as expected at the beginning of the year.

(b) This example illustrates the analysis of insurance revenue required by paragraph 106. See Example 3 for how to determine insurance revenue.

Example 8—Reversal of losses in an onerous group of insurance contracts (paragraphs 49–50 and B123–B124)

IE81 This example illustrates how, for an onerous group of insurance contracts, an entity reverses losses from the loss component of the liability for remaining coverage when the group becomes profitable.

Assumptions

IE82 An entity issues 100 insurance contracts with a coverage period of three years. The coverage period starts when the insurance contracts are issued and the services are provided evenly over the coverage period. It is assumed, for simplicity, that no contracts will lapse before the end of the coverage period.

IE83   The entity expects to receive premiums of CU800 immediately after initial recognition, therefore, the estimates of the present value of cash inflows are CU800.

IE84   The entity estimates annual future cash outflows to be CU400 at the end of each year (total CU1,200). The entity estimates the present value of the future cash outflows to be CU1,089, using a discount rate of 5 per cent a year that reflects the characteristics of nominal cash flows that do not vary based on the returns on any underlying items, determined applying paragraph 36. The entity expects claims will be paid when incurred.

IE85   The risk adjustment for non-financial risk on initial recognition equals CU240 and it is assumed the entity will be released from risk evenly over the coverage period of three years.

IE86   In this example all other amounts, including the investment component are ignored, for simplicity.

IE87   On initial recognition, the entity measures the group of insurance contracts and estimates the fulfilment cash flows at the end of each subsequent year as follows:

	Initial recognition	Year 1	Year 2	Year 3
	CU	CU	CU	CU
Estimates of the present value of future cash inflows	(800)	–	–	–
Estimates of the present value of future cash outflows	1,089	743	381	–
Estimates of the present value of future cash flows	289	743	381	–
Risk adjustment for non-financial risk	240	160	80	–
Fulfilment cash flows	529	903	461	–
Contractual service margin	–			
Insurance contract liability	**529**			

IE88   In Year 1 all events occur as expected on initial recognition.

IE89   At the end of Year 2, the entity revises its estimates of future cash outflows for Year 3 to CU100, instead of CU400 (a decrease in the present value of CU286). The risk adjustment for non-financial risk related to those cash flows remains unchanged.

IE90   In Year 3, all events occur as expected at the end of Year 2.

Analysis

IE91   At the end of Year 1, applying paragraphs B96–B97, the entity analyses the source of changes in the fulfilment cash flows during the year to decide whether each change adjusts the contractual service margin. Using this information, a possible format for the reconciliation of the insurance contract liability required by paragraph 101 is as follows:

	Estimates of the present value of future cash flows	Risk adjustment for non-financial risk	Contractual service margin	Insurance contract liability
	CU	CU	CU	CU
Opening balance	–	–	–	–
Changes related to future service: new contracts	289	240	–	529
Cash inflows	800	–	–	800
Insurance finance expenses	54 (a)	– (b)	–	54
Changes related to current service	–	(80) (b)	– (c)	(80)
Cash outflows	(400)	–	–	(400)
Closing balance	743	160	–	903

(a)   In this example, insurance finance expenses of CU54 are CU1,089 (the sum of the estimates of the present value of the future cash flows on initial recognition of CU289 and the cash inflows of CU800 received at the beginning of Year 1) multiplied by the current discount rate of 5 per cent a year, applying paragraphs 36 and B72(a).

(b)   Applying paragraph 81, the entity chooses not to disaggregate the change in the risk adjustment for non-financial risk between the insurance service result and insurance finance income or expenses; therefore, the entity includes the entire change in the risk adjustment for non-financial risk as part of the insurance service result in the statement of profit or loss.

(c)   Applying paragraph 44(e), the entity does not recognise any contractual service margin in profit or loss for the year because the contractual service margin (before any allocation) equals zero.

IE92   A possible format for a reconciliation between the amounts recognised in the statement of financial position and the statement of profit or loss for Year 1 required by paragraph 100 is as follows:

	Liability for remaining coverage, excluding loss component	Loss component of the liability for remaining coverage	Liability for incurred claims	Insurance contract liability
	CU	CU	CU	CU
Opening balance	–	–	–	–
Cash inflows	800	–	–	800
Insurance service expenses: loss on onerous contracts	–	529 (a)	–	529
Insurance finance expenses	33	21 (b)	–	54 (c)
Insurance revenue	(289) (b)	–	–	(289)
Insurance service expenses: incurred expenses	–	(191) (b)	400	209
Cash outflows	–	–	(400)	(400)
Closing balance	**544**	**359**	**–**	**903**

(a)   Applying paragraph 49, the entity establishes the loss component of the liability for remaining coverage for an onerous group of contracts. The loss component determines the amounts presented in profit or loss as reversals of losses on onerous groups that are consequently excluded from the determination of insurance revenue.

(b)   Changes in fulfilment cash flows are allocated between the liability for remaining coverage excluding the loss component and the loss component of the liability for remaining coverage. See the table after paragraph IE93 and footnotes to that table for the calculation.

(c)   See the table after paragraph IE91 for the calculation. The whole amount of insurance finance expenses is related to the liability for remaining coverage because the liability for incurred claims is paid immediately after the expenses are incurred.

IE93   Applying paragraph 50(a), the entity allocates specified subsequent changes in fulfilment cash flows of the liability for remaining coverage on a systematic basis between the loss component of the liability for remaining coverage and the liability for remaining coverage excluding the loss component. The table below illustrates the systematic allocation of the changes in fulfilment cash flows for the liability for remaining coverage in Year 1.

	Liability for remaining coverage, excluding loss component	Loss component of the liability for remaining coverage	Total
	CU	CU	CU
Release of expected insurance service expenses for the incurred claims for the year	(241)	(159) [a]	(400)
Change in the risk adjustment for non-financial risk caused by the release from risk	(48)	(32) [a]	(80)
Insurance revenue	(289) [b]	–	
Insurance service expenses	–	(191)	

(a) Applying paragraph 50(a), the entity allocates the subsequent changes in the fulfilment cash flows of the liability for remaining coverage on a systematic basis between the loss component of the liability for remaining coverage and the liability for remaining coverage excluding the loss component. In this example the systematic allocation is based on the proportion of 39.8 per cent, calculated on initial recognition of the insurance contracts as the loss component of the liability for remaining coverage of CU529 relative to the total estimate of the present value of the future cash outflows plus risk adjustment for non-financial risk of CU1,329 (CU1,089 + CU240). Consequently, the entity allocates subsequent changes in the fulfilment cash flows to the loss component of the liability for remaining coverage as follows:

(i) the estimates of the future cash flows released from the liability for remaining coverage for the year of CU159, calculated by multiplying the expected insurance service expenses for the incurred claims for the year of CU400 by 39.8 per cent;

(ii) the change in the risk adjustment for non-financial risk caused by the release from risk of CU32, calculated by multiplying the total such change of CU80 by 39.8 per cent; and

(iii) the insurance finance expenses of CU21, calculated by multiplying the total insurance finance expenses of CU54 by 39.8 per cent.

...continued

(b) Insurance revenue of CU289 is:

    (i) determined by the entity applying paragraph B123, as the change in the liability for remaining coverage, excluding:

        1 changes that do not relate to services provided in the period, for example changes resulting from cash inflows from premiums received and changes related to insurance finance income or expenses; and

        2 changes that relate to services but for which the entity does not expect consideration, ie increases and decreases in the loss component of the liability for remaining coverage.

    Thus, in this example insurance revenue of CU289 is the difference between the opening and closing carrying amounts of the liability for remaining coverage of CU544 (CU0 – CU544) excluding insurance finance expenses of CU33 and cash inflows of CU800, ie CU289 = (CU544 – CU800 – CU33).

    (ii) analysed by the entity applying paragraph B124, as the sum of the changes in the liability for remaining coverage in the year that relate to services for which the entity expects to receive consideration. Those changes are:

        1 insurance service expenses incurred in the period (measured at the amounts expected at the beginning of the period), excluding amounts allocated to the loss component of the liability for remaining coverage;

        2 the change in risk adjustment for non-financial risk, excluding changes that adjust the contractual service margin because they relate to future service and amounts allocated to the loss component ie the change caused by the release from risk; and

        3 the amount of the contractual service margin recognised in profit or loss in the period.

    Thus, in this example insurance revenue of CU289 is the sum of the insurance service expenses for the incurred claims for the year of CU400 and the change in the risk adjustment for non-financial risk caused by the release from risk of CU80, minus amounts allocated to the loss component of the liability for remaining coverage of CU191 (CU159 + CU32), ie CU289 = CU400 + CU80 – CU191.

IE94   At the end of Year 2, applying paragraphs B96–B97, the entity analyses the source of changes in the fulfilment cash flows during the year to decide whether each change adjusts the contractual service margin, as follows:

	Estimates of the present value of future cash flows	Risk adjustment for non-financial risk	Contractual service margin	Insurance contract liability
	CU	CU	CU	CU
Opening balance	743	160	–	903
Insurance finance expenses	37 (a)	–	–	37
Changes related to future service	(286) (b)	–	103 (b)	(183)
Changes related to current service	–	(80)	(52) (c)	(132)
Cash outflows	(400)	–	–	(400)
Closing balance	94	80	51	225

(a)   In this example, insurance finance expenses of CU37 are the estimates of the present value of the future cash flows of CU743 at the beginning of Year 2 multiplied by the current discount rate of 5 per cent, determined applying paragraphs 36 and B72(a).

(b)   Applying paragraph 50(b), an entity allocates any subsequent decrease in fulfilment cash flows allocated to the group arising from changes in estimates of the future cash flows relating to future service of CU286 solely to the loss component until that component is reduced to zero (the decrease in fulfilment cash flows of CU183 was allocated to the loss component to reduce it to zero, see the table after paragraph IE95). An entity adjusts the contractual service margin only for the excess of the decrease in fulfilment cash flows over the amount allocated to the loss component of CU103 (CU286 – CU183).

(c)   Applying paragraph B119(b), the entity allocates the contractual service margin at the end of the period (before recognising any amounts in profit or loss) equally to each coverage unit provided in the current period and expected to be provided in the future. Applying paragraph B119(c), the entity recognises in profit or loss the amount allocated to coverage units provided in the period of CU52, which is CU103 divided by two years.

IE95   A possible format for a reconciliation between the amounts recognised in the statement of financial position and the statement of profit or loss for Year 2 required by paragraph 100 is as follows:

	Liability for remaining coverage, excluding loss component	Loss component of the liability for remaining coverage	Liability for incurred claims	Insurance contract liability
	CU	CU	CU	CU
Opening balance	544	359	–	903
Insurance finance expenses	22	15 [(a)]	–	37 [(b)]
Insurance revenue	(341) [(a)]	–	–	(341)
Insurance service expenses: incurred expenses	–	(191) [(a)]	400	209
Insurance service expenses: reversal of loss on onerous contracts	–	(183) [(c)]	–	(183)
Cash flows	–	–	(400)	(400)
Closing balance	**225**	**–**	**–**	**225**

(a)   Applying paragraph 50(a), the entity allocates the subsequent changes in fulfilment cash flows of the liability for remaining coverage on a systematic basis between the loss component of the liability for remaining coverage and the liability for remaining coverage, excluding the loss component. See the table after paragraph IE96 and footnotes to that table for more detailed calculations.

(b)   See the table after paragraph IE94 for the calculation. The whole amount of insurance finance expenses is related to the liability for remaining coverage because the liability for incurred claims is paid immediately after the expenses are incurred.

(c)   Applying paragraph 50(b), the entity allocates any subsequent decrease in fulfilment cash flows allocated to the group arising from changes in estimates of future cash flows relating to future service of CU286 (see the table after paragraph IE94) solely to the loss component until that component is reduced to zero. IFRS 17 does not specify the order in which an entity allocates the fulfilment cash flows in footnote (a) (applying paragraph 50(a)) and the allocation in this footnote (applying paragraph 50(b)). This example illustrates the result of making the allocation required by paragraph 50(a) before the allocation required by paragraph 50(b).

IE96   The table below illustrates the systematic allocation of the changes in fulfilment cash flows for the liability for remaining coverage in Year 2.

	Liability for remaining coverage, excluding loss component	Loss component of the liability for remaining coverage	Total
	CU	CU	CU
Release of expected insurance service expenses for the incurred claims for the year	(241)	(159) [(a)]	(400)
Change in the risk adjustment for non-financial risk caused by the release from risk	(48)	(32) [(a)]	(80)
Contractual service margin recognised in profit or loss for the year	(52)	–	(52)
Insurance revenue	(341) [(b)]	–	
Insurance service expenses	–	(191)	
Insurance finance expenses	22 [(b)]	(15) [(a)]	

(a)   Applying paragraph 50(a), the entity allocates the subsequent changes in the fulfilment cash flows of the liability for remaining coverage on a systematic basis between the loss component of the liability for remaining coverage and the liability for remaining coverage, excluding the loss component. In this example, the systematic allocation is based on the proportion of 39.8 per cent as the opening balance of the loss component of the liability for remaining coverage of CU359, relative to the total of the estimates of the present value of the future cash outflows plus risk adjustment for non-financial risk of CU903 (CU743 + CU160). Consequently, the entity allocates subsequent changes in fulfilment cash flows to the loss component of the liability for remaining coverage as follows:

   (i)   the estimates of the future cash flows released from the liability for remaining coverage for the year of CU159, calculated by multiplying the insurance service expenses for the incurred claims for the year of CU400 by 39.8 per cent;

   (ii)   the change in the risk adjustment for non-financial risk caused by the release from risk of CU32, calculated by multiplying the total such change of CU80 by 39.8 per cent; and

   (iii)   the insurance finance expenses of CU15, calculated by multiplying the total insurance finance expenses of CU37 by 39.8 per cent.

continued...

...continued

(b)   Insurance revenue of CU341 is:

    (i)   determined by the entity applying paragraph B123 as the difference between the opening and closing carrying amounts of the liability for remaining coverage, excluding changes related to the loss component of CU319 (CU544 – CU225), further excluding insurance finance expenses of CU22, ie CU341 = CU319 + CU22; and

    (ii) analysed by the entity applying paragraph B124 as the sum of the insurance service expenses for the incurred claims for the year of CU400, the change in the risk adjustment for non-financial risk caused by the release from risk of CU80 and the amount of the contractual service margin recognised in profit or loss in the period of CU52 minus the reversal of the loss component of the liability for remaining coverage of CU191 (CU159 + CU32), ie CU341 = CU400 + CU80 + CU52 – CU191.

IE97   At the end of Year 3, the coverage period ends and the group of insurance contracts is derecognised. Applying paragraphs B96–B97, the entity analyses the source of changes in the fulfilment cash flows during the year to decide whether each change adjusts the contractual service margin, as follows:

	Estimates of the present value of future cash flows	Risk adjustment for non-financial risk	Contractual service margin	Insurance contract liability
	CU	CU	CU	CU
Opening balance	94	80	51	225
Insurance finance expenses	5 [(a)]	–	3 [(b)]	8
Changes related to current service	–	(80)	(54) [(c)]	(134)
Cash outflows	(100)	–	–	(100)
Rounding difference	1	–	–	1
Closing balance	–	–	–	–

(a)   In this example, insurance finance expenses of CU5 are the estimates of the present value of the future cash flows of CU94 at the beginning of Year 3 multiplied by the current discount rate of 5 per cent, determined applying paragraphs 36 and B72(a).

(b)   Applying paragraph 44(b), the entity calculates interest accreted on the carrying amount of the contractual service margin of CU3 by multiplying the opening balance of CU51 by the discount rate of 5 per cent determined applying paragraphs 44(b) and B72(b).

continued...

...continued

	Estimates of the present value of future cash flows	Risk adjustment for non-financial risk	Contractual service margin	Insurance contract liability
(c)	The full contractual service margin is recognised in profit or loss because Year 3 is the last year of coverage.			

IE98   A possible format for a reconciliation between the amounts recognised in the statement of financial position and the statement of profit or loss for Year 3 required by paragraph 100 is as follows:

	Liability for remaining coverage, excluding loss component	Loss component of the liability for remaining coverage	Liability for incurred claims	Insurance contract liability
	CU	CU	CU	CU
Opening balance	225	–	–	225
Insurance revenue	(233) (a)	–	–	(233)
Insurance service expenses	–	–	100	100
Insurance finance expenses	8 (b)	–	–	8
Cash flows	–	–	(100)	(100)
Closing balance	–	–	–	–

(a)   Insurance revenue of CU233 is:

   (i)   determined by the entity applying paragraph B123 as the difference between the opening and closing carrying amounts of the liability for remaining coverage, excluding changes related to the loss component of CU225 (CU225–CU0), further excluding insurance finance expenses of CU8, ie CU233 = CU225 + CU8; and

   (ii)   analysed by the entity applying paragraph B124 as the sum of the insurance service expenses of CU100, the change in the risk adjustment for non-financial risk caused by the release from risk of CU54 and the contractual service margin recognised in profit or loss of CU54, ie CU233 = CU100 + CU80 + CU54 – CU1 rounding difference.

(b)   See the table after paragraph IE97 for the calculation. The whole amount of insurance finance expenses is related to the liability for remaining coverage because the liability for incurred claims is paid immediately after the expenses are incurred.

Measurement of groups of insurance contracts with direct participation features

Example 9—Measurement on initial recognition and subsequently of groups of insurance contracts with direct participation features (paragraphs 45 and B110–B114)

IE99   This example illustrates the measurement of groups of insurance contracts with direct participation features.

Assumptions

IE100   An entity issues 100 contracts that meet the criteria for insurance contracts with direct participation features applying paragraph B101. The coverage period is three years and starts when the insurance contracts are issued.

IE101   An entity receives a single premium of CU150 for each contract at the beginning of the coverage period. Policyholders will receive either:

(a)   CU170, or the account balance if it is higher, if the insured person dies during the coverage period; or

(b)   the value of the account balance at the end of the coverage period if the insured person survives until the end of the coverage period.

IE102   The entity calculates the account balance for each contract (the underlying items) at the end of each year as follows:

(a)   opening balance; plus

(b)   premiums received (if any); plus

(c)   the change in fair value of a specified pool of assets; minus

(d)   an annual charge equal to 2 per cent of the value of the account balance at the beginning of the year plus the change in fair value; minus

(e)   the value of the remaining account balance when the insured person dies or the coverage period ends.

IE103   The entity purchases the specified pool of assets and measures the assets at fair value through profit or loss. This example assumes that the entity sells assets to collect annual charges and pay claims. Hence, the assets that the entity holds equal the underlying items.

IE104   On initial recognition of the contracts, the entity:

(a)   expects that the fair value of the specified pool of assets will increase by 10 per cent a year;

(b)   determines the discount rate that reflects the characteristics of the nominal cash flows that do not vary based on returns on any underlying items is 6 per cent a year;

    (c)   estimates the risk adjustment for non-financial risk to be CU25 and expects to recognise it in profit or loss in Years 1–3 as follows: CU12, CU8 and CU5;

    (d)   estimates the time value of the guarantee inherent in providing a minimum death benefit;[1] and

    (e)   expects that one insured person will die at the end of each year and claims will be settled immediately.

IE105   During the coverage period, there are changes in the time value of the guarantee and changes in the fair value returns on underlying items, as follows:

    (a)   in Year 1, the fair value of the specified pool of assets increased by 10 per cent, as expected on initial recognition;

    (b)   in Year 2, the increase in fair value was lower than expected on initial recognition and equals 8 per cent; and

    (c)   in Year 3, the increase in fair value goes back to the initially expected 10 per cent.

IE106   In this example all other amounts are ignored, for simplicity.

Analysis

IE107   On initial recognition, the entity measures the group of insurance contracts and estimates the fulfilment cash flows at the end of each subsequent year as follows:

	Initial recognition	Year 1	Year 2	Year 3
	CU	CU	CU	CU
Estimates of the present value of future cash inflows	(15,000)	–	–	–
Estimates of the present value of future cash outflows[(a)]	14,180	15,413	16,757	–
Estimates of the present value of future cash flows	(820)	15,413	16,757	–
Risk adjustment for non-financial risk	25	13	5	–
Fulfilment cash flows	(795)	15,426	16,762	–
Contractual service margin	795			
Insurance contract (asset) / liability on initial recognition	–			

continued...

---

1   There is no prescribed method for the calculation of the time value of a guarantee, and a calculation of an amount separate from the rest of the fulfilment cash flows is not required.

...*continued*

(a) The entity calculates the estimates of the present value of the future cash outflows using current discount rates that reflect the characteristics of the future cash flows, determined applying paragraphs 36 and B72(a). The estimates of the present value of the future cash outflows include an estimate of the time value of the guarantee inherent in providing a minimum death benefit, measured consistently with observable market prices for the guarantee.

IE108 Applying paragraphs 45 and B110–B114, to account for the contractual service margin of the insurance contracts with direct participation features (see the table after paragraph IE111 for the reconciliation of the contractual service margin), the entity needs to:

(a) calculate the fair value of the underlying items in which the policyholders participate to adjust the contractual service margin for those changes; and

(b) analyse the changes in fulfilment cash flows to decide whether each change adjusts the contractual service margin.

IE109 The entity determines the fair value of the underlying items at the end of each reporting period as follows:

Underlying items[a] (the policyholder account balances)	Year 1	Year 2	Year 3	Total
	CU	CU	CU	CU
Opening balance (A)	–	16,008	16,772	N/A
Cash inflows: premiums	15,000	–	–	15,000
Change in fair value (B = 10% × A in Years 1 and 3, 8% × A in Year 2)	1,500	1,281	1,677	4,458
Annual charge (C = 2% × (A + B))	(330)	(346)	(369)	(1,045)
Cash outflows: payments for death claims (1/100, 1/99, 1/98 × (A + B + C))	(162)	(171)	(184)	(517)
Cash outflows: payments on maturity of contracts	–	–	(17,896)	(17,896)
Closing balance	16,008	16,772	–	N/A

(a) In this example, the underlying items equal the assets the entity holds. IFRS 17 defines underlying items as the items that determine some of the amounts payable to a policyholder. Underlying items could comprise any items; for example, a reference portfolio of assets.

IE110   The entity determines the changes in the fulfilment cash flows as follows:

Fulfilment cash flows	Year 1	Year 2	Year 3	Total
	CU	CU	CU	CU
Opening balance	–	15,426	16,461	N/A
Change related to future service: new contracts	(795)	–	–	(795)
Effect of the time value of money and financial risks and the changes therein (a)	1,403	1,214	1,624	4,241
Change related to current service: release from risk	(12)	(8)	(5)	(25)
Cash flows(b)	14,830	(171)	(18,080)	(3,421)
Closing balance	15,426 (c)	16,461 (c)	–	N/A

(a)   The effect of the time value of money and financial risks and the changes therein includes:

(i)   the changes in the time value of the guarantee inherent in providing a minimum death benefit; and

(ii)   the effect of changes in the obligation to the policyholder because of the change in the fair value of the underlying items in Years 2 and 3.

(b)   In Year 1, the entity receives premiums of CU15,000 and pays claims on death of CU170 (CU162 from the account balances and CU8 from the entity's account). In Year 2, the entity pays claims of CU171 only from the account balances because the value of the account balances is higher than the guaranteed amount of CU170. In Year 3, the entity pays claims on death of CU184 from the account balance and amounts at maturity of contracts of CU17,896 (see the table after paragraph IE109 for amounts paid from the account balances).

(c)   The entity determines the estimates of the present value of the future cash outflows using current discount rates that reflect the characteristics of the future cash flows, determined applying paragraphs 36 and B72(a). The estimates of the present value of the future cash outflows include an estimate of the time value of the guarantee inherent in providing a minimum death benefit, measured consistently with observable market prices for the guarantee.

IE111   Applying paragraph 45, the entity determines the carrying amount of the contractual service margin at the end of each reporting period as follows:

Contractual service margin	Year 1	Year 2	Year 3	Total
	CU	CU	CU	CU
Opening balance	–	592	328	N/A
Changes related to future service: new contracts	795	–	–	795
Change in the variable fee[(a)]:				
– change in the fair value of the underlying items	1,500	1,281	1,677	4,458
– effect of the time value of money and financial risks and the changes therein	(1,403)	(1,214)	(1,624)	(4,241)
Change related to current service: recognition in profit or loss[(b)]	(300)	(331)	(381)	(1,012)
Closing balance	**592**	**328**	**–**	**N/A**

(a)   Applying paragraphs B110–B113, the entity adjusts the contractual service margin for the net of changes in:

   (i)   the amount of the entity's share of the fair value of the underlying items; and

   (ii)   the fulfilment cash flows that do not vary based on the returns on underlying items related to future service, determined applying paragraph B96, plus the effect of the time value of money and financial risks and changes therein not arising from the underlying items.

Paragraph B114 permits the entity not to identify each adjustment to the contractual service margin separately, but rather to combine them. In addition, in this example there are no changes in the fulfilment cash flows that do not vary based on the returns on underlying items determined applying paragraph B96. Consequently, the entity could estimate the net adjustment to the contractual service margin as the net of changes in:

   (iii) the fair value of the underlying items (equals (i) plus the obligation to pay to the policyholder an amount equal to the fair value of the underlying items); and

   (iv)   the fulfilment cash flows related to the effect of the time value of money and financial risks and the changes therein (equals (ii) plus the obligation to pay to the policyholder an amount equal to the fair value of the underlying items).

continued...

...continued

Consequently, in this example, the adjustment to the contractual service margin for changes related to future service is the net of the change in fair value of the underlying items and changes in the fulfilment cash flows related to the effect of the time value of money and financial risks and the changes therein.

(b)   Applying paragraphs 45(e) and B119, the entity recognises in profit or loss the amount of contractual service margin determined by allocating the contractual service margin at the end of the period (before recognising any amounts in profit or loss) equally to each coverage unit provided in the current period and expected to be provided in the future, as follows:

(i)   in Year 1, the amount of the contractual service margin immediately before recognition in profit or loss is CU892 (the change related to the new contracts of CU795 plus the net change related to the variable fee of CU97 (CU1,500 – CU1,403));

(ii)   the entity has provided coverage for 100 contracts in Year 1, and expects to provide coverage for 99 contracts in Year 2 and 98 contracts in Year 3 (total coverage units of 297); thus

(iii)   the entity recognises CU300 of the contractual service margin in profit or loss in Year 1 (calculated as the contractual service margin of CU892 multiplied by 100 of the coverage units provided in Year 1 divided by 297 of the total coverage units).

The entity used the same methodology to calculate the amounts recognised in profit or loss in Years 2 and 3. Example 6 illustrates the recognition of the contractual service margin in profit or loss in more detail.

IE112   The amounts recognised in the statement of profit or loss for the period are as follows:

Statement of profit or loss[a]	Year 1	Year 2	Year 3	Total
	CU	CU	CU	CU
Insurance revenue	320 [a]	339	386	1,045 [b]
Insurance service expenses[c]	(8)	–	–	(8)
Insurance service result	**312**	**339**	**386**	**1,037**
Investment income[d]	1,500	1,281	1,677	4,458
Insurance finance expenses[e]	(1,500)	(1,281)	(1,677)	(4,458)
Finance result	**–**	**–**	**–**	**–**
Profit[f]	**312**	**339**	**386**	**1,037**

(a)   The detailed description of the method of the calculation of the insurance revenue is provided in the table after paragraph IE33. For Year 1, insurance revenue of CU320 is:

continued...

...continued

(i) determined by the entity applying paragraph B123 as the difference between the opening and closing carrying amounts of the liability for remaining coverage of CU(16,018), excluding premiums received of CU15,000, insurance finance expenses of CU1,500 and the investment component of CU162 (CU320 = CU(16,018) + CU15,000 + CU1,500 − CU162). The change in the carrying amount of the liability for remaining coverage in Year 1 of CU(16,018) is the opening balance of CU0 minus the closing balance of CU16,018 (the fulfilment cash flows at the end of Year 1 of CU15,426 plus the contractual service margin at the end of Year 1 of CU592). In this example, the liability for remaining coverage equals the total insurance liability because the liability for incurred claims is zero; and

(ii) analysed by the entity applying paragraph B124 as the sum of the expected insurance service expenses for the period of CU8, the change in the risk adjustment for non-financial risk caused by the release from risk of CU12 and the contractual service margin recognised in profit or loss of CU300 (CU320 = CU8 + CU12 + CU300).

(b) Applying paragraph B120, the entity calculates the total insurance revenue of CU1,045 as the amount of premiums paid to the entity of CU15,000 adjusted for the financing effect of CU4,458 (which in this example equals insurance finance expenses) and excluding the investment component paid from the account balances of CU18,413 (CU517 + CU17,896). In this example, total insurance revenue equals the total charges deducted from the policyholder account balances.

(c) Insurance service expenses of CU8 equals the amounts payable to the policyholder in the period of CU170 minus the investment component paid from the account balances of CU162. In Years 2 and 3, insurance service expenses are zero because all the amounts due to the policyholder are paid from the account balance (ie they are repayments of the investment component).

(d) Investment income related to the assets the entity holds is accounted for applying a different Standard.

(e) Applying paragraph B111, changes in the obligation to pay the policyholder an amount equal to the fair value of the underlying items do not relate to future service and do not adjust the contractual service margin. Applying paragraph 87, the entity recognises those changes as insurance finance income or expenses. For example, in Year 1 the change in fair value of the underlying items is CU1,500.

(f) This example assumes that the entity chooses to include all insurance finance income or expenses for the period in profit or loss, applying paragraph 89.

Measurement of groups of insurance contracts using the premium allocation approach

Example 10—Measurement on initial recognition and subsequently of groups of insurance contracts using the premium allocation approach (paragraphs 55–56, 59, 100 and B126)

IE113　This example illustrates the premium allocation approach for simplifying the measurement of the groups of insurance contracts.

Assumptions

IE114　An entity issues insurance contracts on 1 July 20x1. The insurance contracts have a coverage period of 10 months that ends on 30 April 20x2. The entity's annual reporting period ends on 31 December each year and the entity prepares interim financial statements as of 30 June each year.

IE115　On initial recognition the entity expects:

(a)　to receive premiums of CU1,220;

(b)　to pay directly attributable acquisition cash flows of CU20;

(c)　to incur claims and be released from risk evenly over the coverage period; and

(d)　that no contracts will lapse during the coverage period.

IE116　Furthermore, in this example:

(a)　facts and circumstances do not indicate that the group of contracts is onerous, applying paragraph 57; and

(b)　all other amounts, including the investment component, are ignored for simplicity.

IE117　Subsequently:

(a)　immediately after initial recognition the entity receives all the premiums and pays all the acquisition cash flows;

(b)　for the six-month reporting period ending on 31 December 20x1 there were claims incurred of CU600 with a risk adjustment for non-financial risk related to those claims of CU36;

(c)　for the six-month reporting period ending on 30 June 20x2 there were claims incurred of CU400 with a risk adjustment for non-financial risk related to those claims of CU24;

(d)　on 31 August 20x2, the entity revises its estimates related to all claims and settles them by paying CU1,070; and

(e)　for simplicity, the risk adjustment for non-financial risk related to the claims incurred is recognised in profit or loss when the claims are paid.

IE118　　The group of insurance contracts qualifies for the premium allocation approach applying paragraph 53(b). In addition, the entity expects that:

　　　　(a)　　the time between providing each part of the coverage and the related premium due date is no more than a year. Consequently, applying paragraph 56, the entity chooses not to adjust the carrying amount of the liability for remaining coverage to reflect the time value of money and the effect of financial risk (therefore no discounting or interest accretion is applied).

　　　　(b)　　the claims will be paid within one year after the claims are incurred. Consequently, applying paragraph 59(b), the entity chooses not to adjust the liability for incurred claims for the time value of money and the effect of financial risk.

IE119　　Further, applying paragraph 59(a), the entity chooses to recognise the insurance acquisition cash flows as an expense when it incurs the relevant costs.

Analysis

IE120　　The effect of the group of insurance contracts on the statement of financial position is as follows:

Statement of financial position	Dec 20x1	Jun 20x2	Dec 20x2
	CU	CU	CU
Cash	(1,200) [a]	(1,200)	(130) [b]
Insurance contract liability[c]	1,124	1,060	–
Equity	76	140	130

(a)　　The amount of cash at the end of December 20x1 of CU(1,200) equals the premium received of CU(1,220) on 1 July 20x1 plus the acquisition cash flows paid of CU20 on 1 July 20x1.

(b)　　The amount of cash at the end of December 20x2 of CU130 equals the net cash inflow on 1 July 20x1 of CU1,200 minus claims paid on 31 August 20x2 of CU1,070.

(c)　　The insurance contract liability is the sum of the liability for remaining coverage and the liability for incurred claims as illustrated in the table after paragraph IE122.

IE121　　Applying paragraph 100, the entity provides the reconciliation:

　　　　(a)　　between the amounts recognised in the statement of financial position and the statement of profit or loss separately for the liability for remaining coverage and the liability for incurred claims; and

(b) of the liability for incurred claims, disclosing a separate reconciliation for the estimates of the present value of the future cash flows and the risk adjustment for non-financial risk.

IE122   A possible format of the reconciliation required by paragraph 100 is as follows:

	Dec 20x1	Dec 20x1	Jun 20x2	Jun 20x2	Dec 20x2	Dec 20x2
	CU	CU	CU	CU	CU	CU
Liability for remaining coverage						
Opening balance		–		488		–
Cash inflows		1,220		–		–
Insurance revenue		(732) (a)		(488)		–
Closing balance		488 (b)		–		–
Liability for incurred claims						
Estimates of the present value of future cash flows		–	600		1,000	
Risk adjustment for non-financial risk		–	36		60	
Opening balance		–		636		1,060
Estimates of the present value of future cash flows	600		400		70	
Risk adjustment for non-financial risk	36		24		(60)	
Insurance service expenses		636 (c)		424 (d)		10 (e)
Estimates of the present value of future cash flows		–		(1,070)		(1,070)
Cash outflows		–		–		(1,070)
Closing balance		636		1,060		–

(a) See the table after paragraph IE123 for the calculation of insurance revenue.

(b) Applying paragraph 55, the entity measures the liability for remaining coverage at the end of December 20x1 of CU488 as premiums received in the period of CU1,220 minus the insurance revenue of CU732. The entity does not include acquisition cash flows in the liability for remaining coverage because it chooses to expense them when incurred applying paragraph 59(a).

(c) Insurance service expenses of CU636 for the period July 20x1 to December 20x1 comprise the incurred claims of CU600 and a risk adjustment for non-financial risk of CU36.

continued...

...continued

(d) Insurance service expenses of CU424 for the period January 20x2 to June 20x2 comprise the incurred claims of CU400 and a risk adjustment for non-financial risk of CU24.

(e) Insurance service expenses of CU10 comprises:

    (a) a gain of CU60—the risk adjustment for non-financial risk related to the liability for incurred claims recognised in profit or loss because of the release from risk; and

    (b) a loss of CU70—the difference between the previous estimate of claims incurred of CU1,000 and the payment of those claims of CU1,070.

IE123   The amounts included in the statement of profit or loss are as follows:

Statement of profit or loss	Dec 20x1		Jun 20x2		Dec 20x2	
For the 6 months ended						
	CU		CU		CU	
Insurance revenue	732	(a)	488	(a)	–	
Insurance service expenses	(656)	(b)	(424)	(b)	(10)	(b)
Profit / (loss)	**76**		**64**		**(10)**	

(a) Applying paragraph B126, the entity recognises insurance revenue for the period as the amount of expected premium receipts allocated to the period. In this example, the expected premium receipts are allocated to each period of coverage on the basis of the passage of time because the expected pattern of the release of risk during the coverage period does not differ significantly from the passage of time. Consequently, insurance revenue equals CU732 (60 per cent of CU1,220) for the six months ended December 20x1; and CU488 (40 per cent of CU1,220) for the four months ended April 20x2.

(b) See the table after paragraph IE122 for the calculation of insurance service expenses. For the six months ended December 20x1 insurance service expenses comprise CU636 of the amounts recognised from the change in the liability for incurred claims and CU20 of acquisition cash flows recognised in profit or loss as an expense, applying paragraph 59(a).

Measurement of groups of reinsurance contracts held

Example 11—Measurement on initial recognition of groups of reinsurance contracts held (paragraphs 63–65A)

IE124   This example illustrates the measurement on initial recognition of a group of reinsurance contracts that an entity holds.

Assumptions

IE125   An entity enters into a reinsurance contract that in return for a fixed premium covers 30 per cent of each claim from the underlying insurance contracts.

IE126   The entity measures the underlying group of insurance contracts on initial recognition as follows:

	Initial recognition CU
Estimates of the present value of future cash inflows	(1,000)
Estimates of the present value of future cash outflows	900
Estimates of the present value of future cash flows	(100)
Risk adjustment for non-financial risk	60
Fulfilment cash flows	(40)
Contractual service margin	40
Insurance contract (asset) / liability on initial recognition	–

IE127   Applying paragraph 23, the entity establishes a group comprising a single reinsurance contract held. In relation to this reinsurance contract held:

(a)   applying paragraph 63, the entity measures the estimates of the present value of the future cash flows for the group of reinsurance contracts held using assumptions consistent with those used to measure the estimates of the present value of the future cash flows for the group of the underlying insurance contracts. Consequently, the estimates of the present value of the future cash inflows are CU270 (recovery of 30 per cent of the estimates of the present value of the future cash outflows for the underlying group of insurance contracts of CU900);

(b)   applying paragraph 64, the entity determines the risk adjustment for non-financial risk to represent the amount of risk being transferred by the holder of the reinsurance contract to the issuer of this contract. Consequently, the entity estimates the risk adjustment for non-financial risk to be CU18 because the entity expects that it can transfer 30 per cent of the risk from underlying contracts to the reinsurer (30 per cent × CU60); and

(c)   the single reinsurance premium paid to the reinsurer is:

(i)   in Example 11A – CU260; and

(ii)   in Example 11B – CU300.

IE128   In this example the risk of non-performance of the reinsurer and all other amounts are ignored, for simplicity.

Analysis

IE129   The measurement of the reinsurance contract held is as follows:

	Example 11A Reinsurance contract asset	Example 11B Reinsurance contract asset
	CU	CU
Estimates of the present value of future cash inflows (recoveries)	(270)	(270)
Estimates of the present value of future cash outflows (premium paid)	260	300
Estimates of the present value of future cash flows	(10)	30
Risk adjustment for non-financial risk	(18)	(18)
Fulfilment cash flows	(28)	12
Contractual service margin of the reinsurance contract held[a]	28	(12)
Reinsurance contract asset on initial recognition	–	–
The effect on profit or loss will be:		
Profit / (loss) on initial recognition	–	–

(a)   Applying paragraph 65, the entity measures the contractual service margin of the reinsurance contract held at an amount equal to the sum of the fulfilment cash flows and any cash flows arising at that date. For reinsurance contracts held there is no unearned profit as there would be for insurance contracts but instead there is a net cost or net gain on purchasing the reinsurance contract.

Examples 12A and 12B—Measurement subsequent to initial recognition of groups of reinsurance contracts held (paragraph 66)

IE130   This example illustrates the subsequent measurement of the contractual service margin arising from a reinsurance contract held, when the underlying group of insurance contracts is not onerous and, separately, when the underlying group of insurance contracts is onerous.

IE131   This example is not a continuation of Example 11.

Assumptions

IE132   An entity enters into a reinsurance contract that in return for a fixed premium covers 30 per cent of each claim from the underlying insurance contracts (the entity assumes that it could transfer 30 per cent of non-financial risk from the underlying insurance contracts to the reinsurer).

IE133   In this example the effect of discounting, the risk of non-performance of the reinsurer and other amounts are ignored, for simplicity.

IE134   Applying paragraph 23, the entity establishes a group comprising a single reinsurance contract held.

IE135   Immediately before the end of Year 1, the entity measures the group of insurance contracts and the reinsurance contract held as follows:

	Insurance contract liability	Reinsurance contract asset
	CU	CU
Fulfilment cash flows (before the effect of any change in estimates)	300	(90)
Contractual service margin	100	(25) [a]
Insurance contract liability / (reinsurance contract asset) immediately before the end of Year 1	**400**	**(115)**

(a)   In this example, the difference between the contractual service margin for the reinsurance contract held of CU(25) and 30 per cent of the underlying group of insurance contracts of CU30 (30% × CU100) arises because of a different pricing policy between the underlying group of insurance contracts and the reinsurance contract held.

IE136   At the end of Year 1 the entity revises its estimate of the fulfilment cash outflows of the underlying group of insurance contracts as follows:

    (a)   in Example 12A—the entity estimates there is an increase in the fulfilment cash flows of the underlying group of insurance contracts of CU50 and a decrease in the contractual service margin by the same amount (the group of underlying insurance contracts is not onerous).

    (b)   in Example 12B—the entity estimates there is an increase in the fulfilment cash flows of the underlying group of insurance contracts of CU160. This change makes the group of underlying insurance contracts onerous and the entity decreases the contractual service margin by CU100 to zero and recognises the remaining CU60 as a loss in profit or loss.

Analysis

Example 12A—Underlying group of insurance contracts is not onerous

IE137   At the end of Year 1 the entity measures the insurance contract liability and the reinsurance contract asset as follows:

	Insurance contract liability	Reinsurance contract asset
	CU	CU
Fulfilment cash flows (including the effect of the change in estimates)	350	(105) (a)
Contractual service margin	50	(10) (b)
Insurance contract liability / (reinsurance contract asset) at the end of Year 1	**400**	**(115)**
The effect of the change in estimates on profit or loss will be:		
Profit / (loss) at the end of Year 1	–	–

(a)   The entity increases the fulfilment cash flows of the reinsurance contract held by 30 per cent of the change in fulfilment cash flows of the underlying group of insurance contracts (CU15 = 30% of CU50).

(b)   Applying paragraph 66, the entity adjusts the contractual service margin of the reinsurance contract held by the whole amount of the change in the fulfilment cash flows of this reinsurance contract held of CU15 from CU(25) to CU(10). This is because the whole change in the fulfilment cash flows allocated to the group of underlying insurance contracts adjusts the contractual service margin of those underlying insurance contracts.

Example 12B—Underlying group of insurance contracts is onerous

IE138   At the end of Year 1 the entity measures the insurance contract liability and the reinsurance contract asset as follows:

	Insurance contract liability	Reinsurance contract asset
	CU	CU
Fulfilment cash flows (including the effect of the change in estimates)	460	(138) (a)
Contractual service margin	–	5 (b)
Insurance contract liability / (reinsurance contract asset) at the end of Year 1	**460**	**(133)**
The effect on profit or loss will be:		
Profit / (loss) at the end of Year 1	**(60)**	**18** (b)

continued...

...continued

(a) The entity increases the fulfilment cash flows of the reinsurance contract held by CU48, which equals 30 per cent of the change in fulfilment cash flows of the underlying group of insurance contracts (CU48 = 30% of CU160).

(b) Applying paragraph 66, the entity adjusts the contractual service margin of the reinsurance contract held for change in fulfilment cash flows that relate to future service to the extent this change results from a change in fulfilment cash flows of the group of underlying insurance contracts that adjusts the contractual service margin for that group. Consequently, the entity recognises the change in fulfilment cash flows of the reinsurance contract held of CU48 as follows:

    (i) by adjusting the contractual service margin of the reinsurance contract held for CU30 of the change in the fulfilment cash flows. That CU30 is equivalent to the change in the fulfillment cash flows that adjusts the contractual service margin of the underlying contracts of CU100 (CU30 = 30% × CU100). Consequently, the contractual service margin of the reinsurance contract held of CU5 equals the contractual service margin on initial recognition of CU25 adjusted for the part of the change in the fulfilment cash flows of CU30 (CU5 = CU(25) + CU30).

    (ii) by recognising the remaining change in the fulfilment cash flows of the reinsurance contract held of CU18 immediately in profit or loss.

Example 12C—Measurement of a group of reinsurance contracts held that provides coverage for groups of underlying insurance contracts, including an onerous group (paragraphs 66A–66B and B119C–B119F)

IE138A   This example illustrates the initial and subsequent measurement of reinsurance contracts held when one of the groups of underlying insurance contracts is onerous.

Assumptions

IE138B   At the beginning of Year 1, an entity enters into a reinsurance contract that in return for a fixed premium covers 30 per cent of each claim from the groups of underlying insurance contracts. The underlying insurance contracts are issued at the same time as the entity enters into the reinsurance contract.

IE138C   In this example for simplicity it is assumed:

    (a) no contracts will lapse before the end of the coverage period;

    (b) there are no changes in estimates other than that described in paragraph IE138J; and

    (c) all other amounts, including the effect of discounting, the risk adjustments for non-financial risk, and the risk of non-performance of the reinsurer are ignored.

IE138D   Some of the underlying insurance contracts are onerous on initial recognition. Thus, applying paragraph 16, the entity establishes a group comprising the onerous contracts. The remainder of the underlying insurance contracts are expected to be profitable and, applying paragraph 16, in this example the entity establishes a single group comprising the profitable contracts.

IE138E   The coverage period of the underlying insurance contracts and the reinsurance contract held is three years starting from the beginning of Year 1. Services are provided evenly across the coverage periods.

IE138F   The entity expects to receive premiums of CU1,110 on the underlying insurance contracts immediately after initial recognition. Claims on the underlying insurance contracts are expected to be incurred evenly across the coverage period and are paid immediately after the claims are incurred.

IE138G   The entity measures the groups of underlying insurance contracts on initial recognition as follows:

	Profitable group of insurance contracts	Onerous group of insurance contracts	Total
	CU	CU	CU
Estimates of present value of future cash inflows	(900)	(210)	(1,110)
Estimates of present value of future cash outflows	600	300	900
Fulfilment cash flows	(300)	90	(210)
Contractual service margin	300	–	300
Insurance contract liability on initial recognition	–	90	90
Loss on initial recognition	–	(90)	(90)

IE138H   Applying paragraph 61, the entity establishes a group comprising a single reinsurance contract held. The entity pays a premium of CU315 to the reinsurer immediately after initial recognition. The entity expects to receive recoveries of claims from the reinsurer on the same day that the entity pays claims on the underlying insurance contracts.

IE138I   Applying paragraph 63, the entity measures the estimates of the present value of the future cash flows for the group of reinsurance contracts held using assumptions consistent with those used to measure the estimates of the present value of the future cash flows for the groups of underlying insurance contracts. Consequently, the estimate of the present value of the future cash inflows is CU270 (recovery of 30 per cent of the estimates of the present value of the future cash outflows for the groups of underlying insurance contracts of CU900).

IE138J At the end of Year 2, the entity revises its estimates of the remaining fulfilment cash outflows of the groups of underlying insurance contracts. The entity estimates that the fulfilment cash flows of the groups of underlying insurance contracts increase by 10 per cent, from future cash outflows of CU300 to future cash outflows of CU330. Consequently, the entity estimates the fulfilment cash flows of the reinsurance contract held also increase, from future cash inflows of CU90 to future cash inflows of CU99.

Analysis

IE138K The entity measures the group of reinsurance contracts held on initial recognition as follows:

	Initial recognition CU
Estimates of present value of future cash inflows (recoveries)	(270)
Estimates of present value of future cash outflows (premiums)	315
Fulfilment cash flows	**45**
Contractual service margin of the reinsurance contract held (before the loss-recovery adjustment)	(45)
Loss-recovery component	(27) [a]
Contractual service margin of the reinsurance contract held (after the loss-recovery adjustment)	**(72)** [b]
Reinsurance contract asset on initial recognition	**(27)** [c]
Income on initial recognition	**27** [a]

(a) Applying paragraph 66A, the entity adjusts the contractual service margin of the reinsurance contract held and recognises income to reflect the loss recovery. Applying paragraph B119D, the entity determines the adjustment to the contractual service margin and the income recognised as CU27 (the loss of CU90 recognised for the onerous group of underlying insurance contracts multiplied by 30 per cent, the percentage of claims the entity expects to recover).

(b) The contractual service margin of CU45 is adjusted by CU27, resulting in a contractual service margin of CU72, reflecting a net cost on the reinsurance contract held.

(c) The reinsurance contract asset of CU27 comprises the fulfilment cash flows of CU45 (net outflows) and a contractual service margin reflecting a net cost of CU72. Applying paragraph 66B, the entity establishes a loss-recovery component of the asset for remaining coverage of CU27 depicting the recovery of losses recognised applying paragraph 66A.

IE138L At the end of Year 1, the entity measures the insurance contract liability and the reinsurance contract asset as follows:

	Insurance contract liability		Reinsurance contract asset
	Profitable group of insurance contracts	Onerous group of insurance contracts	
	CU	CU	CU
Estimates of present value of future cash inflows (recoveries)	–	–	(180)
Estimates of present value of future cash outflows (claims)	400	200	–
Fulfilment cash flows	400	200	(180)
Contractual service margin	200	–	(48) (a)
Insurance contract liability	**600**	**200**	
Reinsurance contract asset			**(228)**

(a) Applying paragraphs 66(e) and B119, the entity determines the amount of the contractual service margin recognised in profit or loss for the service received in Year 1 as CU24, which is calculated by dividing the contractual service margin on initial recognition of CU72 by the coverage period of three years. Consequently, the contractual service margin of the reinsurance contract held at the end of Year 1 of CU48 equals the contractual service margin on initial recognition of CU72 minus CU24.

IE138M At the end of Year 2, the entity measures the insurance contract liability and the reinsurance contract asset as follows:

	Insurance contract liability		Reinsurance contract asset
	Profitable group of insurance contracts	Onerous group of insurance contracts	
	CU	CU	CU
Estimates of present value of future cash inflows (recoveries)	–	–	(99) (a)
Estimates of present value of future cash outflows (claims)	220 (a)	110 (a)	–
Fulfilment cash flows	220	110	(99)
Contractual service margin	90 (b)	–	(21) (e)
Insurance contract liability	**310**	**110**	
Reinsurance contract asset			**(120)**
Recognition of loss and recovery of loss		**(10) (c)**	**3 (d)**

continued...

...continued

(a)   The entity increases the expected remaining cash outflows of the groups of underlying insurance contracts by 10 per cent for each group (CU30 in total) and increases the expected remaining cash inflows of the reinsurance contract held by 10 per cent of the expected recoveries of CU90 (CU9).

(b)   Applying paragraph 44(c), the entity adjusts the carrying amount of the contractual service margin of CU200 by CU20 for the changes in fulfilment cash flows relating to future service. Applying paragraph 44(e), the entity also adjusts the carrying amount of the contractual service margin by CU90 for the amount recognised as insurance revenue ((CU200 – CU20) ÷ 2). The resulting contractual service margin at the end of Year 2 is CU90 (CU200 – CU20 – CU90).

(c)   Applying paragraph 48, the entity recognises in profit or loss an amount of CU10 for the changes in the fulfilment cash flows relating to future service of the onerous group of underlying insurance contracts.

(d)   Applying paragraph 66(c)(i), the entity adjusts the contractual service margin of the reinsurance contract held for the change in fulfilment cash flows that relate to future service unless the change results from a change in fulfilment cash flows allocated to a group of underlying insurance contracts that does not adjust the contractual service margin for that group. Consequently, the entity recognises the change in the fulfilment cash flows of the reinsurance contract held of CU9 by:

   (i)   recognising immediately in profit or loss CU3 of the change in the fulfilment cash flows of the reinsurance contract held (30 per cent of the CU10 change in the fulfilment cash flows of the onerous group of underlying insurance contracts that does not adjust the contractual service margin of that group); and

   (ii)   adjusting the contractual service margin of the reinsurance contract held by CU6 of the change in the fulfilment cash flows (CU9 – CU3).

(e)   Consequently, the contractual service margin of the reinsurance contract held of CU21 equals the contractual service margin at the end of Year 1 of CU48 adjusted by CU6 and by CU21 of the contractual service margin recognised in profit or loss for the service received in Year 2 (CU21 = (CU48 – CU6) ÷ 2).

IE138N   A possible format of the reconciliation required by paragraph 100 between the amounts recognised in the statement of financial position and the statement of profit or loss for Year 2 is as follows:

	Asset for remaining coverage, excluding loss-recovery component	Loss-recovery component of the asset for remaining coverage	Asset for incurred claims	Reinsurance contract asset
	CU	CU	CU	CU
Opening balance	(210)	(18) [(b)]	–	(228)
Allocation of reinsurance premiums paid[(a)]	102 [(c)]	–	–	102
Amount recovered from the reinsurer[(a)]	–	6 [(d)]	(90)	(84)
Cash flows	–	–	90	90
Closing balance	**(108)**	**(12)**	**–**	**(120)**

(a)   Applying paragraph 86, the entity decides to present separately the amounts recovered from the reinsurer and an allocation of the premiums paid.

(b)   The loss-recovery component of CU18 at the beginning of Year 2 is calculated as the loss-recovery component of CU27 on initial recognition less the reversal of the loss-recovery component of CU9 in Year 1.

(c)   The allocation of reinsurance premiums paid of CU102 is:

   (i)   determined applying paragraph B123 as the difference between the opening and closing carrying amount of the asset for remaining coverage of CU102, ie CU210 – CU108.

   (ii)   analysed applying paragraph B124 as the sum of the recoveries for the incurred claims of the underlying insurance contracts of CU90 less the reversal of the loss-recovery component of CU9 and the contractual service margin of the reinsurance contract held recognised in profit or loss in the period of CU21 (see the table after paragraph IE138M), ie CU102 = CU90 – CU9 + CU21.

(d)   The amount recovered from the reinsurer relating to the loss-recovery component of CU6 is the net of the reversal of the loss-recovery component of CU9 and the additional loss-recovery component of CU3. Applying paragraph 86(ba), amounts recognised relating to the recovery of losses are treated as amounts recovered from the reinsurer.

IE138O   The amounts presented in the statement of profit or loss corresponding to the amounts analysed in the tables above are:

Statement of profit or loss	Year 1	Year 2	Year 3	Total
	CU	CU	CU	CU
Insurance revenue	370	360	380	1,110
Insurance service expenses	(360)	(280)	(290)	(930)
Insurance contracts issued total	10 (b)	80 (d)	90 (f)	180
Allocation of reinsurance premiums paid[(a)]	(105)	(102)	(108)	(315)
Amount recovered from reinsurer[(a)]	108	84	87	279
Reinsurance contracts held total	3 (c)	(18) (e)	(21) (g)	(36)
Insurance service result	13	62	69	144

(a)   Applying paragraph 86, the entity decides to present separately the amounts recovered from the reinsurer and an allocation of the premiums paid.

(b)   For Year 1, the profit of CU10 from the groups of underlying insurance contracts is calculated as follows:

   (i)   insurance revenue of CU370, which is analysed as the sum of the insurance service expenses from the claims incurred of CU270 (CU300 minus the reversal of the loss component of CU30) and the contractual service margin of CU100 recognised in profit or loss in the period (CU370 = CU270 + CU100); minus

   (ii)   insurance service expenses of CU360, which are the sum of the loss component of the onerous group of CU90 and the claims incurred in the period of CU300 minus the reversal of the loss component of CU30 (CU360 = CU90 + CU300 − CU30).

(c)   For Year 1, the income of CU3 from the reinsurance contract held is the net of:

   (i)   the allocation of reinsurance premiums paid of CU105, which is the sum of the recoveries for the incurred claims from the underlying insurance contracts of CU90 less the reversal of the loss-recovery component of CU9 and the contractual service margin of the reinsurance contracts held of CU24 recognised in profit or loss in the period (CU105 = CU90 − CU9 + CU24); and

   (ii)   the amounts recovered from the reinsurer of CU108, which are the income of CU27 on initial recognition and the recoveries for the incurred claims from the underlying insurance contracts of CU90 minus the reversal of the loss-recovery component of CU9 (CU108 = CU27 + CU90 − CU9).

continued...

...continued

(d)   For Year 2, the profit of CU80 from the groups of underlying insurance
        contracts is calculated as follows:

    (i)   insurance revenue of CU360, which is analysed as the sum of the
                insurance service expenses from the claims incurred of CU270 (CU300
                minus the reversal of the loss component of CU30) and the contractual
                service margin of CU90 recognised in profit or loss in the period (CU360
                = CU270 + CU90); minus

    (ii)   insurance service expenses of CU280, which are the sum of the increase
                in the loss component resulting from the changes in the fulfilment cash
                flows of the onerous group of CU10 and the claims incurred of CU300
                minus the reversal of the loss component of CU30 (CU280 = CU10 +
                CU300 − CU30).

(e)   For Year 2, the expense of CU18 from the reinsurance contract held is the net of:

    (i)   the allocation of reinsurance premiums paid of CU102, which is the sum
                of the recoveries for the incurred claims from the underlying insurance
                contracts of CU90 less the reversal of the loss-recovery component of
                CU9 and the contractual service margin of the reinsurance contract held
                of CU21 recognised in profit or loss in the period (CU102 = CU90 − CU9 +
                CU21); and

    (ii)   the amounts recovered from the reinsurer of CU84, which are the sum of
                the recoveries for the incurred claims from the underlying insurance
                contracts of CU90 minus the reversal of the loss-recovery component of
                CU9 and the additional loss-recovery component of CU3 (CU84 = CU90 −
                CU9 + CU3).

(f)   For Year 3, the profit of CU90 from the groups of underlying insurance
        contracts is calculated as follows:

    (i)   insurance revenue of CU380, which is analysed as the sum of the
                insurance service expenses from the claims incurred of CU290 (CU330
                minus the reversal of the loss component of CU40) and the contractual
                service margin of CU90 recognised in profit or loss in the period (CU380
                = CU290 + CU90); minus

    (ii)   insurance service expenses of CU290, which are the claims incurred of
                CU330 minus the reversal of the loss component of CU40 (CU290 =
                CU330 − CU40).

continued...

...continued

(g)		For Year 3, the expense of CU21 from the reinsurance contract held is the net of:
	(i)	the allocation of reinsurance premiums paid of CU108, which is the sum of the recoveries for the incurred claims from the underlying insurance contracts of CU99 less the reversal of the loss-recovery component of CU12 and the contractual service margin of the reinsurance contracts held of CU21 recognised in profit or loss in the period (CU108 = CU99 − CU12 + CU21); and
	(ii)	the amounts recovered from the reinsurer of CU87, which are the recoveries for the incurred claims from the underlying insurance contracts of CU99 minus the reversal of the loss-recovery component of CU12 (CU87 = CU99 − CU12).

Measurement of insurance contracts acquired (paragraphs 38 and B94–B95A)

Example 13—Measurement on initial recognition of insurance contracts acquired in a transfer from another entity

IE139   This example illustrates the initial recognition of a group of insurance contracts acquired in a transfer that is not a business combination.

Assumptions

IE140   An entity acquires insurance contracts in a transfer from another entity. The seller pays CU30 to the entity to take on those insurance contracts.

IE141   Applying paragraph B93 the entity determines that the insurance contracts acquired in a transfer form a group applying paragraphs 14–24, as if it had entered into the contracts on the date of the transaction.

IE142   On initial recognition, the entity estimates the fulfilment cash flows to be:

(a)   in Example 13A — net outflow (or liability) of CU20; and

(b)   in Example 13B — net outflow (or liability) of CU45.

IE143   The entity does not apply the premium allocation approach to the measurement of the insurance contracts.

IE144   In this example all other amounts are ignored, for simplicity.

Analysis

IE145   Applying paragraph B94, the consideration received from the seller is a proxy for the premium received. Consequently, on initial recognition, the entity measures the insurance contract liability as follows:

	Example 13A	Example 13B
	CU	CU
Fulfilment cash flows	20	45
Contractual service margin	10 (a)	– (b)
Insurance contract liability on initial recognition	**30** (c)	**45** (b)
The effect on profit or loss will be:		
Profit / (loss) on initial recognition	–	**(15)** (b)

(a)   Applying paragraph 38, the entity measures the contractual service margin on initial recognition of a group of insurance contracts at an amount that results in no income or expenses arising from the initial recognition of the fulfilment cash flows and any cash flows arising from the contracts in the group at that date. On initial recognition, the fulfilment cash flows are a net inflow (or asset) of CU10 (proxy for the premiums received of CU30 minus the fulfilment cash flows of CU20). Consequently, the contractual service margin is CU10.

(b)   Applying paragraphs 47 and B95A, the entity concludes that the group of insurance contracts is onerous on initial recognition. This is because the total of the fulfilment cash flows of a net outflow of CU45 and cash flows arising at that date (proxy for the premiums of net inflow of CU30) is a net outflow of CU15. The entity recognises a loss in profit or loss for the net outflow of CU15, resulting in the carrying amount of the liability for the group of CU45 being the sum of the fulfilment cash flows of CU45 and the contractual service margin of zero.

(c)   Applying paragraph 32, on initial recognition the entity measures a group of insurance contracts at the total of the fulfilment cash flows and the contractual service margin. Consequently, the entity recognises an insurance contract liability of CU30 as the sum of the fulfilment cash flows of CU20 and the contractual service margin of CU10.

Example 14—Measurement on initial recognition of insurance contracts acquired in a business combination

IE146   This example illustrates the initial recognition of a group of insurance contracts acquired in a business combination within the scope of IFRS 3 *Business Combinations*.

Assumptions

IE147   An entity acquires insurance contracts as part of a business combination within the scope of IFRS 3 and it:

(a)   determines that the transaction results in goodwill applying IFRS 3.

(b)   determines, applying paragraph B93, that those insurance contracts form a group consistent with paragraphs 14–24, as if it had entered into the contracts on the date of the transaction.

IE148   On initial recognition, the entity estimates that the fair value of the group of insurance contracts is CU30 and the fulfilment cash flows are as follows:

(a)   in Example 14A – outflow (or liability) of CU20; and

(b)   in Example 14B – outflow (or liability) of CU45.

IE149   The entity does not apply the premium allocation approach to the measurement of the insurance contracts.

IE150   In this example all other amounts are ignored, for simplicity.

Analysis

IE151   Applying paragraph B94, the fair value of the group of insurance contracts is a proxy for the premium received. Consequently, on initial recognition, the entity measures the liability for the group of insurance contracts as follows:

	Example 14A	Example 14B
	CU	CU
Fulfilment cash flows	20	45
Contractual service margin	10 (a)	– (b)
Insurance contract liability on initial recognition	30 (c)	45 (d)
The effect on profit or loss will be:		
Profit / (loss) on initial recognition	–	– (b)

(a)   Applying paragraph 38, the entity measures the contractual service margin on initial recognition of a group of insurance contracts at an amount that results in no income or expenses arising from the initial recognition of the fulfilment cash flows and any cash flows arising from the contracts in the group at that date. On initial recognition, the fulfilment cash flows are a net inflow (or asset) of CU10 (proxy for the premiums received of CU30 minus the fulfilment cash flows of CU20). Consequently, the contractual service margin equals CU10.

(b)   Applying paragraphs 38 and 47, the entity recognises the contractual service margin as zero because the sum of fulfilment cash flows and cash flows at the date of initial recognition is a net outflow of CU15. Applying paragraph B95A, the entity recognises the excess of CU15 of the fulfilment cash flows of CU45 over the consideration received of CU30 as part of the goodwill on the business combination.

continued...

...continued

(c)   Applying paragraph 32, the entity measures a group of insurance contracts at the total of the fulfilment cash flows and the contractual service margin. Consequently, the entity recognises an insurance contract liability of CU30 on initial recognition as the sum of the fulfilment cash flows (a net outflow) of CU20 and the contractual service margin of CU10.

(d)   Applying paragraph 32, the entity measures a group of insurance contracts at the total of the fulfilment cash flows and the contractual service margin. Consequently, the entity recognises an insurance contract liability of CU45 on initial recognition as the sum of the fulfilment cash flows of CU45 and the contractual service margin of zero.

Insurance finance income or expenses

Example 15—Systematic allocation of the expected total insurance finance income or expenses (paragraphs B130 and B132(a))

IE152   Paragraph 88 allows an entity to make an accounting policy choice to disaggregate insurance finance income or expenses for the period to include in profit or loss an amount determined by a systematic allocation of the expected total finance income or expenses over the duration of the group of insurance contracts.

IE153   This example illustrates the two ways of systematically allocating the expected total insurance finance income or expenses for insurance contracts for which financial risk has a substantial effect on the amounts paid to the policyholders as set out in paragraph B132(a).

Assumptions

IE154   An entity issues 100 insurance contracts with a coverage period of three years. Those contracts:

(a)   meet the definition of insurance contracts because they offer a fixed payment on death. However, to isolate the effects illustrated in this example, and for simplicity, any fixed cash flows payable on death are ignored.

(b)   do not meet the criteria for insurance contracts with direct participation features applying paragraph B101.

IE155   On initial recognition of the group of insurance contracts:

(a)   the entity receives a single premium of CU15 for each contract (the total for the group is CU1,500).

(b)   the entity invests premiums received in fixed income bonds with a duration of two years and expects a return of 10 per cent a year. The entity expects to reinvest the proceeds from the maturity of the bonds in similar financial instruments with a return of 10 per cent a year.

    (c)   the entity expects to pay the policyholders CU1,890 at the end of Year 3 (a present value of CU1,420). This amount is calculated on the basis of the entity's policy for the return paid to the policyholders, as follows:

        (i)   in Example 15A the entity expects to pay 94.54 per cent of the accumulated value of the invested assets at the end of the coverage period; and

        (ii)   in Example 15B the entity expects to increase the account balances of the policyholders by 8 per cent each year (the expected crediting rate).

IE156   At the end of Year 1, the market interest rate falls from 10 per cent a year to 5 per cent a year and the entity revises its expected future cash flows to be paid in Year 3

IE157   In this example all other amounts, including the risk adjustment for non-financial risk, are ignored for simplicity.

IE158   Applying paragraph 88, the entity chooses to disaggregate insurance finance income or expenses for the period to include in profit or loss an amount determined by a systematic allocation of the expected total finance income or expenses over the duration of the contracts, as follows:

    (a)   in Example 15A, the entity uses a rate that allocates the remaining revised expected finance income or expenses over the remaining duration of the group of contracts at a constant rate, applying paragraph B132(a)(i); and

    (b)   in Example 15B, the entity uses an allocation based on the amounts credited in the period and expected to be credited in future periods, applying paragraph B132(a)(ii).

Analysis

Example 15A—Effective yield approach

IE159   Applying paragraph B132(a)(i), the entity uses a rate that allocates the remaining revised expected finance income or expenses over the remaining duration of the group of contracts at a constant rate (an 'effective yield approach'). The effective yield approach is not the same as the effective interest method as defined in IFRS 9 *Financial Instruments*.

IE160   The constant rate at the date of initial recognition of the contracts of 10 per cent a year is calculated as $(CU1,890 \div CU1,420)^{\frac{1}{3}} - 1$. Consequently, the estimates of the present value of the future cash flows included in the carrying amount of the insurance contract liability at the end of Year 1 are CU1,562, calculated as $CU1,420 \times 1.1$.

IE161   At the end of Year 1, the market interest rate falls from 10 per cent a year to 5 per cent a year. Consequently, the entity revises its expectations about future cash flows as follows:

(a)   it expects to achieve a return of 5 per cent in Year 3 (instead of 10 per cent) after reinvesting the maturity proceeds of the fixed income securities that mature at the end of Year 2;

(b)   the fixed income securities it expects to acquire at the end of Year 2 will generate CU1,906 at the end of Year 3; and

(c)   it will pay policyholders CU1,802 at the end of Year 3 (94.54% × CU1,906).

IE162   At the end of Year 1 the entity revises the constant rate used to allocate expected insurance finance income or expenses to reflect the expected reduction in the future cash flows at the end of Year 3 from CU1,890 to CU1,802:

(a)   the entity uses the revised constant rate to accrete the estimates of the present value of the future cash flows included in the carrying amount of the insurance contract liability at the end of Year 1, ie CU1,562, to the revised cash outflow at the end of Year 3 of CU1,802; and

(b)   the revised constant rate of 7.42 per cent a year is calculated as $(1{,}802 \div 1{,}562)^{\frac{1}{2}} - 1$.

IE163   The effect of the change in discount rates on the carrying amounts of the estimates of the present value of the future cash flows, included in the carrying amount of the insurance contract liability, is shown in the table below:

	Initial recognition	Year 1	Year 2	Year 3
	CU	CU	CU	CU
Estimates of the future cash flows at the end of Year 3	1,890	1,802	1,802	1,802
Estimates of the present value of future cash flows at current discount rates (A)	1,420	1,635 [(a)]	1,716	1,802
Estimates of the present value of future cash flows at the constant rate (B)	1,420	1,562 [(b)]	1,678	1,802
Amount accumulated in other comprehensive income (A – B)	–	73	38	–

(a)   CU1,635 equals the estimates of the future cash flows at the end of Year 3 of CU1,802 discounted at the current market rate of 5 per cent a year, ie CU1,802 ÷ 1.05^2 = CU1,635.

(b)   CU1,562 equals the estimates of the future cash flows at the end of Year 3 of CU1,802 discounted at the constant rate of 7.42 per cent a year, ie CU1,802 ÷ 1.0742^2 = CU1,562.

IE164   The insurance finance income and expenses, arising from the fulfilment cash flows, included in profit or loss and other comprehensive income are as follows:

Insurance finance income and expenses arising from the fulfilment cash flows	Year 1	Year 2	Year 3
	CU	CU	CU
In profit or loss	(142) (a)	(116)	(124)
In other comprehensive income	(73) (b)	35	38
In total comprehensive income	(215) (c)	(81)	(86)

(a)   Applying paragraph B132(a)(i), the entity will recognise in profit or loss the insurance finance expenses calculated as the change in estimates of the present value of the future cash flows at the constant rate. In Year 1, the finance expenses of CU142 is the difference between the estimates of the present value of the future cash flows at the original constant rate of 10 per cent at the end of Year 1 of CU1,562 and the corresponding amount at the beginning of the period of CU1,420.

(b)   Applying paragraph B130(b), the entity includes in other comprehensive income the difference between the amount recognised in total comprehensive income and the amount recognised in profit or loss. For example, in Year 1 the amount included in other comprehensive income of CU(73) is CU(215) minus CU(142). In Years 1–3, the total other comprehensive income equals zero (CU0 = CU(73) + CU35 + CU38).

(c)   The entity recognises in total comprehensive income the change in estimates of the present value of the future cash flows at the current discount rate. In Year 1, the total insurance finance expenses of CU(215) is the difference between the estimates of the present value of the future cash flows at the current discount rate at the beginning of Year 1 of CU1,420 and the corresponding amount at the end of Year 1 of CU1,635.

Example 15B—Projected crediting rate approach

IE165   Applying paragraph B132(a)(ii), the entity uses an allocation based on the amounts credited in the period and expected to be credited in future periods (a 'projected crediting rate approach'). In addition, applying paragraph B130(b), the entity needs to ensure that the allocation results in the amounts recognised in other comprehensive income over the duration of the group of contracts totalling to zero. In order to do so, the entity calculates a series of discount rates applicable to each reporting period which, when applied to the initial carrying amount of the liability equals the estimate of future cash flows. This series of discount rates is calculated by multiplying the expected crediting rates in each period by a constant factor (K).

IE166   On initial recognition the entity expects to achieve a return on underlying items of 10 per cent each year and to credit the policyholder account balances by 8 per cent each year (the expected crediting rate). Consequently, the entity expects to pay policyholders CU1,890 at the end of Year 3 (CU1,500 × 1.08 × 1.08 × 1.08 = CU1,890).

IE167   In Year 1, the entity credits the policyholder account balances with a return of 8 per cent a year, as expected at the date of initial recognition.

IE168   At the end of Year 1, the market interest rate falls from 10 per cent a year to 5 per cent a year. Consequently, the entity revises its expectations about cash flows as follows:

    (a)   it will achieve a return of 5 per cent in Year 3 after reinvesting the maturity proceeds of the bonds that mature at the end of Year 2;

    (b)   it will credit the policyholder account balances 8 per cent in Year 2, and 3 per cent in Year 3; and

    (c)   it will pay policyholders CU1,802 at the end of Year 3 (CU1,500 × 1.08 × 1.08 × 1.03 = CU1,802).

IE169   The entity allocates the remaining expected finance income or expenses over the remaining life of the contracts using the series of discount rates calculated as the projected crediting rates multiplied by the constant factor (K). The constant factor (K) and the series of discount rates based on crediting rates at the end of Year 1 are as follows:

    (a)   the product of the actual crediting rate in Year 1 and expected crediting rates in Years 2 and 3 equals 1.20 (1.08 × 1.08 × 1.03);

    (b)   the carrying amount of the liability increases by a factor of 1.269 over three years because of the interest accretion (CU1,802 ÷ CU1,420);

    (c)   consequently, each crediting rate needs to be adjusted by a constant factor (K), as follows: 1.08K × 1.08K × 1.03K = 1.269;

    (d)   the constant K equals 1.0184 calculated as $(1.269 \div 1.20)^{1/3}$; and

    (e)   the resulting accretion rate for Year 1 is 10 per cent (calculated as 1.08 × 1.0184).

IE170   The carrying amount of the liability at the end of Year 1 for the purposes of allocating insurance finance income or expenses to profit or loss is CU1,562 (CU1,420 × 1.08 × 1.0184).

IE171   The actual crediting rates for Years 2 and 3 are as expected at the end of Year 1. The resulting accretion rate for Year 2 is 10 per cent (calculated as (1.08 × 1.0184) − 1) and for Year 3 is 4.9 per cent (calculated as (1.03 × 1.0184) − 1).

	Initial recognition	Year 1	Year 2	Year 3
	CU	CU	CU	CU
Estimates of future cash flows at the end of Year 3	1,890	1,802	1,802	1,802
Estimates of the present value of future cash flows at current discount rates (A)	1,420	1,635	1,716 (a)	1,802
Estimates of the present value of future cash flows at discount rates based on projected crediting (B)	1,420	1,562	1,718 (b)	1,802
Amount accumulated in other comprehensive income (A − B)	–	73	(2) (c)	–

(a)   CU1,716 equals the estimates of the future cash flows at the end of Year 3 of CU1,802 discounted at the current market rate of 5 per cent a year, ie CU1,802 ÷ 1.05 = CU1,716.

(b)   CU1,718 equals the estimates of the future cash flows at the end of Year 3 of CU1,802 discounted at the projected crediting rate of 4.9 per cent a year, ie CU1,802 ÷ 1.049 = CU1,718.

(c)   There is an amount of CU2 accumulated in other comprehensive income at the end of Year 2 because the discount rate based on projected crediting of 4.9 per cent a year (1.03 × K) is different from the current discount rate of 5 per cent a year.

IE172   The insurance finance income and expenses included in profit or loss and other comprehensive income are as follows:

Insurance finance income and expenses arising from fulfilment cash flows	Year 1	Year 2	Year 3
	CU	CU	CU
In profit or loss	(142) (a)	(156)	(84)
In other comprehensive income	(73) (b)	75	(2)
In total comprehensive income	(215) (c)	(81)	(86)

(a)   Applying paragraph B132(a)(ii), the entity will recognise in profit or loss the insurance finance expenses calculated as the change in the estimates of the present value of the future cash flows at the projected crediting rate. In Year 1, the insurance finance expenses of CU142 is the difference between the estimates of the present value of the future cash flows at the original crediting rate of 10 per cent at the end of Year 1 of CU1,562 and the corresponding amount at the beginning of the period of CU1,420.

continued...

...continued

(b)   Applying paragraph B130(b), the entity includes in other comprehensive income the difference between the amount recognised in total comprehensive income and the amount recognised in profit or loss. For example, in Year 1 the amount included in other comprehensive income of CU(73) is CU(215) minus CU(142). In Years 1–3, the total other comprehensive income equals zero (CU0 = CU(73) + CU75 + CU(2)).

(c)   The entity recognises in total comprehensive income the change in estimates of the present value of the future cash flows at the current discount rate. In Year 1, the total insurance finance expenses of CU(215) is the difference between the estimates of the present value of the future cash flows at the current discount rate at the beginning of Year 1 of CU1,420 and the corresponding amount at the end of Year 1 of CU1,635.

Example 16—Amount that eliminates accounting mismatches with finance income or expenses arising on underlying items held (paragraphs 89–90 and B134)

IE173   This example illustrates the presentation of insurance finance income or expenses when an entity applies the approach in paragraph 89(b) ('the current period book yield approach'). This approach applies when an entity holds the underlying items for insurance contracts with direct participation features.

Assumptions

IE174   An entity issues 100 insurance contracts with a coverage period of three years. The coverage period starts when the insurance contracts are issued.

IE175   The contracts in this example:

(a)   meet the definition of insurance contracts because they offer a fixed payment on death. However, to isolate the effects illustrated in this example, and for simplicity, any fixed cash flows payable on death are ignored.

(b)   meet criteria for insurance contracts with direct participation features applying paragraph B101.

IE176   The entity receives a single premium of CU15 for each contract at the beginning of the coverage period (total future cash inflows of CU1,500).

IE177   The entity promises to pay policyholders on maturity of the contract an accumulated amount of returns on a specified pool of bonds minus a charge equal to 5 per cent of the premium and accumulated returns calculated at that date. Thus, policyholders that survive to maturity of the contract receive 95 per cent of the premium and accumulated returns.

IE178   In this example all other amounts, including the risk adjustment for non-financial risk, are ignored for simplicity.

IE179   The entity invests premiums received of CU1,500 in zero coupon fixed income bonds with a duration of three years (the same as the returns promised to policyholders). The bonds return a market interest rate of 10 per cent a year. At the end of Year 1, market interest rates fall from 10 per cent a year to 5 per cent a year.

IE180   The entity measures the bonds at fair value through other comprehensive income applying IFRS 9 *Financial Instruments*. The effective interest rate of the bonds acquired is 10 per cent a year, and that rate is used to calculate investment income in profit or loss. For simplicity, this example excludes the effect of accounting for expected credit losses on financial assets. The value of the bonds held by the entity is illustrated in the table below:

Bonds held	Initial recognition	Year 1	Year 2	Year 3
	CU	CU	CU	CU
Fair value	(1,500)	(1,811)	(1,902)	(1,997)
Amortised cost	(1,500)	(1,650)	(1,815)	(1,997)
Cumulative amounts recognised in other comprehensive income	–	**161**	**87**	–
Change in other comprehensive income		161	(74)	(87)
Investment income recognised in profit or loss (effective interest rate)		150	165	182

IE181   Applying paragraph 89(b), the entity elects to disaggregate insurance finance income or expenses for each period to include in profit or loss an amount that eliminates accounting mismatches with income or expenses included in profit or loss on the underlying items held.

Analysis

IE182   Applying paragraphs 45 and B110–B114 to account for the insurance contracts with direct participation features, the entity needs to analyse the changes in fulfilment cash flows to decide whether each change adjusts the contractual service margin (see the table after paragraph IE184 illustrating the reconciliation of the contractual service margin).

IE183   Applying paragraphs B110–B114, the entity analyses the source of changes in the fulfilment cash flows as follows:

Fulfilment cash flows[a]	Year 1	Year 2	Year 3
	CU	CU	CU
Opening balance	–	1,720	1,806
Change related to future service: new contracts	(75)	–	–
Change in the policyholders' share in the fair value of the underlying items[b]	295	86	90
Cash flows	1,500	–	(1,896)
Closing balance	1,720	1,806	–

(a)   Fulfilment cash flows are the estimate of the present value of the future cash inflows and the estimate of the present value of the future cash outflows (in this example all cash outflows vary based on the returns on underlying items). For example, at initial recognition the fulfilment cash flows of CU(75) are the sum of the estimates of the present value of the future cash inflows of CU(1,500) and the estimates of the present value of the future cash outflows of CU1,425 (the policyholders' share of 95 per cent of the fair value of the underlying items at initial recognition of CU1,500).

(b)   The change in the policyholders' share in the fair value of the underlying items is 95 per cent of the change in fair value of the underlying items. For example, in Year 1 the change in the policyholders' share in the underlying items of CU295 is 95 per cent of the change in fair value in Year 1 of CU311 (CU1,811 – CU1,500). Applying paragraph B111, the entity does not adjust the contractual service margin for the change in the obligation to pay policyholders an amount equal to the fair value of the underlying items because it does not relate to future service.

IE184   Applying paragraph 45, the entity determines the carrying amount of the contractual service margin at the end of each reporting period as follows:

Contractual service margin	Year 1	Year 2	Year 3
	CU	CU	CU
Opening balance	–	61	33
Change related to future service: new contracts	75	–	–
Change in the amount of the entity's share of the fair value of the underlying items[a]	16	5	5
Change related to current service: recognition in profit or loss for the service provided	(30) [b]	(33)	(38)
Closing balance	61	33	–

continued...

...continued

(a) Applying paragraph B112, the entity adjusts the contractual service margin for the change in the amount of the entity's share of the fair value of the underlying items because those changes relate to future service. For example, in Year 1 the change in the amount of the entity's share of the fair value of the underlying items of CU16 is 5 per cent of the change in fair value of the underlying items of CU311 (CU1,811 – CU1,500). This example does not include cash flows that do not vary based on the returns on underlying items. For more details about the changes related to future service that adjust the contractual service margin see Example 10.

(b) Applying paragraphs 45(e) and B119, the entity determines the amount of contractual service margin recognised in profit or loss by allocating the contractual service margin at the end of the period (before recognising any amounts in profit or loss) equally to each coverage unit provided in the current period and expected to be provided in the future. In this example, the coverage provided in each period is the same; hence, the contractual service margin recognised in profit or loss for Year 1 of CU30 is the contractual service margin before allocation of CU91 (CU75 + CU16), divided by three years of coverage.

IE185 The amounts recognised in the statement(s) of financial performance for the period are as follows:

Statement(s) of financial performance	Year 1	Year 2	Year 3
	CU	CU	CU
Profit or loss			
Contractual service margin recognised in profit or loss for the service provided[(a)]	30	33	38
Insurance service result	30	33	38
Investment income	150	165	182
Insurance finance expenses	(150) [(b)]	(165)	(182)
Finance result	–	–	–
Profit	30	33	38
Other comprehensive income			
Gain / (loss) on financial assets measured at fair value through other comprehensive income	161	(74)	(87)
Gain / (loss) on insurance contracts	(161) [(b)]	74	87
Total other comprehensive income	–	–	–

continued...

...continued

(a) This example illustrates the amounts recognised as part of the insurance service result and not presentation requirements. For more details on the presentation requirements see Examples 3 and 9.

(b) Applying paragraph B111, the entity does not adjust the contractual service margin for the changes in the obligation to pay the policyholders an amount equal to the fair value of the underlying items because those changes do not relate to future service. Consequently, applying paragraph 87(c), the entity recognises those changes as insurance finance income or expenses in the statement(s) of financial performance. For example, in Year 1 the change in fair value of the underlying items is CU311 (CU1,811 – CU1,500).

Furthermore, applying paragraphs 89–90 and B134, the entity disaggregates the insurance finance expenses for the period between profit or loss and other comprehensive income to include in profit or loss an amount that eliminates accounting mismatches with the income or expenses included in profit or loss on the underlying items held. This amount exactly matches the income or expenses included in profit or loss for the underlying items, resulting in the net of the two separately presented items being zero. For example in Year 1 the total amount of the insurance finance expenses of CU311 is disaggregated and the entity presents in profit or loss the amount of CU150 that equals the amount of finance income for the underlying items. The remaining amount of insurance finance expenses is recognised in other comprehensive income.

Transition

Example 17—Measurement of groups of insurance contracts without direct participation features applying the modified retrospective approach (paragraphs C11–C15)

IE186 This example illustrates the transition requirements for insurance contracts without direct participation features for which retrospective application is impracticable and an entity chooses to apply the modified retrospective transition approach.

Assumptions

IE187 An entity issues insurance contracts without direct participation features and aggregates those contracts into a group applying paragraphs C9(a) and C10. The entity estimates the fulfilment cash flows at the transition date applying paragraphs 33–37 as the sum of:

(a) an estimate of the present value of the future cash flows of CU620 (including the effect of discounting of CU(150)); and

(b) a risk adjustment for non-financial risk of CU100.

IE188   The entity concludes that it is impracticable to apply IFRS 17 retrospectively. As a result, the entity chooses, applying paragraph C5, to apply the modified retrospective approach to measure the contractual service margin at the transition date. Applying paragraph C6(a), the entity uses reasonable and supportable information to achieve the closest outcome to retrospective application.

Analysis

IE189   The entity determines the contractual service margin at the transition date by estimating the fulfilment cash flows on initial recognition applying paragraphs C12–C15 as follows:

	Transition date	Adjustment to initial recognition	Initial recognition
	CU	CU	CU
Estimates of future cash flows	770	(800)	(30) [a]
Effect of discounting	(150)	(50)	(200) [b]
Estimates of the present value of future cash flows	620	(850)	(230)
Risk adjustment for non-financial risk	100	20	120 [c]
Fulfilment cash flows	**720**	**(830)**	**(110)**

(a)   Applying paragraph C12, the entity estimates the future cash flows at the date of initial recognition of the group of insurance contracts to be the sum of:

   (i)   the estimates of future cash flows of CU770 at the transition date; and

   (ii)   cash flows of CU800 that are known to have occurred between the date of initial recognition of the group of insurance contracts and the transition date (including premiums paid on initial recognition of CU1,000 and cash outflows of CU200 paid during the period). This amount includes cash flows resulting from contracts that ceased to exist before the transition date.

(b)   The entity determines the effect of discounting at the date of initial recognition of the group of insurance contracts to equal CU(200) calculated as the discounting effect on estimates of the future cash flows at the date of initial recognition calculated in footnote (a). Applying paragraph C13(a), the entity determines the effect of discounting by using an observable yield curve that, for at least three years immediately before the transition date, approximates the yield curve estimated applying paragraphs 36 and B72–B85. The entity estimates this amount to equal CU50 reflecting the fact that the premium was received on initial recognition, hence, the discounting effect relates only to the estimate of future cash outflows.

continued...

...continued

(c)   Applying paragraph C14, the entity determines the risk adjustment for non-financial risk on initial recognition of CU120 as the risk adjustment for non-financial risk at the transition date of CU100 adjusted by CU20 to reflect the expected release of risk before the transition date. Applying paragraph C14, the entity determines the expected release of risk by reference to the release of risk for similar insurance contracts that the entity issues at the transition date.

IE190   The contractual service margin at the transition date equals CU20 and is calculated as follows:

(a)   the contractual service margin measured on initial recognition is CU110, an amount that would have resulted in no income or expenses arising from the fulfilment cash flows that would have been estimated on initial recognition of CU110 (see the table after paragraph IE189); minus

(b)   the contractual service margin that would have been recognised in profit or loss before the transition date of CU90, estimated applying paragraph C15.

IE191   As a result, the carrying amount of the insurance contract liability at the transition date equals CU740, which is the sum of the fulfilment cash flows of CU720 and the contractual service margin of CU20.

Example 18—Measurement of groups of insurance contracts with direct participation features applying the modified retrospective approach (paragraph C17)

IE192   This example illustrates the transition requirements for insurance contracts with direct participation features when retrospective application is impracticable and an entity chooses to apply the modified retrospective transition approach.

Assumptions

IE193   An entity issued 100 insurance contracts with direct participation features five years before the transition date and aggregates those contracts into a group, applying paragraphs C9(a) and C10.

IE194   Under the terms of the contracts:

(a)   a single premium is paid at the beginning of the coverage period of 10 years.

(b)   the entity maintains account balances for policyholders and deducts charges from those account balances at the end of each year.

(c)   a policyholder will receive an amount equal to the higher of the account balance and the minimum death benefit if an insured person dies during the coverage period.

(d)   if an insured person survives the coverage period, the policyholder receives the value of the account balance.

IE195   The following events took place in the five year period prior to the transition date:

    (a)   the entity paid death benefits and other expenses of CU239 comprising:

        (i)   CU216 of cash flows that vary based on the returns on underlying items; and

        (ii)   CU23 of cash flows that do not vary based on the returns on underlying items; and

    (b)   the entity deducted charges from the underlying items of CU55.

IE196   Applying paragraphs 33–37, the entity estimates the fulfilment cash flows at the transition date to be CU922, comprising the estimates of the present value of the future cash flows of CU910 and a risk adjustment for non-financial risk of CU12. The fair value of the underlying items at that date is CU948.

IE197   The entity makes the following estimates:

    (a)   based on an analysis of similar contracts that the entity issues at transition date, the estimated change in the risk adjustment for non-financial risk caused by the release from risk in the five-year period before the transition date is CU14; and

    (b)   the units of coverage provided before the transition date is approximately 60 per cent of the total coverage units of the group of contracts.

Analysis

IE198   The entity applies a modified retrospective approach to determine the contractual service margin at the transition date, applying paragraph C17 as follows:

	CU
Fair value of the underlying items at the transition date (paragraph C17(a))	948
Fulfilment cash flows at the transition date (paragraph C17(b))	(922)
Adjustments:	
– Charges deducted from underlying items before the transition date (paragraph C17(c)(i))	55
– Amounts paid before the transition date that would have not varied based on the returns on underlying items (paragraph C17(c)(ii))	(23)
– Estimated change in the risk adjustment for non-financial risk caused by the release from risk before the transition date (paragraph C17(c)(iii))	(14)
Contractual service margin of the group of contracts before recognition in profit or loss	**44**
Estimated amount of the contractual service margin that relates to services provided before the transition date	(26) [a]
Estimated contractual service margin at the transition date	**18**

(a)   Applying paragraph C17(d), the entity determines the contractual service margin that relates to service provided before the transition date of CU26 as the percentage of the coverage units provided before the transition date and the total coverage units of 60 per cent multiplied by the contractual service margin before recognition in profit or loss of CU44.

IE199   Consequently, the carrying amount of the insurance contract liability at the transition date equals CU940, which is the sum of the fulfilment cash flows of CU922 and the contractual service margin of CU18.

Appendix
Amendments to other IFRS Standards

This appendix sets out the amendments to the Illustrative Examples for other IFRS Standards that are a consequence of the International Accounting Standards Board issuing IFRS 17 Insurance Contracts.

* * * * *

The amendments contained in this appendix when this Standard was issued in 2017 have been incorporated into the guidance on the relevant Standards included in this volume.

IFRS 17 *Insurance Contracts*—the accounting model in one page

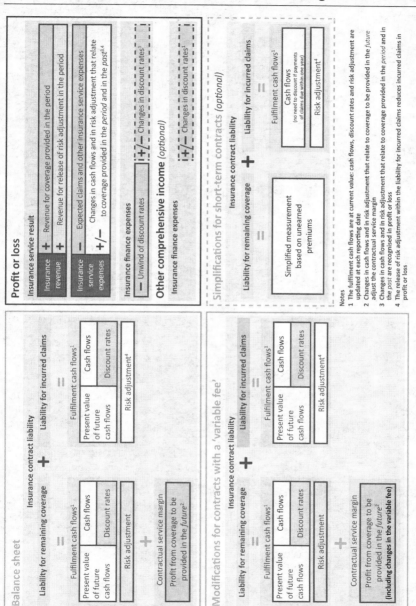

IASB documents published to accompany

IAS 1

Presentation of Financial Statements

The text of the unaccompanied standard, IAS 1, is contained in Part A of this edition. Its effective date when issued was 1 January 2009. The text of the Basis for Conclusions on IAS 1 is contained in Part C of this edition. This part presents the following documents:

IMPLEMENTATION GUIDANCE

APPENDIX

Amendments to guidance on other IFRSs

TABLE OF CONCORDANCE

Guidance on implementing
IAS 1 *Presentation of Financial Statements*

This guidance accompanies, but is not part of, IAS 1.

Illustrative financial statement structure

IG1   IAS 1 sets out the components of financial statements and minimum requirements for disclosure in the statements of financial position, profit or loss and other comprehensive income and changes in equity. It also describes further items that may be presented either in the relevant financial statement or in the notes. This guidance provides simple examples of ways in which the requirements of IAS 1 for the presentation of the statements of financial position, profit or loss and other comprehensive income and changes in equity might be met. An entity should change the order of presentation, the titles of the statements and the descriptions used for line items when necessary to suit its particular circumstances.

IG2   The guidance is in two sections. Paragraphs IG3–IG6 provide examples of the presentation of financial statements. Paragraphs IG7–IG9 have been deleted. Paragraphs IG10 and IG11 provide examples of capital disclosures.

IG3   The illustrative statement of financial position shows one way in which an entity may present a statement of financial position distinguishing between current and non-current items. Other formats may be equally appropriate, provided the distinction is clear.

IG4   The illustrations use the term 'comprehensive income' to label the total of all items of profit or loss and other comprehensive income. The illustrations use the term 'other comprehensive income' to label income and expenses that are included in comprehensive income but excluded from profit or loss. IAS 1 does not require an entity to use those terms in its financial statements.

IG5   Two statements of profit or loss and other comprehensive income are provided, to illustrate the alternative presentations of income and expenses in a single statement or in two statements. The statement of profit or loss and other comprehensive income illustrates the classification of income and expenses within profit or loss by function. The separate statement (in this example, 'the statement or profit or loss') illustrates the classification of income and expenses within profit by nature.

IG5A   Two sets of examples of statements of profit or loss and other comprehensive income are shown. One shows the presentation while IAS 39 *Financial Instruments: Recognition and Measurement* remains effective and is applied; the other shows presentation when IFRS 9 *Financial Instruments* is applied.

IG6   The examples are not intended to illustrate all aspects of IFRSs, nor do they constitute a complete set of financial statements, which would also include a statement of cash flows, disclosures about material accounting policy information and other explanatory information.

Part I: Illustrative presentation of financial statements

**XYZ Group – Statement of financial position as at 31 December 20X7
(in thousands of currency units)**

	31 Dec 20X7	31 Dec 20X6
ASSETS		
Non-current assets		
Property, plant and equipment	350,700	360,020
Goodwill	80,800	91,200
Other intangible assets	227,470	227,470
Investments in associates	100,150	110,770
Investments in equity instruments	142,500	156,000
	901,620	945,460
Current assets		
Inventories	135,230	132,500
Trade receivables	91,600	110,800
Other current assets	25,650	12,540
Cash and cash equivalents	312,400	322,900
	564,880	578,740
Total assets	1,466,500	1,524,200

**XYZ Group – Statement of financial position as at 31 December 20X7
(in thousands of currency units)**

	31 Dec 20X7	31 Dec 20X6
EQUITY AND LIABILITIES		
Equity attributable to owners of the parent		
Share capital	650,000	600,000
Retained earnings	243,500	161,700
Other components of equity	10,200	21,200
	903,700	782,900
Non-controlling interests	70,050	48,600
Total equity	973,750	831,500

continued...

...continued

XYZ Group – Statement of financial position as at 31 December 20X7
(in thousands of currency units)

	31 Dec 20X7	31 Dec 20X6
Non-current liabilities		
Long-term borrowings	120,000	160,000
Deferred tax	28,800	26,040
Long-term provisions	28,850	52,240
Total non-current liabilities	177,650	238,280
Current liabilities		
Trade and other payables	115,100	187,620
Short-term borrowings	150,000	200,000
Current portion of long-term borrowings	10,000	20,000
Current tax payable	35,000	42,000
Short-term provisions	5,000	4,800
Total current liabilities	315,100	454,420
Total liabilities	492,750	692,700
Total equity and liabilities	1,466,500	1,524,200

Examples of statement of profit or loss and other comprehensive income when
IAS 39 *Financial Instruments: Recognition and Measurement* is applied
XYZ Group – Statement of profit or loss and other comprehensive income for the year
ended 31 December 20X7
(illustrating the presentation of profit or loss and other comprehensive income in one
statement and the classification of expenses within profit or loss by function)
(in thousands of currency units)

	20X7	20X6
Revenue	390,000	355,000
Cost of sales	(245,000)	(230,000)
Gross profit	145,000	125,000
Other income	20,667	11,300
Distribution costs	(9,000)	(8,700)
Administrative expenses	(20,000)	(21,000)
Other expenses	(2,100)	(1,200)
Finance costs	(8,000)	(7,500)
Share of profit of associates[(a)]	35,100	30,100
Profit before tax	161,667	128,000
Income tax expense	(40,417)	(32,000)
Profit for the year from continuing operations	121,250	96,000
Loss for the year from discontinued operations	–	(30,500)
PROFIT FOR THE YEAR	121,250	65,500

continued...

...continued

Examples of statement of profit or loss and other comprehensive income when IAS 39 *Financial Instruments: Recognition and Measurement* **is applied**
XYZ Group – Statement of profit or loss and other comprehensive income for the year ended 31 December 20X7
(illustrating the presentation of profit or loss and other comprehensive income in one statement and the classification of expenses within profit or loss by function)
(in thousands of currency units)

	20X7	20X6
Other comprehensive income:		
Items that will not be reclassified to profit or loss [Refer: paragraph 82A(a)(i)]:		
Gains on property revaluation	933	3,367
Remeasurements of defined benefit pension plans	(667)	1,333
Share of other comprehensive income of associates[b]	400	(700)
Income tax relating to items that will not be reclassified[c]	(166)	(1,000)
	500	3,000
Items that may be reclassified subsequently to profit or loss [Refer: paragraph 82A(a)(ii)]:		
Exchange differences on translating foreign operations[d]	5,334	10,667
Available-for-sale financial assets[d]	(24,000)	26,667
Cash flow hedges[d]	(667)	(4,000)
Income tax relating to items that may be reclassified[c]	4,833	(8,334)
	(14,500)	25,000
Other comprehensive income for the year, net of tax	(14,000)	28,000
TOTAL COMPREHENSIVE INCOME FOR THE YEAR	107,250	93,500

continued...

...continued

Examples of statement of profit or loss and other comprehensive income when IAS 39 *Financial Instruments: Recognition and Measurement* is applied
XYZ Group – Statement of profit or loss and other comprehensive income for the year ended 31 December 20X7
(illustrating the presentation of profit or loss and other comprehensive income in one statement and the classification of expenses within profit or loss by function)
(in thousands of currency units)

	20X7	20X6
Profit attributable to:		
Owners of the parent	97,000	52,400
Non-controlling interests	24,250	13,100
	121,250	65,500
Total comprehensive income attributable to:		
Owners of the parent	85,800	74,800
Non-controlling interests	21,450	18,700
	107,250	93,500
Earnings per share (in currency units):		
Basic and diluted	0.46	0.30

Alternatively, items of other comprehensive income could be presented in the statement of profit or loss and other comprehensive income net of tax.

Other comprehensive income for the year, after tax:	20X7	20X6
Items that will not be reclassified to profit or loss:		
Gains on property revaluation	600	2,700
Remeasurements of defined benefit pension plans	(500)	1,000
Share of other comprehensive income of associates	400	(700)

continued...

...continued

**Examples of statement of profit or loss and other comprehensive income when
IAS 39 *Financial Instruments: Recognition and Measurement* is applied
XYZ Group – Statement of profit or loss and other comprehensive income for the year
ended 31 December 20X7
(illustrating the presentation of profit or loss and other comprehensive income in one
statement and the classification of expenses within profit or loss by function)
(in thousands of currency units)**

	20X7	20X6
	500	3,000
Items that may be reclassified subsequently to profit or loss:		
Exchange differences on translating foreign operations	4,000	8,000
Investments in equity instruments	(18,000)	20,000
Cash flow hedges	(500)	(3,000)
	(14,500)	25,000
Other comprehensive income for the year, net of tax[(c)]	(14,000)	28,000

(a) This means the share of associates' profit attributable to owners of the associates, ie it is after tax and non-controlling interests in the associates.

(b) This means the share of associates' other comprehensive income attributable to owners of the associates, ie it is after tax and non-controlling interests in the associates. In this example, the other comprehensive income of associates consists only of items that will not be subsequently reclassified to profit or loss. **[Refer: paragraph 82A(b)(i)]** Entities whose associates' other comprehensive income includes items that may be subsequently reclassified to profit or loss are required by paragraph 82A(b) to present that amount in a separate line.

(c) The income tax relating to each item of other comprehensive income is disclosed in the notes.

(d) This illustrates the aggregated presentation, with disclosure of the current year gain or loss and reclassification adjustment presented in the notes. Alternatively, a gross presentation can be used.

XYZ Group – Statement of profit or loss for the year ended 31 December 20X7 (illustrating the presentation of profit or loss and other comprehensive income in two statements and the classification of expenses within profit or loss by nature) (in thousands of currency units)

	20X7	20X6
Revenue	390,000	355,000
Other income	20,667	11,300
Changes in inventories of finished goods and work in progress	(115,100)	(107,900)
Work performed by the entity and capitalised	16,000	15,000
Raw material and consumables used	(96,000)	(92,000)
Employee benefits expense	(45,000)	(43,000)
Depreciation and amortisation expense	(19,000)	(17,000)
Impairment of property, plant and equipment	(4,000)	–
Other expenses	(6,000)	(5,500)
Finance costs	(15,000)	(18,000)
Share of profit of associates[a]	35,100	30,100
Profit before tax	161,667	128,000
Income tax expense	(40,417)	(32,000)
Profit for the year from continuing operations	121,250	96,000
Loss for the year from discontinued operations	–	(30,500)
PROFIT FOR THE YEAR	121,250	65,500
Profit attributable to:		
Owners of the parent	97,000	52,400
Non-controlling interests	24,250	13,100
	121,250	65,500
Earnings per share (in currency units):		
Basic and diluted	0.46	0.30

(a) This means the share of associates' profit attributable to owners of the associates, ie it is after tax and non-controlling interests in the associates.

XYZ Group – Statement of profit or loss and other comprehensive income for the year ended 31 December 20X7
(illustrating the presentation of profit or loss and other comprehensive income in two statements)
(in thousands of currency units)

	20X7	20X6
Profit for the year	121,250	65,500
Other comprehensive income:		
Items that will not be reclassified to profit or loss [Refer: paragraph 82A(a)(i)]:		
Gains on property revaluation	933	3,367
Remeasurements of defined benefit pension plans	(667)	1,333
Share of other comprehensive income of associates[a]	400	(700)
Income tax relating to items that will not be reclassified[b]	(166)	(1,000)
	500	3,000
Items that may be reclassified subsequently to profit or loss [Refer: paragraph 82A(a)(ii)]:		
Exchange differences on translating foreign operations	5,334	10,667
Investments in equity instruments	(24,000)	26,667
Cash flow hedges	(667)	(4,000)
Income tax relating to items that may be reclassified[b]	4,833	(8,334)
	(14,500)	25,000
Other comprehensive income for the year, net of tax	(14,000)	28,000
TOTAL COMPREHENSIVE INCOME FOR THE YEAR	107,250	93,500
Total comprehensive income attributable to:		
Owners of the parent	85,800	74,800
Non-controlling interests	21,450	18,700
	107,250	93,500

Alternatively, items of other comprehensive income could be presented, net of tax. Refer to the statement of profit or loss and other comprehensive income illustrating the presentation of income and expenses in one statement.

(a) This means the share of associates' other comprehensive income attributable to owners of the associates, ie it is after tax and non-controlling interests in the associates. In this example, the other comprehensive income of associates consists only of items that will not be subsequently reclassified to profit or loss. [Refer: paragraph 82A(b)(i)] Entities whose associates' other comprehensive income includes items that may be subsequently reclassified to profit or loss are required by paragraph 82A(b) to present that amount in a separate line.

(b) The income tax relating to each item of other comprehensive income is disclosed in the notes.

© IFRS Foundation

Examples of statement of profit or loss and other comprehensive income when
IFRS 9 *Financial Instruments* is applied
XYZ Group – Statement of profit or loss and other comprehensive income for the year
ended 31 December 20X7
(illustrating the presentation of profit or loss and other comprehensive income in one
statement and the classification of expenses within profit or loss by function)
(in thousands of currency units)

	20X7	20X6
Revenue	390,000	355,000
Cost of sales	(245,000)	(230,000)
Gross profit	145,000	125,000
Other income	20,667	11,300
Distribution costs	(9,000)	(8,700)
Administrative expenses	(20,000)	(21,000)
Other expenses	(2,100)	(1,200)
Finance costs	(8,000)	(7,500)
Share of profit of associates[a]	35,100	30,100
Profit before tax	161,667	128,000
Income tax expense	(40,417)	(32,000)
Profit for the year from continuing operations	121,250	96,000
Loss for the year from discontinued operations	–	(30,500)
PROFIT FOR THE YEAR	121,250	65,500
Other comprehensive income:		
Items that will not be reclassified to profit or loss [Refer: paragraph 82A(a)(i)]:		
Gains on property revaluation	933	3,367
Investments in equity instruments	(24,000)	26,667
Remeasurements of defined benefit pension plans	(667)	1,333
Share of other comprehensive income of associates[b]	400	(700)
Income tax relating to items that will not be reclassified[c]	5,834	(7,667)
	(17,500)	23,000

continued...

...continued

Examples of statement of profit or loss and other comprehensive income when IFRS 9 *Financial Instruments* is applied
XYZ Group – Statement of profit or loss and other comprehensive income for the year ended 31 December 20X7
(illustrating the presentation of profit or loss and other comprehensive income in one statement and the classification of expenses within profit or loss by function)
(in thousands of currency units)

	20X7	20X6
Items that may be reclassified subsequently to profit or loss [Refer: paragraph 82A(a)(ii)]:		
Exchange differences on translating foreign operations[d]	5,334	10,667
Cash flow hedges[d]	(667)	(4,000)
Income tax relating to items that may be reclassified[c]	(1,167)	(1,667)
	3,500	5,000
Other comprehensive income for the year, net of tax	(14,000)	28,000
TOTAL COMPREHENSIVE INCOME FOR THE YEAR	107,250	93,500
Profit attributable to:		
Owners of the parent	97,000	52,400
Non-controlling interests	24,250	13,100
	121,250	65,500
Total comprehensive income attributable to:		
Owners of the parent	85,800	74,800
Non-controlling interests	21,450	18,700
	107,250	93,500
Earnings per share (in currency units):		
Basic and diluted	0.46	0.30

continued...

...continued

Examples of statement of profit or loss and other comprehensive income when IFRS 9 *Financial Instruments* is applied

XYZ Group – Statement of profit or loss and other comprehensive income for the year ended 31 December 20X7

(illustrating the presentation of profit or loss and other comprehensive income in one statement and the classification of expenses within profit or loss by function)

(in thousands of currency units)

	20X7	20X6
Alternatively, items of other comprehensive income could be presented in the statement of profit or loss and other comprehensive income net of tax.		
Other comprehensive income for the year, after tax:		
Items that will not be reclassified to profit or loss:		
Gains on property revaluation	600	2,700
Investments in equity instruments	(18,000)	20,000
Remeasurements of defined benefit pension plans	(500)	1,000
Share of other comprehensive income of associates	400	(700)
	(17,500)	23,000
Items that may be reclassified subsequently to profit or loss:		
Exchange differences on translating foreign operations	4,000	8,000
Cash flow hedges	(500)	(3,000)
	3,500	5,000
Other comprehensive income for the year, net of tax[(c)]	(14,000)	28,000

(a) This means the share of associates' profit attributable to owners of the associates, ie it is after tax and non-controlling interests in the associates.

(b) This means the share of associates' other comprehensive income attributable to owners of the associates, ie it is after tax and non-controlling interests in the associates. In this example, the other comprehensive income of associates consists only of items that will not be subsequently reclassified to profit or loss. **[Refer: paragraph 82A(b)(i)]** Entities whose associates' other comprehensive income includes items that may be subsequently reclassified to profit or loss are required by paragraph 82A(b) to present that amount in a separate line.

(c) The income tax relating to each item of other comprehensive income is disclosed in the notes.

(d) This illustrates the aggregated presentation, with disclosure of the current year gain or loss and reclassification adjustment presented in the notes. Alternatively, a gross presentation can be used.

**XYZ Group – Statement of profit or loss for the year ended 31 December 20X7
(illustrating the presentation of profit or loss and other comprehensive income in two
statements and the classification of expenses within profit or loss by nature)
(in thousands of currency units)**

	20X7	20X6
Revenue	390,000	355,000
Other income	20,667	11,300
Changes in inventories of finished goods and work in progress	(115,100)	(107,900)
Work performed by the entity and capitalised	16,000	15,000
Raw material and consumables used	(96,000)	(92,000)
Employee benefits expense	(45,000)	(43,000)
Depreciation and amortisation expense	(19,000)	(17,000)
Impairment of property, plant and equipment	(4,000)	–
Other expenses	(6,000)	(5,500)
Finance costs	(15,000)	(18,000)
Share of profit of associates[a]	35,100	30,100
Profit before tax	161,667	128,000
Income tax expense	(40,417)	(32,000)
Profit for the year from continuing operations	121,250	96,000
Loss for the year from discontinued operations	–	(30,500)
PROFIT FOR THE YEAR	121,250	65,500
Profit attributable to:		
Owners of the parent	97,000	52,400
Non-controlling interests	24,250	13,100
	121,250	65,500
Earnings per share (in currency units):		
Basic and diluted	0.46	0.30

(a) This means the share of associates' profit attributable to owners of the associates, ie it is after
tax and non-controlling interests in the associates.

XYZ Group – Statement of profit or loss and other comprehensive income for the year ended 31 December 20X7
(illustrating the presentation of profit or loss and other comprehensive income in two statements)
(in thousands of currency units)

	20X7	20X6
Profit for the year	121,250	65,500
Other comprehensive income:		
Items that will not be reclassified to profit or loss [Refer: paragraph 82A(a)(i)]:		
Gains on property revaluation	933	3,367
Investments in equity instruments	(24,000)	26,667
Remeasurements of defined benefit pension plans	(667)	1,333
Share of other comprehensive income of associates[(a)]	400	(700)
Income tax relating to items that will not be reclassified[(b)]	5,834	(7,667)
	(17,500)	23,000
Items that may be reclassified subsequently to profit or loss [Refer: paragraph 82A(a)(ii)]:		
Exchange differences on translating foreign operations	5,334	10,667
Cash flow hedges	(667)	(4,000)
Income tax relating to items that may be reclassified[(b)]	(1,167)	(1,667)
	3,500	5,000
Other comprehensive income for the year, net of tax	(14,000)	28,000
TOTAL COMPREHENSIVE INCOME FOR THE YEAR	107,250	93,500

continued...

...continued

XYZ Group – Statement of profit or loss and other comprehensive income for the year ended 31 December 20X7
(illustrating the presentation of profit or loss and other comprehensive income in two statements)
(in thousands of currency units)

	20X7	20X6
Total comprehensive income attributable to:		
Owners of the parent	85,800	74,800
Non-controlling interests	21,450	18,700
	107,250	93,500

Alternatively, items of other comprehensive income could be presented, net of tax. Refer to the statement of profit or loss and other comprehensive income illustrating the presentation of income and expenses in one statement.

(a) This means the share of associates' other comprehensive income attributable to owners of the associates, ie it is after tax and non-controlling interests in the associates. In this example, the other comprehensive income of associates consists only of items that will not be subsequently reclassified to profit or loss. [Refer: paragraph 82A(b)(i)] Entities whose associates' other comprehensive income includes items that may be subsequently reclassified to profit or loss are required by paragraph 82A(b) to present that amount in a separate line.

(b) The income tax relating to each item of other comprehensive income is disclosed in the notes.

XYZ Group
Disclosure of components of other comprehensive income[(a)]
Notes
Year ended 31 December 20X7
(in thousands of currency units)

	20X7		20X6
Other comprehensive income:			
Exchange differences on translating foreign operations[(b)]	5,334		10,667
Investments in equity instruments	(24,000)		26,667
Cash flow hedges:			
Gains (losses) arising during the year	(4,667)	(4,000)	
Less: Reclassification adjustments for gains (losses) included in profit or loss	4,000	(667)	–	(4,000)
Gains on property revaluation	933		3,367
Remeasurements of defined benefit pension plans	(667)		1,333
Share of other comprehensive income of associates	400		(700)
Other comprehensive income	(18,667)		37,334
Income tax relating to components of other comprehensive income[(c)]	4,667		(9,334)
Other comprehensive income for the year	**(14,000)**		**28,000**

(a) When an entity chooses an aggregated presentation in the statement of comprehensive income, the amounts for reclassification adjustments and current year gain or loss are presented in the notes.

(b) There was no disposal of a foreign operation. Therefore, there is no reclassification adjustment for the years presented.

(c) The income tax relating to each component of other comprehensive income is disclosed in the notes.

XYZ Group
Disclosure of tax effects relating to each component of other comprehensive income
Notes
Year ended 31 December 20X7
(in thousands of currency units)

	20X7			20X6		
	Before-tax amount	Tax (expense) benefit	Net-of-tax amount	Before-tax amount	Tax (expense) benefit	Net-of-tax amount
Exchange differences on translating foreign operations	5,334	(1,334)	4,000	10,667	(2,667)	8,000
Investments in equity instruments	(24,000)	6,000	(18,000)	26,667	(6,667)	20,000
Cash flow hedges	(667)	167	(500)	(4,000)	1,000	(3,000)
Gains on property revaluation	933	(333)	600	3,367	(667)	2,700
Remeasurements of defined benefit pension plans	(667)	167	(500)	1,333	(333)	1,000
Share of other comprehensive income of associates	400	–	400	(700)	–	(700)
Other comprehensive income	(18,667)	4,667	(14,000)	37,334	(9,334)	28,000

XYZ Group – Statement of changes in equity for the year ended 31 December 20X7
(in thousands of currency units)

	Share capital	Retained earnings	Translation of foreign operations	Investments in equity instruments	Cash flow hedges	Revaluation surplus	Total	Non-controlling interests	Total equity
Balance at 1 January 20X6	600,000	118,100	(4,000)	1,600	2,000	–	717,700	29,800	747,500
Changes in accounting policy	–	400	–	–	–	–	400	100	500
Restated balance	600,000	118,500	(4,000)	1,600	2,000	–	718,100	29,900	748,000
Changes in equity for 20X6									
Dividends	–	(10,000)	–	–	–	–	(10,000)		(10,000)
Total comprehensive income for the year(a)	–	53,200	6,400	16,000	(2,400)	1,600	74,800	18,700	93,500
Balance at 31 December 20X6	600,000	161,700	2,400	17,600	(400)	1,600	782,900	48,600	831,500

continued...

...continued

XYZ Group – Statement of changes in equity for the year ended 31 December 20X7
(in thousands of currency units)

Changes in equity for 20X7	Share capital	Retained earnings	Translation of foreign operations	Investments in equity instruments	Cash flow hedges	Revaluation surplus	Total	Non-controlling interests	Total equity
Issue of share capital	50,000	–	–	–	–	–	50,000	–	50,000
Dividends	–	(15,000)	–	–	–	–	(15,000)	–	(15,000)
Total comprehensive income for the year(b)	–	96,600	3,200	(14,400)	(400)	800	85,800	21,450	107,250
Transfer to retained earnings	–	200	–	–	–	(200)	–	–	–
Balance at 31 December 20X7	650,000	243,500	5,600	3,200	(800)	2,200	903,700	70,050	973,750

(a) The amount included in retained earnings for 20X6 of 53,200 represents profit attributable to owners of the parent of 52,400 plus remeasurements of defined benefit pension plans of 800 (1,333, less tax 333, less non-controlling interests 200).

The amount included in the translation, investments in equity instruments and cash flow hedge reserves represent other comprehensive income for each component, net of tax and non-controlling interests, eg other comprehensive income related to investments in equity instruments for 20X6 of 16,000 is 26,667, less tax 6,667, less non-controlling interests 4,000.

The amount included in the revaluation surplus of 1,600 represents the share of other comprehensive income of associates of 2,300 (3,367, less tax 667, less non-controlling interests 400). Other comprehensive income of associates relates solely to gains or losses on property revaluation.

(b) The amount included in retained earnings for 20X7 of 96,600 represents profit attributable to owners of the parent of 97,000 plus remeasurements of defined benefit pension plans of 400 (667, less tax 167, less non-controlling interests 100).

The amount included in the translation, investments in equity instruments and cash flow hedge reserves represents other comprehensive income for each component, net of tax and non-controlling interests, eg other comprehensive income related to the translation of foreign operations for 20X7 of 3,200 is 5,334, less tax 1,334, less non-controlling interests 800.

The amount included in the revaluation surplus of 800 represents the share of other comprehensive income of associates of 400 plus gains on property revaluation of 400 (933, less tax 333, less non-controlling interests 200). Other comprehensive income of associates relates solely to gains or losses on property revaluation.

IG7–IG9   [Deleted]

Part III: Illustrative examples of capital disclosures (paragraphs 134–136)

An entity that is not a regulated financial institution

IG10   The following example illustrates the application of paragraphs 134 and 135 for an entity that is not a financial institution and is not subject to an externally imposed capital requirement. In this example, the entity monitors capital using a debt-to-adjusted capital ratio. Other entities may use different methods to monitor capital. The example is also relatively simple. An entity decides, in the light of its circumstances, how much detail it provides to satisfy the requirements of paragraphs 134 and 135. In determining the form and content of the disclosure to satisfy those requirements, an entity also considers the disclosure requirements set out in paragraphs 44A–44E of IAS 7 *Statement of Cash Flows*.

Facts

Group A manufactures and sells cars. Group A includes a finance subsidiary that provides finance to customers, primarily in the form of leases. Group A is not subject to any externally imposed capital requirements.

Example disclosure

The Group's objectives when managing capital are:

- to safeguard the entity's ability to continue as a going concern, so that it can continue to provide returns for shareholders and benefits for other stakeholders, and

- to provide an adequate return to shareholders by pricing products and services commensurately with the level of risk.

The Group sets the amount of capital in proportion to risk. The Group manages the capital structure and makes adjustments to it in the light of changes in economic conditions and the risk characteristics of the underlying assets. In order to maintain or adjust the capital structure, the Group may adjust the amount of dividends paid to shareholders, return capital to shareholders, issue new shares, or sell assets to reduce debt.

Consistently with others in the industry, the Group monitors capital on the basis of the debt-to-adjusted capital ratio. This ratio is calculated as net debt ÷ adjusted capital. Net debt is calculated as total debt (as shown in the statement of financial position) less cash and cash equivalents. Adjusted capital comprises all components of equity (ie share capital, share premium, non-controlling interests, retained earnings, and revaluation surplus) other than amounts accumulated in equity relating to cash flow hedges, and includes some forms of subordinated debt.

continued...

...continued

During 20X4, the Group's strategy, which was unchanged from 20X3, was to maintain the debt-to-adjusted capital ratio at the lower end of the range 6:1 to 7:1, in order to secure access to finance at a reasonable cost by maintaining a BB credit rating. The debt-to-adjusted capital ratios at 31 December 20X4 and at 31 December 20X3 were as follows:

	31 Dec 20X4	31 Dec 20X3
	CU million	CU million
Total debt	1,000	1,100
Less: cash and cash equivalents	(90)	(150)
Net debt	910	950
Total equity	110	105
Add: subordinated debt instruments	38	38
Less: amounts accumulated in equity relating to cash flow hedges	(10)	(5)
Adjusted capital	138	138
Debt-to-adjusted capital ratio	6.6	6.9

The decrease in the debt-to-adjusted capital ratio during 20X4 resulted primarily from the reduction in net debt that occurred on the sale of subsidiary Z. As a result of this reduction in net debt, improved profitability and lower levels of managed receivables, the dividend payment was increased to CU2.8 million for 20X4 (from CU2.5 million for 20X3).

An entity that has not complied with externally imposed capital requirements

IG11   The following example illustrates the application of paragraph 135(e) when an entity has not complied with externally imposed capital requirements during the period. Other disclosures would be provided to comply with the other requirements of paragraphs 134 and 135.

Facts

Entity A provides financial services to its customers and is subject to capital requirements imposed by Regulator B. During the year ended 31 December 20X7, Entity A did not comply with the capital requirements imposed by Regulator B. In its financial statements for the year ended 31 December 20X7, Entity A provides the following disclosure relating to its non-compliance.

...continued

Example disclosure

Entity A filed its quarterly regulatory capital return for 30 September 20X7 on 20 October 20X7. At that date, Entity A's regulatory capital was below the capital requirement imposed by Regulator B by CU1 million. As a result, Entity A was required to submit a plan to the regulator indicating how it would increase its regulatory capital to the amount required. Entity A submitted a plan that entailed selling part of its unquoted equities portfolio with a carrying amount of CU11.5 million in the fourth quarter of 20X7. In the fourth quarter of 20X7, Entity A sold its fixed interest investment portfolio for CU12.6 million and met its regulatory capital requirement.

Appendix
Amendments to guidance on other IFRSs

The following amendments to guidance on other IFRSs are necessary in order to ensure consistency with the revised IAS 1. In the amended paragraphs, new text is underlined and deleted text is struck through.

* * * * *

The amendments contained in this appendix when IAS 1 was revised in 2007 have been incorporated into the guidance on the relevant IFRSs, published in this volume.

Table of Concordance

This table shows how the contents of IAS 1 (revised 2003 and amended in 2005) and IAS 1 (as revised in 2007) correspond. Paragraphs are treated as corresponding if they broadly address the same matter even though the guidance may differ.

Superseded IAS 1 paragraph	IAS 1 (revised 2007) paragraph
1	1, 3
2	2
3	4, 7
4	None
5	5
6	6
7	9
8	10
9, 10	13, 14
11	7
12	7
None	8
None	11, 12
13–22	15–24
23, 24	25, 26
25, 26	27, 28
27, 28	45, 46
29–31	29–31
32–35	32–35
36	38
None	39
37–41	40–44
42, 43	47, 48
44–48	49–53
49, 50	36, 37
51–67	60–76
68	54
68A	54
69–73	55–59
74–77	77–80

continued...

...*continued*

Superseded IAS 1 paragraph	IAS 1 (revised 2007) paragraph
None	81
78	88
79	89
80	89
81	82
82	83
None	84
83–85	85–87
None	90–96
86–94	97–105
95	107
None	108
96, 97	106, 107
98	109
101	None
102	111
103–107	112–116
108–115	117–124
116–124	125–133
124A–124C	134–136
125, 126	137, 138
127	139
127A	None
127B	None
128	140
IG1	IG1
None	IG2
IG2	IG3
None	IG4
IG3, IG4	IG5, IG6
None	IG7
None	IG8
None	IG9

continued...

© IFRS Foundation

...continued

Superseded IAS 1 paragraph	IAS 1 (revised 2007) paragraph
IG5, IG6	IG10, IG11

IASB documents published to accompany

IAS 7

Statement of Cash Flows

The text of the unaccompanied standard, IAS 7, is contained in Part A of this edition. Its effective date when issued was 1 January 1994. The text of the Basis for Conclusions on IAS 7 is contained in Part C of this edition. This part presents the following documents:

ILLUSTRATIVE EXAMPLES

A Statement of cash flows for an entity other than a financial institution

B Statement of cash flows for a financial institution

C Reconciliation of liabilities arising from financing activities

Illustrative Examples

These illustrative examples accompany, but are not part of, IAS 7.

A Statement of cash flows for an entity other than a financial institution

1   The examples show only current period amounts. Corresponding amounts for the preceding period are required to be presented in accordance with IAS 1 *Presentation of Financial Statements*.

2   Information from the statement of comprehensive income and statement of financial position is provided to show how the statements of cash flows under the direct method and indirect method have been derived. Neither the statement of comprehensive income nor the statement of financial position is presented in conformity with the disclosure and presentation requirements of other Standards.

3   The following additional information is also relevant for the preparation of the statements of cash flows:

- all of the shares of a subsidiary were acquired for 590. The fair values of assets acquired and liabilities assumed were as follows:

Inventories	100
Accounts receivable	100
Cash	40
Property, plant and equipment	650
Trade payables	100
Long-term debt	200

- 250 was raised from the issue of share capital and a further 250 was raised from long-term borrowings.

- interest expense was 400, of which 170 was paid during the period. Also, 100 relating to interest expense of the prior period was paid during the period.

- dividends paid were 1,200.

- the liability for tax at the beginning and end of the period was 1,000 and 400 respectively. During the period, a further 200 tax was provided for. Withholding tax on dividends received amounted to 100.

- during the period, the group acquired property, plant and equipment and right-of-use assets relating to property, plant and equipment with an aggregate cost of 1,250, of which 900 related to right-of-use assets. Cash payments of 350 were made to purchase property, plant and equipment.

- plant with original cost of 80 and accumulated depreciation of 60 was sold for 20.

- accounts receivable as at the end of 20X2 include 100 of interest receivable.

Consolidated statement of comprehensive income for the period ended 20X2[(a)]

Sales	30,650
Cost of sales	(26,000)
Gross profit	4,650
Depreciation	(450)
Administrative and selling expenses	(910)
Interest expense	(400)
Investment income	500
Foreign exchange loss	(40)
Profit before taxation	3,350
Taxes on income	(300)
Profit	3,050

(a) The entity did not recognise any components of other comprehensive income in the period ended 20X2

Consolidated statement of financial position as at end of 20X2

	20X2	20X1
Assets		
Cash and cash equivalents	230	160
Accounts receivable	1,900	1,200
Inventory	1,000	1,950
Portfolio investments	2,500	2,500
Property, plant and equipment at cost	3,730	1,910
Accumulated depreciation	(1,450)	(1,060)
Property, plant and equipment net	2,280	850
Total assets	7,910	6,660
Liabilities		
Trade payables	250	1,890
Interest payable	230	100
Income taxes payable	400	1,000
Long-term debt	2,300	1,040
Total liabilities	3,180	4,030
Shareholders' equity		
Share capital	1,500	1,250
Retained earnings	3,230	1,380
Total shareholders' equity	4,730	2,630
Total liabilities and shareholders' equity	7,910	6,660

Direct method statement of cash flows (paragraph 18(a))

	20X2
Cash flows from operating activities [Refer: paragraph 10]	
Cash receipts from customers [Refer: paragraph 14]	30,150
Cash paid to suppliers and employees [Refer: paragraph 14]	(27,600)
Cash generated from operations	2,550
Interest paid [Refer: paragraphs 31–33]	(270)
Income taxes paid [Refer: paragraphs 35 and 36]	(900)
Net cash from operating activities	1,380
Cash flows from investing activities [Refer: paragraph 10]	
Acquisition of subsidiary X, net of cash acquired (Note A) [Refer: paragraphs 39 and 42]	(550)
Purchase of property, plant and equipment (Note B) [Refer: paragraph 21]	(350)
Proceeds from sale of equipment [Refer: paragraph 21]	20
Interest received [Refer: paragraphs 31 and 33]	200
Dividends received [Refer: paragraphs 31 and 33]	200
Net cash used in investing activities	(480)

continued...

...continued

Direct method statement of cash flows (paragraph 18(a))

	20X2
Cash flows from financing activities **[Refer: paragraph 10]**	
Proceeds from issue of share capital **[Refer: paragraph 21]**	250
Proceeds from long-term borrowings **[Refer: paragraph 21]**	250
Payment of lease liabilities **[Refer: paragraph 21]**	(90)
Dividends paid[(a)] **[Refer: paragraphs 31 and 34]**	(1,200)
Net cash used in financing activities	(790)
Net increase in cash and cash equivalents	110
Cash and cash equivalents at beginning of period (Note C)	120
Cash and cash equivalents at end of period (Note C)	230

(a) This could also be shown as an operating cash flow.

Indirect method statement of cash flows (paragraph 18(b))

	20X2

Cash flows from operating activities
[Refer: paragraph 10]

Profit before taxation [Refer: paragraph 20]	3,350
Adjustments for:	
Depreciation [Refer: paragraph 20(b)]	450
Foreign exchange loss [Refer: paragraph 20(b) and (c)]	40
Investment income [Refer: paragraph 20(c)]	(500)
Interest expense	400
	3,740
Increase in trade and other receivables [Refer: paragraph 20(a)]	(500)
Decrease in inventories [Refer: paragraph 20(a)]	1,050
Decrease in trade payables [Refer: paragraph 20(a)]	(1,740)
Cash generated from operations [Refer: paragraph 20]	2,550
Interest paid [Refer: paragraphs 31–33]	(270)
Income taxes paid [Refer: paragraphs 35 and 36]	(900)
Net cash from operating activities	1,380

Cash flows from investing activities
[Refer: paragraph 10]

Acquisition of subsidiary X net of cash acquired (Note A) [Refer: paragraphs 39 and 42]	(550)
Purchase of property, plant and equipment (Note B) [Refer: paragraph 21]	(350)
Proceeds from sale of equipment [Refer: paragraph 21]	20
Interest received [Refer: paragraphs 31 and 33]	200
Dividends received [Refer: paragraphs 31 and 33]	200
Net cash used in investing activities	(480)

continued...

...continued

Indirect method statement of cash flows (paragraph 18(b))

	20X2
Cash flows from financing activities [Refer: paragraph 10]	
Proceeds from issue of share capital [Refer: paragraph 21]	250
Proceeds from long-term borrowings [Refer: paragraph 21]	250
Payment of lease liabilities [Refer: paragraph 21]	(90)
Dividends paid(a) [Refer: paragraphs 31 and 34]	(1,200)
Net cash used in financing activities	(790)
Net increase in cash and cash equivalents	110
Cash and cash equivalents at beginning of period (Note C)	120
Cash and cash equivalents at end of period (Note C)	230

(a) This could also be shown as an operating cash flow.

Notes to the statement of cash flows (direct method and indirect method)

A. Obtaining control of subsidiary

During the period the Group obtained control of subsidiary X. The fair values of assets acquired and liabilities assumed were as follows [Refer: paragraph 40]:

Cash	40
Inventories	100
Accounts receivable	100
Property, plant and equipment	650
Trade payables	(100)
Long-term debt	(200)
Total purchase price paid in cash	590
Less: Cash of subsidiary X acquired	(40)
Cash paid to obtain control net of cash acquired	550

B. Property, plant and equipment

During the period, the Group acquired property, plant and equipment and right-of-use assets relating to property, plant and equipment with an aggregate cost of 1,250, of which 900 related to right-of-use assets. Cash payments of 350 were made to purchase property, plant and equipment [Refer: paragraphs 43 and 44].

C. Cash and cash equivalents

Cash and cash equivalents consist of cash on hand and balances with banks, and investments in money market instruments. Cash and cash equivalents included in the statement of cash flows comprise the following amounts in the statement of financial position [Refer: paragraphs 45–47]:

	20X2	20X1
Cash on hand and balances with banks	40	25
Short-term investments	190	135
Cash and cash equivalents as previously reported	230	160
Effect of exchange rate changes	–	(40)
Cash and cash equivalents as restated	230	120

Cash and cash equivalents at the end of the period include deposits with banks of 100 held by a subsidiary which are not freely remissible to the holding company because of currency exchange restrictions. [Refer: paragraph 48]

The Group has undrawn borrowing facilities of 2,000 of which 700 may be used only for future expansion. [Refer: paragraphs 48 and 50(a)]

D. Segment information

[Refer: paragraphs 50(d) and 52]

	Segment A	Segment B	Total
Cash flows from:			
Operating activities	1,520	(140)	1,380
Investing activities	(640)	160	(480)
Financing activities	(570)	(220)	(790)
	310	(200)	110

E. Reconciliation of liabilities arising from financing activities

[Refer: paragraphs 44A and 44B]

	20X1	Cash flows	Non-cash changes		20X2
			Acquisition	New leases	
Long-term borrowings	1,040	250	200	–	1,490
Lease liabilities	–	(90)	–	900	810
Long-term debt	1,040	160	200	900	2,300

Alternative presentation (indirect method)

[Refer: paragraph 20]

As an alternative, in an indirect method statement of cash flows, operating profit before working capital changes is sometimes presented as follows:

Revenues excluding investment income	30,650
Operating expense excluding depreciation	(26,910)
Operating profit before working capital changes	3,740

B Statement of cash flows for a financial institution

1   The example shows only current period amounts. Comparative amounts for the preceding period are required to be presented in accordance with IAS 1 *Presentation of Financial Statements*.

2   The example is presented using the direct method.

Cash flows from operating activities
[Refer: paragraph 10]

Interest and commission receipts [Refer: paragraph 33]	28,447
Interest payments [Refer: paragraph 33]	(23,463)
Recoveries on loans previously written off [Refer: paragraph 14]	237
Cash payments to employees and suppliers [Refer: paragraph 14]	(997)
	4,224

(Increase) decrease in operating assets:

Short-term funds [Refer: paragraphs 15 and 24]	(650)
Deposits held for regulatory or monetary control purposes [Refer: paragraphs 15 and 24]	234
Funds advanced to customers [Refer: paragraphs 15 and 24]	(288)
Net increase in credit card receivables [Refer: paragraphs 15 and 24]	(360)
Other short-term negotiable securities [Refer: paragraphs 15 and 24]	(120)

Increase (decrease) in operating liabilities:

Deposits from customers [Refer: paragraphs 15 and 24]	600	
Negotiable certificates of deposit [Refer: paragraphs 15 and 24]	(200)	
Net cash from operating activities before income tax	3,440	
Income taxes paid [Refer: paragraphs 35 and 36]	(100)	
Net cash from operating activities		3,340

continued...

...continued

	20X2
Cash flows from investing activities [Refer: paragraph 10]	
Disposal of subsidiary Y [Refer: paragraphs 39–42B]	50
Dividends received [Refer: paragraphs 31 and 33]	200
Interest received [Refer: paragraphs 31 and 33]	300
Proceeds from sales of non-dealing securities [Refer: paragraph 21]	1,200
Purchase of non-dealing securities [Refer: paragraph 21]	(600)
Purchase of property, plant and equipment [Refer: paragraph 21]	(500)
Net cash from investing activities	650
Cash flows from financing activities [Refer: paragraph 10]	
Issue of loan capital [Refer: paragraph 21]	1,000
Issue of preference shares by subsidiary undertaking [Refer: paragraph 21]	800
Repayment of long-term borrowings [Refer: paragraph 21]	(200)
Net decrease in other borrowings [Refer: paragraph 21]	(1,000)
Dividends paid [Refer: paragraphs 31 and 34]	(400)
Net cash from financing activities	200
Effects of exchange rate changes on cash and cash equivalents [Refer: paragraph 28]	600
Net increase in cash and cash equivalents	4,790
Cash and cash equivalents at beginning of period	4,050
Cash and cash equivalents at end of period	8,840

C Reconciliation of liabilities arising from financing activities

[Refer: paragraphs 44A and 44B]

1   This example illustrates one possible way of providing the disclosures required by paragraphs 44A–44E.

2   The example shows only current period amounts. Corresponding amounts for the preceding period are required to be presented in accordance with IAS 1 *Presentation of Financial Statements*.

	20X1	Cash flows	Acquisition	Foreign exchange movement	Fair value changes	20X2
			Non-cash changes			
Long-term borrowings	22,000	(1,000)	–	–	–	21,000
Short-term borrowings	10,000	(500)	–	200	–	9,700
Lease liabilities	4,000	(800)	300	–	–	3,500
Assets held to hedge long-term borrowings	(675)	150	–	–	(25)	(550)
Total liabilities from financing activities	35,325	(2,150)	300	200	(25)	33,650

IASB documents published to accompany

IAS 8

Accounting Policies, Changes in Accounting Estimates and Errors

The text of the unaccompanied standard, IAS 8, is contained in Part A of this edition. Its effective date when issued was 1 January 2005. The text of the Basis for Conclusions on IAS 8 is contained in Part C of this edition. This part presents the following document:

IMPLEMENTATION GUIDANCE

Guidance on implementing
IAS 8 *Accounting Policies, Changes in Accounting Estimates and Errors*

This guidance accompanies, but is not part of, IAS 8.

Example 1 – Retrospective restatement of errors

[Refer: paragraph 42]

1.1   During 20X2, Beta Co discovered that some products that had been sold during 20X1 were incorrectly included in inventory at 31 December 20X1 at CU6,500.[1]

1.2   Beta's accounting records for 20X2 show sales of CU104,000, cost of goods sold of CU86,500 (including CU6,500 for the error in opening inventory), and income taxes of CU5,250.

1.3   In 20X1, Beta reported:

	CU
Sales	73,500
Cost of goods sold	(53,500)
Profit before income taxes	20,000
Income taxes	(6,000)
Profit	14,000

1.4   20X1 opening retained earnings was CU20,000 and closing retained earnings was CU34,000.

1.5   Beta's income tax rate was 30 per cent for 20X2 and 20X1. It had no other income or expenses.

1.6   Beta had CU5,000 of share capital throughout, and no other components of equity except for retained earnings. Its shares are not publicly traded and it does not disclose earnings per share.

---

1   In these examples, monetary amounts are denominated in 'currency units (CU)'.

Beta Co Extract from the statement of comprehensive income

	20X2	(restated) 20X1
	CU	CU
Sales	104,000	73,500
Cost of goods sold	(80,000)	(60,000)
Profit before income taxes	24,000	13,500
Income taxes	(7,200)	(4,050)
Profit	16,800	9,450

Beta Co Statement of changes in equity

	Share capital	Retained earnings	Total
	CU	CU	CU
Balance at 31 December 20X0	5,000	20,000	25,000
Profit for the year ended 31 December 20X1 as restated		9,450	9,450
Balance at 31 December 20X1	5,000	29,450	34,450
Profit for the year ended 31 December 20X2		16,800	16,800
Balance at 31 December 20X2	5,000	46,250	51,250

Extracts from the notes

1   Some products that had been sold in 20X1 were incorrectly included in inventory at 31 December 20X1 at CU6,500. **[Refer: paragraph 49(a)]** The financial statements of 20X1 have been restated to correct this error. The effect of the restatement on those financial statements is summarised below. There is no effect in 20X2.
[Refer: paragraph 49(b)(i)]

	Effect on 20X1
	CU
(Increase) in cost of goods sold	(6,500)
Decrease in income tax expense	1,950
(Decrease) in profit	(4,550)
(Decrease) in inventory	(6,500)
Decrease in income tax payable	1,950
(Decrease) in equity	(4,550)

Example 2 – Change in accounting policy with retrospective application

[Deleted]

Example 3 – Prospective application of a change in accounting policy when retrospective application is not practicable

[Deleted]

[Refer: Basis for Conclusions paragraph BC54]

Example 4 – Applying the definition of accounting estimates—Fair value of an investment property

[Refer: Basis for Conclusions paragraph BC55]

Fact pattern

4.1 Entity A owns an investment property that it accounts for by applying the fair value model in IAS 40 *Investment Property*. Since it acquired the investment property, Entity A has been measuring the investment property's fair value using a valuation technique consistent with the income approach described in IFRS 13 *Fair Value Measurement*.

4.2 However, because of changes in market conditions since the previous reporting period, Entity A changes the valuation technique it uses to a valuation technique consistent with the market approach described in IFRS 13. Entity A has concluded that the resulting measurement is more representative of the investment property's fair value in the circumstances existing at the end of the current reporting period and, therefore, that IFRS 13 permits such a change. Entity A has also concluded that the change in the valuation technique is not a correction of a prior period error.

Applying the definition of accounting estimates

4.3 The fair value of the investment property is an accounting estimate because:

(a) the fair value of the investment property is a monetary amount in the financial statements that is subject to measurement uncertainty. Fair value reflects the price that would be received or paid in a hypothetical sale or purchase transaction between market participants — accordingly, it cannot be observed directly and must instead be estimated.

(b) the fair value of the investment property is an output of a measurement technique (a valuation technique) used in applying the accounting policy (fair value model).

(c) in developing its estimate of the fair value of the investment property, Entity A uses judgements and assumptions, for example, in:

(i) selecting the measurement technique — selecting the valuation technique that is appropriate in the circumstances; and

(ii) applying the measurement technique – developing the inputs that market participants would use in applying the valuation technique, such as information generated by market transactions involving comparable assets.

[Refer: paragraph 5 (definition of accounting estimates) and paragraphs 32–32A]

4.4 In this fact pattern, the change in the valuation technique is a change in the measurement technique applied to estimate the fair value of the investment property. The effect of this change is a change in an accounting estimate because the accounting policy – to measure the investment property at fair value – has not changed.

[Refer: paragraph 34A]

Example 5 – Applying the definition of accounting estimates—Fair value of a cash-settled share-based payment liability

[Refer: Basis for Conclusions paragraph BC55]

Fact pattern

5.1 On 1 January 20X0, Entity A grants 100 share appreciation rights (SARs) to each of its employees, provided the employee remains in the entity's employment for the next three years. The SARs entitle the employees to a future cash payment based on the increase in the entity's share price over the three-year vesting period starting on 1 January 20X0.

5.2 Applying IFRS 2 *Share-based Payment*, Entity A accounts for the grant of the SARs as cash-settled share-based payment transactions – in doing so it recognises a liability for the SARs and measures that liability at its fair value (as defined by IFRS 2). Entity A applies the Black–Scholes–Merton formula (an option pricing model) to measure the fair value of the liability for the SARs at 1 January 20X0 and at the end of the reporting period.

5.3 At 31 December 20X1, because of changes in market conditions since the end of the previous reporting period, Entity A changes its estimate of the expected volatility of the share price – an input to the option pricing model – in estimating the fair value of the liability for the SARs at that date. Entity A has concluded that the change in that input is not a correction of a prior period error.

Applying the definition of accounting estimates

5.4 The fair value of the liability is an accounting estimate because:

(a) the fair value of the liability is a monetary amount in the financial statements that is subject to measurement uncertainty. That fair value is the amount for which the liability could be settled in a hypothetical transaction – accordingly, it cannot be observed directly and must instead be estimated.

    (b)   the fair value of the liability is an output of a measurement technique (option pricing model) used in applying the accounting policy (measuring a liability for a cash-settled share-based payment at fair value).

    (c)   to estimate the fair value of the liability, Entity A uses judgements and assumptions, for example, in:

        (i)   selecting the measurement technique — selecting the option pricing model; and

        (ii)   applying the measurement technique — developing the inputs that market participants would use in applying that option pricing model, such as the expected volatility of the share price and dividends expected on the shares.

[Refer: paragraph 5 (definition of accounting estimates) and paragraphs 32–32A]

5.5   In this fact pattern, the change in the expected volatility of the share price is a change in an input used to measure the fair value of the liability for the SARs at 31 December 20X1. The effect of this change is a change in accounting estimate because the accounting policy — to measure the liability at fair value — has not changed.

[Refer: paragraph 34A]

IASB documents published to accompany

IAS 12

Income Taxes

The text of the unaccompanied standard, IAS 12, is contained in Part A of this edition. Its effective date when issued was 1 January 1998. The text of the Basis for Conclusions on IAS 12 is contained in Part C of this edition. This part presents the following documents:

ILLUSTRATIVE EXAMPLES

Examples of temporary differences

Illustrative computations and presentation

Illustrative Examples

These illustrative examples accompany, but are not part of, IAS 12.

Examples of temporary differences

A. Examples of circumstances that give rise to taxable temporary differences

All taxable temporary differences give rise to a deferred tax liability.
[Refer: paragraph 15]

Transactions that affect profit or loss

1   Interest revenue is received in arrears and is included in accounting profit on a time apportionment basis but is included in taxable profit on a cash basis.

2   Revenue from the sale of goods is included in accounting profit when goods are delivered **[Refer: IFRS 15 paragraph 31]** but is included in taxable profit when cash is collected. *(note: as explained in B3 below, there is also a **deductible** temporary difference associated with any related inventory).*

3   Depreciation of an asset is accelerated for tax purposes.

4   Development costs have been capitalised **[Refer: IAS 38 paragraphs 57–67]** and will be amortised to the statement of comprehensive income but were deducted in determining taxable profit in the period in which they were incurred.

5   Prepaid expenses have already been deducted on a cash basis in determining the taxable profit of the current or previous periods.

Transactions that affect the statement of financial position

6   Depreciation of an asset is not deductible for tax purposes and no deduction will be available for tax purposes when the asset is sold or scrapped. *(note: paragraph 15(b) of the Standard prohibits recognition of the resulting deferred tax liability unless the asset was acquired in a business combination, see also paragraph 22 of the Standard.)*

7   A borrower records a loan at the proceeds received (which equal the amount due at maturity), less transaction costs. **[Refer: IFRS 9 paragraph 5.1.1]** Subsequently, the carrying amount of the loan is increased by amortisation of the transaction costs to accounting profit. **[Refer: IFRS 9 Appendix A (definition of effective interest rate)]** The transaction costs were deducted for tax purposes in the period when the loan was first recognised. *(notes: (1) the taxable temporary difference is the amount of transaction costs already deducted in determining the taxable profit of current or prior periods, less the cumulative amount amortised to accounting profit; and (2) as the initial recognition of the loan affects taxable profit, the exception in paragraph 15(b) of the Standard does not apply. Therefore, the borrower recognises the deferred tax liability.)*

8   A loan payable was measured on initial recognition at the amount of the net proceeds, net of transaction costs. The transaction costs are amortised to accounting profit over the life of the loan. [Refer: IFRS 9 Appendix A (definition of effective interest rate)] Those transaction costs are not deductible in determining the taxable profit of future, current or prior periods. *(notes: (1) the taxable temporary difference is the amount of unamortised transaction costs; and (2) paragraph 15(b) of the Standard prohibits recognition of the resulting deferred tax liability.)*

9   The liability component of a compound financial instrument (for example a convertible bond) is measured at a discount to the amount repayable on maturity (see IAS 32 *Financial Instruments: Presentation*). [Refer: IAS 32 paragraphs 28–32] The discount is not deductible in determining taxable profit (tax loss).

[Refer: Illustrative computations and presentation example 4]

Fair value adjustments and revaluations

10   Financial assets [Refer: IFRS 9 paragraph 5.2.1] or investment property [Refer: IAS 40 paragraph 30] are carried at fair value which exceeds cost but no equivalent adjustment is made for tax purposes. [Refer: Illustrative computations and presentation example 7]

11   An entity revalues property, plant and equipment (under the revaluation model treatment in IAS 16 *Property, Plant and Equipment*) [Refer: IAS 16 paragraphs 29 and 31–42] but no equivalent adjustment is made for tax purposes. *(note: paragraph 61A of the Standard requires the related deferred tax to be recognised in other comprehensive income.)*

Business combinations and consolidation

12   The carrying amount of an asset is increased to fair value in a business combination [Refer: IFRS 3 paragraph 18] and no equivalent adjustment is made for tax purposes. *(Note that on initial recognition, the resulting deferred tax liability increases goodwill or decreases the amount of any bargain purchase gain recognised. See paragraph 66 of the Standard.)*

13   Reductions in the carrying amount of goodwill are not deductible in determining taxable profit and the cost of the goodwill would not be deductible on disposal of the business. *(Note that paragraph 15(a) of the Standard prohibits recognition of the resulting deferred tax liability.)*

14   Unrealised losses resulting from intragroup transactions are eliminated by inclusion in the carrying amount of inventory or property, plant and equipment.

[Refer: IFRS 10 paragraph B86(c)]

15   Retained earnings of subsidiaries, branches, associates and joint ventures are included in consolidated retained earnings, but income taxes [Refer: paragraph 2] will be payable if the profits are distributed to the reporting parent. *(note: paragraph 39 of the Standard prohibits recognition of the resulting deferred tax liability if the parent, investor or venturer is able to control the*

timing of the reversal of the temporary difference and it is probable that the temporary difference will not reverse in the foreseeable future.)

16   Investments in foreign subsidiaries, branches or associates or interests in foreign joint ventures are affected by changes in foreign exchange rates. *(notes: (1) there may be either a taxable temporary difference or a deductible temporary difference; and (2) paragraph 39 of the Standard prohibits recognition of the resulting deferred tax liability if the parent, investor or venturer is able to control the timing of the reversal of the temporary difference and it is probable that the temporary difference will not reverse in the foreseeable future.)*

17   The non-monetary assets and liabilities of an entity are measured in its functional currency but the taxable profit or tax loss is determined in a different currency. **[Refer: IAS 21 paragraphs 21 and 23]** *(notes: (1) there may be either a taxable temporary difference or a deductible temporary difference; (2) where there is a taxable temporary difference, the resulting deferred tax liability is recognised (paragraph 41 of the Standard); and (3) the deferred tax is recognised in profit or loss, see paragraph 58 of the Standard.)*

Hyperinflation

18   Non-monetary assets are restated in terms of the measuring unit current at the end of the reporting period (see IAS 29 *Financial Reporting in Hyperinflationary Economies*) **[Refer: IAS 29 paragraph 8]** and no equivalent adjustment is made for tax purposes. *(notes: (1) the deferred tax is recognised in profit or loss; and (2) if, in addition to the restatement, the non-monetary assets are also revalued, the deferred tax relating to the revaluation is recognised in other comprehensive income and the deferred tax relating to the restatement is recognised in profit or loss.)*

B. Examples of circumstances that give rise to deductible temporary differences

All deductible temporary differences give rise to a deferred tax asset. However, some deferred tax assets may not satisfy the recognition criteria in paragraph 24 of the Standard.

Transactions that affect profit or loss

1   Retirement benefit costs are deducted in determining accounting profit as service is provided by the employee, **[Refer: IAS 19 paragraphs 26–130]** but are not deducted in determining taxable profit until the entity pays either retirement benefits or contributions to a fund. *(note: similar deductible temporary differences arise where other expenses, such as product warranty costs or interest, are deductible on a cash basis in determining taxable profit.)*

2   Accumulated depreciation of an asset in the financial statements is greater than the cumulative depreciation allowed up to the end of the reporting period for tax purposes.

3   The cost of inventories sold before the end of the reporting period is deducted in determining accounting profit when goods or services are delivered but is deducted in determining taxable profit when cash is collected. *(note: as explained in A2 above, there is also a* **taxable** *temporary difference associated with the related trade receivable.)*

4   The net realisable value of an item of inventory, **[Refer: IAS 2 paragraph 9]** or the recoverable amount of an item of property, plant or equipment, **[Refer: IAS 36 paragraph 59]** is less than the previous carrying amount and an entity therefore reduces the carrying amount of the asset, but that reduction is ignored for tax purposes until the asset is sold.

5   Research costs (or organisation or other start-up costs) are recognised as an expense in determining accounting profit **[Refer: IAS 38 paragraphs 54–56]** but are not permitted as a deduction in determining taxable profit until a later period.

6   Income is deferred in the statement of financial position but has already been included in taxable profit in current or prior periods.

7   A government grant which is included in the statement of financial position as deferred income **[Refer: IAS 20 paragraph 24]** will not be taxable in future periods. *(note: paragraph 24 of the Standard prohibits the recognition of the resulting deferred tax asset, see also paragraph 33 of the Standard.)*

Fair value adjustments and revaluations

8   Financial assets or investment property are carried at fair value which is less than cost, but no equivalent adjustment is made for tax purposes. **[Refer: Illustrative computations and presentation example 7]**

Business combinations and consolidation

9   A liability is recognised at its fair value in a business combination, **[Refer: IFRS 3 paragraph 18]** but none of the related expense is deducted in determining taxable profit until a later period. *(Note that the resulting deferred tax asset decreases goodwill or increases the amount of any bargain purchase gain recognised. See paragraph 66 of the Standard.)*

10   [Deleted]

11   Unrealised profits resulting from intragroup transactions are eliminated from the carrying amount of assets, such as inventory or property, plant or equipment, but no equivalent adjustment is made for tax purposes. **[Refer: IFRS 10 paragraph B86(c)]**

12   Investments in foreign subsidiaries, branches or associates or interests in foreign joint ventures are affected by changes in foreign exchange rates. *(notes: (1) there may be a taxable temporary difference or a deductible temporary difference; and (2) paragraph 44 of the Standard requires recognition of the resulting deferred tax asset to the extent, and only to the extent, that it is probable that: (a) the temporary difference will reverse in the foreseeable future; and (b) taxable profit will be available against which the temporary difference can be utilised).* **[Refer: paragraphs 27–31 and 34–36]**

13　The non-monetary assets and liabilities of an entity are measured in its functional currency but the taxable profit or tax loss is determined in a different currency. *(notes: (1) there may be either a taxable temporary difference or a deductible temporary difference; (2) where there is a deductible temporary difference, the resulting deferred tax asset is recognised to the extent that it is probable* **[Refer: paragraphs 27–31]** *that sufficient taxable profit will be available (paragraph 41 of the Standard); and (3) the deferred tax is recognised in profit or loss, see paragraph 58 of the Standard.)*

C. Examples of circumstances where the carrying amount of an asset or liability is equal to its tax base

1　Accrued expenses have already been deducted in determining an entity's current tax liability for the current or earlier periods.

2　A loan payable is measured at the amount originally received and this amount is the same as the amount repayable on final maturity of the loan.

3　Accrued expenses will never be deductible for tax purposes.

4　Accrued income will never be taxable.

[Refer: paragraphs 7 and 8]

Illustrative computations and presentation

Extracts from statements of financial position and statements of comprehensive income are provided to show the effects on these financial statements of the transactions described below. These extracts do not necessarily conform with all the disclosure and presentation requirements of other Standards.

All the examples below assume that the entities concerned have no transaction other than those described.

Example 1 – Depreciable assets

An entity buys equipment for 10,000 and depreciates it on a straight-line basis over its expected useful life of five years. For tax purposes, the equipment is depreciated at 25% a year on a straight-line basis. Tax losses may be carried back against taxable profit of the previous five years. In year 0, the entity's taxable profit was 5,000. The tax rate [Refer: paragraphs 46–52A] is 40%.

The entity will recover the carrying amount of the equipment by using it to manufacture goods for resale. [Refer: paragraph 51] Therefore, the entity's current tax computation is as follows:

	Year				
	1	2	3	4	5
Taxable income	2,000	2,000	2,000	2,000	2,000
Depreciation for tax purposes	2,500	2,500	2,500	2,500	0
Taxable profit (tax loss)	(500)	(500)	(500)	(500)	2,000
Current tax expense (income) at 40%	(200)	(200)	(200)	(200)	800

[Refer: paragraph 58]

The entity recognises a current tax asset at the end of years 1 to 4 because it recovers the benefit of the tax loss against the taxable profit of year 0.

[Refer: paragraph 14]

The temporary differences associated with the equipment and the resulting deferred tax asset and liability and deferred tax expense and income are as follows:

	Year				
	1	2	3	4	5
Carrying amount	8,000	6,000	4,000	2,000	0
Tax base	7,500	5,000	2,500	0	0
Taxable temporary difference	500	1,000	1,500	2,000	0
Opening deferred tax liability	0	200	400	600	800
Deferred tax expense (income)	200	200	200	200	(800)
Closing deferred tax liability	200	400	600	800	0

[Refer: paragraphs 7, 15, 47, 51, 53 and 58]

The entity recognises the deferred tax liability in years 1 to 4 because the reversal of the taxable temporary difference will create taxable income in subsequent years. The entity's statement of comprehensive income includes the following:

	Year				
	1	2	3	4	5
Income	2,000	2,000	2,000	2,000	2,000
Depreciation	2,000	2,000	2,000	2,000	2,000
Profit before tax	0	0	0	0	0
Current tax expense (income)	(200)	(200)	(200)	(200)	800
Deferred tax expense (income)	200	200	200	200	(800)
Total tax expense (income)	0	0	0	0	0
Profit for the period	0	0	0	0	0

[Refer: paragraphs 58 and 77]

Example 2 – Deferred tax assets and liabilities

The example deals with an entity over the two-year period, X5 and X6. In X5 the enacted income tax rate was 40% of taxable profit. In X6 the enacted income tax rate was 35% of taxable profit.
[Refer: paragraphs 47–52A]

Charitable donations are recognised as an expense when they are paid and are not deductible for tax purposes.

In X5, the entity was notified by the relevant authorities that they intend to pursue an action against the entity with respect to sulphur emissions. Although as at December X6 the action had not yet come to court the entity recognised a liability of 700 in X5 being its best estimate of the fine arising from the action. [Refer: IAS 37 paragraphs 14 and 36–40] Fines are not deductible for tax purposes.

In X2, the entity incurred 1,250 of costs in relation to the development of a new product. These costs were deducted for tax purposes in X2. For accounting purposes, the entity capitalised this expenditure and amortised it on the straight-line basis over five years. [Refer: IAS 38 paragraphs 57–67 and 74] At 31/12/X4, the unamortised balance of these product development costs was 500.

In X5, the entity entered into an agreement with its existing employees to provide healthcare benefits to retirees. The entity recognises as an expense the cost of this plan as employees provide service. [Refer: IAS 19 paragraphs 26–130] No payments to retirees were made for such benefits in X5 or X6. Healthcare costs are deductible for tax purposes when payments are made to retirees. The entity has determined that it is probable [Refer: paragraphs 27–31] that taxable profit will be available against which any resulting deferred tax asset can be utilised.

Buildings are depreciated for accounting purposes at 5% a year on a straight-line basis and at 10% a year on a straight-line basis for tax purposes. Motor vehicles are depreciated for accounting purposes at 20% a year on a straight-line basis and at 25% a year on a straight-line basis for tax purposes. [Refer: IAS 16 paragraphs 43–62] A full year's depreciation is charged for accounting purposes in the year that an asset is acquired.

At 1/1/X6, the building was revalued to 65,000 and the entity estimated that the remaining useful life of the building was 20 years from the date of the revaluation. [Refer: IAS 16 paragraph 31] The revaluation did not affect taxable profit in X6 and the taxation authorities did not adjust the tax base of the building to reflect the revaluation. In X6, the entity transferred 1,033 from revaluation surplus to retained earnings. This represents the difference of 1,590 between the actual depreciation on the building (3,250) and equivalent depreciation based on the cost of the building (1,660, which is the book value at 1/1/X6 of 33,200 divided by the remaining useful life of 20 years), less the related deferred tax of 557 (see paragraph 64 of the Standard).

Current tax expense

	X5	X6
Accounting profit	8,775	8,740
Add		
Depreciation for accounting purposes	4,800	8,250
Charitable donations	500	350
Fine for environmental pollution	700	–
Product development costs	250	250
Healthcare benefits	2,000	1,000
	17,025	18,590
Deduct		
Depreciation for tax purposes	(8,100)	(11,850)
Taxable profit	8,925	6,740
Current tax expense at 40%	3,570	
Current tax expense at 35%		2,359

[Refer: paragraph 58]

Carrying amounts of property, plant and equipment

	Building	Motor vehicles	Total
Balance at 31/12/X4	50,000	10,000	60,000
Additions X5	6,000	–	6,000
Balance at 31/12/X5	56,000	10,000	66,000
Elimination of accumulated depreciation on revaluation at 1/1/X6	(22,800)	–	(22,800)
Revaluation at 1/1/X6	31,800	–	31,800
Balance at 1/1/X6	65,000	10,000	75,000
Additions X6	–	15,000	15,000
	65,000	25,000	90,000
Accumulated depreciation	5%	20%	
Balance at 31/12/X4	20,000	4,000	24,000
Depreciation X5	2,800	2,000	4,800
Balance at 31/12/X5	22,800	6,000	28,800
Revaluation at 1/1/X6	(22,800)	–	(22,800)
Balance at 1/1/X6	–	6,000	6,000
Depreciation X6	3,250	5,000	8,250
Balance at 31/12/X6	3,250	11,000	14,250
Carrying amount			
31/12/X4	30,000	6,000	36,000
31/12/X5	33,200	4,000	37,200
31/12/X6	61,750	14,000	75,750

[Refer: IAS 16]

Tax base of property, plant and equipment

	Building	Motor vehicles	Total
Cost			
Balance at 31/12/X4	50,000	10,000	60,000
Additions X5	6,000	–	6,000
Balance at 31/12/X5	56,000	10,000	66,000
Additions X6	–	15,000	15,000
Balance at 31/12/X6	56,000	25,000	81,000
Accumulated depreciation	10%	25%	
Balance at 31/12/X4	40,000	5,000	45,000
Depreciation X5	5,600	2,500	8,100
Balance at 31/12/X5	45,600	7,500	53,100
Depreciation X6	5,600	6,250	11,850
Balance 31/12/X6	51,200	13,750	64,950
Tax base			
31/12/X4	10,000	5,000	15,000
31/12/X5	10,400	2,500	12,900
31/12/X6	4,800	11,250	16,050

[Refer: paragraphs 7–10]

Deferred tax assets, liabilities and expense at 31/12/X4

	Carrying amount	Tax base	Temporary differences
Accounts receivable	500	500	–
Inventory	2,000	2,000	–
Product development costs	500	–	500
Investments	33,000	33,000	–
Property, plant & equipment	36,000	15,000	21,000
TOTAL ASSETS	72,000	50,500	21,500
Current income taxes payable	3,000	3,000	–
Accounts payable	500	500	–
Fines payable	–	–	–
Liability for healthcare benefits	–	–	–
Long-term debt	20,000	20,000	–
Deferred income taxes	8,600	8,600	–
TOTAL LIABILITIES	32,100	32,100	
Share capital	5,000	5,000	–
Revaluation surplus	–	–	–
Retained earnings	34,900	13,400	
TOTAL LIABILITIES/EQUITY	72,000	50,500	
TEMPORARY DIFFERENCES			21,500
Deferred tax liability	21,500 at 40%		8,600
Deferred tax asset	–		–
Net deferred tax liability			
[Refer: paragraphs 15–33 and 46–60]			8,600

Deferred tax assets, liabilities and expense at 31/12/X5

	Carrying amount	Tax base	Temporary differences
Accounts receivable	500	500	–
Inventory	2,000	2,000	–
Product development costs	250	–	250
Investments	33,000	33,000	–
Property, plant & equipment	37,200	12,900	24,300
TOTAL ASSETS	72,950	48,400	24,550
Current income taxes payable	3,570	3,570	–
Accounts payable	500	500	–
Fines payable	700	700	–
Liability for healthcare benefits	2,000	–	(2,000)
Long-term debt	12,475	12,475	–
Deferred income taxes	9,020	9,020	–
TOTAL LIABILITIES	28,265	26,265	(2,000)
Share capital	5,000	5,000	–
Revaluation surplus	–	–	–
Retained earnings	39,685	17,135	
TOTAL LIABILITIES/EQUITY	72,950	48,400	
TEMPORARY DIFFERENCES			22,550

Deferred tax liability	24,550 at 40%	9,820
Deferred tax asset	2,000 at 40%	(800)
Net deferred tax liability		9,020
Less: Opening deferred tax liability		(8,600)
Deferred tax expense (income) related to the origination and reversal of temporary differences		
[Refer: paragraphs 15–33 and 46–60]		420

Deferred tax assets, liabilities and expense at 31/12/X6

	Carrying amount	Tax base	Temporary differences
Accounts receivable	500	500	–
Inventory	2,000	2,000	–
Product development costs	–	–	
Investments	33,000	33,000	–
Property, plant & equipment	75,750	16,050	59,700
TOTAL ASSETS	111,250	51,550	59,700
Current income taxes payable	2,359	2,359	–
Accounts payable	500	500	
Fines payable	700	700	
Liability for healthcare benefits	3,000	–	(3,000)
Long-term debt	12,805	12,805	–
Deferred income taxes	19,845	19,845	–
TOTAL LIABILITIES	39,209	36,209	(3,000)
Share capital	5,000	5,000	–
Revaluation surplus	19,637	–	
Retained earnings	47,404	10,341	
TOTAL LIABILITIES/EQUITY	111,250	51,550	

TEMPORARY DIFFERENCES		56,700
Deferred tax liability	59,700 at 35%	20,895
Deferred tax asset	3,000 at 35%	(1,050)
Net deferred tax liability		19,845
Less: Opening deferred tax liability		(9,020)
Adjustment to opening deferred tax liability resulting from reduction in tax rate	22,550 at 5%	1,127
Deferred tax attributable to revaluation surplus	31,800 at 35%	(11,130)
Deferred tax expense (income) related to the origination and reversal of temporary differences		
[Refer: paragraphs 15–33 and 46–65]		822

Illustrative disclosure

The amounts to be disclosed in accordance with the Standard are as follows:

Major components of tax expense (income) (paragraph 79)

	X5	X6
Current tax expense	3,570	2,359
Deferred tax expense relating to the origination and reversal of temporary differences:	420	822
Deferred tax expense (income) resulting from reduction in tax rate	–	(1,127)
Tax expense	3,990	2,054

Income tax relating to the components of other comprehensive income (paragraph 81(ab))

Deferred tax relating to revaluation of building	–	(11,130)

In addition, deferred tax of 557 was transferred in X6 from retained earnings to revaluation surplus. This relates to the difference between the actual depreciation on the building and equivalent depreciation based on the cost of the building.

Explanation of the relationship between tax expense and accounting profit (paragraph 81(c))

The Standard permits two alternative methods of explaining the relationship between tax expense (income) and accounting profit. Both of these formats are illustrated below.

(i)   a numerical reconciliation between tax expense (income) and the product of accounting profit multiplied by the applicable tax rate(s), disclosing also the basis on which the applicable tax rate(s) is (are) computed

	X5	X6
Accounting profit	8,775	8,740
Tax at the applicable tax rate of 35% (X5: 40%)	3,510	3,059
Tax effect of expenses that are not deductible in determining taxable profit:		
Charitable donations	200	122
Fines for environmental pollution	280	–
Reduction in opening deferred taxes resulting from reduction in tax rate	–	(1,127)
Tax expense	3,990	2,054

The applicable tax rate is the aggregate of the national income tax rate of 30% (X5: 35%) and the local income tax rate of 5%.

(ii)   a numerical reconciliation between the average effective tax rate and the applicable tax rate, disclosing also the basis on which the applicable tax rate is computed

	X5	X6
	%	%
Applicable tax rate	40.0	35.0
Tax effect of expenses that are not deductible for tax purposes:		
Charitable donations	2.3	1.4
Fines for environmental pollution	3.2	–
Effect on opening deferred taxes of reduction in tax rate	–	(12.9)
Average effective tax rate (tax expense divided by profit before tax)	45.5	23.5

The applicable tax rate **[Refer: paragraphs 46–52A]** is the aggregate of the national income tax rate of 30% (X5: 35%) and the local income tax rate of 5%.

An explanation of changes in the applicable tax rate(s) compared to the previous accounting period (paragraph 81(d))

In X6, the government enacted a change in the national income tax rate from 35% to 30%.

In respect of each type of temporary difference, and in respect of each type of unused tax losses and unused tax credits:

(i)   the amount of the deferred tax assets and liabilities recognised in the statement of financial position for each period presented;

(ii)   the amount of the deferred tax income or expense recognised in profit or loss for each period presented, if this is not apparent from the changes in the amounts recognised in the statement of financial position (paragraph 81(g)).

	X5	X6
Accelerated depreciation for tax purposes	9,720	10,322
Liabilities for healthcare benefits that are deducted for tax purposes only when paid	(800)	(1,050)
Product development costs deducted from taxable profit in earlier years	100	–
Revaluation, net of related depreciation	–	10,573
Deferred tax liability	9,020	19,845

(note: the amount of the deferred tax income or expense recognised in profit or loss for the current year is apparent from the changes in the amounts recognised in the statement of financial position)

Example 3 – Business combinations

On 1 January X5 entity A acquired 100 per cent of the shares of entity B at a cost of 600. At the acquisition date, the tax base in A's tax jurisdiction of A's investment in B is 600. Reductions in the carrying amount of goodwill are not deductible for tax purposes, and the cost of the goodwill would also not be deductible if B were to dispose of its underlying business. The tax rate in A's tax jurisdiction is 30 per cent and the tax rate in B's tax jurisdiction is 40 per cent.

The fair value of the identifiable assets acquired and liabilities assumed (excluding deferred tax assets and liabilities) by A is set out in the following table, together with their tax bases in B's tax jurisdiction and the resulting temporary differences.

	Amount recognised at acquisition [Refer: IFRS 3 paragraphs 10–40]	Tax base	Temporary differences
Property, plant and equipment	270	155	115
Accounts receivable	210	210	–
Inventory	174	124	50
Retirement benefit obligations	(30)	–	(30)
Accounts payable	(120)	(120)	–
Identifiable assets acquired and liabilities assumed, excluding deferred tax	504	369	135

The deferred tax asset arising from the retirement benefit obligations is offset against the deferred tax liabilities arising from the property, plant and equipment and inventory (see paragraph 74 of the Standard).

No deduction is available in B's tax jurisdiction for the cost of the goodwill. Therefore, the tax base of the goodwill in B's jurisdiction is nil. However, in accordance with paragraph 15(a) of the Standard, A recognises no deferred tax liability for the taxable temporary difference associated with the goodwill in B's tax jurisdiction.

The carrying amount, in A's consolidated financial statements, of its investment in B is made up as follows:

Fair value of identifiable assets acquired and liabilities assumed, excluding deferred tax	504
Deferred tax liability (135 at 40%)	(54)
Fair value of identifiable assets acquired and liabilities assumed	450
Goodwill	150
Carrying amount	600

Because, at the acquisition date, the tax base in A's tax jurisdiction, of A's investment in B is 600, no temporary difference is associated in A's tax jurisdiction with the investment.

During X5, B's equity (incorporating the fair value adjustments made as a result of the business combination) changed as follows:

At 1 January X5	450
Retained profit for X5 (net profit of 150, less dividend payable of 80)	70
At 31 December X5	520

A recognises a liability for any withholding tax or other taxes that it will incur on the accrued dividend receivable of 80.

At 31 December X5, the carrying amount of A's underlying investment in B, excluding the accrued dividend receivable, is as follows:

Net assets of B	520
Goodwill	150
Carrying amount	670

The temporary difference associated with A's underlying investment is 70. This amount is equal to the cumulative retained profit since the acquisition date.

If A has determined that it will not sell the investment in the foreseeable future and that B will not distribute its retained profits in the foreseeable future, no deferred tax liability is recognised in relation to A's investment in B (see paragraphs 39 and 40 of the Standard). Note that this exception would apply for an investment in an associate only if there is an agreement requiring that the profits of the associate will not be distributed in the foreseeable future (see paragraph 42 of the Standard). A discloses the amount of the temporary difference for which no deferred tax is recognised, ie 70 (see paragraph 81(f) of the Standard).

If A expects to sell the investment in B, or that B will distribute its retained profits in the foreseeable future, A recognises a deferred tax liability to the extent that the temporary difference is expected to reverse. The tax rate reflects the manner in which A expects to recover the carrying amount of its investment (see paragraph 51 of the Standard). A recognises the deferred tax in other comprehensive income to the extent that the deferred tax results from foreign exchange translation differences that have been recognised in other comprehensive income (paragraph 61A of the Standard). A discloses separately:

(a) the amount of deferred tax that has been recognised in other comprehensive income (paragraph 81(ab) of the Standard); and

(b) the amount of any remaining temporary difference which is not expected to reverse in the foreseeable future and for which, therefore, no deferred tax is recognised (see paragraph 81(f) of the Standard).

Example 4 – Compound financial instruments

An entity receives a non-interest-bearing convertible loan of 1,000 on 31 December X4 repayable at par on 1 January X8. In accordance with IAS 32 *Financial Instruments: Presentation* the entity classifies the instrument's liability component as a liability and the equity component as equity. **[Refer: IAS 32 paragraphs 28–32]** The entity assigns an initial carrying amount of 751 to the liability component of the convertible loan and 249 to the equity component. Subsequently, the entity recognises imputed discount as interest expense at an annual rate of 10% on the carrying amount of the liability component at the beginning of the year. The tax authorities do not allow the entity to claim any deduction for the imputed discount on the liability component of the convertible loan. The tax rate **[Refer: paragraphs 47–52A]** is 40%.

The temporary differences associated with the liability component and the resulting deferred tax liability and deferred tax expense and income are as follows:

	Year			
	X4	X5	X6	X7
Carrying amount of liability component	751	826	909	1,000
Tax base	1,000	1,000	1,000	1,000
Taxable temporary difference	249	174	91	–
Opening deferred tax liability at 40%	0	100	70	37
Deferred tax charged to equity	100	–	–	–
Deferred tax expense (income)	–	(30)	(33)	(37)
Closing deferred tax liability at 40%	100	70	37	–

As explained in paragraph 23 of the Standard, at 31 December X4, the entity recognises the resulting deferred tax liability by adjusting the initial carrying amount of the equity component of the convertible liability. Therefore, the amounts recognised at that date are as follows:

Liability component	751
Deferred tax liability	100
Equity component (249 less 100)	149
	1,000

Subsequent changes in the deferred tax liability are recognised in profit or loss as tax income (see paragraph 23 of the Standard). Therefore, the entity's profit or loss includes the following:

	Year			
	X4	X5	X6	X7
Interest expense (imputed discount)	–	75	83	91
Deferred tax expense (income)	–	(30)	(33)	(37)
	–	45	50	54

Example 5 – Share-based payment transactions

In accordance with IFRS 2 *Share-based Payment*, an entity has recognised an expense for the consumption of employee services received as consideration for share options granted. [Refer: IFRS 2 paragraph 7] A tax deduction will not arise until the options are exercised, and the deduction is based on the options' intrinsic value at exercise date.

As explained in paragraph 68B of the Standard, the difference between the tax base of the employee services received to date (being the amount the taxation authorities will permit as a deduction in future periods in respect of those services), and the carrying amount of nil, is a deductible temporary difference that results in a deferred tax asset. Paragraph 68B requires that, if the amount the taxation authorities will permit as a deduction in future periods is not known at the end of the period, it should be estimated, based on information available at the end of the period. If the amount that the taxation authorities will permit as a deduction in future periods is dependent upon the entity's share price at a future date, the measurement of the deductible temporary difference should be based on the entity's share price at the end of the period. Therefore, in this example, the estimated future tax deduction (and hence the measurement of the deferred tax asset) should be based on the options' intrinsic value at the end of the period.

As explained in paragraph 68C of the Standard, if the tax deduction (or estimated future tax deduction) exceeds the amount of the related cumulative remuneration expense, this indicates that the tax deduction relates not only to remuneration expense but also to an equity item. In this situation, paragraph 68C requires that the excess of the associated current or deferred tax should be recognised directly in equity.

The entity's tax rate [Refer: paragraphs 46–52A] is 40 per cent. The options were granted at the start of year 1, vested at the end of year 3 and were exercised at the end of year 5. Details of the expense recognised for employee services received and consumed in each accounting period, the number of options outstanding at each year-end, and the intrinsic value of the options at each year-end, are as follows:

	Employee services expense	Number of options at year-end	Intrinsic value per option
Year 1	188,000	50,000	5
Year 2	185,000	45,000	8
Year 3	190,000	40,000	13
Year 4	0	40,000	17
Year 5	0	40,000	20

The entity recognises a deferred tax asset and deferred tax income in years 1–4 and current tax income in year 5 as follows. In years 4 and 5, some of the deferred and current tax income is recognised directly in equity, because the estimated (and actual) tax deduction exceeds the cumulative remuneration expense.

Year 1

Deferred tax asset and deferred tax income:

$(50,000 \times 5 \times 1/3^{(a)} \times 0.40) =$ ⟶ 33,333

(a) The tax base of the employee services received is based on the intrinsic value of the options, and those options were granted for three years' services. Because only one year's services have been received to date, it is necessary to multiply the option's intrinsic value by one-third to arrive at the tax base of the employee services received in year 1.

The deferred tax income is all recognised in profit or loss, because the estimated future tax deduction of 83,333 (50,000 × 5 × $1/3$) is less than the cumulative remuneration expense of 188,000.

[Refer: paragraphs 9, 24, 47, 53, 58 and 68A–68C]

Year 2

Deferred tax asset at year-end:

$(45,000 \times 8 \times 2/3 \times 0.40) =$ ⟶ 96,000

Less deferred tax asset at start of year ⟶ (33,333)

Deferred tax income for year ⟶ 62,667*

* This amount consists of the following:

Deferred tax income for the temporary difference between the tax base of the employee services received during the year and their carrying amount of nil:

$(45,000 \times 8 \times 1/3 \times 0.40)$ ⟶ 48,000

Tax income resulting from an adjustment to the tax base of employee services received in previous years:

(a) increase in intrinsic value: $(45,000 \times 3 \times 1/3 \times 0.40)$ ⟶ 18,000

(b) decrease in number of options: $(5,000 \times 5 \times 1/3 \times 0.40)$ ⟶ (3,333)

Deferred tax income for year ⟶ 62,667

The deferred tax income is all recognised in profit or loss, because the estimated future tax deduction of 240,000 (45,000 × 8 × $2/3$) is less than the cumulative remuneration expense of 373,000 (188,000 + 185,000).

[Refer: paragraphs 9, 24, 47, 53, 58 and 68A–68C]

Year 3

Deferred tax asset at year-end:

$(40,000 \times 13 \times 0.40) =$ ⟶ 208,000

Less deferred tax asset at start of year ⟶ (96,000)

Deferred tax income for year ⟶ 112,000

The deferred tax income is all recognised in profit or loss, because the estimated future tax deduction of 520,000 (40,000 × 13) is less than the cumulative remuneration expense of 563,000 (188,000 + 185,000 + 190,000).

[Refer: paragraphs 9, 24, 47, 53, 58 and 68A–68C]

Year 4

Deferred tax asset at year-end:

(40,000 × 17 × 0.40) =	272,000	
Less deferred tax asset at start of year	(208,000)	
Deferred tax income for year		64,000

The deferred tax income is recognised partly in profit or loss and partly directly in equity as follows:

Estimated future tax deduction (40,000 × 17) =	680,000	
Cumulative remuneration expense	563,000	
Excess tax deduction		117,000
Deferred tax income for year	64,000	
Excess recognised directly in equity (117,000 × 0.40) =	46,800	
Recognised in profit or loss		17,200

[Refer: paragraphs 9, 24, 47, 53, 58, 61 and 68A–68C]

Year 5

Deferred tax expense (reversal of deferred tax asset)	272,000	
Amount recognised directly in equity (reversal of cumulative deferred tax income recognised directly in equity)	46,800	
Amount recognised in profit or loss		225,200
Current tax income based on intrinsic value of options at exercise date (40,000 × 20 × 0.40) =	320,000	
Amount recognised in profit or loss (563,000 × 0.40) =	225,200	
Amount recognised directly in equity		94,800

[Refer: paragraphs 9, 24, 47, 53, 58, 61 and 68A–68C]

Summary

	Statement of comprehensive income				Statement of financial position	
	Employee services expense	Current tax expense (income)	Deferred tax expense (income)	Total tax expense (income)	Equity	Deferred tax asset
Year 1	188,000	0	(33,333)	(33,333)	0	33,333
Year 2	185,000	0	(62,667)	(62,667)	0	96,000
Year 3	190,000	0	(112,000)	(112,000)	0	208,000
Year 4	0	0	(17,200)	(17,200)	(46,800)	272,000
Year 5	0	(225,200)	225,200	0	46,800	0
					(94,800)	
Totals	563,000	(225,200)	0	(225,200)	(94,800)	0

[Refer: paragraphs 9, 24, 47, 53, 58, 61 and 68A–68C]

Example 6 – Replacement awards in a business combination

On 1 January 20X1 Entity A acquired 100 per cent of Entity B. Entity A pays cash consideration of CU400 to the former owners of Entity B.

At the acquisition date Entity B had outstanding employee share options with a market-based measure of CU100. The share options were fully vested. As part of the business combination Entity B's outstanding share options are replaced by share options of Entity A (replacement awards) with a market-based measure of CU100 and an intrinsic value of CU80. The replacement awards are fully vested. In accordance with paragraphs B56–B62 of IFRS 3 *Business Combinations* (as revised in 2008), the replacement awards are part of the consideration transferred for Entity B. A tax deduction for the replacement awards will not arise until the options are exercised. The tax deduction will be based on the share options' intrinsic value at that date. Entity A's tax rate is 40 per cent. Entity A recognises a deferred tax asset of CU32 (CU80 intrinsic value × 40%) on the replacement awards at the acquisition date.

Entity A measures the identifiable net assets obtained in the business combination (excluding deferred tax assets and liabilities) at CU450. [Refer: IFRS 3 paragraphs 10 and 18] The tax base of the identifiable net assets obtained is CU300. Entity A recognises a deferred tax liability of CU60 ((CU450 – CU300) × 40%) on the identifiable net assets at the acquisition date.

Goodwill is calculated as follows:

	CU
Cash consideration [Refer: IFRS 3 paragraphs 37 and 38]	400
Market-based measure of replacement awards [Refer: IFRS 3 paragraphs B56–B61]	100
Total consideration transferred [Refer: IFRS 3 paragraph 32(a)]	500
Identifiable net assets, excluding deferred tax assets and liabilities [Refer: IFRS 3 paragraphs 10 and 18]	(450)
Deferred tax asset [Refer: IFRS 3 paragraph B62]	32
Deferred tax liability [Refer: IFRS 3 paragraph 24]	60
Goodwill [Refer: IFRS 3 paragraph 32]	78

Reductions in the carrying amount of goodwill are not deductible for tax purposes. In accordance with paragraph 15(a) of the Standard, Entity A recognises no deferred tax liability for the taxable temporary difference associated with the goodwill recognised in the business combination.

The accounting entry for the business combination is as follows:

		CU	CU
Dr	Goodwill	78	
Dr	Identifiable net assets	450	
Dr	Deferred tax asset	32	
	Cr Cash		400
	Cr Equity (replacement awards)		100
	Cr Deferred tax liability		60

On 31 December 20X1 the intrinsic value of the replacement awards is CU120. Entity A recognises a deferred tax asset of CU48 (CU120 × 40%). Entity A recognises deferred tax income of CU16 (CU48 – CU32) from the increase in the intrinsic value of the replacement awards. The accounting entry is as follows:

		CU	CU
Dr	Deferred tax asset	16	
	Cr Deferred tax income		16

If the replacement awards had not been tax-deductible under current tax law, Entity A would not have recognised a deferred tax asset on the acquisition date. Entity A would have accounted for any subsequent events that result in a tax deduction related to the replacement award in the deferred tax income or expense of the period in which the subsequent event occurred.

Paragraphs B56–B62 of IFRS 3 provide guidance on determining which portion of a replacement award is part of the consideration transferred in a business combination and which portion is attributable to future service and thus a post-combination remuneration expense. Deferred tax assets and liabilities on replacement awards that are post-combination expenses are accounted for in accordance with the general principles as illustrated in Example 5.

Example 7—Debt instruments measured at fair value

Debt instruments

At 31 December 20X1, Entity Z holds a portfolio of three debt instruments:

Debt Instrument	Cost (CU)	Fair value (CU)	Contractual interest rate
A	2,000,000	1,942,857	2.00%
B	750,000	778,571	9.00%
C	2,000,000	1,961,905	3.00%

Entity Z acquired all the debt instruments on issuance for their nominal value. The terms of the debt instruments require the issuer to pay the nominal value of the debt instruments on their maturity on 31 December 20X2.

Interest is paid at the end of each year at the contractually fixed rate, which equalled the market interest rate when the debt instruments were acquired. At the end of 20X1, the market interest rate is 5 per cent, which has caused the fair value of Debt Instruments A and C to fall below their cost and the fair value of Debt Instrument B to rise above its cost. It is probable that Entity Z will receive all the contractual cash flows if it continues to hold the debt instruments.

At the end of 20X1, Entity Z expects that it will recover the carrying amounts of Debt Instruments A and B through use, ie by continuing to hold them and collecting contractual cash flows, and Debt Instrument C by sale at the beginning of 20X2 for its fair value on 31 December 20X1. It is assumed that no other tax planning opportunity is available to Entity Z that would enable it to sell Debt Instrument B to generate a capital gain against which it could offset the capital loss arising from selling Debt Instrument C. [Refer: paragraph 29(b)]

The debt instruments are measured at fair value through other comprehensive income in accordance with IFRS 9 *Financial Instruments* (or IAS 39 *Financial Instruments: Recognition and Measurement*[1]). [Refer: IFRS 9 paragraph 4.1.2A]

Tax law

The tax base of the debt instruments is cost, which tax law allows to be offset either on maturity when principal is paid or against the sale proceeds when the debt instruments are sold [Refer: paragraph 7]. Tax law specifies that gains (losses) on the debt instruments are taxable (deductible) only when realised.

Tax law distinguishes ordinary gains and losses from capital gains and losses. Ordinary losses can be offset against both ordinary gains and capital gains. Capital losses can only be offset against capital gains. Capital losses can be carried forward for 5 years and ordinary losses can be carried forward for 20 years.

1   IFRS 9 replaced IAS 39. IFRS 9 applies to all items that were previously within the scope of IAS 39.

Ordinary gains are taxed at 30 per cent and capital gains are taxed at 10 per cent.

Tax law classifies interest income from the debt instruments as 'ordinary' and gains and losses arising on the sale of the debt instruments as 'capital'. Losses that arise if the issuer of the debt instrument fails to pay the principal on maturity are classified as ordinary by tax law.

General

On 31 December 20X1, Entity Z has, from other sources, taxable temporary differences of CU50,000 and deductible temporary differences of CU430,000, which will reverse in ordinary taxable profit (or ordinary tax loss) in 20X2.

At the end of 20X1, it is probable that Entity Z will report to the tax authorities an ordinary tax loss of CU200,000 for the year 20X2. This tax loss includes all taxable economic benefits and tax deductions for which temporary differences exist on 31 December 20X1 and that are classified as ordinary by tax law. These amounts contribute equally to the loss for the period according to tax law.

Entity Z has no capital gains against which it can utilise capital losses arising in the years 20X1–20X2.

Except for the information given in the previous paragraphs, there is no further information that is relevant to Entity Z's accounting for deferred taxes in the period 20X1–20X2.

Temporary differences

At the end of 20X1, Entity Z identifies the following temporary differences:

	Carrying amount (CU)	Tax base (CU)	Taxable temporary differences (CU) [Refer: paragraphs 15 and 20]	Deductible temporary differences (CU) [Refer: paragraphs 24 and 26(d)]
Debt Instrument A	1,942,857	2,000,000		57,143
Debt Instrument B	778,571	750,000	28,571	
Debt Instrument C	1,961,905	2,000,000		38,095
Other sources	Not specified		50,000	430,000

The difference between the carrying amount of an asset or liability and its tax base gives rise to a deductible (taxable) temporary difference (see paragraphs 20 and 26(d) of the Standard). This is because deductible (taxable) temporary differences are differences between the carrying amount of an asset or liability in the statement of financial position and its tax base, which will result in amounts that are deductible (taxable) in determining taxable profit (tax loss) of future periods when the carrying amount of the asset or liability is recovered or settled (see paragraph 5 of the Standard).

Utilisation of deductible temporary differences

With some exceptions, deferred tax assets arising from deductible temporary differences are recognised to the extent that sufficient future taxable profit will be available against which the deductible temporary differences are utilised (see paragraph 24 of the Standard).

Paragraphs 28–29 of IAS 12 identify the sources of taxable profits against which an entity can utilise deductible temporary differences. They include:

(a)   future reversal of existing taxable temporary differences;

(b)   taxable profit in future periods; and

(c)   tax planning opportunities.

The deductible temporary difference that arises from Debt Instrument C is assessed separately for utilisation. This is because tax law classifies the loss resulting from recovering the carrying amount of Debt Instrument C by sale as capital and allows capital losses to be offset only against capital gains (see paragraph 27A of the Standard).

The separate assessment results in not recognising a deferred tax asset for the deductible temporary difference that arises from Debt Instrument C because Entity Z has no source of taxable profit available that tax law classifies as capital.

In contrast, the deductible temporary difference that arises from Debt Instrument A and other sources are assessed for utilisation in combination with one another. This is because their related tax deductions would be classified as ordinary by tax law.

The tax deductions represented by the deductible temporary differences related to Debt Instrument A are classified as ordinary because the tax law classifies the effect on taxable profit (tax loss) from deducting the tax base on maturity as ordinary.

In assessing the utilisation of deductible temporary differences on 31 December 20X1, the following two steps are performed by Entity Z.

Step 1: Utilisation of deductible temporary differences because of the reversal of taxable temporary differences (see paragraph 28 of the Standard)

Entity Z first assesses the availability of taxable temporary differences as follows:

	(CU)
Expected reversal of deductible temporary differences in 20X2	
From Debt Instrument A	57,143
From other sources	430,000
Total reversal of deductible temporary differences	487,143
Expected reversal of taxable temporary differences in 20X2	
From Debt Instrument B	(28,571)
From other sources	(50,000)

continued...

...continued

Total reversal of taxable temporary differences	(78,571)
Utilisation because of the reversal of taxable temporary differences (Step 1)	78,571
Remaining deductible temporary differences to be assessed for utilisation in Step 2 (487,143 - 78,571)	408,572

In Step 1, Entity Z can recognise a deferred tax asset in relation to a deductible temporary difference of CU78,571.

Step 2: Utilisation of deductible temporary differences because of future taxable profit (see paragraph 29(a) of the Standard)

In this step, Entity Z assesses the availability of future taxable profit as follows:

	(CU)
Probable future tax profit (loss) in 20X2 (upon which income taxes are payable (recoverable))	(200,000)
Add back: reversal of deductible temporary differences expected to reverse in 20X2	487,143
Less: reversal of taxable temporary differences (utilised in Step 1)	(78,571)
Probable taxable profit excluding tax deductions for assessing utilisation of deductible temporary differences in 20X2	208,572
Remaining deductible temporary differences to be assessed for utilisation from Step 1	408,572
Utilisation because of future taxable profit (Step 2)	208,572
Utilisation because of the reversal of taxable temporary differences (Step 1)	78,571
Total utilisation of deductible temporary differences	287,143

The tax loss of CU200,000 includes the taxable economic benefit of CU2 million from the collection of the principal of Debt Instrument A and the equivalent tax deduction, because it is probable that Entity Z will recover the debt instrument for more than its carrying amount (see paragraph 29A of the Standard).

The utilisation of deductible temporary differences is not, however, assessed against probable future taxable profit for a period upon which income taxes are payable (see paragraph 5 of the Standard). Instead, the utilisation of deductible temporary differences is assessed against probable future taxable profit that excludes tax deductions resulting from the reversal of deductible temporary differences (see paragraph 29(a) of the Standard). Assessing the utilisation of deductible temporary differences against probable future taxable profits without excluding those deductions would lead to double counting the deductible temporary differences in that assessment.

In Step 2, Entity Z determines that it can recognise a deferred tax asset in relation to a future taxable profit, excluding tax deductions resulting from the reversal of deductible temporary differences, of CU208,572. Consequently, the total utilisation of deductible temporary differences amounts to CU287,143 (CU78,571 (Step 1) + CU208,572 (Step 2)).

Measurement of deferred tax assets and deferred tax liabilities

Entity Z presents the following deferred tax assets and deferred tax liabilities in its financial statements on 31 December 20X1:

	(CU)
Total taxable temporary differences	78,571
Total utilisation of deductible temporary differences	287,143
Deferred tax liabilities (78,571 at 30%)	23,571
Deferred tax assets (287,143 at 30%)	86,143

The deferred tax assets and the deferred tax liabilities are measured using the tax rate for ordinary gains of 30 per cent, in accordance with the expected manner of recovery (settlement) of the underlying assets (liabilities) (see paragraph 51 of the Standard).

Allocation of changes in deferred tax assets between profit or loss and other comprehensive income

Changes in deferred tax that arise from items that are recognised in profit or loss are recognised in profit or loss (see paragraph 58 of the Standard). Changes in deferred tax that arise from items that are recognised in other comprehensive income are recognised in other comprehensive income (see paragraph 61A of the Standard).

Entity Z did not recognise deferred tax assets for all of its deductible temporary differences at 31 December 20X1, and according to tax law all the tax deductions represented by the deductible temporary differences contribute equally to the tax loss for the period. Consequently, the assessment of the utilisation of deductible temporary differences does not specify whether the taxable profits are utilised for deferred tax items that are recognised in profit or loss (ie the deductible temporary differences from other sources) or whether instead the taxable profits are utilised for deferred tax items that are recognised in other comprehensive income (ie the deductible temporary differences related to debt instruments classified as fair value through other comprehensive income).

For such situations, paragraph 63 of the Standard requires the changes in deferred taxes to be allocated to profit or loss and other comprehensive income on a reasonable pro rata basis or by another method that achieves a more appropriate allocation in the circumstances.

Example 8—Leases

Lease

An entity (Lessee) enters into a five-year lease of a building. The annual lease payments are CU100 payable at the end of each year. Before the commencement date of the lease, Lessee makes a lease payment of CU15 (advance lease payment) and pays initial direct costs of CU5. The interest rate implicit in the lease cannot be readily determined. Lessee's incremental borrowing rate is 5% per year.

At the commencement date, applying IFRS 16 *Leases*, Lessee recognises a lease liability of CU435 (measured at the present value of the five lease payments of CU100, discounted at the interest rate of 5% per year). Lessee measures the right-of-use asset (lease asset) at CU455, comprising the initial measurement of the lease liability (CU435), the advance lease payment (CU15) and the initial direct costs (CU5).
[Refer: IFRS 16 paragraphs 22–28]

Tax law

The tax law allows tax deductions for lease payments (including those made before the commencement date) and initial direct costs when an entity makes those payments. Economic benefits that will flow to Lessee when it recovers the carrying amount of the lease asset will be taxable.

A tax rate of 20% is expected to apply to the period(s) when Lessee will recover the carrying amount of the lease asset and will settle the lease liability.
[Refer: paragraph 47]

After considering the applicable tax law, Lessee concludes that the tax deductions it will receive for lease payments relate to the repayment of the lease liability.[2]
[Refer: Basis for Conclusions paragraphs BC74–BC75]

Deferred tax on the advance lease payment and initial direct costs
[Refer: Basis for Conclusions paragraphs BC90–BC91]

Lessee recognises the advance lease payment (CU15) and initial direct costs (CU5) as components of the lease asset's cost. The tax base of these components is nil because Lessee already received tax deductions for the advance lease payment and initial direct costs when it made those payments. The difference between the tax base (nil) and the carrying amount of each component results in taxable temporary differences of CU15 (related to the advance lease payment) and CU5 (related to the initial direct costs).

The exemption from recognising a deferred tax liability in paragraph 15 does not apply because the temporary differences arise from transactions that, at the time of the transactions, affect Lessee's taxable profit (that is, the tax deductions Lessee received when it made the advance lease payment and paid initial direct costs reduced its taxable profit). Accordingly, Lessee recognises a deferred tax liability of CU3 (CU15 × 20%) and CU1 (CU5 × 20%) for the taxable temporary differences related to the advance lease payment and initial direct costs, respectively.

---

2   Depending on the applicable tax law, an entity might alternatively conclude that the tax deductions it will receive for lease payments relate to the lease asset, in which case temporary differences would not arise on initial recognition of the lease liability and the related component of the lease asset's cost. Accordingly, the entity would not recognise deferred tax on initial recognition but would do so if and when temporary differences arise after initial recognition.

Deferred tax on the lease liability and related component of the lease asset's cost
[Refer: paragraphs 15(b)(iii), 22A and 24(c)]

At the commencement date, the tax base of the lease liability is nil because Lessee will receive tax deductions equal to the carrying amount of the lease liability (CU435). The tax base of the related component of the lease asset's cost is also nil because Lessee will receive no tax deductions from recovering the carrying amount of that component of the lease asset's cost (CU435).

The differences between the carrying amounts of the lease liability and the related component of the lease asset's cost (CU435) and their tax bases of nil result in the following temporary differences at the commencement date:

(a)   a taxable temporary difference of CU435 associated with the lease asset; and

(b)   a deductible temporary difference of CU435 associated with the lease liability.

The exemption from recognising a deferred tax asset and liability in paragraphs 15 and 24 does not apply because the transaction gives rise to equal taxable and deductible temporary differences. Lessee concludes that it is probable that taxable profit will be available against which the deductible temporary difference can be utilised. Accordingly, Lessee recognises a deferred tax asset and a deferred tax liability, each of CU87 (CU435 × 20%), for the deductible and taxable temporary differences.

Summary of recognised deferred tax

The table below summarises the deferred tax that Lessee recognises on initial recognition of the lease (including the advance lease payment and initial direct costs):

	Carrying amount	Tax base	Deductible / (taxable) temporary difference	Deferred tax asset / (liability)
Lease asset				
– advance lease payment	15	—	(15)	(3)
– initial direct costs	5	—	(5)	(1)
– the amount of the initial measurement of the lease liability	435	—	(435)	(87)
Lease liability	435	—	435	87

Applying paragraph 22(b) of IAS 12, Lessee recognises deferred tax assets and liabilities as illustrated in this example and recognises the resulting deferred tax income or expense in profit or loss.

IASB documents published to accompany

IAS 19

Employee Benefits

The text of the unaccompanied standard, IAS 19, is contained in Part A of this edition. Its effective date when issued was 1 January 1999. The text of the Basis for Conclusions on IAS 19 is contained in Part C of this edition. This part presents the following documents:

TABLE OF CONCORDANCE

AMENDMENTS TO GUIDANCE ON OTHER IFRSS

Table of Concordance

This table shows how the contents of the superseded version of IAS 19 (as revised in 2004) and IAS 19 as amended in 2011 correspond. Paragraphs are treated as corresponding if they broadly address the same matter even though the guidance may differ.

Superseded IAS 19 paragraph	IAS 19 (2011) paragraph
Objective	1
1–6	2–7
7	8
8	9
9	None
10	11, 12
11–23	13–25
24	26
25	27, 28
26–28	29–31
29	32, 33
30	34 and 148
31	35
32	36
32A	37
32B	None
33	38
34–34B	40–42 and 149
35	Deleted in a previous amendment of IAS 19
36–38	43–45
39–42	46–49
43–47	50–54
48–50	55–57
51	60
52, 53	61, 62
54	63
55	None
56, 57	58, 59
58	64

continued...

...continued

Superseded IAS 19 paragraph	IAS 19 (2011) paragraph
58A, 58B	None
59	65
60	None
61, 62	120, 121
63	66
64–66	67–69
67–71	70–74
72–77	75–80
78–81	83–86
82	None
83	87
84	90
85	88
86	89
87	95
88–90	96–98
91	92–94
92–93D	None
94	128
95	None
96, 97	None
98	108
99, 100	None
101	107
102–104	113–115
104A–104D	116–119
105, 106	None
107	130
108	None
109	109, 110
110	99
111	105
111A	None

continued...

...continued

Superseded IAS 19 paragraph	IAS 19 (2011) paragraph
112	111
113	112
114	101
115	None
116–119	131–134
120	135
120A(a)	None
120A(b)	139(a)
120A(c), (e), (g), (h)	140, 141
120A(d)	138
120A(f), (i)	None
120A(j), (k)	142, 143
120A(l), (m)	None
120A(n)	144
120A(o), (p)	None
120A(q)	147(b)
121	139(a)
122	138
123	148
124, 125	151, 152
126–131	153–158
132	159
133, 134	165–167
135	161
136	160 and 164
137	None
138	168
139, 141	None
142, 143	171
144–152	Deleted in a previous amendment of IAS 19
153–161	None

continued...

...continued

Superseded IAS 19 paragraph	IAS 19 (2011) paragraph
None	10, 39, 81, 82, 91, 100, 102–104, 106, 122, 123–126, 127, 129, 136, 137, 139(b), 139(c), 145, 146, 147(a), 147(c), 150, 162, 163, 169, 170, 172, 173

Amendments to guidance on other IFRSs

These amendments to guidance on IFRSs are necessary in order to ensure consistency with the amendments to IAS 19. In the amended paragraphs, new text is underlined and deleted text is struck through.

* * * * *

The amendments contained in this appendix when IAS 19, as amended in 2011, was issued have been incorporated into the guidance on implementing IFRS 1 and IAS 1 and the illustrative examples accompanying IAS 34 and IFRIC 14, as published at 16 June 2011.

IASB documents published to accompany

IAS 23

Borrowing Costs

The text of the unaccompanied standard, IAS 23, is contained in Part A of this edition. Its effective date when issued was 1 January 2009. The text of the Basis for Conclusions on IAS 23 is contained in Part C of this edition. This part presents the following documents:

TABLE OF CONCORDANCE

AMENDMENTS TO GUIDANCE ON OTHER PRONOUNCEMENTS

Table of Concordance

This table shows how the contents of the superseded version of IAS 23 and the revised version of IAS 23 correspond. Paragraphs are treated as corresponding if they broadly address the same matter even though the guidance may differ.

Superseded IAS 23 paragraph	Revised IAS 23 paragraph
Objective	1
1	2
2	None
3	3
4	5
5	6
6	7
7	None
8	None
9	None
10	8
11	None
12	9
13	10
14	11
15	12
16	13
17	14
18	15
19	16
20	17
21	18
22	19
23	20
24	21
25	22
26	23
27	24
28	25
29	26

continued...

...continued

Superseded IAS 23 paragraph	Revised IAS 23 paragraph
30	None
31	None
None	4
None	27, 28
None	29
None	30

Amendments to guidance on other pronouncements

The following amendments to guidance on other pronouncements are necessary in order to ensure consistency with the revised IAS 23. In the amended paragraphs, new text is underlined and deleted text is struck through.

* * * * *

The amendments contained in this appendix when IAS 23 was issued in 2007 have been applied in the guidance on implementing IFRS 1 and IAS 8 and the illustrative examples accompanying IFRIC 12.

IASB documents published to accompany

IAS 24

Related Party Disclosures

The text of the unaccompanied standard, IAS 24, is contained in Part A of this edition. Its effective date when issued was 1 January 2011. The text of the Basis for Conclusions on IAS 24 is contained in Part C of this edition. This part presents the following documents:

ILLUSTRATIVE EXAMPLES

TABLE OF CONCORDANCE

Illustrative Examples

The following examples accompany, but are not part of, IAS 24 Related Party Disclosures. They illustrate:

- *the partial exemption for government-related entities; and*

- *how the definition of a related party would apply in specified circumstances.*

In the examples, references to 'financial statements' relate to the individual, separate or consolidated financial statements.

Partial exemption for government-related entities

Example 1 – Exemption from disclosure (paragraph 25)

IE1   Government G directly or indirectly controls Entities 1 and 2 and Entities A, B, C and D. Person X is a member of the key management personnel of Entity 1.

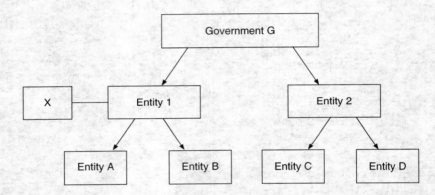

IE2   For Entity A's financial statements, the exemption in paragraph 25 applies to:

(a)   transactions with Government G; and

(b)   transactions with Entities 1 and 2 and Entities B, C and D.

However, that exemption does not apply to transactions with Person X.

Disclosure requirements when exemption applies (paragraph 26)

IE3   In Entity A's financial statements, an example of disclosure to comply with paragraph 26(b)(i) for **individually** significant transactions could be:

Example of disclosure for individually significant transaction carried out on **non-market terms**

On 15 January 20X1 Entity A, a utility company in which Government G indirectly owns 75 per cent of outstanding shares, sold a 10 hectare piece of land to another government-related utility company for CU5 million.[1] On 31 December 20X0 a plot of land in a similar location, of a similar size and with similar characteristics, was sold for CU3 million. There had not been any appreciation or depreciation of the land in the intervening period. See note X [of the financial statements] for disclosure of government assistance as required by IAS 20 *Accounting for Government Grants and Disclosure of Government Assistance* and notes Y and Z [of the financial statements] for compliance with other relevant IFRSs.

Example of disclosure for individually significant transaction because of **size** of transaction

In the year ended December 20X1 Government G provided Entity A, a utility company in which Government G indirectly owns 75 per cent of outstanding shares, with a loan equivalent to 50 per cent of its funding requirement, repayable in quarterly instalments over the next five years. Interest is charged on the loan at a rate of 3 per cent, which is comparable to that charged on Entity A's bank loans.[2] See notes Y and Z [of the financial statements] for compliance with other relevant IFRSs.

Example of disclosure of collectively significant transactions

In Entity A's financial statements, an example of disclosure to comply with paragraph 26(b)(ii) for **collectively** significant transactions could be:

Government G, indirectly, owns 75 per cent of Entity A's outstanding shares. Entity A's significant transactions with Government G and other entities controlled, jointly controlled or significantly influenced by Government G are [a large portion of its sales of goods and purchases of raw materials] or [about 50 per cent of its sales of goods and about 35 per cent of its purchases of raw materials].

The company also benefits from guarantees by Government G of the company's bank borrowing. See note X [of the financial statements] for disclosure of government assistance as required by IAS 20 *Accounting for Government Grants and Disclosure of Government Assistance* and notes Y and Z [of the financial statements] for compliance with other relevant IFRSs.

---

1   In these examples monetary amounts are denominated in 'currency units (CU)'.

2   If the reporting entity had concluded that this transaction constituted government assistance it would have needed to consider the disclosure requirements in IAS 20.

Definition of a related party

*The references are to subparagraphs of the definition of a **related party** in paragraph 9 of IAS 24.*

Example 2 – Associates and subsidiaries

IE4   Parent entity has a controlling interest in Subsidiaries A, B and C and has significant influence over Associates 1 and 2. Subsidiary C has significant influence over Associate 3.

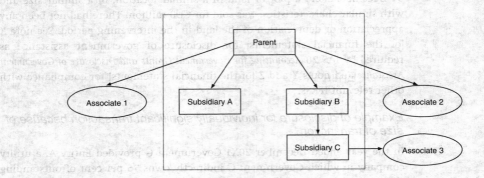

IE5   For Parent's separate financial statements, Subsidiaries A, B and C and Associates 1, 2 and 3 are related parties. *[Paragraph 9(b)(i) and (ii)]*

IE6   For Subsidiary A's financial statements, Parent, Subsidiaries B and C and Associates 1, 2 and 3 are related parties. For Subsidiary B's separate financial statements, Parent, Subsidiaries A and C and Associates 1, 2 and 3 are related parties. For Subsidiary C's financial statements, Parent, Subsidiaries A and B and Associates 1, 2 and 3 are related parties. *[Paragraph 9(b)(i) and (ii)]*

IE7   For the financial statements of Associates 1, 2 and 3, Parent and Subsidiaries A, B and C are related parties. Associates 1, 2 and 3 are not related to each other. *[Paragraph 9(b)(ii)]*

IE8   For Parent's consolidated financial statements, Associates 1, 2 and 3 are related to the Group. *[Paragraph 9(b)(ii)]*

Example 3 – Key management personnel

IE9   A person, X, has a 100 per cent investment in Entity A and is a member of the key management personnel of Entity C. Entity B has a 100 per cent investment in Entity C.

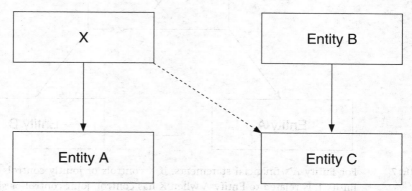

IE10   For Entity C's financial statements, Entity A is related to Entity C because X controls Entity A and is a member of the key management personnel of Entity C. [Paragraph 9(b)(vi)–(a)(iii)]

IE11   For Entity C's financial statements, Entity A is also related to Entity C if X is a member of the key management personnel of Entity B and not of Entity C. [Paragraph 9(b)(vi)–(a)(iii)]

IE12   Furthermore, the outcome described in paragraphs IE10 and IE11 will be the same if X has joint control over Entity A. [Paragraph 9(b)(vi)–(a)(iii)] (If X had only significant influence over Entity A and not control or joint control, then Entities A and C would not be related to each other.)

IE13   For Entity A's financial statements, Entity C is related to Entity A because X controls A and is a member of Entity C's key management personnel. [Paragraph 9(b)(vii)–(a)(i)]

IE14   Furthermore, the outcome described in paragraph IE13 will be the same if X has joint control over Entity A. The outcome will also be the same if X is a member of key management personnel of Entity B and not of Entity C. [Paragraph 9(b)(vii)–(a)(i)]

IE15   For Entity B's consolidated financial statements, Entity A is a related party of the Group if X is a member of key management personnel of the Group. [Paragraph 9(b)(vi)–(a)(iii)]

Example 4 – Person as investor

IE16   A person, X, has an investment in Entity A and Entity B.

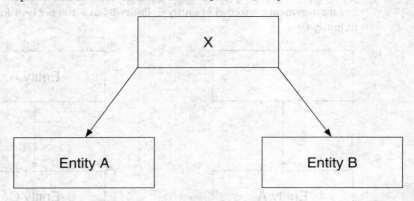

IE17   For Entity A's financial statements, if X controls or jointly controls Entity A, Entity B is related to Entity A when X has control, joint control or significant influence over Entity B. [*Paragraph 9(b)(vi)–(a)(i) and 9(b)(vii)–(a)(i)*]

IE18   For Entity B's financial statements, if X controls or jointly controls Entity A, Entity A is related to Entity B when X has control, joint control or significant influence over Entity B. [*Paragraph 9(b)(vi)–(a)(i) and 9(b)(vi)–(a)(ii)*]

IE19   If X has significant influence over both Entity A and Entity B, Entities A and B are not related to each other.

Example 5 – Close members of the family holding investments

IE20   A person, X, is the domestic partner of Y. X has an investment in Entity A and Y has an investment in Entity B.

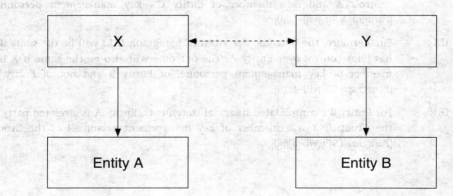

IE21   For Entity A's financial statements, if X controls or jointly controls Entity A, Entity B is related to Entity A when Y has control, joint control or significant influence over Entity B. [*Paragraph 9(b)(vi)–(a)(i) and 9(b)(vii)–(a)(i)*]

IE22   For Entity B's financial statements, if X controls or jointly controls Entity A, Entity A is related to Entity B when Y has control, joint control or significant influence over Entity B. [*Paragraph 9(b)(vi)–(a)(i) and 9(b)(vi)–(a)(ii)*]

IE23   If X has significant influence over Entity A and Y has significant influence over Entity B, Entities A and B are not related to each other.

Example 6 – Entity with joint control

IE24   Entity A has both (i) joint control over Entity B and (ii) joint control or significant influence over Entity C.

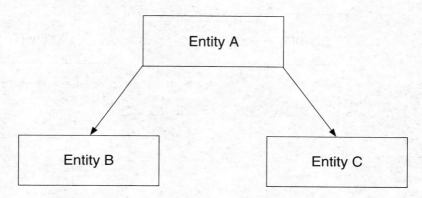

IE25   For Entity B's financial statements, Entity C is related to Entity B. [*Paragraph 9(b)(iii) and (iv)*]

IE26   Similarly, for Entity C's financial statements, Entity B is related to Entity C. [*Paragraph 9(b)(iii) and (iv)*]

Table of Concordance

This table shows how the contents of the superseded version of IAS 24 and the revised version of IAS 24 correspond. Paragraphs are treated as corresponding if they broadly address the same matter even though the guidance may differ.

Superseded IAS 24 paragraph	Revised IAS 24 paragraph
1	1
2	2
3	3
4	4
5	5
6	6
7	7
8	8
9	9
10	10
11	11
None	12
12	13
13	14
14	15
15	16
16	17
17	18
18	19
19	20
20	21
20	22
21	23
22	24
None	25
None	26
None	27
23	28
23A	None
24	29

IASB documents published to accompany

IAS 27

Separate Financial Statements

The text of the unaccompanied standard, IAS 27, is contained in Part A of this edition. Its effective date when issued was 1 January 2013. The text of the Basis for Conclusions on IAS 27 is contained in Part C of this edition. This part presents the following document:

TABLE OF CONCORDANCE

Table of Concordance

This table shows how the contents of IAS 27 *Consolidated and Separate Financial Statements* (the 'superseded IAS 27') and IAS 27 *Separate Financial Statements* (the 'amended IAS 27') correspond. Some requirements in the superseded version of IAS 27 were incorporated into IFRS 10 and IFRS 12; this table also shows how those paragraphs correspond. Paragraphs are treated as corresponding if they broadly address the same matter even though the requirements may differ.

The main change made in May 2011 was that IFRS 10 *Consolidated Financial Statements* replaced the consolidation requirements in IAS 27. Only accounting and disclosure requirements for the preparation of separate financial statements remained in IAS 27; the Standard was therefore renamed *Separate Financial Statements*.

Superseded IAS 27 paragraph	Amended IAS 27 paragraph	IFRS 10 paragraph	IFRS 12 paragraph
1		1	
2		3	
3	2		
4	4, 5	Appendix A	
5			
6–8	6–8		
9		1, 2	
10		4(a)	
11			
12		Appendix A	
13		7	
14		B47	
15		B48, B49	
16, 17			
18		B86	
19		B89	
20, 21		B86(c)	
22, 23		B92, B93	
24		19	
25, 26		B87, B88	
27		22	
28, 29		B94, B95	
30		23	

continued...

...continued

Superseded IAS 27 paragraph	Amended IAS 27 paragraph	IFRS 10 paragraph	IFRS 12 paragraph
31		B96	
32		B83	
33–35		B97–B99	
36		25(b)	
37		25(b)	
38	10		
38A–38C	12–14		
39	3		
40	11		
41			10–19
42, 43	16, 17		
44–45E	18		
46	20		
None	1, 9, 15, 19		

IASB documents published to accompany

IAS 28

Investments in Associates and Joint Ventures

The text of the unaccompanied standard, IAS 28, is contained in Part A of this edition. Its effective date when issued was 1 January 2013. The text of the Basis for Conclusions on IAS 28 is contained in Part C of this edition. This part presents the following document:

TABLE OF CONCORDANCE

IAS 28 SUPPORTING MATERIAL

Example published by the Board to accompany *Long-term Interests in Associates and Joint Ventures* (Amendments to IAS 28) in October 2017

Table of Concordance

This table shows how the contents of the superseded version of IAS 28 (as revised in 2003) and the amended version of IAS 28 in 2011 correspond. Some requirements in the superseded version of IAS 28 were incorporated into IFRS 12 *Disclosure of Interests in Other Entities*; this table also shows how those paragraphs correspond. Paragraphs are treated as corresponding if they broadly address the same matter even though the guidance may differ.

Superseded IAS 28 paragraph	Amended IAS 28 paragraph	IFRS 12 paragraph	Amended IAS 27 paragraph
1	2, 18, 19		
2	3, 4		
3			7
4			6
5			8
6	5		
7	6		
8	7		
9	8		
10	9		
11	10		
12	12		
13	17		
14	20		
15	21		
16	11		
17	22		
18	22		
19	22		
19A	23		
20	26		
21	27		
22	28		
23	32		
24	33		
25	34		

continued...

© IFRS Foundation

...continued

Superseded IAS 28 paragraph	Amended IAS 28 paragraph	IFRS 12 paragraph	Amended IAS 27 paragraph
26	35		
27	36		
28	37		
29	38		
30	39		
31	40		
32	41		
33	42		
34	43		
35	44		
36			3
37		21–24	
38		21–24	
39		21–24	
40		21–24	
41	45		
41A–41E			
42	47		
43	47		
None	1, 13–16, 24, 25, 29–31, 46		

Illustrative Example—Long-term Interests in Associates and Joint Ventures

This example portrays a hypothetical situation illustrating how an entity (investor) accounts for long-term interests that, in substance, form part of the entity's net investment in an associate (long-term interests) applying IFRS 9 and IAS 28 based on the assumptions presented. [Refer: IAS 28 paragraph 14A] The entity applies IFRS 9 in accounting for long-term interests. The entity applies IAS 28 to its net investment in the associate, which includes long-term interests. The analysis in this example is not intended to represent the only manner in which the requirements in IAS 28 could be applied.

Assumptions

The investor has the following three types of interests in the associate:

(a)   O Shares—ordinary shares representing a 40% ownership interest to which the investor applies the equity method. This interest is the least senior of the three interests, based on their relative priority in liquidation.

(b)   P Shares—non-cumulative preference shares that form part of the net investment in the associate and that the investor measures at fair value through profit or loss applying IFRS 9.

(c)   LT Loan—a long-term loan that forms part of the net investment in the associate and that the investor measures at amortised cost applying IFRS 9, with a stated interest rate and an effective interest rate of 5% a year. The associate makes interest-only payments to the investor each year. The LT Loan is the most senior of the three interests.

The LT Loan is not an originated credit-impaired loan. Throughout the years illustrated, there has not been any objective evidence that the net investment in the associate is impaired applying IAS 28, nor does the LT Loan become credit-impaired applying IFRS 9.

The associate does not have any outstanding cumulative preference shares classified as equity, as described in paragraph 37 of IAS 28. Throughout the years illustrated, the associate neither declares nor pays dividends on O Shares or P Shares.

The investor has not incurred any legal or constructive obligations, nor made payments on behalf of the associate, as described in paragraph 39 of IAS 28. Accordingly, the investor does not recognise its share of the associate's losses once the carrying amount of its net investment in the associate is reduced to zero.

The amount of the investor's initial investment in O Shares is CU200,[1] in P Shares is CU100 and in the LT Loan is CU100. On acquisition of the investment, the cost of the

---

1   In this Illustrative Example, currency amounts are denominated in currency units (CU).

investment equals the investor's share of the net fair value of the associate's identifiable assets and liabilities.

This table summarises the carrying amount at the end of each year for P Shares and the LT Loan applying IFRS 9 but before applying IAS 28, and the associate's profit (loss) for each year. The amounts for the LT Loan are shown net of the loss allowance.

At the end of	P Shares applying IFRS 9 (fair value)	LT Loan applying IFRS 9 (amortised cost)	Profit (Loss) of the associate
Year 1	CU110	CU90	CU50
Year 2	CU90	CU70	CU(200)
Year 3	CU50	CU50	CU(500)
Year 4	CU40	CU50	CU(150)
Year 5	CU60	CU60	–
Year 6	CU80	CU70	CU500
Year 7	CU110	CU90	CU500

Analysis

Year 1

The investor recognises the following in Year 1:

Investments in the associate:

DR. O Shares … CU200
DR. P Shares … CU100
DR. LT Loan … CU100
　　CR. Cash … CU400

To recognise the initial investment in the associate

DR. P Shares … CU10
　　CR. Profit or loss … CU10

To recognise the change in fair value (CU110 – CU100)

DR. Profit or loss … CU10
　　CR. Loss allowance (LT Loan) … CU10

To recognise an increase in the loss allowance (CU90 – CU100)

DR. O Shares … CU20
　　CR. Profit or loss … CU20

To recognise the investor's share of the associate's profit (CU50 × 40%)

At the end of Year 1, the carrying amount of O Shares is CU220, P Shares is CU110 and the LT Loan (net of loss allowance) is CU90.

Year 2

The investor recognises the following in Year 2:

DR. Profit or loss   CU20

    CR. P Shares   CU20

To recognise the change in fair value (CU90 – CU110)

DR. Profit or loss   CU20

    CR. Loss allowance (LT Loan)   CU20

To recognise an increase in the loss allowance (CU70 – CU90)

DR. Profit or loss   CU80

    CR. O Shares   CU80

To recognise the investor's share of the associate's loss (CU200 × 40%)

At the end of Year 2, the carrying amount of O Shares is CU140, P Shares is CU90 and the LT Loan (net of loss allowance) is CU70.

Year 3

Applying paragraph 14A of IAS 28, the investor applies IFRS 9 to P Shares and the LT Loan before it applies paragraph 38 of IAS 28. Accordingly, the investor recognises the following in Year 3:

DR. Profit or loss   CU40

    CR. P Shares   CU40

To recognise the change in fair value (CU50 – CU90)

DR. Profit or loss   CU20

    CR. Loss allowance (LT Loan)   CU20

To recognise an increase in the loss allowance (CU50 – CU70)

DR. Profit or loss   CU200

    CR. O Shares   CU140

    CR. P Shares   CU50

    CR. LT Loan   CU10

To recognise the investor's share of the associate's loss in reverse order of seniority as specified in paragraph 38 of IAS 28 (CU500 × 40%)

At the end of Year 3, the carrying amount of O Shares is zero, P Shares is zero and the LT Loan (net of loss allowance) is CU40.

Year 4

Applying IFRS 9 to its interests in the associate, the investor recognises the following in Year 4:

DR. Profit or loss	CU10
CR. P Shares	CU10

To recognise the change in fair value (CU40 – CU50)

Recognition of the change in fair value of CU10 in Year 4 results in the carrying amount of P Shares being negative CU10. Consequently, the investor recognises the following to reverse a portion of the associate's losses previously allocated to P Shares:

DR. P Shares	CU10
CR. Profit or loss	CU10

To reverse a portion of the associate's losses previously allocated to P Shares

Applying paragraph 38 of IAS 28, the investor limits the recognition of the associate's losses to CU40 because the carrying amount of its net investment in the associate is then zero. Accordingly, the investor recognises the following:

DR. Profit or loss	CU40
CR. LT Loan	CU40

To recognise the investor's share of the associate's loss

At the end of Year 4, the carrying amount of O Shares is zero, P Shares is zero and the LT Loan (net of loss allowance) is zero. There is also an unrecognised share of the associate's losses of CU30 (the investor's share of the associate's cumulative losses of CU340 – CU320 losses recognised cumulatively + CU10 losses reversed).

Year 5

Applying IFRS 9 to its interests in the associate, the investor recognises the following in Year 5:

DR. P Shares	CU20
CR. Profit or loss	CU20

To recognise the change in fair value (CU60 – CU40)

DR. Loss allowance (LT Loan)	CU10
CR. Profit or loss	CU10

To recognise a decrease in the loss allowance (CU60 – CU50)

After applying IFRS 9 to P Shares and the LT Loan, these interests have a positive carrying amount. Consequently, the investor allocates the previously unrecognised share of the associate's losses of CU30 to these interests.

DR. Profit or loss		CU30
CR. P Shares		CU20
CR. LT Loan		CU10

To recognise the previously unrecognised share of the associate's losses

At the end of Year 5, the carrying amount of O Shares is zero, P Shares is zero and the LT Loan (net of loss allowance) is zero.

Year 6

Applying IFRS 9 to its interests in the associate, the investor recognises the following in Year 6:

DR. P Shares		CU20
CR. Profit or loss		CU20

To recognise the change in fair value (CU80 – CU60)

DR. Loss allowance (LT Loan)		CU10
CR. Profit or loss		CU10

To recognise a decrease in the loss allowance (CU70 – CU60)

The investor allocates the associate's profit to each interest in the order of seniority. The investor limits the amount of the associate's profit it allocates to P Shares and the LT Loan to the amount of equity method losses previously allocated to those interests, which in this example is CU60 for both interests.

DR. O Shares		CU80
DR. P Shares		CU60
DR. LT Loan		CU60
CR. Profit or loss		CU200

To recognise the investor's share of the associate's profit (CU500 × 40%)

At the end of Year 6, the carrying amount of O Shares is CU80, P Shares is CU80 and the LT Loan (net of loss allowance) is CU70.

Year 7

The investor recognises the following in Year 7:

DR. P Shares		CU30
CR. Profit or loss		CU30

To recognise the change in fair value (CU110 – CU80)

| DR. Loss allowance (LT Loan) | CU20 | |
| CR. Profit or loss | | CU20 |

To recognise a decrease in the loss allowance (CU90 – CU70)

| DR. O Shares | CU200 | |
| CR. Profit or loss | | CU200 |

To recognise the investor's share of the associate's profit (CU500 × 40%)

At the end of Year 7, the carrying amount of O Shares is CU280, P Shares is CU110 and the LT Loan (net of loss allowance) is CU90.

Years 1–7

When recognising interest revenue on the LT Loan in each year, the investor does not take account of any adjustments to the carrying amount of the LT Loan that arose from applying IAS 28 (paragraph 14A of IAS 28). Accordingly, the investor recognises the following in each year:

| DR. Cash | CU5 | |
| CR. Profit or loss | | CU5 |

To recognise interest revenue on LT Loan based on the effective interest rate of 5%

Summary of amounts recognised in profit or loss

This table summarises the amounts recognised in the investor's profit or loss.

Items recognised During	Impairment (losses), including reversals, applying IFRS 9	Gains (losses) of P Shares applying IFRS 9	Share of profit (loss) of the associate recognised applying the equity method	Interest revenue applying IFRS 9
Year 1	CU(10)	CU10	CU20	CU5
Year 2	CU(20)	CU(20)	CU(80)	CU5
Year 3	CU(20)	CU(40)	CU(200)	CU5
Year 4	–	CU(10)	CU(30)	CU5
Year 5	CU10	CU20	CU(30)	CU5
Year 6	CU10	CU20	CU200	CU5
Year 7	CU20	CU30	CU200	CU5

IASB documents published to accompany

IAS 32

Financial Instruments: Presentation

The text of the unaccompanied standard, IAS 32, is contained in Part A of this edition. Its effective date when issued was 1 January 2005. The text of the Basis for Conclusions on IAS 32 is contained in Part C of this edition. This part presents the following document:

ILLUSTRATIVE EXAMPLES

CONTENTS

IAS 32 *Financial Instruments: Presentation*
Illustrative Examples

These examples accompany, but are not part of, IAS 32.

Accounting for contracts on equity instruments of an entity

IE1   The following examples[1] illustrate the application of paragraphs 15–27 and IFRS 9 to the accounting for contracts on an entity's own equity instruments (other than the financial instruments specified in paragraphs 16A and 16B or paragraphs 16C and 16D).

Example 1: Forward to buy shares

IE2   This example illustrates the journal entries for forward purchase contracts on an entity's own shares that will be settled (a) net in cash, (b) net in shares or (c) by delivering cash in exchange for shares. It also discusses the effect of settlement options (see (d) below). To simplify the illustration, it is assumed that no dividends are paid on the underlying shares (ie the 'carry return' is zero) so that the present value of the forward price equals the spot price when the fair value of the forward contract is zero. The fair value of the forward has been computed as the difference between the market share price and the present value of the fixed forward price.

Assumptions:

Contract date	1 February 20X2
Maturity date	31 January 20X3
Market price per share on 1 February 20X2	CU100
Market price per share on 31 December 20X2	CU110
Market price per share on 31 January 20X3	CU106
Fixed forward price to be paid on 31 January 20X3	CU104
Present value of forward price on 1 February 20X2	CU100
Number of shares under forward contract	1,000
Fair value of forward on 1 February 20X2	CU0
Fair value of forward on 31 December 20X2	CU6,300
Fair value of forward on 31 January 20X3	CU2,000

---

1   In these examples, monetary amounts are denominated in 'currency units (CU)'.

(a) Cash for cash ('net cash settlement')

IE3 In this subsection, the forward purchase contract on the entity's own shares will be settled net in cash, ie there is no receipt or delivery of the entity's own shares upon settlement of the forward contract.

On 1 February 20X2, Entity A enters into a contract with Entity B to receive the fair value of 1,000 of Entity A's own outstanding ordinary shares as of 31 January 20X3 in exchange for a payment of CU104,000 in cash (ie CU104 per share) on 31 January 20X3. The contract will be settled net in cash. Entity A records the following journal entries.

1 February 20X2

The price per share when the contract is agreed on 1 February 20X2 is CU100. The initial fair value of the forward contract on 1 February 20X2 is zero.

No entry is required because the fair value of the derivative is zero and no cash is paid or received.

31 December 20X2

On 31 December 20X2, the market price per share has increased to CU110 and, as a result, the fair value of the forward contract has increased to CU6,300.

Dr Forward asset	CU6,300	
Cr Gain		CU6,300

To record the increase in the fair value of the forward contract.

[Refer: paragraphs 11 (definition of a financial asset) and AG27(c)]

31 January 20X3

On 31 January 20X3, the market price per share has decreased to CU106. The fair value of the forward contract is CU2,000 ([CU106 × 1,000] – CU104,000).

On the same day, the contract is settled net in cash. Entity A has an obligation to deliver CU104,000 to Entity B and Entity B has an obligation to deliver CU106,000 (CU106 × 1,000) to Entity A, so Entity B pays the net amount of CU2,000 to Entity A.

Dr Loss	CU4,300	
Cr Forward asset		CU4,300

To record the decrease in the fair value of the forward contract (ie CU4,300 = CU6,300 – CU2,000).

Dr Cash	CU2,000	
Cr Forward asset		CU2,000

To record the settlement of the forward contract.

(b) Shares for shares ('net share settlement')

IE4   Assume the same facts as in (a) except that settlement will be made net in shares instead of net in cash. Entity A's journal entries are the same as those shown in (a) above, except for recording the settlement of the forward contract, as follows:

[Refer: paragraph AG27(d)]

31 January 20X3

The contract is settled net in shares. Entity A has an obligation to deliver CU104,000 (CU104 × 1,000) worth of its shares to Entity B and Entity B has an obligation to deliver CU106,000 (CU106 × 1,000) worth of shares to Entity A. Thus, Entity B delivers a net amount of CU2,000 (CU106,000 − CU104,000) worth of shares to Entity A, ie 18.9 shares (CU2,000/CU106).

Dr	Equity	CU2,000
	Cr Forward asset	CU2,000

To record the settlement of the forward contract.

[Refer: paragraphs 33 and AG36]

(c) Cash for shares ('gross physical settlement')

IE5   Assume the same facts as in (a) except that settlement will be made by delivering a fixed amount of cash and receiving a fixed number of Entity A's shares. Similarly to (a) and (b) above, the price per share that Entity A will pay in one year is fixed at CU104. Accordingly, Entity A has an obligation to pay CU104,000 in cash to Entity B (CU104 × 1,000) and Entity B has an obligation to deliver 1,000 of Entity A's outstanding shares to Entity A in one year. Entity A records the following journal entries.

1 February 20X2

Dr	Equity	CU100,000
	Cr Liability	CU100,000

To record the obligation to deliver CU104,000 in one year at its present value of CU100,000 discounted using an appropriate interest rate (see IFRS 9, paragraph B5.1.1).

[Refer: paragraphs 16, 22, 23 and AG27(a)]

31 December 20X2

Dr	Interest expense	CU3,660
	Cr Liability	CU3,660

To accrue interest in accordance with the effective interest method on the liability for the share redemption amount.

31 January 20X3

Dr	Interest expense	CU340	
	Cr	Liability	CU340

To accrue interest in accordance with the effective interest method on the liability for the share redemption amount.

Entity A delivers CU104,000 in cash to Entity B and Entity B delivers 1,000 of Entity A's shares to Entity A.

Dr	Liability	CU104,000	
	Cr	Cash	CU104,000

To record the settlement of the obligation to redeem Entity A's own shares for cash.

(d) Settlement options

IE6 The existence of settlement options (such as net in cash, net in shares or by an exchange of cash and shares) has the result that the forward repurchase contract is a financial asset or a financial liability. If one of the settlement alternatives is to exchange cash for shares ((c) above), Entity A recognises a liability for the obligation to deliver cash, as illustrated in (c) above. Otherwise, Entity A accounts for the forward contract as a derivative.
[Refer: paragraph 26]

Example 2: Forward to sell shares

IE7 This example illustrates the journal entries for forward sale contracts on an entity's own shares that will be settled (a) net in cash, (b) net in shares or (c) by receiving cash in exchange for shares. It also discusses the effect of settlement options (see (d) below). To simplify the illustration, it is assumed that no dividends are paid on the underlying shares (ie the 'carry return' is zero) so that the present value of the forward price equals the spot price when the fair value of the forward contract is zero. The fair value of the forward has been computed as the difference between the market share price and the present value of the fixed forward price.

Assumptions:

Contract date	1 February 20X2
Maturity date	31 January 20X3
Market price per share on 1 February 20X2	CU100
Market price per share on 31 December 20X2	CU110
Market price per share on 31 January 20X3	CU106
Fixed forward price to be paid on 31 January 20X3	CU104
Present value of forward price on 1 February 20X2	CU100
Number of shares under forward contract	1,000
Fair value of forward on 1 February 20X2	CU0
Fair value of forward on 31 December 20X2	(CU6,300)
Fair value of forward on 31 January 20X3	(CU2,000)

(a) Cash for cash ('net cash settlement')

IE8   On 1 February 20X2, Entity A enters into a contract with Entity B to pay the
fair value of 1,000 of Entity A's own outstanding ordinary shares as of
31 January 20X3 in exchange for CU104,000 in cash (ie CU104 per share) on
31 January 20X3. The contract will be settled net in cash. Entity A records the
following journal entries.

1 February 20X2

No entry is required because the fair value of the derivative is zero and no cash is paid or received.

31 December 20X2

Dr Loss	CU6,300	
Cr Forward liability		CU6,300

To record the decrease in the fair value of the forward contract.

[Refer: paragraphs 11 (definition of a financial liability) and AG27(c)]

31 January 20X3

Dr Forward liability	CU4,300	
Cr Gain		CU4,300

To record the increase in the fair value of the forward contract (ie CU4,300 = CU6,300 − CU2,000).

The contract is settled net in cash. Entity B has an obligation to deliver CU104,000 to Entity A, and Entity A has an obligation to deliver CU106,000 (CU106 × 1,000) to Entity B. Thus, Entity A pays the net amount of CU2,000 to Entity B.

Dr	Forward liability	CU2,000	
	Cr Cash		C2,000

To record the settlement of the forward contract.

(b) Shares for shares ('net share settlement')

IE9   Assume the same facts as in (a) except that settlement will be made net in shares instead of net in cash. Entity A's journal entries are the same as those shown in (a), except:
[Refer: paragraph AG27(d)]

31 January 20X3

The contract is settled net in shares. Entity A has a right to receive CU104,000 (CU104 × 1,000) worth of its shares and an obligation to deliver CU106,000 (CU106 × 1,000) worth of its shares to Entity B. Thus, Entity A delivers a net amount of CU2,000 (CU106,000 – CU104,000) worth of its shares to Entity B, ie 18.9 shares (CU2,000/CU106).

Dr	Forward liability	CU2,000	
	Cr Equity		CU2,000

To record the settlement of the forward contract. The issue of the entity's own shares is treated as an equity transaction.

(c) Shares for cash ('gross physical settlement')

IE10   Assume the same facts as in (a), except that settlement will be made by receiving a fixed amount of cash and delivering a fixed number of the entity's own shares. Similarly to (a) and (b) above, the price per share that Entity A will receive in one year is fixed at CU104. Accordingly, Entity A has a right to receive CU104,000 in cash (CU104 × 1,000) and an obligation to deliver 1,000 of its own shares in one year. Entity A records the following journal entries.

1 February 20X2

No entry is made on 1 February. No cash is paid or received because the forward has an initial fair value of zero. A forward contract to deliver a fixed number of Entity A's own shares in exchange for a fixed amount of cash or another financial asset meets the definition of an equity instrument because it cannot be settled otherwise than through the delivery of shares in exchange for cash.

[Refer: paragraphs 22 and AG27(a)]

31 December 20X2

No entry is made on 31 December because no cash is paid or received and a contract to deliver a fixed number of Entity A's own shares in exchange for a fixed amount of cash meets the definition of an equity instrument of the entity.

[Refer: paragraph 22]

31 January 20X3

On 31 January 20X3, Entity A receives CU104,000 in cash and delivers 1,000 shares.

Dr Cash	CU104,000	
Cr Equity		CU104,000

To record the settlement of the forward contract.

[Refer: paragraphs 11 (definition of an equity instrument) and 16]

(d) Settlement options

IE11   The existence of settlement options (such as net in cash, net in shares or by an exchange of cash and shares) has the result that the forward contract is a financial asset or a financial liability. It does not meet the definition of an equity instrument because it can be settled otherwise than by Entity A repurchasing a fixed number of its own shares in exchange for paying a fixed amount of cash or another financial asset. Entity A recognises a derivative asset or liability, as illustrated in (a) and (b) above. The accounting entry to be made on settlement depends on how the contract is actually settled.

[Refer: paragraph 26]

Example 3: Purchased call option on shares

IE12   This example illustrates the journal entries for a purchased call option right on the entity's own shares that will be settled (a) net in cash, (b) net in shares or (c) by delivering cash in exchange for the entity's own shares. It also discusses the effect of settlement options (see (d) below):

Assumptions:

Contract date	1 February 20X2
Exercise date	31 January 20X3
	(European terms, ie it can be exercised only at maturity)
Exercise right holder	Reporting entity
	(Entity A)
Market price per share on 1 February 20X2	CU100
Market price per share on 31 December 20X2	CU104
Market price per share on 31 January 20X3	CU104
Fixed exercise price to be paid on 31 January 20X3	CU102
Number of shares under option contract	1,000
Fair value of option on 1 February 20X2	CU5,000
Fair value of option on 31 December 20X2	CU3,000
Fair value of option on 31 January 20X3	CU2,000

(a) Cash for cash ('net cash settlement')

IE13   On 1 February 20X2, Entity A enters into a contract with Entity B that gives Entity B the obligation to deliver, and Entity A the right to receive the fair value of 1,000 of Entity A's own ordinary shares as of 31 January 20X3 in exchange for CU102,000 in cash (ie CU102 per share) on 31 January 20X3, if Entity A exercises that right. The contract will be settled net in cash. If Entity A does not exercise its right, no payment will be made. Entity A records the following journal entries.

1 February 20X2

The price per share when the contract is agreed on 1 February 20X2 is CU100. The initial fair value of the option contract on 1 February 20X2 is CU5,000, which Entity A pays to Entity B in cash on that date. On that date, the option has no intrinsic value, only time value, because the exercise price of CU102 exceeds the market price per share of CU100 and it would therefore not be economic for Entity A to exercise the option. In other words, the call option is out of the money.

Dr	Call option asset	CU5,000	
	Cr Cash		CU5,000

To recognise the purchased call option.

[Refer: paragraphs 11 (definition of a financial asset) and AG27(c)]

31 December 20X2

On 31 December 20X2, the market price per share has increased to CU104. The fair value of the call option has decreased to CU3,000, of which CU2,000 is intrinsic value ([CU104 − CU102] × 1,000), and CU1,000 is the remaining time value.

Dr	Loss	CU2,000	
	Cr Call option asset		CU2,000

To record the decrease in the fair value of the call option.

31 January 20X3

On 31 January 20X3, the market price per share is still CU104. The fair value of the call option has decreased to CU2,000, which is all intrinsic value ([CU104 − CU102] × 1,000) because no time value remains.

Dr	Loss	CU1,000	
	Cr Call option asset		CU1,000

To record the decrease in the fair value of the call option.

On the same day, Entity A exercises the call option and the contract is settled net in cash. Entity B has an obligation to deliver CU104,000 (CU104 × 1,000) to Entity A in exchange for CU102,000 (CU102 × 1,000) from Entity A, so Entity A receives a net amount of CU2,000.

Dr	Cash	CU2,000	
	Cr Call option asset		CU2,000

To record the settlement of the option contract.

(b) Shares for shares ('net share settlement')

IE14 Assume the same facts as in (a) except that settlement will be made net in shares instead of net in cash. Entity A's journal entries are the same as those shown in (a) except for recording the settlement of the option contract as follows:

[Refer: paragraphs 11 (definition of a financial asset) and AG27(d)]

31 January 20X3

Entity A exercises the call option and the contract is settled net in shares. Entity B has an obligation to deliver CU104,000 (CU104 × 1,000) worth of Entity A's shares to Entity A in exchange for CU102,000 (CU102 × 1,000) worth of Entity A's shares. Thus, Entity B delivers the net amount of CU2,000 worth of shares to Entity A, ie 19.2 shares (CU2,000/CU104).

Dr	Equity	CU2,000	
	Cr Call option asset		CU2,000

To record the settlement of the option contract. The settlement is accounted for as a treasury share transaction (ie no gain or loss).

[Refer: paragraphs 33 and AG36]

(c) Cash for shares ('gross physical settlement')

IE15   Assume the same facts as in (a) except that settlement will be made by receiving a fixed number of shares and paying a fixed amount of cash, if Entity A exercises the option. Similarly to (a) and (b) above, the exercise price per share is fixed at CU102. Accordingly, Entity A has a right to receive 1,000 of Entity A's own outstanding shares in exchange for CU102,000 (CU102 × 1,000) in cash, if Entity A exercises its option. Entity A records the following journal entries.

1 February 20X2

Dr	Equity	CU5,000	
	Cr Cash		CU5,000

To record the cash paid in exchange for the right to receive Entity A's own shares in one year for a fixed price. The premium paid is recognised in equity.

[Refer: paragraphs 16, 22 and AG14]

31 December 20X2

No entry is made on 31 December because no cash is paid or received and a contract that gives a right to receive a fixed number of Entity A's own shares in exchange for a fixed amount of cash meets the definition of an equity instrument of the entity.

31 January 20X3

Entity A exercises the call option and the contract is settled gross. Entity B has an obligation to deliver 1,000 of Entity A's shares in exchange for CU102,000 in cash.

Dr	Equity	CU102,000	
	Cr Cash		CU102,000

To record the settlement of the option contract.

[Refer: paragraphs 33 and AG36]

(d) Settlement options

IE16   The existence of settlement options (such as net in cash, net in shares or by an exchange of cash and shares) has the result that the call option is a financial asset. It does not meet the definition of an equity instrument because it can be settled otherwise than by Entity A repurchasing a fixed number of its own shares in exchange for paying a fixed amount of cash or another financial asset. Entity A recognises a derivative asset, as illustrated in (a) and (b) above. The accounting entry to be made on settlement depends on how the contract is actually settled.

[Refer: paragraphs 11 (definition of a financial asset), 26 and 27]

Example 4: Written call option on shares

IE17   This example illustrates the journal entries for a written call option obligation on the entity's own shares that will be settled (a) net in cash, (b) net in shares or (c) by delivering cash in exchange for shares. It also discusses the effect of settlement options (see (d) below).

Assumptions:

Contract date	1 February 20X2
Exercise date	31 January 20X3
	(European terms, ie it can be exercised only at maturity)
Exercise right holder	Counterparty
	(Entity B)
Market price per share on 1 February 20X2	CU100
Market price per share on 31 December 20X2	CU104
Market price per share on 31 January 20X3	CU104
Fixed exercise price to be paid on 31 January 20X3	CU102
Number of shares under option contract	1,000
Fair value of option on 1 February 20X2	CU5,000
Fair value of option on 31 December 20X2	CU3,000
Fair value of option on 31 January 20X3	CU2,000

(a) Cash for cash ('net cash settlement')

IE18   Assume the same facts as in Example 3(a) above except that Entity A has written a call option on its own shares instead of having purchased a call option on them. Accordingly, on 1 February 20X2 Entity A enters into a contract with Entity B that gives Entity B the right to receive and Entity A the obligation to pay the fair value of 1,000 of Entity A's own ordinary shares as of

31 January 20X3 in exchange for CU102,000 in cash (ie CU102 per share) on 31 January 20X3, if Entity B exercises that right. The contract will be settled net in cash. If Entity B does not exercise its right, no payment will be made. Entity A records the following journal entries.

1 February 20X2

Dr	Cash	CU5,000
	Cr Call option obligation	CU5,000

To recognise the written call option.

[Refer: paragraphs 11 (definition of a financial liability) and AG27(c)]

31 December 20X2

Dr	Call option obligation	CU2,000
	Cr Gain	CU2,000

To record the decrease in the fair value of the call option.

31 January 20X3

Dr	Call option obligation	CU1,000
	Cr Gain	CU1,000

To record the decrease in the fair value of the option.

On the same day, Entity B exercises the call option and the contract is settled net in cash. Entity A has an obligation to deliver CU104,000 (CU104 × 1,000) to Entity B in exchange for CU102,000 (CU102 × 1,000) from Entity B, so Entity A pays a net amount of CU2,000.

Dr	Call option obligation	CU2,000
	Cr Cash	CU2,000

To record the settlement of the option contract.

(b) Shares for shares ('net share settlement')

IE19   Assume the same facts as in (a) except that settlement will be made net in shares instead of net in cash. Entity A's journal entries are the same as those shown in (a), except for recording the settlement of the option contract, as follows:

[Refer: paragraph AG27(d)]

31 December 20X3

Entity B exercises the call option and the contract is settled net in shares. Entity A has an obligation to deliver CU104,000 (CU104 × 1,000) worth of Entity A's shares to Entity B in exchange for CU102,000 (CU102 × 1,000) worth of Entity A's shares. Thus, Entity A delivers the net amount of CU2,000 worth of shares to Entity B, ie 19.2 shares (CU2,000/CU104).

Dr Call option obligation	CU2,000	
Cr Equity		CU2,000

To record the settlement of the option contract. The settlement is accounted for as an equity transaction.

(c) Cash for shares ('gross physical settlement')

IE20 Assume the same facts as in (a) except that settlement will be made by delivering a fixed number of shares and receiving a fixed amount of cash, if Entity B exercises the option. Similarly to (a) and (b) above, the exercise price per share is fixed at CU102. Accordingly, Entity B has a right to receive 1,000 of Entity A's own outstanding shares in exchange for CU102,000 (CU102 × 1,000) in cash, if Entity B exercises its option. Entity A records the following journal entries.

1 February 20X2

Dr Cash	CU5,000	
Cr Equity		CU5,000

To record the cash received in exchange for the obligation to deliver a fixed number of Entity A's own shares in one year for a fixed price. The premium received is recognised in equity. Upon exercise, the call would result in the issue of a fixed number of shares in exchange for a fixed amount of cash.
[Refer: paragraphs 22 and AG27(a)]

31 December 20X2

No entry is made on 31 December because no cash is paid or received and a contract to deliver a fixed number of Entity A's own shares in exchange for a fixed amount of cash meets the definition of an equity instrument of the entity.

[Refer: paragraph 22]

31 January 20X3

Entity B exercises the call option and the contract is settled gross. Entity A has an obligation to deliver 1,000 shares in exchange for CU102,000 in cash.

Dr Cash	CU102,000	
Cr Equity		CU102,000

To record the settlement of the option contract.

[Refer: paragraphs 11 (definition of an equity instrument) and 16]

(d) Settlement options

IE21 The existence of settlement options (such as net in cash, net in shares or by an exchange of cash and shares) has the result that the call option is a financial liability. It does not meet the definition of an equity instrument because it can be settled otherwise than by Entity A issuing a fixed number of its own shares in exchange for receiving a fixed amount of cash or another financial asset. Entity A recognises a derivative liability, as illustrated in (a) and (b) above. The accounting entry to be made on settlement depends on how the contract is actually settled.

[Refer: paragraph 26]

Example 5: Purchased put option on shares

IE22   This example illustrates the journal entries for a purchased put option on the entity's own shares that will be settled (a) net in cash, (b) net in shares or (c) by delivering cash in exchange for shares. It also discusses the effect of settlement options (see (d) below).

Assumptions:

Contract date	1 February 20X2
Exercise date	31 January 20X3
	(European terms, ie it can be exercised only at maturity)
Exercise right holder	Reporting entity (Entity A)
Market price per share on 1 February 20X2	CU100
Market price per share on 31 December 20X2	CU95
Market price per share on 31 January 20X3	CU95
Fixed exercise price to be paid on 31 January 20X3	CU98
Number of shares under option contract	1,000
Fair value of option on 1 February 20X2	CU5,000
Fair value of option on 31 December 20X2	CU4,000
Fair value of option on 31 January 20X3	CU3,000

(a) Cash for cash ('net cash settlement')

IE23   On 1 February 20X2, Entity A enters into a contract with Entity B that gives Entity A the right to sell, and Entity B the obligation to buy the fair value of 1,000 of Entity A's own outstanding ordinary shares as of 31 January 20X3 at a strike price of CU98,000 (ie CU98 per share) on 31 January 20X3, if Entity A exercises that right. The contract will be settled net in cash. If Entity A does not exercise its right, no payment will be made. Entity A records the following journal entries.

© IFRS Foundation

1 February 20X2

The price per share when the contract is agreed on 1 February 20X2 is CU100. The initial fair value of the option contract on 1 February 20X2 is CU5,000, which Entity A pays to Entity B in cash on that date. On that date, the option has no intrinsic value, only time value, because the exercise price of CU98 is less than the market price per share of CU100. Therefore it would not be economic for Entity A to exercise the option. In other words, the put option is out of the money.

Dr Put option asset	CU5,000	
Cr Cash		CU5,000

To recognise the purchased put option.

[Refer: paragraphs 11 (definition of a financial asset) and AG27(c)]

31 December 20X2

On 31 December 20X2 the market price per share has decreased to CU95. The fair value of the put option has decreased to CU4,000, of which CU3,000 is intrinsic value ([CU98 − CU95] × 1,000) and CU1,000 is the remaining time value.

Dr Loss	CU1,000	
Cr Put option asset		CU1,000

To record the decrease in the fair value of the put option.

31 January 20X3

On 31 January 20X3 the market price per share is still CU95. The fair value of the put option has decreased to CU3,000, which is all intrinsic value ([CU98 − CU95] × 1,000) because no time value remains.

Dr Loss	CU1,000	
Cr Put option asset		CU1,000

To record the decrease in the fair value of the option.

On the same day, Entity A exercises the put option and the contract is settled net in cash. Entity B has an obligation to deliver CU98,000 to Entity A and Entity A has an obligation to deliver CU95,000 (CU95 × 1,000) to Entity B, so Entity B pays the net amount of CU3,000 to Entity A.

Dr Cash	CU3,000	
Cr Put option asset		CU3,000

To record the settlement of the option contract.

(b) Shares for shares ('net share settlement')

IE24 Assume the same facts as in (a) except that settlement will be made net in shares instead of net in cash. Entity A's journal entries are the same as shown in (a), except:

[Refer: paragraph AG27(d)]

31 January 20X3

Entity A exercises the put option and the contract is settled net in shares. In effect, Entity B has an obligation to deliver CU98,000 worth of Entity A's shares to Entity A, and Entity A has an obligation to deliver CU95,000 worth of Entity A's shares (CU95 × 1,000) to Entity B, so Entity B delivers the net amount of CU3,000 worth of shares to Entity A, ie 31.6 shares (CU3,000/CU95).

Dr Equity	CU3,000	
Cr Put option asset		CU3,000

To record the settlement of the option contract.

(c) Cash for shares ('gross physical settlement')

IE25 Assume the same facts as in (a) except that settlement will be made by receiving a fixed amount of cash and delivering a fixed number of Entity A's shares, if Entity A exercises the option. Similarly to (a) and (b) above, the exercise price per share is fixed at CU98. Accordingly, Entity B has an obligation to pay CU98,000 in cash to Entity A (CU98 × 1,000) in exchange for 1,000 of Entity A's outstanding shares, if Entity A exercises its option. Entity A records the following journal entries.

1 February 20X2

Dr Equity	CU5,000	
Cr Cash		CU5,000

To record the cash received in exchange for the right to deliver Entity A's own shares in one year for a fixed price. The premium paid is recognised directly in equity. Upon exercise, it results in the issue of a fixed number of shares in exchange for a fixed price.

[Refer: paragraphs 16, 22 and AG27(a)]

31 December 20X2

No entry is made on 31 December because no cash is paid or received and a contract to deliver a fixed number of Entity A's own shares in exchange for a fixed amount of cash meets the definition of an equity instrument of Entity A.

[Refer: paragraph 22]

31 January 20X3

Entity A exercises the put option and the contract is settled gross. Entity B has an obligation to deliver CU98,000 in cash to Entity A in exchange for 1,000 shares.

Dr Cash	CU98,000	
Cr Equity		CU98,000

To record the settlement of the option contract.

[Refer: paragraphs 11 (definition of an equity instrument) and 16]

(d) Settlement options

IE26   The existence of settlement options (such as net in cash, net in shares or by an exchange of cash and shares) has the result that the put option is a financial asset. It does not meet the definition of an equity instrument because it can be settled otherwise than by Entity A issuing a fixed number of its own shares in exchange for receiving a fixed amount of cash or another financial asset. Entity A recognises a derivative asset, as illustrated in (a) and (b) above. The accounting entry to be made on settlement depends on how the contract is actually settled.

[Refer: paragraph 26]

Example 6: Written put option on shares

IE27   This example illustrates the journal entries for a written put option on the entity's own shares that will be settled (a) net in cash, (b) net in shares or (c) by delivering cash in exchange for shares. It also discusses the effect of settlement options (see (d) below).

Assumptions:

Contract date	1 February 20X2
Exercise date	31 January 20X3
	(European terms, ie it can be exercised only at maturity)
Exercise right holder	Counterparty (Entity B)
Market price per share on 1 February 20X2	CU100
Market price per share on 31 December 20X2	CU95
Market price per share on 31 January 20X3	CU95
Fixed exercise price to be paid on 31 January 20X3	CU98
Present value of exercise price on 1 February 20X2	CU95
Number of shares under option contract	1,000
Fair value of option on 1 February 20X2	CU5,000
Fair value of option on 31 December 20X2	CU4,000
Fair value of option on 31 January 20X3	CU3,000

(a) Cash for cash ('net cash settlement')

IE28   Assume the same facts as in Example 5(a) above, except that Entity A has written a put option on its own shares instead of having purchased a put option on its own shares. Accordingly, on 1 February 20X2, Entity A enters into a contract with Entity B that gives Entity B the right to receive and Entity A the obligation to pay the fair value of 1,000 of Entity A's outstanding ordinary shares as of 31 January 20X3 in exchange for CU98,000 in cash (ie CU98 per share) on 31 January 20X3, if Entity B exercises that right. The contract will be settled net in cash. If Entity B does not exercise its right, no payment will be made. Entity A records the following journal entries.

1 February 20X2

Dr	Cash	CU5,000
	Cr Put option liability	CU5,000

To recognise the written put option.

[Refer: paragraphs 11 (definition of a financial liability) and AG27(c)]

31 December 20X2

Dr	Put option liability	CU1,000
	Cr Gain	CU1,000

To record the decrease in the fair value of the put option.

31 January 20X3

Dr	Put option liability	CU1,000
	Cr Gain	CU1,000

To record the decrease in the fair value of the put option.

On the same day, Entity B exercises the put option and the contract is settled net in cash. Entity A has an obligation to deliver CU98,000 to Entity B, and Entity B has an obligation to deliver CU95,000 (CU95 × 1,000) to Entity A. Thus, Entity A pays the net amount of CU3,000 to Entity B.

Dr	Put option liability	CU3,000
	Cr Cash	CU3,000

To record the settlement of the option contract.

(b) Shares for shares ('net share settlement')

IE29   Assume the same facts as in (a) except that settlement will be made net in shares instead of net in cash. Entity A's journal entries are the same as those in (a), except for the following:

[Refer: paragraph AG27(d)]

31 January 20X3

Entity B exercises the put option and the contract is settled net in shares. In effect, Entity A has an obligation to deliver CU98,000 worth of shares to Entity B, and Entity B has an obligation to deliver CU95,000 worth of Entity A's shares (CU95 × 1,000) to Entity A. Thus, Entity A delivers the net amount of CU3,000 worth of Entity A's shares to Entity B, ie 31.6 shares (3,000/95).

Dr	Put option liability	CU3,000
	Cr Equity	CU3,000

To record the settlement of the option contract. The issue of Entity A's own shares is accounted for as an equity transaction.

[Refer: paragraphs 11 (definition of an equity instrument) and 16]

(c) Cash for shares ('gross physical settlement')

IE30   Assume the same facts as in (a) except that settlement will be made by delivering a fixed amount of cash and receiving a fixed number of shares, if Entity B exercises the option. Similarly to (a) and (b) above, the exercise price per share is fixed at CU98. Accordingly, Entity A has an obligation to pay CU98,000 in cash to Entity B (CU98 × 1,000) in exchange for 1,000 of Entity A's outstanding shares, if Entity B exercises its option. Entity A records the following journal entries.

1 February 20X2

Dr	Cash	CU5,000	
	Cr Equity		CU5,000

To recognise the option premium received of CU5,000 in equity.

[Refer: paragraphs 22 and AG27(a)]

Dr	Equity	CU95,000	
	Cr Liability		CU95,000

To recognise the present value of the obligation to deliver CU98,000 in one year, ie CU95,000, as a liability.

[Refer: paragraphs 23 and AG13]

31 December 20X2

Dr	Interest expense	CU2,750	
	Cr Liability		CU2,750

To accrue interest in accordance with the effective interest method on the liability for the share redemption amount.

31 January 20X3

Dr	Interest expense	CU250	
	Cr Liability		CU250

To accrue interest in accordance with the effective interest method on the liability for the share redemption amount.

On the same day, Entity B exercises the put option and the contract is settled gross. Entity A has an obligation to deliver CU98,000 in cash to Entity B in exchange for CU95,000 worth of shares (CU95 × 1,000).

Dr	Liability	CU98,000	
	Cr Cash		CU98,000

To record the settlement of the option contract.

(d) Settlement options

IE31   The existence of settlement options (such as net in cash, net in shares or by an exchange of cash and shares) has the result that the written put option is a financial liability. If one of the settlement alternatives is to exchange cash for shares ((c) above), Entity A recognises a liability for the obligation to deliver cash, as illustrated in (c) above. Otherwise, Entity A accounts for the put option as a derivative liability.
[Refer: paragraph 26]

Entities such as mutual funds and co-operatives whose share capital is not equity as defined in IAS 32

Example 7: Entities with no equity
[Refer: paragraph 18(b)]

IE32   The following example illustrates a format of a statement of comprehensive income and statement of financial position that may be used by entities such as mutual funds that do not have equity as defined in IAS 32. Other formats are possible.

Statement of comprehensive income for the year ended 31 December 20X1

	20X1	20X0
	CU	CU
Revenue	2,956	1,718
Expenses (classified by nature or function)	(644)	(614)
Profit from operating activities	2,312	1,104
Finance costs		
– other finance costs	(47)	(47)
– distributions to unitholders **[Refer: paragraphs 35 and 36]**	(50)	(50)
Change in net assets attributable to unitholders	2,215	1,007

Statement of financial position at 31 December 20X1

	20X1	20X1	20X0	20X0
	CU	CU	CU	CU
ASSETS				
Non-current assets (classified in accordance with IAS 1)	91,374		78,484	
Total non-current assets		91,374		78,484
Current assets (classified in accordance with IAS 1)	1,422		1,769	
Total current assets		1,422		1,769
Total assets		92,796		80,253
LIABILITIES				
Current liabilities (classified in accordance with IAS 1)	647		66	
Total current liabilities		(647)		(66)
Non-current liabilities excluding net assets attributable to unitholders (classified in accordance with IAS 1)	280		136	
		(280)		(136)
Net assets attributable to unitholders		91,869		80,051

Example 8: Entities with some equity
[Refer: paragraph 18(b)]

IE33   The following example illustrates a format of a statement of comprehensive income and statement of financial position that may be used by entities whose share capital is not equity as defined in IAS 32 because the entity has an obligation to repay the share capital on demand but does not have all the features or meet the conditions in paragraphs 16A and 16B or paragraphs 16C and 16D. Other formats are possible.

Statement of comprehensive income for the year ended 31 December 20X1

	20X1	20X0
	CU	CU
Revenue	472	498
Expenses (classified by nature or function)	(367)	(396)
Profit from operating activities	105	102
Finance costs		
– other finance costs	(4)	(4)
– distributions to members [Refer: paragraphs 35 and 36]	(50)	(50)
Change in net assets attributable to members	51	48

Statement of financial position at 31 December 20X1

	20X1		20X0	
	CU	CU	CU	CU
ASSETS				
Non-current assets (classified in accordance with IAS 1)	908		830	
Total non-current assets		908		830
Current assets (classified in accordance with IAS 1)	383		350	
Total current assets		383		350
Total assets		1,291		1,180
LIABILITIES				
Current liabilities (classified in accordance with IAS 1)	372		338	
Share capital repayable on demand	202		161	
Total current liabilities		(574)		(499)
Total assets less current liabilities		717		681
Non-current liabilities (classified in accordance with IAS 1)	187		196	
		(187)		(196)

continued...

...continued

Statement of financial position at 31 December 20X1

	20X1		20X0	
	CU	CU	CU	CU
OTHER COMPONENTS OF EQUITY(a)				
Reserves eg revaluation surplus, retained earnings etc	530		485	
		530		485
		717		681

MEMORANDUM NOTE – Total members' interests

Share capital repayable on demand	202	161
Reserves	530	485
	732	646

(a) In this example, the entity has no obligation to deliver a share of its reserves to its members.

Accounting for compound financial instruments

Example 9: Separation of a compound financial instrument on initial recognition

IE34   Paragraph 28 describes how the components of a compound financial instrument are separated by the entity on initial recognition. The following example illustrates how such a separation is made.

IE35   An entity issues 2,000 convertible bonds at the start of year 1. The bonds have a three-year term, and are issued at par with a face value of CU1,000 per bond, giving total proceeds of CU2,000,000. Interest is payable annually in arrears at a nominal annual interest rate of 6 per cent. Each bond is convertible at any time up to maturity into 250 ordinary shares. When the bonds are issued, the prevailing market interest rate for similar debt without conversion options is 9 per cent.

IE36   The liability component is measured first, and the difference between the proceeds of the bond issue and the fair value of the liability is assigned to the equity component. The present value of the liability component is calculated using a discount rate of 9 per cent, the market interest rate for similar bonds having no conversion rights, as shown below.

© IFRS Foundation

	CU
Present value of the principal – CU2,000,000 payable at the end of three years	1,544,367
Present value of the interest – CU120,000 payable annually in arrears for three years	303,755
Total liability component	1,848,122
Equity component (by deduction)	151,878
Proceeds of the bond issue	2,000,000

[Refer: paragraphs 28, AG30 and AG31]

Example 10: Separation of a compound financial instrument with multiple embedded derivative features

IE37 The following example illustrates the application of paragraph 31 to the separation of the liability and equity components of a compound financial instrument with multiple embedded derivative features.

IE38 Assume that the proceeds received on the issue of a callable convertible bond are CU60. The value of a similar bond without a call or equity conversion option is CU57. Based on an option pricing model, it is determined that the value to the entity of the embedded call feature in a similar bond without an equity conversion option is CU2. In this case, the value allocated to the liability component under paragraph 31 is CU55 (CU57 – CU2) and the value allocated to the equity component is CU5 (CU60 – CU55).
[Refer: paragraph 31]

Example 11: Repurchase of a convertible instrument

IE39 The following example illustrates how an entity accounts for a repurchase of a convertible instrument. For simplicity, at inception, the face amount of the instrument is assumed to be equal to the aggregate carrying amount of its liability and equity components in the financial statements, ie no original issue premium or discount exists. Also, for simplicity, tax considerations have been omitted from the example.

IE40 On 1 January 20X0, Entity A issued a 10 per cent convertible debenture with a face value of CU1,000 maturing on 31 December 20X9. The debenture is convertible into ordinary shares of Entity A at a conversion price of CU25 per share. Interest is payable half-yearly in cash. At the date of issue, Entity A could have issued non-convertible debt with a ten-year term bearing a coupon interest rate of 11 per cent.

IE41   In the financial statements of Entity A the carrying amount of the debenture was allocated on issue as follows:

	CU
Liability component	
Present value of 20 half-yearly interest payments of CU50, discounted at 11%	597
Present value of CU1,000 due in 10 years, discounted at 11%, compounded half-yearly	343
	940
Equity component	
(difference between CU1,000 total proceeds and CU940 allocated above)	60
Total proceeds	1,000

[Refer: paragraphs 28, 29, 31 and AG31]

IE42   On 1 January 20X5, the convertible debenture has a fair value of CU1,700.

IE43   Entity A makes a tender offer to the holder of the debenture to repurchase the debenture for CU1,700, which the holder accepts. At the date of repurchase, Entity A could have issued non-convertible debt with a five-year term bearing a coupon interest rate of 8 per cent.

IE44   The repurchase price is allocated as follows:

	Carrying value	Fair value	Difference
Liability component:	CU	CU	CU
Present value of 10 remaining half-yearly interest payments of CU50, discounted at 11% and 8%, respectively	377	405	
Present value of CU1,000 due in 5 years, discounted at 11% and 8%, compounded half-yearly, respectively	585	676	
	962	1,081	(119)
Equity component	60	619[a]	(559)
Total	1,022	1,700	(678)

(a) This amount represents the difference between the fair value amount allocated to the liability component and the repurchase price of CU1,700.

[Refer: paragraph AG33]

IE45   Entity A recognises the repurchase of the debenture as follows:

Dr	Liability component	CU962	
Dr	Debt settlement expense (profit or loss)	CU119	
	Cr Cash		CU1,081

To recognise the repurchase of the liability component.

[Refer: paragraphs AG33 and AG34]

Dr	Equity	CU619	
	Cr Cash		CU619

To recognise the cash paid for the equity component.

[Refer: paragraphs AG33 and AG34]

IE46   The equity component remains as equity, but may be transferred from one line item within equity to another.

Example 12: Amendment of the terms of a convertible instrument to induce early conversion

IE47   The following example illustrates how an entity accounts for the additional consideration paid when the terms of a convertible instrument are amended to induce early conversion.

IE48   On 1 January 20X0, Entity A issued a 10 per cent convertible debenture with a face value of CU1,000 with the same terms as described in Example 11. On 1 January 20X1, to induce the holder to convert the convertible debenture promptly, Entity A reduces the conversion price to CU20 if the debenture is converted before 1 March 20X1 (ie within 60 days).

IE49   Assume the market price of Entity A's ordinary shares on the date the terms are amended is CU40 per share. The fair value of the incremental consideration paid by Entity A is calculated as follows:

*Number of ordinary shares to be issued to debenture holders under **amended** conversion terms:*

Face amount	CU1,000	
New conversion price	/CU20	per share
Number of ordinary shares to be issued on conversion	50	shares

continued...

...continued

*Number of ordinary shares to be issued to debenture holders
under **original** conversion terms:*

Face amount	CU1,000
Original conversion price	/CU25 per share
Number of ordinary shares to be issued on conversion	40 shares

*Number of incremental ordinary shares issued upon
conversion*

	10 shares

*Value of **incremental** ordinary shares issued upon conversion*

CU40 per share x 10 incremental shares	CU400

IE50   The incremental consideration of CU400 is recognised as a loss in profit or loss.

IASB documents published to accompany

IAS 33

Earnings per Share

The text of the unaccompanied standard, IAS 33, is contained in Part A of this edition. Its effective date when issued was 1 January 2005. The text of the Basis for Conclusions on IAS 33 is contained in Part C of this edition. This part presents the following document:

ILLUSTRATIVE EXAMPLES

IAS 33 SUPPORTING MATERIAL

Example published by the IFRS Interpretations Committee to accompany the Agenda Decision *IAS 33 Earnings per Share–Tax arising from payments on participating equity instruments* in June 2017

CONTENTS

IAS 33 *EARNINGS PER SHARE*
ILLUSTRATIVE EXAMPLES

IAS 33 *Earnings per Share*
Illustrative Examples

These examples accompany, but are not part of, IAS 33.

Example 1 Increasing rate preference shares

Reference: IAS 33, paragraphs 12 and 15

Entity D issued non-convertible, non-redeemable class A cumulative preference shares of CU100 par value on 1 January 20X1. The class A preference shares are entitled to a cumulative annual dividend of CU7 per share starting in 20X4.

At the time of issue, the market rate dividend yield on the class A preference shares was 7 per cent a year. Thus, Entity D could have expected to receive proceeds of approximately CU100 per class A preference share if the dividend rate of CU7 per share had been in effect at the date of issue.

In consideration of the dividend payment terms, however, the class A preference shares were issued at CU81.63 per share, ie at a discount of CU18.37 per share. The issue price can be calculated by taking the present value of CU100, discounted at 7 per cent over a three-year period.

Because the shares are classified as equity, the original issue discount is amortised to retained earnings using the effective interest method **[Refer: IFRS 9 Appendix A (definition of effective interest method) and paragraphs B5.4.1–B5.4.7]** and treated as a preference dividend for earnings per share purposes. To calculate basic earnings per share, the following imputed dividend per class A preference share is deducted to determine the profit or loss attributable to ordinary equity holders of the parent entity: **[Refer: paragraphs 12–18, A1, A13 and A14]**

Year	Carrying amount of class A preference shares 1 January	Imputed[a] dividend	Carrying[b] amount of class A preference shares 31 December	Dividend paid
	CU	CU	CU	CU
20X1	81.63	5.71	87.34	–
20X2	87.34	6.12	93.46	–
20X3	93.46	6.54	100.00	–
Thereafter:	100.00	7.00	107.00	(7.00)

(a) at 7%

(b) This is before dividend payment.

Example 2 Weighted average number of ordinary shares

Reference: IAS 33, paragraphs 19–21

		Shares issued	Treasury[a] shares	Shares outstanding
1 January 20X1	Balance at beginning of year	2,000	300	1,700
31 May 20X1	Issue of new shares for cash	800	–	2,500
1 December 20X1	Purchase of treasury shares for cash	–	250	2,250
31 December 20X1	Balance at year-end	2,800	550	2,250

Calculation of weighted average:

$(1{,}700 \times {}^5/_{12}) + (2{,}500 \times {}^6/_{12}) + (2{,}250 \times {}^1/_{12}) = 2{,}146$ shares *or*

$(1{,}700 \times {}^{12}/_{12}) + (800 \times {}^7/_{12}) - (250 \times {}^1/_{12}) = 2{,}146$ shares

(a) Treasury shares are equity instruments reacquired and held by the issuing entity itself or by its subsidiaries.

Example 3 Bonus issue

Reference: IAS 33, paragraphs 26, 27(a) and 28

Profit attributable to ordinary equity holders of the parent entity 20X0	CU180
Profit attributable to ordinary equity holders of the parent entity 20X1	CU600
Ordinary shares outstanding until 30 September 20X1	200
Bonus issue 1 October 20X1	2 ordinary shares for each ordinary share outstanding at 30 September 20X1
	$200 \times 2 = 400$

Basic earnings per share 20X1
$$\frac{CU600}{(200 + 400)} = CU1.00$$

Basic earnings per share 20X0
$$\frac{CU180}{(200 + 400)} = CU0.30$$

Because the bonus issue was without consideration, it is treated as if it had occurred before the beginning of 20X0, the earliest period presented.

Example 4 Rights issue

Reference: IAS 33, paragraphs 26, 27(b) and A2

	20X0	20X1	20X2
Profit attributable to ordinary equity holders of the parent entity	CU1,100	CU1,500	CU1,800

Shares outstanding before rights issue	500 shares
Rights issue	One new share for each five outstanding shares
	(100 new shares total)
	Exercise price: CU5.00
	Date of rights issue: 1 January 20X1
	Last date to exercise rights: 1 March 20X1
Market price of one ordinary share immediately before exercise on 1 March 20X1:	CU11.00
Reporting date	31 December

Calculation of theoretical ex-rights value per share

$$\frac{\text{Fair value of all outstanding shares before the exercise of rights} + \text{total amount received from exercise of rights}}{\text{Number of shares outstanding before exercise} + \text{number of shares issued in the exercise}}$$

$$\frac{(CU11.00 \times 500 \text{ shares}) + (CU5.00 \times 100 \text{ shares})}{500 \text{ shares} + 100 \text{ shares}}$$

Theoretical ex-rights value per share = CU10.00

Calculation of adjustment factor

$$\frac{\text{Fair value per share before exercise of rights}}{\text{Theoretical ex-rights value per share}} \qquad \frac{CU11.00}{CU10.00} = 1.10$$

continued...

...continued

Calculation of basic earnings per share

		20X0	20X1	20X2
20X0 basic EPS as originally reported:	CU1,100 ÷ 500 shares	CU2.20		
20X0 basic EPS restated for rights issue:	$\dfrac{\text{CU1,100}}{(500 \text{ shares} \times 1.1)}$	CU2.00		
20X1 basic EPS including effects of rights issue:	$\dfrac{\text{CU1,500}}{(500 \times 1.1 \times {}^{2}/_{12}) + (600 \times {}^{10}/_{12})}$		CU2.54	
20X2 basic EPS:	CU1,800 ÷ 600 shares			CU3.00

Example 5 Effects of share options on diluted earnings per share

Reference: IAS 33, paragraphs 45–47

Profit attributable to ordinary equity holders of the parent entity for year 20X1	CU1,200,000
Weighted average number of ordinary shares outstanding during year 20X1	500,000 shares
Average market price of one ordinary share during year 20X1	CU20.00
Weighted average number of shares under option during year 20X1	100,000 shares
Exercise price for shares under option during year 20X1	CU15.00

continued...

...continued

Calculation of earnings per share

	Earnings	Shares	Per share
Profit attributable to ordinary equity holders of the parent entity for year 20X1	CU1,200,000		
Weighted average shares outstanding during year 20X1		500,000	
Basic earnings per share			CU2.40
Weighted average number of shares under option		100,000	
Weighted average number of shares that would have been issued at average market price: (100,000 × CU15.00) ÷ CU20.00		(75,000)	(a)
Diluted earnings per share	CU1,200,000	525,000	CU2.29

(a) Earnings have not increased because the total number of shares has increased only by the number of shares (25,000) deemed to have been issued for no consideration (see paragraph 46(b) of the Standard).

Example 5A Determining the exercise price of employee share options

[Refer: paragraph 47A]

Weighted average number of unvested share options per employee	1,000
Weighted average amount per employee to be recognised over the remainder of the vesting period for employee services to be rendered as consideration for the share options, determined in accordance with IFRS 2 *Share-based Payment*	CU1,200
Cash exercise price of unvested share options	CU15

Calculation of adjusted exercise price

Fair value of services yet to be rendered per employee:	CU1,200
Fair value of services yet to be rendered per option: (CU1,200 ÷ 1,000)	CU1.20
Total exercise price of share options: (CU15.00 + CU1.20)	CU16.20

Example 6 Convertible bonds[1]

Reference: IAS 33, paragraphs 33, 34, 36 and 49

Profit attributable to ordinary equity holders of the parent entity	CU1,004
Ordinary shares outstanding	1,000
Basic earnings per share	CU1.00
Convertible bonds	100
Each block of 10 bonds is convertible into three ordinary shares	
Interest expense for the current year relating to the liability component of the convertible bonds	CU10
Current and deferred tax relating to that interest expense	CU4

Note: the interest expense includes amortisation of the discount arising on initial recognition of the liability component (see IAS 32 Financial Instruments: Presentation).

Adjusted profit attributable to ordinary equity holders of the parent entity	CU1,004 + CU10 – CU4 = CU1,010
Number of ordinary shares resulting from conversion of bonds	30
Number of ordinary shares used to calculate diluted earnings per share	1,000 + 30 = 1,030
Diluted earnings per share	$\frac{CU1,010}{1,030}$ = CU0.98

---

1   This example does not illustrate the classification of the components of convertible financial instruments as liabilities and equity or the classification of related interest and dividends as expenses and equity as required by IAS 32.

Example 7 Contingently issuable shares

Reference: IAS 33, paragraphs 19, 24, 36, 37, 41–43 and 52

Ordinary shares outstanding during 20X1	1,000,000 (there were no options, warrants or convertible instruments outstanding during the period)

An agreement related to a recent business combination provides for the issue of additional ordinary shares based on the following conditions:

	5,000 additional ordinary shares for each new retail site opened during 20X1
	1,000 additional ordinary shares for each CU1,000 of consolidated profit in excess of CU2,000,000 for the year ended 31 December 20X1
Retail sites opened during the year:	one on 1 May 20X1
	one on 1 September 20X1
Consolidated year-to-date profit attributable to ordinary equity holders of the parent entity:	CU1,100,000 as of 31 March 20X1
	CU2,300,000 as of 30 June 20X1
	CU1,900,000 as of 30 September 20X1 (including a CU450,000 loss from a discontinued operation)
	CU2,900,000 as of 31 December 20X1

Basic earnings per share

	First quarter	Second quarter	Third quarter	Fourth quarter	Full year
Numerator (CU)	1,100,000	1,200,000	(400,000)	1,000,000	2,900,000
Denominator:					
Ordinary shares outstanding	1,000,000	1,000,000	1,000,000	1,000,000	1,000,000
Retail site contingency	–	3,333[a]	6,667[b]	10,000	5,000[c]
Earnings contingency[d]	–	–	–	–	–
Total shares	1,000,000	1,003,333	1,006,667	1,010,000	1,005,000
Basic earnings per share (CU)	1.10	1.20	(0.40)	0.99	2.89

(a) 5,000 shares × $^2/_3$

(b) 5,000 shares + (5,000 shares × $^1/_3$)

(c) (5,000 shares × $^8/_{12}$) + (5,000 shares × $^4/_{12}$)

(d) The earnings contingency has no effect on basic earnings per share because it is not certain that the condition is satisfied until the end of the contingency period. The effect is negligible for the fourth-quarter and full-year calculations because it is not certain that the condition is met until the last day of the period.

Diluted earnings per share

	First quarter	Second quarter	Third quarter	Fourth quarter	Full year
Numerator (CU)	1,100,000	1,200,000	(400,000)	1,000,000	2,900,000
Denominator:					
Ordinary shares outstanding	1,000,000	1,000,000	1,000,000	1,000,000	1,000,000
Retail site contingency	–	5,000	10,000	10,000	10,000
Earnings contingency	–[a]	300,000[b]	–[c]	900,000[d]	900,000[d]
Total shares	1,000,000	1,305,000	1,010,000	1,910,000	1,910,000
Diluted earnings per share (CU)	1.10	0.92	(0.40)[e]	0.52	1.52

(a) Company A does not have year-to-date profit exceeding CU2,000,000 at 31 March 20X1. The Standard does not permit projecting future earnings levels and including the related contingent shares.

(b) [(CU2,300,000 – CU2,000,000) ÷ 1,000] × 1,000 shares = 300,000 shares.

(c) Year-to-date profit is less than CU2,000,000.

(d) [(CU2,900,000 – CU2,000,000) ÷ 1,000] × 1,000 shares = 900,000 shares.

(e) Because the loss during the third quarter is attributable to a loss from a discontinued operation, the antidilution rules do not apply. The control number (ie profit or loss from, continuing operations attributable to the equity holders of the parent entity) is positive. Accordingly, the effect of potential ordinary shares is included in the calculation of diluted earnings per share.

Example 8 Convertible bonds settled in shares or cash at the issuer's option

Reference: IAS 33, paragraphs 31–33, 36, 58 and 59

An entity issues 2,000 convertible bonds at the beginning of Year 1. The bonds have a three-year term, and are issued at par with a face value of CU1,000 per bond, giving total proceeds of CU2,000,000. Interest is payable annually in arrears at a nominal annual interest rate of 6 per cent. Each bond is convertible at any time up to maturity into 250 ordinary shares. The entity has an option to settle the principal amount of the convertible bonds in ordinary shares or in cash.

When the bonds are issued, the prevailing market interest rate for similar debt without a conversion option is 9 per cent. At the issue date, the market price of one ordinary share is CU3. Income tax is ignored.

Profit attributable to ordinary equity holders of the parent entity Year 1	CU1,000,000
Ordinary shares outstanding	1,200,000
Convertible bonds outstanding	2,000
Allocation of proceeds of the bond issue:	
Liability component	CU1,848,122[a]
Equity component	CU151,878
	CU2,000,000

(a) This represents the present value of the principal and interest discounted at 9% – CU2,000,000 payable at the end of three years; CU120,000 payable annually in arrears for three years.

The liability and equity components would be determined in accordance with IAS 32 *Financial Instruments: Presentation*. These amounts are recognised as the initial carrying amounts of the liability and equity components. The amount assigned to the issuer conversion option equity element is an addition to equity and is not adjusted.

Basic earnings per share Year 1:

$$\frac{CU1,000,000}{1,200,000} = CU0.83 \text{ per ordinary share}$$

Diluted earnings per share Year 1:

It is presumed that the issuer will settle the contract by the issue of ordinary shares. The dilutive effect is therefore calculated in accordance with paragraph 59 of the Standard.

$$\frac{CU1,000,000 + CU166,331^{(a)}}{1,200,000 + 500,000^{(b)}} = CU0.69 \text{ per ordinary share}$$

(a) Profit is adjusted for the accretion of CU166,331 (CU1,848,122 × 9%) of the liability because of the passage of time.

(b) 500,000 ordinary shares = 250 ordinary shares × 2,000 convertible bonds

Example 9 Calculation of weighted average number of shares: determining the order in which to include dilutive instruments[2]

Primary reference: IAS 33, paragraph 44

Secondary reference: IAS 33, paragraphs 10, 12, 19, 31–33, 36, 41–47, 49 and 50

Earnings	CU
Profit from continuing operations attributable to the parent entity	16,400,000
Less dividends on preference shares	(6,400,000)
Profit from continuing operations attributable to ordinary equity holders of the parent entity	10,000,000
Loss from discontinued operations attributable to the parent entity	(4,000,000)
Profit attributable to ordinary equity holders of the parent entity	6,000,000
Ordinary shares outstanding	2,000,000
Average market price of one ordinary share during year	CU75.00

Potential ordinary shares

Options	100,000 with exercise price of CU60
Convertible preference shares	800,000 shares with a par value of CU100 entitled to a cumulative dividend of CU8 per share. Each preference share is convertible to two ordinary shares.
5% convertible bonds	Nominal amount CU100,000,000. Each CU1,000 bond is convertible to 20 ordinary shares. There is no amortisation of premium or discount affecting the determination of interest expense.
Tax rate	40%

---

2   This example does not illustrate the classification of the components of convertible financial instruments as liabilities and equity or the classification of related interest and dividends as expenses and equity as required by IAS 32.

Increase in earnings attributable to ordinary equity holders on conversion of potential ordinary shares

		Increase in earnings	Increase in number of ordinary shares	Earnings per incremental share
		CU		CU
Options				
Increase in earnings		Nil		
Incremental shares issued for no consideration	100,000 × (CU75 – CU60) ÷ CU75		20,000	Nil
Convertible preference shares				
Increase in profit	CU800,000 × 100 × 0.08	6,400,000		
Incremental shares	2 × 800,000		1,600,000	4.00
5% convertible bonds				
Increase in profit	CU100,000,000 × 0.05 × (1 – 0.40)	3,000,000		
Incremental shares	100,000 × 20		2,000,000	1.50

The order in which to include the dilutive instruments is therefore:

1   Options

2   5% convertible bonds

3   Convertible preference shares

Calculation of diluted earnings per share

	Profit from continuing operations attributable to ordinary equity holders of the parent entity (control number)	Ordinary shares	Per share	
	CU		CU	
As reported	10,000,000	2,000,000	5.00	
Options	–	20,000		
	10,000,000	2,020,000	4.95	Dilutive
5% convertible bonds	3,000,000	2,000,000		
	13,000,000	4,020,000	3.23	Dilutive
Convertible preference shares	6,400,000	1,600,000		
	19,400,000	5,620,000	3.45	Antidilutive

Because diluted earnings per share is increased when taking the convertible preference shares into account (from CU3.23 to CU3.45), the convertible preference shares are antidilutive and are ignored in the calculation of diluted earnings per share. Therefore, diluted earnings per share for profit from continuing operations is CU3.23:

	Basic EPS	Diluted EPS
	CU	CU
Profit from continuing operations attributable to ordinary equity holders of the parent entity	5.00	3.23
Loss from discontinued operations attributable to ordinary equity holders of the parent entity	(2.00)[a]	(0.99)[b]
Profit attributable to ordinary equity holders of the parent entity	3.00[c]	2.24[d]

(a) (CU4,000,000) ÷ 2,000,000 = (CU2.00)
(b) (CU4,000,000) ÷ 4,020,000 = (CU0.99)
(c) CU6,000,000 ÷ 2,000,000 = CU3.00
(d) (CU6,000,000 + CU3,000,000) ÷ 4,020,000 = CU2.24

Example 10 Instruments of a subsidiary: calculation of basic and diluted earnings per share[3]

Reference: IAS 33, paragraphs 40, A11 and A12

Parent:

Profit attributable to ordinary equity holders of the parent entity	CU12,000 (excluding any earnings of, or dividends paid by, the subsidiary)
Ordinary shares outstanding	10,000
Instruments of subsidiary owned by the parent	800 ordinary shares
	30 warrants exercisable to purchase ordinary shares of subsidiary
	300 convertible preference shares

Subsidiary:

Profit	CU5,400
Ordinary shares outstanding	1,000
Warrants	150, exercisable to purchase ordinary shares of the subsidiary
Exercise price	CU10
Average market price of one ordinary share	CU20
Convertible preference shares	400, each convertible into one ordinary share
Dividends on preference shares	CU1 per share

No inter-company eliminations or adjustments were necessary except for dividends.

For the purposes of this illustration, income taxes have been ignored.

---

3   This example does not illustrate the classification of the components of convertible financial instruments as liabilities and equity or the classification of related interest and dividends as expenses and equity as required by IAS 32.

Subsidiary's earnings per share

Basic EPS   CU5.00 calculated:
$$\frac{CU5,400^{(a)} - CU400^{(b)}}{1,000^{(c)}}$$

Diluted EPS   CU3.66 calculated:
$$\frac{CU5,400^{(d)}}{(1,000 + 75^{(e)} + 400^{(f)})}$$

(a) Subsidiary's profit attributable to ordinary equity holders.
(b) Dividends paid by subsidiary on convertible preference shares.
(c) Subsidiary's ordinary shares outstanding.
(d) Subsidiary's profit attributable to ordinary equity holders (CU5,000) increased by CU400 preference dividends for the purpose of calculating diluted earnings per share.
(e) Incremental shares from warrants, calculated: $[(CU20 - CU10) \div CU20] \times 150$.
(f) Subsidiary's ordinary shares assumed outstanding from conversion of convertible preference shares, calculated: 400 convertible preference shares × conversion factor of 1.

Consolidated earnings per share

Basic EPS   CU1.63 calculated:
$$\frac{CU12,000^{(a)} + CU4,300^{(b)}}{10,000^{(c)}}$$

Diluted EPS   CU1.61 calculated:
$$\frac{CU12,000 + CU2,928^{(d)} + CU55^{(e)} + CU1,098^{(f)}}{10,000}$$

(a) Parent's profit attributable to ordinary equity holders of the parent entity.
(b) Portion of subsidiary's profit to be included in consolidated basic earnings per share, calculated: $(800 \times CU5.00) + (300 \times CU1.00)$.
(c) Parent's ordinary shares outstanding.
(d) Parent's proportionate interest in subsidiary's earnings attributable to ordinary shares, calculated: $(800 \div 1,000) \times (1,000$ shares × CU3.66 per share).
(e) Parent's proportionate interest in subsidiary's earnings attributable to warrants, calculated: $(30 \div 150) \times (75$ incremental shares × CU3.66 per share).
(f) Parent's proportionate interest in subsidiary's earnings attributable to convertible preference shares, calculated: $(300 \div 400) \times (400$ shares from conversion × CU3.66 per share).

Example 11 Participating equity instruments and two-class ordinary shares[4]

Reference: IAS 33, paragraphs A13 and A14

Profit attributable to equity holders of the parent entity	CU100,000
Ordinary shares outstanding	10,000
Non-convertible preference shares	6,000
Non-cumulative annual dividend on preference shares (before any dividend is paid on ordinary shares)	CU5.50 per share

After ordinary shares have been paid a dividend of CU2.10 per share, the preference shares participate in any additional dividends on a 20:80 ratio with ordinary shares (ie after preference and ordinary shares have been paid dividends of CU5.50 and CU2.10 per share, respectively, preference shares participate in any additional dividends at a rate of one-fourth of the amount paid to ordinary shares on a per-share basis).

Dividends on preference shares paid	CU33,000	(CU5.50 per share)
Dividends on ordinary shares paid	CU21,000	(CU2.10 per share)

Basic earnings per share is calculated as follows:

	CU	CU
Profit attributable to equity holders of the parent entity		100,000
Less dividends paid:		
Preference	33,000	
Ordinary	21,000	
		(54,000)
Undistributed earnings		46,000

continued...

---

4   This example does not illustrate the classification of the components of convertible financial instruments as liabilities and equity or the classification of related interest and dividends as expenses and equity as required by IAS 32.

...continued

Allocation of undistributed earnings:

Allocation per ordinary share = A

Allocation per preference share = B; B = $^1/_4$ A

$$(A \times 10,000) + (^1/_4 \times A \times 6,000) = CU46,000$$

$$A = CU46,000 \div (10,000 + 1,500)$$

$$A = CU4.00$$

$$B = ^1/_4 A$$

$$B = CU1.00$$

Basic per share amounts:

	Preference shares	Ordinary shares
Distributed earnings	CU5.50	CU2.10
Undistributed earnings	CU1.00	CU4.00
Totals	CU6.50	CU6.10

Example 12 Calculation and presentation of basic and diluted earnings per share (comprehensive example)[5]

This example illustrates the quarterly and annual calculations of basic and diluted earnings per share in the year 20X1 for Company A, which has a complex capital structure. The control number is profit or loss from continuing operations attributable to the parent entity. Other facts assumed are as follows:

Average market price of ordinary shares: The average market prices of ordinary shares for the calendar year 20X1 were as follows:

First quarter	CU49
Second quarter	CU60
Third quarter	CU67
Fourth quarter	CU67

The average market price of ordinary shares from 1 July to 1 September 20X1 was CU65.

Ordinary shares: The number of ordinary shares outstanding at the beginning of 20X1 was 5,000,000. On 1 March 20X1, 200,000 ordinary shares were issued for cash.

---

5   This example does not illustrate the classification of the components of convertible financial instruments as liabilities and equity or the classification of related interest and dividends as expenses and equity as required by IAS 32.

Convertible bonds: In the last quarter of 20X0, 5 per cent convertible bonds with a principal amount of CU12,000,000 due in 20 years were sold for cash at CU1,000 (par). Interest is payable twice a year, on 1 November and 1 May. Each CU1,000 bond is convertible into 40 ordinary shares. No bonds were converted in 20X0. The entire issue was converted on 1 April 20X1 because the issue was called by Company A.

Convertible preference shares: In the second quarter of 20X0, 800,000 convertible preference shares were issued for assets in a purchase transaction. The quarterly dividend on each convertible preference share is CU0.05, payable at the end of the quarter for shares outstanding at that date. Each share is convertible into one ordinary share. Holders of 600,000 convertible preference shares converted their preference shares into ordinary shares on 1 June 20X1.

Warrants: Warrants to buy 600,000 ordinary shares at CU55 per share for a period of five years were issued on 1 January 20X1. All outstanding warrants were exercised on 1 September 20X1.

Options: Options to buy 1,500,000 ordinary shares at CU75 per share for a period of 10 years were issued on 1 July 20X1. No options were exercised during 20X1 because the exercise price of the options exceeded the market price of the ordinary shares.

Tax rate: The tax rate was 40 per cent for 20X1.

20X1	Profit (loss) from continuing operations attributable to the parent entity[a]	Profit (loss) attributable to the parent entity
	CU	CU
First quarter	5,000,000	5,000,000
Second quarter	6,500,000	6,500,000
Third quarter	1,000,000	(1,000,000)[b]
Fourth quarter	(700,000)	(700,000)
Full year	11,800,000	9,800,000

(a) This is the control number (before adjusting for preference dividends).
(b) Company A had a CU2,000,000 loss (net of tax) from discontinued operations in the third quarter.

First Quarter 20X1

Basic EPS calculation			CU
Profit from continuing operations attributable to the parent entity			5,000,000
Less: preference share dividends			(40,000)[a]
Profit attributable to ordinary equity holders of the parent entity			4,960,000

Dates	Shares outstanding	Fraction of period	Weighted-average shares
1 January–28 February	5,000,000	$^2/_3$	3,333,333
Issue of ordinary shares on 1 March			
1 March–31 March	200,000	$^1/_3$	1,733,333
Weighted-average shares	5,200,000		5,066,666
Basic EPS			**CU0.98**

continued...

...continued

Diluted EPS calculation

Profit attributable to ordinary equity holders of the parent entity		CU4,960,000
Plus: profit impact of assumed conversions		
Preference share dividends	CU40,000 (a)	
Interest on 5% convertible bonds	CU90,000 (b)	
Effect of assumed conversions		CU130,000
Profit attributable to ordinary equity holders of the parent entity including assumed conversions		CU5,090,000
Weighted-average shares		5,066,666
Plus: incremental shares from assumed conversions		
Warrants	0 (c)	
Convertible preference shares	800,000	
5% convertible bonds	480,000	
Dilutive potential ordinary shares		1,280,000
Adjusted weighted-average shares		6,346,666
Diluted EPS		***CU0.80***

(a) 800,000 shares × CU0.05

(b) (CU12,000,000 × 5%) ÷ 4; less taxes at 40%

(c) The warrants were not assumed to be exercised because they were antidilutive in the period (CU55 [exercise price] > CU49 [average price]).

Second Quarter 20X1

Basic EPS calculation			CU
Profit from continuing operations attributable to the parent entity			6,500,000
Less: preference share dividends			(10,000)[a]
Profit attributable to ordinary equity holders of the parent entity			6,490,000

Dates	Shares outstanding	Fraction of period	Weighted-average shares
1 April	5,200,000		
Conversion of 5% bonds on 1 April	480,000		
1 April–31 May	5,680,000	$2/3$	3,786,666
Conversion of preference shares 1 June	600,000		
1 June–30 June	6,280,000	$1/3$	2,093,333
Weighted-average shares			5,880,000
Basic EPS			**CU1.10**

continued...

...continued

Diluted EPS calculation

Profit attributable to ordinary equity holders of the parent entity	CU6,490,000
Plus: profit impact of assumed conversions	
Preference share dividends	CU10,000[a]
Effect of assumed conversions	CU10,000
Profit attributable to ordinary equity holders of the parent entity including assumed conversions	CU6,500,000
Weighted-average shares	5,880,000
Plus: incremental shares from assumed conversions	
Warrants	50,000[b]
Convertible preference shares	600,000[c]
Dilutive potential ordinary shares	650,000
Adjusted weighted-average shares	6,530,000
Diluted EPS	***CU1.00***

(a) 200,000 shares × CU0.05

(b) CU55 × 600,000 = CU33,000,000; CU33,000,000 ÷ CU60 = 550,000; 600,000 − 550,000 = 50,000 shares OR [(CU60 − CU55) ÷ CU60] × 600,000 shares = 50,000 shares

(c) (800,000 shares × $^2/_3$) + (200,000 shares × $^1/_3$)

Third Quarter 20X1

Basic EPS calculation			<u>CU</u>
Profit from continuing operations attributable to the parent entity			1,000,000
Less: preference share dividends			(10,000)
Profit from continuing operations attributable to ordinary equity holders of the parent entity			990,000
Loss from discontinued operations attributable to the parent entity			(2,000,000)
Loss attributable to ordinary equity holders of the parent entity			(1,010,000)

Dates	*Shares outstanding*	*Fraction of period*	*Weighted-average shares*
1 July–31 August	6,280,000	$^2/_3$	4,186,666
Exercise of warrants on 1 September	600,000		
1 September–30 September	6,880,000	$^1/_3$	2,293,333
Weighted-average shares			6,480,000

Basic EPS

Profit from continuing operations	**CU0.15**
Loss from discontinued operations	**(CU0.31)**
Loss	**(CU0.16)**

continued...

...continued

Diluted EPS calculation

Profit from continuing operations attributable to ordinary equity holders of the parent entity		CU990,000
Plus: profit impact of assumed conversions		
Preference share dividends	CU10,000	
Effect of assumed conversions		CU10,000
Profit from continuing operations attributable to ordinary equity holders of the parent entity including assumed conversions		CU1,000,000
Loss from discontinued operations attributable to the parent entity		(CU2,000,000)
Loss attributable to ordinary equity holders of the parent entity including assumed conversions		(CU1,000,000)
Weighted-average shares		6,480,000
Plus: incremental shares from assumed conversions		
Warrants	61,538[(a)]	
Convertible preference shares	200,000	
Dilutive potential ordinary shares		261,538
Adjusted weighted-average shares		6,741,538

Diluted EPS	
Profit from continuing operations	*CU0.15*
Loss from discontinued operations	*(CU0.30)*
Loss	*(CU0.15)*

(a) [(CU65 – CU55) ÷ CU65] × 600,000 = 92,308 shares; 92,308 × $^2/_3$ = 61,538 shares

Note: The incremental shares from assumed conversions are included in calculating the diluted per-share amounts for the loss from discontinued operations and loss even though they are antidilutive. This is because the control number (profit from continuing operations attributable to ordinary equity holders of the parent entity, adjusted for preference dividends) was positive (ie profit, rather than loss).

[Refer: paragraphs 41–44 and A3]

Fourth Quarter 20X1

Basic EPS calculation	CU
Loss from continuing operations attributable to the parent entity	(700,000)
Add: preference share dividends	(10,000)
Loss attributable to ordinary equity holders of the parent entity	(710,000)

Dates	Shares outstanding	Fraction of period	Weighted-average shares
1 October–31 December	6,880,000	$^3/_3$	6,880,000
Weighted-average shares			6,880,000

Basic and diluted EPS

Loss attributable to ordinary equity holders of the parent entity	*(CU0.10)*

Note: The incremental shares from assumed conversions are not included in calculating the diluted per-share amounts because the control number (loss from continuing operations attributable to ordinary equity holders of the parent entity adjusted for preference dividends) was negative (ie a loss, rather than profit).

Full Year 20X1

Basic EPS calculation			CU
Profit from continuing operations attributable to the parent entity			11,800,000
Less: preference share dividends			(70,000)
Profit from continuing operations attributable to ordinary equity holders of the parent entity			11,730,000
Loss from discontinued operations attributable to the parent entity			(2,000,000)
Profit attributable to ordinary equity holders of the parent entity			9,730,000

Dates	Shares outstanding	Fraction of period	Weighted-average shares
1 January–28 February	5,000,000	$^2/_{12}$	833,333
Issue of ordinary shares on 1 March	200,000		
1 March–31 March	5,200,000	$^1/_{12}$	433,333
Conversion of 5% bonds on 1 April	480,000		
1 April–31 May	5,680,000	$^2/_{12}$	946,667
Conversion of preference shares on 1 June	600,000		
1 June–31 August	6,280,000	$^3/_{12}$	1,570,000
Exercise of warrants on 1 September	600,000		
1 September–31 December	6,880,000	$^4/_{12}$	2,293,333
Weighted-average shares			6,076,667

Basic EPS

Profit from continuing operations			*CU1.93*
Loss from discontinued operations			*(CU0.33)*
Profit			*CU1.60*

continued...

...continued

Diluted EPS calculation

Profit from continuing operations attributable to ordinary equity holders of the parent entity		CU11,730,000
Plus: profit impact of assumed conversions		
Preference share dividends	CU70,000	
Interest on 5% convertible bonds	CU90,000[(a)]	
Effect of assumed conversions		CU160,000
Profit from continuing operations attributable to ordinary equity holders of the parent entity including assumed conversions		CU11,890,000
Loss from discontinued operations attributable to the parent entity		(CU2,000,000)
Profit attributable to ordinary equity holders of the parent entity including assumed conversions		CU9,890,000
Weighted-average shares		6,076,667
Plus: incremental shares from assumed conversions		
Warrants	14,880[(b)]	
Convertible preference shares	450,000[(c)]	
5% convertible bonds	120,000[(d)]	
Dilutive potential ordinary shares		584,880
Adjusted weighted-average shares		6,661,547

Diluted EPS	
Profit from continuing operations	***CU1.78***
Loss from discontinued operations	***(CU0.30)***
Profit	***CU1.48***

(a) (CU12,000,000 × 5%) ÷ 4; less taxes at 40%.
(b) [(CU57.125* − CU55) ÷ CU57.125] × 600,000 = 22,320 shares; 22,320 × $^8/_{12}$ = 14,880 shares*.
     The average market price from 1 January 20X1 to 1 September 20X1.
(c) (800,000 shares × $^5/_{12}$) + (200,000 shares × $^7/_{12}$).
(d) 480,000 shares × $^3/_{12}$.

The following illustrates how Company A might present its earnings per share data in its statement of comprehensive income. Note that the amounts per share for the loss from discontinued operations are not required to be presented in the statement of comprehensive income. **[Refer: paragraph 66]**

	For the year ended 20X1
	CU
Earnings per ordinary share	
Profit from continuing operations	1.93
Loss from discontinued operations	(0.33)
Profit	1.60
Diluted earnings per ordinary share	
Profit from continuing operations	1.78
Loss from discontinued operations	(0.30)
Profit	1.48

The following table includes the quarterly and annual earnings per share data for Company A. The purpose of this table is to illustrate that the sum of the four quarters' earnings per share data will not necessarily equal the annual earnings per share data. The Standard does not require disclosure of this information.

	First quarter	*Second quarter*	*Third quarter*	*Fourth quarter*	*Full year*
	CU	**CU**	**CU**	**CU**	**CU**
Basic EPS					
Profit (loss) from continuing operations	0.98	1.10	0.15	(0.10)	1.93
Loss from discontinued operations	–	–	(0.31)	–	(0.33)
Profit (loss)	0.98	1.10	(0.16)	(0.10)	1.60
Diluted EPS					
Profit (loss) from continuing operations	0.80	1.00	0.15	(0.10)	1.78
Loss from discontinued operations	–	–	(0.30)	–	(0.30)
Profit (loss)	0.80	1.00	(0.15)	(0.10)	1.48

Note: The Agenda Decision *IAS 33 Earnings per Share—Tax arising from payments on participating equity instruments* is reproduced in this edition beneath paragraph A14 of IAS 33.

The following example was published by the IFRS Interpretations Committee as education material to accompany that Agenda Decision. This example is not part of IAS 33.

Illustrative example accompanying agenda decision *IAS 33 Earnings per Share—Tax arising from payments on participating equity instruments*

Reference—IAS 33, paragraphs A13 and A14

This example illustrates how an entity (Entity Y) determines profit or loss attributable to ordinary shareholders (ie the numerator in the basic earnings per share (EPS) calculation) over three reporting periods. Entity Y has two classes of equity instruments outstanding —ordinary shares and participating equity instruments. Other facts assumed are as follows:

Participation rights: Participating equity holders participate in dividends with ordinary shareholders according to a 10:1 ratio (except for any distribution relating to the tax benefit—see **Tax deductibility** and **Attribution of the tax benefit** assumptions below).

Tax deductibility: The dividends on participating equity instruments are deductible for tax purposes. Accordingly, such payments reduce taxable income and thus reduce income taxes payable to the taxation authority ('tax benefit').

Attribution of the tax benefit: Ordinary shareholders, not participating equity holders, benefit from the tax benefit.

Tax rate: The tax rate is 30 per cent.

Profit for the year: Entity Y's profit applying IFRS Standards for years 1, 2 and 3 are CU330, CU550 and CU110 respectively—before considering any tax benefit that arises from paying dividends to participating equity holders.

Dividends declared:

Year 1—Entity Y does not declare or pay dividends.

Year 2—at the end of year 2, Entity Y declares and pays dividends for (a) all the profit in year 1 of CU330 and (b) the tax benefit that arises from paying dividends to the participating equity holders.

Year 3—at the end of year 3, Entity Y declares and pays dividends for (a) all the profit in years 2 and 3 and (b) the tax benefit that arises from paying dividends to the participating equity holders.

This table summarises Entity Y's profit, dividends paid and tax benefit in each of the three years:

	Year 1	Year 2	Year 3	Total
	CU	CU	CU	CU
Profit (before tax benefit)	330	550	110	990
Dividends declared and paid (before considering the tax benefit):				
To participating equity holders (in ratio of 10:1) [A]	0	300	600	900
To ordinary shareholders (in ratio of 10:1)	0	30	60	90
	0	330	660	990
Tax benefit from paying dividends [A x 30%]	0	90	180	270
Dividends declared and paid relating to the tax benefit:				
To participating equity holders	0	0	0	0
To ordinary shareholders(a)	0	90	180	270
	0	90	180	270
Total dividends declared and paid:				
To participating equity holders	0	300	600	900
To ordinary shareholders	0	120	240	360
	0	420	840	1,260

(a) In this example, ordinary shareholders (and not participating equity holders) benefit from the tax benefit. However, if that were not the case, and ordinary shareholders and participating equity holders were to share the tax benefit according to the same ratio as other dividend payments (for example, 10:1 ratio), an entity would allocate the dividend related to the tax benefit using the relevant ratio.

Step 1 — adjust profit for the dividends declared

Paragraph A14(a) of IAS 33 states:

(a)   profit or loss attributable to ordinary equity holders of the parent entity is adjusted (a profit reduced and a loss increased) by the amount of dividends declared in the period for each class of shares and by the contractual amount of dividends (or interest on participating bonds) that must be paid for the period (for example, unpaid cumulative dividends).

This table illustrates how Entity Y applies this requirement:

	Year 1 CU	Year 2 CU	Year 3 CU	Total CU
Profit (before tax benefit)	330	550	110	990
Tax benefit from paying dividends	0	90	180	270
Profit (after tax benefit)[(a)]	330	640	290	1,260
Less total dividends declared and paid (including the tax benefit):				
To participating equity holders	0	(300)	(600)	(900)
To ordinary shareholders	0	(120)	(240)	(360)
	0	(420)	(840)	(1,260)
Remaining profit	330	220	(550)	0

(a)   In this example, Entity Y recognises the tax benefit arising from the payment of dividends in profit or loss. If an entity were to recognise the tax benefit directly in equity, the entity would adjust profit or loss for the period by the amount of the tax benefit when calculating basic EPS. Paragraph 11 of IAS 33 states: 'The objective of basic earnings per share information is to provide a measure of the interests of each ordinary share of a parent entity in the performance of the entity over the reporting period.' Adjusting profit or loss by the amount of any tax benefit is consistent with the view that the tax benefit represents an interest of the ordinary shareholder.

Step 2 — allocate the remaining profit

Paragraph A14(b) of IAS 33 states:

(b)   the remaining profit or loss is allocated to ordinary shares and participating equity instruments to the extent that each instrument shares in earnings as if all of the profit or loss for the period had been distributed....

This table illustrates how Entity Y applies this requirement:

	Year 1	Year 2	Year 3	Total
	CU	CU	CU	CU
Remaining profit	330	220	(550)	0
Allocation:				
To participating equity holders (in ratio of 10:1) [B]	300	200	(500)	0
To ordinary shareholders:				
Allocation of remaining profit (in ratio of 10:1)	30	20	(50)	0
Add—tax benefit on hypothetical distribution of profit to participating equity holders[(a)] [B x 30%]	90	60	(150)	0
	120	80	(200)	0

(a) Adjustment to reflect the Committee's conclusion that Entity Y adjusts profit or loss attributable to ordinary shareholders for the portion of any tax benefit attributable to those ordinary shareholders. This tax benefit would arise on the hypothetical distribution of profit to the participating equity holders if all the profit or loss for the period had been distributed. The tax benefit is calculated as the hypothetical distribution to participating equity holders multiplied by the tax rate (ie 30%).

Step 3—add the amount allocated for dividends and for a participation feature

Paragraph A14(b) of IAS 33 states:

(b)   …The total profit or loss allocated to each class of equity instrument is determined by adding together the amount allocated for dividends and the amount allocated for a participation feature.

This table illustrates how Entity Y applies this requirement to calculate profit or loss attributable to ordinary shareholders (ie the numerator for calculating basic EPS):

	Year 1	Year 2	Year 3	Total
	CU	CU	CU	CU
Profit or loss attributable to ordinary shareholders:				
Dividends declared	0	120	240	360
Remaining profit allocated	120	80	(200)	0
	120	200	40	360

Profit or loss attributable to ordinary shareholders

The total profit or loss attributable to ordinary shareholders in each year reflects the ordinary shareholders' share of (i) profit for the year plus (ii) the tax benefit that would arise on the hypothetical distribution of profit for the year to the participating equity holders.

This table illustrates the outcome:

	Year 1	Year 2	Year 3	Total
	CU	CU	CU	CU
Profit or loss attributable to ordinary shareholders:				
(i) Ordinary shareholders' share of profit for the year	30	50	10	90
(ii) Tax benefit on hypothetical distribution of profit to participating equity holders[a]	90	150	30	270
	120	200	40	360

(a) Calculated as participating equity holder's share of profits of CU300, CU500 and CU100 in years 1, 2 and 3 respectively multiplied by the tax rate of 30%.

IASB documents published to accompany

IAS 34

Interim Financial Reporting

The text of the unaccompanied standard, IAS 34, is contained in Part A of this edition. Its effective date when issued was 1 January 1999. The text of the Basis for Conclusions on IAS 34 is contained in Part C of this edition. This part presents the following document:

ILLUSTRATIVE EXAMPLES

Illustrative Examples

These illustrative examples accompany, but are not part of, IAS 34.

A Illustration of periods required to be presented

The following examples illustrate application of the principle in paragraph 20.

Entity publishes interim financial reports half-yearly

A1   The entity's financial year ends 31 December (calendar year). The entity will present the following financial statements (condensed or complete) in its half-yearly interim financial report as of 30 June 20X1:

Statement of financial position:
[Refer: paragraph 20(a)]

At	30 June 20X1	31 December 20X0

Statement of comprehensive income:
[Refer: paragraph 20(b)]

6 months ending	30 June 20X1	30 June 20X0

Statement of cash flows:
[Refer: paragraph 20(d)]

6 months ending	30 June 20X1	30 June 20X0

Statement of changes in equity:
[Refer: paragraph 20(c)]

6 months ending	30 June 20X1	30 June 20X0

Entity publishes interim financial reports quarterly

A2   The entity's financial year ends 31 December (calendar year). The entity will present the following financial statements (condensed or complete) in its quarterly interim financial report as of 30 June 20X1:

© IFRS Foundation

Statement of financial position:

[Refer: paragraph 20(a)]

	30 June 20X1	31 December 20X0
At		

Statement of comprehensive income:

[Refer: paragraph 20(b)]

	30 June 20X1	30 June 20X0
6 months ending	30 June 20X1	30 June 20X0
3 months ending	30 June 20X1	30 June 20X0

Statement of cash flows:

[Refer: paragraph 20(d)]

	30 June 20X1	30 June 20X0
6 months ending	30 June 20X1	30 June 20X0

Statement of changes in equity:

[Refer: paragraph 20(c)]

	30 June 20X1	30 June 20X0
6 months ending	30 June 20X1	30 June 20X0

B Examples of applying the recognition and measurement principles

The following are examples of applying the general recognition and measurement principles set out in paragraphs 28–39.

Employer payroll taxes and insurance contributions

B1   If employer payroll taxes or contributions to government-sponsored insurance funds are assessed on an annual basis, the employer's related expense is recognised in interim periods using an estimated average annual effective payroll tax or contribution rate, even though a large portion of the payments may be made early in the financial year. A common example is an employer payroll tax or insurance contribution that is imposed up to a certain maximum level of earnings per employee. For higher income employees, the maximum income is reached before the end of the financial year, and the employer makes no further payments through the end of the year.

Major planned periodic maintenance or overhaul

B2   The cost of a planned major periodic maintenance or overhaul or other seasonal expenditure that is expected to occur late in the year is not anticipated for interim reporting purposes unless an event has caused the entity to have a legal or constructive obligation. The mere intention or necessity to incur expenditure related to the future is not sufficient to give rise to an obligation.

[Refer: IAS 37]

Provisions

B3   A provision is recognised when an entity has no realistic alternative but to make a transfer of economic benefits as a result of an event that has created a legal or constructive obligation. The amount of the obligation is adjusted upward or downward, with a corresponding loss or gain recognised in profit or loss, if the entity's best estimate of the amount of the obligation changes.

B4   The Standard requires that an entity apply the same criteria for recognising and measuring a provision at an interim date as it would at the end of its financial year. The existence or non-existence of an obligation to transfer benefits is not a function of the length of the reporting period. It is a question of fact.

[Refer: IAS 37]

Year-end bonuses

B5   The nature of year-end bonuses varies widely. Some are earned simply by continued employment during a time period. Some bonuses are earned based on a monthly, quarterly, or annual measure of operating result. They may be purely discretionary, contractual, or based on years of historical precedent.

B6   A bonus is anticipated for interim reporting purposes if, and only if, (a) the bonus is a legal obligation or past practice would make the bonus a constructive obligation for which the entity has no realistic alternative but to make the payments, and (b) a reliable estimate of the obligation can be made. IAS 19 *Employee Benefits* provides guidance.

Variable lease payments

B7   Variable lease payments based on sales can be an example of a legal or constructive obligation that is recognised as a liability. If a lease provides for variable payments based on the lessee achieving a certain level of annual sales, an obligation can arise in the interim periods of the financial year before the required annual level of sales has been achieved, if that required level of sales is expected to be achieved and the entity, therefore, has no realistic alternative but to make the future lease payment.

[Refer: IFRS 16 paragraph 38(b)]

Intangible assets

B8   An entity will apply the definition and recognition criteria for an intangible asset in the same way in an interim period as in an annual period. Costs incurred before the recognition criteria for an intangible asset are met are recognised as an expense. Costs incurred after the specific point in time at which the criteria are met are recognised as part of the cost of an intangible asset. 'Deferring' costs as assets in an interim statement of financial position in the hope that the recognition criteria will be met later in the financial year is not justified.

[Refer: IAS 38]

Pensions

B9   Pension cost for an interim period is calculated on a year-to-date basis by using the actuarially determined pension cost rate at the end of the prior financial year, adjusted for significant market fluctuations **[Refer: IAS 19 Basis for Conclusions paragraph BC173F]** since that time and for significant one-off events, such as plan amendments, curtailments and settlements.
[Refer: IAS 19 Basis for Conclusions paragraph BC64]

Vacations, holidays, and other short-term compensated absences

B10   Accumulating paid absences are those that are carried forward and can be used in future periods if the current period's entitlement is not used in full. IAS 19 *Employee Benefits* requires that an entity measure the expected cost of and obligation for accumulating paid absences at the amount the entity expects to pay as a result of the unused entitlement that has accumulated at the end of the reporting period. That principle is also applied at the end of interim financial reporting periods. Conversely, an entity recognises no expense or liability for non-accumulating paid absences at the end of an interim reporting period, just as it recognises none at the end of an annual reporting period.

Other planned but irregularly occurring costs

B11   An entity's budget may include certain costs expected to be incurred irregularly during the financial year, such as charitable contributions and employee training costs. Those costs generally are discretionary even though they are planned and tend to recur from year to year. Recognising an obligation at the end of an interim financial reporting period for such costs that have not yet been incurred generally is not consistent with the definition of a liability.

Measuring interim income tax expense

B12   Interim period income tax expense is accrued using the tax rate that would be applicable to expected total annual earnings, that is, the estimated average annual effective income tax rate applied to the pre-tax income of the interim period.

B13   This is consistent with the basic concept set out in paragraph 28 that the same accounting recognition and measurement principles shall be applied in an interim financial report as are applied in annual financial statements **[Refer: IAS 1 paragraphs 36 and 37]**. Income taxes are assessed on an annual basis. Interim period income tax expense is calculated by applying to an interim period's pre-tax income the tax rate that would be applicable to expected total annual earnings, that is, the estimated average annual effective income tax rate. That estimated average annual rate would reflect a blend of the progressive tax rate structure expected to be applicable to the full year's earnings including enacted or substantively enacted changes in the income tax rates scheduled to take effect later in the financial year. IAS 12 *Income*

Taxes provides guidance on substantively enacted changes in tax rates. The estimated average annual income tax rate would be re-estimated on a year-to-date basis, consistent with paragraph 28 of the Standard. Paragraph 16A requires disclosure of a significant change in estimate.

B14 To the extent practicable, a separate estimated average annual effective income tax rate is determined for each taxing jurisdiction and applied individually to the interim period pre-tax income of each jurisdiction. Similarly, if different income tax rates apply to different categories of income (such as capital gains or income earned in particular industries), to the extent practicable a separate rate is applied to each individual category of interim period pre-tax income. While that degree of precision is desirable, it may not be achievable in all cases, and a weighted average of rates across jurisdictions or across categories of income is used if it is a reasonable approximation of the effect of using more specific rates.

B15 To illustrate the application of the foregoing principle, an entity reporting quarterly expects to earn 10,000 pre-tax each quarter and operates in a jurisdiction with a tax rate of 20 per cent on the first 20,000 of annual earnings and 30 per cent on all additional earnings. Actual earnings match expectations. The following table shows the amount of income tax expense that is reported in each quarter:

	1st Quarter	2nd Quarter	3rd Quarter	4th Quarter	Annual
Tax expense	2,500	2,500	2,500	2,500	10,000

10,000 of tax is expected to be payable for the full year on 40,000 of pre-tax income.

B16 As another illustration, an entity reports quarterly, earns 15,000 pre-tax profit in the first quarter but expects to incur losses of 5,000 in each of the three remaining quarters (thus having zero income for the year), and operates in a jurisdiction in which its estimated average annual income tax rate is expected to be 20 per cent. The following table shows the amount of income tax expense that is reported in each quarter:

	1st Quarter	2nd Quarter	3rd Quarter	4th Quarter	Annual
Tax expense	3,000	(1,000)	(1,000)	(1,000)	0

Difference in financial reporting year and tax year

B17 If the financial reporting year and the income tax year differ, income tax expense for the interim periods of that financial reporting year is measured using separate weighted average estimated effective tax rates for each of the income tax years applied to the portion of pre-tax income earned in each of those income tax years.

B18 To illustrate, an entity's financial reporting year ends 30 June and it reports quarterly. Its taxable year ends 31 December. For the financial year that begins 1 July, Year 1 and ends 30 June, Year 2, the entity earns 10,000 pre-tax each quarter. The estimated average annual income tax rate is 30 per cent in Year 1 and 40 per cent in Year 2.

	Quarter ending 30 Sept Year 1	Quarter ending 31 Dec Year 1	Quarter ending 31 Mar Year 2	Quarter ending 30 June Year 2	Year ending 30 June Year 2
Tax expense	3,000	3,000	4,000	4,000	14,000

Tax credits

B19 Some tax jurisdictions give taxpayers credits against the tax payable based on amounts of capital expenditures, exports, research and development expenditures, or other bases. Anticipated tax benefits of this type for the full year are generally reflected in computing the estimated annual effective income tax rate, because those credits are granted and calculated on an annual basis under most tax laws and regulations. On the other hand, tax benefits that relate to a one-off event are recognised in computing income tax expense in that interim period, in the same way that special tax rates applicable to particular categories of income are not blended into a single effective annual tax rate. Moreover, in some jurisdictions tax benefits or credits, including those related to capital expenditures and levels of exports, while reported on the income tax return, are more similar to a government grant and are recognised in the interim period in which they arise.

Tax loss and tax credit carrybacks and carryforwards

B20 The benefits of a tax loss carryback are reflected in the interim period in which the related tax loss occurs. IAS 12 provides that 'the benefit relating to a tax loss that can be carried back to recover current tax of a previous period shall be recognised as an asset'. A corresponding reduction of tax expense or increase of tax income is also recognised.

B21 IAS 12 provides that 'a deferred tax asset shall be recognised for the carryforward of unused tax losses and unused tax credits to the extent that it is probable that future taxable profit will be available against which the unused tax losses and unused tax credits can be utilised'. IAS 12 provides criteria for assessing the probability of taxable profit against which the unused tax losses and credits can be utilised. Those criteria are applied at the end of each interim period and, if they are met, the effect of the tax loss carryforward is reflected in the computation of the estimated average annual effective income tax rate.

B22 To illustrate, an entity that reports quarterly has an operating loss carryforward of 10,000 for income tax purposes at the start of the current financial year for which a deferred tax asset has not been recognised. The entity earns 10,000 in the first quarter of the current year and expects to earn

10,000 in each of the three remaining quarters. Excluding the carryforward, the estimated average annual income tax rate is expected to be 40 per cent. Tax expense is as follows:

	1st Quarter	2nd Quarter	3rd Quarter	4th Quarter	Annual
Tax expense	3,000	3,000	3,000	3,000	12,000

Contractual or anticipated purchase price changes

B23　Volume rebates or discounts and other contractual changes in the prices of raw materials, labour, or other purchased goods and services are anticipated in interim periods, by both the payer and the recipient, if it is probable that they have been earned or will take effect. Thus, contractual rebates and discounts are anticipated but discretionary rebates and discounts are not anticipated because the resulting asset or liability would not satisfy the conditions in the *Conceptual Framework*[1] that an asset must be a resource controlled by the entity as a result of a past event and that a liability must be a present obligation whose settlement is expected to result in an outflow of resources.

Depreciation and amortisation

B24　Depreciation and amortisation for an interim period is based only on assets owned during that interim period. It does not take into account asset acquisitions or dispositions planned for later in the financial year.

Inventories

B25　Inventories are measured for interim financial reporting by the same principles as at financial year-end. IAS 2 *Inventories* establishes standards for recognising and measuring inventories. Inventories pose particular problems at the end of any financial reporting period because of the need to determine inventory quantities, costs, and net realisable values. Nonetheless, the same measurement principles are applied for interim inventories. To save cost and time, entities often use estimates to measure inventories at interim dates to a greater extent than at the end of annual reporting periods. Following are examples of how to apply the net realisable value test at an interim date and how to treat manufacturing variances at interim dates.

Net realisable value of inventories

B26　The net realisable value of inventories is determined by reference to selling prices and related costs to complete and dispose at interim dates. An entity will reverse a write-down to net realisable value in a subsequent interim period only if it would be appropriate to do so at the end of the financial year.

B27　[Deleted]

1　The reference to the *Conceptual Framework* is to the *Conceptual Framework for Financial Reporting*, issued in 2010.

Interim period manufacturing cost variances

B28   Price, efficiency, spending, and volume variances of a manufacturing entity are recognised in income at interim reporting dates to the same extent that those variances are recognised in income at financial year-end. Deferral of variances that are expected to be absorbed by year-end is not appropriate because it could result in reporting inventory at the interim date at more or less than its portion of the actual cost of manufacture.

Foreign currency translation gains and losses

B29   Foreign currency translation gains and losses are measured for interim financial reporting by the same principles as at financial year-end.

B30   IAS 21 *The Effects of Changes in Foreign Exchange Rates* specifies how to translate the financial statements for foreign operations into the presentation currency, including guidelines for using average or closing foreign exchange rates and guidelines for recognising the resulting adjustments in profit or loss, or in other comprehensive income. Consistently with IAS 21, the actual average and closing rates for the interim period are used. Entities do not anticipate some future changes in foreign exchange rates in the remainder of the current financial year in translating foreign operations at an interim date.

B31   If IAS 21 requires translation adjustments to be recognised as income or expense in the period in which they arise, that principle is applied during each interim period. Entities do not defer some foreign currency translation adjustments at an interim date if the adjustment is expected to reverse before the end of the financial year.

Interim financial reporting in hyperinflationary economies

B32   Interim financial reports in hyperinflationary economies **[Refer: IAS 29 paragraphs 2–4]** are prepared by the same principles as at financial year-end.

B33   IAS 29 *Financial Reporting in Hyperinflationary Economies* requires that the financial statements of an entity that reports in the currency of a hyperinflationary economy **[Refer: IAS 29 paragraphs 2–4]** be stated in terms of the measuring unit current at the end of the reporting period, and the gain or loss on the net monetary position is included in net income. Also, comparative financial data reported for prior periods are restated to the current measuring unit.

B34   Entities follow those same principles at interim dates, thereby presenting all interim data in the measuring unit as of the end of the interim period, with the resulting gain or loss on the net monetary position included in the interim period's net income. Entities do not annualise the recognition of the gain or loss. Nor do they use an estimated annual inflation rate in preparing an interim financial report in a hyperinflationary economy **[Refer: IAS 29 paragraphs 2–4]**.

Impairment of assets

B35 IAS 36 *Impairment of Assets* requires that an impairment loss be recognised if the recoverable amount has declined below carrying amount.

B36 This Standard requires that an entity apply the same impairment testing, recognition, and reversal criteria at an interim date as it would at the end of its financial year. That does not mean, however, that an entity must necessarily make a detailed impairment calculation at the end of each interim period. Rather, an entity will review for indications of significant impairment since the end of the most recent financial year to determine whether such a calculation is needed.

C Examples of the use of estimates

The following examples illustrate application of the principle in paragraph 41.

C1 **Inventories:** Full stock-taking and valuation procedures may not be required for inventories at interim dates, although it may be done at financial year-end. It may be sufficient to make estimates at interim dates based on sales margins.

C2 **Classifications of current and non-current assets and liabilities:** Entities may do a more thorough investigation for classifying assets and liabilities as current or non-current [Refer: IAS 1 paragraphs 60–76] at annual reporting dates than at interim dates.

C3 **Provisions:** Determination of the appropriate amount of a provision (such as a provision for warranties, environmental costs, and site restoration costs) may be complex and often costly and time-consuming. Entities sometimes engage outside experts to assist in the annual calculations. Making similar estimates at interim dates often entails updating of the prior annual provision rather than the engaging of outside experts to do a new calculation.

C4 **Pensions:** IAS 19 *Employee Benefits* requires an entity to determine the present value of defined benefit obligations and the fair value of plan assets at the end of each reporting period and encourages an entity to involve a professionally qualified actuary in measurement of the obligations. For interim reporting purposes, reliable measurement is often obtainable by extrapolation of the latest actuarial valuation.

C5 **Income taxes:** Entities may calculate income tax expense and deferred income tax liability at annual dates by applying the tax rate for each individual jurisdiction to measures of income for each jurisdiction. Paragraph B14 acknowledges that while that degree of precision is desirable at interim reporting dates as well, it may not be achievable in all cases, and a weighted average of rates across jurisdictions or across categories of income is used if it is a reasonable approximation of the effect of using more specific rates.

C6 **Contingencies:** The measurement of contingencies [Refer: IAS 37 paragraphs 36–52] may involve the opinions of legal experts or other advisers. Formal reports from independent experts are sometimes obtained with respect to contingencies. Such opinions about litigation, claims, assessments, and other contingencies and uncertainties may or may not also be needed at interim dates.

C7 **Revaluations and fair value accounting:** IAS 16 *Property, Plant and Equipment* allows an entity to choose as its accounting policy the revaluation model whereby items of property, plant and equipment are revalued to fair value. **[Refer: IAS 16 paragraphs 29 and 31–42]** IFRS 16 *Leases* allows a lessee to measure right-of-use assets applying the revaluation model in IAS 16 if those right-of-use assets relate to a class of property, plant and equipment to which the lessee applies the revaluation model in IAS 16. **[Refer: IFRS 16 paragraph 35]** Similarly, IAS 40 *Investment Property* requires an entity to measure the fair value of investment property. **[Refer: IAS 40 paragraphs 30 and 33–55]** For those measurements, an entity may rely on professionally qualified valuers at annual reporting dates though not at interim reporting dates.

C8 **Intercompany reconciliations:** Some intercompany balances that are reconciled on a detailed level in preparing consolidated financial statements at financial year-end might be reconciled at a less detailed level in preparing consolidated financial statements at an interim date.

C9 **Specialised industries:** Because of complexity, costliness, and time, interim period measurements in specialised industries might be less precise than at financial year-end.

IASB documents published to accompany

IAS 36

Impairment of Assets

The text of the unaccompanied standard, IAS 36, is contained in Part A of this edition. Its effective date when issued was 31 March 2004. The text of the Basis for Conclusions on IAS 36 is contained in Part C of this edition. This part presents the following document:

ILLUSTRATIVE EXAMPLES

Contents

IAS 36 *Impairment of Assets*
Illustrative Examples

These examples accompany, but are not part of, IAS 36. All the examples assume that the entities concerned have no transactions other than those described. In the examples monetary amounts are denominated in 'currency units (CU)'.

Example 1 Identification of cash-generating units

The purpose of this example is:

(a)   *to indicate how cash-generating units are identified in various situations; and*

(b)   *to highlight certain factors that an entity may consider in identifying the cash-generating unit to which an asset belongs.*

A Retail store chain

Background

IE1   Store X belongs to a retail store chain M. X makes all its retail purchases through M's purchasing centre. Pricing, marketing, advertising and human resources policies (except for hiring X's cashiers and sales staff) are decided by M. M also owns five other stores in the same city as X (although in different neighbourhoods) and 20 other stores in other cities. All stores are managed in the same way as X. X and four other stores were purchased five years ago and goodwill was recognised.

What is the cash-generating unit for X (X's cash-generating unit)?

Analysis

IE2   In identifying X's cash-generating unit, an entity considers whether, for example:

(a)   internal management reporting is organised to measure performance on a store-by-store basis; and

(b)   the business is run on a store-by-store profit basis or on a region/city basis.

IE3   All M's stores are in different neighbourhoods and probably have different customer bases. So, although X is managed at a corporate level, X generates cash inflows that are largely independent of those of M's other stores. Therefore, it is likely that X is a cash-generating unit.

IE4   If X's cash-generating unit represents the lowest level within M at which the goodwill is monitored for internal management purposes, M applies to that cash-generating unit the impairment test described in paragraph 90 of IAS 36. If information about the carrying amount of goodwill is not available and monitored for internal management purposes at the level of X's cash-generating unit, M applies to that cash-generating unit the impairment test described in paragraph 88 of IAS 36.

B Plant for an intermediate step in a production process

Background

IE5   A significant raw material used for plant Y's final production is an intermediate product bought from plant X of the same entity. X's products are sold to Y at a transfer price that passes all margins to X. Eighty per cent of Y's final production is sold to customers outside of the entity. Sixty per cent of X's final production is sold to Y and the remaining 40 per cent is sold to customers outside of the entity.

For each of the following cases, what are the cash-generating units for X and Y?

Case 1: X could sell the products it sells to Y in an active market. Internal transfer prices are higher than market prices.

Case 2: There is no active market for the products X sells to Y.

Analysis

Case 1

IE6   X could sell its products in an active market and, so, generate cash inflows that would be largely independent of the cash inflows from Y. Therefore, it is likely that X is a separate cash-generating unit, although part of its production is used by Y (see paragraph 70 of IAS 36).

IE7   It is likely that Y is also a separate cash-generating unit. Y sells 80 per cent of its products to customers outside of the entity. Therefore, its cash inflows can be regarded as largely independent.

IE8   Internal transfer prices do not reflect market prices for X's output. Therefore, in determining value in use of both X and Y, the entity adjusts financial budgets/forecasts to reflect management's best estimate of future prices that could be achieved in arm's length transactions for those of X's products that are used internally (see paragraph 70 of IAS 36).

Case 2

IE9   It is likely that the recoverable amount of each plant cannot be assessed independently of the recoverable amount of the other plant because:

(a)   the majority of X's production is used internally and could not be sold in an active market. So, cash inflows of X depend on demand for Y's products. Therefore, X cannot be considered to generate cash inflows that are largely independent of those of Y.

(b)   the two plants are managed together.

IE10   As a consequence, it is likely that X and Y together are the smallest group of assets that generates cash inflows that are largely independent.

C Single product entity

Background

IE11 Entity M produces a single product and owns plants A, B and C. Each plant is located in a different continent. A produces a component that is assembled in either B or C. The combined capacity of B and C is not fully utilised. M's products are sold worldwide from either B or C. For example, B's production can be sold in C's continent if the products can be delivered faster from B than from C. Utilisation levels of B and C depend on the allocation of sales between the two sites.

For each of the following cases, what are the cash-generating units for A, B and C?

Case 1: There is an active market for A's products.

Case 2: There is no active market for A's products.

Analysis

Case 1

IE12 It is likely that A is a separate cash-generating unit because there is an active market for its products (see Example B - Plant for an intermediate step in a production process, Case 1).

IE13 Although there is an active market for the products assembled by B and C, cash inflows for B and C depend on the allocation of production across the two sites. It is unlikely that the future cash inflows for B and C can be determined individually. Therefore, it is likely that B and C together are the smallest identifiable group of assets that generates cash inflows that are largely independent.

IE14 In determining the value in use of A and B plus C, M adjusts financial budgets/forecasts to reflect its best estimate of future prices that could be achieved in arm's length transactions for A's products (see paragraph 70 of IAS 36).

Case 2

IE15 It is likely that the recoverable amount of each plant cannot be assessed independently because:

(a) there is no active market for A's products. Therefore, A's cash inflows depend on sales of the final product by B and C.

(b) although there is an active market for the products assembled by B and C, cash inflows for B and C depend on the allocation of production across the two sites. It is unlikely that the future cash inflows for B and C can be determined individually.

IE16 As a consequence, it is likely that A, B and C together (ie M as a whole) are the smallest identifiable group of assets that generates cash inflows that are largely independent.

D Magazine titles

Background

IE17   A publisher owns 150 magazine titles of which 70 were purchased and 80 were self-created. The price paid for a purchased magazine title is recognised as an intangible asset. The costs of creating magazine titles and maintaining the existing titles are recognised as an expense when incurred. Cash inflows from direct sales and advertising are identifiable for each magazine title. Titles are managed by customer segments. The level of advertising income for a magazine title depends on the range of titles in the customer segment to which the magazine title relates. Management has a policy to abandon old titles before the end of their economic lives and replace them immediately with new titles for the same customer segment.

What is the cash-generating unit for an individual magazine title?

Analysis

IE18   It is likely that the recoverable amount of an individual magazine title can be assessed. Even though the level of advertising income for a title is influenced, to a certain extent, by the other titles in the customer segment, cash inflows from direct sales and advertising are identifiable for each title. In addition, although titles are managed by customer segments, decisions to abandon titles are made on an individual title basis.

IE19   Therefore, it is likely that individual magazine titles generate cash inflows that are largely independent of each other and that each magazine title is a separate cash-generating unit.

E Building half-rented to others and half-occupied for own use

Background

IE20   M is a manufacturing company. It owns a headquarters building that used to be fully occupied for internal use. After down-sizing, half of the building is now used internally and half rented to third parties. The lease agreement with the tenant is for five years.

What is the cash-generating unit of the building?

Analysis

IE21   The primary purpose of the building is to serve as a corporate asset, supporting M's manufacturing activities. Therefore, the building as a whole cannot be considered to generate cash inflows that are largely independent of the cash inflows from the entity as a whole. So, it is likely that the cash-generating unit for the building is M as a whole.

IE22   The building is not held as an investment. Therefore, it would not be appropriate to determine the value in use of the building based on projections of future market related rents.

Example 2 Calculation of value in use and recognition of an impairment loss

In this example, tax effects are ignored.

Background and calculation of value in use

IE23 At the end of 20X0, entity T acquires entity M for CU10,000. M has manufacturing plants in three countries.

Schedule 1. Data at the end of 20X0

End of 20X0	Allocation of purchase price	Fair value of identifiable assets	Goodwill[a]
	CU	CU	CU
Activities in Country A	3,000	2,000	1,000
Activities in Country B	2,000	1,500	500
Activities in Country C	5,000	3,500	1,500
Total	10,000	7,000	3,000

(a) Activities in each country represent the lowest level at which the goodwill is monitored for internal management purposes (determined as the difference between the purchase price of the activities in each country, as specified in the purchase agreement, and the fair value of the identifiable assets).

IE23A Because goodwill has been allocated to the activities in each country, each of those activities must be tested for impairment annually or more frequently if there is any indication that it may be impaired (see paragraph 90 of IAS 36).

IE24 The recoverable amounts (ie higher of value in use and fair value less costs of disposal) of the cash-generating units are determined on the basis of value in use calculations. At the end of 20X0 and 20X1, the value in use of each cash-generating unit exceeds its carrying amount. Therefore the activities in each country and the goodwill allocated to those activities are regarded as not impaired.

IE25 At the beginning of 20X2, a new government is elected in Country A. It passes legislation significantly restricting exports of T's main product. As a result, and for the foreseeable future, T's production in Country A will be cut by 40 per cent.

IE26 The significant export restriction and the resulting production decrease require T also to estimate the recoverable amount of the Country A operations at the beginning of 20X2.

IE27 T uses straight-line depreciation over a 12-year life for the Country A identifiable assets and anticipates no residual value.

IE28   To determine the value in use for the Country A cash-generating unit (see Schedule 2), T:

    (a)   prepares cash flow forecasts derived from the most recent financial budgets/forecasts for the next five years (years 20X2–20X6) approved by management.

    (b)   estimates subsequent cash flows (years 20X7–20Y2) based on declining growth rates. The growth rate for 20X7 is estimated to be 3 per cent. This rate is lower than the average long-term growth rate for the market in Country A.

    (c)   selects a 15 per cent discount rate, which represents a pre-tax rate that reflects current market assessments of the time value of money and the risks specific to the Country A cash-generating unit.

Recognition and measurement of impairment loss

IE29   The recoverable amount of the Country A cash-generating unit is CU1,360.

IE30   T compares the recoverable amount of the Country A cash-generating unit with its carrying amount (see Schedule 3).

IE31   Because the carrying amount exceeds the recoverable amount by CU1,473, T recognises an impairment loss of CU1,473 immediately in profit or loss. The carrying amount of the goodwill that relates to the Country A operations is reduced to zero before reducing the carrying amount of other identifiable assets within the Country A cash-generating unit (see paragraph 104 of IAS 36).

IE32   Tax effects are accounted for separately in accordance with IAS 12 *Income Taxes* (see Illustrative Example 3A).

     Schedule 2. Calculation of the value in use of the Country A cash-generating unit at the beginning of 20X2

Year	Long-term growth rates	Future cash flows	Present value factor at 15% discount rate[a]	Discounted future cash flows
		CU		CU
20X2 (n=1)		230[b]	0.86957	200
20X3		253[b]	0.75614	191
20X4		273[b]	0.65752	180
20X5		290[b]	0.57175	166
20X6		304[b]	0.49718	151
20X7	3%	313 [c]	0.43233	135
20X8	(2%)	307[c]	0.37594	115
20X9	(6%)	289[c]	0.32690	94
20Y0	(15%)	245[c]	0.28426	70
20Y1	(25%)	184[c]	0.24719	45
20Y2	(67%)	61[c]	0.21494	13
Value in use				1,360

(a) The present value factor is calculated as $k = 1/(1+a)^n$, where a = discount rate and n = period of discount.

(b) Based on management's best estimate of net cash flow projections (after the 40% cut).

(c) Based on an extrapolation from preceding year cash flow using declining growth rates.

Schedule 3. Calculation and allocation of the impairment loss for the Country A cash-generating unit at the beginning of 20X2

Beginning of 20X2	Goodwill	Identifiable assets	Total
	CU	CU	CU
Historical cost	1,000	2,000	3,000
Accumulated depreciation (20X1)	–	(167)	(167)
Carrying amount	1,000	1,833	2,833
Impairment loss	(1,000)	(473)	(1,473)
Carrying amount after impairment loss	–	1,360	1,360

Example 3 Deferred tax effects

Use the data for entity T as presented in Example 2, with supplementary information as provided in this example.

A Deferred tax effects of the recognition of an impairment loss

IE33 At the beginning of 20X2, the tax base of the identifiable assets of the Country A cash-generating unit is CU900. Impairment losses are not deductible for tax purposes. The tax rate is 40 per cent.

IE34 The recognition of an impairment loss on the assets of the Country A cash-generating unit reduces the taxable temporary difference related to those assets. The deferred tax liability is reduced accordingly.

Beginning of 20X2	Identifiable assets before impairment loss	Impairment loss	Identifiable assets after impairment loss
	CU	CU	CU
Carrying amount (Example 2)	1,833	(473)	1,360
Tax base	900	–	900
Taxable temporary difference	933	(473)	460
Deferred tax liability at 40%	373	(189)	184

IE35 In accordance with IAS 12 *Income Taxes*, no deferred tax relating to the goodwill was recognised initially. [Refer: IAS 12 paragraph 15(a)] Therefore, the impairment loss relating to the goodwill does not give rise to a deferred tax adjustment.

B Recognition of an impairment loss creates a deferred tax asset

IE36 An entity has an identifiable asset with a carrying amount of CU1,000. Its recoverable amount is CU650. The tax rate is 30 per cent and the tax base of the asset is CU800. Impairment losses are not deductible for tax purposes. The effect of the impairment loss is as follows:

	Before impairment	Effect of impairment	After impairment
	CU	CU	CU
Carrying amount	1,000	(350)	650
Tax base	800	–	800
Taxable (deductible) temporary difference	200	(350)	(150)
Deferred tax liability (asset) at 30%	60	(105)	(45)

IE37　　In accordance with IAS 12, the entity recognises the deferred tax asset to the extent that it is probable that taxable profit will be available against which the deductible temporary difference can be utilised.

Example 4　Reversal of an impairment loss

Use the data for entity T as presented in Example 2, with supplementary information as provided in this example. In this example, tax effects are ignored.

Background

IE38　　In 20X3, the government is still in office in Country A, but the business situation is improving. The effects of the export laws on T's production are proving to be less drastic than initially expected by management. As a result, management estimates that production will increase by 30 per cent. This favourable change requires T to re-estimate the recoverable amount of the net assets of the Country A operations (see paragraphs 110 and 111 of IAS 36). The cash-generating unit for the net assets of the Country A operations is still the Country A operations.

IE39　　Calculations similar to those in Example 2 show that the recoverable amount of the Country A cash-generating unit is now CU1,910.

Reversal of impairment loss

IE40　　T compares the recoverable amount and the net carrying amount of the Country A cash-generating unit.

Schedule 1. Calculation of the carrying amount of the Country A cash-generating unit at the end of 20X3

	Goodwill	Identifiable assets	Total
	CU	CU	CU
Beginning of 20X2 (Example 2)			
Historical cost	1,000	2,000	3,000
Accumulated depreciation	–	(167)	(167)
Impairment loss	(1,000)	(473)	(1,473)
Carrying amount after impairment loss	–	1,360	1,360

continued...

...continued

	Goodwill	Identifiable assets	Total
	CU	**CU**	**CU**
End of 20X3			
Additional depreciation (2 years) (a)	–	(247)	(247)
Carrying amount	–	1,113	1,113
Recoverable amount			1,910
Excess of recoverable amount over carrying amount			797

(a) After recognition of the impairment loss at the beginning of 20X2, T revised the depreciation charge for the Country A identifiable assets (from CU166.7 per year to CU123.6 per year), based on the revised carrying amount and remaining useful life (11 years).

IE41 There has been a favourable change in the estimates used to determine the recoverable amount of the Country A net assets since the last impairment loss was recognised. Therefore, in accordance with paragraph 114 of IAS 36, T recognises a reversal of the impairment loss recognised in 20X2.

IE42 In accordance with paragraphs 122 and 123 of IAS 36, T increases the carrying amount of the Country A identifiable assets by CU387 (see Schedule 3), ie up to the lower of recoverable amount (CU1,910) and the identifiable assets' depreciated historical cost (CU1,500) (see Schedule 2). This increase is recognised immediately in profit or loss.

IE43 In accordance with paragraph 124 of IAS 36, the impairment loss on goodwill is not reversed.

Schedule 2. Determination of the depreciated historical cost of the Country A identifiable assets at the end of 20X3

End of 20X3	*Identifiable assets*
	CU
Historical cost	2,000
Accumulated depreciation *(166.7 × 3 years)*	(500)
Depreciated historical cost	1,500
Carrying amount (Schedule 1)	1,113
Difference	387

Schedule 3. Carrying amount of the Country A assets at the end of 20X3

End of 20X3	Goodwill	Identifiable assets	Total
	CU	CU	CU
Gross carrying amount	1,000	2,000	3,000
Accumulated amortisation	–	(414)	(414)
Accumulated impairment loss	(1,000)	(473)	(1,473)
Carrying amount	–	1,113	1,113
Reversal of impairment loss	0	387	387
Carrying amount after reversal of impairment loss	–	1,500	1,500

Example 5 Treatment of a future restructuring

In this example, tax effects are ignored.

Background

IE44   At the end of 20X0, entity K tests a plant for impairment. The plant is a cash-generating unit. The plant's assets are carried at depreciated historical cost. The plant has a carrying amount of CU3,000 and a remaining useful life of 10 years.

IE45   The plant's recoverable amount (ie higher of value in use and fair value less costs of disposal) is determined on the basis of a value in use calculation. Value in use is calculated using a pre-tax discount rate of 14 per cent.

IE46   Management approved budgets reflect that:

(a)   at the end of 20X3, the plant will be restructured at an estimated cost of CU100. Since K is not yet committed to the restructuring, a provision has not been recognised for the future restructuring costs.

(b)   there will be future benefits from this restructuring in the form of reduced future cash outflows.

IE47   At the end of 20X2, K becomes committed to the restructuring. The costs are still estimated to be CU100 and a provision is recognised accordingly. The plant's estimated future cash flows reflected in the most recent management approved budgets are given in paragraph IE51 and a current discount rate is the same as at the end of 20X0.

IE48   At the end of 20X3, actual restructuring costs of CU100 are incurred and paid. Again, the plant's estimated future cash flows reflected in the most recent management approved budgets and a current discount rate are the same as those estimated at the end of 20X2.

At the end of 20X0

Schedule 1. Calculation of the plant's value in use at the end of 20X0

Year	Future cash flows	Discounted at 14%
	CU	CU
20X1	300[a]	263
20X2	280[b]	215
20X3	420[b]	283
20X4	520[b]	308
20X5	350[b]	182
20X6	420[b]	191
20X7	480[b]	192
20X8	480[b]	168
20X9	460[b]	141
20X10	400[b]	108
		2,051

(a) Excludes estimated restructuring costs reflected in management budgets.
(b) Excludes estimated benefits expected from the restructuring reflected in management budgets.

IE49   The plant's recoverable amount (ie value in use) is less than its carrying amount. Therefore, K recognises an impairment loss for the plant.

Schedule 2. Calculation of the impairment loss at the end of 20X0

	Plant CU
Carrying amount before impairment loss	3,000
Recoverable amount (Schedule 1)	2,051
Impairment loss	(949)
Carrying amount after impairment loss	2,051

At the end of 20X1

IE50   No event occurs that requires the plant's recoverable amount to be re-estimated. Therefore, no calculation of the recoverable amount is required to be performed.

At the end of 20X2

IE51　The entity is now committed to the restructuring. Therefore, in determining the plant's value in use, the benefits expected from the restructuring are considered in forecasting cash flows. This results in an increase in the estimated future cash flows used to determine value in use at the end of 20X0. In accordance with paragraphs 110 and 111 of IAS 36, the recoverable amount of the plant is re-determined at the end of 20X2.

Schedule 3. Calculation of the plant's value in use at the end of 20X2

Year	Future cash flows	Discounted at 14%
	CU	CU
20X3	420[(a)]	368
20X4	570[(b)]	439
20X5	380[(b)]	256
20X6	450[(b)]	266
20X7	510[(b)]	265
20X8	510[(b)]	232
20X9	480[(b)]	192
20X10	410[(b)]	144
		2,162

(a) Excludes estimated restructuring costs because a liability has already been recognised.
(b) Includes estimated benefits expected from the restructuring reflected in management budgets.

IE52　The plant's recoverable amount (value in use) is higher than its carrying amount (see Schedule 4). Therefore, K reverses the impairment loss recognised for the plant at the end of 20X0.

Schedule 4. Calculation of the reversal of the impairment loss at the end of 20X2

	Plant CU
Carrying amount at the end of 20X0 (Schedule 2)	2,051
End of 20X2	
Depreciation charge (for 20X1 and 20X2–Schedule 5)	(410)
Carrying amount before reversal	1,641
Recoverable amount (Schedule 3)	2,162
Reversal of the impairment loss	521
Carrying amount after reversal	2,162
Carrying amount: depreciated historical cost (Schedule 5)	2,400[a]

(a) The reversal does not result in the carrying amount of the plant exceeding what its carrying amount would have been at depreciated historical cost. Therefore, the full reversal of the impairment loss is recognised.

At the end of 20X3

IE53 There is a cash outflow of CU100 when the restructuring costs are paid. Even though a cash outflow has taken place, there is no change in the estimated future cash flows used to determine value in use at the end of 20X2. Therefore, the plant's recoverable amount is not calculated at the end of 20X3.

Schedule 5. Summary of the carrying amount of the plant

End of year	Depreciated historical cost	Recoverable amount	Adjusted depreciation charge	Impairment loss	Carrying amount after impairment
	CU	CU	CU	CU	CU
20X0	3,000	2,051	0	(949)	2,051
20X1	2,700	nc	(205)	0	1,846
20X2	2,400	2,162	(205)	521	2,162
20X3	2,100	nc	(270)	0	1,892

nc = not calculated as there is no indication that the impairment loss may have increased/decreased.

Example 6   Treatment of future costs

In this example, tax effects are ignored.

Background

IE54 At the end of 20X0, entity F tests a machine for impairment. The machine is a cash-generating unit. It is carried at depreciated historical cost and its carrying amount is CU150,000. It has an estimated remaining useful life of 10 years.

IE55   The machine's recoverable amount (ie higher of value in use and fair value less costs of disposal) is determined on the basis of a value in use calculation. Value in use is calculated using a pre-tax discount rate of 14 per cent.

IE56   Management approved budgets reflect:

(a)   estimated costs necessary to maintain the level of economic benefit expected to arise from the machine in its current condition; and

(b)   that in 20X4, costs of CU25,000 will be incurred to enhance the machine's performance by increasing its productive capacity.

IE57   At the end of 20X4, costs to enhance the machine's performance are incurred. The machine's estimated future cash flows reflected in the most recent management approved budgets are given in paragraph IE60 and a current discount rate is the same as at the end of 20X0.

At the end of 20X0

Schedule 1. Calculation of the machine's value in use at the end of 20X0

Year	Future cash flows	Discounted at 14%
	CU	CU
20X1	22,165[a]	19,443
20X2	21,450[a]	16,505
20X3	20,550[a]	13,871
20X4	24,725[a],[b]	14,639
20X5	25,325[a],[c]	13,153
20X6	24,825[a],[c]	11,310
20X7	24,123[a],[c]	9,640
20X8	25,533[a],[c]	8,951
20X9	24,234[a],[c]	7,452
20X10	22,850[a],[c]	6,164
Value in use		121,128

(a) Includes estimated costs necessary to maintain the level of economic benefit expected to arise from the machine in its current condition.
(b) Excludes estimated costs to enhance the machine's performance reflected in management budgets.
(c) Excludes estimated benefits expected from enhancing the machine's performance reflected in management budgets.

IE58   The machine's recoverable amount (value in use) is less than its carrying amount. Therefore, F recognises an impairment loss for the machine.

Schedule 2. Calculation of the impairment loss at the end of 20X0

	Machine CU
Carrying amount before impairment loss	150,000
Recoverable amount (Schedule 1)	121,128
Impairment loss	(28,872)
Carrying amount after impairment loss	121,128

Years 20X1–20X3

IE59   No event occurs that requires the machine's recoverable amount to be re-estimated. Therefore, no calculation of recoverable amount is required to be performed.

At the end of 20X4

IE60   The costs to enhance the machine's performance are incurred. Therefore, in determining the machine's value in use, the future benefits expected from enhancing the machine's performance are considered in forecasting cash flows. This results in an increase in the estimated future cash flows used to determine value in use at the end of 20X0. As a consequence, in accordance with paragraphs 110 and 111 of IAS 36, the recoverable amount of the machine is recalculated at the end of 20X4.

Schedule 3. Calculation of the machine's value in use at the end of 20X4

Year	Future cash flows[a] CU	Discounted at 14% CU
20X5	30,321	26,597
20X6	32,750	25,200
20X7	31,721	21,411
20X8	31,950	18,917
20X9	33,100	17,191
20X10	27,999	12,756
Value in use		122,072

(a) Includes estimated benefits expected from enhancing the machine's performance reflected in management budgets.

IE61   The machine's recoverable amount (ie value in use) is higher than the machine's carrying amount and depreciated historical cost (see Schedule 4). Therefore, K reverses the impairment loss recognised for the machine at the end of 20X0 so that the machine is carried at depreciated historical cost.

Schedule 4. Calculation of the reversal of the impairment loss at the end of 20X4

	Machine
	CU
Carrying amount at the end of 20X0 (Schedule 2)	121,128
End of 20X4	
Depreciation charge (20X1 to 20X4 – Schedule 5)	(48,452)
Costs to enhance the asset's performance	25,000
Carrying amount before reversal	97,676
Recoverable amount (Schedule 3)	122,072
Reversal of the impairment loss	17,324
Carrying amount after reversal	115,000
Carrying amount: depreciated historical cost (Schedule 5)	115,000[a]

(a)   The value in use of the machine exceeds what its carrying amount would have been at depreciated historical cost. Therefore, the reversal is limited to an amount that does not result in the carrying amount of the machine exceeding depreciated historical cost.

Schedule 5. Summary of the carrying amount of the machine

Year	Depreciated histori-cal cost	Recoverable amount	Adjusted depreci-ated charge	Impairment loss	Carrying amount after impairment
	CU	CU	CU	CU	CU
20X0	150,000	121,128	0	(28,872)	121,128
20X1	135,000	nc	(12,113)	0	109,015
20X2	120,000	nc	(12,113)	0	96,902
20X3	105,000	nc	(12,113)	0	84,789
20X4	90,000		(12,113)		
enhancement	25,000		—		
	115,000	122,072	(12,113)	17,324	115,000
20X5	95,833	nc	(19,167)	0	95,833

nc = not calculated as there is no indication that the impairment loss may have increased/decreased.

Example 7 Impairment testing cash-generating units with goodwill and non-controlling interests

Example 7A Non-controlling interests measured initially as a proportionate share of the net identifiable assets

In this example, tax effects are ignored.

Background

IE62   Parent acquires an 80 per cent ownership interest in Subsidiary for CU2,100 on 1 January 20X3. At that date, Subsidiary's net identifiable assets have a fair value of CU1,500. Parent chooses to measure the non-controlling interests as the proportionate interest of Subsidiary's net identifiable assets of CU300 (20% of CU1,500). Goodwill of CU900 is the difference between the aggregate of the consideration transferred and the amount of the non-controlling interests (CU2,100 + CU300) and the net identifiable assets (CU1,500).

IE63   The assets of Subsidiary together are the smallest group of assets that generate cash inflows that are largely independent of the cash inflows from other assets or groups of assets. Therefore Subsidiary is a cash-generating unit. Because other cash-generating units of Parent are expected to benefit from the synergies of the combination, the goodwill of CU500 related to those synergies has been allocated to other cash-generating units within Parent. Because the cash-generating unit comprising Subsidiary includes goodwill within its carrying amount, it must be tested for impairment annually, or more frequently if there is an indication that it may be impaired (see paragraph 90 of IAS 36).

IE64   At the end of 20X3, Parent determines that the recoverable amount of cash-generating unit Subsidiary is CU1,000. The carrying amount of the net assets of Subsidiary, excluding goodwill, is CU1,350.

Testing Subsidiary (cash-generating unit) for impairment

IE65   Goodwill attributable to non-controlling interests is included in Subsidiary's recoverable amount of CU1,000 but has not been recognised in Parent's consolidated financial statements. Therefore, in accordance with paragraph C4 of Appendix C of IAS 36, the carrying amount of Subsidiary is grossed up to include goodwill attributable to the non-controlling interests, before being compared with the recoverable amount of CU1,000. Goodwill attributable to Parent's 80 per cent interest in Subsidiary at the acquisition date is CU400 after allocating CU500 to other cash-generating units within Parent. Therefore, goodwill attributable to the 20 per cent non-controlling interests in Subsidiary at the acquisition date is CU100.

Schedule 1. Testing Subsidiary for impairment at the end of 20X3

End of 20X3	Goodwill of Subsidiary	Net identifiable assets	Total
	CU	CU	CU
Carrying amount	400	1,350	1,750
Unrecognised non-controlling interests	100	–	100
Adjusted carrying amount	500	1,350	1,850
Recoverable amount			1,000
Impairment loss			850

Allocating the impairment loss

IE66 In accordance with paragraph 104 of IAS 36, the impairment loss of CU850 is allocated to the assets in the unit by first reducing the carrying amount of goodwill.

IE67 Therefore, CU500 of the CU850 impairment loss for the unit is allocated to the goodwill. In accordance with paragraph C6 of Appendix C of IAS 36, if the partially-owned subsidiary is itself a cash-generating unit, the goodwill impairment loss is allocated to the controlling and non-controlling interests on the same basis as that on which profit or loss is allocated. In this example, profit or loss is allocated on the basis of relative ownership interests. Because the goodwill is recognised only to the extent of Parent's 80 per cent ownership interest in Subsidiary, Parent recognises only 80 per cent of that goodwill impairment loss (ie CU400).

IE68 The remaining impairment loss of CU350 is recognised by reducing the carrying amounts of Subsidiary's identifiable assets (see Schedule 2).

Schedule 2. Allocation of the impairment loss for Subsidiary at the end of 20X3

End of 20X3	Goodwill	Net identifiable assets	Total
	CU	CU	CU
Carrying amount	400	1,350	1,750
Impairment loss	(400)	(350)	(750)
Carrying amount after impairment loss	–	1,000	1,000

Example 7B Non-controlling interests measured initially at fair value and the related subsidiary is a stand-alone cash-generating unit

In this example, tax effects are ignored.

Background

IE68A   Parent acquires an 80 per cent ownership interest in Subsidiary for CU2,100 on 1 January 20X3. At that date, Subsidiary's net identifiable assets have a fair value of CU1,500. Parent chooses to measure the non-controlling interests at fair value, which is CU350. Goodwill of CU950 is the difference between the aggregate of the consideration transferred and the amount of the non-controlling interests (CU2,100 + CU350) and the net identifiable assets (CU1,500).

IE68B   The assets of Subsidiary together are the smallest group of assets that generate cash inflows that are largely independent of the cash inflows from other assets or groups of assets. Therefore, Subsidiary is a cash-generating unit. Because other cash-generating units of Parent are expected to benefit from the synergies of the combination, the goodwill of CU500 related to those synergies has been allocated to other cash-generating units within Parent. Because Subsidiary includes goodwill within its carrying amount, it must be tested for impairment annually, or more frequently if there is an indication that it might be impaired (see paragraph 90 of IAS 36).

Testing Subsidiary for impairment

IE68C   At the end of 20X3, Parent determines that the recoverable amount of cash-generating unit Subsidiary is CU1,650. The carrying amount of the net assets of Subsidiary, excluding goodwill, is CU1,350.

Schedule 1. Testing Subsidiary for impairment at the end of 20X3

End of 20X3	Goodwill	Net identifiable assets	Total
	CU	**CU**	**CU**
Carrying amount	450	1,350	1,800
Recoverable amount			1,650
Impairment loss			150

Allocating the impairment loss

IE68D   In accordance with paragraph 104 of IAS 36, the impairment loss of CU150 is allocated to the assets in the unit by first reducing the carrying amount of goodwill.

IE68E   Therefore, the full amount of impairment loss of CU150 for the unit is allocated to the goodwill. In accordance with paragraph C6 of Appendix C of IAS 36, if the partially-owned subsidiary is itself a cash-generating unit, the goodwill impairment loss is allocated to the controlling and non-controlling interests on the same basis as that on which profit or loss is allocated.

Example 7C Non-controlling interests measured initially at fair value and the related subsidiary is part of a larger cash-generating unit

In this example, tax effects are ignored.

Background

IE68F   Suppose that, for the business combination described in paragraph IE68A of Example 7B, the assets of Subsidiary will generate cash inflows together with other assets or groups of assets of Parent. Therefore, rather than Subsidiary being the cash-generating unit for the purposes of impairment testing, Subsidiary becomes part of a larger cash-generating unit, Z. Other cash-generating units of Parent are also expected to benefit from the synergies of the combination. Therefore, goodwill related to those synergies, in the amount of CU500, has been allocated to those other cash-generating units. Z's goodwill related to previous business combinations is CU800.

IE68G   Because Z includes goodwill within its carrying amount, both from Subsidiary and from previous business combinations, it must be tested for impairment annually, or more frequently if there is an indication that it might be impaired (see paragraph 90 of IAS 36).

Testing Subsidiary for impairment

IE68H   At the end of 20X3, Parent determines that the recoverable amount of cash-generating unit Z is CU3,300. The carrying amount of the net assets of Z, excluding goodwill, is CU2,250.

Schedule 3. Testing Z for impairment at the end of 20X3

End of 20X3	Goodwill	Net identifiable assets	Total
	CU	CU	CU
Carrying amount	1,250	2,250	3,500
Recoverable amount			3,300
Impairment loss			200

Allocating the impairment loss

IE68I   In accordance with paragraph 104 of IAS 36, the impairment loss of CU200 is allocated to the assets in the unit by first reducing the carrying amount of goodwill. Therefore, the full amount of impairment loss of CU200 for cash-generating unit Z is allocated to the goodwill. In accordance with paragraph C7 of Appendix C of IAS 36, if the partially-owned Subsidiary forms part of a larger cash-generating unit, the goodwill impairment loss would be allocated first to the parts of the cash-generating unit, Z, and then to the controlling and non-controlling interests of the partially-owned Subsidiary.

IE68J   Parent allocates the impairment loss to the parts of the cash-generating unit on the basis of the relative carrying values of the goodwill of the parts before the impairment. In this example Subsidiary is allocated 36 per cent of the impairment (450/1,250). The impairment loss is then allocated to the controlling and non-controlling interests on the same basis as that on which profit or loss is allocated.

Example 8   Allocation of corporate assets

In this example, tax effects are ignored.

Background

IE69   Entity M has three cash-generating units: A, B and C. The carrying amounts of those units do not include goodwill. There are adverse changes in the technological environment in which M operates. Therefore, M conducts impairment tests of each of its cash-generating units. At the end of 20X0, the carrying amounts of A, B and C are CU100, CU150 and CU200 respectively.

IE70   The operations are conducted from a headquarters. The carrying amount of the headquarters is CU200: a headquarters building of CU150 and a research centre of CU50. The relative carrying amounts of the cash-generating units are a reasonable indication of the proportion of the headquarters building devoted to each cash-generating unit. The carrying amount of the research centre cannot be allocated on a reasonable basis to the individual cash-generating units.

IE71   The remaining estimated useful life of cash-generating unit A is 10 years. The remaining useful lives of B, C and the headquarters are 20 years. The headquarters is depreciated on a straight-line basis.

IE72   The recoverable amount (ie higher of value in use and fair value less costs of disposal) of each cash-generating unit is based on its value in use. Value in use is calculated using a pre-tax discount rate of 15 per cent.

Identification of corporate assets

IE73   In accordance with paragraph 102 of IAS 36, M first identifies all the corporate assets that relate to the individual cash-generating units under review. The corporate assets are the headquarters building and the research centre.

IE74   M then decides how to deal with each of the corporate assets:

(a)   the carrying amount of the headquarters building can be allocated on a reasonable and consistent basis to the cash-generating units under review; and

(b)   the carrying amount of the research centre cannot be allocated on a reasonable and consistent basis to the individual cash-generating units under review.

Allocation of corporate assets

IE75 The carrying amount of the headquarters building is allocated to the carrying amount of each individual cash-generating unit. A weighted allocation basis is used because the estimated remaining useful life of A's cash-generating unit is 10 years, whereas the estimated remaining useful lives of B and C's cash-generating units are 20 years.

Schedule 1. Calculation of a weighted allocation of the carrying amount of the headquarters building

End of 20X0	A	B	C	Total
	CU	CU	CU	CU
Carrying amount	100	150	200	450
Useful life	10 years	20 years	20 years	
Weighting based on useful life	1	2	2	
Carrying amount after weighting	100	300	400	800
Pro-rata allocation of the building	12% (100/800)	38% (300/800)	50% (400/800)	100%
Allocation of the carrying amount of the building (based on pro-rata above)	19	56	75	150
Carrying amount (after allocation of the building)	119	206	275	600

Determination of recoverable amount and calculation of impairment losses

IE76 Paragraph 102 of IAS 36 requires first that the recoverable amount of each individual cash-generating unit be compared with its carrying amount, including the portion of the carrying amount of the headquarters building allocated to the unit, and any resulting impairment loss recognised. Paragraph 102 of IAS 36 then requires the recoverable amount of M as a whole (ie the smallest group of cash-generating units that includes the research centre) to be compared with its carrying amount, including both the headquarters building and the research centre.

Schedule 2. Calculation of A, B, C and M's value in use at the end of 20X0

Year	A Future cash flows	A Discount at 15%	B Future cash flows	B Discount at 15%	C Future cash flows	C Discount at 15%	M Future cash flows	M Discount at 15%
	CU	CU	CU	CU	CU	CU	CU	CU
1	18	16	9	8	10	9	39	34
2	31	23	16	12	20	15	72	54
3	37	24	24	16	34	22	105	69
4	42	24	29	17	44	25	128	73
5	47	24	32	16	51	25	143	71
6	52	22	33	14	56	24	155	67
7	55	21	34	13	60	22	162	61
8	55	18	35	11	63	21	166	54
9	53	15	35	10	65	18	167	48
10	48	12	35	9	66	16	169	42
11			36	8	66	14	132	28
12			35	7	66	12	131	25
13			35	6	66	11	131	21
14			33	5	65	9	128	18
15			30	4	62	8	122	15
16			26	3	60	6	115	12
17			22	2	57	5	108	10
18			18	1	51	4	97	8
19			14	1	43	3	85	6
20			10	1	35	2	71	4
Value in use		199		164		271		720[a]

(a) It is assumed that the research centre generates additional future cash flows for the entity as a whole. Therefore, the sum of the value in use of each individual cash-generating unit is less than the value in use of the business as a whole. The additional cash flows are not attributable to the headquarters building.

Schedule 3. Impairment testing A, B and C

End of 20X0	A	B	C
	CU	CU	CU
Carrying amount (after allocation of the building) (Schedule 1)	119	206	275
Recoverable amount (Schedule 2)	199	164	271
Impairment loss	0	(42)	(4)

IE77   The next step is to allocate the impairment losses between the assets of the cash-generating units and the headquarters building.

Schedule 4. Allocation of the impairment losses for cash-generating units B and C

Cash-generating unit	B		C	
	CU		CU	
To headquarters building	(12)	$(42 \times {}^{56}/_{206})$	(1)	$(4 \times {}^{75}/_{275})$
To assets in cash-generating unit	(30)	$(42 \times {}^{150}/_{206})$	(3)	$(4 \times {}^{200}/_{275})$
	(42)		(4)	

IE78   Because the research centre could not be allocated on a reasonable and consistent basis to A, B and C's cash-generating units, M compares the carrying amount of the smallest group of cash-generating units to which the carrying amount of the research centre can be allocated (ie M as a whole) to its recoverable amount.

Schedule 5. Impairment testing the smallest group of cash-generating units to which the carrying amount of the research centre can be allocated (ie M as a whole)

End of 20X0	A	B	C	Building	Research centre	M
	CU	CU	CU	CU	CU	CU
Carrying amount	100	150	200	150	50	650
Impairment loss arising from the first step of the test	–	(30)	(3)	(13)	–	(46)
Carrying amount after the first step of the test	100	120	197	137	50	604
Recoverable amount (Schedule 2)						720
Impairment loss for the 'larger' cash-generating unit						0

IE79 Therefore, no additional impairment loss results from the application of the impairment test to M as a whole. Only an impairment loss of CU46 is recognised as a result of the application of the first step of the test to A, B and C.

Example 9 Disclosures about cash-generating units with goodwill or intangible assets with indefinite useful lives

The purpose of this example is to illustrate the disclosures required by paragraphs 134 and 135 of IAS 36.

Background

IE80 Entity M is a multinational manufacturing firm that uses geographical segments for reporting segment information. M's three reportable segments are Europe, North America and Asia. Goodwill has been allocated for impairment testing purposes to three individual cash-generating units—two in Europe (units A and B) and one in North America (unit C)—and to one group of cash-generating units (comprising operation XYZ) in Asia. Units A, B and C and operation XYZ each represent the lowest level within M at which the goodwill is monitored for internal management purposes.

IE81 M acquired unit C, a manufacturing operation in North America, in December 20X2. Unlike M's other North American operations, C operates in an industry with high margins and high growth rates, and with the benefit of a 10-year patent on its primary product. The patent was granted to C just before M's acquisition of C. As part of accounting for the acquisition of C, M recognised, in addition to the patent, goodwill of CU3,000 and a brand name of CU1,000. M's management has determined that the brand name has an indefinite useful life [Refer: IAS 38 paragraph 88]. M has no other intangible assets with indefinite useful lives.

© IFRS Foundation

IE82   The carrying amounts of goodwill and intangible assets with indefinite useful lives **[Refer: IAS 38 paragraph 88]** allocated to units A, B and C and to operation XYZ are as follows:

	Goodwill	Intangible assets with indefinite useful lives
	CU	CU
A	350	
B	450	
C	3,000	1,000
XYZ	1,200	
Total	5,000	1,000

IE83   During the year ending 31 December 20X3, M determines that there is no impairment of any of its cash-generating units or group of cash-generating units containing goodwill or intangible assets with indefinite useful lives **[Refer: IAS 38 paragraph 88]**. The recoverable amounts (ie higher of value in use and fair value less costs of disposal) of those units and group of units are determined on the basis of value in use calculations. M has determined that the recoverable amount calculations are most sensitive to changes in the following assumptions:

Units A and B	Unit C	Operation XYZ
Gross margin during the budget period (budget period is 4 years)	5-year US government bond rate during the budget period (budget period is 5 years)	Gross margin during the budget period (budget period is 5 years)
Raw materials price inflation during the budget period	Raw materials price inflation during the budget period	Japanese yen/US dollar exchange rate during the budget period
Market share during the budget period	Market share during the budget period	Market share during the budget period
Growth rate used to extrapolate cash flows beyond the budget period	Growth rate used to extrapolate cash flows beyond the budget period	Growth rate used to extrapolate cash flows beyond the budget period

IE84   Gross margins during the budget period for A, B and XYZ are estimated by M based on average gross margins achieved in the period immediately before the start of the budget period, increased by 5 per cent per year for anticipated efficiency improvements. A and B produce complementary products and are operated by M to achieve the same gross margins.

IE85   Market shares during the budget period are estimated by M based on average market shares achieved in the period immediately before the start of the budget period, adjusted each year for any anticipated growth or decline in market shares. M anticipates that:

(a)   market shares for A and B will differ, but will each grow during the budget period by 3 per cent per year as a result of ongoing improvements in product quality.

(b)   C's market share will grow during the budget period by 6 per cent per year as a result of increased advertising expenditure and the benefits from the protection of the 10-year patent on its primary product.

(c)   XYZ's market share will remain unchanged during the budget period as a result of the combination of ongoing improvements in product quality and an anticipated increase in competition.

IE86   A and B purchase raw materials from the same European suppliers, whereas C's raw materials are purchased from various North American suppliers. Raw materials price inflation during the budget period is estimated by M to be consistent with forecast consumer price indices published by government agencies in the relevant European and North American countries.

IE87   The 5-year US government bond rate during the budget period is estimated by M to be consistent with the yield on such bonds at the beginning of the budget period. The Japanese yen/US dollar exchange rate is estimated by M to be consistent with the average market forward exchange rate over the budget period.

IE88   M uses steady growth rates to extrapolate beyond the budget period cash flows for A, B, C and XYX. The growth rates for A, B and XYZ are estimated by M to be consistent with publicly available information about the long-term average growth rates for the markets in which A, B and XYZ operate. However, the growth rate for C exceeds the long-term average growth rate for the market in which C operates. M's management is of the opinion that this is reasonable in the light of the protection of the 10-year patent on C's primary product.

IE89   M includes the following disclosure in the notes to its financial statements for the year ending 31 December 20X3.

Impairment Tests for Goodwill and Intangible Assets with Indefinite Lives

Goodwill has been allocated for impairment testing purposes to three individual cash-generating units—two in Europe (units A and B) and one in North America (unit C)—and to one group of cash-generating units (comprising operation XYZ) in Asia. The carrying amount of goodwill allocated to unit C and operation XYZ is significant in comparison with the total carrying amount of goodwill, but the carrying amount of goodwill allocated to each of units A and B is not. Nevertheless, the recoverable amounts of units A and B are based on some of the same key assumptions, and the aggregate carrying amount of goodwill allocated to those units is significant.

          © IFRS Foundation

Operation XYZ

The recoverable amount of operation XYZ has been determined based on a value in use calculation. That calculation uses cash flow projections based on financial budgets approved by management covering a five-year period, and a discount rate of 8.4 per cent. Cash flows beyond that five-year period have been extrapolated using a steady 6.3 per cent growth rate. This growth rate does not exceed the long-term average growth rate for the market in which XYZ operates. Management believes that any reasonably possible change in the key assumptions on which XYZ's recoverable amount is based would *not* cause XYZ's carrying amount to exceed its recoverable amount.

Unit C

The recoverable amount of unit C has also been determined based on a value in use calculation. That calculation uses cash flow projections based on financial budgets approved by management covering a five-year period, and a discount rate of 9.2 per cent. C's cash flows beyond the five-year period are extrapolated using a steady 12 per cent growth rate. This growth rate exceeds by 4 percentage points the long-term average growth rate for the market in which C operates. However, C benefits from the protection of a 10-year patent on its primary product, granted in December 20X2. Management believes that a 12 per cent growth rate is reasonable in the light of that patent. Management also believes that any reasonably possible change in the key assumptions on which C's recoverable amount is based would *not* cause C's carrying amount to exceed its recoverable amount.

Units A and B

The recoverable amounts of units A and B have been determined on the basis of value in use calculations. Those units produce complementary products, and their recoverable amounts are based on some of the same key assumptions. Both value in use calculations use cash flow projections based on financial budgets approved by management covering a four-year period, and a discount rate of 7.9 per cent. Both sets of cash flows beyond the four-year period are extrapolated using a steady 5 per cent growth rate. This growth rate does not exceed the long-term average growth rate for the market in which A and B operate. Cash flow projections during the budget period for both A and B are also based on the same expected gross margins during the budget period and the same raw materials price inflation during the budget period. Management believes that any reasonably possible change in any of these key assumptions would *not* cause the aggregate carrying amount of A and B to exceed the aggregate recoverable amount of those units.

	Operation XYZ	Unit C	Units A and B (in aggregate)
Carrying amount of goodwill	CU1,200	CU3,000	CU800
Carrying amount of brand name with indefinite useful life	–	CU1,000	–
Key assumptions used in value in use calculations[(a)]			
Key assumption	Budgeted gross margins	5-year US government bond rate	Budgeted gross margins
Basis for determining value(s) assigned to key assumption	Average gross margins achieved in period immediately before the budget period, increased for expected efficiency improvements.	Yield on 5-year US government bonds at the beginning of the budget period.	Average gross margins achieved in period immediately before the budget period, increased for expected efficiency improvements.
	Values assigned to key assumption reflect past experience, except for efficiency improvements. Management believes improvements of 5% per year are reasonably achievable.	Value assigned to key assumption is consistent with external sources of information.	Values assigned to key assumption reflect past experience, except for efficiency improvements. Management believes improvements of 5% per year are reasonably achievable.

continued...

...continued

Key assumption	Japanese yen/ US dollar exchange rate during the budget period	Raw materials price inflation	Raw materials price inflation
Basis for determining value(s) assigned to key assumption	Average market forward exchange rate over the budget period.	Forecast consumer price indices during the budget period for North American countries from which raw materials are purchased.	Forecast consumer price indices during the budget period for European countries from which raw materials are purchased.
	Value assigned to key assumption is consistent with external sources of information.	Value assigned to key assumption is consistent with external sources of information.	Value assigned to key assumption is consistent with external sources of information.
Key assumption	Budgeted market share	Budgeted market share	
Basis for determining value(s) assigned to key assumption	Average market share in period immediately before the budget period.	Average market share in period immediately before the budget period, increased each year for anticipated growth in market share.	

continued...

...continued

	Value assigned to key assumption reflects past experience. No change in market share expected as a result of ongoing product quality improvements coupled with anticipated increase in competition.	Management believes market share growth of 6% per year is reasonably achievable due to increased advertising expenditure, the benefits from the protection of the 10-year patent on C's primary product, and the expected synergies to be achieved from operating C as part of M's North American segment.

(a) The key assumptions shown in this table for units A and B are only those that are used in the recoverable amount calculations for both units.

IASB documents published to accompany

IAS 37

Provisions, Contingent Liabilities and Contingent Assets

The text of the unaccompanied standard, IAS 37, is contained in Part A of this edition. Its effective date when issued was 1 July 1999. The text of the Basis for Conclusions on IAS 37 is contained in Part C of this edition. This part presents the following documents:

IMPLEMENTATION GUIDANCE

A Tables – Provisions, contingent liabilities, contingent assets and reimbursements

B Decision tree

C Examples: recognition

D Examples: disclosures

Guidance on implementing
IAS 37 *Provisions, Contingent Liabilities and Contingent Assets*

This guidance accompanies, but is not part of, IAS 37.

A Tables – Provisions, contingent liabilities, contingent assets and reimbursements

The purpose of these tables is to summarise the main requirements of the Standard.

Provisions and contingent liabilities

Where, as a result of past events, there may be an outflow of resources embodying future economic benefits in settlement of: (a) a present obligation; or (b) a possible obligation whose existence will be confirmed only by the occurrence or non-occurrence of one or more uncertain future events not wholly within the control of the entity.		
There is a present obligation that probably requires an outflow of resources.	There is a possible obligation or a present obligation that may, but probably will not, require an outflow of resources.	There is a possible obligation or a present obligation where the likelihood of an outflow of resources is remote.
A provision is recognised (paragraph 14).	No provision is recognised (paragraph 27).	No provision is recognised (paragraph 27).
Disclosures are required for the provision (paragraphs 84 and 85).	Disclosures are required for the contingent liability (paragraph 86).	No disclosure is required (paragraph 86).

A contingent liability also arises in the extremely rare case where there is a liability that cannot be recognised because it cannot be measured reliably. Disclosures are required for the contingent liability.

Contingent assets

Where, as a result of past events, there is a possible asset whose existence will be confirmed only by the occurrence or non-occurrence of one or more uncertain future events not wholly within the control of the entity.		
The inflow of economic benefits is virtually certain.	The inflow of economic benefits is probable, but not virtually certain.	The inflow is not probable.
The asset is not contingent (paragraph 33).	No asset is recognised (paragraph 31).	No asset is recognised (paragraph 31).
	Disclosures are required (paragraph 89).	No disclosure is required (paragraph 89).

Reimbursements

Some or all of the expenditure required to settle a provision is expected to be reimbursed by another party.		
The entity has no obligation for the part of the expenditure to be reimbursed by the other party.	The obligation for the amount expected to be reimbursed remains with the entity and it is virtually certain that reimbursement will be received if the entity settles the provision.	The obligation for the amount expected to be reimbursed remains with the entity and the reimbursement is not virtually certain if the entity settles the provision.
The entity has no liability for the amount to be reimbursed (paragraph 57).	The reimbursement is recognised as a separate asset in the statement of financial position and may be offset against the expense in the statement of comprehensive income. The amount recognised for the expected reimbursement does not exceed the liability (paragraphs 53 and 54).	The expected reimbursement is not recognised as an asset (paragraph 53).
No disclosure is required.	The reimbursement is disclosed together with the amount recognised for the reimbursement (paragraph 85(c)).	The expected reimbursement is disclosed (paragraph 85(c)).

B Decision tree

The purpose of this diagram is to summarise the main recognition requirements of the Standard for provisions and contingent liabilities.

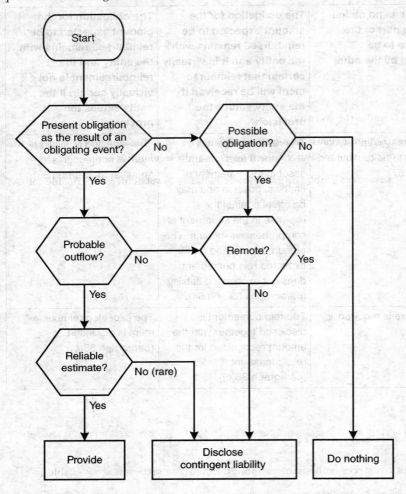

Note: In rare cases, it is not clear whether there is a present obligation. In these cases, a past event is deemed to give rise to a present obligation if, taking account of all available evidence, it is more likely than not that a present obligation exists at the end of the reporting period (paragraph 15 of the Standard).

[Refer: paragraph 16]

C Examples: recognition

All the entities in the examples have 31 December year-ends. In all cases, it is assumed that a reliable estimate can be made of any outflows expected. In some examples the circumstances described may have resulted in impairment of the assets — this aspect is not dealt with in the examples.

The cross-references provided in the examples indicate paragraphs of the Standard that are particularly relevant.

References to 'best estimate' **[Refer: paragraphs 36–44]** *are to the present value* **[Refer: paragraphs 45–47]** *amount, where the effect of the time value of money is material.*

Example 1 Warranties

A manufacturer gives warranties at the time of sale to purchasers of its product. Under the terms of the contract for sale the manufacturer undertakes to make good, by repair or replacement, manufacturing defects that become apparent within three years from the date of sale. On past experience, it is probable (ie more likely than not) that there will be some claims under the warranties.

Present obligation as a result of a past obligating event – The obligating event is the sale of the product with a warranty, which gives rise to a legal obligation.

An outflow of resources embodying economic benefits in settlement – Probable for the warranties as a whole (see paragraph 24).

Conclusion – A provision is recognised for the best estimate of the costs of making good under the warranty products sold before the end of the reporting period (see paragraphs 14 and 24).

Example 2A Contaminated land – legislation virtually certain to be enacted

An entity in the oil industry causes contamination but cleans up only when required to do so under the laws of the particular country in which it operates. One country in which it operates has had no legislation requiring cleaning up, and the entity has been contaminating land in that country for several years. At 31 December 20X0 it is virtually certain that a draft law requiring a clean-up of land already contaminated will be enacted shortly after the year-end.

Present obligation as a result of a past obligating event – The obligating event is the contamination of the land because of the virtual certainty of legislation requiring cleaning up.

An outflow of resources embodying economic benefits in settlement – Probable.

Conclusion – A provision is recognised for the best estimate of the costs of the clean-up (see paragraphs 14 and 22).

Example 2B Contaminated land and constructive obligation

An entity in the oil industry causes contamination and operates in a country where there is no environmental legislation. However, the entity has a widely published environmental policy in which it undertakes to clean up all contamination that it causes. The entity has a record of honouring this published policy.

Present obligation as a result of a past obligating event – The obligating event is the contamination of the land, which gives rise to a constructive obligation because the conduct of the entity has created a valid expectation on the part of those affected by it that the entity will clean up contamination.

An outflow of resources embodying economic benefits in settlement – Probable.

Conclusion – A provision is recognised for the best estimate of the costs of clean-up (see paragraphs 10 (the definition of a constructive obligation), 14 and 17).

Example 3 Offshore oilfield

An entity operates an offshore oilfield where its licensing agreement requires it to remove the oil rig at the end of production and restore the seabed. Ninety per cent of the eventual costs relate to the removal of the oil rig and restoration of damage caused by building it, and 10 per cent arise through the extraction of oil. At the end of the reporting period, the rig has been constructed but no oil has been extracted.

Present obligation as a result of a past obligating event – The construction of the oil rig creates a legal obligation under the terms of the licence to remove the rig and restore the seabed and is thus an obligating event. At the end of the reporting period, however, there is no obligation to rectify the damage that will be caused by extraction of the oil.

An outflow of resources embodying economic benefits in settlement – Probable.

Conclusion – A provision is recognised for the best estimate of ninety per cent of the eventual costs that relate to the removal of the oil rig and restoration of damage caused by building it (see paragraph 14). These costs are included as part of the cost of the oil rig. The 10 per cent of costs that arise through the extraction of oil are recognised as a liability when the oil is extracted.

Example 4 Refunds policy

A retail store has a policy of refunding purchases by dissatisfied customers, even though it is under no legal obligation to do so. Its policy of making refunds is generally known.

Present obligation as a result of a past obligating event – The obligating event is the sale of the product, which gives rise to a constructive obligation because the conduct of the store has created a valid expectation on the part of its customers that the store will refund purchases.

An outflow of resources embodying economic benefits in settlement – Probable, a proportion of goods are returned for refund (see paragraph 24).

Conclusion – A provision is recognised for the best estimate of the costs of refunds (see paragraphs 10 (the definition of a constructive obligation), 14, 17 and 24).

Example 5A Closure of a division – no implementation before end of the reporting period

On 12 December 20X0 the board of an entity decided to close down a division. Before the end of the reporting period (31 December 20X0) the decision was not communicated to any of those affected and no other steps were taken to implement the decision.

Present obligation as a result of a past obligating event – There has been no obligating event and so there is no obligation.

Conclusion – No provision is recognised (see paragraphs 14 and 72).

Example 5B Closure of a division – communication/ implementation before end of the reporting period

On 12 December 20X0, the board of an entity decided to close down a division making a particular product. On 20 December 20X0 a detailed plan for closing down the division was agreed by the board; letters were sent to customers warning them to seek an alternative source of supply and redundancy notices were sent to the staff of the division.

Present obligation as a result of a past obligating event – The obligating event is the communication of the decision to the customers and employees, which gives rise to a constructive obligation from that date, because it creates a valid expectation that the division will be closed.

An outflow of resources embodying economic benefits in settlement – Probable.

Conclusion – A provision is recognised at 31 December 20X0 for the best estimate of the costs of closing the division (see paragraphs 14 and 72).

Example 6 Legal requirement to fit smoke filters

Under new legislation, an entity is required to fit smoke filters to its factories by 30 June 20X1. The entity has not fitted the smoke filters.

(a)   At 31 December 20X0, the end of the reporting period

Present obligation as a result of a past obligating event – There is no obligation because there is no obligating event either for the costs of fitting smoke filters or for fines under the legislation.

Conclusion – No provision is recognised for the cost of fitting the smoke filters (see paragraphs 14 and 17–19).

(b)   At 31 December 20X1, the end of the reporting period

Present obligation as a result of a past obligating event – There is still no obligation for the costs of fitting smoke filters because no obligating event has occurred (the fitting of the filters). However, an obligation might arise to pay fines or penalties under the legislation because the obligating event has occurred (the non-compliant operation of the factory).

An outflow of resources embodying economic benefits in settlement – Assessment of probability of incurring fines and penalties by non-compliant operation depends on the details of the legislation and the stringency of the enforcement regime.

Conclusion – No provision is recognised for the costs of fitting smoke filters. However, a provision is recognised for the best estimate of any fines and penalties that are more likely than not to be imposed (see paragraphs 14 and 17–19).

Example 7 Staff retraining as a result of changes in the income tax system

The government introduces a number of changes to the income tax system. As a result of these changes, an entity in the financial services sector will need to retrain a large proportion of its administrative and sales workforce in order to ensure continued compliance with financial services regulation. At the end of the reporting period, no retraining of staff has taken place.

Present obligation as a result of a past obligating event – There is no obligation because no obligating event (retraining) has taken place.

Conclusion – No provision is recognised (see paragraphs 14 and 17–19).

Example 8 An onerous contract

[Deleted]

Example 9 A single guarantee

[Deleted]

Example 10 A court case

After a wedding in 20X0, ten people died, possibly as a result of food poisoning from products sold by the entity. Legal proceedings are started seeking damages from the entity but it disputes liability. Up to the date of authorisation of the financial statements for the year to 31 December 20X0 for issue, the entity's lawyers advise that it is probable that the entity will not be found liable. However, when the entity prepares the financial statements for the year to 31 December 20X1, its lawyers advise that, owing to developments in the case, it is probable that the entity will be found liable.

(a)   At 31 December 20X0

Present obligation as a result of a past obligating event – On the basis of the evidence available when the financial statements were approved, there is no obligation as a result of past events.

Conclusion – No provision is recognised (see paragraphs 15 and 16). The matter is disclosed as a contingent liability unless the probability of any outflow is regarded as remote (paragraph 86).

(b)   At 31 December 20X1

Present obligation as a result of a past obligating event – On the basis of the evidence available, there is a present obligation.

An outflow of resources embodying economic benefits in settlement – Probable.

Conclusion – A provision is recognised for the best estimate of the amount to settle the obligation (paragraphs 14–16).

Example 11 Repairs and maintenance

Some assets require, in addition to routine maintenance, substantial expenditure every few years for major refits or refurbishment and the replacement of major components. IAS 16 *Property, Plant and Equipment* gives guidance on allocating expenditure on an asset to its component parts where these components have different useful lives or provide benefits in a different pattern.

Example 11A Refurbishment costs – no legislative requirement

A furnace has a lining that needs to be replaced every five years for technical reasons. At the end of the reporting period, the lining has been in use for three years.

Present obligation as a result of a past obligating event – There is no present obligation.

Conclusion – No provision is recognised (see paragraphs 14 and 17–19).

The cost of replacing the lining is not recognised because, at the end of the reporting period, no obligation to replace the lining exists independently of the company's future actions – even the intention to incur the expenditure depends on the company deciding to continue operating the furnace or to replace the lining. Instead of a provision being recognised, the depreciation of the lining takes account of its consumption, ie it is depreciated over five years. The re-lining costs then incurred are capitalised with the consumption of each new lining shown by depreciation over the subsequent five years.

Example 11B Refurbishment costs – legislative requirement

An airline is required by law to overhaul its aircraft once every three years.

Present obligation as a result of a past obligating event – There is no present obligation.

Conclusion – No provision is recognised (see paragraphs 14 and 17–19).

The costs of overhauling aircraft are not recognised as a provision for the same reasons as the cost of replacing the lining is not recognised as a provision in example 11A. Even a legal requirement to overhaul does not make the costs of overhaul a liability, because no obligation exists to overhaul the aircraft independently of the entity's future actions – the entity could avoid the future expenditure by its future actions, for example by selling the aircraft. Instead of a provision being recognised, the depreciation of the aircraft takes account of the future incidence of maintenance costs, ie an amount equivalent to the expected maintenance costs is depreciated over three years.

D Examples: disclosures

Two examples of the disclosures required by paragraph 85 are provided below.

Example 1 Warranties

A manufacturer gives warranties at the time of sale to purchasers of its three product lines. Under the terms of the warranty, the manufacturer undertakes to repair or replace items that fail to perform satisfactorily for two years from the date of sale. At the end of the reporting period, a provision of 60,000 has been recognised. The provision has not been discounted as the effect of discounting is not material. The following information is disclosed:

A provision of 60,000 has been recognised for expected warranty claims on products sold during the last three financial years. It is expected that the majority of this expenditure will be incurred in the next financial year, and all will be incurred within two years after the reporting period.

Example 2 Decommissioning costs

In 2000, an entity involved in nuclear activities recognises a provision for decommissioning costs of 300 million. The provision is estimated using the assumption that decommissioning will take place in 60–70 years' time. However, there is a possibility that it will not take place until 100–110 years' time, in which case the present value of the costs will be significantly reduced. The following information is disclosed:

A provision of 300 million has been recognised for decommissioning costs. These costs are expected to be incurred between 2060 and 2070; however, there is a possibility that decommissioning will not take place until 2100–2110. If the costs were measured based upon the expectation that they would not be incurred until 2100–2110 the provision would be reduced to 136 million. The provision has been estimated using existing technology, at current prices, and discounted using a real discount rate of 2 per cent.

An example is given below of the disclosures required by paragraph 92 where some of the information required is not given because it can be expected to prejudice seriously the position of the entity.

Example 3 Disclosure exemption

An entity is involved in a dispute with a competitor, who is alleging that the entity has infringed patents and is seeking damages of 100 million. The entity recognises a provision for its best estimate of the obligation, but discloses none of the information required by paragraphs 84 and 85 of the Standard. The following information is disclosed:

Litigation is in process against the company relating to a dispute with a competitor who alleges that the company has infringed patents and is seeking damages of 100 million. The information usually required by IAS 37 Provisions, Contingent Liabilities and Contingent Assets *is not disclosed on the grounds that it can be expected to prejudice seriously the outcome of the litigation. The directors are of the opinion that the claim can be successfully resisted by the company.*

IASB documents published to accompany

IAS 38

Intangible Assets

The text of the unaccompanied standard, IAS 38, is contained in Part A of this edition. Its effective date when issued was 31 March 2004. The text of the Basis for Conclusions on IAS 38 is contained in Part C of this edition. This part presents the following documents:

ILLUSTRATIVE EXAMPLES
Assessing the useful lives of intangible assets

IAS 38 *Intangible Assets*
Illustrative Examples

These examples accompany, but are not part of, IAS 38.

Assessing the useful lives of intangible assets

The following guidance provides examples on determining the useful life of an intangible asset in accordance with IAS 38.

Each of the following examples describes an acquired intangible asset, the facts and circumstances surrounding the determination of its useful life, and the subsequent accounting based on that determination.

Example 1 An acquired customer list

A direct-mail marketing company acquires a customer list and expects that it will be able to derive benefit from the information on the list for at least one year, but no more than three years.

The customer list would be amortised **[Refer: paragraphs 97–106]** over management's best estimate of its useful life, **[Refer: paragraphs 88–96]** say 18 months. Although the direct-mail marketing company may intend to add customer names and other information to the list in the future, the expected benefits of the acquired customer list relate only to the customers on that list at the date it was acquired. The customer list also would be reviewed for impairment in accordance with IAS 36 *Impairment of Assets* by assessing at the end of each reporting period whether there is any indication that the customer list may be impaired. **[Refer: paragraph 111]**

Example 2 An acquired patent that expires in 15 years

The product protected by the patented technology is expected to be a source of net cash inflows for at least 15 years. The entity has a commitment from a third party to purchase that patent in five years for 60 per cent of the fair value of the patent at the date it was acquired, and the entity intends to sell the patent in five years.

The patent would be amortised **[Refer: paragraphs 97–106]** over its five-year useful life **[Refer: paragraphs 88–96]** to the entity, with a residual value **[Refer: paragraphs 100–103]** equal to the present value of 60 per cent of the patent's fair value at the date it was acquired. The patent would also be reviewed for impairment in accordance with IAS 36 by assessing at the end of each reporting period whether there is any indication that it may be impaired. **[Refer: paragraph 111]**

Example 3 An acquired copyright that has a remaining legal life of 50 years

An analysis of consumer habits and market trends provides evidence that the copyrighted material will generate net cash inflows for only 30 more years.

The copyright would be amortised [Refer: paragraphs 97–106] over its 30-year estimated useful life [Refer: paragraphs 88–96]. The copyright also would be reviewed for impairment in accordance with IAS 36 by assessing at the end of each reporting period whether there is any indication that it may be impaired. [Refer: paragraph 111]

Example 4 An acquired broadcasting licence that expires in five years

The broadcasting licence is renewable every 10 years if the entity provides at least an average level of service to its customers and complies with the relevant legislative requirements. The licence may be renewed indefinitely at little cost and has been renewed twice before the most recent acquisition. The acquiring entity intends to renew the licence indefinitely and evidence supports its ability to do so. Historically, there has been no compelling challenge to the licence renewal. The technology used in broadcasting is not expected to be replaced by another technology at any time in the foreseeable future. Therefore, the licence is expected to contribute to the entity's net cash inflows indefinitely.

The broadcasting licence would be treated as having an indefinite useful life because it is expected to contribute to the entity's net cash inflows indefinitely [Refer: paragraphs 88–96]. Therefore, the licence would not be amortised until its useful life is determined to be finite. [Refer: paragraphs 107–110] The licence would be tested for impairment in accordance with IAS 36 annually and whenever there is an indication that it may be impaired. [Refer: paragraph 108]

Example 5 The broadcasting licence in Example 4

The licensing authority subsequently decides that it will no longer renew broadcasting licences, but rather will auction the licences. At the time the licensing authority's decision is made, the entity's broadcasting licence has three years until it expires. The entity expects that the licence will continue to contribute to net cash inflows until the licence expires.

Because the broadcasting licence can no longer be renewed, its useful life is no longer indefinite. [Refer: paragraph 109] Thus, the acquired licence would be amortised [Refer: paragraphs 97–106] over its remaining three-year useful life and immediately tested for impairment in accordance with IAS 36. [Refer: paragraph 110]

Example 6 An acquired airline route authority between two European cities that expires in three years

The route authority may be renewed every five years, and the acquiring entity intends to comply with the applicable rules and regulations surrounding renewal. Route authority renewals are routinely granted at a minimal cost and historically have been renewed when the airline has complied with the applicable rules and regulations. The acquiring entity expects to provide service indefinitely between the two cities from its hub airports and expects that the related supporting infrastructure (airport gates, slots, and terminal facility leases) will remain in place at those airports for as long as it has the route authority. An analysis of demand and cash flows supports those assumptions.

Because the facts and circumstances support the acquiring entity's ability to continue providing air service indefinitely between the two cities, the intangible asset related to the route authority is treated as having an indefinite useful life. [Refer: paragraphs 88–96] Therefore, the route authority would not be amortised until its useful life is determined to be finite. [Refer: paragraphs 107–110] It would be tested for impairment in accordance with IAS 36 annually and whenever there is an indication that it may be impaired. [Refer: paragraph 108]

Example 7 An acquired trademark used to identify and distinguish a leading consumer product that has been a market-share leader for the past eight years

The trademark has a remaining legal life of five years but is renewable every 10 years at little cost. The acquiring entity intends to renew the trademark continuously and evidence supports its ability to do so. An analysis of (1) product life cycle studies, (2) market, competitive and environmental trends, and (3) brand extension opportunities provides evidence that the trademarked product will generate net cash inflows for the acquiring entity for an indefinite period.

The trademark would be treated as having an indefinite useful life because it is expected to contribute to net cash inflows indefinitely [Refer: paragraphs 88–96]. Therefore, the trademark would not be amortised until its useful life is determined to be finite. [Refer: paragraphs 107–110] It would be tested for impairment in accordance with IAS 36 annually and whenever there is an indication that it may be impaired. [Refer: paragraph 108]

Example 8 A trademark acquired 10 years ago that distinguishes a leading consumer product

The trademark was regarded as having an indefinite useful life when it was acquired because the trademarked product was expected to generate net cash inflows indefinitely. [Refer: paragraphs 88–96] However, unexpected competition has recently entered the market and will reduce future sales of the product. Management estimates that net cash inflows generated by the product will be 20 per cent less for the foreseeable future. However, management expects that the product will continue to generate net cash inflows indefinitely at those reduced amounts. [Refer: paragraph 109]

As a result of the projected decrease in future net cash inflows, the entity determines that the estimated recoverable amount of the trademark is less than its carrying amount, and an impairment loss is recognised. [Refer: paragraph 108] Because it is still regarded as having an indefinite useful life, [Refer: paragraphs 88–96] the trademark would continue not to be amortised but would be tested for impairment in accordance with IAS 36 annually and whenever there is an indication that it may be impaired. [Refer: paragraphs 107–110]

Example 9 A trademark for a line of products that was acquired several years ago in a business combination

At the time of the business combination the acquiree had been producing the line of products for 35 years with many new models developed under the trademark. At the acquisition date the acquirer expected to continue producing the line, and an analysis of various economic factors indicated there was no limit to the period the trademark would contribute to net cash inflows. [Refer: paragraphs 88–96] Consequently, the trademark was not amortised by the acquirer. [Refer: paragraph 107] However, management has recently decided that production of the product line will be discontinued over the next four years. [Refer: paragraph 109]

Because the useful life of the acquired trademark is no longer regarded as indefinite, the carrying amount of the trademark would be tested for impairment in accordance with IAS 36 [Refer: paragraph 110] and amortised over its remaining four-year useful life. [Refer: paragraphs 97–106]

IASB documents published to accompany

IAS 39

Financial Instruments: Recognition and Measurement

The text of the unaccompanied standard, IAS 39, is contained in Part A of this edition. Its effective date when issued was 1 January 2005. The text of the Basis for Conclusions on IAS 39 is contained in Part C of this edition. This part presents the following documents:

ILLUSTRATIVE EXAMPLE

IMPLEMENTATION GUIDANCE

IAS 39 *Financial Instruments: Recognition and Measurement*
Illustrative Examples

This example accompanies, but is not part of, IAS 39.

Facts

IE1   On 1 January 20X1, Entity A identifies a portfolio comprising assets and liabilities whose interest rate risk it wishes to hedge. The liabilities include demandable deposit liabilities that the depositor may withdraw at any time without notice. For risk management purposes, the entity views all of the items in the portfolio as fixed rate items.

IE2   For risk management purposes, Entity A analyses the assets and liabilities in the portfolio into repricing time periods based on expected repricing dates. The entity uses monthly time periods and schedules items for the next five years (ie it has 60 separate monthly time periods).[1] The assets in the portfolio are prepayable assets that Entity A allocates into time periods based on the expected prepayment dates, by allocating a percentage of all of the assets, rather than individual items, into each time period. The portfolio also includes demandable liabilities that the entity expects, on a portfolio basis, to repay between one month and five years and, for risk management purposes, are scheduled into time periods on this basis. On the basis of this analysis, Entity A decides what amount it wishes to hedge in each time period.

[Refer: paragraph 78]

IE3   This example deals only with the repricing time period expiring in three months' time, ie the time period maturing on 31 March 20X1 (a similar procedure would be applied for each of the other 59 time periods). Entity A has scheduled assets of CU100 million[2] and liabilities of CU80 million into this time period. All of the liabilities are repayable on demand.

IE4   Entity A decides, for risk management purposes, to hedge the net position of CU20 million and accordingly enters into an interest rate swap[3] on 1 January 20X1 to pay a fixed rate and receive LIBOR, with a notional principal amount of CU20 million and a fixed life of three months.

[Refer: paragraph 81A]

IE5   This example makes the following simplifying assumptions:

        (a)   the coupon on the fixed leg of the swap is equal to the fixed coupon on the asset;

---

1   In this example principal cash flows have been scheduled into time periods but the related interest cash flows have been included when calculating the change in the fair value of the hedged item. Other methods of scheduling assets and liabilities are also possible. Also, in this example, monthly repricing time periods have been used. An entity may choose narrower or wider time periods.

2   In this example monetary amounts are denominated in 'currency units (CU)'.

3   The example uses a swap as the hedging instrument. An entity may use forward rate agreements or other derivatives as hedging instruments.

(b)   the coupon on the fixed leg of the swap becomes payable on the same
        dates as the interest payments on the asset; and

(c)   the interest on the variable leg of the swap is the overnight LIBOR rate.
        As a result, the entire fair value change of the swap arises from the
        fixed leg only, because the variable leg is not exposed to changes in fair
        value due to changes in interest rates.

In cases when these simplifying assumptions do not hold, greater
ineffectiveness will arise. (The ineffectiveness arising from (a) could be
eliminated by designating as the hedged item a portion of the cash flows on
the asset that are equivalent to the fixed leg of the swap.)

IE6   It is also assumed that Entity A tests effectiveness on a monthly basis.

IE7   The fair value of an equivalent non-prepayable asset of CU20 million, ignoring
        changes in value that are not attributable to interest rate movements, at
        various times during the period of the hedge is as follows:

	1 Jan 20X1	31 Jan 20X1	1 Feb 20X1	28 Feb 20X1	31 Mar 20X1
Fair value (asset) (CU)	20,000,000	20,047,408	20,047,408	20,023,795	Nil

IE8   The fair value of the swap at various times during the period of the hedge is as
        follows:

	1 Jan 20X1	31 Jan 20X1	1 Feb 20X1	28 Feb 20X1	31 Mar 20X1
Fair value (liability) (CU)	Nil	(47,408)	(47,408)	(23,795)	Nil

Accounting treatment

IE9   On 1 January 20X1, Entity A designates as the hedged item an amount of
        CU20 million of assets in the three-month time period. It designates as the
        hedged risk the change in the value of the hedged item (ie the CU20 million of
        assets) that is attributable to changes in LIBOR. It also complies with the other
        designation requirements set out in paragraphs 88(d) and AG119 of the
        Standard.

        [Refer: paragraphs 81A and AG114]

IE10   Entity A designates as the hedging instrument the interest rate swap described
        in paragraph IE4.

        End of month 1 (31 January 20X1)

IE11   On 31 January 20X1 (at the end of month 1) when Entity A tests effectiveness,
        LIBOR has decreased. Based on historical prepayment experience, Entity A
        estimates that, as a consequence, prepayments will occur faster than
        previously estimated. As a result it re-estimates the amount of assets

scheduled into this time period (excluding new assets originated during the month) as CU96 million.

IE12   The fair value of the designated interest rate swap with a notional principal of CU20 million is (CU47,408)[4] (the swap is a liability).

IE13   Entity A computes the change in the fair value of the hedged item, taking into account the change in estimated prepayments, as follows.

   (a)   First, it calculates the percentage of the initial estimate of the assets in the time period that was hedged. This is 20 per cent (CU20 million ÷ CU100 million).

   (b)   Second, it applies this percentage (20 per cent) to its revised estimate of the amount in that time period (CU96 million) to calculate the amount that is the hedged item based on its revised estimate. This is CU19.2 million.

   (c)   Third, it calculates the change in the fair value of this revised estimate of the hedged item (CU19.2 million) that is attributable to changes in LIBOR. This is CU45,511 (CU47,408[5] × (CU19.2 million ÷ CU20 million)).

[Refer: paragraph AG126]

IE14   Entity A makes the following accounting entries relating to this time period:

Dr Cash	CU172,097	
Cr Profit or loss (interest income)[(a)]		CU172,097

To recognise the interest received on the hedged amount (CU19.2 million).

Dr Profit or loss (interest expense)	CU179,268	
Cr Profit or loss (interest income)		CU179,268
Cr Cash		Nil

To recognise the interest received and paid on the swap designated as the hedging instrument.

Dr Profit or loss (loss)	CU47,408	
Cr Derivative liability		CU47,408

To recognise the change in the fair value of the swap. **[Refer: paragraphs 89(a) and AG114(h)]**

continued...

---

4   see paragraph IE8
5   ie CU20,047,408 – CU20,000,000. See paragraph IE7.

...continued

Dr	Separate line item in the statement of financial position	CU45,511
	Cr Profit or loss (gain)	CU45,511

To recognise the change in the fair value of the hedged amount.
[Refer: paragraphs 89(b), 89A and AG114(g)]

    (a) This example does not show how amounts of interest income and interest expense are calculated.

IE15   The net result on profit or loss (excluding interest income and interest expense) is to recognise a loss of (CU1,897). This represents ineffectiveness in the hedging relationship that arises from the change in estimated prepayment dates.
[Refer: paragraphs AG114(h) and (i) and AG126(b)(iv)]

Beginning of month 2

IE16   On 1 February 20X1 Entity A sells a proportion of the assets in the various time periods. Entity A calculates that it has sold $8^1/_3$ per cent of the entire portfolio of assets. Because the assets were allocated into time periods by allocating a percentage of the assets (rather than individual assets) into each time period, Entity A determines that it cannot ascertain into which specific time periods the sold assets were scheduled. Hence it uses a systematic and rational basis of allocation. Based on the fact that it sold a representative selection of the assets in the portfolio, Entity A allocates the sale proportionately over all time periods.
[Refer: paragraph AG128]

IE17   On this basis, Entity A computes that it has sold $8^1/_3$ per cent of the assets allocated to the three-month time period, ie CU8 million ($8^1/_3$ per cent of CU96 million). The proceeds received are CU8,018,400, equal to the fair value of the assets.[6] On derecognition of the assets, Entity A also removes from the separate line item in the statement of financial position an amount that represents the change in the fair value of the hedged assets that it has now sold. This is $8^1/_3$ per cent of the total line item balance of CU45,511, ie CU3,793.
[Refer: paragraph AG128]

IE18   Entity A makes the following accounting entries to recognise the sale of the asset and the removal of part of the balance in the separate line item in the statement of financial position:

---

6   The amount realised on sale of the asset is the fair value of a prepayable asset, which is less than the fair value of the equivalent non-prepayable asset shown in paragraph IE7.

Dr	Cash	CU8,018,400	
	Cr	Asset	CU8,000,000
	Cr	Separate line item in the statement of financial position	CU3,793
	Cr	Profit or loss (gain)	CU14,607

To recognise the sale of the asset at fair value and to recognise a gain on sale.

Because the change in the amount of the assets is not attributable to a change in the hedged interest rate no ineffectiveness arises.
[Refer: paragraphs 89A and AG128]

IE19 Entity A now has CU88 million of assets and CU80 million of liabilities in this time period. Hence the net amount Entity A wants to hedge is now CU8 million and, accordingly, it designates CU8 million as the hedged amount.
[Refer:

paragraphs 81A and AG127

Basis for Conclusions paragraph BC205]

IE20 Entity A decides to adjust the hedging instrument by designating only a proportion of the original swap as the hedging instrument. Accordingly, it designates as the hedging instrument CU8 million or 40 per cent of the notional amount of the original swap with a remaining life of two months and a fair value of CU18,963.[7] It also complies with the other designation requirements in paragraphs 88(a) and AG119 of the Standard. The CU12 million of the notional amount of the swap that is no longer designated as the hedging instrument is either classified as held for trading with changes in fair value recognised in profit or loss, or is designated as the hedging instrument in a different hedge.[8]
[Refer:

paragraphs 75 and AG127

Basis for Conclusions paragraph BC205]

IE21 As at 1 February 20X1 and after accounting for the sale of assets, the separate line item in the statement of financial position is CU41,718 (CU45,511 − CU3,793), which represents the cumulative change in fair value of CU17.6 million[9] of assets. However, as at 1 February 20X1, Entity A is hedging only CU8 million of assets that have a cumulative change in fair value of CU18,963.[10] The remaining separate line item in the statement of financial position of CU22,755[11] relates to an amount of assets that Entity A still holds

---

7 CU47,408 × 40 per cent

8 The entity could instead enter into an offsetting swap with a notional principal of CU12 million to adjust its position and designate as the hedging instrument all CU20 million of the existing swap and all CU12 million of the new offsetting swap. **[Refer: paragraph 77]**

9 CU19.2 million − (8$^1/_3$% × CU19.2 million)

10 CU41,718 × (CU8 million ÷ CU17.6 million)

11 CU41,718 − CU18,963

© IFRS Foundation

but is no longer hedging. Accordingly Entity A amortises this amount over the remaining life of the time period, ie it amortises CU22,755 over two months. **[Refer: paragraphs 91, 92 and AG131]**

IE22   Entity A determines that it is not practicable to use a method of amortisation based on a recalculated effective yield and hence uses a straight-line method. **[Refer: paragraph 92]**

End of month 2 (28 February 20X1)

IE23   On 28 February 20X1 when Entity A next tests effectiveness, LIBOR is unchanged. Entity A does not revise its prepayment expectations. The fair value of the designated interest rate swap with a notional principal of CU8 million is (CU9,518)[12] (the swap is a liability). Also, Entity A calculates the fair value of the CU8 million of the hedged assets as at 28 February 20X1 as CU8,009,518.[13]

IE24   Entity A makes the following accounting entries relating to the hedge in this time period:

Dr Cash	CU71,707	
Cr Profit or loss (interest income)		CU71,707

To recognise the interest received on the hedged amount (CU8 million).

Dr Profit or loss (interest expense)	CU71,707	
Cr Profit or loss (interest income)		CU62,115
Cr Cash		CU9,592

To recognise the interest received and paid on the portion of the swap designated as the hedging instrument (CU8 million).

Dr Derivative liability	CU9,445	
Cr Profit or loss (gain)		CU9,445

To recognise the change in the fair value of the portion of the swap designated as the hedging instrument (CU8 million) (CU9,518 – CU18,963). **[Refer: paragraphs 89(a) and AG114(h)]**

Dr Profit or loss (loss)	CU9,445	
Cr Separate line item in the statement of financial position		CU9,445

To recognise the change in the fair value of the hedged amount (CU8,009,518 – CU8,018,963). **[Refer: paragraphs 89(b), 89A and AG114(g)]**

---

12 CU23,795 [see paragraph IE8] × (CU8 million ÷ CU20 million)

13 CU20,023,795 [see paragraph IE7] × (CU8 million ÷ CU20 million)

IE25   The net effect on profit or loss (excluding interest income and interest expense) is nil reflecting that the hedge is fully effective.

IE26   Entity A makes the following accounting entry to amortise the line item balance for this time period:

Dr	Profit or loss (loss)	CU11,378
	Cr Separate line item in the statement of financial position	CU11,378[(a)]

To recognise the amortisation charge for the period. **[Refer: paragraphs 92 and AG131]**

(a) CU22,755 ÷ 2

End of month 3

IE27   During the third month there is no further change in the amount of assets or liabilities in the three-month time period. On 31 March 20X1 the assets and the swap mature and all balances are recognised in profit or loss.

IE28   Entity A makes the following accounting entries relating to this time period:

Dr	Cash	CU8,071,707
	Cr Asset (statement of financial position)	CU8,000,000
	Cr Profit or loss (interest income)	CU71,707

To recognise the interest and cash received on maturity of the hedged amount (CU8 million).

Dr	Profit or loss (interest expense)	CU71,707
	Cr Profit or loss (interest income)	CU62,115
	Cr Cash	CU9,592

To recognise the interest received and paid on the portion of the swap designated as the hedging instrument (CU8 million).

Dr	Derivative liability	CU9,518
	Cr Profit or loss (gain)	CU9,518

To recognise the expiry of the portion of the swap designated as the hedging instrument (CU8 million). **[Refer: paragraphs 89(a) and AG114(h)]**

Dr	Profit or loss (loss)	CU9,518
	Cr Separate line item in the statement of financial position	CU9,518

To remove the remaining line item balance on expiry of the time period.
[Refer: paragraphs 89(b), 89A, 91 and AG114(g)]

IE29   The net effect on profit or loss (excluding interest income and interest expense) is nil reflecting that the hedge is fully effective.

IE30   Entity A makes the following accounting entry to amortise the line item balance for this time period:

Dr   Profit or loss (loss)   CU11,377
      Cr   Separate line item in the statement of
            financial position   CU11,377[a]

To recognise the amortisation charge for the period. **[Refer: paragraphs 92 and AG131]**

(a) CU22,755 ÷ 2

Summary

IE31   The tables below summarise:

(a)   changes in the separate line item in the statement of financial position;

(b)   the fair value of the derivative;

(c)   the profit or loss effect of the hedge for the entire three-month period of the hedge; and

(d)   interest income and interest expense relating to the amount designated as hedged.

Description	1 Jan 20X1	31 Jan 20X1	1 Feb 20X1	28 Feb 20X1	31 Mar 20X1
	CU	CU	CU	CU	CU
Amount of asset hedged	20,000,000	19,200,000	8,000,000	8,000,000	8,000,000

(a) Changes in the separate line item in the statement of financial position

	1 Jan 20X1	31 Jan 20X1	1 Feb 20X1	28 Feb 20X1	31 Mar 20X1
Brought forward:					
Balance to be amortised	Nil	Nil	Nil	22,755	11,377
Remaining balance	Nil	Nil	45,511	18,963	9,518
Less: Adjustment on sale of asset	Nil	Nil	(3,793)	Nil	Nil
Adjustment for change in fair value of the hedged asset	Nil	45,511	Nil	(9,445)	(9,518)
Amortisation	Nil	Nil	Nil	(11,378)	(11,377)
Carried forward:					
Balance to be amortised	Nil	Nil	22,755	11,377	Nil
Remaining balance	Nil	45,511	18,963	9,518	Nil

(b) The fair value of the derivative

	1 Jan 20X1	31 Jan 20X1	1 Feb 20X1	28 Feb 20X1	31 Mar 20X1
CU20,000,000	Nil	47,408	—	—	—
CU12,000,000	Nil	—	28,445	No longer designated as the hedging instrument.	
CU8,000,000	Nil	—	18,963	9,518	Nil
Total	Nil	47,408	47,408	9,518	Nil

continued...

...continued

(c) Profit or loss effect of the hedge

	1 Jan 20X1	31 Jan 20X1	1 Feb 20X1	28 Feb 20X1	31 Mar 20X1
Change in line item: asset	Nil	45,511	N/A	(9,445)	(9,518)
Change in derivative fair value	Nil	(47,408)	N/A	9,445	9,518
Net effect	**Nil**	**(1,897)**	**N/A**	**Nil**	**Nil**
Amortisation	**Nil**	**Nil**	**N/A**	**(11,378)**	**(11,377)**

In addition, there is a gain on sale of assets of CU14,607 at 1 February 20X1.

(d) Interest income and interest expense relating to the amount designated as hedged

Profit or loss recognised for the amount hedged	1 Jan 20X1	31 Jan 20X1	1 Feb 20X1	28 Feb 20X1	31 Mar 20X1
Interest income					
– on the asset	Nil	172,097	N/A	71,707	71,707
– on the swap	Nil	179,268	N/A	62,115	62,115
Interest expense					
– on the swap	Nil	(179,268)	N/A	(71,707)	(71,707)

Guidance on implementing
IAS 39 *Financial Instruments: Recognition and Measurement*

This guidance accompanies, but is not part of, IAS 39.

Sections A–G

[Deleted]

IASB documents published to accompany

IAS 41

Agriculture

The text of the unaccompanied standard, IAS 41, is contained in Part A of this edition. Its effective date when issued was 1 January 2003. The text of the Basis for Conclusions on IAS 41 is contained in Part C of this edition. This part presents the following document:

ILLUSTRATIVE EXAMPLES

Illustrative Examples

These examples, which were prepared by the IASC staff but were not approved by the IASC Board, accompany, but are not part of, IAS 41. They have been updated to take account of the changes made by IAS 1 Presentation of Financial Statements *(as revised in 2007) and* Improvements to IFRSs *issued in 2008.*

A1   Example 1 illustrates how the disclosure requirements of this Standard might be put into practice for a dairy farming entity. This Standard encourages the separation of the change in fair value less costs to sell of an entity's biological assets into physical change and price change. That separation is reflected in Example 1. Example 2 illustrates how to separate physical change and price change.

A2   The financial statements in Example 1 do not conform to all of the disclosure and presentation requirements of other Standards. Other approaches to presentation and disclosure may also be appropriate.

Example 1 XYZ Dairy Ltd

Statement of financial position

XYZ Dairy Ltd Statement of financial position	Notes	31 December 20X1	31 December 20X0
ASSETS			
Non-current assets [Refer: IAS 1 paragraphs 60–68]			
Dairy livestock – immature[a] **[Refer: paragraphs 41–45]**		52,060	47,730
Dairy livestock – mature[a] **[Refer: paragraphs 41–45]**		372,990	411,840
Subtotal – biological assets **[Refer: IAS 1 paragraph 54(f)]**	3	425,050	459,570
Property, plant and equipment **[Refer: IAS 1 paragraph 54(a)]**		1,462,650	1,409,800
Total non-current assets		**1,887,700**	**1,869,370**
Current assets [Refer: IAS 1 paragraphs 66–68]			
Inventories **[Refer: IAS 1 paragraph 54(g)]**		82,950	70,650
Trade and other receivables **[Refer: IAS 1 paragraph 54(h)]**		88,000	65,000
Cash **[Refer: IAS 1 paragraph 54(i)]**		10,000	10,000
Total current assets		**180,950**	**145,650**
Total assets		**2,068,650**	**2,015,020**

continued...

...*continued*

XYZ Dairy Ltd Statement of financial position	Notes	31 December 20X1	31 December 20X0
EQUITY AND LIABILITIES			
Equity			
Issued capital		1,000,000	1,000,000
Retained earnings		902,828	865,000
Total equity		**1,902,828**	**1,865,000**
Current liabilities [Refer: IAS 1 paragraphs 69–76]			
Trade and other payables [Refer: IAS 1 paragraph 54(k)]		165,822	150,020
Total current liabilities		**165,822**	**150,020**
Total equity and liabilities		**2,068,650**	**2,015,020**

(a) An entity is encouraged, but not required, to provide a quantified description of each group of biological assets, distinguishing between consumable and bearer biological assets or between mature and immature biological assets, as appropriate. An entity discloses the basis for making any such distinctions.

Statement of comprehensive income[1]

XYZ Dairy Ltd Statement of comprehensive income	Notes	Year ended 31 December 20X1
Fair value of milk produced [Refer: paragraph 40]		518,240
Gains arising from changes in fair value less costs to sell of dairy livestock [Refer: paragraph 40]	3	39,930
		558,170
Inventories used		(137,523)
Staff costs		(127,283)
Depreciation expense		(15,250)
Other operating expenses		(197,092)
		(477,148)
Profit from operations		**81,022**
Income tax expense [Refer: IAS 1 paragraph 82(d)]		(43,194)
Profit/comprehensive income for the year [Refer: IAS 1 paragraph 82(f)]		**37,828**

Statement of changes in equity

XYZ Dairy Ltd Statement of changes in equity			Year ended 31 December 20X1

	Share capital	Retained earnings	Total
Balance at 1 January 20X1	1,000,000	865,000	**1,865,000**
	[Refer: IAS 1 paragraph 106(d)]	[Refer: IAS 1 paragraph 106(d)]	
Profit/comprehensive income for the year [Refer: IAS 1 paragraph 106(a)]		37,828	**37,828**
		[Refer: IAS 1 paragraph 106(d)]	
Balance at 31 December 20X1	**1,000,000**	**902,828**	
	[Refer: IAS 1 paragraph 106(d)]	[Refer: IAS 1 paragraph 106(d)]	**1,902,828**

1 This statement of comprehensive income presents an analysis of expenses using a classification based on the nature of expenses. IAS 1 *Presentation of Financial Statements* requires that an entity present, either in the statement of comprehensive income or in the notes, an analysis of expenses using a classification based on either the nature of expenses or their function within the entity. IAS 1 encourages presentation of an analysis of expenses in the statement of comprehensive income.

Statement of cash flows[2]

XYZ Dairy Ltd Statement of cash flows	Notes	Year ended 31 December 20X1
Cash flows from operating activities [Refer: IAS 7 paragraph 10]		
Cash receipts from sales of milk [Refer: IAS 7 paragraph 14]		498,027
Cash receipts from sales of livestock [Refer: IAS 7 paragraph 14]		97,913
Cash paid for supplies and to employees [Refer: IAS 7 paragraph 14]		(460,831)
Cash paid for purchases of livestock [Refer: IAS 7 paragraph 14]		(23,815)
		111,294
Income taxes paid [Refer: IAS 7 paragraphs 35 and 36]		(43,194)
Net cash from operating activities		68,100
Cash flows from investing activities [Refer: IAS 7 paragraph 10]		
Purchase of property, plant and equipment [Refer: IAS 7 paragraph 21]		(68,100)
Net cash used in investing activities		**(68,100)**
Net increase in cash		0
Cash at beginning of the year		10,000
Cash at end of the year		10,000

---

2   This statement of cash flows reports cash flows from operating activities using the direct method. IAS 7 *Statement of Cash Flows* requires that an entity report cash flows from operating activities using either the direct method or the indirect method. IAS 7 encourages use of the direct method.

Notes

1	**Operations and principal activities**

XYZ Dairy Ltd ('the Company') is engaged in milk production for supply to various customers. **[Refer: paragraph 46(a)]** At 31 December 20X1, the Company held 419 cows **[Refer: paragraph 46(b)(i)]** able to produce milk (mature assets) and 137 heifers **[Refer: paragraph 46(b)(i)]** being raised to produce milk in the future (immature assets). The Company produced 157,584kg of milk **[Refer: paragraph 46(b)(ii)]** with a fair value **[Refer: paragraph 8]** less costs to sell **[Refer: paragraph 5]** of 518,240 **[Refer: paragraph 48]** (at the time of milking) in the year ended 31 December 20X1.
[Refer: paragraphs 41–45]

2	**Accounting policies**

Livestock and milk

Livestock are measured at their fair value **[Refer: paragraph 8 (definition of fair value)]** less costs to sell **[Refer: paragraph 5 (definition of costs to sell)]**. The fair value of livestock is based on quoted prices of livestock of similar age, breed, and genetic merit in the principal (or most advantageous) market for the livestock. Milk is initially measured at its fair value less costs to sell at the time of milking. The fair value of milk is based on quoted prices in the local area in the principal (or most advantageous) market for the milk.
[Refer: paragraph 47]

3	**Biological assets**

Reconciliation of carrying amounts of dairy livestock	20X1
Carrying amount at 1 January 20X1 [Refer: paragraph 50]	459,570
Increases due to purchases [Refer: paragraph 50(b)]	26,250
Gain arising from changes in fair value less costs to sell attributable to physical changes[(a)] [Refer: paragraphs 50(a), 51 and 52]	15,350
Gain arising from changes in fair value less costs to sell attributable to price changes[(a)] [Refer: paragraphs 50(a) and 51]	24,580
Decreases due to sales [Refer: paragraph 50(c)]	(100,700)
Carrying amount at 31 December 20X1 [Refer: paragraph 50]	**425,050**

(a) Separating the increase in fair value less costs to sell between the portion attributable to physical changes and the portion attributable to price changes is encouraged but not required by this Standard.

4	**Financial risk management strategies**

The Company is exposed to financial risks arising from changes in milk prices. The Company does not anticipate that milk prices will decline significantly in the foreseeable future and, therefore, has not entered into derivative or other contracts to manage the risk of a decline in milk prices. The Company reviews its outlook for milk prices regularly in considering the need for active financial risk management.

[Refer: paragraph 49(c)]

Example 2 Physical change and price change

[Refer: paragraphs 50(a), 51 and 52]

The following example illustrates how to separate physical change and price change. Separating the change in fair value [Refer: paragraph 8 (definition of fair value)] less costs to sell [Refer: paragraph 5 (definition of costs to sell)] between the portion attributable to physical changes and the portion attributable to price changes is encouraged but not required by this Standard.

A herd of 10 2 year old animals was held at 1 January 20X1. One animal aged 2.5 years was purchased on 1 July 20X1 for 108, and one animal was born on 1 July 20X1. No animals were sold or disposed of during the period. Per-unit fair values less costs to sell were as follows:

2 year old animal at 1 January 20X1	100
Newborn animal at 1 July 20X1	70
2.5 year old animal at 1 July 20X1	108
Newborn animal at 31 December 20X1	72
0.5 year old animal at 31 December 20X1	80
2 year old animal at 31 December 20X1	105
2.5 year old animal at 31 December 20X1	111
3 year old animal at 31 December 20X1	120

Fair value [Refer: paragraph 8 (definition of fair value)] less costs to sell [Refer: paragraph 5 (definition of costs to sell)] of herd at 1 January 20X1 (10 × 100)		1,000
Purchase on 1 July 20X1 (1 × 108)		108
Increase in fair value less costs to sell due to price change:		
10 × (105 – 100)	50	
1 × (111 – 108)	3	
1 × (72 – 70)	2	55

continued...

...continued

Increase in fair value less costs to sell due to physical change:
[Refer: paragraph 52]

10 × (120 − 105)	150	
1 × (120 − 111)	9	
1 × (80 − 72)	8	
1 × 70	70	237

Fair value less costs to sell of herd at 31 December 20X1

11 × 120	1,320	
1 × 80	80	1,400

Documents published to accompany

IFRIC 1

Changes in Existing Decommissioning, Restoration and Similar Liabilities

The text of the unaccompanied Interpretation, IFRIC 1, is contained in Part A of this edition. Its effective date when issued was 1 September 2004. The text of the Basis for Conclusions on IFRIC 1 is contained in Part C of this edition. This part presents the following documents:

ILLUSTRATIVE EXAMPLES

Example 1: Cost model

Example 2: Revaluation model

Example 3: Transition

IFRIC Interpretation 1
Illustrative Examples

These examples accompany, but are not part of, IFRIC 1.

Common facts

IE1   An entity has a nuclear power plant and a related decommissioning liability. The nuclear power plant started operating on 1 January 2000. The plant has a useful life of 40 years. Its initial cost was CU120,000;[1] this included an amount for decommissioning costs of CU10,000, which represented CU70,400 in estimated cash flows payable in 40 years discounted at a risk-adjusted rate of 5 per cent. The entity's financial year ends on 31 December.

Example 1: Cost model

IE2   On 31 December 2009, the plant is 10 years old. Accumulated depreciation is CU30,000 (CU120,000 × $^{10}/_{40}$ years). Because of the unwinding of discount (5 per cent) over the 10 years, the decommissioning liability has grown from CU10,000 to CU16,300.

IE3   On 31 December 2009, the discount rate has not changed. However, the entity estimates that, as a result of technological advances, the net present value of the decommissioning liability has decreased by CU8,000. Accordingly, the entity adjusts the decommissioning liability from CU16,300 to CU8,300. On this date, the entity makes the following journal entry to reflect the change:

	CU	CU
Dr decommissioning liability	8,000	
Cr cost of asset		8,000

[Refer: paragraphs 4 and 5]

IE4   Following this adjustment, the carrying amount of the asset is CU82,000 (CU120,000 − CU8,000 − CU30,000), which will be depreciated over the remaining 30 years of the asset's life giving a depreciation expense for the next year of CU2,733 (CU82,000 ÷ 30). The next year's finance cost for the unwinding of the discount will be CU415 (CU8,300 × 5 per cent).
[Refer: paragraphs 7 and 8]

IE5   If the change in the liability had resulted from a change in the discount rate, instead of a change in the estimated cash flows, the accounting for the change would have been the same but the next year's finance cost would have reflected the new discount rate.
[Refer: paragraphs 4, 5, 7 and 8]

---

1   In these examples, monetary amounts are denominated in 'currency units (CU)'.

Example 2: Revaluation model

IE6   The entity adopts the revaluation model in IAS 16 whereby the plant is revalued with sufficient regularity that the carrying amount does not differ materially from fair value. The entity's policy is to eliminate accumulated depreciation at the revaluation date against the gross carrying amount of the asset.

    [Refer: IAS 16 paragraphs 31–42]

IE7   When accounting for revalued assets to which decommissioning liabilities attach, it is important to understand the basis of the valuation obtained. For example:

      (a)   if an asset is valued on a discounted cash flow basis, some valuers may value the asset without deducting any allowance for decommissioning costs (a 'gross' valuation), whereas others may value the asset after deducting an allowance for decommissioning costs (a 'net' valuation), because an entity acquiring the asset will generally also assume the decommissioning obligation. For financial reporting purposes, the decommissioning obligation is recognised as a separate liability, and is not deducted from the asset. Accordingly, if the asset is valued on a net basis, it is necessary to adjust the valuation obtained by adding back the allowance for the liability, so that the liability is not counted twice.[2]

      (b)   if an asset is valued on a depreciated replacement cost basis, the valuation obtained may not include an amount for the decommissioning component of the asset. If it does not, an appropriate amount will need to be added to the valuation to reflect the depreciated replacement cost of that component.

IE8   Assume that a market-based discounted cash flow valuation of CU115,000 is obtained at 31 December 2002. It includes an allowance of CU11,600 for decommissioning costs, which represents no change to the original estimate, after the unwinding of three years' discount. The amounts included in the statement of financial position at 31 December 2002 are therefore:

	CU
Asset at valuation (1) **[Refer: IAS 16 paragraph 31]**	126,600
Accumulated depreciation **[Refer: IAS 16 paragraph 35(b)]**	nil
Decommissioning liability **[Refer: IAS 37 paragraph 60]**	(11,600)
Net assets	115,000
Retained earnings (2)	(10,600)
Revaluation surplus (3)	15,600

continued...

---

2   For examples of this principle, see IAS 36 *Impairment of Assets* and IAS 40 *Investment Property*.

...continued

Notes:

1   Valuation obtained of CU115,000 plus decommissioning costs of CU11,600, allowed for in the valuation but recognised as a separate liability = CU126,600. **[Refer: Illustrative Examples paragraph IE7(a)]**

2   Three years' depreciation on original cost CU120,000 × $^3/_{40}$ = CU9,000 **[Refer: IAS 16 paragraph 31]** plus cumulative discount on CU10,000 at 5 per cent compound = CU1,600; **[Refer: IAS 37 paragraph 60]** total CU10,600.

3   Revalued amount CU126,600 less previous net book value of CU111,000 (cost CU120,000 less accumulated depreciation CU9,000). **[Refer: IAS 16 paragraph 39]**

IE9   The depreciation expense for 2003 is therefore CU3,420 (CU126,600 × $^1/_{37}$) and the discount expense for 2003 is CU600 (5 per cent of CU11,600). **[Refer: paragraphs 7 and 8]** On 31 December 2003, the decommissioning liability (before any adjustment) is CU12,200 and the discount rate has not changed. However, on that date, the entity estimates that, as a result of technological advances, the present value of the decommissioning liability has decreased by CU5,000. Accordingly, the entity adjusts the decommissioning liability from CU12,200 to CU7,200. **[Refer: IAS 37 paragraph 60]**

IE10   The whole of this adjustment is taken to revaluation surplus, because it does not exceed the carrying amount that would have been recognised had the asset been carried under the cost model. **[Refer: paragraph 6(a)(i)]** If it had done, the excess would have been taken to profit or loss in accordance with paragraph 6(b). The entity makes the following journal entry to reflect the change:

	CU	CU
Dr decommissioning liability	5,000	
Cr revaluation surplus		5,000

IE11   The entity decides that a full valuation of the asset is needed at 31 December 2003, in order to ensure that the carrying amount does not differ materially from fair value. **[Refer: paragraph 6(c)]** Suppose that the asset is now valued at CU107,000, which is net of an allowance of CU7,200 for the reduced decommissioning obligation that should be recognised as a separate liability. The valuation of the asset for financial reporting purposes, before deducting this allowance, is therefore CU114,200. The following additional journal entry is needed:

	CU	CU
Dr accumulated depreciation (1)	3,420	
Cr asset at valuation		3,420
Dr revaluation surplus (2)	8,980	
Cr asset at valuation (3)		8,980

Notes:

1   Eliminating accumulated depreciation of CU3,420 in accordance with the entity's accounting policy. **[Refer: IAS 16 paragraph 35(b)]**

2   The debit is to revaluation surplus because the deficit arising on the revaluation does not exceed the credit balance existing in the revaluation surplus in respect of the asset. **[Refer: IAS 16 paragraph 40]**

3   Previous valuation (before allowance for decommissioning costs) CU126,600, less cumulative depreciation CU3,420, less new valuation (before allowance for decommissioning costs) CU114,200. **[Refer: IAS 16 paragraph 31]**

IE12   Following this valuation, the amounts included in the statement of financial position are:

	CU
Asset at valuation	114,200
Accumulated depreciation	nil
Decommissioning liability	(7,200)
Net assets	107,000
Retained earnings (1)	(14,620)
Revaluation surplus (2)	11,620

Notes:

1   CU10,600 at 31 December 2002 plus 2003's depreciation expense of CU3,420 and discount expense of CU600 = CU14,620. **[Refer: paragraphs 7 and 8]**

2   CU15,600 at 31 December 2002, plus CU5,000 arising on the decrease in the liability, **[Refer: paragraph 6(a)]** less CU8,980 deficit on revaluation **[Refer: IAS 16 paragraph 40]** = CU11,620.

Example 3: Transition
[Refer: paragraph 10]

IE13 The following example illustrates retrospective application of the Interpretation for preparers that already apply IFRSs. Retrospective application is required by IAS 8 *Accounting Policies, Changes in Accounting Estimates and Errors*, where practicable, [Refer: IAS 8 paragraphs 19–27 and 50–53] and is the benchmark treatment in the previous version of IAS 8. The example assumes that the entity:

(a) adopted IAS 37 on 1 July 1999;

(b) adopts the Interpretation on 1 January 2005; and

(c) before the adoption of the Interpretation, recognised changes in estimated cash flows to settle decommissioning liabilities as income or expense.

IE14 On 31 December 2000, because of the unwinding of the discount (5 per cent) for one year, the decommissioning liability has grown from CU10,000 to CU10,500. In addition, based on recent facts, the entity estimates that the present value of the decommissioning liability has increased by CU1,500 and accordingly adjusts it from CU10,500 to CU12,000. In accordance with its then policy, the increase in the liability is recognised in profit or loss.

IE15 On 1 January 2005, the entity makes the following journal entry to reflect the adoption of the Interpretation:

	CU	CU
Dr cost of asset	1,500	
Cr accumulated depreciation		154
Cr opening retained earnings		1,346

IE16 The cost of the asset is adjusted to what it would have been if the increase in the estimated amount of decommissioning costs at 31 December 2000 had been capitalised on that date. This additional cost would have been depreciated over 39 years. Hence, accumulated depreciation on that amount at 31 December 2004 would be CU154 (CU1,500 × $^4/_{39}$ years).

IE17 Because, before adopting the Interpretation on 1 January 2005, the entity recognised changes in the decommissioning liability in profit or loss, the net adjustment of CU1,346 is recognised as a credit to opening retained earnings. This credit is not required to be disclosed in the financial statements, because of the restatement described below.

IE18 IAS 8 requires the comparative financial statements to be restated [Refer: IAS 8 paragraphs 19 and 22] and the adjustment to opening retained earnings at the start of the comparative period to be disclosed. [Refer: IAS 8 paragraph 28] The equivalent journal entries at 1 January 2004 are shown below. In addition, depreciation expense for the year ended 31 December 2004 is increased by CU39 from the amount previously reported:

		CU	CU
Dr	cost of asset	1,500	
	Cr accumulated depreciation		115
	Cr opening retained earnings		1,385

Documents published to accompany

IFRIC 7

Applying the Restatement Approach under IAS 29 Financial Reporting in Hyperinflationary Economies

The text of the unaccompanied Interpretation, IFRIC 7, is contained in Part A of this edition. Its effective date when issued was 1 March 2006. The text of the Basis for Conclusions on IFRIC 7 is contained in Part C of this edition. This part presents the following document:

ILLUSTRATIVE EXAMPLE

IFRIC Interpretation 7
Illustrative Examples

This example accompanies, but is not part of, IFRIC 7.

IE1   This example illustrates the restatement of deferred tax items when an entity restates for the effects of inflation under IAS 29 *Financial Reporting in Hyperinflationary Economies*. As the example is intended only to illustrate the mechanics of the restatement approach in IAS 29 for deferred tax items, it does not illustrate an entity's complete IFRS financial statements.

Facts

IE2   An entity's IFRS statement of financial position at 31 December 20X4 (before restatement) is as follows:

Note	Statement of financial position	20X4[a]	20X3
		CU million	CU million
	ASSETS		
1	Property, plant and equipment	300	400
	Other assets	XXX	XXX
	Total assets	XXX	XXX
	EQUITY AND LIABILITIES		
	Total equity	XXX	XXX
	Liabilities		
2	Deferred tax liability	30	20
	Other liabilities	XXX	XXX
	Total liabilities	XXX	XXX
	Total equity and liabilities	XXX	XXX

(a) In this example, monetary amounts are denominated in 'currency units (CU)'.

> **Notes**
>
> *Property, plant and equipment*
>
> All items of property, plant and equipment were acquired in December 20X2. Property, plant and equipment are depreciated over their useful life, which is five years.
>
> *Deferred tax liability*
>
> The deferred tax liability at 31 December 20X4 of CU30 million is measured as the taxable temporary difference between the carrying amount of property, plant and equipment of 300 and their tax base of 200. The applicable tax rate is 30 per cent. Similarly, the deferred tax liability at 31 December 20X3 of CU20 million is measured as the taxable temporary difference between the carrying amount of property, plant and equipment of CU400 and their tax base of CU333.

IE3   Assume that the entity identifies the existence of hyperinflation [Refer: IAS 29 paragraphs 2 and 3] in, for example, April 20X4 and therefore applies IAS 29 from the beginning of 20X4. The entity restates its financial statements on the basis of the following general price indices and conversion factors:

	General price indices	Conversion factors at 31 Dec 20X4
December 20X2(a)	95	2.347
December 20X3	135	1.652
December 20X4	223	1.000

(a)   For example, the conversion factor for December 20X2 is 2.347 = 223/95.

Restatement

IE4   The restatement of the entity's 20X4 financial statements is based on the following requirements:

- Property, plant and equipment are restated by applying the change in a general price index from the date of acquisition to the end of the reporting period to their historical cost and accumulated depreciation.

- Deferred taxes should be accounted for in accordance with IAS 12 *Income Taxes*.

- Comparative figures for property, plant and equipment for the previous reporting period are presented in terms of the measuring unit current at the end of the reporting period.

- Comparative deferred tax figures should be measured in accordance with paragraph 4 of the Interpretation.

IE5   Therefore the entity restates its statement of financial position at
31 December 20X4 as follows:

Note	Statement of financial position (restated)	20X4	20X3
		CU million	CU million
	ASSETS		
1	Property, plant and equipment	704	939
	Other assets	XXX	XXX
	Total assets	XXX	XXX
	EQUITY AND LIABILITIES		
	Total equity	XXX	XXX
	Liabilities		
2	Deferred tax liability	151	117
	Other liabilities	XXX	XXX
	Total liabilities	XXX	XXX
	Total equity and liabilities	XXX	XXX

Notes

1   *Property, plant and equipment*

All items of property, plant and equipment were purchased in
December 20X2 and depreciated over a five-year period. The cost of
property, plant and equipment is restated to reflect the change in
the general price level since acquisition, ie the conversion factor is
2.347 (223/95).

	Historical CU million	Restated CU million
Cost of property, plant and equipment	500	1,174
Depreciation 20X3	(100)	(235)
Carrying amount 31 December 20X3	400	939
Depreciation 20X4	(100)	(235)
Carrying amount 31 December 20X4	300	704

continued...

...continued

2   *Deferred tax liability*

The nominal deferred tax liability at 31 December 20X4 of CU30 million is measured as the taxable temporary difference between the carrying amount of property, plant and equipment of CU300 and their tax base of CU200. Similarly, the deferred tax liability at 31 December 20X3 of CU20 million is measured as the taxable temporary difference between the carrying amount of property, plant and equipment of CU400 and their tax base of CU333. The applicable tax rate is 30 per cent.

In its restated financial statements, at the end of the reporting period the entity remeasures deferred tax items in accordance with the general provisions in IAS 12, ie on the basis of its restated financial statements. However, because deferred tax items are a function of carrying amounts of assets or liabilities and their tax bases, an entity cannot restate its comparative deferred tax items by applying a general price index. Instead, in the reporting period in which an entity applies the restatement approach under IAS 29, it (a) remeasures its comparative deferred tax items in accordance with IAS 12 after it has restated the nominal carrying amounts of its non-monetary items **[Refer: IAS 29 paragraphs 12–14]** at the date of the opening statement of financial position of the current reporting period by applying the measuring unit at that date, and (b) restates the remeasured deferred tax items for the change in the measuring unit from the date of the opening statement of financial position of the current period up to the end of the reporting period.

In the example, the restated deferred tax liability is calculated as follows:

	CU million
At the end of the reporting period:	
Restated carrying amount of property, plant and equipment (see note 1)	704
Tax base	(200)
Temporary difference	504
@ 30 per cent tax rate = Restated deferred tax liability 31 December 20X4	151

continued...

...continued

Comparative deferred tax figures:	
Restated carrying amount of property, plant and equipment [either 400 × 1.421 (conversion factor 1.421 = 135/95), or 939/1.652 (conversion factor 1.652 = 223/135)]	568
Tax base	(333)
Temporary difference	235
@ 30 per cent tax rate = Restated deferred tax liability 31 December 20X3 at the general price level at the end of 20X3	71
Restated deferred tax liability 31 December 20X3 at the general price level at the end of 20X4 (conversion factor 1.652 = 223/135)	117

IE6   In this example, the restated deferred tax liability is increased by CU34 to CU151 from 31 December 20X3 to 31 December 20X4. That increase, which is included in profit or loss in 20X4, reflects (a) the effect of a change in the taxable temporary difference of property, plant and equipment, and (b) a loss of purchasing power on the tax base of property, plant and equipment. The two components can be analysed as follows:

	CU million
Effect on deferred tax liability because of a decrease in the taxable temporary difference of property, plant and equipment ((CU235) + CU133) × 30%	31
Loss on tax base because of inflation in 20X4 (CU333 × 1.652 − CU333) × 30%	(65)
Net increase of deferred tax liability	(34)
Debit to profit or loss in 20X4	34

The loss on tax base is a monetary loss. Paragraph 28 of IAS 29 explains this as follows:

> The gain or loss on the net monetary position is included in net income. The adjustment to those assets and liabilities linked by agreement to changes in prices made in accordance with paragraph 13 is offset against the gain or loss on net monetary position. Other income and expense items, such as interest income and expense, and foreign exchange differences related to invested or borrowed funds, are also associated with the net monetary position. Although such items are separately disclosed, it may be helpful if they are presented together with

the gain or loss on net monetary position in the statement of comprehensive income.

Documents published to accompany

IFRIC 12

Service Concession Arrangements

The text of the unaccompanied Interpretation, IFRIC 12, is contained in Part A of this edition. Its effective date when issued was 1 January 2008. The text of the Basis for Conclusions on IFRIC 12 is contained in Part C of this edition. This part presents the following documents:

INFORMATION NOTES

1 Accounting framework for public-to-private service arrangements

2 References to IFRSs that apply to typical types of public-to-private arrangements

ILLUSTRATIVE EXAMPLES

Information note 1

Accounting framework for public-to-private service arrangements

This note accompanies, but is not part of, IFRIC 12.

The diagram below summarises the accounting for service arrangements established by IFRIC 12.

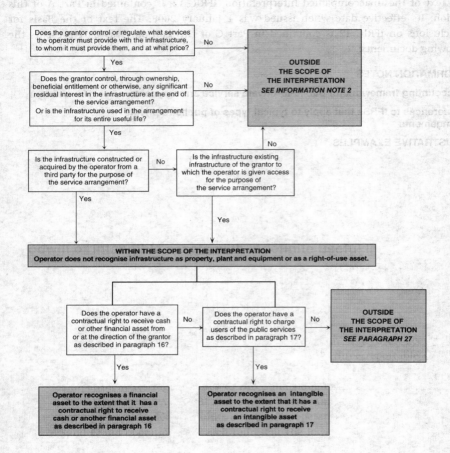

© IFRS Foundation

Information note 2

References to IFRSs that apply to typical types of public-to-private arrangements

This note accompanies, but is not part of, IFRIC 12.

The table sets out the typical types of arrangements for private sector participation in the provision of public sector services and provides references to IFRSs that apply to those arrangements. The list of arrangements types is not exhaustive. The purpose of the table is to highlight the continuum of arrangements. It is not the IFRIC's intention to convey the impression that bright lines exist between the accounting requirements for public-to-private arrangements.

Category	Lessee	Service provider			Owner	
Typical arrangement types	Lease (eg Operator leases assets from grantor)	Service and/or maintenance contract (specific tasks eg debt collection)	Rehabilitate-operate-transfer	Build-operate-transfer	Build-own-operate	100% Divestment/ Privatisation/ Corporation
Asset ownership	Grantor				Operator	
Capital investment	Grantor		Operator			
Demand risk	Shared	Grantor	Operator and/or Grantor		Operator	
Typical duration	8–20 years	1–5 years	25–30 years			Indefinite (or may be limited by licence)
Residual interest	Grantor				Operator	
Relevant IFRSs	IFRS 16	IFRS 15	IFRIC 12		IAS 16	

Illustrative Examples

These examples accompany, but are not part of, IFRIC 12.

Example 1: The grantor gives the operator a financial asset

Arrangement terms

IE1 The terms of the arrangement require an operator to construct a road—completing construction within two years—and maintain and operate the road to a specified standard for eight years (ie years 3–10). The terms of the arrangement also require the operator to resurface the road at the end of year 8. At the end of year 10, the arrangement will end. Assume that the operator identifies three performance obligations for construction services, operation services and road resurfacing. The operator estimates that the costs it will incur to fulfil its obligations will be:

Table 1.1 *Contract costs*

	Year	CU[(a)]
Construction services	1	500
	2	500
Operation services (per year)	3–10	10
Road resurfacing	8	100
(a) in this example, monetary amounts are denominated in 'currency units (CU)'.		

IE2 The terms of the arrangement require the grantor to pay the operator 200 currency units (CU200) per year in years 3–10 for making the road available to the public.

IE3 For the purpose of this illustration, it is assumed that all cash flows take place at the end of the year.

Revenue

IE4 The operator recognises revenue in accordance with IFRS 15 *Revenue from Contracts with Customers*. Revenue—the amount of consideration to which the operator expects to be entitled from the grantor for the services provided—is recognised when (or as) the performance obligations are satisfied. **[Refer: IFRS 15 paragraph 31]** Under the terms of the arrangement the operator is obliged to resurface the road at the end of year 8. In year 8 the operator will be reimbursed by the grantor for resurfacing the road.

IE5   The total expected consideration (CU200 in each of years 3–10) is allocated to the performance obligations based on the relative stand-alone selling prices **[Refer: IFRS 15 paragraph 74]** of the construction services, operation services and road resurfacing, taking into account the significant financing component, as follows:

Table 1.2 *Transaction price allocated to each performance obligation*

	Transaction price allocation (including effect of the significant financing component)
	CU
Construction services (over two years)[a]	1,050
Operation services (over 8 years)[b]	96
Road resurfacing services (in year 8)[c]	110
Total	1,256
Implied interest rate[d]	6.18% per year

(a) The operator estimates the relative stand-alone selling price by reference to the forecast cost plus 5 per cent.

(b) The operator estimates the relative stand-alone selling price by reference to the forecast cost plus 20 per cent.

(c) The operator estimates the relative stand-alone selling price by reference to the forecast cost plus 10 per cent.

(d) The implied interest rate is assumed to be the rate that would be reflected in a financing transaction between the operator and the grantor.

IE6   In year 1, for example, construction costs of CU500, construction revenue of CU525, and hence construction profit of CU25 are recognised in profit or loss.

[Refer: paragraphs 13 and 14]

Financial asset
[Refer: paragraphs 23–25]

IE7   During the first two years, the entity recognises a contract asset and accounts for the significant financing component in the arrangement in accordance with IFRS 15. Once the construction is complete, the amounts due from the grantor are accounted for in accordance with IFRS 9 *Financial Instruments* as receivables.

IE8   If the cash flows and fair values remain the same as those forecast, the effective interest rate is 6.18 per cent per year [Refer: IFRS 9 Appendix A (definition of effective interest rate)] and the receivable recognised at the end of years 1–3 will be:

Table 1.3 *Measurement of contract asset/receivable*

	CU
Amount due for construction in year 1	525
Contract asset at end of year 1[a]	**525**
Effective interest in year 2 on contract asset at the end of year 1 (6.18% × CU525)	32
Amount due for construction in year 2	525
Receivable at end of year 2	**1,082**
Effective interest in year 3 on receivable at the end of year 2 (6.18% × CU1,082)	67
Amount due for operation in year 3 (CU10 x (1 + 20%))	12
Cash receipts in year 3	(200)
Receivable at end of year 3	**961**

(a) No effective interest arises in year 1 because the cash flows are assumed to take place at the end of the year.

Overview of cash flows, statement of comprehensive income and statement of financial position

IE9   For the purpose of this illustration, it is assumed that the operator finances the arrangement wholly with debt and retained profits. It pays interest at 6.7 per cent per year on outstanding debt. If the cash flows and fair values remain the same as those forecast, the operator's cash flows, statement of comprehensive income and statement of financial position over the duration of the arrangement will be:

Table 1.4 *Cash flows (currency units)*

Year	1	2	3	4	5	6	7	8	9	10	Total
Receipts	-	-	200	200	200	200	200	200	200	200	1,600
Contract costs[a]	(500)	(500)	(10)	(10)	(10)	(10)	(10)	(110)	(10)	(10)	(1,180)
Borrowing costs[b]	-	(34)	(69)	(61)	(53)	(43)	(33)	(23)	(19)	(7)	(342)
Net inflow/(outflow)	(500)	(534)	121	129	137	147	157	67	171	183	78

(a) Table 1.1
(b) Debt at start of year (table 1.6) x 6.7%

Table 1.5 *Statement of comprehensive income (currency units)*

Year	1	2	3	4	5	6	7	8	9	10	Total
Revenue	525	525	12	12	12	12	12	122	12	12	1,256
Contract costs	(500)	(500)	(10)	(10)	(10)	(10)	(10)	(110)	(10)	(10)	(1,180)
Finance income(a)	-	32	67	59	51	43	34	25	22	11	344
Borrowing costs(b)	-	(34)	(69)	(61)	(53)	(43)	(33)	(23)	(19)	(7)	(342)
Net profit	25	23	-	-	-	2	3	14	5	6	78

(a) Amount due from grantor at start of year (table 1.6) × 6.18%
(b) Cash/(debt) (table 1.6) × 6.7%

Table 1.6 *Statement of financial position (currency units)*

End of year	1	2	3	4	5	6	7	8	9	10
Amount due from grantor(a)	525	1,082	961	832	695	550	396	343	177	-
Cash/(debt)(b)	(500)	(1,034)	(913)	(784)	(647)	(500)	(343)	(276)	(105)	78
Net assets	25	48	48	48	48	50	53	67	72	78

(a) Amount due from grantor at start of year, plus revenue and finance income earned in year (table 1.5), less receipts in year (table 1.4).
(b) Debt at start of year plus net cash flow in year (table 1.4).

IE10 This example deals with only one of many possible types of arrangements. Its purpose is to illustrate the accounting treatment for some features that are commonly found in practice. To make the illustration as clear as possible, it has been assumed that the arrangement period is only ten years and that the operator's annual receipts are constant over that period. In practice, arrangement periods may be much longer and annual revenues may increase with time. In such circumstances, the changes in net profit from year to year could be greater.

Example 2: The grantor gives the operator an intangible asset (a licence to charge users)

Arrangement terms

IE11 The terms of a service arrangement require an operator to construct a road—completing construction within two years—and maintain and operate the road to a specified standard for eight years (ie years 3–10). The terms of the arrangement also require the operator to resurface the road when the original surface has deteriorated below a specified condition. The operator estimates that it will have to undertake the resurfacing at the end of year 8. At the end of year 10, the service arrangement will end. Assume that the operator identifies a single performance obligation for construction services. **[Refer: IFRS 15 paragraph 22]** The operator estimates that the costs it will incur to fulfil its obligations will be:

Table 2.1 *Contract costs*

	Year	CU[(a)]
Construction services	1	500
	2	500
Operating the road (per year)	3–10	10
Road resurfacing	8	100
(a) in this example, monetary amounts are denominated in 'currency units (CU)'.		

IE12   The terms of the arrangement allow the operator to collect tolls from drivers using the road. The operator forecasts that vehicle numbers will remain constant over the duration of the contract and that it will receive tolls of 200 currency units (CU200) in each of years 3–10.

IE13   For the purpose of this illustration, it is assumed that all cash flows take place at the end of the year.

Intangible asset

IE14   The operator provides construction services to the grantor in exchange for an intangible asset, ie a right to collect tolls from road users in years 3–10. In accordance with IFRS 15, the operator measures this non-cash consideration at fair value. **[Refer: IFRS 15 paragraph 66]** In this case, the operator determines the fair value indirectly by reference to the stand-alone selling price **[Refer: IFRS 15 paragraph 67]** of the construction services delivered.

[Refer: paragraph 26]

IE15   During the construction phase of the arrangement the operator's contract asset (representing its accumulating right to be paid for providing construction services) is presented as an intangible asset (licence to charge users of the infrastructure). The operator estimates the stand-alone selling price of the construction services to be equal to the forecast construction costs plus 5 per cent margin, which the operator concludes is consistent with the rate that a market participant would require as compensation for providing the construction services and for assuming the risk associated with the construction costs. It is also assumed that, in accordance with IAS 23 *Borrowing Costs*, the operator capitalises the borrowing costs, estimated at 6.7 per cent, during the construction phase of the arrangement:

[Refer: paragraph 22]

Table 2.2 *Initial measurement of intangible asset*

	CU
Construction services in year 1	525
Capitalisation of borrowing costs (table 2.4)	34
Construction services in year 2	525
Intangible asset at end of year 2	**1,084**

IE16   In accordance with IAS 38, the intangible asset is amortised over the period in which it is expected to be available for use by the operator, ie years 3–10. The depreciable amount of the intangible asset (CU1,084) is allocated using a straight-line method. The annual amortisation charge is therefore CU1,084 divided by 8 years, ie CU135 per year.
[Refer: IAS 38 paragraph 97]

Construction costs and revenue

IE17   The operator accounts for the construction services in accordance with IFRS 15. It measures revenue at the fair value of the non-cash consideration received or receivable. **[Refer: IFRS 15 paragraph 66]** Thus in each of years 1 and 2 it recognises in its profit or loss construction costs of CU500, construction revenue of CU525 and, hence, construction profit of CU25.
[Refer: paragraph 14]

Toll revenue

IE18   The road users pay for the public services at the same time as they receive them, ie when they use the road. The operator therefore recognises toll revenue when it collects the tolls.

Resurfacing obligations

IE19   The operator's resurfacing obligation arises as a consequence of use of the road during the operating phase. It is recognised and measured in accordance with IAS 37 *Provisions, Contingent Liabilities and Contingent Assets*, ie at the best estimate of the expenditure required to settle the present obligation at the end of the reporting period.
[Refer: paragraph 21]

IE20   For the purpose of this illustration, it is assumed that the terms of the operator's contractual obligation are such that the best estimate of the expenditure required to settle the obligation at any date is proportional to the number of vehicles that have used the road by that date and increases by CU17 (discounted to a current value) each year. The operator discounts the provision to its present value in accordance with IAS 37. The charge recognised each period in profit or loss is:

Table 2.3 *Resurfacing obligation (currency units)*

Year	3	4	5	6	7	8	Total
Obligation arising in year (CU17 discounted at 6%)	12	13	14	15	16	17	87
Increase in earlier years' provision arising from passage of time	0	1	1	2	4	5	13
Total expense recognised in profit or loss	12	14	15	17	20	22	100

Overview of cash flows, statement of comprehensive income and statement of financial position

IE21 For the purposes of this illustration, it is assumed that the operator finances the arrangement wholly with debt and retained profits. It pays interest at 6.7 per cent per year on outstanding debt. If the cash flows and fair values remain the same as those forecast, the operator's cash flows, statement of comprehensive income and statement of financial position over the duration of the arrangement will be:

Table 2.4 *Cash flows (currency units)*

Year	1	2	3	4	5	6	7	8	9	10	Total
Receipts	-	-	200	200	200	200	200	200	200	200	1,600
Contract costs(a)	(500)	(500)	(10)	(10)	(10)	(10)	(10)	(110)	(10)	(10)	(1,180)
Borrowing costs(b)	-	(34)	(69)	(61)	(53)	(43)	(33)	(23)	(19)	(7)	(342)
Net inflow/ (outflow)	(500)	(534)	121	129	137	147	157	67	171	183	78

(a) Table 2.1
(b) Debt at start of year (table 2.6) × 6.7%

Table 2.5 *Statement of comprehensive income (currency units)*

Year	1	2	3	4	5	6	7	8	9	10	Total
Revenue	525	525	200	200	200	200	200	200	200	200	2,650
Amortisation	-	-	(135)	(135)	(136)	(136)	(136)	(136)	(135)	(135)	(1,084)
Resurfacing expense	-	-	(12)	(14)	(15)	(17)	(20)	(22)	-	-	(100)
Other contract costs	(500)	(500)	(10)	(10)	(10)	(10)	(10)	(10)	(10)	(10)	(1,080)
Borrowing costs(a),(b)	-	-	(69)	(61)	(53)	(43)	(33)	(23)	(19)	(7)	(308)
Net profit	25	25	(26)	(20)	(14)	(6)	1	9	36	48	78

(a) Borrowing costs are capitalised during the construction phase.
(b) Table 2.4

Table 2.6 *Statement of financial position (currency units)*

End of year	1	2	3	4	5	6	7	8	9	10
Intangible asset	525	1,084	949	814	678	542	406	270	135	-
Cash/(debt)(a)	(500)	(1,034)	(913)	(784)	(647)	(500)	(343)	(276)	(105)	78
Resurfacing obligation	-	-	(12)	(26)	(41)	(58)	(78)	-	-	-
Net assets	25	50	24	4	(10)	(16)	(15)	(6)	30	78

(a) Debt at start of year plus net cash flow in year (table 2.4)

IE22 This example deals with only one of many possible types of arrangements. Its purpose is to illustrate the accounting treatment for some features that are commonly found in practice. To make the illustration as clear as possible, it has been assumed that the arrangement period is only ten years and that the operator's annual receipts are constant over that period. In practice, arrangement periods may be much longer and annual revenues may increase with time. In such circumstances, the changes in net profit from year to year could be greater.

Example 3: The grantor gives the operator a financial asset and an intangible asset

Arrangement terms

IE23 The terms of a service arrangement require an operator to construct a road—completing construction within two years—and to operate the road and maintain it to a specified standard for eight years (ie years 3–10). The terms of the arrangement also require the operator to resurface the road when the original surface has deteriorated below a specified condition. The operator estimates that it will have to undertake the resurfacing at the end of year 8. At the end of year 10, the arrangement will end. Assume that the operator identifies a single performance obligation for construction services. [Refer: IFRS 15 paragraph 22] The operator estimates that the costs it will incur to fulfil its obligations will be:

Table 3.1 *Contract costs*

	Year	CU(a)
Construction services	1	500
	2	500
Operating the road (per year)	3–10	10
Road resurfacing	8	100

(a) in this example, monetary amounts are denominated in 'currency units (CU)'.

IE24 The operator estimates the consideration in respect of construction services to be CU1,050 by reference to the stand-alone selling price [Refer: IFRS 15 paragraph 74] of those services (which it estimates at forecast costs plus 5 per cent).

IE25 The terms of the arrangement allow the operator to collect tolls from drivers using the road. In addition, the grantor guarantees the operator a minimum amount of CU700 and interest at a specified rate of 6.18 per cent to reflect the timing of cash receipts. The operator forecasts that vehicle numbers will remain constant over the duration of the contract and that it will receive tolls of CU200 in each of years 3–10.

IE26 For the purpose of this illustration, it is assumed that all cash flows take place at the end of the year.

Dividing the arrangement

IE27 The contractual right to receive cash from the grantor for the services and the right to charge users for the public services should be regarded as two separate assets under IFRSs. Therefore in this arrangement it is necessary to divide the operator's contract asset during the construction phase into two components — a financial asset component based on the guaranteed amount and an intangible asset for the remainder. When the construction services are completed, the two components of the contract asset would be classified and measured as a financial asset and an intangible asset accordingly.
[Refer: paragraph 18]

Table 3.2 *Dividing the operator's consideration*

Year	Total	Financial asset	Intangible asset
Construction services in year 1	525	350	175
Construction services in year 2	525	350	175
Total construction services	1,050	700	350
	100%	*67%*[(a)]	*33%*
Finance income, at specified rate of 6.18% on receivable (see table 3.3)	22	22	-
Borrowing costs capitalised (interest paid in years 1 and 2 × 33%) (see table 3.7)	11	-	11
Total fair value of the operator's consideration	1,083	722	361

(a) Amount guaranteed by the grantor as a proportion of the construction services

Financial asset
[Refer: paragraphs 23–25]

IE28 During the first two years, the entity recognises a contract asset and accounts for the significant financing component in the arrangement in accordance with IFRS 15. Once the construction is complete, the amount due from, or at the direction of, the grantor in exchange for the construction services is accounted for in accordance with IFRS 9 as a receivable.

IE29   On this basis the receivable recognised at the end of years 2 and 3 will be:

Table 3.3 *Measurement of contract asset/receivable*

	CU
Construction services in year 1 allocated to the contract asset	350
Contract asset at end of year 1	350
Construction services in year 2 allocated to the contract asset	350
Interest in year 2 on contract asset at end of year 1 (6.18% × CU350)	22
Receivable at end of year 2	722
Interest in year 3 on receivable at end of year 2 (6.18% × CU722)	45
Cash receipts in year 3 (see table 3.5)	(117)
Receivable at end of year 3	650

Intangible asset
[Refer: paragraph 26]

IE30   In accordance with IAS 38 *Intangible Assets*, the operator recognises the intangible asset at cost, ie the fair value of the consideration received or receivable.

IE31   During the construction phase of the arrangement the portion of the operator's contract asset that represents its accumulating right to be paid amounts in excess of the guaranteed amount for providing construction services is presented as a right to receive a licence to charge users of the infrastructure. The operator estimates the stand-alone selling price of the construction services as equal to the forecast construction costs plus 5 per cent, which the operator concludes is consistent with the rate that a market participant would require as compensation for providing the construction services and for assuming the risk associated with the construction costs. It is also assumed that, in accordance with IAS 23 *Borrowing Costs*, the operator capitalises the borrowing costs, estimated at 6.7 per cent, during the construction phase:

Table 3.4 *Initial measurement of intangible asset*

	CU
Construction services in year 1	175
Borrowing costs (interest paid in years 1 and 2 × 33%) (see table 3.7)	11
Construction services in year 2	175
Intangible asset at the end of year 2	361

IE32 In accordance with IAS 38, the intangible asset is amortised over the period in which it is expected to be available for use by the operator, ie years 3–10. The depreciable amount of the intangible asset (CU361 including borrowing costs) is allocated using a straight-line method. The annual amortisation charge is therefore CU361 divided by 8 years, ie CU45 per year.

Revenue and costs

IE33 The operator provides construction services to the grantor in exchange for a financial asset and an intangible asset. Under both the financial asset model and intangible asset model, the operator accounts for the construction services in accordance with IFRS 15. Thus in each of years 1 and 2 it recognises in profit or loss construction costs of CU500 and construction revenue of CU525.

[Refer: paragraph 14]

Toll revenue

IE34 The road users pay for the public services at the same time as they receive them, ie when they use the road. Under the terms of this arrangement the cash flows are allocated to the financial asset and intangible asset in proportion, so the operator allocates the receipts from tolls between repayment of the financial asset and revenue earned from the intangible asset:
[Refer: paragraph 18]

Table 3.5 *Allocation of toll receipts*

Year	CU
Guaranteed receipt from grantor	700
Finance income (see table 3.8)	237
Total	937
Cash allocated to realisation of the financial asset per year (CU937/8 years)	**117**
Receipts attributable to intangible asset (CU200 x 8 years – CU937)	663
Annual receipt from intangible asset (CU663/8 years)	**83**

Resurfacing obligations
[Refer: paragraph 21]

IE35 The operator's resurfacing obligation arises as a consequence of use of the road during the operation phase. It is recognised and measured in accordance with IAS 37 *Provisions, Contingent Liabilities and Contingent Assets*, ie at the best estimate of the expenditure required to settle the present obligation at the end of the reporting period.

IE36 For the purpose of this illustration, it is assumed that the terms of the operator's contractual obligation are such that the best estimate of the expenditure required to settle the obligation at any date is proportional to the number of vehicles that have used the road by that date and increases by

CU17 each year. The operator discounts the provision to its present value in accordance with IAS 37. The charge recognised each period in profit or loss is:

Table 3.6 *Resurfacing obligation (currency units)*

Year	3	4	5	6	7	8	Total
Obligation arising in year (CU17 discounted at 6%)	12	13	14	15	16	17	87
Increase in earlier years' provision arising from passage of time	0	1	1	2	4	5	13
Total expense recognised in profit or loss	12	14	15	17	20	22	100

Overview of cash flows, statement of comprehensive income and statement of financial position

IE37   For the purposes of this illustration, it is assumed that the operator finances the arrangement wholly with debt and retained profits. It pays interest at 6.7 per cent per year on outstanding debt. If the cash flows and fair values remain the same as those forecast, the operator's cash flows, statement of comprehensive income and statement of financial position over the duration of the arrangement will be:

Table 3.7 *Cash flows (currency units)*

Year	1	2	3	4	5	6	7	8	9	10	Total
Receipts	-	-	200	200	200	200	200	200	200	200	1,600
Contract costs[(a)]	(500)	(500)	(10)	(10)	(10)	(10)	(10)	(110)	(10)	(10)	(1,180)
Borrowing costs[(b)]	-	(34)	(69)	(61)	(53)	(43)	(33)	(23)	(19)	(7)	(342)
Net inflow/(outflow)	(500)	(534)	121	129	137	147	157	67	171	183	78

(a)   Table 3.1
(b)   Debt at start of year (table 3.9) × 6.7%

Table 3.8 *Statement of comprehensive income (currency units)*

Year	1	2	3	4	5	6	7	8	9	10	Total
Revenue on construction	525	525	-	-	-	-	-	-	-	-	1,050
Revenue from intangible asset	-	-	83	83	83	83	83	83	83	83	663
Finance income[(a)]	-	22	45	40	35	30	25	19	13	7	237
Amortisation	-	-	(45)	(45)	(45)	(45)	(45)	(45)	(45)	(46)	(361)
Resurfacing expense	-	-	(12)	(14)	(15)	(17)	(20)	(22)	-	-	(100)
Construction costs	(500)	(500)									(1,000)
Other contract costs[(b)]			(10)	(10)	(10)	(10)	(10)	(10)	(10)	(10)	(80)
Borrowing costs (table 3.7)[(c)]	-	(23)	(69)	(61)	(53)	(43)	(33)	(23)	(19)	(7)	(331)
Net profit	25	24	(8)	(7)	(5)	(2)	0	2	22	27	78

(a) Interest on receivable
(b) Table 3.1
(c) In year 2, borrowing costs are stated net of amount capitalised in the intangible (see table 3.4).

Table 3.9 *Statement of financial position (currency units)*

End of year	1	2	3	4	5	6	7	8	9	10
Receivable	350	722	650	573	491	404	312	214	110	-
Intangible asset	175	361	316	271	226	181	136	91	46	-
Cash/(debt)[(a)]	(500)	(1,034)	(913)	(784)	(647)	(500)	(343)	(276)	(105)	78
Resurfacing obligation	-	-	(12)	(26)	(41)	(58)	(78)	-	-	-
Net assets	25	49	41	34	29	27	27	29	51	78

(a) Debt at start of year plus net cash flow in year (table 3.7)

IE38   This example deals with only one of many possible types of arrangements. Its purpose is to illustrate the accounting treatment for some features that are commonly found in practice. To make the illustration as clear as possible, it has been assumed that the arrangement period is only ten years and that the operator's annual receipts are constant over that period. In practice, arrangement periods may be much longer and annual revenues may increase with time. In such circumstances, the changes in net profit from year to year could be greater.

Documents published to accompany

IFRIC 14

IAS 19 — The Limit on a Defined Benefit Asset, Minimum Funding Requirements and their Interaction

The text of the unaccompanied Interpretation, IFRIC 14, is contained in Part A of this edition. Its effective date when issued was 1 January 2008. The text of the Basis for Conclusions on IFRIC 14 is contained in Part C of this edition. This part presents the following document:

ILLUSTRATIVE EXAMPLES

Illustrative Examples

These examples accompany, but are not part of, IFRIC 14.

Example 1—Effect of the minimum funding requirement when there is an IAS 19 surplus and the minimum funding contributions payable are fully refundable to the entity

IE1   An entity has a funding level on the minimum funding requirement basis (which is measured on a different basis from that required under IAS 19) of 82 per cent in Plan A. Under the minimum funding requirements, the entity is required to increase the funding level to 95 per cent immediately. As a result, the entity has a statutory obligation at the end of the reporting period to contribute 200 to Plan A immediately. The plan rules permit a full refund of any surplus to the entity at the end of the life of the plan. The year-end valuations for Plan A are set out below.

Fair value of assets	1,200
Present value of defined benefit obligation under IAS 19	(1,100)
Surplus	100

Application of requirements

IE2   Paragraph 24 of IFRIC 14 requires the entity to recognise a liability to the extent that the contributions payable are not fully available. Payment of the contributions of 200 will increase the IAS 19 surplus from 100 to 300. Under the rules of the plan this amount will be fully refundable to the entity with no associated costs. Therefore, no liability is recognised for the obligation to pay the contributions and the net defined benefit asset is 100.

Example 2—Effect of a minimum funding requirement when there is an IAS 19 deficit and the minimum funding contributions payable would not be fully available

IE3   An entity has a funding level on the minimum funding requirement basis (which is measured on a different basis from that required under IAS 19) of 77 per cent in Plan B. Under the minimum funding requirements, the entity is required to increase the funding level to 100 per cent immediately. As a result, the entity has a statutory obligation at the end of the reporting period to pay additional contributions of 300 to Plan B. The plan rules permit a maximum refund of 60 per cent of the IAS 19 surplus to the entity and the entity is not permitted to reduce its contributions below a specified level which happens to equal the IAS 19 service cost. The year-end valuations for Plan B are set out below.

Fair value of assets	1,000
Present value of defined benefit obligation under IAS 19	(1,100)
Deficit	(100)

Application of requirements

IE4   The payment of 300 would change the IAS 19 deficit of 100 to a surplus of 200. Of this 200, 60 per cent (120) is refundable.

IE5   Therefore, of the contributions of 300, 100 eliminates the IAS 19 deficit and 120 (60 per cent of 200) is available as an economic benefit. The remaining 80 (40 per cent of 200) of the contributions paid is not available to the entity.

IE6   Paragraph 24 of IFRIC 14 requires the entity to recognise a liability to the extent that the additional contributions payable are not available to it.

IE7   Therefore, the net defined benefit liability is 180, comprising the deficit of 100 plus the additional liability of 80 resulting from the requirements in paragraph 24 of IFRIC 14. No other liability is recognised in respect of the statutory obligation to pay contributions of 300.

Summary

Fair value of assets	1,000
Present value of defined benefit obligation under IAS 19	(1,100)
Deficit	(100)
Effect of the asset ceiling	(80)
Net defined benefit liability	(180)

IE8   When the contributions of 300 are paid, the net defined benefit asset will be 120.

Example 3—Effect of a minimum funding requirement when the contributions payable would not be fully available and the effect on the economic benefit available as a future contribution reduction

IE9   An entity has a funding level on the minimum funding basis (which it measures on a different basis from that required by IAS 19) of 95 per cent in Plan C. The minimum funding requirements require the entity to pay contributions to increase the funding level to 100 per cent over the next three years. The contributions are required to make good the deficit on the minimum funding basis (shortfall) and to cover future service.

IE10   Plan C also has an IAS 19 surplus at the end of the reporting period of 50, which cannot be refunded to the entity under any circumstances.

IE11   The nominal amounts of contributions required to satisfy the minimum funding requirements in respect of the shortfall and the future service for the next three years are set out below.

Year	Total contributions for minimum funding requirement	Contributions required to make good the shortfall	Contributions required to cover future service
1	135	120	15
2	125	112	13
3	115	104	11

Application of requirements

IE12   The entity's present obligation in respect of services already received includes the contributions required to make good the shortfall but does not include the contributions required to cover future service.

IE13   The present value of the entity's obligation, assuming a discount rate of 6 per cent per year, is approximately 300, calculated as follows:

$$[120/(1.06) + 112/(1.06)^2 + 104/(1.06)^3]$$

IE14   When these contributions are paid into the plan, the IAS 19 surplus (ie the fair value of assets less the present value of the defined benefit obligation) would, other things being equal, increase from 50 to 350 (300 + 50).

IE15   However, the surplus is not refundable although an asset may be available as a future contribution reduction.

IE16   In accordance with paragraph 20 of IFRIC 14, the economic benefit available as a reduction in future contributions is the sum of:

(a)   any amount that reduces future minimum funding requirement contributions for future service because the entity made a prepayment (ie paid the amount before being required to do so); and

(b)   the estimated future service cost in each period in accordance with paragraphs 16 and 17, less the estimated minimum funding requirement contributions that would be required for future service in those periods if there were no prepayment as described in (a).

IE17   In this example there is no prepayment as described in paragraph 20(a). The amounts available as a reduction in future contributions when applying paragraph 20(b) are set out below.

Year	IAS 19 service cost	Minimum contributions required to cover future service	Amount available as contribution reduction
1	13	15	(2)
2	13	13	0
3	13	11	2
4+	13	9	4

IE18   Assuming a discount rate of 6 per cent, the present value of the economic benefit available as a future contribution reduction is therefore equal to:

$$(2)/(1.06) + 0/(1.06)^2 + 2/(1.06)^3 + 4/(1.06)^4 \ldots = 56$$

Thus in accordance with paragraph 58(b) of IAS 19, the present value of the economic benefit available from future contribution reductions is limited to 56.

IE19   Paragraph 24 of IFRIC 14 requires the entity to recognise a liability to the extent that the additional contributions payable will not be fully available. Therefore, the effect of the asset ceiling is 294 (50 + 300 − 56).

IE20   The entity recognises a net defined benefit liability of 244 in the statement of financial position. No other liability is recognised in respect of the obligation to make contributions to fund the minimum funding shortfall.

Summary

Surplus	50
Net defined benefit asset (before consideration of the minimum funding requirement)	50
Effect of the asset ceiling	(294)
Net defined benefit liability	(244)

IE21   When the contributions of 300 are paid into the plan, the net defined benefit asset will become 56 (300 − 244).

Example 4—Effect of a prepayment when a minimum funding requirement exceeds the expected future service charge

IE22   An entity is required to fund Plan D so that no deficit arises on the minimum funding basis. The entity is required to pay minimum funding requirement contributions to cover the service cost in each period determined on the minimum funding basis.

IE23   Plan D has an IAS 19 surplus of 35 at the beginning of 20X1. This example assumes that the discount rate and expected return on assets are 0 per cent, and that the plan cannot refund the surplus to the entity under any circumstances but can use the surplus for reductions of future contributions.

IE24   The minimum contributions required to cover future service are 15 for each of the next five years. The expected IAS 19 service cost is 10 in each year.

IE25   The entity makes a prepayment of 30 at the beginning of 20X1 in respect of years 20X1 and 20X2, increasing its surplus at the beginning of 20X1 to 65. That prepayment reduces the future contributions it expects to make in the following two years, as follows:

Year	IAS 19 service cost	Minimum funding requirement contribution before prepayment	Minimum funding requirement contribution after prepayment
20X1	10	15	0
20X2	10	15	0
20X3	10	15	15
20X4	10	15	15
20X5	10	15	15
Total	50	75	45

Application of requirements

IE26   In accordance with paragraphs 20 and 22 of IFRIC 14, at the beginning of 20X1, the economic benefit available as a reduction in future contributions is the sum of:

(a)   30, being the prepayment of the minimum funding requirement contributions; and

(b)   nil. The estimated minimum funding requirement contributions required for future service would be 75 if there was no prepayment. Those contributions exceed the estimated future service cost (50); therefore the entity cannot use any part of the surplus of 35 noted in paragraph IE23 (see paragraph 22).

IE27 Assuming a discount rate of 0 per cent, the present value of the economic benefit available as a reduction in future contributions is equal to 30. Thus in accordance with paragraph 64 of IAS 19 the entity recognises a net defined benefit asset of 30 (because this is lower than the IAS 19 surplus of 65).

Documents published to accompany

IFRIC 16

Hedges of a Net Investment in a Foreign Operation

The text of the unaccompanied Interpretation, IFRIC 16, is contained in Part A of this edition. Its effective date when issued was 1 October 2008. The text of the Basis for Conclusions on IFRIC 16 is contained in Part C of this edition. This part presents the following document:

ILLUSTRATIVE EXAMPLE

Illustrative Examples

This example accompanies, but is not part of, IFRIC 16.

Disposal of a foreign operation (paragraphs 16 and 17)

IE1   This example illustrates the application of paragraphs 16 and 17 in connection with the reclassification adjustment on the disposal of a foreign operation.

Background

IE2   This example assumes the group structure set out in the application guidance and that Parent used a USD borrowing in Subsidiary A to hedge the EUR/USD risk of the net investment in Subsidiary C in Parent's consolidated financial statements. Parent uses the step-by-step method of consolidation. Assume the hedge was fully effective and the full USD/EUR accumulated change in the value of the hedging instrument before disposal of Subsidiary C is €24 million (gain). This is matched exactly by the fall in value of the net investment in Subsidiary C, when measured against the functional currency of Parent (euro).

IE3   If the direct method of consolidation is used, the fall in the value of Parent's net investment in Subsidiary C of €24 million would be reflected totally in the foreign currency translation reserve relating to Subsidiary C in Parent's consolidated financial statements. However, because Parent uses the step-by-step method, this fall in the net investment value in Subsidiary C of €24 million would be reflected both in Subsidiary B's foreign currency translation reserve relating to Subsidiary C and in Parent's foreign currency translation reserve relating to Subsidiary B.

IE4   The aggregate amount recognised in the foreign currency translation reserve in respect of Subsidiaries B and C is not affected by the consolidation method. Assume that using the direct method of consolidation, the foreign currency translation reserves for Subsidiaries B and C in Parent's consolidated financial statements are €62 million gain and €24 million loss respectively; using the step-by-step method of consolidation those amounts are €49 million gain and €11 million loss respectively.

Reclassification

IE5   When the investment in Subsidiary C is disposed of, IFRS 9 requires the full €24 million gain on the hedging instrument to be reclassified to profit or loss. Using the step-by-step method, the amount to be reclassified to profit or loss in respect of the net investment in Subsidiary C would be only €11 million loss. Parent could adjust the foreign currency translation reserves of both Subsidiaries B and C by €13 million in order to match the amounts reclassified in respect of the hedging instrument and the net investment as would have been the case if the direct method of consolidation had been used, if that was its accounting policy. An entity that had not hedged its net investment could make the same reclassification.

Documents published to accompany

IFRIC 17

Distributions of Non-cash Assets to Owners

The text of the unaccompanied Interpretation, IFRIC 17, is contained in Part A of this edition. Its effective date when issued was 1 July 2009. The text of the Basis for Conclusions on IFRIC 17 is contained in Part C of this edition. This part presents the following document:

ILLUSTRATIVE EXAMPLES

Illustrative Examples

These examples accompany, but are not part of, IFRIC 17.

Scope of the Interpretation (paragraphs 3–8)

CHART 1 (distribution of available-for-sale securities)

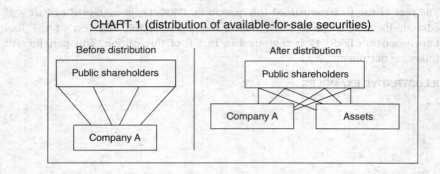

CHART 1 (distribution of available-for-sale securities)

| Before distribution | After distribution |

IE1   Assume Company A is owned by public shareholders. No single shareholder controls Company A and no group of shareholders is bound by a contractual agreement to act together to control Company A jointly. Company A distributes certain assets (eg available-for-sale securities) pro rata to the shareholders. This transaction is within the scope of the Interpretation.

IE2   However, if one of the shareholders (or a group bound by a contractual agreement to act together) controls Company A both before and after the transaction, the entire transaction (including the distributions to the non-controlling shareholders) is not within the scope of the Interpretation. This is because in a pro rata distribution to all owners of the same class of equity instruments, the controlling shareholder (or group of shareholders) will continue to control the non-cash assets after the distribution.

CHART 2 (distribution of shares of subsidiaries)

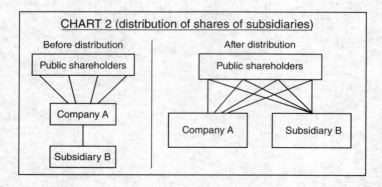

CHART 2 (distribution of shares of subsidiaries)

IE3   Assume Company A is owned by public shareholders. No single shareholder controls Company A and no group of shareholders is bound by a contractual agreement to act together to control Company A jointly. Company A owns all of the shares of Subsidiary B. Company A distributes all of the shares of Subsidiary B pro rata to its shareholders, thereby losing control of Subsidiary B. This transaction is within the scope of the Interpretation.

IE4   However, if Company A distributes to its shareholders shares of Subsidiary B representing only a non-controlling interest in Subsidiary B and retains control of Subsidiary B, the transaction is not within the scope of the Interpretation. Company A accounts for the distribution in accordance with IFRS 10 *Consolidated Financial Statements*. Company A controls Company B both before and after the transaction.

Documents published to accompany

IFRIC 21

Levies

The text of the unaccompanied Interpretation, IFRIC 21, is contained in Part A of this edition. Its effective date when issued was 1 January 2014. The text of the Basis for Conclusions on IFRIC 21 is contained in Part C of this edition. This part presents the following document:

ILLUSTRATIVE EXAMPLES

IFRIC Interpretation 21
Illustrative Examples

These examples accompany, but are not part of, IFRIC 21.

IE1   The objective of these examples is to illustrate how an entity should account for a liability to pay a levy in its annual financial statements and in its interim financial report.

Example 1—A levy is triggered progressively as the entity generates revenue

Entity A has an annual reporting period that ends on 31 December. In accordance with legislation, a levy is triggered progressively as an entity generates revenue in 20X1. The amount of the levy is calculated by reference to revenue generated by the entity in 20X1.

In this example, the liability is recognised progressively during 20X1 as Entity A generates revenue, because the obligating event, as identified by the legislation, is the generation of revenue during 20X1. At any point in 20X1, Entity A has a present obligation to pay a levy on revenue generated to date. Entity A has no present obligation to pay a levy that will arise from generating revenue in the future.

In the interim financial report (if any), the liability is recognised progressively as Entity A generates revenue. Entity A has a present obligation to pay the levy on revenue generated from 1 January 20X1 to the end of the interim period.

Example 2—A levy is triggered in full as soon as the entity generates revenue

Entity B has an annual reporting period that ends on 31 December. In accordance with legislation, a levy is triggered in full as soon as an entity generates revenue in 20X1. The amount of the levy is calculated by reference to revenue generated by the entity in 20X0. Entity B generated revenue in 20X0 and in 20X1 starts to generate revenue on 3 January 20X1.

In this example, the liability is recognised in full on 3 January 20X1 because the obligating event, as identified by the legislation, is the first generation of revenue in 20X1. The generation of revenue in 20X0 is necessary, but not sufficient, to create a present obligation to pay a levy. Before 3 January 20X1, Entity B has no present obligation to pay a levy. In other words, the activity that triggers the payment of the levy, as identified by the legislation, is the point at which Entity B first generates revenue in 20X1. The generation of revenue in 20X0 is not the activity that triggers the payment of the levy and the recognition of the liability. The amount of revenue generated in 20X0 only affects the measurement of the liability.

In the interim financial report (if any), the liability is recognised in full in the first interim period of 20X1 because the liability is recognised in full on 3 January 20X1.

Example 3—A levy is triggered in full if the entity operates as a bank at a specified date

Entity C is a bank and has an annual reporting period that ends on 31 December. In accordance with legislation, a levy is triggered in full only if an entity operates as a bank at the end of the annual reporting period. The amount of the levy is calculated by reference to the amounts in the statement of financial position of the entity at the end of the annual reporting period. The end of the annual reporting period of Entity C is 31 December 20X1.

In this example, the liability is recognised on 31 December 20X1 because the obligating event, as identified by the legislation, is Entity C operating as a bank at the end of the annual reporting period. Before that point, Entity C has no present obligation to pay a levy, even if it is economically compelled to continue to operate as a bank in the future. In other words, the activity that triggers the payment of the levy, as identified by the legislation, is the entity operating as a bank at the end of the annual reporting period, which does not occur until 31 December 20X1. The conclusion would not change even if the amount of the liability is based on the length of the reporting period, because the obligating event is the entity operating as a bank at the end of the annual reporting period.

In the interim financial report (if any), the liability is recognised in full in the interim period in which 31 December 20X1 falls because the liability is recognised in full on that date.

Example 4—A levy is triggered if the entity generates revenue above a minimum amount of revenue

Entity D has an annual reporting period that ends on 31 December. In accordance with legislation, a levy is triggered if an entity generates revenue above CU50 million in 20X1.[a] The amount of the levy is calculated by reference to revenue generated above CU50 million, with the levy rate at 0 per cent for the first CU50 million revenue generated (below the threshold) and 2 per cent above CU50 million revenue. Entity D's revenue reaches the revenue threshold of CU50 million on 17 July 20X1.

In this example, the liability is recognised between 17 July 20X1 and 31 December 20X1 as Entity D generates revenue above the threshold because the obligating event, as identified by the legislation, is the activity undertaken after the threshold is reached (ie the generation of revenue after the threshold is reached). The amount of the liability is based on the revenue generated to date that exceeds the threshold of CU50 million revenue.

In the interim financial report (if any), the liability is recognised between 17 July 20X1 and 31 December 20X1 as Entity D generates revenue above the threshold.

continued...

...continued

Example 4—A levy is triggered if the entity generates revenue above a minimum amount of revenue

---

Variation:

Same fact pattern as above (ie a levy is triggered if Entity D generates revenue above CU50 million in 20X1), except that the amount of the levy is calculated by reference to all revenue generated by Entity D in 20X1 (ie including the first CU50 million revenue generated in 20X1).

In this example, the liability for the payment of the levy related to the first CU50 million revenue is recognised on 17 July 20X1 when the threshold is met, because the obligating event, as identified by the legislation, for the payment of that amount is the reaching of the threshold. The liability for the payment of the levy related to revenue generated above the threshold is recognised between 17 July 20X1 and 31 December 20X1 as the entity generates revenue above the threshold, because the obligating event, as identified by the legislation, is the activity undertaken after the threshold is reached (ie the generation of revenue after the threshold is reached). The amount of the liability is based on the revenue generated to date, including the first CU50 million revenue. The same recognition principles apply in the interim financial report (if any) as in the annual financial statements.

(a)   In this Interpretation, currency amounts are denominated in 'currency units' (CU).

Documents published to accompany

IFRIC 22

Foreign Currency Transactions and Advance Consideration

The text of the unaccompanied Interpretation, IFRIC 22, is contained in Part A of this edition. Its effective date when issued was 1 January 2018. The text of the Basis for Conclusions on IFRIC 22 is contained in Part C of this edition. This part presents the following document:

ILLUSTRATIVE EXAMPLES

IFRIC 22 *Foreign Currency Transactions and Advance Consideration*
Illustrative Examples

These Illustrative Examples accompany, but are not part of, IFRIC 22.

In these Illustrative Examples, foreign currency amounts are 'Foreign Currency' (FC) and functional currency amounts are 'Local Currency' (LC).

IE1   The objective of these examples is to illustrate how an entity determines the date of the transaction when it recognises a non-monetary asset or non-monetary liability arising from advance consideration in a foreign currency before it recognises the related asset, expense or income (or part of it) applying relevant IFRS Standards.

Example 1—A single advance payment for the purchase of a single item of property, plant and equipment

[Refer: paragraph 8]

IE2   On 1 March 20X1, Entity A entered into a contract with a supplier to purchase a machine for use in its business. Under the terms of the contract, Entity A pays the supplier a fixed purchase price of FC1,000 on 1 April 20X1. On 15 April 20X1, Entity A takes delivery of the machine.

IE3   Entity A initially recognises a non-monetary asset translating FC1,000 into its functional currency at the spot exchange rate between the functional currency and the foreign currency on 1 April 20X1. Applying paragraph 23(b) of IAS 21 *The Effects of Changes in Foreign Exchange Rates*, Entity A does not update the translated amount of that non-monetary asset.

IE4   On 15 April 20X1, Entity A takes delivery of the machine. Entity A derecognises the non-monetary asset and recognises the machine as property, plant and equipment applying IAS 16 *Property, Plant and Equipment*. On initial recognition of the machine, Entity A recognises the cost of the machine using the exchange rate at the date of the transaction, which is 1 April 20X1 (the date of initial recognition of the non-monetary asset).

Example 2—Multiple receipts for revenue recognised at a single point in time

[Refer: paragraph 9]

IE5   On 1 June 20X2, Entity B entered into a contract with a customer to deliver goods on 1 September 20X2. The total fixed contract price is an amount of FC100, of which FC40 is due and received on 1 August 20X2 and the balance is receivable on 30 September 20X2.

IE6   Entity B initially recognises a non-monetary contract liability translating FC40 into its functional currency at the spot exchange rate between the functional currency and the foreign currency on 1 August 20X2. Applying paragraph 23(b) of IAS 21, Entity B does not update the translated amount of that non-monetary liability.

IE7   Applying paragraph 31 of IFRS 15 *Revenue from Contracts with Customers*, Entity B recognises revenue on 1 September 20X2, the date on which it transfers the goods to the customer.

IE8   Entity B determines that the date of the transaction for the revenue relating to the advance consideration of FC40 is 1 August 20X2. Applying paragraph 22 of IAS 21, Entity B determines that the date of the transaction for the remainder of the revenue is 1 September 20X2.

IE9   On 1 September 20X2, Entity B:

   (a)   derecognises the contract liability of FC40 and recognises revenue using the exchange rate on 1 August 20X2; and

   (b)   recognises revenue of FC60 and a corresponding receivable using the exchange rate on that date (1 September 20X2).

IE10 The receivable of FC60 recognised on 1 September 20X2 is a monetary item. Entity B updates the translated amount of the receivable until the receivable is settled.

Example 3—Multiple payments for purchases of services over a period of time

[Refer: paragraph 9]

IE11 On 1 May 20X3, Entity C entered into a contract with a supplier for services. The supplier will provide the services to Entity C evenly over the period from 1 July 20X3 to 31 December 20X3. The contract requires Entity C to pay the supplier FC200 on 15 June 20X3 and FC400 on 31 December 20X3. Entity C has determined that, for this contract, the payment of FC200 on 15 June 20X3 relates to the services to be received in the period 1 July–31 August 20X3, and the payment of FC400 on 31 December 20X3 relates to the services to be received in the period 1 September–31 December 20X3.

IE12 Entity C initially recognises a non-monetary asset translating FC200 into its functional currency at the spot exchange rate between the functional currency and the foreign currency on 15 June 20X3.

IE13 In the period 1 July–31 August 20X3, Entity C derecognises the non-monetary asset and recognises an expense of FC200 in profit or loss as it receives the services from the supplier. Entity C determines that the date of the transaction for the expense related to the advance consideration of FC200 is 15 June 20X3 (the date of initial recognition of the non-monetary asset).

IE14   In the period 1 September–31 December 20X3, Entity C initially recognises the expense in profit or loss as it receives the services from the supplier. In principle, the dates of the transaction are each day in the period 1 September–31 December 20X3. However, if exchange rates do not fluctuate significantly, Entity C may use a rate that approximates the actual rates as permitted by paragraph 22 of IAS 21. If that is the case, Entity C may, for example, translate each month's expense of FC100 (FC400 ÷ 4) into its functional currency using the average exchange rate for each month for the period 1 September–31 December 20X3.

IE15   As Entity C recognises the expense in the period 1 September–31 December 20X3, it recognises a corresponding liability in respect of its obligation to pay the supplier. The liability is a monetary item. Entity C updates the translated amount of the liability until the liability is settled.

Example 4—Multiple receipts for revenue recognised at multiple points in time

[Refer: paragraph 9]

IE16   On 1 January 20X4, Entity D enters into a contract to sell two products to a customer. Entity D transfers one product on 1 March 20X4 and the second on 1 June 20X4. As required by the contract, the customer pays a fixed purchase price of FC1,000, of which FC200 is due and received in advance on 31 January 20X4 and the balance is due and received on 1 June 20X4.

IE17   The following facts are relevant:

(a)   applying IFRS 15, Entity D allocates FC450 of the transaction price to the first product and FC550 to the second product.

(b)   Entity D has determined that, for this contract, the consideration of FC200 received on 31 January 20X4 relates to the first product transferred on 1 March 20X4. On transfer of that product to the customer, Entity D has an unconditional right to FC250 of the remaining consideration.

IE18   The spot exchange rates are:

Date	Spot exchange rate FC:LC
31 January 20X4	1:1.5
1 March 20X4	1:1.7
1 June 20X4	1:1.9

IE19   The following journal entries illustrate how Entity D accounts for the foreign currency aspects of the contract:

(a)   Entity D receives the advance payment of FC200 on 31 January 20X4, which it translates into its functional currency using the exchange rate at 31 January 20X4.

Dr Cash (FC200)	LC300	
Cr Contract liability (FC200)		LC300

(b) Applying paragraph 23(b) of IAS 21, Entity D does not update the translated amount of the non-monetary contract liability.

(c) Entity D transfers the first product with a transaction price of FC450 on 1 March 20X4. Entity D derecognises the contract liability and recognises revenue of LC300. Entity D recognises the remaining revenue of FC250 relating to the first product and a corresponding receivable, both of which it translates at the exchange rate at the date that it initially recognises the remaining revenue of FC250, ie 1 March 20X4.

Dr Contract liability (FC200)	LC300	
Dr Receivable (FC250)	LC425	
Cr Revenue (FC450)		LC725

(d) The receivable of FC250 is a monetary item. Entity D updates the translated amount of the receivable until the receivable is settled (1 June 20X4). At 1 June 20X4, the receivable of FC250 is equivalent to LC475. As required by paragraph 28 of IAS 21 Entity D recognises an exchange gain of LC50 in profit or loss.

Dr Receivable	LC50	
Cr Foreign exchange gain		LC50

(e) Entity D transfers the second product with a transaction price of FC550 on 1 June 20X4. Entity D recognises revenue of FC550 using the exchange rate at the date of the transaction, which is the date that Entity D first recognises this part of the transaction in its financial statements, ie 1 June 20X4.

(f) Entity D also receives the remaining consideration of FC800 on 1 June 20X4. FC250 of the consideration received settles the receivable of FC250 arising on the transfer of the first product. Entity D translates the cash at the exchange rate at 1 June 20X4.

Dr Cash (FC800)	LC1,520	
Cr Receivable (FC250)		LC475
Cr Revenue (FC550)		LC1,045

Documents published to accompany

IFRIC 23

Uncertainty over Income Tax Treatments

The text of the unaccompanied Interpretation, IFRIC 23, is contained in Part A of this edition. Its effective date when issued was 1 January 2019. The text of the Basis for Conclusions on IFRIC 23 is contained in Part C of this edition. This part presents the following document:

ILLUSTRATIVE EXAMPLES

IFRIC 23 *Uncertainty over Income Tax Treatments* Illustrative Examples

These examples accompany, but are not part of, IFRIC 23.

IE1   These examples portray hypothetical situations illustrating how an entity might apply some of the requirements in IFRIC 23 based on the limited facts presented. In all the examples, as required by paragraph 8 of IFRIC 23, the entity has assumed that the taxation authority will examine amounts it has a right to examine and have full knowledge of all related information when making those examinations.

Example 1—The expected value method is used to reflect the effect of uncertainty for tax treatments considered together

[Refer: paragraph 11(b)]

IE2   Entity A's income tax filing in a jurisdiction includes deductions related to transfer pricing. The taxation authority may challenge those tax treatments. In the context of applying IAS 12, the uncertain tax treatments affect only the determination of taxable profit for the current period.

IE3   Entity A notes that the taxation authority's decision on one transfer pricing matter would affect, or be affected by, the other transfer pricing matters. Applying paragraph 6 of IFRIC 23, Entity A concludes that considering the tax treatments of all transfer pricing matters in the jurisdiction together better predicts the resolution of the uncertainty. Entity A also concludes it is not probable that the taxation authority will accept the tax treatments. Consequently, Entity A reflects the effect of the uncertainty in determining its taxable profit applying paragraph 11 of IFRIC 23. [Refer: paragraph 6]

IE4   Entity A estimates the probabilities of the possible additional amounts that might be added to its taxable profit, as follows:

	Estimated additional amount, CU[(a)]	Probability, %	Estimate of expected value, CU
Outcome 1	–	5%	–
Outcome 2	200	5%	10
Outcome 3	400	20%	80
Outcome 4	600	20%	120
Outcome 5	800	30%	240
Outcome 6	1,000	20%	200
		100%	650

(a) In these Illustrative Examples, currency amounts are denominated in 'currency units' (CU)

IE5   Outcome 5 is the most likely outcome. However, Entity A observes that there is a range of possible outcomes that are neither binary nor concentrated on one value. Consequently, Entity A concludes that the expected value of CU650 better predicts the resolution of the uncertainty.

IE6   Accordingly, Entity A recognises and measures its current tax liability applying IAS 12 based on taxable profit that includes CU650 to reflect the effect of the uncertainty. The amount of CU650 is in addition to the amount of taxable profit reported in its income tax filing.

Example 2—The most likely amount method is used to reflect the effect of uncertainty when recognising and measuring deferred tax and current tax

[Refer: paragraph 11(a)]

IE7   Entity B acquires for CU100 a separately identifiable intangible asset that has an indefinite life and, therefore, is not amortised applying IAS 38 *Intangible Assets*. The tax law specifies that the full cost of the intangible asset is deductible for tax purposes, but the timing of deductibility is uncertain. Applying paragraph 6 of IFRIC 23, Entity B concludes that considering this tax treatment separately better predicts the resolution of the uncertainty. **[Refer: paragraph 6]**

IE8   Entity B deducts CU100 (the cost of the intangible asset) in calculating taxable profit for Year 1 in its income tax filing. At the end of Year 1, Entity B concludes it is not probable that the taxation authority will accept the tax treatment. Consequently, Entity B reflects the effect of the uncertainty in determining its taxable profit and the tax base of the intangible asset applying paragraph 11 of IFRIC 23. Entity B concludes the most likely amount that the taxation authority will accept as a deductible amount for Year 1 is CU10 and that the most likely amount better predicts the resolution of the uncertainty.

IE9   Accordingly, in recognising and measuring its deferred tax liability applying IAS 12 at the end of Year 1, Entity B calculates a taxable temporary difference based on the most likely amount of the tax base of CU90 (CU100 – CU10) to reflect the effect of the uncertainty, instead of the tax base calculated based on Entity B's income tax filing (CU0).

IE10   Similarly, as required by paragraph 12 of IFRIC 23, Entity B reflects the effect of the uncertainty in determining taxable profit for Year 1 using judgements and estimates that are consistent with those used to calculate the deferred tax liability. Entity B recognises and measures its current tax liability applying IAS 12 based on taxable profit that includes CU90 (CU100 – CU10). The amount of CU90 is in addition to the amount of taxable profit included in its income tax filing. This is because Entity B deducted CU100 in calculating taxable profit for Year 1, whereas the most likely amount of the deduction is CU10.

Material published to accompany

SIC-32

Intangible Assets — Web Site Costs

The text of the unaccompanied Interpretation, SIC-32, is contained in Part A of this edition. Its effective date when issued was 25 March 2002. The text of the Basis for Conclusions on SIC-32 is contained in Part C of this edition. This part presents the following document:

ILLUSTRATIVE EXAMPLE

Illustrative Examples

This example accompanies, but is not part of, SIC-32. Its purpose is to illustrate examples of expenditure that occur during each of the stages described in paragraphs 2 and 3 of SIC-32 and illustrate application of SIC-32 to assist in clarifying its meaning. It is not intended to be a comprehensive checklist of expenditure that might be incurred.

Example application of SIC-32

Stage/nature of expenditure	Accounting treatment
Planning • undertaking feasibility studies • defining hardware and software specifications • evaluating alternative products and suppliers • selecting preferences	Recognise as an expense when incurred in accordance with IAS 38.54
Application and infrastructure development • purchasing or developing hardware	Apply the requirements of IAS 16
• obtaining a domain name • developing operating software (eg operating system and server software) • developing code for the application • installing developed applications on the web server • stress testing	Recognise as an expense when incurred, unless the expenditure can be directly attributed to preparing the web site to operate in the manner intended by management, and the web site meets the recognition criteria in IAS 38.21 and IAS 38.57[a]
Graphical design development • designing the appearance (eg layout and colour) of web pages	Recognise as an expense when incurred, unless the expenditure can be directly attributed to preparing the web site to operate in the manner intended by management, and the web site meets the recognition criteria in IAS 38.21 and IAS 38.57[a]

continued...

...continued

Stage/nature of expenditure	Accounting treatment
Content development	
• creating, purchasing, preparing (eg creating links and identifying tags), and uploading information, either textual or graphical in nature, on the web site before the completion of the web site's development. Examples of content include information about an entity, products or services offered for sale, and topics that subscribers access	Recognise as an expense when incurred in accordance with IAS 38.69(c) to the extent that content is developed to advertise and promote an entity's own products and services (eg digital photographs of products). Otherwise, recognise as an expense when incurred, unless the expenditure can be directly attributed to preparing the web site to operate in the manner intended by management, and the web site meets the recognition criteria in IAS 38.21 and IAS 38.57[a]
Operating	
• updating graphics and revising content • adding new functions, features and content • registering the web site with search engines • backing up data • reviewing security access • analysing usage of the web site	Assess whether it meets the definition of an intangible asset and the recognition criteria set out in IAS 38 18, in which case the expenditure is recognised in the carrying amount of the web site asset
Other	
• selling, administrative and other general overhead expenditure unless it can be directly attributed to preparing the web site for use to operate in the manner intended by management • clearly identified inefficiencies and initial operating losses incurred before the web site achieves planned performance [eg false start testing] • training employees to operate the web site	Recognise as an expense when incurred in accordance with IAS 38.65–.70

(a) All expenditure on developing a web site solely or primarily for promoting and advertising an entity's own products and services is recognised as an expense when incurred in accordance with IAS 38.68.

[Refer: paragraphs 7–10]

IFRS Practice Statement 1

Management Commentary
A framework for presentation

IFRS Practice Statement 1 *Management Commentary* was issued in December 2010 for application from 8 December 2010. The text of the Basis for Conclusions is contained in Part C of this edition.

Other Standards have made minor consequential amendments to IFRS Practice Statement 1 *Management Commentary*, including *Amendments to References to the Conceptual Framework in IFRS Standards* (issued March 2018).

FOR THE BASIS FOR CONCLUSIONS, SEE PART C OF THIS EDITION

BASIS FOR CONCLUSIONS

IFRS Practice Statement 1 *Management Commentary* is set out in paragraphs 1–41 and the Appendix. Terms defined in the Appendix are in *italics* the first time they appear in the Practice Statement. Definitions of other terms are given in the Glossary for International Financial Reporting Standards. The Practice Statement should be read in the context of its objective and the Basis for Conclusions, the *Preface to IFRS Standards* and the *Conceptual Framework for Financial Reporting*.

Introduction

Purpose of the Practice Statement

IN1   The IFRS Practice Statement *Management Commentary* provides a broad, non-binding framework for the presentation of management commentary that relates to financial statements that have been prepared in accordance with International Financial Reporting Standards (IFRSs).

     [Refer:

     paragraphs 1–4

     Basis for Conclusions paragraphs BC12–BC17]

IN2   The Practice Statement is not an IFRS. Consequently, entities applying IFRSs are not required to comply with the Practice Statement, unless specifically required by their jurisdiction. Furthermore, non-compliance with the Practice Statement will not prevent an entity's financial statements from complying with IFRSs, if they otherwise do so.

     [Refer: Basis for Conclusions paragraph BC17]

What is management commentary?

IN3   Management commentary is a narrative report that provides a context within which to interpret the financial position, financial performance and cash flows of an entity. It also provides management with an opportunity to explain its objectives and its strategies for achieving those objectives. Users routinely use the type of information provided in management commentary to help them evaluate an entity's prospects and its general risks, as well as the success of management's strategies for achieving its stated objectives. For many entities, management commentary is already an important element of their communication with the capital markets, supplementing as well as complementing the financial statements.

     [Refer:

     Appendix (definition of management commentary)

     Basis for Conclusions paragraphs BC3–BC5]

How to apply the Practice Statement

IN4   The Practice Statement is prepared on the basis that management commentary lies within the boundaries of financial reporting because it meets the definition of other financial reporting in paragraph 7 of the *Preface to International Financial Reporting Standards*.[1] Therefore management commentary is within the scope of the *Conceptual Framework for Financial Reporting*. Consequently, the Statement should be read in the context of the *Conceptual Framework*.

     [Refer: Basis for Conclusions paragraph BC7–BC11]

---

1   *Preface to International Financial Reporting Standards* renamed *Preface to IFRS Standards* in December 2018. The reference to paragraph 7 remains unchanged.

IN5   The Practice Statement sets out the principles, **[Refer: paragraphs 8–19 and Basis for Conclusions paragraphs BC22–BC41]** qualitative characteristics **[Refer: paragraphs 20 and 21 and Basis for Conclusions paragraphs BC42–BC44]** and elements **[Refer: paragraphs 24–40]** of management commentary that are necessary to provide users of financial reports with useful information. However, the form and content of management commentary may vary by entity. Thus, the Statement also provides principles to enable entities to adapt the information they provide to the particular circumstances of their business, including the legal and economic circumstances of individual jurisdictions. This flexible approach will generate more meaningful disclosure by encouraging entities that choose to present management commentary to discuss those matters that are most relevant to their individual circumstances. **[Refer:**

paragraphs 22 and 23

Basis for Conclusions paragraphs BC14 and BC45–BC47]

IN6   The Practice Statement refers to 'management' as the persons responsible for the decision-making and oversight of the entity. They may include executive employees, key management personnel and members of a governing body.[2] **[Refer: Basis for Conclusions paragraphs BC29–BC32]**

---

2   See paragraphs BC31 and BC32 for additional information.

IFRS Practice Statement
Management Commentary
A framework for presentation

Objective

[Refer: Basis for Conclusions paragraphs BC12–BC14]

1   The objective of the Practice Statement is to assist management in presenting useful *management commentary* that relates to financial statements that have been prepared in accordance with International Financial Reporting Standards (IFRSs).

Scope

[Refer: Basis for Conclusions paragraphs BC15–BC17]

2   The Practice Statement applies only to management commentary and not to other information presented in either the financial statements or the broader financial reports.

3   The Practice Statement should be applied by entities that present management commentary that relates to financial statements prepared in accordance with IFRSs.

4   The Practice Statement does not mandate which entities should be required to publish management commentary, how frequently an entity should do so or the level of assurance to which management commentary should be subjected.

Identification of management commentary

[Refer: Basis for Conclusions paragraphs BC18–BC21]

5   When management commentary relates to financial statements, an entity should either make the financial statements available with the commentary or identify in the commentary the financial statements to which it relates.

6   Management **[Refer: Introduction paragraph IN6]** should identify clearly what it is presenting as management commentary and distinguish it from other information.

7   When management commentary is presented, management should explain the extent to which the Practice Statement has been followed. An assertion that management commentary complies with the Practice Statement can be made only if it complies with the Statement in its entirety.

Users of management commentary

[Refer: Basis for Conclusions paragraphs BC22–BC25]

8 Management **[Refer: Introduction paragraph IN6]** should determine the information to include in management commentary considering the needs of the primary users of financial reports. Those users are existing and potential investors, lenders and other creditors. **[Refer: *Conceptual Framework* paragraph 1.5]**

Framework for the presentation of management commentary

Purpose
[Refer: Basis for Conclusions paragraphs BC26–BC28]

9 Management commentary should provide users of financial statements with integrated information that provides a context for the related financial statements. Such information explains management's view not only about what has happened, including both positive and negative circumstances, but also why it has happened and what the implications are for the entity's future.

10 Management commentary complements and supplements the financial statements by communicating integrated information about the entity's resources and the claims against the entity and its resources, and the transactions and other events that change them.

11 Management commentary should also explain the main trends and factors that are likely to affect the entity's future performance, position and *progress*. Consequently, management commentary looks not only at the present, but also at the past and the future.

Principles
[Refer: Basis for Conclusions paragraphs BC29–BC44]

12 Management should present commentary that is consistent with the following principles:

(a) to provide management's view **[Refer: Introduction paragraph IN6]** of the entity's performance, position and progress; **[Refer: paragraph 15]** and

(b) to supplement and complement information presented in the financial statements. **[Refer: paragraph 16]**

[Refer: Introduction paragraph IN3]

13 In aligning with those principles, management commentary should include:

(a) *forward-looking information*; **[Refer: paragraphs 17–19]** and

(b) information that possesses the qualitative characteristics described in the *Conceptual Framework for Financial Reporting*. **[Refer: paragraphs 20 and 21]**

14   Management commentary should provide information to help users
        [Refer: paragraph 8] of the financial reports to assess the performance of the
        entity and the actions of its management relative to stated strategies and
        plans for progress. That type of commentary will help users of the financial
        reports to understand, for example:

        (a)   the entity's risk exposures, its strategies for managing risks and the
                effectiveness of those strategies;

        (b)   how resources that are not presented in the financial statements could
                affect the entity's operations; and

        (c)   how non-financial factors have influenced the information presented
                in the financial statements.

Management's view
[Refer:

Introduction paragraph IN6

paragraph 12(a)

Basis for Conclusions paragraphs BC29–BC32]

15   Management commentary should provide management's perspective of the
        entity's performance, position and progress. Management commentary should
        derive from the information that is important to management in managing
        the business.

Supplement and complement the financial statement information
[Refer:

paragraph 12(b)

Basis for Conclusions paragraphs BC33 and BC34]

16   Management commentary should supplement and complement the financial
        statements with explanations of the amounts presented in the financial
        statements and the conditions and events that shaped that information.
        Management commentary should also include information about the entity
        and its performance that is not presented in the financial statements but is
        important to the management of the entity.

Forward-looking information
[Refer:

paragraph 13(a)

Basis for Conclusions paragraphs BC35–BC41]

17   Management commentary should communicate management's perspective of
        the entity's direction. Such information does not predict the future, but
        instead sets out management's objectives for the entity and its strategies for
        achieving those objectives. The extent to which management commentary
        looks forward will be influenced by the regulatory and legal environment
        within which the entity operates.

18   Management should include forward-looking information when it is aware of trends, uncertainties or other factors that could affect the entity's liquidity, capital resources, revenues and the results of its operations. Such information should focus on the extent to which the entity's financial position, liquidity and performance may change in the future and why, and include management's assessment of the entity's prospects in the light of current period results. Management should provide forward-looking information through narrative explanations or through quantified data, which may—but are not required to—include projections or forecasts. Management should disclose the assumptions used in providing forward-looking information.

19   Management should explain how and why the performance of the entity is short of, meets or exceeds forward-looking disclosures made in the prior period management commentary. For example, if management stated targets for future performance in previous reporting periods, it should report the entity's actual performance in the current reporting period and analyse and explain significant variances from its previously stated targets as well as the implications of those variances for management's expectations for the entity's future performance.

Qualitative characteristics of useful information
[Refer: Basis for Conclusions paragraphs BC42–BC44]

20   Information in management commentary should possess the fundamental qualitative characteristics of *relevance* and *faithful representation*. [Refer: *Conceptual Framework* paragraphs 2.5–2.22] Information in management commentary should also maximise the enhancing qualitative characteristics of *comparability*, [Refer: *Conceptual Framework* paragraphs 2.24–2.29] *verifiability*, [Refer: *Conceptual Framework* paragraphs 2.30–2.32] *timeliness* [Refer: *Conceptual Framework* paragraph 2.33] and *understandability* [Refer: *Conceptual Framework* paragraphs 2.34–2.36].

[Refer: *Conceptual Framework* paragraphs 2.37 and 2.38]

Materiality

21   Management should include information that is material to the entity in management commentary. *Materiality* will be different for each entity. Materiality is an 'entity-specific aspect of relevance'; thus information that is relevant for an entity will also be material.

[Refer: *Conceptual Framework* paragraph 2.11]

Presentation

[Refer:

Introduction paragraph IN5

Basis for Conclusions paragraphs BC45 and BC46]

22   Management commentary should be clear and straightforward. The form and content of management commentary will vary between entities, reflecting the nature of their business, the strategies adopted by management and the regulatory environment in which they operate.

23   Management commentary should be presented with a focus on the most important information in a manner intended to address the principles described in this Practice Statement. Specifically:

(a)   Management commentary should be consistent with its related financial statements. If the financial statements include segment information, the information presented in the management commentary should reflect that segmentation.

(b)   When practicable, management should avoid duplicating in its management commentary the disclosures made in the notes to its financial statements. Reciting financial statement information without analysis, or presenting boilerplate discussions that do not provide insight into the entity's past performance or prospects, is unlikely to provide information that is useful to users of the financial reports and may create an obstacle for users to identify and understand the most significant matters facing the entity.

(c)   Management should also avoid generic disclosures that do not relate to the practices and circumstances of the entity and immaterial disclosures that make the more important information difficult to find.

Elements of management commentary

[Refer: Basis for Conclusions paragraphs BC47–BC49]

24   Although the particular focus of management commentary will depend on the facts and circumstances of the entity, management commentary should include information that is essential to an understanding of:

(a)   the nature of the business; [Refer: paragraph 26]

(b)   management's objectives and its strategies for meeting those objectives; [Refer: paragraphs 27 and 28]

(c)   the entity's most significant resources, risks and relationships; [Refer: paragraphs 29–33]

(d)   the results of operations and prospects; [Refer: paragraphs 34–36] and

(e)   the critical performance measures and indicators that management uses to evaluate the entity's performance against stated objectives. [Refer: paragraphs 37–40]

25   The elements are not listed in a specific order. They are, however, related and should not be presented in isolation. Management should provide its perspective on the business and its analysis of the interaction of the elements to help users to understand the entity's financial statements and to understand management's objectives and strategies for achieving those objectives.

Nature of the business
[Refer:

paragraph 24(a)

Basis for Conclusions paragraph BC48]

26   Management should provide a description of the business to help users of the financial reports to gain an understanding of the entity and of the external environment in which it operates. That information serves as a starting point for assessing and understanding an entity's performance, strategic options and prospects. Depending on the nature of the business, management commentary may include an integrated discussion of the following types of information:

    (a)   the industries in which the entity operates;

    (b)   the entity's main markets and competitive position within those markets;

    (c)   significant features of the legal, regulatory and macro-economic environments that influence the entity and the markets in which the entity operates;

    (d)   the entity's main products, services, business processes and distribution methods; and

    (e)   the entity's structure and how it creates value.

Objectives and strategies
[Refer:

paragraph 24(b)

Basis for Conclusions paragraph BC48]

27   Management should disclose its objectives and strategies in a way that enables users of the financial reports to understand the priorities for action as well as to identify the resources that must be managed to deliver results. For example, information about how management intends to address market trends and the threats and opportunities those market trends represent provides users of the financial reports with insight that may shape their expectations about the entity's future performance. Management should also explain how success will be measured and over what period of time it should be assessed.

28   Management should discuss significant changes in an entity's objectives and strategies from the previous period or periods. Discussion of the relationship between objectives, strategy, management actions and executive remuneration is also helpful.

Resources, risks and relationships

[Refer:
paragraph 24(c)
Basis for Conclusions paragraph BC48]

29   Management commentary should include a clear description of the most important resources, risks and relationships that management believes can affect the entity's value and how those resources, risks and relationships are managed.

Resources

30   Management commentary should set out the critical financial and non-financial resources available to the entity and how those resources are used in meeting management's stated objectives for the entity. Disclosure about resources depends on the nature of the entity and on the industries in which the entity operates. Analysis of the adequacy of the entity's capital structure, financial arrangements (whether or not recognised in the statement of financial position), liquidity and cash flows, and human and intellectual capital resources, as well as plans to address any surplus resources or identified and expected inadequacies, are examples of disclosures that can provide useful information.

Risks

31   Management should disclose an entity's principal risk exposures and changes in those risks, together with its plans and strategies for bearing or mitigating those risks, as well as disclosure of the effectiveness of its risk management strategies. This disclosure helps users to evaluate the entity's risks as well as its expected outcomes. Management should distinguish the principal risks and uncertainties facing the entity, rather than listing all possible risks and uncertainties.

32   Management should disclose its principal strategic, commercial, operational and financial risks, which are those that may significantly affect the entity's strategies and progress of the entity's value. The description of the principal risks facing the entity should cover both exposures to negative consequences and potential opportunities. Management commentary provides useful information when it discusses the principal risks and uncertainties necessary to understand management's objectives and strategies for the entity. The principal risks and uncertainties can constitute either a significant external or internal risk to the entity.

Relationships

33   Management should identify the significant relationships that the entity has with stakeholders, how those relationships are likely to affect the performance and value of the entity, and how those relationships are managed. This type of disclosure helps users of the financial reports to understand how an entity's relationships influence the nature of its business and whether an entity's relationships expose the business to substantial risk.

Results and prospects
[Refer:

paragraph 24(d)

Basis for Conclusions paragraph BC48]

34   Management commentary should include a clear description of the entity's financial and non-financial performance, the extent to which that performance may be indicative of future performance and management's assessment of the entity's prospects. Useful disclosure on those matters can help users to make their own assessments about the entity's performance, position, progress and prospects.

Results

35   Management commentary should include explanations of the performance and progress of the entity during the period and its position at the end of that period. Those explanations provide users of the financial reports with insight into the main trends and factors affecting the business. In providing those explanations, management should describe the relationship between the entity's results, management's objectives and management's strategies for achieving those objectives. In addition, management should provide discussion and analysis of significant changes in financial position, liquidity and performance compared with those of the previous period or periods, as this can help users to understand the extent to which past performance may be indicative of future performance.

Prospects

36   Management should provide an analysis of the prospects of the entity, which may include targets for financial and non-financial measures. This information can help users of the financial reports to understand how management intends to implement its strategies for the entity over the long term. When targets are quantified, management should explain the risks and assumptions necessary for users to assess the likelihood of achieving those targets.

Performance measures and indicators
[Refer:

paragraph 24(e)

Basis for Conclusions paragraph BC48]

37   Performance measures are quantified measurements that reflect the critical success factors of an entity. Indicators can be narrative evidence describing how the business is managed or quantified measures that provide indirect evidence of performance. Management should disclose performance measures and indicators (both financial and non-financial) that are used by management to assess progress against its stated objectives. Management should explain why the results from performance measures have changed over the period or how the indicators have changed. This disclosure can help users of the financial reports assess the extent to which goals and objectives are being achieved.

38   The performance measures and indicators that are most important to understanding an entity are those that management uses to manage that entity. The performance measures and indicators will usually reflect the industry in which the entity operates. Comparability is enhanced if the performance measures and indicators are accepted and used widely, either within an industry or more generally. Management should explain why the performance measures and indicators used are relevant.

39   Consistent reporting of performance measures and indicators increases the comparability of management commentary over time. However, management should consider whether the performance measures and indicators used in the previous period continue to be relevant. As strategies and objectives change, management might decide that the performance measures and indicators presented in the previous period's management commentary are no longer relevant. When management changes the performance measures and indicators used, the changes should be identified and explained.

40   If information from the financial statements has been adjusted for inclusion in management commentary, that fact should be disclosed. If financial performance measures that are not required or defined by IFRSs are included within management commentary, those measures should be defined and explained, including an explanation of the relevance of the measure to users. When financial performance measures are derived or drawn from the financial statements, those measures should be reconciled to measures presented in the financial statements that have been prepared in accordance with IFRSs.

Application date

41   An entity may apply this Practice Statement to management commentary presented prospectively from **8 December 2010**.

Appendix
Defined terms

This appendix is an integral part of the Practice Statement.

forward-looking information	Information about the future. It includes information about the future (for example, information about prospects and plans) that may later be presented as historical information (ie results). It is subjective and its preparation requires the exercise of professional judgement.
	[Refer: Basis for Conclusions paragraphs BC35–BC41]
management commentary	A narrative report that relates to financial statements that have been prepared in accordance with IFRSs. Management commentary provides users with historical explanations of the amounts presented in the financial statements, specifically the entity's financial position, financial performance and cash flows. It also provides commentary on an entity's prospects and other information not presented in the financial statements. Management commentary also serves as a basis for understanding management's objectives and its strategies for achieving those objectives.
	[Refer:
	Introduction paragraph IN3
	Basis for Conclusions paragraphs BC26–BC32]
progress	Reflects how the entity has grown or changed in the current year, as well as how it expects to grow or change in the future.
	[Refer: Basis for Conclusions paragraph BC28]

The following terms are used in the Practice Statement with the meanings specified in the *Conceptual Framework for Financial Reporting*:

(a)   comparability **[Refer: *Conceptual Framework* paragraphs 2.24–2.29]**

(b)   faithful representation **[Refer: *Conceptual Framework* paragraphs 2.12–2.19]**

(c)   materiality **[Refer: *Conceptual Framework* paragraph 2.11]**

(d)   relevance **[Refer: *Conceptual Framework* paragraphs 2.6–2.10]**

(e)   timeliness **[Refer: *Conceptual Framework* paragraph 2.33]**

(f)   understandability **[Refer: *Conceptual Framework* paragraphs 2.34–2.36]**

(g)   verifiability **[Refer: *Conceptual Framework* paragraphs 2.30–2.32]**.

IFRS Practice Statement 2

Making Materiality Judgements

IFRS Practice Statement 2 *Making Materiality Judgements* was issued in September 2017 for application from 14 September 2017. The text of the Basis for Conclusions is contained in Part C of this edition.

In February 2021 the Board issued *Disclosure of Accounting Policies* which amended IAS 1 *Presentation of Financial Statements* and IFRS Practice Statement 2. The amendment amended IFRS Practice Statement 2 to add guidance to help entities apply the definition of material in making decisions about accounting policy disclosures.

Other Standards have made minor consequential amendments to IFRS Practice Statement 2 *Making Materiality Judgements*, including *Amendments to References to the Conceptual Framework in IFRS Standards* (issued March 2018) and *Definition of Material* (Amendments to IAS 1 and IAS 8) issued October 2018.

Contents

continued...

...continued

APPROVAL BY THE BOARD OF AMENDMENTS TO IFRS PRACTICE STATEMENT 2:

Disclosure of Accounting Policies issued in February 2021

FOR THE BASIS FOR CONCLUSIONS, SEE PART C OF THIS EDITION

BASIS FOR CONCLUSIONS

IFRS Practice Statement 2 *Making Materiality Judgements* (Practice Statement) is set out in paragraphs 1–89. This Practice Statement should be read in the context of its objective and Basis for Conclusions, as well as in the context of the *Preface to IFRS Standards*, the *Conceptual Framework for Financial Reporting* and IFRS Standards.

Introduction

IN1   The objective of general purpose financial statements is to provide financial information about a reporting entity that is useful to existing and potential investors, lenders and other creditors in making decisions about providing resources to the entity. The entity identifies the information necessary to meet that objective by making appropriate materiality judgements. **[Refer: paragraph 7]**

IN2   The aim of this IFRS Practice Statement 2 *Making Materiality Judgements* (Practice Statement) is to provide reporting entities with guidance on making materiality judgements when preparing general purpose financial statements in accordance with IFRS Standards. **[Refer: paragraph 1]** While some of the guidance in this Practice Statement may be useful to entities applying the *IFRS for SMEs*® Standard, the Practice Statement is not intended for those entities. **[Refer: paragraph 3]**

IN3   The need for materiality judgements is pervasive in the preparation of financial statements. An entity makes materiality judgements when making decisions about recognition and measurement as well as presentation and disclosure. Requirements in IFRS Standards only need to be applied if their effect is material to the complete set of financial statements. **[Refer: paragraph 8]**

IN4   This Practice Statement:

     (a)   provides an overview of the general characteristics of materiality. **[Refer: paragraphs 5–26]**

     (b)   presents a four-step process an entity may follow in making materiality judgements when preparing its financial statements (materiality process). The description of the materiality process provides an overview of the role materiality plays in the preparation of financial statements, with a focus on the factors the entity should consider when making materiality judgements. **[Refer: paragraphs 29–65]**

     (c)   provides guidance on how to make materiality judgements in specific circumstances, namely, how to make materiality judgements about prior-period information, **[Refer: paragraphs 66–71]** errors **[Refer: paragraphs 72–80]** and covenants, **[Refer: paragraphs 81–83]** and in the context of interim reporting. **[Refer: paragraphs 84–88]**

IN5   Whether information is material is a matter of judgement and depends on the facts involved and the circumstances of a specific entity. This Practice Statement illustrates the types of factors that the entity should consider when judging whether information is material. **[Refer: paragraphs 42–55]**

IN6   A Practice Statement is non-mandatory guidance developed by the International Accounting Standards Board. It is not a Standard. Therefore, its application is not required to state compliance with IFRS Standards. **[Refer: paragraph 4]**

IN7   This Practice Statement includes examples illustrating how an entity might apply some of the guidance in the Practice Statement based on the limited facts presented. The analysis in each example is not intended to represent the only manner in which the guidance could be applied.

IFRS Practice Statement 2
Making Materiality Judgements

Objective

[Refer:

Basis for Conclusions paragraphs BC1–BC4 (reasons for issuing the Practice Statement)]

[Link to Basis for Conclusions paragraphs BC42–BC45 for likely effects of this Practice Statement]

1   This IFRS Practice Statement 2 *Making Materiality Judgements* (Practice Statement) provides reporting entities with non-mandatory guidance **[Refer: Basis for Conclusions paragraphs BC5–BC8]** on making materiality judgements when preparing general purpose financial statements in accordance with IFRS Standards.
[Refer: Basis for Conclusions paragraph BC11]

2   The guidance may also help other parties involved in financial reporting to understand how an entity makes materiality judgements when preparing such financial statements. **[Refer: Basis for Conclusions paragraph BC11]**

Scope

3   The Practice Statement is applicable when preparing financial statements in accordance with IFRS Standards. It is not intended for entities applying the *IFRS for SMEs*® Standard. **[Refer: Basis for Conclusions paragraph BC12]**

4   The Practice Statement provides non-mandatory guidance; **[Refer: Basis for Conclusions paragraphs BC5–BC8]** therefore, its application is not required to state compliance with IFRS Standards.

General characteristics of materiality

Definition of material

5   The *Conceptual Framework for Financial Reporting* (*Conceptual Framework*) provides the following definition of material information (paragraph 7 of IAS 1 *Presentation of Financial Statements* provides a similar definition[1]):

> Information is material if omitting, misstating or obscuring it could reasonably be expected to influence decisions that the primary users of general purpose financial reports make on the basis of those reports, which provide financial information about a specific reporting entity. In other words, materiality is an entity-specific aspect of relevance based on the nature or magnitude, or both, of the items to which the information relates in the context of an individual entity's financial report.[2]

[Refer: Basis for Conclusions paragraphs BC14–BC15]

---

1   See paragraph 7 of IAS 1 *Presentation of Financial Statements*.
2   Paragraph 2.11 of the *Conceptual Framework for Financial Reporting* (*Conceptual Framework*).

6 When making materiality judgements, an entity needs to take into account how information could reasonably be expected to influence the primary users of its financial statements—its primary users—when they make decisions[3] on the basis of those statements (see paragraphs 13–23).[4]

7 The objective of financial statements is to provide financial information about a reporting entity that is useful to existing and potential investors, lenders and other creditors in making decisions about providing resources to the entity.[5] The entity identifies the information necessary to meet that objective by making appropriate materiality judgements.

Materiality judgements are pervasive
[Refer: Basis for Conclusions paragraph BC16]

8 The need for materiality judgements is pervasive in the preparation of financial statements. An entity makes materiality judgements when making decisions about recognition, measurement, presentation and disclosure. Requirements in IFRS Standards only need to be applied if their effect is material to the complete set of financial statements,[6] which includes the primary financial statements[7] and the notes. However, it is inappropriate for the entity to make, or leave uncorrected, immaterial departures from IFRS Standards to achieve a particular presentation of its financial position, financial performance or cash flows.[8]

Recognition and measurement

9 IFRS Standards set out reporting requirements that the International Accounting Standards Board (Board) has concluded will lead to financial statements that provide information about the financial position, financial performance and cash flows of an entity that is useful to the primary users of those statements. The entity is only required to apply recognition and measurement requirements when the effect of applying them is material.
[Refer: IAS 8 paragraph 8]

---

3 Throughout this Practice Statement, the term 'decisions' refers to decisions about providing resources to the entity, unless specifically indicated otherwise.
4 See paragraph 7 of IAS 1.
5 See paragraph 1.2 of the *Conceptual Framework*.
6 In this Practice Statement the phrases 'complete set of financial statements' and 'financial statements as a whole' are used interchangeably.
7 For the purposes of this Practice Statement, the primary financial statements comprise the statement of financial position, statement(s) of financial performance, statement of changes in equity and statement of cash flows.
8 See paragraph 8 of IAS 8 *Accounting Policies, Changes in Accounting Estimates and Errors*.

Example A—materiality judgements on the application of accounting policies

Background

An entity has a policy of capitalising expenditures on items of property, plant and equipment (PP&E) in excess of a specified threshold and recognising any smaller amounts as an expense.

Application

IAS 16 *Property, Plant and Equipment* requires that the cost of an item of PP&E is recognised as an asset when the criteria in paragraph 7 of IAS 16 are met.

The entity has assessed that its accounting policy—not capitalising expenditure below a specific threshold—will not have a material effect on the current-period financial statements or on future financial statements, because information reflecting the capitalisation and amortisation of such expenditure could not reasonably be expected to influence decisions made by the primary users of the entity's financial statements.

Provided that such a policy does not have a material effect on the financial statements and was not set to intentionally achieve a particular presentation of the entity's financial position, financial performance or cash flows, the entity's financial statements comply with IAS 16. Such a policy is nevertheless reassessed each reporting period to ensure that its effect on the entity's financial statements remains immaterial.

Presentation and disclosure

10   An entity need not provide a disclosure specified by an IFRS Standard if the information resulting from that disclosure is not material. This is the case even if the Standard contains a list of specific disclosure requirements or describes them as 'minimum requirements'. Conversely, the entity must consider whether to provide information not specified by IFRS Standards if that information is necessary for primary users to understand the impact of particular transactions, other events and conditions on the entity's financial position, financial performance and cash flows.[9]

Example B—materiality judgements on disclosures specified by IFRS Standards

Background

An entity presents property, plant and equipment (PP&E) as a separate line item in its statement of financial position.

Application

IAS 16 *Property, Plant and Equipment* sets out specific disclosure requirements for PP&E, including the disclosure of the amount of contractual commitments for the acquisition of PP&E (paragraph 74(c) of IAS 16).

---

continued...

---

9   See paragraphs 17(c) and 31 of IAS 1.

...continued

When preparing its financial statements, the entity assesses whether disclosures specified in IAS 16 are material information. Even if PP&E is presented as a separate line item in the statement of financial position, not all disclosures specified in IAS 16 will automatically be required. In the absence of any qualitative considerations (see paragraphs 46–51), if the amount of contractual commitments for the acquisition of PP&E is not material, the entity is not required to disclose this information.

Example C—materiality judgements that lead to the disclosure of information in addition to the specific disclosure requirements in IFRS Standards

Background

An entity has its main operations in a country that, as part of an international agreement, is committed to introducing regulations to reduce the use of carbon-based energy. The regulations had not yet been enacted in the national legislation of that country at the end of the reporting period.

The entity owns a coal-fired power station in that country. During the reporting period, the entity recorded an impairment loss on its coal-fired power station, reducing the carrying amount of the power station to its recoverable amount. No goodwill or intangible assets with an indefinite useful life were included in the cash-generating unit.

Application

Paragraph 132 of IAS 36 *Impairment of Assets* does not require an entity to disclose the assumptions used to determine the recoverable amount of a tangible asset, unless goodwill or intangible assets with an indefinite useful life are included in the carrying amount of the cash-generating unit.

Nevertheless, the entity has concluded that the assumptions about the likelihood of national enactment of regulations to reduce the use of carbon-based energy, as well as about the enactment plan, it considered in measuring the recoverable amount of its coal-fired power station could reasonably be expected to influence decisions primary users make on the basis of the entity's financial statements. Hence, information about those assumptions is necessary for primary users to understand the impact of the impairment on the entity's financial position, financial performance and cash flows. Therefore, even though not specifically required by IAS 36, the entity concludes that its assumptions about the likelihood of national enactment of regulations to reduce the use of carbon-based energy, as well as about the enactment plan, constitute material information and discloses those assumptions in its financial statements.

Judgement

11   When assessing whether information is material to the financial statements, an entity applies judgement to decide whether the information could reasonably be expected to influence decisions that primary users make on the basis of those financial statements. When applying such judgement, the entity considers both its specific circumstances and how the information provided in the financial statements responds to the information needs of primary users.

12   Because an entity's circumstances change over time, materiality judgements are reassessed at each reporting date in the light of those changed circumstances.

Primary users and their information needs

13   When making materiality judgements, an entity needs to consider the impact information could reasonably be expected to have on the primary users of its financial statements. Those primary users are existing and potential investors, lenders and other creditors—those users who cannot require entities to provide information directly to them and must rely on general purpose financial statements for much of the financial information they need.[10] In addition to those primary users, other parties, such as the entity's management, regulators and members of the public, may be interested in financial information about the entity and may find the financial statements useful. However, the financial statements are not primarily directed at these other parties.[11]

[Refer: Basis for Conclusions paragraph BC17]

14   Because primary users include potential investors, lenders and other creditors, it would be inappropriate for an entity to narrow the information provided in its financial statements by focusing only on the information needs of existing investors, lenders and other creditors.

[Refer: Basis for Conclusions paragraph BC18]

---

10 See paragraph 1.5 of the *Conceptual Framework*.
11 See paragraphs 1.9 and 1.10 of the *Conceptual Framework*.

Example D—existing and potential investors, lenders and other creditors

Background

An entity is 100 per cent owned by its parent. Its parent provides the entity with semi-finished products that the entity assembles and sells back to the parent. The entity is entirely financed by its parent. The current users of the entity's financial statements include the parent and the entity's creditors (mainly local suppliers).

Application

The entity refers to the *Conceptual Framework for Financial Reporting* to identify the primary users of its financial statements—existing and potential investors, lenders and other creditors who cannot require the entity to provide information directly to them and must rely on general purpose financial statements. When making materiality judgements in the preparation of its financial statements, the entity does not reduce its disclosures to only those of interest to its parent or its existing creditors. The entity also considers the information needs of potential investors, lenders and other creditors when making those judgements.

---

15   When making materiality judgements, an entity also considers that primary users are expected to have a reasonable knowledge of business and economic activities and to review and analyse the information included in the financial statements diligently.[12]

Decisions made by primary users
[Refer: Basis for Conclusions paragraph BC19]

16   An entity needs to consider what type of decisions its primary users make on the basis of the financial statements and, consequently, what information they need to make those decisions.

17   The primary users of an entity's financial statements make decisions about providing resources to the entity. Those decisions involve: buying, selling or holding equity and debt instruments, providing or settling loans and other forms of credit, and exercising rights while holding investments (such as the right to vote on or otherwise influence management's actions that affect the use of the entity's economic resources).[13] Such decisions depend on the returns that primary users expect from an investment in those instruments.

18   The expectations existing and potential investors, lenders and other creditors have about returns, in turn, depend on their assessment of the amount, timing and uncertainty of the future net cash inflows to an entity,[14] together with their assessment of management's stewardship of the entity's resources.

---

12 See paragraph 2.36 of the *Conceptual Framework*.

13 See paragraph 1.2 of the *Conceptual Framework*.

14 See paragraph 1.3 of the *Conceptual Framework*.

© IFRS Foundation

19　　　Consequently, an entity's primary users need information about:

　　(a)　the resources of the entity (assets), claims against the entity (liabilities and equity) and changes in those resources and claims (income and expenses); and

　　(b)　how efficiently and effectively the entity's management and governing board have discharged their responsibility to use the entity's resources.[15]

20　　　Financial information can make a difference in decisions if it has predictive value, confirmatory value or both.[16] When making materiality judgements, an entity needs to assess whether information could reasonably be expected to influence primary users' decisions, rather than assessing whether that information alone could reasonably be expected to change their decisions.

Meeting primary users' information needs
[Refer: Basis for Conclusions paragraph BC20]

21　　　The objective of financial statements is to provide primary users with financial information that is useful to them in making decisions about providing resources to an entity. However, general purpose financial statements do not, and cannot, provide all the information that primary users need.[17] Therefore, the entity aims to meet the common information needs of its primary users. It does not aim to address specialised information needs—information needs that are unique to particular users.

Example E—primary users' unique or individual information requests

Background

Twenty investors each hold 5 per cent of an entity's voting rights. One of these investors is particularly interested in information about the entity's expenditure in a specific location because that investor operates another business in that location. Such information could not reasonably be expected to influence decisions that other primary users make on the basis of the entity's financial statements.

Application

In making its materiality judgements, the entity does not need to consider the specific information needs of that single investor. The entity concludes that information about its expenditure in the specific location is immaterial information for its primary users as a group and therefore decides not to provide it in its financial statements.

22　　　To meet the common information needs of its primary users, an entity first separately identifies the information needs that are shared by users within one of the three categories of primary users defined in the *Conceptual Framework*—for example investors (existing and potential)—then repeats the

---

15　See paragraph 1.4 of the *Conceptual Framework*.

16　See paragraph 2.7 of the *Conceptual Framework*.

17　See paragraph 1.6 of the *Conceptual Framework*.

assessment for the two remaining categories—namely lenders (existing and potential) and other creditors (existing and potential). The total of the information needs identified is the set of common information needs the entity aims to meet.

23   In other words, the assessment of common information needs does not require identifying information needs shared across all existing and potential investors, lenders and other creditors. Some of the identified information needs will be common to all three categories, but others may be specific to only one or two of those categories. If an entity were to focus only on those information needs that are common to all categories of primary users, it might exclude information that meets the needs of only one category.

Impact of publicly available information

24   The primary users of financial statements generally consider information from sources other than just the financial statements. For example, they might also consider other sections of the annual report, information about the industry an entity operates in, its competitors and the state of the economy, the entity's press releases as well as other documents the entity has published.

25   However, the financial statements are required to be a comprehensive document that provides information about the financial position, financial performance and cash flows of an entity that is useful to primary users in making decisions about providing resources to the entity. Consequently, the entity assesses whether information is material to the financial statements, regardless of whether such information is also publicly available from another source.

26   Moreover, public availability of information does not relieve an entity of the obligation to provide material information in its financial statements.

Example F—impact of an entity's press release on materiality judgements

Background

An entity undertook a business combination in the reporting period. The acquisition doubled the size of the entity's operations in one of its main markets. On the acquisition date, the entity issued a press release providing an extensive explanation of the primary reasons for the business combination and a description of how it obtained control over the acquired business, together with other information related to the acquisition.

Application

In preparing its financial statements, the entity first considered the disclosure requirements in IFRS 3 *Business Combinations*. Paragraph B64(d) of IFRS 3 requires an entity to disclose, for each business combination that occurs during the reporting period, 'the primary reasons for the business combination and a description of how the acquirer obtained control of the acquiree'.

continued...

...continued

> The entity concludes that information about the business combination is material because the acquisition is expected to have a significant impact on the entity's operations, due to the overall size of the transaction compared with the size of the entity. In these circumstances, even though information relating to the primary reasons for the business combination and the description of how it obtained control is already included in a public statement, the entity needs to provide the information in its financial statements.

Interaction with local laws and regulations

[Refer: Basis for Conclusions paragraphs BC21–BC23]

27   An entity's financial statements must comply with the requirements in IFRS Standards, including requirements related to materiality (materiality requirements), for the entity to state its compliance with those Standards. Hence, an entity that wishes to state compliance with IFRS Standards cannot provide less information than the information required by the Standards, even if local laws and regulations permit otherwise. **[Refer: paragraph 69]**

28   Nevertheless, local laws and regulations may specify requirements that affect what information is provided in the financial statements. In such circumstances, providing information to meet local legal or regulatory requirements is permitted by IFRS Standards, even if that information is not material according to the materiality requirements in the Standards. However, such information must not obscure information that is material according to IFRS Standards.[18]

> **Example G—information that is immaterial according to IFRS Standards required by local laws and regulations**
>
> **Background**
>
> An entity is a food retailer operating in country ABC. In country ABC, investments in research and development (R&D) are generally limited across the industry; nonetheless, the government requires all entities to disclose, in their financial statements, the aggregate amount of R&D expenditure incurred during the period.
>
> In the current reporting period, the entity recognised a small amount of expenditure on R&D activities as an expense. No R&D expenditure was capitalised during the period.
>
> When preparing its financial statements, the entity assessed the disclosure of information about R&D expenditure incurred during the period as immaterial, for IFRS purposes.
>
> *continued...*

18   See paragraph 30A of IAS 1 and paragraph BC30F of the Basis for Conclusions on IAS 1.

...continued

Application

To comply with local regulations, the entity discloses in its financial statements information about R&D expenditure incurred during the period. IFRS Standards permit the entity to disclose that information in its financial statements, but the entity needs to organise its disclosures to ensure that material information is not obscured.

Example H—information that is material according to IFRS Standards not required by local laws and regulations

Background

An entity operates in a country where the government requires the disclosure of the details of property, plant and equipment (PP&E) disposals, but only if their carrying amounts exceed a specified percentage of total assets.

In the current reporting period, the entity disposed of PP&E below the threshold specified in the local regulation. This transaction was with a related party, which paid the entity less than the fair value of the item disposed.

When preparing its financial statements, the entity applied judgement and concluded that information about the details of the disposal was material, mainly because of the terms of the transaction and the fact it was with a related party.

Application

To comply with IFRS Standards, the entity discloses details of that disposal even though local regulations require disclosure of PP&E disposals only if their carrying amount exceeds a specified percentage of total assets.

Making materiality judgements

Overview of the materiality process

29   An entity may find it helpful to follow a systematic process in making materiality judgements when preparing its financial statements. **[Refer: Basis for Conclusions paragraph BC24]** The four-step process described in the following paragraphs is an example of such a process. This description provides an overview of the role materiality plays in the preparation of financial statements, with a focus on the factors **[Refer: paragraphs 44–55]** the entity should consider when making materiality judgements. In this Practice Statement, this four-step process is called the 'materiality process'.

[Refer: Basis for Conclusions paragraph BC26]

30   The materiality process describes how an entity could assess whether information is material for the purposes of presentation and disclosure, as well as for recognition and measurement. The process illustrates one possible way to make materiality judgements, but it incorporates the materiality

requirements an entity must apply to state compliance with IFRS Standards. **[Refer: Basis for Conclusions paragraph BC25]** The materiality process considers potential omission and potential misstatement of information, as well as unnecessary inclusion of immaterial information and whether immaterial information obscures material information. In all cases, the entity needs to focus on how the information could reasonably be expected to influence decisions of the primary users of its financial statements.

31   Judgement is involved in assessing materiality when preparing financial statements. The materiality process is designed as a practice guide to help an entity apply judgement in an efficient and effective way.

32   The materiality process is not intended to describe the assessment of materiality for local legal and regulatory purposes. An entity refers to its local requirements to assess whether it is compliant with local laws and regulations.

A four-step materiality process

33   The steps identified as a possible approach to the assessment of materiality in the preparation of the financial statements are, in summary:

(a)   Step 1—identify. Identify information that has the potential to be material. **[Refer: paragraphs 35–39]**

(b)   Step 2—assess. Assess whether the information identified in Step 1 is, in fact, material. **[Refer: paragraphs 40–55]**

(c)   Step 3—organise. Organise the information within the draft financial statements in a way that communicates the information clearly and concisely to primary users. **[Refer: paragraphs 56–59]**

(d)   Step 4—review. Review the draft financial statements to determine whether all material information has been identified and materiality considered from a wide perspective and in aggregate, on the basis of the complete set of financial statements. **[Refer: paragraphs 60–65]**

34   When preparing its financial statements, an entity may rely on materiality assessments from prior periods, provided that it reconsiders them in the light of any change in circumstances and of any new or updated information.

Diagram 1—the four-step materiality process

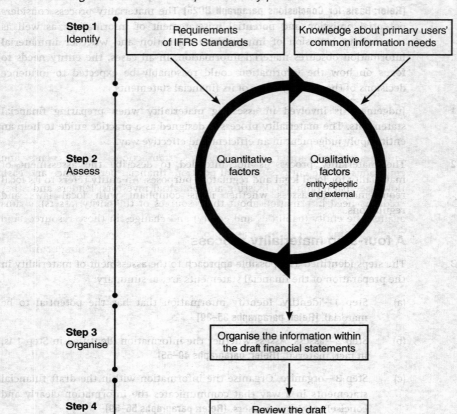

Step 1
Identify

Requirements
of IFRS Standards

Knowledge about primary users'
common information needs

Step 2
Assess

Quantitative
factors

Qualitative
factors
entity-specific
and external

Step 3
Organise

Organise the information within
the draft financial statements

Step 4
Review

Review the draft
financial statements

Step 1—identify
[Refer: Basis for Conclusions paragraph BC27]

35   An entity identifies information about its transactions, other events and
      conditions that primary users might need to understand to make decisions
      about providing resources to the entity.

36   In identifying this information, an entity considers, as a starting point, the
      requirements of the IFRS Standards applicable to its transactions, other events
      and conditions. This is the starting point because, when developing a
      Standard, the Board identifies the information it expects will meet the needs
      of a broad range of primary users for a wide variety of entities in a range of
      circumstances.[19]

---

19   See paragraph 1.8 of the *Conceptual Framework*.

37　　　　When the Board develops a Standard, it also considers the balance between the benefits of providing information and the costs of complying with the requirements in that Standard. **[Refer: *Conceptual Framework* paragraph 2.42]** However, the cost of applying the requirements in the Standards is not a factor for an entity to consider when making materiality judgements—the entity should not consider the cost of complying with requirements in IFRS Standards, unless there is explicit permission in the Standards.

38　　　　An entity also considers its primary users' common information needs (as explained in paragraphs 21–23) to identify any information—in addition to that specified in IFRS Standards—necessary to enable primary users to understand the impact of the entity's transactions, other events and conditions on the entity's financial position, financial performance and cash flows (see paragraph 10). Existing and potential investors, lenders and other creditors need information about the resources of the entity (assets), claims against the entity (liabilities and equity) and changes in those resources and claims (income and expenses), and information that will help them assess how efficiently and effectively the entity's management and governing board have discharged their responsibility to use the entity's resources.[20]

39　　　　The output of Step 1 is a set of potentially material information.

Step 2—assess
[Refer: Basis for Conclusions paragraph BC28]

40　　　　An entity assesses whether the potentially material information identified in Step 1 is, in fact, material. In making this assessment, the entity needs to consider whether its primary users could reasonably be expected to be influenced by the information when making decisions about providing resources to the entity on the basis of the financial statements. The entity performs this assessment in the context of the financial statements as a whole.

41　　　　An entity might conclude that an item of information is material for various reasons. Those reasons include the item's nature or magnitude, or a combination of both, judged in relation to the particular circumstances of the entity.[21] Therefore, making materiality judgements involves both quantitative and qualitative considerations. It would not be appropriate for the entity to rely on purely numerical guidelines or to apply a uniform quantitative threshold for materiality (see paragraphs 53–55).

42　　　　The following paragraphs describe some common 'materiality factors' that an entity should use to help identify when an item of information is material. These factors are organised into the following categories:

　　　　(a)　　quantitative; **[Refer: paragraphs 44 and 45]** and

　　　　(b)　　qualitative—either entity-specific or external. **[Refer: paragraphs 46–51]**

20　See paragraph 1.4 of the *Conceptual Framework*.

21　See paragraph 7 of IAS 1.

43   The output of Step 2 is a preliminary set of material information. For presentation and disclosure, this involves decisions about what information an entity needs to provide in its financial statements, and in how much detail[22] (including identifying appropriate levels of aggregation an entity provides in the financial statements). For recognition and measurement, the output of Step 2 involves the identification of information that, if not recognised or otherwise misstated, could reasonably be expected to influence primary users' decisions.

Quantitative factors

44   An entity ordinarily assesses whether information is quantitatively material by considering the size of the impact of the transaction, other event or condition against measures of the entity's financial position, financial performance and cash flows. The entity makes this assessment by considering not only the size of the impact it recognises in its primary financial statements but also any unrecognised items that could ultimately affect primary users' overall perception of the entity's financial position, financial performance and cash flows (eg contingent liabilities or contingent assets). The entity needs to assess whether the impact is of such a size that information about the transaction, other event or condition could reasonably be expected to influence its primary users' decisions about providing resources to the entity.

45   Identifying the measures against which an entity makes this quantitative assessment is a matter of judgement. That judgement depends on which measures are of great interest to the primary users of the entity's financial statements. Examples include measures of the entity's revenues, the entity's profitability, financial position ratios and cash flow measures.

Qualitative factors

46   For the purposes of this Practice Statement, qualitative factors are characteristics of an entity's transactions, other events or conditions, or of their context, that, if present, make information more likely to influence the decisions of the primary users of the entity's financial statements. The mere presence of a qualitative factor will not necessarily make the information material, but is likely to increase primary users' interest in that information.

47   In making materiality judgements, an entity considers both entity-specific [Refer: paragraph 48] and external [Refer: paragraphs 49–51] qualitative factors. These factors are described separately in the following paragraphs. However, in practice, the entity may need to consider them together.

48   An entity-specific qualitative factor is a characteristic of the entity's transaction, other event or condition. Examples of such factors include, but are not limited to:

(a)   involvement of a related party of the entity;

---

22   See paragraph 29 of IAS 1.

(b)   uncommon, or non-standard, features of a transaction or other event or condition; or

(c)   unexpected variation or unexpected changes in trends. In some circumstances, the entity might consider a quantitatively immaterial amount as material because of the unexpected variation compared to the prior-period amount provided in its financial statements.

49   The relevance of information to the primary users of an entity's financial statements can also be affected by the context in which the entity operates. An external qualitative factor is a characteristic of the context in which the entity's transaction, other event or condition occur that, if present, makes information more likely to influence the primary users' decisions. Characteristics of the entity's context that might represent external qualitative factors include, but are not limited to, the entity's geographical location, its industry sector, or the state of the economy or economies in which the entity operates.

50   Due to the nature of external qualitative factors, entities operating in the same context might share a number of external qualitative factors. Moreover, external qualitative factors could remain constant over time or could vary.

51   In some circumstances, if an entity is not exposed to a risk to which other entities in its industry are exposed, that fact could reasonably be expected to influence its primary users' decisions; that is, information about the lack of exposure to that particular risk could be material information.

Interaction of qualitative and quantitative factors

52   An entity could identify an item of information as material on the basis of one or more materiality factors. In general, the more factors that apply to a particular item, or the more significant those factors are, the more likely it is that the item is material.

53   Although there is no hierarchy among materiality factors, assessing an item of information from a quantitative perspective first could be an efficient approach to assessing materiality. If an entity identifies an item of information as material solely on the basis of the size of the impact of the transaction, other event or condition, the entity does not need to assess that item of information further against other materiality factors. In these circumstances, a quantitative threshold—a specified level, rate or amount of one of the measures used in assessing size—can be a helpful tool in making a materiality judgement. However, a quantitative assessment alone is not always sufficient to conclude that an item of information is not material. The entity should further assess the presence of qualitative factors.

54   The presence of a qualitative factor lowers the thresholds for the quantitative assessment. The more significant the qualitative factors, the lower those quantitative thresholds will be. However, in some cases an entity might decide that, despite the presence of qualitative factors, an item of information is not material because its effect on the financial statements is so small that it could not reasonably be expected to influence primary users' decisions.

55   In some other circumstances, an item of information could reasonably be expected to influence primary users' decisions regardless of its size—a quantitative threshold could even reduce to zero. This might happen when information about a transaction, other event or condition is highly scrutinised by the primary users of an entity's financial statements. Moreover, a quantitative assessment is not always possible: non-numeric information might only be assessed from a qualitative perspective.

Example I—information about a related party transaction assessed as material

Background

An entity has identified measures of its profitability as the measures of great interest to the primary users of its financial statements. In the current reporting period, the entity signed a five-year contract with company ABC. Company ABC will provide the entity with maintenance services for the entity's offices for an annual fee. Company ABC is controlled by a member of the entity's key management personnel. Hence, company ABC is a related party of the entity.

Application

IAS 24 *Related Party Disclosures* requires an entity to disclose, for each related party transaction that occurred during the period, the nature of the related party relationship as well as information about the transaction and outstanding balances, including commitments, necessary for users to understand the potential effect of the relationship on the financial statements. **[Refer: IAS 24 paragraph 18]**

When preparing its financial statements, the entity assessed whether information about the transaction with company ABC was material.

The entity started its assessment from a quantitative perspective and evaluated the impact of the related party transaction against measures of the entity's profitability. Having initially concluded that the impact of the related party transaction was not material from a purely quantitative perspective, the entity further assessed the presence of any qualitative factors. **[Refer: paragraph 53]**

As the Board noted in developing IAS 24, related parties may enter into transactions that unrelated parties would not enter into, and the transactions may be priced at amounts that differ from the price for transactions between unrelated parties. **[Refer: IAS 24 paragraph 6]**

The entity identified the fact that the maintenance agreement was concluded with a related party as a characteristic that makes information about that transaction more likely to influence the decisions of its primary users.

continued...

...continued

The entity further assessed the transaction from a quantitative perspective to determine whether the impact of the transaction could reasonably be expected to influence primary users' decisions when considered with the fact that the transaction was with a related party (ie the presence of a qualitative factor lowers the quantitative threshold). Having considered that the transaction was with a related party, the entity concluded that the impact was large enough to reasonably be expected to influence primary users' decisions. Hence, the entity assessed information about the transaction with company ABC as material and disclosed that information in its financial statements.

Example J—information about a related party transaction assessed as immaterial

Background

An entity has identified measures of its profitability as the measures of great interest to the primary users of its financial statements. The entity owns a large fleet of vehicles. In the current reporting period, the entity sold an almost fully depreciated vehicle to company DEF. The entity transferred the vehicle for total consideration consistent with its market value and its carrying amount. Company DEF is controlled by a member of the entity's key management personnel. Hence, company DEF is a related party of the entity.

Application

When preparing its financial statements, the entity assessed whether information about the transaction with company DEF was material.

As in **Example I**, the entity started its assessment from a quantitative perspective and evaluated the impact of the related party transaction against measures of the entity's profitability. Having initially concluded that the impact of the related party transaction was not material from a purely quantitative perspective, the entity further assessed the presence of any qualitative factors.

[Refer: paragraph 53]

The entity transferred the vehicle for a total consideration consistent with its market value and its carrying amount. However, the entity identified the fact that the vehicle was sold to a related party as a characteristic that makes information about that transaction more likely to influence the decisions of its primary users.

The entity further assessed the transaction from a quantitative perspective but concluded that its impact was too small to reasonably be expected to influence primary users' decisions, even when considered with the fact that the transaction was with a related party. Information about the transaction with company DEF was consequently assessed as immaterial and not disclosed in the entity's financial statements.

> **Example K—influence of external qualitative factors on materiality judgements**
>
> **Background**
>
> An international bank holds a very small amount of debt originating from a country whose national economy is currently experiencing severe financial difficulties. Other international banks that operate in the same sector as the entity hold significant amounts of debt originating from that country and, hence, are significantly affected by the financial difficulties in that country.
>
> **Application**
>
> Paragraph 31 of IFRS 7 *Financial Instruments: Disclosures* requires an entity to disclose information that enables users of its financial statements to evaluate the nature and extent of risk arising from financial instruments to which the entity is exposed at the end of the reporting period.
>
> When preparing its financial statements, the bank assessed whether the fact that it holds a very small amount of debt originating from that country was material information.
>
> In making that assessment, the bank considered the exposure to that particular debt faced by other international banks operating in the same sector (external qualitative factor). **[Refer: paragraph 51]**
>
> In these circumstances, the fact that the bank is holding a very small amount of debt (or even no debt at all) originating from that country, while other international banks operating in the same sector have significant holdings, provides the entity's primary users with useful information about how effective management has been at protecting the bank's resources from unfavourable effects of the economic conditions in that country.
>
> The bank assessed the information about the lack of exposure to that particular debt as material and disclosed that information in its financial statements.

Step 3—organise
[Refer: Basis for Conclusions paragraph BC29]

56   Classifying, characterising and presenting information clearly and concisely makes it understandable.[23] An entity exercises judgement when deciding how to communicate information clearly and concisely. For example, the entity is more likely to clearly and concisely communicate the material information identified in Step 2 by organising it to:

    (a)   emphasise material matters;

    (b)   tailor information to the entity's own circumstances;

    (c)   describe the entity's transactions, other events and conditions as simply and directly as possible without omitting material information and without unnecessarily increasing the length of the financial statements;

---

23   See paragraph 2.34 of the *Conceptual Framework*.

    (d)   highlight relationships between different pieces of information;

    (e)   provide information in a format that is appropriate for its type, eg tabular or narrative;

    (f)   provide information in a way that maximises, to the extent possible, comparability among entities and across reporting periods;

    (g)   avoid or minimise duplication of information in different parts of the financial statements; and

    (h)   ensure material information is not obscured by immaterial information. **[Refer: IAS 1 paragraph 30A]**

57   Financial statements are less understandable for primary users if information is organised in an unclear manner. Similarly, financial statements are less understandable if an entity aggregates material items that have different natures or functions, or if material information is obscured,[24] for example, by an excessive amount of immaterial information.

58   Furthermore, an entity considers the different roles of primary financial statements and notes in deciding whether to present an item of information separately in the primary financial statements, to aggregate it with other information or to disclose the information in the notes.

59   The output of Step 3 is the draft financial statements.

Step 4—review
[Refer: Basis for Conclusions paragraph BC30]

60   An entity needs to assess whether information is material both individually and in combination with other information[25] in the context of its financial statements as a whole. Even if information is judged not to be material on its own, it might be material when considered in combination with other information in the complete set of financial statements.

61   When reviewing its draft financial statements, an entity draws on its knowledge and experience of its transactions, other events and conditions to identify whether all material information has been provided in the financial statements, and with appropriate prominence.

62   This review gives an entity the opportunity to 'step back' and consider the information provided from a wider perspective and in aggregate. This enables the entity to consider the overall picture of its financial position, financial performance and cash flows. In performing this review, the entity also considers whether:

    (a)   all relevant relationships between different items of information have been identified. Identifying new relationships between information might lead to that information being identified as material for the first time.

---

24 See paragraph 30A of IAS 1.

25 See paragraph 7 of IAS 1.

    (b)   items of information that are individually immaterial, when considered together, could nevertheless reasonably be expected to influence primary users' decisions. **[Refer: IAS 8 paragraph 5 and IAS 1 paragraph 7]**

    (c)   the information in the financial statements is communicated in an effective and understandable way, and organised to avoid obscuring material information.

    (d)   the financial statements provide a fair presentation of the entity's financial position, financial performance and cash flows.[26]

63   The review may lead to:

    (a)   additional information being provided in the financial statements;

    (b)   greater disaggregation of information that had already been identified as material;

    (c)   information that had already been identified as immaterial being removed from the financial statements to avoid obscuring material information; or

    (d)   information being reorganised within the financial statements.

64   The review in Step 4 may also lead an entity to question the assessment performed in Step 2 and decide to re-perform that assessment. As a result of re-performing its assessment in Step 2, the entity might conclude that information previously identified as material is, in fact, immaterial, and remove it from the financial statements.

65   The output of Step 4 is the final financial statements.

Specific topics

Prior-period information
[Refer: Basis for Conclusions paragraphs BC31–BC33]

66   An entity makes materiality judgements on the complete set of financial statements, including prior-period[27] information provided in the financial statements.

67   IFRS Standards require an entity to present information in respect of the preceding period for all amounts reported in the current-period financial statements.[28] Furthermore, the Standards require the entity to provide prior-period information for narrative and descriptive information if it is relevant to understanding the current-period financial statements.[29] Finally, the Standards require the entity to present, as a minimum, two statements of

---

26 See paragraph 15 of IAS 1.

27 For this Practice Statement, 'prior-period' should be read as 'prior-periods' if financial statements include amounts and disclosures for more than one prior period.

28 Except when IFRS Standards permit or require otherwise. See paragraph 38 of IAS 1.

29 See paragraph 38 of IAS 1.

            © IFRS Foundation

financial position, two statements of profit or loss and other comprehensive income, two statements of profit or loss (if presented separately), two statements of cash flows, two statements of changes in equity, and related notes.[30] These requirements are the minimum comparative information identified by the Standards.[31]

68   Assessing whether prior-period information is material to the current-period financial statements might lead an entity to:

(a)   provide more prior-period information than was provided in the prior-period financial statements (see paragraph 70); or

(b)   provide less prior-period information than was provided in the prior-period financial statements (see paragraph 71).

69   An entity also needs to consider any local laws or regulations, in respect of the prior-period information to be provided in financial statements, when making decisions on what prior-period information to provide in the current-period financial statements. Those local laws or regulations might require the entity to provide in the financial statements prior-period information in addition to the minimum comparative information required by the Standards. The Standards permit the inclusion of such additional information, but require that it is prepared in accordance with the Standards[32] and does not obscure material information.[33] However, an entity that wishes to state compliance with IFRS Standards cannot provide less information than required by the Standards, even if local laws and regulations permit otherwise. **[Refer: paragraph 27]**

Prior-period information not previously provided

70   An entity must provide prior-period information needed to understand the current-period financial statements,[34] regardless of whether that information was provided in the prior-period financial statements—this requirement is not conditional on whether the prior-period information was provided in the prior-period financial statements. Consequently, the inclusion of prior-period information not previously included would be required if this is necessary for the primary users to understand the current-period financial statements.

---

30   See paragraph 38A of IAS 1.

31   Paragraph 10(f) of IAS 1 also requires an entity to provide a statement of financial position as at the beginning of the preceding period when the entity applies an accounting policy retrospectively or makes a retrospective restatement of items in its financial statements, or when it reclassifies items in its financial statements in accordance with paragraphs 40A–40D of IAS 1.

32   See paragraph 38C of IAS 1.

33   See paragraph 30A of IAS 1 and paragraph BC30F of the Basis for Conclusions on IAS 1.

34   See paragraph 38 of IAS 1.

> **Example L—prior-period information not previously provided**
>
> **Background**
>
> In the prior period, an entity had a very small amount of debt outstanding. Information about this debt was appropriately assessed as immaterial in the prior period, and so the entity did not disclose any maturity analysis showing the remaining contractual maturities or other information that would otherwise be required by paragraph 39(a) of IFRS 7 *Financial Instruments: Disclosures*.
>
> In the current period, the entity issued a large amount of debt. The entity concluded that information about debt maturity was material information and disclosed it, in the form of a table, in the current-period financial statements.
>
> **Application**
>
> The entity might conclude that including a prior-period debt maturity analysis in the financial statements would be necessary for primary users to understand the current-period financial statements. In these circumstances, a narrative description of the maturity of the prior-period balances of the outstanding debt might be sufficient.

Summarising prior-period information

71 Except to the extent required to comply with any local laws or regulations affecting the preparation of financial statements or their audit, **[Refer: paragraph 69]** an entity does not automatically reproduce in the current-period financial statements all the information provided in the prior-period financial statements. Instead, the entity may summarise prior-period information, retaining the information necessary for primary users to understand the current-period financial statements.

Example M—summarising prior-period information

Background

An entity disclosed, in the prior-period financial statements, details of a legal dispute which led to the recognition, in that period, of a provision. In accordance with IAS 37 *Provisions, Contingent Liabilities and Contingent Assets* the entity disclosed in the prior-period financial statements a detailed description of uncertainties about the amount and timing of possible cash outflows, in respect of the dispute, together with the major assumptions made concerning future events.

Most of the uncertainties have been resolved in the current period, and, even though the liability has not been settled, a court pronouncement confirmed the amount already recognised in the financial statements by the entity.

The entity considered the relevant local laws, regulations and other reporting requirements and concluded that there were no locally prescribed obligations relating to the inclusion of prior-period information in the current-period financial statements.

Application

In these circumstances, on the basis of the requirements in IFRS Standards, the entity may not need to reproduce in the current-period financial statements all of the information about the legal dispute provided in the prior-period financial statements. Because most of the uncertainties have been resolved, users of the financial statements for the current period may no longer need detailed information about those uncertainties. Instead, information about those uncertainties might be summarised and updated to reflect the current-period events and circumstances and the resolution of previously reported uncertainties.

Errors

72 Errors are omissions from and/or misstatements in an entity's financial statements arising from a failure to use, or misuse of, reliable information that is available, or could reasonably be expected to be obtained.[35] Material errors are errors that individually or collectively could reasonably be expected to influence decisions that primary users make on the basis of those financial statements. Errors may affect narrative descriptions disclosed in the notes as well as amounts reported in the primary financial statements or in the notes.

73 An entity must correct all material errors, as well as any immaterial errors made intentionally to achieve a particular presentation of its financial position, financial performance or cash flows, to ensure compliance with IFRS Standards.[36] **[Refer: Basis for Conclusions paragraph BC37]** The entity should refer to IAS 8 *Accounting Policies, Changes in Accounting Estimates and Errors* for guidance on how to correct an error. **[Refer: IAS 8 paragraph 42]**

---

35 See paragraph 5 of IAS 8 (derived from the definition of prior-period errors).

36 See paragraph 41 of IAS 8.

74   Immaterial errors, if not made intentionally to achieve a particular presentation, do not need to be corrected to ensure compliance with IFRS Standards. However, correcting all errors (including those that are not material) in the preparation of the financial statements lowers the risk that immaterial errors will accumulate over reporting periods and become material.

75   An entity assesses whether an error is material by applying the same considerations as outlined in the description of the materiality process. [Refer: paragraphs 33–65] Making materiality judgements about errors involves both quantitative and qualitative considerations. The entity identifies information that, if misstated or omitted, could reasonably be expected to influence primary users' decisions (as described in Step 1 and Step 2 of the materiality process). The entity also considers whether any identified errors are material on a collective basis (as described in Step 4 of the materiality process).

      [Refer: Basis for Conclusions paragraph BC34]

76   If an error is judged not to be material on its own, it might be regarded as material when considered in combination with other information. However, in general, if an error is individually assessed as material to an entity's financial statements, the existence of other errors that affect the entity's financial position, financial performance or cash flows in the opposite way, does not make the error immaterial, nor does it eliminate the need to correct the error.

Example N—individual and collective assessment of errors

Background

An entity has identified measures of its profitability as the measures of great interest to the primary users of its financial statements. During the current reporting period, the entity recognised:

(a)   an expense accrual of CU100[a] that should not have been recognised. The accrual affected the line item 'cost of services'.

(b)   the reversal of a provision of CU80 recognised in the previous period that should not have been reversed. The reversal affected the line item 'other operating income (expense)'.

Application

In assessing whether these errors are material to its financial statements, the entity did not identify the presence of any qualitative factors [Refer: paragraphs 46–51] and thus made its materiality judgement solely from a quantitative perspective. [Refer: paragraphs 44 and 45] The entity concluded that both errors were individually material because of their impact on its profit.

continued...

...continued

> In these circumstances, it would be inappropriate to consider the quantitative effect of the errors on a net basis, ie as a CU20 overstatement of expenses, thereby concluding that the identified errors do not need to be corrected. If an error is individually assessed as material to the entity's financial statements, the existence of other errors that affect the entity's financial position, financial performance or cash flows in an opposite way, does not eliminate the need to correct it, or make the error immaterial.
>
> (a) In this example, currency amounts are denominated in 'currency units' (CU).

Cumulative errors

77   An entity may, over a number of reporting periods, accumulate errors that were immaterial, both in individual prior periods and cumulatively over all prior periods. Uncorrected errors that have accumulated over more than one period are sometimes called 'cumulative errors'.

78   Materiality judgements about cumulative errors in prior-period financial statements that an entity made at the time those statements were authorised for issue need not be revisited in subsequent periods unless the entity failed to use, or misused, information that:

(a)   was available when financial statements for those periods were authorised for issue; and

(b)   could reasonably be expected to have been obtained and taken into account in the preparation of those financial statements.[37]

[Refer: Basis for Conclusions paragraphs BC35(a)]

79   To assess whether a cumulative error has become material to the current-period financial statements, an entity considers whether, in the current period:

(a)   the entity's circumstances have changed, leading to a different materiality assessment for the current period; or

(b)   further accumulation of a current-period error onto the cumulative error has occurred.

[Refer: Basis for Conclusions paragraphs BC35(b)]

80   An entity must correct cumulative errors if they have become material to the current-period financial statements.

[Refer: Basis for Conclusions paragraphs BC36]

---

37 See paragraph 5 of IAS 8.

Example O—current-period assessment of cumulative errors

Background

An entity, three years ago, purchased a plant. The plant has a useful life of 50 years and a residual value amounting to 20 per cent of the plant cost. The entity started to use the plant three years ago, but has not recognised any depreciation for it (cumulative error). In each prior period, the entity assessed the error of not depreciating its plant as being individually and cumulatively immaterial to the financial statements for that period. There is no indication that the materiality judgements of prior periods were wrong.

In the current period, the entity started depreciating the plant.

In the same period, the entity experienced a significant reduction in profitability (the type of circumstance referred to in paragraph 79(a) of the Practice Statement).

Application

When making its materiality judgements in the preparation of the current-period financial statements, the entity concluded that the cumulative error was material to the current-period financial statements.

In this scenario, the entity does not need to revisit the materiality assessments it made in prior periods. **[Refer: paragraph 78]** However, because in the current period the cumulative error has become material to the current-period financial statements, the entity must apply the requirements in IAS 8 to correct it. **[Refer: paragraph 80]**

Information about covenants

81   An entity assesses the materiality of information about the existence and terms of a loan agreement clause (covenant), or of a covenant breach, to decide whether to provide information related to the covenant in the financial statements. This assessment is made in the same way as for other information, that is, by considering whether that information could reasonably be expected to influence decisions that its primary users make on the basis of the entity's financial statements (see 'A four-step materiality process', from paragraph 33).

82   In particular, when a covenant exists, an entity considers both:

(a)   the consequences of a breach occurring, that is, the impact a covenant breach would have on the entity's financial position, financial performance and cash flows. If those consequences would affect the entity's financial position, financial performance or cash flows in a way that could reasonably be expected to influence primary users' decisions, then the information about the existence of the covenant and its terms is likely to be material. Conversely, if the consequences of a covenant breach would not affect the entity's financial position, financial performance or cash flows in such a way, then disclosures about the covenant might not be needed.

(b)   the likelihood of a covenant breach occurring. The more likely it is that a covenant breach would occur, the more likely it is that information about the existence and terms of the covenant would be material.

[Refer: Basis for Conclusions paragraph BC39]

83   In assessing whether information about a covenant is material, a combination of the considerations in paragraph 82(a)–82(b) applies. Information about a covenant for which the consequences of a breach would affect an entity's financial position, financial performance or cash flows in a way that could reasonably be expected to influence primary users' decisions, but for which there is only a remote likelihood of the breach occurring, is not material.

[Refer: Basis for Conclusions paragraph BC39]

Example P—assessing whether information about covenants is material

Background

An entity has rapidly grown over the past five years and recently suffered some liquidity problems. A long-term loan was granted to the entity in the current reporting period. The loan agreement includes a clause that requires the entity to maintain a ratio of debt to equity below a specified threshold, to be measured at each reporting date (the covenant). According to the loan agreement, the debt-to-equity ratio has to be calculated on the basis of debt and equity figures as presented in the entity's IFRS financial statements. If the entity breaches the covenant, the entire loan becomes payable on demand. The disclosure of covenant terms in an entity's financial statements is not required by any local laws or regulations.

Application

Paragraph 31 of IFRS 7 *Financial Instruments: Disclosures* requires an entity to disclose information that enables users of its financial statements to evaluate the nature and extent of risk arising from financial instruments to which the entity is exposed at the end of the reporting period.

In the preparation of its financial statements, the entity assesses whether information about the existence of the covenant and its terms is material information, considering both the consequences [Refer: paragraph 82(a)] and the likelihood of a breach occurring. [Refer: paragraph 82(b)]

In these circumstances, the entity concluded that, considering its recent liquidity problem, any acceleration of the long-term loan repayment plan (the consequence of the covenant breach occurring) would affect the entity's financial position and cash flows in a way that could reasonably be expected to influence primary users' decisions.

The entity also considered the likelihood of a breach occurring.

continued...

...continued

> **Scenario 1 – the lender defined the covenant threshold on the basis of the three-year business plan prepared by the entity, adding a 10 per cent tolerance to the forecast figures**
>
> In this scenario, even though the entity has historically met its past business plans, it assessed the likelihood of a breach occurring as higher than remote. Therefore, information about the existence of the covenant and its terms was assessed as material and disclosed in the entity's financial statements.
>
> **Scenario 2 – the lender defined the covenant threshold on the basis of the three-year business plan prepared by the entity, adding a 200 per cent tolerance to the forecast figures**
>
> In this scenario, the entity assessed the likelihood of a breach occurring as remote, on the basis of its historical track record of meeting its past business plans and the magnitude of the tolerance included in the covenant threshold. Therefore, although the consequences of the covenant breach would affect the entity's financial position and cash flows in a way that could reasonably be expected to influence primary users' decisions, the entity concluded that information about the existence of the covenant and its terms was not material.
>
> **[Refer: paragraph 83]**

Materiality judgements for interim reporting
[Refer: Basis for Conclusions paragraph BC41]

84   An entity makes materiality judgements in preparing both annual financial statements and interim financial reports prepared in accordance with IAS 34 *Interim Financial Reporting*. In either case, the entity could apply the materiality process described in paragraphs 29–65. For its interim financial report, the entity considers the same materiality factors as in its annual assessment. However, it takes into consideration that the time period and the purpose of an interim financial report differ from those of the annual financial statements.

85   In making materiality judgements on its interim financial report, an entity focuses on the period covered by that report, that is:

(a)   it assesses whether information in the interim financial report is material in relation to the interim period financial data, not annual data.[38]

(b)   it applies the materiality factors on the basis of both the current interim period data and also, whenever there is more than one interim period (eg in the case of quarterly reporting), the data for the current financial year to date.[39]

---

38   See paragraphs 23 and 25 of IAS 34 *Interim Financial Reporting*.

39   Paragraph 20 of IAS 34 requires an entity to include in the interim financial report the statements of profit or loss and other comprehensive income for both periods, the current interim period and the current financial year to date.

(c)   it may consider whether to provide in the interim financial report information that is expected to be material to the annual financial statements. However, information that is expected to be material to the annual financial statements need not be provided in the interim financial report if it is not material to the interim financial report.

Example Q—information that is expected to be material to the annual financial statements

Background

An entity sells mainly standardised products to private customers in its home market. In the first half of the reporting period, 98 per cent of the entity's revenue was generated by sales of Product X. The remaining revenue was principally derived from a pilot sale of a new product line — Product Y — that the entity planned to launch in the third quarter of the year. The entity expects revenue from Product Y to increase significantly by the end of the annual reporting period, so that Product Y will provide approximately 20 per cent of the entity's revenue for the full annual period.

Application

Paragraph 114 of IFRS 15 *Revenue from Contracts with Customers* requires an entity to disaggregate revenue recognised from contracts into categories that depict how the nature, amount, timing and uncertainty of revenue and cash flows are affected by economic factors.

The entity did not identify any qualitative factors **[Refer: paragraphs 46–51]** that made the amount of revenues from Product Y material to the interim period.

In these circumstances, the entity concluded that the information about disaggregation of revenue by product lines was not material to the interim financial report and did not disclose it. In the preparation of the interim financial report, the entity is not required to disaggregate its revenue by product lines even if a greater level of disaggregation is expected to be required for the subsequent annual financial statements. In other words, although the entity expects that revenue by product lines will be material information for the annual financial statements, that fact does not influence the materiality assessment in the preparation of the entity's interim financial report.

---

86   Similarly, an entity may consider whether to provide information in the annual financial statements that is only material to the interim financial report. However, if information is material to the interim financial report, it need not be presented or disclosed subsequently in the annual financial statements if it is not material to those statements.

Example R—information that is only material to the interim financial report

Background

An entity has identified measures of its profitability and cash flows as the measures of great interest to the primary users of its financial statements. During the interim period, the entity constructed a new chemical handling process to enable it to comply with environmental requirements for the production and storage of dangerous chemicals. Such an item of property, plant and equipment (PP&E) qualifies for recognition as an asset in accordance with paragraph 11 of IAS 16 *Property, Plant and Equipment*.

Application

Paragraph 74(b) of IAS 16 requires the disclosure of the expenditure recognised in the carrying amount of an item of PP&E in the course of its construction.

In the preparation of the interim financial report, the entity assessed, both from a quantitative and qualitative perspective, the information about expenditure recognised in the carrying amount of the chemical handling process, concluded that information was material to the interim financial report and disclosed it. **[Refer: paragraph 85(a)]**

The entity incurred no further expenditure related to the chemical handling process in the second half of the annual reporting period. In the preparation of its annual financial statements, the entity assessed the expenditure recognised in the carrying amount of the chemical handling process against its annual profitability and cash flow measures and concluded that this information was not material to the annual financial statements. In reaching that conclusion, the entity did not identify any qualitative factors leading to a different assessment.

The entity is not required to disclose information about the expenditure recognised in the carrying amount of its chemical handling process in its annual financial statements.

---

87   In assessing materiality, an entity also considers the purpose of interim financial reports, which differs from the purpose of annual financial statements. An interim financial report is intended to provide an update on the latest complete set of annual financial statements.[40] Information that is material to the interim period, but was already provided in the latest annual financial statements, does not need to be reproduced in the interim financial report, unless something new occurs or an update is needed.[41]

---

40   See paragraph 6 of IAS 34.

41   See paragraphs 15–15A of IAS 34.

Interim reporting estimates

88   When an entity concludes that information about estimation uncertainty is material, the entity needs to disclose that information. **[Refer: IAS 1 paragraph 125]** Measurements included in interim financial reports often rely more on estimates than measurements included in the annual financial statements.[42] That fact does not, in itself, make the estimated measurements material. Nevertheless, relying on estimates for interim financial data to a greater extent than for annual financial data might result in more disclosures about such uncertainties being material, and thus being provided in the interim financial report, compared with the annual financial statements.

Information about accounting policies
[Refer: Basis of Conclusions paragraphs BC41A-BC41F]

88A   Paragraph 117 of IAS 1 requires an entity to disclose material accounting policy information.

    [Refer: Basis for Conclusions paragraph BC41A]

88B   Accounting policy information relating to immaterial transactions, other events or conditions is immaterial and need not be disclosed. Accounting policy information may nevertheless be material because of the nature of the related transactions, other events or conditions, even if the amounts are immaterial. An entity is required to disclose accounting policy information relating to material transactions, other events or conditions if that information is material to the financial statements.

88C   In assessing whether accounting policy information is material to its financial statements, an entity considers whether users of the entity's financial statements would need that information to understand other material information in the financial statements. An entity makes this assessment in the same way it assesses other information: by considering qualitative and quantitative factors, as described in paragraphs 44–55. Diagram 2 illustrates how an entity assesses whether accounting policy information is material and, therefore, shall be disclosed.

    [Refer: Basis for Conclusions paragraph BC41C]

---

42 See paragraph 41 of IAS 34.

Diagram 2 — determining whether accounting policy information is material

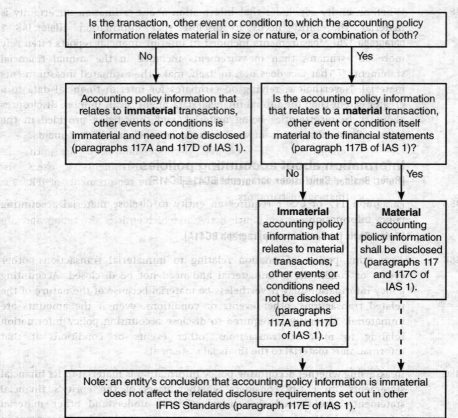

88D   Paragraph 117B of IAS 1 includes examples of circumstances in which an entity is likely to consider accounting policy information to be material to its financial statements. The list is not exhaustive, but provides guidance on when an entity would normally consider accounting policy information to be material.

       [Refer: Basis for Conclusions paragraph BC41C]

88E   Paragraph 117C of IAS 1 describes the type of material accounting policy information that users of financial statements find most useful. Users generally find information about the characteristics of an entity's transactions, other events or conditions — entity-specific information — more useful than disclosures that only include standardised information, or information that duplicates or summarises the requirements of the IFRS Standards. Entity-specific accounting policy information is particularly useful when that information relates to an area for which an entity has exercised judgement — for example, when an entity applies an IFRS Standard differently from similar entities in the same industry.

       [Refer: Basis for Conclusions paragraph BC41C]

88F   Although entity-specific accounting policy information is generally more useful, material accounting policy information could sometimes include information that is standardised, or that duplicates or summarises the requirements of the IFRS Standards. Such information may be material if, for example:

(a)   users of the entity's financial statements need that information to understand other material information provided in the financial statements. Such a scenario might arise when an entity applying IFRS 9 *Financial Instruments* has no choice regarding the classification of its financial instruments. In such scenarios, users of that entity's financial statements may only be able to understand how the entity has accounted for its material financial instruments if users also understand how the entity has applied the requirements of IFRS 9 to its financial instruments.

(b)   an entity reports in a jurisdiction in which entities also report applying local accounting standards.

(c)   the accounting required by the IFRS Standards is complex, and users of financial statements need to understand the required accounting. Such a scenario might arise when an entity accounts for a material class of transactions, other events or conditions by applying more than one IFRS Standard.

[Refer: Basis for Conclusions paragraph BC41E]

88G   Paragraph 117D of IAS 1 states that if an entity discloses immaterial accounting policy information, such information shall not obscure material information. Paragraphs 56–59 provide guidance about how to communicate information clearly and concisely in the financial statements.

Example S—making materiality judgements and focusing on entity-specific information while avoiding standardised (boilerplate) accounting policy information
[Refer: Basis for Conclusions paragraphs BC41C and BC41D]

Background

An entity operates within the telecommunications industry. It has entered into contracts with retail customers to deliver mobile phone handsets and data services. In a typical contract, the entity provides a customer with a handset and data services over three years. The entity applies IFRS 15 *Revenue from Contracts with Customers* and recognises revenue when, or as, the entity satisfies its performance obligations in line with the terms of the contract.

continued...

...continued

The entity has identified two performance obligations and related considerations:

(a)   the handset—the customer makes monthly payments for the handset over three years; and

(b)   data—the customer pays a fixed monthly charge to use a specified monthly amount of data over three years.

For the handset, the entity concludes that it should recognise revenue when it satisfies the performance obligation (when it provides the handset to the customer). For the provision of data, the entity concludes that it should recognise revenue as it satisfies the performance obligation (as the entity provides data services to the customer over the three-year life of the contract).

The entity notes that, in accounting for revenue it has made judgements about:

(a)   the allocation of the transaction price to the performance obligations; and

(b)   the timing of satisfaction of the performance obligations.

The entity has concluded that revenue generated from these contracts is material to the reporting period.

Application

The entity notes that for contracts of this type it applies separate accounting policies for two sources of revenue, namely revenue from:

(a)   the sale of handsets; and

(b)   the provision of data services.

Having identified revenue from contracts of this type as material to the financial statements, the entity assesses whether accounting policy information for revenue from these contracts is, in fact, material.

continued...

...*continued*

The entity evaluates the effect of disclosing the accounting policy information by considering the presence of qualitative factors. The entity noted that its revenue recognition accounting policies:

(a)   were unchanged during the reporting period;

(b)   were not chosen from accounting policy options available in the IFRS Standards;

(c)   were not developed in accordance with IAS 8 *Accounting Policies, Changes in Accounting Estimates and Errors* in the absence of an IFRS Standard that specifically applies; and

(d)   are not so complex that primary users will be unable to understand the related revenue transactions without standardised descriptions of the requirements of IFRS 15.

However, some of the entity's revenue recognition accounting policies relate to an area for which the entity has made significant judgements in applying its accounting policies—for example, in deciding how to allocate the transaction price to the performance obligations, and the timing of revenue recognition.

The entity considers that, in addition to disclosing the information required by paragraphs 123–126 of IFRS 15 about the significant judgements made in applying IFRS 15, primary users of its financial statements are likely to need to understand related accounting policy information. Consequently, the entity concludes that such accounting policy information could reasonably be expected to influence the decisions of the primary users of its financial statements. For example, understanding:

(a)   how the entity allocates the transaction price to its performance obligations is likely to help users understand how each component of the transaction contributes to the entity's revenue and cash flows; and

(b)   that some revenue is recognised at a point in time and some is recognised over time is likely to help users understand how reported cash flows relate to revenue.

The entity also notes that the judgements it made are specific to the entity. Consequently, material accounting policy information would include information about how the entity has applied the requirements of IFRS 15 to its specific circumstances.

The entity, therefore, assesses that accounting policy information about revenue recognition is material and should be disclosed. Such disclosure would include information about how the entity allocates the transaction price to its performance obligations and when the entity recognises revenue.

Example T—making materiality judgements on accounting policy information that only duplicates requirements in the IFRS Standards
[Refer: Basis for Conclusions paragraphs BC41C and BC41D]

Background

Property, plant and equipment are material to an entity's financial statements.

The entity has no intangible assets or goodwill and has not recognised an impairment loss on its property, plant or equipment in either the current or comparative reporting periods.

In previous reporting periods, the entity disclosed accounting policy information relating to impairment of non-current assets which duplicates the requirements of IAS 36 *Impairment of Assets* and provides no entity-specific information. The entity disclosed that:

> The carrying amounts of the group's intangible assets and its property, plant and equipment are reviewed at each reporting date to determine whether there is any indication of impairment. If any such indication exists, the asset's recoverable amount is estimated. For goodwill and intangibles with an indefinite useful life, the recoverable amount is estimated at least annually.

> An impairment loss is recognised in the statement of profit or loss whenever the carrying amount of an asset or its cash-generating unit exceeds its recoverable amount.

> The recoverable amount of assets is the greater of their fair value less costs to sell and their value in use. In measuring value in use, estimated future cash flows are discounted to present value using a pre-tax discount rate that reflects current market assessments of the time value of money and the risks specific to the asset. For an asset that does not generate largely independent cash inflows, the recoverable amount is determined for the cash-generating unit to which the asset belongs.

> Impairment losses recognised in respect of cash-generating units are allocated first to reduce the carrying amount of any goodwill allocated to that cash-generating unit and then to reduce the carrying amount of the other assets in the unit on a pro rata basis.

> An impairment loss in respect of goodwill is not subsequently reversed. For other assets, an impairment loss is reversed if there has been a change in the estimates used to determine the recoverable amount, but only to the extent that the new carrying amount does not exceed the carrying amount that would have been determined, net of depreciation and amortisation, if no impairment loss had been recognised.

continued...

© IFRS Foundation

...continued

Application

Having identified assets subject to impairment testing as being material to the financial statements, the entity assesses whether the accounting policy information for impairment is, in fact, material.

As part of its assessment, the entity considers that an impairment or a reversal of an impairment had not occurred in the current or comparative reporting periods. Consequently, accounting policy information about how the entity recognises and allocates impairment losses is unlikely to be material to its primary users. Similarly, because the entity has no intangible assets or goodwill, information about its accounting policy for impairments of intangible assets and goodwill is unlikely to provide its primary users with material information.

However, the entity's impairment accounting policy relates to an area for which the entity is required to make significant judgements or assumptions, as described in paragraphs 122 and 125 of IAS 1. Given the entity's specific circumstances, it concludes that information about its significant judgements and assumptions related to its impairment assessments could reasonably be expected to influence the decisions of the primary users of the entity's financial statements. The entity notes that its disclosures about significant judgements and assumptions already include information about the significant judgements and assumptions used in its impairment assessments.

The entity decides that the primary users of its financial statements would be unlikely to need to understand the recognition and measurement requirements of IAS 36 to understand related information in the financial statements.

Consequently, the entity concludes that disclosing a summary of the requirements in IAS 36 in a separate accounting policy for impairment would not provide information that could reasonably be expected to influence decisions made by the primary users of its financial statements. Instead, the entity discloses material accounting policy information related to the significant judgements and assumptions the entity has applied in its impairment assessments elsewhere in the financial statements.

Although the entity assesses some accounting policy information for impairments of assets as immaterial, the entity still assesses whether other disclosure requirements of IAS 36 provide material information that should be disclosed.

Application date

89   This Practice Statement does not change any requirements in IFRS Standards or introduce any new requirements. An entity that chooses to apply the guidance in the Practice Statement is permitted to apply it to financial statements prepared from 14 September 2017.

Appendix
References to the *Conceptual Framework for Financial Reporting* and IFRS Standards

Extracts from the *Conceptual Framework for Financial Reporting*

Paragraph 1.2

Referred to in paragraphs 7 and 17 of the Practice Statement

The objective of general purpose financial reporting is to provide financial information about the reporting entity that is useful to existing and potential investors, lenders and other creditors in making decisions relating to providing resources to the entity. Those decisions involve decisions about:

(a)   buying, selling or holding equity and debt instruments;

(b)   providing or settling loans and other forms of credit; or

(c)   exercising rights to vote on, or otherwise influence, management's actions that affect the use of the entity's economic resources.

Paragraph 1.3

Referred to in paragraph 18 of the Practice Statement

The decisions described in paragraph 1.2 depend on the returns that existing and potential investors, lenders and other creditors expect, for example, dividends, principal and interest payments or market price increases. Investors', lenders' and other creditors' expectations about returns depend on their assessment of the amount, timing and uncertainty of (the prospects for) future net cash inflows to the entity and on their assessment of management's stewardship of the entity's economic resources. Existing and potential investors, lenders and other creditors need information to help them make those assessments.

Paragraph 1.4

Referred to in paragraphs 19 and 38 of the Practice Statement

To make the assessments described in paragraph 1.3, existing and potential investors, lenders and other creditors need information about:

(a)   the economic resources of the entity, claims against the entity and changes in those resources and claims (see paragraphs 1.12–1.21); and

(b)   how efficiently and effectively the entity's management and governing board have discharged their responsibilities to use the entity's economic resources (see paragraphs 1.22–1.23).

Paragraph 1.5

Referred to in paragraph 13 of the Practice Statement

Many existing and potential investors, lenders and other creditors cannot require reporting entities to provide information directly to them and must rely on general purpose financial reports for much of the financial information they need. Consequently, they are the primary users to whom general purpose financial reports are directed.

Paragraph 1.6

Referred to in paragraph 21 of the Practice Statement

However, general purpose financial reports do not and cannot provide all of the information that existing and potential investors, lenders and other creditors need. Those users need to consider pertinent information from other sources, for example, general economic conditions and expectations, political events and political climate, and industry and company outlooks.

Paragraph 1.8

Referred to in paragraph 36 of the Practice Statement

Individual primary users have different, and possibly conflicting, information needs and desires. The Board, in developing Standards, will seek to provide the information set that will meet the needs of the maximum number of primary users. However, focusing on common information needs does not prevent the reporting entity from including additional information that is most useful to a particular subset of primary users.

Paragraph 1.9

Referred to in paragraph 13 of the Practice Statement

The management of a reporting entity is also interested in financial information about the entity. However, management need not rely on general purpose financial reports because it is able to obtain the financial information it needs internally.

Paragraph 1.10

Referred to in paragraph 13 of the Practice Statement

Other parties, such as regulators and members of the public other than investors, lenders and other creditors, may also find general purpose financial reports useful. However, those reports are not primarily directed to these other groups.

Paragraph 2.7

Referred to in paragraph 20 of the Practice Statement

Financial information is capable of making a difference in decisions if it has predictive value, confirmatory value or both.

Paragraph 2.11

Referred to in paragraph 5 of the Practice Statement

Information is material if omitting, misstating or obscuring it could reasonably be expected to influence decisions that the primary users of general purpose financial reports (see paragraph 1.5) make on the basis of those reports, which provide financial information about a specific reporting entity. In other words, materiality is an entity-specific aspect of relevance based on the nature or magnitude, or both, of the items to which the information relates in the context of an individual entity's financial report. Consequently, the Board cannot specify a uniform quantitative threshold for materiality or predetermine what could be material in a particular situation.

Paragraph 2.34

Referred to in paragraph 56 of the Practice Statement

Classifying, characterising and presenting information clearly and concisely makes it understandable.

Paragraph 2.36

Referred to in paragraph 15 of the Practice Statement

Financial reports are prepared for users who have a reasonable knowledge of business and economic activities and who review and analyse the information diligently. At times, even well-informed and diligent users may need to seek the aid of an adviser to understand information about complex economic phenomena.

Extracts from IAS 1 *Presentation of Financial Statements*

Paragraph 7

Referred to in paragraphs 5, 41 and 60 of the Practice Statement

Material:

Information is material if omitting, misstating or obscuring it could reasonably be expected to influence decisions that the primary users of general purpose financial statements make on the basis of those financial statements which provide financial information about a specific reporting entity.

Materiality depends on the nature or magnitude of information, or both. An entity assesses whether information, either individually or in combination with other information, is material in the context of its financial statements taken as a whole.

Paragraph 7

Referred to in paragraph 6 of the Practice Statement

Assessing whether information could reasonably be expected to influence decisions made by the primary users of a specific reporting entity's general purpose financial statements requires an entity to consider the characteristics of those users while also considering the entity's own circumstances. [...] At times, even well informed and diligent users may need to seek the aid of an adviser to understand information about complex economic phenomena.

Paragraph 15

Referred to in paragraph 62 of the Practice Statement

Financial statements shall present fairly the financial position, financial performance and cash flows of an entity. Fair presentation requires the faithful representation of the effects of transactions, other events and conditions in accordance with the definitions and recognition criteria for assets, liabilities, income and expenses set out in the *Conceptual Framework for Financial Reporting* (*Conceptual Framework*). The application of IFRSs, with additional disclosure when necessary, is presumed to result in financial statements that achieve a fair presentation.

Paragraph 17

Referred to in paragraph 10 of the Practice Statement

In virtually all circumstances, an entity achieves a fair presentation by compliance with applicable IFRSs. A fair presentation also requires an entity:

(a)   to select and apply accounting policies in accordance with IAS 8 *Accounting Policies, Changes in Accounting Estimates and Errors*. IAS 8 sets out a hierarchy of authoritative guidance that management considers in the absence of an IFRS that specifically applies to an item.

(b)   to present information, including accounting policies, in a manner that provides relevant, reliable, comparable and understandable information.

(c)   to provide additional disclosures when compliance with the specific requirements in IFRSs is insufficient to enable users to understand the impact of particular transactions, other events and conditions on the entity's financial position and financial performance.

Paragraph 29

Referred to in paragraph 43 of the Practice Statement

An entity shall present separately each material class of similar items. An entity shall present separately items of a dissimilar nature or function unless they are immaterial.

Paragraph 30A

Referred to in paragraphs 28, 57 and 69 of the Practice Statement

When applying this and other IFRSs an entity shall decide, taking into consideration all relevant facts and circumstances, how it aggregates information in the financial statements, which include the notes. An entity shall not reduce the understandability of its financial statements by obscuring material information with immaterial information or by aggregating material items that have different natures or functions.

Paragraph 31

Referred to in paragraph 10 of the Practice Statement

Some IFRSs specify information that is required to be included in the financial statements, which include the notes. An entity need not provide a specific disclosure required by an IFRS if the information resulting from that disclosure is not material. This is the case even if the IFRS contains a list of specific requirements or describes them as minimum requirements. An entity shall also consider whether to provide additional disclosures when compliance with the specific requirements in IFRS is insufficient to enable users of financial statements to understand the impact of particular transactions, other events and conditions on the entity's financial position and financial performance.

Paragraph 38

Referred to in paragraphs 67 and 70 of the Practice Statement

Except when IFRSs permit or require otherwise, an entity shall present comparative information in respect of the preceding period for all amounts reported in the current period's financial statements. An entity shall include comparative information for narrative and descriptive information if it is relevant to understanding the current period's financial statements.

Paragraph 38A

Referred to in paragraph 67 of the Practice Statement

An entity shall present, as a minimum, two statements of financial position, two statements of profit or loss and other comprehensive income, two separate statements of profit or loss (if presented), two statements of cash flows and two statements of changes in equity, and related notes.

Paragraph 38C

Referred to in paragraph 69 of the Practice Statement

An entity may present comparative information in addition to the minimum comparative financial statements required by IFRSs, as long as that information is prepared in accordance with IFRSs. This comparative information may consist of one or more statements referred to in paragraph 10, but need not comprise a complete set of financial statements. When this is the case, the entity shall present related note information for those additional statements.

Paragraph 117

Referred to in paragraphs 88A and 88C of the Practice Statement

An entity shall disclose material accounting policy information (see paragraph 7). Accounting policy information is material if, when considered together with other information included in an entity's financial statements, it can reasonably be expected to influence decisions that the primary users of general purpose financial statements make on the basis of those financial statements.

Paragraph 117A

Referred to in paragraph 88C of the Practice Statement

Accounting policy information that relates to immaterial transactions, other events or conditions is immaterial and need not be disclosed. Accounting policy information may nevertheless be material because of the nature of the related transactions, other events or conditions, even if the amounts are immaterial. However, not all accounting policy information relating to material transactions, other events or conditions is itself material.

Paragraph 117B

Referred to in paragraphs 88C and 88D of the Practice Statement

Accounting policy information is expected to be material if users of an entity's financial statements would need it to understand other material information in the financial statements. For example, an entity is likely to consider accounting policy information material to its financial statements if that information relates to material transactions, other events or conditions and:

(a)   the entity changed its accounting policy during the reporting period and this change resulted in a material change to the information in the financial statements;

(b)   the entity chose the accounting policy from one or more options permitted by IFRSs — such a situation could arise if the entity chose to measure investment property at historical cost rather than fair value;

(c)   the accounting policy was developed in accordance with IAS 8 in the absence of an IFRS that specifically applies;

(d)   the accounting policy relates to an area for which an entity is required to make significant judgements or assumptions in applying an accounting policy, and the entity discloses those judgements or assumptions in accordance with paragraphs 122 and 125; or

(e)   the accounting required for them is complex and users of the entity's financial statements would otherwise not understand those material transactions, other events or conditions — such a situation could arise if an entity applies more than one IFRS to a class of material transactions.

Paragraph 117C

Referred to in paragraphs 88C and 88E of the Practice Statement

Accounting policy information that focuses on how an entity has applied the requirements of the IFRSs to its own circumstances provides entity-specific information that is more useful to users of financial statements than standardised information, or information that only duplicates or summarises the requirements of the IFRSs.

Paragraph 117D

Referred to in paragraphs 88C and 88G of the Practice Statement

If an entity discloses immaterial accounting policy information, such information shall not obscure material accounting policy information.

Paragraph 117E

Referred to in paragraph 88C of the Practice Statement

An entity's conclusion that accounting policy information is immaterial does not affect the related disclosure requirements set out in other IFRSs.

Paragraph BC30F of the Basis for Conclusions

Referred to in paragraphs 28 and 69 of the Practice Statement

Paragraph 30A was added to IAS 1 to highlight that when an entity decides how it aggregates information in the financial statements, it should take into consideration all relevant facts and circumstances. Paragraph 30A emphasises that an entity should not reduce the understandability of its financial statements by providing immaterial information that obscures the material information in financial statements or by aggregating material items that have different natures or functions. Obscuring material information with immaterial information in financial statements makes the material information less visible and therefore makes the financial statements less understandable. The amendments do not actually prohibit entities from disclosing immaterial information, because the Board thinks that such a requirement would not be operational; however, the amendments emphasise that disclosure should not result in material information being obscured.

Extracts from IAS 8 *Accounting Policies, Changes in Accounting Estimates and Errors*

Paragraph 5

Referred to in paragraphs 72 and 78 of the Practice Statement

Prior period errors are omissions from, and misstatements in, the entity's financial statements for one or more prior periods arising from a failure to use, or misuse of, reliable information that:

(a) was available when financial statements for those periods were authorised for issue; and

(b) could reasonably be expected to have been obtained and taken into account in the preparation and presentation of those financial statements.

Such errors include the effects of mathematical mistakes, mistakes in applying accounting policies, oversights or misinterpretations of facts, and fraud.

Paragraph 8

Referred to in paragraph 8 of the Practice Statement

IFRSs set out accounting policies that the IASB has concluded result in financial statements containing relevant and reliable information about the transactions, other events and conditions to which they apply. Those policies need not be applied when the effect of applying them is immaterial. However, it is inappropriate to make, or leave uncorrected, immaterial departures from IFRSs to achieve a particular presentation of an entity's financial position, financial performance or cash flows.

Paragraph 41

Referred to in paragraph 73 of the Practice Statement

Errors can arise in respect of the recognition, measurement, presentation or disclosure of elements of financial statements. Financial statements do not comply with IFRSs if they contain either material errors or immaterial errors made intentionally to achieve a particular presentation of an entity's financial position, financial performance or cash flows. Potential current period errors discovered in that period are corrected before the financial statements are authorised for issue. However, material errors are sometimes not discovered until a subsequent period, and these prior period errors are corrected in the comparative information presented in the financial statements for that subsequent period (see paragraphs 42–47).

Extracts from IAS 34 *Interim Financial Reporting*

Paragraph 6

Referred to in paragraph 87 of the Practice Statement

In the interest of timeliness and cost considerations and to avoid repetition of information previously reported, an entity may be required to or may elect to provide less information at interim dates as compared with its annual financial statements. This Standard defines the minimum content of an interim financial report as including condensed financial statements and selected explanatory notes. The interim financial report is intended to provide an update on the latest complete set of annual financial statements. Accordingly, it focuses on new activities, events, and circumstances and does not duplicate information previously reported.

Paragraph 15

Referred to in paragraph 87 of the Practice Statement

An entity shall include in its interim financial report an explanation of events and transactions that are significant to an understanding of the changes in financial position and performance of the entity since the end of the last annual reporting period. Information disclosed in relation to those events and transactions shall update the relevant information presented in the most recent annual financial report.

Paragraph 15A

Referred to in paragraph 87 of the Practice Statement

A user of an entity's interim financial report will have access to the most recent annual financial report of that entity. Therefore, it is unnecessary for the notes to an interim financial report to provide relatively insignificant updates to the information that was reported in the notes in the most recent annual financial report.

Paragraph 20

Referred to in paragraph 85 of the Practice Statement

Interim reports shall include interim financial statements (condensed or complete) for periods as follows:

(a) statement of financial position as of the end of the current interim period and a comparative statement of financial position as of the end of the immediately preceding financial year.

(b) statements of profit or loss and other comprehensive income for the current interim period and cumulatively for the current financial year to date, with comparative statements of profit or loss and other comprehensive income for the comparable interim periods (current and year-to-date) of the immediately preceding financial year. As permitted by IAS 1 (as amended in 2011), an interim report may present for each period a statement or statements of profit or loss and other comprehensive income.

(c) statement of changes in equity cumulatively for the current financial year to date, with a comparative statement for the comparable year-to-date period of the immediately preceding financial year.

(d) statement of cash flows cumulatively for the current financial year to date, with a comparative statement for the comparable year-to-date period of the immediately preceding financial year.

Paragraph 23

Referred to in paragraph 85 of the Practice Statement

> In deciding how to recognise, measure, classify, or disclose an item for interim financial reporting purposes, materiality shall be assessed in relation to the interim period financial data. In making assessments of materiality, it shall be recognised that interim measurements may rely on estimates to a greater extent than measurements of annual financial data.

Paragraph 25

Referred to in paragraph 85 of the Practice Statement

> While judgement is always required in assessing materiality, this Standard bases the recognition and disclosure decision on data for the interim period by itself for reasons of understandability of the interim figures. Thus, for example, unusual items, changes in accounting policies or estimates, and errors are recognised and disclosed on the basis of materiality in relation to interim period data to avoid misleading inferences that might result from non-disclosure. The overriding goal is to ensure that an interim financial report includes all information that is relevant to understanding an entity's financial position and performance during the interim period.

Paragraph 41

Referred to in paragraph 88 of the Practice Statement

> The measurement procedures to be followed in an interim financial report shall be designed to ensure that the resulting information is reliable and that all material financial information that is relevant to an understanding of the financial position or performance of the entity is appropriately disclosed. While measurements in both annual and interim financial reports are often based on reasonable estimates, the preparation of interim financial reports generally will require a greater use of estimation methods than annual financial reports.

Approval by the Board of the IFRS Practice Statement 2 *Making Materiality Judgements* issued in September 2017

The IFRS Practice Statement 2 *Making Materiality Judgements* was approved for issue by 12 of 12 members of the International Accounting Standards Board.[43]

Hans Hoogervorst	Chairman
Suzanne Lloyd	Vice-Chair
Stephen Cooper	
Martin Edelmann	
Françoise Flores	
Amaro Luiz De Oliveira Gomes	
Gary Kabureck	
Takatsugu Ochi	
Darrel Scott	
Thomas Scott	
Chungwoo Suh	
Mary Tokar	

---

[43] Stephen Cooper was a member of the Board when the IFRS Practice Statement 2 *Making Materiality Judgements* was balloted.

Approval by the Board of *Disclosure of Accounting Policies* issued in February 2021

Disclosure of Accounting Policies, which amends IAS 1 and IFRS Practice Statement 2, was approved for issue by 10 of 13 members of the International Accounting Standards Board (Board). Ms Flores dissented. Her dissent is set out after the Basis for Conclusions. Messrs Gast and Mackenzie abstained in view of their recent appointment to the Board.

Hans Hoogervorst	Chairman
Suzanne Lloyd	Vice-Chair
Nick Anderson	
Tadeu Cendon	
Martin Edelmann	
Françoise Flores	
Zach Gast	
Jianqiao Lu	
Bruce Mackenzie	
Thomas Scott	
Rika Suzuki	
Ann Tarca	
Mary Tokar	

NOTES

NOTES

NOTES

NOTES

NOTES

NOTES

NOTES

NOTES

NOTES

NOTES

NOTES

NOTES

NOTES

NOTES

NOTES

NOTES

NOTES

NOTES

NOTES

NOTES

NOTES